WOMEN'S
PERIODICALS
IN THE
UNITED STATES

D0169082

Recent Titles in
Historical Guides to the World's Periodicals and Newspapers

This series provides historically focused narrative and analytical profiles of periodicals and newspapers with accompanying bibliographical data.

Index to City and Regional Magazines of the United States
Sam G. Riley and Gary W. Selnow, compilers

International Music Journals
Linda M. Fidler and Richard S. James, editors

American Mass-Market Magazines
Alan Nourie and Barbara Nourie, editors

Military Periodicals: United States and Selected International Journals and Newspapers
Michael E. Unsworth

Regional Interest Magazines of the United States
Sam G. Riley and Gary W. Selnow, editors

Business Journals of the United States
William Fisher, editor

Corporate Magazines of the United States
Sam G. Riley, editor

American Literary Magazines: The Twentieth Century
Edward E. Chielens, editor

Consumer Magazines of the British Isles
Sam G. Riley, editor

Trade, Industrial, and Professional Periodicals of the United States
Kathleen L. Endres, editor

Popular Religious Magazines of the United States
Mark P. Fackler and Charles H. Lippy, editors

Women's Periodicals in the United States: Consumer Magazines
Kathleen L. Endres and Therese L. Lueck, editors

WOMEN'S PERIODICALS IN THE UNITED STATES

SOCIAL AND POLITICAL ISSUES

Edited by
Kathleen L. Endres and Therese L. Lueck

Historical Guides to the World's Periodicals and Newspapers

Greenwood Press
Westport, Connecticut • London

Library of Congress Cataloging-in-Publication Data

Women's periodicals in the United States : social and political issues
/ edited by Kathleen L. Endres and Therese L. Lueck.
      p.   cm. — (Historical guides to the world's periodicals and
newspapers, ISSN 0742–5538)
   Includes bibliographical references and index.
   ISBN 0–313–28632–9 (alk. paper)
   1. Women's periodicals, American—History. I. Endres, Kathleen
L. II. Lueck, Therese L. III. Series.
PN4879.W614   1996
051'.082—dc20   96–7144

British Library Cataloguing in Publication Data is available.

Library of Congress Catalog Card Number: 96–7144
ISBN: 0–313–28632–9
ISSN: 0742–5538

First published in 1996

Greenwood Press, 88 Post Road West, Westport, CT 06881
An imprint of Greenwood Publishing Group, Inc.

Printed in the United States of America

The paper used in this book complies with the
Permanent Paper Standard issued by the National
Information Standards Organization (Z39.48–1984).

10 9 8 7 6 5 4 3 2 1

Contents

Preface

This volume is a work in progress. It is not designed to cover every women's periodical that has ever dealt with social, economic, or political issues. Rather, this volume is designed to be a beginning point, an entry into the field of women's publishing on this topic. It is designed to provide a hint of the rich diversity of approaches and voices that have characterized the women's periodicals that dealt with social, political, and economic issues. Some of the publications profiled in this book could be categorized as reactionary; others might be called radical; somewhere in between have been many, many others. This volume is designed to offer a glimpse into the history of women's periodicals that dealt with social, economic, and political issues.

Literally thousands of women have published magazines, newspapers, and newsletters dedicated to some form of social, economic, or political change; others opposed such measures and began their own periodicals to react to the proposed changes. Chronicling all these publications would be an impossible task. Therefore, some hard decisions had to be made.

Several approaches were considered as this book was planned. One called for this book to deal solely with the currently published feminist periodicals, a much-needed volume. Another suggested a focus on suffrage and antisuffrage periodicals only—again, while more is written on this topic, still a needed book. Another plan called for looking at the women's reform periodicals of the nineteenth century. All represented interesting, needed approaches. Each, however, was rejected because each, in its way, failed to suggest the rich diversity of thought and ideas that has characterized the women's periodicals over the generations.

The approach eventually adopted is eclectic; some might argue, unfocused. This volume attempts to cover a wide range of social, economic, and political issues—from abolitionism to temperance, from moral reform to birth control, from suffragism to antisuffragism, from pacifism to feminism. Women represented a constant in each of these areas. They were working together to bring about change (or in the case of antisuffrage, to reverse the flood of sentiment toward the vote). As such they needed voices, their own voices. Many of those voices are presented in this book.

Given this broad-based approach, literally thousands of periodicals could have been profiled in this book. A quick count will reveal that only seventy-six are actually included. The selection process went through a number of different stages. The first attempted to locate what were perceived to be the leading women's periodicals in the various social, economic, and political reform movements of the nineteenth and twentieth centuries. A search of standard reference books, textbooks, specialized histories, and interviews with experts in the field yielded the names of about five hundred publications. Then the hard part began, discarding periodicals from the list. Two publications might be dropped because another was clearly the most important one because of the editor, the editorial approach, or the size of the circulation. Another might be discarded because it more clearly fell under the title of a consumer magazine, covered in a previous volume. Still others were taken off the list because, upon closer evaluation, they did not seem appropriate for this volume.

During the selection process, attempts were made to include women's periodicals that reflected the racial and cultural diversity in the field. These publications could be identified, but locating complete holdings proved to be a different matter. This editor alone requested twelve periodicals edited by African-American and Latino-American women. Only two were eventually located, and, then, there were not sufficient holdings to allow the development of a profile of either.

The shortcomings of holdings help explain other reasons that certain publications were not profiled. Several individuals had to drop out of this project because other commitments did not permit them the search and travel allowances to access the periodicals. This meant that several periodicals that were scheduled to be included in this volume had to be dropped.

A quick look at the chronology appendix reveals that the publications profiled in this volume do cover a range of issues over both the nineteenth and twentieth centuries. They also cover all parts of the country—from the big eastern cities to small towns in Kansas and Nebraska.

Readers are directed to the contributors list. These are the individuals who truly have made this book possible. These individuals had a daunting, twofold task. Not only did they have to profile specific periodicals, but they also had to place each publication within its respective reform movement or organization. Each entry reveals that the contributors to this book did an excellent job. Contributors completed their tasks, even though they faced monumental obstacles. Many related tales of woe as they tried to track down complete holdings of each periodical. One researcher explained her dismay—and the horror of the librarians—when the drawer that was supposed to hold a complete run of a rare periodical was empty. No one could explain just what had happened to that publication. This horror story was not the only occurrence of physical checks revealing a far different story from the records. One library that was said to have a run of a periodical could turn up only one tattered issue. In another instance, just days before a researcher inquired, a total of twenty years of a publication was dumped to make storage space. No one had been notified; the move was not noted in the records.

Other contributors had stories of success when they related how certain libraries had committed funds to the acquisition of women's reform periodicals. These libraries represent treasure troves for those interested in doing research on women's publications. They include the library of Texas Woman's University; the library of Northwestern University; the library of Oberlin College (Ohio); the Peace Collection at Swarthmore College; the New York Public Library; the State Historical Society of Wisconsin (Madison); the Schlesinger Library, Radcliffe College; the Sophia Smith Collection, Smith College; the library at the University of California at Santa Barbara; the library at the University of Illinois; and the Library of Congress. Selected women's reform periodicals have also been reproduced on microfilm in six principal collections: American Periodical Series, Gerritsen Collection, Greenwood Microform, Herstory, History of Women, and Underground Press Collection.

The contributors, then, should be thanked for all their work in the preparation of this volume. Other individuals should also be thanked as well. Librarians from many institutions have helped the contributors in the preparation of their work. The staffs of many libraries should be thanked for their cooperation with the researchers. The Library of Congress, New York Public Library, William Paterson College Library, Oberlin College library, University of Western Ontario Library, and the University of Colorado library immediately come to mind. At my own institution, Sarah Akers, who is in charge of interlibrary loan at the University of Akron's Bierce Library, should be especially thanked. She has displayed infinite patience, ingenuity, and encouragement, no matter what periodical I requested.

In addition, I thank Linda Miller and Luberta Rookard for their assistance during the preparation of this book. Both my coeditor and I would like to thank our families for their patience during the preparation of this work.

This volume offers much technical information that needs to be explained. Circulation is an important part of any periodical's story, but the numbers reflect only a moment in time. Thus, most of the circulation figures are preceded by a source as well as a date so the reader can chronicle changes over time. The exact source can be found by checking the bibliography that precedes the Publication History. A caution should be attached to some of the circulation figures. When there are no sources indicated, the figures have been provided by the periodical itself. These are not necessarily audited circulation figures. Also, these figures do not necessarily indicate a paid circulation. A number of the periodicals profiled had a substantial nonpaid circulation. That information is provided when available.

Another problem that needs to be addressed is page numbers. A few entries do not provide page numbers in the notes. The authors of these entries used microfilmed reproductions; and, in several cases, the page numbers could not be deciphered. Volume and issue data also represented a problem, particularly for the more recent periodicals. A number of these publications never used volume numbers. Thus, the number of issues is noted.

Frequencies cited are as exact as possible. However, because of incomplete holdings in libraries as well as incomplete records on these periodicals, it is often difficult to provide exact information on frequency and sometimes even information on the last issue published.

Asterisks that appear throughout this volume denote the periodicals that are profiled elsewhere in this book.

As in other books in this Greenwood series, the periodical titles are arranged in alphabetical order. Each entry offers a historical essay that covers the publication's founding, editorial development, and content. The Information Sources section offers a *selected* bibliography, index sources, and locations where the publication can be found. The Publication History section provides the publication title and title changes, volume and issue data, publisher and place of publication, editors, and circulation. In instances where a collective edits the periodical, that information is noted, but the exact names of all collective members are not included.

It is this editor's hope that this volume will represent a useful beginning point for the study of women's periodicals that address social, economic, and political issues of the United States.

Kathleen L. Endres

Introduction

For a group that has lacked the vote—the male-defined instrument of political and social power—until relatively recently, women have long affected American life.[1] This book is a testament to that fact.

Throughout American history women have worked in reform organizations, informal community groups, and consciousness-raising "cells" to change their neighborhoods, their state, their nation, and their society. In their organization, their focus, and their strategies, women have not necessarily followed male hierarchical models of organization.[2] Although many women's groups have been as hierarchical in organization as any men's association (e.g., Carrie Chapman Catt's Woman Suffrage Party in New York City or the current National Organization for Women), other women's groups have skirted such patterns and adopted a collaborative, cooperative approach in their organization (e.g., Cell 16, the Women Strike for Peace, and New York Radical Feminists).[3]

Much the same can be said of women's communication networks. Women have always had communication networks. Often, they were as informal as morning coffee with friends. Other times, they might be words exchanged among women about shared problems at work. More recently, they might e-mail unseen "friends" a continent or an office away. But, in order to effect extensive social, political, and economic change, women have had to reach beyond their immediate circle of friends and acquaintances and reach a "mass" audience.

To do this, women needed the media. In the print media, women could choose any number of options, from submitting letters and articles to the "mainstream" press (primarily male-owned newspapers and magazines marketed to appeal to the general reading public), to working on the staff of the "alternative" press (primarily male-controlled newspapers and magazines committed to a specific cause and distributed to those already sympathetic to that cause). Neither of these options was necessarily effective or satisfying to women. Although many women thrived in the male-dominated media, others became frustrated and searched for other outlets.[4] They came to share reformer Susan B. Anthony's suspicion of the male-controlled and male-operated media:

> Just as long as newspapers and magazines are controlled by men, every woman upon them must write articles which are reflections of men's ideas. As long as that continues, women's ideas and deepest convictions will never go before the public.[5]

This distrust, combined with a personal commitment to a particular reform that promised to bring about social, political, or economic change—as opposed to monetary reward—led women to establish the newspapers, magazines, and newsletters that are profiled in this book. It was fortuitous that these women did not start their periodicals with plans of making large sums of money, for seldom did these publications break even—much less make money. More likely, the women soon discovered that they had to rely on their own financial resources or the generosity of "friends" to keep their periodicals going. As can be seen on the pages of this book, women-owned, -operated, and -edited periodicals that proposed social and political change faced a precarious future. Whether they were started in the nineteenth century as an abolitionist newspaper or in the twentieth century as a voice of feminism, these periodicals shared a common financial future: bleak.

The average life span for the publications profiled was 19.9 years. That average is artificially high because of a few long-publishing periodicals. The *Union Signal** has survived (at this writing) 112 years; *The Advocate and Family Guardian** tried to change American sexual morals for 106 years before giving up in 1941; the General Federation of Women's Clubs' periodical (under various titles) has published for 75 years; and the *Women Lawyers Journal** has celebrated 84 years of life. Indeed, the publications that have endured so many years have all been underwritten by large, financially stable women's organizations. (The *Union Signal* was published by the Woman's Christian Temperance Union; *The Advocate and Family Guardian* was underwritten by the American Female Guardian Society and Home for the Friendless; and the National Association of Women Lawyers has financially supported the *Women Lawyers Journal* since 1911.)

Most of the periodicals profiled in this book could not draw on the resources of large, established national women's associations. The largest number of the publications profiled—more than one-third of those included in this volume (N = 34)—had a life span of fewer than ten years. Many suffered because they offered an editorial product that embraced controversial social, economic, and political issues. Many women's periodicals were committed to such radical causes as abolitionism (*Pittsburgh Saturday Visiter**), dress reform (*The Sibyl** and *The Lily**), suffrage (*National Citizen and Ballot Box** and *New North-*

*west**), abortion/birth control (*Woman Rebel** and *Birth Control Review**) or feminism (*New Women's Times** and *Prime Time**).

Most of the women's periodicals profiled in this book also faced harsh publishing realities. Most were undercapitalized and had to rely on the financial resources of an individual woman or a small women's association. In either instance, the periodical quickly became a drain on financial resources. These periodicals never seemed to be able to draw the advertising revenue or the readership base needed to be financially self-sufficient.

A combination of factors explains the lack of advertising. Perhaps the most obvious was the organization of the advertising industry itself. In both the nineteenth and twentieth centuries, the advertising industry has been primarily male-controlled. Although women have joined the ranks of media buyers, men have—and still do—ultimately make most of the final media buying decisions.[6] Research has indicated that small periodicals that embrace "unpopular" positions do not attract large amounts of advertising.[7] This situation may be more complex than simple male hostility[8] or advertising industry practices.

Often, the women who ran the publications profiled in this book lacked the business background and expertise to develop a marketing package that would attract advertisers.[9] Starting their publications in order to express a point of view, the woman or women who started many of the periodicals profiled in this book lacked a substantial business or journalistic background. For example, the first collective of *off our backs* had only one woman who had journalistic experience; neither Harriet Desmoines nor Catherine Nicholson had any experience in publishing when they started *Sinister Wisdom.** This situation was not peculiar to the recent feminist periodicals but can be seen in the nineteenth-century periodicals as well. For example, Amelia Bloomer had contributed only a few pieces to a local temperance newspaper before she started *The Lily*[10]; Susan B. Anthony had no experience in publishing when she became proprietor of *The Revolution**; Paulina Wright Davis had no journalistic experience prior to starting *The Una.** Of course, there were notable exceptions to this tendency. Ida B. Wells had been extensively involved in journalism prior to her involvement in the *Free Speech and Headlight,** and Jane Grey Swisshelm had not only contributed to the local Pittsburgh papers but also briefly been a reporter for the *New York Tribune* before starting the *Pittsburgh Saturday Visiter.* But even journalism and editing experience could not assure success—or an ability to bring sufficient advertising to their newspapers. Both Wells and Swisshelm found that their newspapers were short-lived. No doubt the controversial nature of both of these publications had something to do with their longevity—and lack of advertising. Wells, an African-American woman,[11] was challenging many southern white beliefs and practices (most notably lynching). Swisshelm was an ardent abolitionist and woman's rights advocate. Swisshelm, particularly, often complained about her inability to get *paid* advertising (political and otherwise) in her newspaper.

Whatever the explanation, many of the woman-owned, -operated, and -edited publications profiled in this book have had to rely on small—primarily local—

advertising, even when the periodical had a national circulation. In the feminist publications of the second half of the twentieth century, much of the advertising seems to have been placed by women-owned businesses or small ventures designed specifically to appeal to women.[12]

The second component of the abysmal finances of so many of the periodicals profiled in this book was the lack of a substantial circulation base. Although circulation information is not available for twenty-six publications and the figures are suspect in a number of other instances,[13] it appears that the greatest number of periodicals profiled in this book could not draw a large-enough circulation base to make them financially stable. The average circulation of the periodicals profiled in this book was 12,230.[14] Several factors have worked against these periodicals. In the consumer magazine field, publishers rent "lists," or compilations of names of individuals who represent the demographic mixture a magazine hopes to reach. Lists of "feminists," "liberal feminists," or "radical feminists" have not generally been available. The launch of *off our backs* illustrated this principle. *off our backs* founder Marilyn Webb had been involved in Vietnam Summer, a national antiwar group. Accordingly, she had access to the membership list for this association. The *off our backs* collective sent subscription solicitations to each of these members. The initial mailing to this group—as well as mailings to women involved in antiwar groups in Chicago, San Francisco, and other cities—elicited a response rate of almost 100 percent, a figure virtually unheard of in publishing. Although this pointed to the demand for such publications, feminist periodicals did not always have access to such a successful "list."[15] A number of feminist publications had access only to their own association's membership lists and attempted to reach out to potential subscribers through single-copy sales in the relatively small network of feminist bookstores across the country.[16]

In a sense, the earlier women's periodicals (such as *The Revolution, Woman's Tribune,* * *The National Citizen and Ballot Box,* * and *Pittsburgh Saturday Visiter,*) may have been better equipped to increase their circulation than today's feminist publications. Not only did these publications have access to the membership lists of the group with which they were formally affiliated, but they also had access to sympathetic women across the country. Editors of woman's rights/suffrage periodicals were popular speakers at the various woman's rights/suffrage conventions across the country. At the same time that editors exhorted woman's progress politically, socially, educationally, and economically, they also solicited subscriptions to the sympathetic audience. For example, Susan B. Anthony solicited subscriptions for *The National Citizen and Ballot Box* during her speeches. Indeed, that help was so vital to the success of that periodical that it was suspended shortly after Anthony retired from the lecture circuit. Clara Bewick Colby, editor of the *Woman's Tribune*, was a popular speaker both on the lecture circuit and at conventions. She solicited subscriptions at the same time she stumped for woman suffrage.[17]

Later suffrage periodicals benefited from the growth in support for woman suffrage. Organizations grew in size and strength. The circulation of the periodicals affiliated with these organizations grew apace. In fact, at least one—*The Woman Voter*—was even sold on New York City newsstands. However, this represented an exception. Most women's periodicals that were committed to social, political, or economic change (such as those found in this book) were not sold at commercial newsstands.[18] Those that did make it to the newsstands often found that they were not prominently displayed. For instance, *Majority Report** stated that it was on "hundreds" of newsstands in greater New York City but also reported that many of these newsstands "keep it discreetly hidden under last week's Irish Echo."[19]

Recent feminist publications have found an alternative method to survive in today's publishing environment. Some are taking advantage of the U.S. government tax codes. *Ms* was probably the first feminist periodical to become a nonprofit organization and take advantage of the benefits of that status. Subsequently, *Big Mama Rag* followed suit. However, that publication found its tax-free status has brought a snarl of legal problems. The Internal Revenue Service (IRS) challenged the publication's nonprofit status as an "educational organization." Although the lower court upheld the IRS interpretation, the Washington, D.C., Circuit Court reversed that ruling, concluding that the government standards for educational organizations are vague.[20] But nonprofit status did not save *Big Mama Rag;* the periodical ceased publication in 1984.[21]

As the *Big Mama Rag* lawsuit indicated, nonprofit status is not necessarily the answer to the financial problems facing these feminist periodicals. When *off our backs* (*oob*) considered applying for nonprofit status, collective members became deeply concerned about their future editorial independence. One of the benefits of the nonprofit status is eligibility for grants, but the *oob* collective members were concerned about strings that might be attached to grant money.[22]

The finances of the largest number of periodicals profiled in this book tell a pessimistic story. But finances are only one part of the story of the women-owned, -operated, and -edited periodicals profiled in this book. The larger story here is one of tremendous hope, optimism, confidence, and energy. The women who began these periodicals did so because they believed that they could change society. This is one theme that transcends time and reform. Whether the woman was starting a newspaper to work for abolitionism and woman's rights in antebellum Pittsburgh or beginning a newsletter to fight against ageism in twentieth-century America, whether the woman was setting out to change the Constitution to allow women to vote or launching a magazine to fight that "dangerous" cause, whether the woman was starting periodicals that promoted racial, ethnic, or religious equality, whether the woman was putting together periodicals that endorsed birth control or editorially denouncing it, these editors did so because they believed that they could change American society.

The second trend that transcended time and the type of reform was the desire to communicate, to convince others of the merit of their cause. Some of these women (e.g., Charlotte Perkins Gilman, Jane Grey Swisshelm, Emma Pack, and

Ida B. Wells) wrote periodically for male-edited publications. Nonetheless, that did not diminish their desire to start their own publications so that these women could speak in a voice not edited (or mediated) by men. The women associated with feminist periodicals, especially, found that option preferable to working on male-owned, -operated, and -edited publications. As the *off our back* collective explained in that publication's first issue, male-dominated media "consistently denied us the space and freedom necessary to develop our journalistic talents and sharpen our political and economic analyses."[23]

Although many women had lost confidence in male-dominated media, they never seemed to lose faith in women to effect change. This is the third trend that seemed to transcend time and cause. The editors of these newspapers, magazines, and newsletters wanted to reach out to other women to inform them and to convince them to work for change. As Rosa Sonneschein wrote in the first edition of *The American Jewess,*

> We invite all to follow us to the goals of universal sisterhood. We need diligent workers and warm friends. . . . Every Jewess in America ought to assist us as best she can, either with word or pen . . . to join us to build up a journal worthy of American Judaism.[24]

Along with this desire to reach out to other women in the spirit of that "universal sisterhood" that Rosa Sonneschein discussed was an enormous confidence in the ability of women—once informed—to reform American society. Editors of the periodicals profiled in this book seemed driven by this idea. No matter what the reform, women seemed to be the key to its success. Whether the publication invoked traditional appeals as wives and mothers (as was the case in the *La Wisp*'s work for peace and *The Anti-Suffragist*'s work against the proposed amendment) or radical feminist demands (as was the case in *No More Fun and Games* and *Notes from the First Year*), these editors were confident that informed, aware women could work together to bring lasting change. Or, as *New Directions for Women* explained in its premier edition, "New Directions is convinced that when women understand sex discrimination, they will reach for the tools to combat it."[25]

In addition to these common threads,[26] the periodicals profiled in this book reflect a rich diversity of cause, point of view, editorial organization, and medium employed.

Over the course of American history, women have been involved in a range of reform movements. From temperance to abolitionism, from woman's rights to suffrage, from feminism to pacifism, women have worked within reform groups to change American society. Among these reform-minded women, an informal communication network developed. Sometimes these were as informal as conversations among like-minded women at the various reform meetings held in the nineteenth century.[27] The temperance, abolitionist, and woman's rights movements were especially marked by this type of activity.[28] Between meetings, women were forced to rely on the mails to retain these informal communication networks.[29] As technology improved, women employed all the new advances to keep their informal communication networks alive. The telephone, for example, aided these informal exchanges tremendously.[30] More recently, the advance of computer technology has allowed women to communicate more effectively and less expensively across long distances via the Internet.[31] In general, these communication networks have been informal and have served women on a personal level, providing information, inspiration, and motivation.

To effectively and efficiently communicate with larger numbers of women, to reach beyond the small circle of friends and acquaintances, individual women—and groups of women—began their own newspapers, magazines, and newsletters. These publications were started as voices for change—women's voices for change.

These voices came in a number of different tones. Some cried out for temperance (*Union Signal*); others called for abolitionism (*Pittsburgh Saturday Visiter*); a few pointed to dress reform (*The Sibyl* and *The Lily*); more dealt with suffrage and woman's rights (*New Northwest,* * *The Pioneer,* * *Queen Bee,* * *The Revolution,* and *Woman's Journal*); others spoke against the idea (*Anti-Suffragist* * and *Remonstrance* *). A few outlined the plight of working-class women (*Far and Near* * and *Life and Labor* *). Some endorsed peace (*Four Lights,* * *Peace and Freedom,* * *La Wisp,* and *N.Y. Peaceletter* *); while others advocated violent revolution (*Red Star* *). Some dealt with the ethereal (*Thesmorphia* * and *Womanspirit* *). Others spoke from the perspective of an established church (*Daughters of Sarah* *). A number spoke with the authority of a large, national organization (*GFWC Clubwoman* * and *9to5 Newsline* *); others voiced the perspective of small, radical "cells" (*No More Fun and Games,* and *Notes from the First Year*). Some spoke from the perspective of racial minorities (*Free Speech and Headlight*). Others represented a range of sexual preferences, from lesbianism (*Sinister Wisdom, The Ladder,* * and *Focus* *) to celibacy (*The Celibate Woman* *). Still others pushed for moral reform (*The Friend of Virtue* * and *The Advocate and Family Guardian*). The causes espoused were as diverse as the women who edited the periodicals.

The women who edited these publications did not always speak in a "feminist" voice. Just as the causes that the women espoused seemed to run the gamut, so to did their perspectives.

Some based their arguments on a traditional, conservative view of women's role in society (e.g., wife and mother). For example, that perspective was offered by both sides on the suffrage question. Obviously, those opposed to suffrage emphasized the traditional roles of women as wives and mothers and how the vote might disrupt those functions (see *Anti-Suffragist* and *Remonstance*). Those traditional appeals, however, were also used to support suffrage. Women should get the vote because they were wives and mothers who needed suffrage to protect their homes and their children. Or, as *The Woman Voter* emphasized: "It is woman's right that she should have a voice in the government of the state, since every act of government . . . touches her personal welfare and that of the children, in the schools, in the playgrounds, in the streets, in the factories, in the markets and in the home.''[32]

The appeal to the traditional roles of women was also used in peace publications. The Women Strike for Peace, particularly, framed its appeals in those terms. Women, as wives and mothers, had to protect their children by working to stop the proliferation of nuclear weapons and the Vietnam War. Or, as one appeal implored: ''save the children—save our sons—save our souls— STOP THE BARBAROUS WAR.''[33]

Other publications framed their arguments in a variety of feminist terms. This was not necessarily a twentieth-century development. Indeed, many of the early woman's rights/suffrage periodicals offered a feminist point of view. The most obvious example of this was *The Revolution.* Susan B. Anthony and her newspaper called for ''new constructions, not reconstructions. Old foundations as well as old fabrics must be removed.''[34]

The editorial point of view of *The Forerunner,* Charlotte Perkins Gilman's early twentieth-century magazine, could be categorized as ''radical feminist.'' Gilman would not appreciate the label. She preferred to call herself a ''humanist'': ''I am not primarily a 'feminist,' but a humanist. My interest in the position of woman, in the child, in the home, is altogether with a view to their influence upon human life, happiness and progress.''[35] Nonetheless, Gilman defined the philosophical base of ''radical feminism'' and identified the differing perspectives that would eventually split the feminist movement decades later.[36]

Thus, generalizations with regard to the editorial point of view of the periodicals profiled in this book must reflect the diversity of the voices. Some editors accepted the traditional roles of women within society. Some of these publications used arguments invoking traditional roles and responsibilities of women to actually enlarge their sphere from the home to the ''larger household.'' Some emphasized feminist perspectives, calling for changes to the social, economic, and political fabric of the nation. To understand the women's periodicals profiled in this book is to accept the differing points of view, the diversity of voices.

There was also a certain amount of diversity in the organization of the editorial staffs. Martha Allen in her dissertation on women's communication networks from 1963 to 1983 emphasized the preference for the collective.[37] Certainly, some of the more recent periodicals profiled in this book do back up that conclusion. However, it appears that the preference for the collective is a recent development. The largest number of periodicals profiled in this book— and all the periodicals prior to 1960—had editorial staffs organized along traditional, hierarchical lines. An editor, working alone, made the editorial decisions on what would appear in the periodical. It is unclear if this was simply the editor's preference or a situation dictated by staffing realities. Other women may not have been interested in spending the time, energy, and money producing a periodical. Nonetheless, most of these enterprises were the products of one woman working alone, according to the staff listed in the periodicals. Even when a number of women were involved in the publication, a hierarchical editorial organization was employed by most of the periodicals.

A feminist label did not necessarily equate with a collective editorial organization, as *New Directions for Women, Media Report to Women,* and *Plainswoman** illustrated. In general, the collective on the editorial side seemed to reflect the ''New Left'' roots of the publication's founders.[38] *off our backs, No More Fun and Games,* and *Notes from the First Year* all seemed to illustrate that principle. In each case, the founders of these periodicals had come from the ''New Left,'' as opposed to the civil rights movement.

Finally, there was a good deal of variety in the medium eventually employed. Women had three options with regard to printed publications: magazines, newspapers, and newsletters. Nineteenth-century editors seemed to prefer the newspaper as their medium. No doubt financial considerations entered into this. Newspapers published on cheap paper were less expensive to produce than the only other real alternative of the period, the magazine.[39]

The twentieth century brought more variety. The newsletter was the least expensive to produce and became the popular alternative for organizations that were not well funded. Local chapters of Women Strike for Peace relied on newsletters to promote their ideas. The newspaper, although more expensive to produce, remained a viable option and became the selected format for many voices (e.g., *New Women's Times, off our backs, New Directions for Women*). The magazine format was the most expensive option. Yet it offered certain benefits not afforded newsletters or newspapers; the magazine allowed for greater graphic creativity, a ''longer life'' with the reader, and more room for editorial comment. For this reason, Charlotte Perkins Gilman, although lacking financial support from any outside group, opted for the magazine format for her *Forerunner.* In general, the magazine has been the format of preference for national women's organizations (e.g., *GFWC Clubwoman* and *The Advocate of Family Guardian*).

Finally, this volume suggests other trends that need to be more fully researched. For example, individual publication profiles point toward certain women's networks that helped launch and sustain reform periodicals. One of the most obvious is the Allen family. Mother, Donna, launched *Media Report to Women;* daughters Dana Densmore and Martha Allen were also involved in launching or sustaining other feminist periodicals. Dana was a force in *No More Fun and Games;* Martha started *The Celibate Woman* and edited *Index/Directory of Women's Media,* a product of Women's Institute for Freedom of the Press In turn, Donna contributed to *No More Fun and Games.* Thus, the Allen family might be one focus for such research.

Familial networks in publishing were not peculiar to the feminist periodicals. The best-known familial relationship in reform publishing was Lucy Stone and Alice Blackwell, mother– daughter reformers of the woman suffrage movement. Both had been involved with the *Woman's Journal.* Blackwell went on to edit the *Woman's Column* and contribute to many other suffrage publications of the day. Both Stone and Blackwell shared the more conservative position with regard to suffrage and women's role in society. A shared fundamental philosophy may be a characteristic of the familial networks. The Allen family was clearly more radical feminist in its writings.

These networks were not necessarily familial in origin. Some appeared to grow out of friendships and shared perceptions of the role women should play in society. This was especially apparent in the early woman's rights periodicals. Certain events helped these friendship networks to develop. The woman's rights activists saw each other at the various woman's rights conventions held throughout the United States, and these meetings seemed to be conducive to the development and reinforcement of friendships. This process appeared to work on two levels: first, women contributed editorially to publications, and second, women sustained publications by soliciting subscriptions. The more radical within the woman's rights/suffrage movement appeared to be the most active in combining these strategies. After the demise of *The Revolution,* Susan B. Anthony made it a point to solicit subscriptions for *The National Citizen and Ballot Box,* a radical (by nineteenth-century standards) newspaper that began in Toledo, Ohio. Anthony, likewise, supported the periodical editorially by contributing letters to it, as did Elizabeth Cady Stanton. But *The National Citizen and Ballot Box* was not the only publication that benefited from Stanton and Anthony's help. A number of other radical periodicals, including the *The Woman's Tribune* benefited from friendship relationships with Stanton and Anthony. Stanton, especially, supported the *Tribune* editorially by contributing letters regularly to that newspaper.[40]

Less clear is how friendship networks within the community may have helped individual periodicals. Because so many of the publications had to rely on local advertising for revenue, "friends" within the community may have helped to arrange this much-needed revenue.

Friendship networks may be difficult to chart; but a careful reading of the publications and manuscript collections left behind by the women in question, as well as standard historical works, might help trace the relationships.

Many other research projects are suggested in this volume. Some might look at women editors as a distinct group sharing certain characteristics and how those characteristics may have changed over time or with the editorial perspective and the reform. Another might look at the rhetorical appeals presented in these periodicals. Hopefully, these analyses will extend beyond a single publication and look at a number of periodicals in a single reform or across reforms to gauge similarities and differences. Others might look at the "business" of reform, or companies that advertised in these periodicals. Along these lines, also, surely a closer examination of the nonprofit status and its ramifications for feminist periodicals is needed.

It is this editor's hope that this volume will be a resource in this future research on editors and periodicals of social and political issues.

Kathleen L. Endres

Notes

1. Many histories have chronicles the contributions women have made to American life. Among the best are those that deal with the campaign for suffrage and the effects of that campaign. See, for example, William H. Chafe, *The American Woman: Her Changing Social, Economic and Political Roles 1920–1970* (New York: Oxford University Press, 1972); Ellen C. DuBois, *Feminism and Suffrage: The Emergence of an Independent Women's Movement in America 1848–1860* (Ithaca, N.Y.: Cornell University Press, 1978); Eleanor Flexner, *Century of Struggle: The Woman's Rights Movement in the United States* (New York: Athenaeum, 1975 repr.); William P. O'Neill, *Everyone Was Brave: A History of Feminism in America* (Chicago: Quadrangle, 1969); J. Stanley Lemons, *The Woman Citizen: Social Feminism in the 1920s* (Urbana: University of Illinois Press, 1973).

2. See, for example, Joan Acker, "Hierarchies, Jobs, Bodies: A Theory of Gendered Organizations," *Gender & Society,* 4:2, June 1990, pp. 139–158.

3. The organization of feminist groups has been the subject of much discussion among researchers. Many of the more recent feminist researchers have emphasized the need for an ideology of inclusiveness and democracy, as opposed to bureaucracy and hierarchy, in the organization of feminist groups. See, for example, Acker, "Hierarchies, Jobs, Bodies," pp. 139–158; Kathleen Ferguson, *The Feminist Case against Bureaucracy* (Philadelphia: Temple University Press, 1984); and Ann Bookman and Sandra Morgen, eds., *Women and the Politics of Empowerment* (Philadelphia: Temple University Press, 1988).

4. The collective of *off our backs* probably spoke for a number of women when it observed that "existing institutions and channels for communication have ceased to meet the growing needs of women's struggles. Women who have worked in the media are well acquainted with the patterns of discrimination which define and confine their news within the 'Style' and 'Fashion' section. Serious and competent women journalists soon learn that they can expect to remain research assistants or be satisfied with the dullest and least important assignments. So-called radical and movement periodicals usually retain token articles while vital issues wind up on back pages or in wastebaskets" ("dear sisters," *off our backs,* February 27, 1970, p. 2).

5. As reprinted in "The Need for Women's Publishing," *New Women's Times,* January 4–17, 1980, p. 2.

6. The most recent study outlining the role women currently play in the advertising industry can be found in *Advertising Age.* Even in today's advertising industry, men still outnumber women in all executive positions except agency account executive and media director (Mark Gaines, "Women Stymied by Sharp Salary Gender Gap," *Advertising Age,* December 5, 1994, pp. S1, S12). Another study done the year before also outlined the strength of the so-called old boys' network within broadcasting, publishing, and advertising (Fred Danzig and Melanie Wells, " 'Old Boys' Network' Still Alive," *Advertising Age,* May 24, 1993, p. 40).

7. In large part, this is due to an advertising concept called "qualitative media value." In short, this means that an advertisement "shares" the "environment" with the editorial. Thus, the "controversial" nature of the editorial material in any alternative publication, including those that are women-owned and-operated, can "rub off" on the advertiser. Many advertisers who might be interested in reaching the audience of a specific periodical might shy away from that publication because of its controversial editorial nature. See Jack Z. Sissors and E. Reynold Petray, *Advertising Media Planning* (Chicago: Crain Books, 1976), pp. 142–148. For a full discussion on how this principle affected at least one feminist periodical, see Amy Erdman Farrell, "A Social Experiment in Publishing: Ms. Magazine, 1972–1989," *Human Relations* 47:6, June 1994, p. 723. Lauren Kessler also talked about this issue in the dissident press in general. She pointed out that, while many publications of this class refused to accept advertising, those that did found that they could not attract much advertising. She argued that the audience of such periodicals may not have been appealing to advertisers. "Not only was the audience small," Kessler concluded, "it was often comprised of readers who could not afford the goods and services advertisers had to sell" (Lauren Kessler, *The Dissident Press: Alternative Journalism in American History* [Beverly Hills, Calif.: Sage, 1984], p. 157).

8. Male hostility, however, should not be discounted. As Amy Erdman Farrell reported in her study of *Ms.* magazine, when that periodical first started as a feminist commercial enterprise, a sales representative from that organization was "literally spit on while making her presentation" (Farrell, "A Social Experiment in Publishing," p. 723).

9. In keeping with this point, these underfinanced periodicals also were not likely to be able to afford the type of research materials that many advertising agencies have come to expect. With regard to the more recently published periodicals, these publications were not likely to hire audit bureaus (e.g., Audit Bureau of Circulation or Business Publications Audit of Circulations), research firms (e.g., Simmons or Mediamark Research Inc.), or outside consultants to provide demographic or psychographic profiles of readers. Without this material, the women were not able to put together a convincing media kit that would appeal to advertisers. Leonard Mogel discusses the requirements needed to convince a potential advertiser in Leonard Mogel, *The Magazine,* 2d ed. (Chester, Conn.: Globe Pequot Press, 1988), pp. 48–63.

10. Her husband, however, did have publishing experience. He had been coeditor of the *Seneca County* (New York) *Courier.*

11. African-American newspapers often had difficulty gaining advertising from white-owned businesses, especially in the South. Robert L. Allen talked about Ida B. Wells' newspaper and explained that it was "successful." No doubt its success was based on the African-American community that financially supported it through advertising and subscriptions (Robert L. Allen, *Reluctant Reformers: Racism and Social Reform Movements in the United States* [Washington, D.C.: Howard University Press, 1974], p. 57). Market segmentation that includes the African-American media has been a relatively recent development. Advertising for products that are owned by mainstream corporations are beginning to feature African-American and Latino models. Since the 1970s, especially, certain advertising campaigns have also included African-American-and Latino-owned periodicals (Clint C. Wilson II and Felix Gutierrez, *Race, Multiculturalism, and the Media: From Mass to Class Communication,* 2d ed. [Thousand Oaks, Calif.: Sage, 1995], pp. 125–132).

12. However, it is possible that women editors and women publishers might have

used their friendship "networks" to obtain the advertising that did appear in their publications.

13. Some of these circulation figures may be inflated. Few of the publications profiled in this book ever had their circulations audited by any outside group. Thus, most of the figures provided in this book were offered by the publication itself.

14. N = 48. This included figures on unverified and suspect circulation numbers.

15. In the 1960s and early 1970s, radical groups themselves may have been reluctant to release membership lists to outsiders in light of the paranoia of the day. As many subsequent histories of this period have shown, many radical organizations, including feminist groups, were spied on and infiltrated. Todd Gitlin outlined the situation in *The Sixties: Years of Hope, Days of Rage* (New York: Bantam, 1987). For a discussion of Federal Bureau of Investigation (FBI) surveillance of the women's liberation movement, see Letty Cottin Pogrebrin, "The FBI Was Watching You," *Ms.,* June 1977, p. 42, and Frank J. Donner, *The Age of Surveillance: The Aims and Methods of America's Political Intelligence System* (New York: Random House, 1981), pp. 150–155. Two members of the *off our backs (oob)* collective outlined personal experience with government harassment. As Carol Anne Douglas and Fran Moira related, after *oob* published a Weather Underground "communiqué," *oob* offices were broken into, and its paperwork was rifled, but no money was taken. Collective members talked about using code names because they assumed their phones were tapped. However, the collective members never actually took those measures. See Carol Anne Douglas and Fran Moira, *"off our backs.* The First Decade 1970–1980," in Ken Wachsberger, ed., *Voices from the Underground Vol. 1 Insider Histories of the Vietnam Era Underground Press* (Tempe, Ariz.: Mica Press, 1993), pp. 107–123.

16. A full discussion of feminist bookstores and their role in distributing feminist books and periodicals can be found in Kirsten Grimstad and Susan Rennie, *The New Woman's Survival Sourcebook* (New York: Knopf, 1975), pp. 139–145.

17. Olympia (Brown) Willis, ed., *Democratic Ideals: A Memorial Sketch of Clara B. Colby* (n.p.: Federal Suffrage Association, 1917), p. 34.

18. Women's periodicals that were committed to social, political, or economic change have tended to be categorized as "underground" or "alternative" publication, terms that cover a wide range of causes. In general, "underground" or "alternative" publications— no matter what the gender of the publisher, editor, or anticipated audience—have not been handled by most commercial newsstands. Feminist bookstores, however, have been distribution points for women-opened and -operated periodicals that express a feminist point of view. Guidelines on newsstand distribution can be found in Mogel, *The Magazine,* pp. 106–111.

19. "How to Find This Paper," *Majority Report,* June 1973, p. 2.

20. Peter H. Winslow, "Effects of the Big Mama Rag Decision on Exempt Education Organizations: An Analysis," *Journal of Taxation* 55.1, July 1981, pp. 20–24.

21. "Welcome to OFF OUR BACKS," *off our backs,* June 1985, p. 1.

22. Jennie Ruby, "Off our backs," in Cynthia M. Lont, ed., *Women and Media: Content. Careers and Criticism* (Belmont, Calif.: Wadsworth, 1995), pp. 41–53.

23. "dear sisters," *off our backs,* February 27, 1970, p. 2.

24. *American Jewess,* April 1895, p. 20.

25. "Statement of Purpose," *New Directions for Women.* January 1972, p. 1.

26. Martha Allen noted a number of characteristics that the women periodicals between 1963 and 1983 shared. They included women speaking for themselves, not re-

porting for others; a preference for the collective rather than the hierarchical; a sharing instead of a competitive approach; an analysis of mass media's role relative to women and women's media; a nonattack approach toward different views; an emphasis on an "open forum"; a coverage of information not reported in mass media; and an activist orientation (Martha L. Allen, *The Development of Communication Networks among Women. 1963–1983* (Ann Arbor, Mich.: University Microfilms International, 1989).

27. Perhaps the best example of this occurred after the American women delegates were not recognized and not allowed to participate in the World Anti-Slavery Convention in London in 1840. At that time, Lucretia Mott and Elizabeth Cady Stanton spent time together discussing the broader issue of woman's rights. The seeds of the first woman's rights convention in Seneca Falls, New York, were sown at that convention. See Eleanor Flexner, *Century of Struggle: The Woman's Rights Movement in the United States* (Cambridge, Mass.: Belknap Press, 1975 repr.), pp. 72–77.

28. Flexner pointed to church sewing circles as the "earliest rudimentary women's organizations." Early in the nineteenth century, women were involved in specific reform movements. As early as 1833, women organized the Philadelphia Female Anti-Slavery Society after the American Anti-Slavery Society allowed some women to attend its meeting but refused to let them join the association or sign its Declaration of Sentiments and Purpose. The first National Female Anti-Slavery Society convention was held in New York in 1837 with eighty-one delegates from twelve states. Earlier, local female groups had meetings and often faced mobs (Flexner, *Century of Struggle,* pp. 41–43). Women were similarly involved in the temperance reform movement. These women participated in both gender-specific organizations (twenty-four women's societies were reported in 1831) and the general American Temperance Society (ATS) locals. According to Jack S. Blocker Jr., the typical ATS local society contained a membership that was between 35 and 60 percent female. The first women's temperance convention was held in 1835 in Montpelier, Vermont. The Daughters of Temperance were active in the 1840s, and this represented, according to Blocker, "a more woman-centered view of temperance activity than was evident during the 1820s and 1830s." This organization even had its own newspaper, *New York Olive Plant* (Jack S. Blocker Jr., *American Temperance Movements: Cycles of Reform* [Boston: Twayne, 1989], pp. 18–19, 49).

29. Flexner noted that after the World Anti-Slavery Convention exclusion, Lucretia Mott and Elizabeth Cady Stanton continued their discussion of woman's rights through correspondence. This was not the only example of letter writing as the communication between meetings and conventions. From 1850 to 1860, national woman's rights conventions were held annually, supplemented by local and regional gatherings, especially in Ohio, Indiana, New York, Pennsylvania, and Massachusetts. Individual correspondence among activists was supplemented by such early woman's rights publications as *The Lily, The Una,* and *Saturday Visiter* (Flexner, *Century of Struggle,* pp. 73–81).

30. Few researchers have looked at the role of the telephone within women's communications networks. One notable exception was Lana Rakow, who has argued that the telephone was "not a neutral, but a gendered, technology." Rakow outlined how women used the telephone in a different manner from men, that the telephone was used to carry out their gender roles and responsibilities. While Rakow mentions only in passing the role of the telephone for the work of reform, specifically the National Organization for Women's "telephone trees used to alert members to important information," her research represented an important beginning point in understanding how women use the telephone

(Lana Rakow, *Gender on the Line: Women, the Telephone, and Community Life* [Urbana: University of Illinois Press, 1992], pp. 1, 34–58, 61–79, 149).

31. See, for example, Bryn Austin, "The Irreverent (Under) World of 'Zines," *Ms.* January 1993, p. 68.

32. "An Open Letter to the Legislature by a Voter," *Women Voter,* March 1910, p. 4.

33. *Peaceletter,* February 1967, p. 3.

34. Susan B. Anthony, "The Work of the Hour," *The Revolution,* August 6, 1886, p. 72.

35. "On Ellen Key and the Woman Movement," *The Forerunner,* February 1913, p. 35.

36. Nancy F. Cott discusses Gilman's contributions to modern feminism in *The Grounding of Modern Feminism* (New Haven, Conn.: Yale University Press, 1987), pp. 41–42, 48–49, 163–164, 192. Her public quarrel with Ellen Key that was waged on the pages of *The Forerunner* helped define the split between liberal and radical feminism two generations later. The radical feminist "holds that sex is a minor department of life; that the main lines of human development have nothing to do with sex, and that what women need most is the development of human characteristics." Gilman called these individuals "human feminists." The liberal feminist "considers sex as paramount as underlying or covering all phases of life, and that what woman needs is an even fuller exercise, development and recognition of her sex." Gilman termed these "female feminists" ("The Conflict between 'Human' and 'Female' Feminism," *The Forerunner,* April 1914, p. 291).

37. Allen, *The Development of Communication Networks 1963–1983.*

38. Historian Alice Echols made that point about the organization of radical feminist groups. However, the "new left" heritage toward the collective also seemed to spill over to the staffing of the periodicals (Echols, *Daring to Be Bad,* pp. 16–18).

39. The newsletter format gained great popularity during the twentieth century.

40. In a number of instances, Clara Bewick Colby used the "Stanton connection" to solicit subscriptions. She emphasized that Stanton would be regularly contributing to the newspaper. See, for example, *Woman's Tribune,* December 1, 1888, p. 4.

A

THE ADVOCATE AND FAMILY GUARDIAN

A "wide-awake" women's periodical was keeping New Yorkers informed while many of that city's news giants still "slumbered." *The Advocate of Moral Reform* was begun in 1835; the same year as the *New York Herald* and predating the *Tribune* (1840) and the *Times* (1851). Although the *New York Sun* was established in 1833, that same year the *Advocate*'s predecessor, *McDowall's Journal,* was also created.

The New York Female Moral Reform Society was founded—and it began publication of the *Advocate*—during an era known as the "Second Great Awakening." This was a time when "a millennial spirit pervaded efforts at transforming United States society," and reformers "sought not merely social change but spiritual transformation, the moral regeneration of the world."[1]

The foremost messenger in the crusade for moral reform from the mid-nineteenth to the mid-twentieth centuries, the *Advocate* was the official publication of the New York Female Moral Reform Society. This women's society later became the American Female Moral Reform Society, and the *Advocate* was its national organ. The magazine had two specific missions: to convert prostitutes and to broadcast the occasions of seduction. It did not blame women for prostitution. Rather, it laid a full measure of responsibility on the men who perpetrated acts of seduction. It also educated children against becoming either victims or future perpetrators of lewd behavior.

The eight-page publication, tight with print, disseminated these messages as *The Advocate of Moral Reform* when it superseded *McDowall's Journal* in 1835. It continued its mission, although it changed its name to *The Advocate of Moral Reform and Family Guardian* (in 1847) and, in 1849, to *The Advocate and Family Guardian,* which it remained until ceasing publication in 1941.

A group of women banded together to follow the example of missionary John

McDowall, who had issued a controversial report in 1832 on the need for reform
of New York society. In the journal he started a year later, McDowall outlined
his strategy for reform as one of prevention, "persuading the virtuous to maintain their integrity, and [to] pluck from ruin as many of the degraded as possible." He cited his journal's mission:

> The principal design of the Journal is to expose public immorality, to elicit
> public sentiment, and to devise and carry into effect the means of pre-
> venting licentiousness and vice.
>   It is desirable, for the public good, that a copy of each number should
> be placed in every family in the land.[2]

Through his writings, McDowall documented the evils of the city. "[H]e
meant to alarm a slumbering ministry, a slumbering church, and a slumbering
world, if words or facts could do it, whatever might be the sacrifice." Despite
the uproar caused by McDowall's report and subsequent disbanding of his society, women continued working for moral reform. "[H]is name a proverb and
a byword on earth. . . . He originated all that has since been done in the cause
to which he fell a martyr."[3]

In spite of the public censure McDowall incurred, the women sought further
inspiration in the revivals of theologian and reformer Charles G. Finney and
formed their own society, the New York Female Moral Reform Society, on May
12, 1834.[4] Through this society they endeavored to carry on the mission
McDowall had defined. In the fall of 1834, the society voted to purchase
McDowall's Journal and "transform it into a national women's paper with an
exclusively female staff."[5] The journal was named *The Advocate of Moral Reform* and was begun at the start of the year.

> [A] little band of Christian women, whose attention had been directed to
> an agency of Satan that was operating unchecked . . . decided to combine
> their labors, and seek the co-operation of others in a work of PREVEN-
> TION.
>   Among their first efforts was the commencement of a periodical, whose
> design was to exalt the law of God, and thus *prevent* its violation—to
> guard the domestic hearth from the invasion of the Spoiler, thus *preventing*
> the fall of the innocent; and, as far as practicable, to produce such a reform
> in the public sentiment, that the morally debased should be estimated
> according to their true character, and made to feel that access to the favor
> of the virtuous could only be secured by being *pure in heart.*[6]

Journalism historian Susan Henry cited the *Advocate* as an excellent example
of "the journalism produced by the women who lived and believed most fervently in the values" of women's culture, a separate sphere in which women
"developed shared, female-identified values, rituals, relationships, and modes of

communication that were sources of satisfaction and strength."[7] The magazine was a valuable asset to the women's moral reform society. Without the journal

> there is every reason to believe the usefulness of the Society would have been greatly circumscribed, perhaps . . . wholly suspended. . . .
>
> The sole aim of all its publications has been to carry out a specific object of the Society, viz.; the formation of a correct public sentiment, relative to the prevention of vice, the discharge of Christian duty in meeting the claims of the young, friendless, destitute and exposed, and the obligations of the family to extend its guardianship and moral influence over those within its reach.[8]

Impassioned by their cause of reforming society's morals, these women expanded their influence beyond their domestic sphere. Historian Carroll Smith-Rosenberg postulated that the women were able to carry with them the legitimation of their authority by their belief in the "Cult of True Womanhood."[9]

Editors allowed many women's voices to be heard. Readers submitted accounts of seduction, which they could share nowhere else. Most reader contributions ran with the headline "To the *Advocate*." Editors made efforts to check information before printing it, as is evidenced by a note that ran as an apology for delaying one submission. "The facts were of such a character, that the Executive Committee deemed it best, at the time, to defer their publication till further information was received." The story was about a woman who was raped while traveling alone by coach. The note also contained this caution: "Let those of the weaker sex who may read it, be admonished never to travel *alone* in a public conveyance, till a renovated state of society is apparent."[10]

Readers spoke through the pages of the *Advocate,* sometimes self-consciously using the publication as a soapbox, as in this example about a secular magazine's immodest frontispiece, which typifies the sense of duty felt by the women readers as well as the editors:

> As your paper professes to be a "Family Guardian," I wish to say a few words through its pages about a late No. of a Monthly Periodical taken in my family. . . . I feel prompted by a sense of duty, as a friend to the young, as a friend to good morals, as a friend to purity, as the rightful guardian of my daughter's chastity, "in *thought,* speech and behavior," to protest against such exquisitely immodest prints.[11]

Reports from female reform associations ran regularly; sometimes a collection of various reports was put into a general abstract. Some of these groups also used the *Advocate* as their mouthpiece, as did this group, whose sentiment typifies the ostracism of women who attempted to broach issues of rape, incest, or prostitution:

As a society of a little band of females, we are surrounded by discour-
agements; we have not the hearty co-operation of our ministers. . . .

We regard the Advocate as well calculated to enlighten and instruct and
believe it may be, in many instances, the monitor and protector of the
unwary and innocent.[12]

The *Advocate* boldly spoke out about matters ministers hesitated to address,
and often with a decidedly feminist perspective. In an account of a woman
acquitted of stabbing a man to death, the *Advocate* came out on the side of the
woman, not advocating killing, it explained, but glad that the man was recognized as a seducer.[13]

As radical as such a perspective was, the society did not "openly espouse"
woman's rights. But—more than a decade earlier than the 1848 Seneca Falls
Convention, which is traditionally recognized as the beginning of the U.S. woman's rights movement—the society was advocating that, for a good cause,
women should enlarge their sphere of influence. Historian Carroll Smith-
Rosenberg credited the moral reform movement with being the forerunner of
the woman's rights movement in the United States.

Both groups found women's traditionally passive role intolerable. Both
wished to assert female worth and values in a heretofore entirely male
world. Both welcomed the creation of a sense of feminine loyalty and
sisterhood that could give emotional strength and comfort to women isolated within their homes. . . . And it can hardly be assumed that the demand for votes for women was appreciably more radical than a moral
absolutism which encouraged women to invade bordellos, befriend harlots,
and publicly discuss rape, seduction, and prostitution.[14]

Researcher Barbara Berg took this analysis further, stating that, especially in the
1840s and 1850s, the *Advocate* "continuously and explicitly refuted the traditional role assigned to antebellum women and urged a feminist critique of society."[15]

However, in reflecting the female moral reform movement itself, the *Advocate*
presented what researcher Mary Ryan viewed as contradictory tendencies. While
it exposed the double standard of sexual morality, it also "reveled in portraying
the . . . nineteenth-century stereotype of " 'true womanhood.' ' "[16]

The *Advocate* ran reprints from other papers, secular as well as evangelical.
Controversy would run in its entirety, for instance, a scandal from Oberlin, Ohio,
on the discovery of the poor moral character of the *Oberlin Evangelist*'s late
editor, H. C. Taylor, who was found to have embezzled contributions, seduced
women, and advised abortion.[17] Building further on their audience's right to
know, the editors sometimes ran reprints that had a feminist cast. In an unchar-
acteristically jaunty reprint, foremothers—the forgotten of history—were
praised.

> We hear enough about our forefathers. They were nice old fellows, no doubt. . . . But where are their companions—their "chums"—who, as their helpmates, urged them along? . . .
>
> We wish not to detract . . . but . . . we wish to speak a word in season for women generally, and especially for our noble and self-sacrificing foremothers, lest time and the one-sided page of history shall blot them forever from our memories.[18]

Although atypical in tone, the article does carry a characteristic statement of advocacy for women and their frustration with second-class status in a male-dominated society.

A core of educated, morally righteous women, the editors recognized the vast number of ignorant people to be the cause of much of what was wrong in society. For instance, in addition to the "partial silence on the pulpit," wrong training in childhood was shown to be one of the primary causes of crime.[19] The journal gave much space to addressing what was to be done about the destitute. Women were to expand their familial roles by educating destitute children. The society housed victims, later adding to the masthead of the *Advocate*, "Home for the Friendless."

Most of the target audience were mothers, who were held responsible for the formation of the moral character of their children. Pages were filled with cautionary tales, such as the analysis of a news item sent in by a reader. A man had just been imprisoned for molesting children on their way home from school. The reader pointed out that in the case of two of the girls molested, the crime was not known until their mothers noticed they had contracted a disease and began asking questions. The court nearly set the man free because the children did not cry out at the time of the offense. Keeping silent on improper but crucial matters was seen as the culprit.

> Is it not a duty that mothers owe their children to teach them, if insulted in this way, *to scream?* Should they not, as they value their safety, teach them to distinguish between *right* and *wrong on all subjects that they may need to understand,* and never suffer them to go in the streets . . . till they can have full confidence that in case of any emergency, they would obey their wishes implicitly?[20]

Editors most often spoke directly to women, but some pieces were thought to be of particular interest to children, such as memoirs of saintly children who had died or wretched victims of unfortunate circumstances. One place that poetry was often included was in the "Children's Department." For instance, a poem about a dead child was printed, its title gathered from his prayer shortly before his death, "May I go to heaven when I die, and have a golden harp."[21]

Books known to be instructive and of good moral character, often by women authors, were advertised and reviewed in the pages of the *Advocate*. However, those were not to be confused with the common novels of the day, which would waste the time of a discriminating reader and, by making light of virtues, would endanger a reader's morals.[22]

The editorial staff was all female, and it was important that readers knew that the editor was a "lady."

> The Advocate is, as it professes to be, EXCLUSIVELY under the direction of the American Female Moral Reform Society—it is edited entirely by a lady, under the control and supervision of a Publishing Committee, composed from the Board of Managers of the Society.[23]

The *Advocate,* the "eldest offspring of the Society,"[24] being so successful, the society developed a publishing department and reported its profits regularly until the early 1860s, after which time regular space was not give for the society's business report. Circulation was shown to have increased fairly steadily. This trend persisted throughout the Civil War, although the high price of paper forced some thinner issues during that time.[25] There was a slight decline in circulation in the postwar years.[26] Even though as many as half of the issues printed of the *Advocate* were circulated without cost,[27] much of the profit from the *Advocate* and the other tracts that the society published went toward the society's home for the destitute.

Perhaps spawned by the women's recognition that they were disrupting an economic livelihood when they discouraged prostitution, these Protestant, mainly middle-class women became interested in women's economy and soon began addressing female labor on the pages of the *Advocate.* "Females must be better paid for their labor. . . . A great deal of light work that is performed by men might be given to females."[28] The publication took a stance that the sewing machine was evil, because it deprived women who hand-sewed at home of employment. In 1859, the society developed a sewing machine fund through which they could supply the "most worthy with sewing machines."[29] They bought sewing machines from manufacturers and sold them to the independent seamstresses, receiving installment payments of three dollars to five dollars a month. After one year, the fund had distributed forty-two sewing machines, and most of the money had been repaid.[30]

The society housed victimized women. In this House of Industry, women were offered employment training, such as typesetting and printing. By June 1859, the publisher's box ran the line "Printed at the Home of Industry." By 1861 the paper was entirely produced by women. Although powerful testimony to the precept of the society that women could do many tasks heretofore relegated only to males, editors felt constrained to answer often-posed questions of social impropriety:

> To the inquiry, "Why should a benevolent society publish and print on their own premises, in a charitable institution?" we reply, the Society has

issued a paper, as its organ with the public, during the twenty-five years of its existence, which facts without number have proved indispensable to the success of the enterprise. . . .

The measure of printing the journal, etc. at the Institution, is of recent origin; the erection of the Home Chapel furnished basement rooms well adapted to the purpose.

The consolidation of operations being convenient and less expensive, the society also found the "experiment" of encouraging young girls "to live honestly by the work of their hands . . . not only self-sustaining but advantageous."[31] After four years of being printed at the Home Chapel basement, the publication enumerated its successes and those workers performing the duties, stating that "every branch of the business is satisfactorily performed" by the females in the home,

not merely the *type-setting* . . . but the more difficult processes of the art, including the proof-reading and other complex details, being subject only to the general oversight of the superintendent of this department. There are now eight female employees regularly engaged, with two assisting occasionally. *Three* of these are deaf-mutes, who have already attained a satisfactory proficiency in those branches for which previous education had fitted them. This "corps" of laborers prepare the pages of the *Advocate* for stereotyping—it now being printed by steam from plates—print the wrappers, and fold the papers ready for mailing. . . .

. . . [W]e expect to graduate a number of young women as proficients in the course of a few years.[32]

From the standpoint both of providing skills training for women and of producing publications at reasonable cost, the "experiment" of using in-house labor for printing the paper was deemed successful and was continued as normal practice.

Although the society initially addressed its influence to the domestic sphere, it expanded to address affairs of state. "The Family takes precedence. It was instituted in the Garden of Eden. The State is of later origin."[33] Of particular note was the push for legislation against the men who seduced women, as opposed to merely sanctioning the women involved. Problems of the nation were personalized, as the family was used as a natural stepping-stone to the nation and even the world.

The condition of our own beloved country—its national sins, that are assuming greater prominence year by year, its high-handed oppression—its soul-ruining licentiousness . . . may well affect our hearts. Other lands, too, with their teeming millions—most of whom are in the darkness of heathenism—demand of us a *faith* that can embrace a world.[34]

In the 1860s, the publication reflected the strife of the Civil War. Its society lost members with "the decided stand taken by the majority for the Union side."[35] The *Advocate* commented that America was a "nation of mourners," since many family circles had been broken, in great part because of lives given to the country.[36] These rents in the social fabric of the nation were seen as the great evil of the Civil War, and, thus, the reuniting of the nation was the great triumph. Despite the society's passion for social reform, it was a white interest; the division of the nation through secession was seen as a far greater evil than slavery.[37] A reunited nation was celebrated on the *Advocate*'s pages.

> For four long years treason has done her utmost to rend [the republic] in twain, to ruin if it could not rule it, and, lo! to-day it stands firmer than ever before. . . .
>
> And so we are now, as never before, a free people. Slavery having proved the main inciter and supporter of rebellion, a death-blow was struck at it, that the nation might not perish.[38]

In 1847, the name of the publication was changed to *The Advocate of Moral Reform and Family Guardian* to downplay the phrase "moral reform," which many people still found objectionable.[39] The next year, the society renamed itself the American Female Moral Reform and Guardian Society. The Home for the Friendless was also opened in July 1847,[40] and soon it was incorporated into the title of the society. Both the name of the publication and the name of the society were further modified until *The Advocate and Family Guardian* was the official organ of the American Female Guardian Society and Home for the Friendless.[41]

As the times changed, the society continued to refocus its mission on housing the "friendless." During the depression of the 1870s, a women's shelter was opened; with other institutions closing over the following decade, the society accepted the overflow. Affluent summer homes were donated; funds were started to house homeless children, and the society bought buildings and playgrounds.[42] In 1902 the society moved into a new home, and in 1929 construction was completed on a building that would serve as a dormitory for older boys and a recreation facility for all the children.[43] During World War I, despite a lack of charitable gifts and an increase in the price of commodities, the society remained solvent.[44]

Adding the phrase "Home for the Friendless" symbolized the shift in the society's mission. A print of the imposing Home for the Friendless on Woody Crest Avenue[45] served as a logo for the society and the publication. Increasingly, the mission of the society shifted from reforming women to housing children, providing a home for them until they graduated from high school and were ready to support themselves.[46] The society eventually became the Woodycrest Youth Service.[47] With the changing of the times and the recentering of its mission, the society ceased publication of the *Advocate* in 1941.

Notes

1. Lori D. Ginzberg, " 'Moral Suasion Is Moral Balderdash': Women, Politics, and Social Activism in the 1850s," *Journal of American History* 73.3, December 1986, p. 601.
2. "Extracts from Journal, No. 1, 1833," *McDowall's Journal,* January 1834, pp. 1, 2.
3. "Who Was McDowall?" March 1, 1844, pp. 36–37.
4. Carroll Smith-Rosenberg, *Disorderly Conduct: Visions of Gender in Victorian America* (New York: Knopf, 1985), pp. 111, 112.
5. Smith-Rosenberg, *Disorderly Conduct,* p. 115.
6. "Thirteenth Annual Report of the American Female Moral Reform Society," June 1, 1847, p. [81].
7. Susan Henry, "Changing Media History through Women's History," in Pamela J. Creedon, ed., *Women in Mass Communication,* 2d ed. (Newbury Park, Calif.: Sage, 1993), p. 349.
8. June 1, 1859, p. 167.
9. Smith-Rosenberg, *Disorderly Conduct,* p. 109.
10. Ed., January 15, 1844, p. 15.
11. A Plain Countrywoman, "For the Advocate and Guardian. Common Sense Comments," letter, December 1, 1847, p. 179.
12. Mrs. H. Newhall, secretary, Conway, Massachusetts, Society, "Abstract of Annual Reports," January 15, 1844, p. 15.
13. "Trial and Acquittal of Amelia Norman," February 1, 1844, p. 21.
14. Smith-Rosenberg, *Disorderly Conduct,* p. 127
15. Barbara J. Berg, *The Remembered Gate: Origins of American Feminism: The Woman and the City, 1800–1860* (New York: Oxford University Press, 1978), n. 45, p. 291.
16. Mary Ryan, "The Power of Women's Networks: A Case Study of Female Moral Reform in Antebellum America," *Feminist Studies* 5, Spring 1979, p. 67.
17. A. Mahan, H. Cowles, J. A. Thome, and G. Whipple, "From the Oberlin Evangelist," January 1, 1844, p. 4. The *Advocate* would soon have its own troubles: in 1845, editor Sarah Martyn resigned in sympathy with a treasurer who was expelled. See Flora L. Northrup, *The Record of a Century, 1834–1934* (New York: American Female Guardian Society and Home for the Friendless, 1934), p. 27, and "Sarah Towne Smith Martyn," in Dumas Malone, ed., *Dictionary of American Biography,* vol. 12 (New York: Charles Scribner's Sons, 1933), p. 353.
18. *Selected,* "Our Foremothers," January 1, 1860, p. 6.
19. "The Cause and the Remedy. No. VI. To Understand an Ill Is Half Its Cure," February 15, 1844, p. 28.
20. H—S, "A Caution to Mothers," January 15, 1844, p. 11.
21. H., "May I Go to Heaven When I Die, and Have a Golden Harp," January 1, 1844, p. 4.
22. T. E., "From the American Messenger. Put Down That Novel!" January 15, 1848, p. 11.
23. Publisher's box, January 1, 1844, p. [1].
24. "Twenty-Sixth Annual Report of the American Female Guardian Society: Publishing Department," June 1, 1860, p. 168.

10 THE ADVOCATE AND FAMILY GUARDIAN

25. "Our Paper," editorial, January 1, 1863, p. 9.

26. The annual report of 1868 showed a circulation of thirty-eight thousand, a drop of three thousand from a peak of forty-one thousand in 1864.

27. "Thirteenth Annual Report of the American Female Moral Reform Society. Publications of the Society," June 1, 1847, p. [81].

28. "Female Labor, *Portland Tribune,*" January 1, 1844, p. 7.

29. "The Sewing Machine Fund," June 1, 1860, p. 167.

30. Northrup, *The Record of a Century,* p. 45.

31. June 1, 1859, p. 167.

32. S. Angell, "Home Industrial Schools. Printing Department," June 1, 1861, pp. 168–169.

33. "Anniversary Meeting," editorial, June 1, 1847, p. 84.

34. "Thoughts for the Season," editorial, January 1, 1844, p. 5.

35. Northrup, *The Record of a Century,* p. 44.

36. "The New Year," editorial, January 2, 1865, p. 8.

37. "Partial Review of the Year," editorial, January 1, 1862, p. 13.

38. "Long Live the Republic!" editorial, May 16, 1865, p. 116.

39. "To the Patrons of the Advocate," editorial, December 15, 1846, p. 188.

40. Northrup, *The Record of a Century,* p. 30.

41. January 1, 1859, p. [1].

42. Northrup, *The Record of a Century,* pp. 55–61.

43. Ibid., pp. 84, 88.

44. Ibid., p. 82.

45. Ibid., frontispiece.

46. Ibid., pp. 78, 83.

47. Jonathan W. Zophy, "Moral Reform," in Angela Howard Zophy, ed., *Handbook of American Women's History* (New York: Garland, 1990), pp. 385–386.

Information Sources

BIBLIOGRAPHY:

Berg, Barbara J. *The Remembered Gate: Origins of American Feminism: The Woman and the City, 1800–1860.* New York: Oxford University Press, 1978.

Ginzberg, Lori D. " 'Moral Suasion Is Moral Balderdash': Women, Politics, and Social Activism in the 1850s." *Journal of American History* 73.3, December 1986, pp. 601–622.

Henry, Susan. "Changing Media History through Women's History." In Pamela J. Creedon, ed., *Women in Mass Communication,* 2d ed. Newbury Park, Calif.: Sage, 1993.

Northrup, Flora L. *The Record of a Century, 1834–1934.* New York: American Female Guardian Society and Home for the Friendless, 1934.

Ryan, Mary. "The Power of Women's Networks: A Case Study of Female Moral Reform in Antebellum America." *Feminist Studies* 5, Spring 1979, pp. 66–85.

"Sarah Towne Smith Martyn." In Dumas Malone, ed., *Dictionary of American Biography,* Vol. 12. New York: Charles Scribner's Sons, 1933, pp. 352–353.

Smith-Rosenberg, Carroll. *Disorderly Conduct: Visions of Gender in Victorian America.* New York: Knopf, 1985.

Zophy, Jonathan W. "Moral Reform." In Angela Howard Zophy, ed., *Handbook of American Women's History.* New York: Garland, 1990, pp. 385–386.

INDEX SOURCES: Union List of Serials.
LOCATION SOURCES: Library of Congress, Oberlin College (Ohio), and other libraries.

Publication History

PERIODICAL TITLE AND TITLE CHANGES: (*McDowall's Journal,* predecessor, 1833–1834.) *The Advocate of Moral Reform* (1835–1846), *The Advocate of Moral Reform and Family Guardian* (1847–1849), *The Advocate and Family Guardian* (1849–1941).

VOLUME AND ISSUE DATA: Vols. 1–109 (January 1835–June 1941). Monthly (1835–1840?); biweekly (1840?–1890?); monthly (1890?–1941).

PUBLISHER AND PLACE OF PUBLICATION: American Female Guardian Society (name changes: New York Female Moral Reform Society, 1834–1839; American Female Moral Reform Society, 1839–1849; American Female Guardian Society, 1849–1887; American Female Guardian Society and Home for the Friendless, 1887–1941). New York.

EDITORS: Mrs. Hawkins (1835–1836); Miss Sarah Towne Smith (later, Mrs. S. T. Martyn) (1836–1842); Mrs. S. R. Ingraham (later, Mrs. Sarah R. I. Bennett) (1842–1877); Mrs. Helen E. Brown (1877–1893); Flora L. Northrup (1893–1941).

CIRCULATION: Annual report, 1864: 41,000.

Therese L. Lueck

THE AMERICAN JEWESS

The American Jewess remains important as the sole English-language, nineteenth-century publication of Jewish women's thought. Indeed, it was the only national Jewish publication in America and the only one in the world devoted to the interests of Jewish women. Considered by people of the time to be radical and even militant in its tone, it addressed issues of concern to Jewish women, such as the unionization of women workers, protective labor legislation, the establishment of settlement houses for new immigrants, and the woman suffrage movement. *The American Jewess* is *Lilith*'s illustrious, though short-lived, predecessor. *Lilith** is a feminist journal by any standard, with roots in the publication under consideration.

Starting in Chicago and later moving to New York City, Rosa Sonneschein's monthly magazine, *The American Jewess,* ran from April 1895 to May 1899.[1] The magazine went from monthly to quarterly publication in May 1899, appearing in August for a final issue. The sixty-one issues produced averaged fifty-eight pages per issue.[2]

The American Jewess began publication at a time when Jewish women were moving from parochial ladies' benevolent societies to city, state, and national organizations.[3] It reflected the "new" role and status of Jewish women in America.[4] In club activities, Jewish women challenged traditional assumptions, although they could not break entirely with those values of home and family.

Nevertheless, they began a new kind of participation for women within Jewish communal life, and Rosa Sonneschein's magazine championed this new role and status.[5]

This represented a break from Jewish traditions, which saw women's primary responsibility as attending to family needs. This work exempted women from all positive religious obligations, an exemption that is the theoretical basis for an oft-quoted blessing recited daily by Orthodox Jewish men. They thank the Almighty for not having made them women. Therefore, women received a religious and communal status inferior to that of men. Women could visit the synagogue to pray, but only in the curtained-off section or in a balcony of the structure. Thus, the synagogue was like a men's club.

In marriage, Jewish women had second-class status, also. In a traditional marriage ceremony, the groom took a wife; she remained passive. Moreover, the husband legally could dissolve a marriage, his prerogative to initiate Jewish divorce proceedings. Not until the Middle Ages, when the Jewish woman's status rose along with her economic power, was it declared that a husband could not divorce his wife against her will. Then, as now, a husband refusing to grant a divorce or disappearing or dying without witness, left his wife forever forbidden under Jewish law to remarry.[6]

Further, in their own households, women had to eat in the kitchen when there were male guests. Such isolation, therefore, closed off a significant portion of worldly experience from most women's reach, at least until modern times.[7] A shtetl saying summed up this attitude: "Many daughters, many troubles; many sons, many honors."[8]

Nevertheless, by the end of the eighteenth century, Jews of the Germanic lands had heard the call of the Enlightenment, the liberal ideological movement that introduced the concepts of equality, natural law, and democracy into modern political thought. The Enlightenment promised equality if only Jews shed their traditional ways. Thus, many Jews attempted to purge themselves of their ghetto mentality and to prove themselves worthy of citizenship. Many accepted as their own the values and standards of modern German culture and began to evaluate their Jewish tradition by those new criteria—classical liberalism and enlightenment—of Western culture.[9]

As German Jews assimilated Western ideals and culture, they also adopted Western attitudes toward women. Jewish women grasped modernization more rapidly than their male counterparts. Those from well-to-do families benefited from the Enlightenment by learning "the social graces that enabled them to move in a society not limited to Jews."[10]

Therefore, Jewish women rebelled against their status in traditional Judaism. Western society offered the bourgeois Jewish woman a social and intellectual status denied her within the confines of the traditional Jewish community.

Keeping the loyalty of the modern Jewish woman, then, became worrisome to Jewish leadership. An 1846 rabbinical synod did not publicly discuss the status of women, although it accepted the need to ratify proposals for reforming

Judaism brought to it. Moreover, Reform (liberal) congregations in Berlin on their own had taken the lead already in introducing changes proposed at the synod. Those changes essentially introduced religious equality for female laity.[11]

The first Jewish women to escape from the traditional Jewish definition of what a woman should be and do, therefore, were the Jewish women of Western Europe, who began to arrive in the United States in large numbers beginning in the 1840s. The Jews who immigrated to the United States in the nineteenth century sought to modify themselves in accordance with the tasteful and refined standards of the American Protestant middle class. Besides helping to build the American Jewish community, the Jews became models of the successful American Jewish woman for the Eastern European immigrants who followed them to the American shores as the nineteenth century drew to a close.[12]

Jewish immigrants arrived not as prosperous merchants; rather, they possessed little money, started as peddlers, carried merchandise to customers in the countryside, and after acquiring sufficient capital, purchased horses and wagons to carry on their enterprises. Later the successful ones began shops and became settled merchants, or "store princes," as they were popularly known.[13]

From the beginning, American Jews sought to demonstrate that they were 100 percent Americans. They wanted to integrate into the American society as well as maintain loyalty to their religious traditions, demonstrating that Jews could be good Americans, and Americans could be good Jews. Judaism in America accepted the aesthetic standards and cultural patterns of Protestantism. Immigrant Jews delighted in the American climate of equality and sought to be as much like their neighbors as possible.[14] American Jews' desire to conform, coupled with the overwhelming pull of the environment, led them to adapt themselves completely to the American social pattern in dress, language, demeanor, and even the names they bore.

One of the Jewish women adapting to American culture was Rosa Fassel Sonneschein, born in Hungary on March 12, 1847.[15] She rejected the first two men her father wanted her to marry but then was forced to accept the third, since she was almost seventeen. At age seventeen, she married Rabbi Solomon Hirsch Sonneschein. After marrying, they moved to Prague, then to America in the early 1870s. She bore him four children, the youngest in St. Louis, where the rabbi assumed a pulpit.[16]

In 1878, a group of fifteen Jewish women in town formed a club promoting culture and general knowledge, the Pioneers. Rosa belonged; no men could join.[17] She began her writing career with a history of the group.

The couple was incompatible. Indeed, the marriage proved to be a disaster.[18] The rabbi drank to excess and abused his wife. Moreover, when he was in a state of drunkenness, he beat their children. She left him in September 1891, after the children were grown.[19] She received no alimony. Their divorce became final in January 1893, when she was forty-six. He remarried; she did not.[20] He moved to Des Moines, Iowa, and assumed another pulpit.[21]

Left alone, Rosa Sonneschein moved to Chicago and started a magazine, *The*

American Jewess. While there are no financial records available, it appears this was a solo effort; Sonneschein did not receive economic assistance from anyone.[22] The magazine was able to attract luxury advertisers, who created magnificent full-page ads for her periodical. She was not the first to start a magazine for Jewish women, although it was the first English-language Jewish women's publication that was independent of any organizational or religious ties. The first publication for Jewish women, *Die Deborah,* in German, had been founded in 1855 by Rabbi Isaac Mayer Wise in Cincinnati.[23]

Subtitled "The Only Publication in the World Devoted to the Interests of Jewish Women," *The American Jewess* appeared in April 1895, published by the Rosa Sonneschein Company, winning words of praise from the *Reform Advocate,* the *Milwaukee Journal,* the *Chicago Staats-Zeitung,* and the *Chicago Times-Herald.* The magazine contained material about social, religious, and literary subjects. An attractive publication, it included beautiful portraits, woodcuts, and engravings.

Rosa Sonneschein's publication came about when men of the Jewish community had left their peddler roots and were solidly upper-middle-class. They included wealthy financiers, bankers, and department store owners, bonded to each other by means of financial, social, and marital ties. In fact, these Jews became visibly successful, with more than 25 percent of Jewish firms being capitalized over one hundred thousand dollars, and sixty of them in New York City became millionaires.[24] In practice, group members sought to copy the culture as well as lifestyle of their Protestant peers.[25] Hired household help, slackened religious observance, and use of laborsaving technological innovations gave women the time necessary for personal philanthropy in the late nineteenth century.

The American Jewess came out of that philanthropic empire; the publication's founder attended the Columbian Exposition held in Chicago in 1893, the year that saw the establishment of the National Council of Jewish Women (NCJW). Wrote the editor, the NCJW is "the beacon of light for the Jewesses of America."[26] The NCJW was but one of many new voluntary associations, involving women to "do good" for others.[27] It became a Jewish women's organization that addressed human needs. For instance, NCJW projects included organizing schools for slum children and vocational and industrial classes, managing model tenements and offering free baths to slum dwellers, starting free libraries, running employment bureaus, and providing summer outings for children. In addition, they met and cared for incoming single girls and were the first group to serve at Ellis Island in 1904, to assist immigrant girls and protect them from white slavery. The organization sought to deal with social welfare problems in the Jewish and general communities. Thus, German Jewish women joined their Gentile sisters in the movement to reform American society.

In establishing the magazine in April 1895, Sonneschein wrote positively of the organization and urged women to join. She reviewed the work of the NCJW,

even offered them columns in the magazine (but the group never took her up on it), and wanted to make the magazine "the official organ of the Council."[28]
The theme of sisterhood was stated in the opening editorial:

> We invite all to follow us to the goals of universal sisterhood. We need diligent workers and warm friends. . . . Every Jewess in America ought to assist us as best she can, either with word or pen . . . to join us to build up a journal worthy of American Judaism.[29]

The magazine, both political and literary, contained poems, historical sketches, and short stories, as well as articles on fashion, music, art, and the care of children. Nearly all articles were written by women.[30]

The first issue of April 1895 was fifty-five pages long with ten pages of advertising. Like other women's magazines of the period, *The American Jewess* was divided into departments on science and medicine, juvenile entertainment, music and the arts, and fashion. The ads featured articles for women: corsets, malt extract, jewelry, footwear, cosmetics, wines, restaurants—and interestingly, investment securities and banks in Chicago and St. Louis. These last ads reflected the philosophy of the editor.

The American Jewess addressed issues for the "New Woman" through the use of role models. The inaugural issue featured Hannah G(reenbaum) Solomon, founder and president of the NCJW. The second issue described "Successful Business Women," Zerlina and Laura Rosenfield, owners of the largest stenographic and typewriting service in the country. The second issue offered a biographical sketch and photo of Rebekah Kohut, president of the New York section of the NCJW, who inspired women to achieve greater things. She was the widow of Rabbi Alexander Kohut.[31]

The editor sang the praises of woman's rights leader Susan B. Anthony in several issues and lauded the accomplishments of Kate Chopin in a profile accompanying the writer's short story.[32] A message of the role models was simple and sobering: a woman should use her time to work for humanity, yet she should not neglect the home. Such a life could be lived with servants, who were often poor Eastern European girls arriving by the thousands. Jewish matrons of the earlier German wave of immigration thought they could save the girls from white slavery.[33] Indeed, *The American Jewess* assisted readers in becoming experts in "domestic science" by running brief articles containing household tips, information on how to treat servants, and material about how to run a house.[34]

The American Jewess produced countless household tips in a department titled "The Woman Who Talks." Thus, "Dress in the Kitchen" called for neat, becoming, appropriate dress, a cap and gloves for sweeping and dusting. "Get gloves two–three sizes too large to slip on easily." No slippers, for they offered little support, but leather or cloth shoes were preferable.[35] Another set of tips gave advice on how to take out tar, remove fruit stains from table linen, clean unvarnished furniture, get rid of sewing machine oil, clean tan shoes.[36] Advice in a different issue told readers how to clean walls, buy meat for soup, use salt water for gargle, treat silk and lace in the wash, eat horseradish for coughs after la grippe, clean sponges, treat bilious dyspepsia with stewed fruit and milk puddings.[37] In yet another, guidance concerned complexion paste for the face and costumes lined with fiber chamois.[38]

The American Jewess also addressed readers to remain feminine but to take on male virtues of courage, persistence, reliance, and resoluteness. "Girls have it in their power to-day to assert and achieve self-dependence."[39] Women should be able to ride bicycles and wear bloomers.[40] In fact, full-page ads for bicycle manufacturing companies ran throughout the publication, and the editor's youngest son, Monroe, wrote a lengthy article, complete with photographs, about how bicycles are made.[41]

Contributors included prominent writers, such as Kate Chopin, as well as various women whose names are bylined in the magazine but without further identity.

The American Jewess also advocated equality in religious observance. The editor reported a list of 102 congregations with more than twenty thousand names, but all memberships were in "Mr." only, never "Mr. and Mrs." Women could not be admitted to meetings. In fact, even if a widow owned a pew and paid her dues or taxes, she was not allowed to vote, the June 1895 issue reported.[42] The magazine promoted Jewish women's being able to attend synagogue and share equally ecclesiastically as well as socially, since they are the "active spirit in benevolent organizations" and the "light and life in every movement that elevates the Jewish world."[43] The Jewish woman should be proud of her position in America, proud of her status.

The magazine apparently prospered and after only three years of publication claimed 29,000 subscribers. A few months later, it boasted "almost 31,000."[44] The May 1899 issue, for example, was eighty pages long; seven pages of advertising promoted liqueurs, fancy chocolates, diamond rings, corsets, a Great Book series, tapestries, and health spas. Clearly, the audience was "uptown." The American Tapestry Decorative Company on Fifth Avenue in New York told readers, "If you intend Decorating, . . . call and see what we are doing and for whom."[45] The ads reflected the interests of an upper-middle or upper class, those sincerely trying to help the poor, working-class East Europeans who crowded into Lower East Side tenements, a kind of noblesse oblige toward the oppressed.

A children's story department, hints on how to write a business letter, a description of the latest styles in kitchen fashion, fashions from Paris and London, and book reviews also ran in the magazine.

Of special significance was the journal's important contribution to both Jewish and Zionist affairs. Serious European thinkers like Theodor Herzl and Max Nordau found their first American audiences in the pages of her journal.[46] Herzl was a Hungarian Jew who founded modern political Zionism, first expressed in *The Jewish State* in 1896. He obtained his doctorate in law from the University of Vienna, then wrote numerous plays and works of fiction, served as Paris correspondent for the *Neue Freie Presse* from 1891 to 1895, and organized the first World Zionist Congress in Switzerland in August 1897. Nordau, a philosopher, writer, orator, and physician, cofounded with Herzl the World Zionist Organization.

By 1898, a strong Zionist presence had emerged in America, and Rosa Sonneschein and her journal were in the midst of the political and cultural events of the time. Articles on persecutions in Eastern Europe, growing anti-Semitism in France, the woman suffrage movement, political muckrakers, and reformers of the Progressive Era ran in the magazine.[47] Pieces on Herzl and on the show trial of French captain Alfred Dreyfus appeared.[48]

The year 1898 also saw America's entrance into the war with Spain, and the magazine made a special appeal: the magazine sought a permanent fund "for the immediate alleviation . . . not alone to our country, but also to other countries" since this was the "age of philanthropy."[49] The magazine caught the war spirit, as could be seen in the May 1898 issue, with a poem, "To the Dead of the Battleship Maine." The November 1898 issue carried a proud piece, "Jews in the Army."[50]

Yet, *The American Jewess* lasted only from April 1895 through August 1899. It died for financial reasons as advertising declined, and its editor increasingly had less to do with the publication. The December 1898 issue noted that on November 10 Rosa Sonneschein had returned to Chicago. "New management," that is, other Jewish women, had taken over the magazine as of July–August 1898.[51]

Another, more tragic explanation for ending her magazine may have been that Rosa Sonneschein was losing her hearing; a few years after the demise of her magazine, she was completely deaf. She became reclusive after 1900 and died thirty-two years later, March 5, 1932.[52]

The American Jewess, far more than merely a woman's magazine, maintained a balance of items appealing to the new Jewish women in America. Rosa Sonneschein must be remembered, too, as a woman who, though shaped by outmoded practices and attitudes, perceived herself in a new, American light. While she was a product of the traditions of Jewish historical experience, she became a product of Americanization, too.

Notes

1. No business records of the magazine are extant. Moreover, no other material relating to Rosa Sonneschein or the magazine—aside from the publication itself—seems to exist. As a result, she has received little attention from researchers about the role of women in American Jewish life. For example, see Anita Lebeson, *Recall to Life: the Jewish Woman in America* (South Brunswick, N.J.: Thomas Yoseloff, 1970).

2. No personal or professional papers of Rosa Sonneschein exist. A humorous history she wrote is on file in St. Louis, and an interview with her grandson is on file in Cincinnati at the American Jewish Archives, from which the sociologist Jack Nusan Porter

took the material for his article, cited in note 16. Thus, with these sole exceptions, nothing seems to remain except for her magazine, her legacy.

3. The title of their new organizations bore the word "women," not "ladies," and "club" or "council," not "society."

4. Deborah Grand Golomb, "The 1893 Congress of Jewish Women: Evolution or Revolution in American Jewish Women's History?" *American Jewish History* 70, September 1980, pp. 52–67; Charlotte Baum, Paula Hyman, and Sonya Michel, *The Jewish Woman in America* (New York: New American Library, 1976), pp. 46–52.

5. Nancy B. Sinkoff, "Education for 'Proper' Jewish Womanhood: A Case Study in Domesticity and Vocational Training, 1897–1926," *American Jewish History* 77, June 1988, pp. 572–599; Joan Kelly, *Women, History, and Theory* (Chicago: University of Chicago Press, 1984), p. 130.

6. Leo Trepp, *A History of the Jewish Experience* (New York: Behrman House, 1973), pp. 227–231.

7. Robert M. Seltzer, *Jewish People, Jewish Thought* (New York: Macmillan, 1980).

8. See, for example, Mark Zborowski and Elizabeth Herzog, *Life Is with People: The Jewish Little-Town of Eastern Europe* (New York: International Universities Press, 1952). See Chapter 4, "The Woman's Share," pp. 124–141.

9. Trepp, *A History of the Jewish Experience,* pp. 291–298.

10. Jacob Katz, *Tradition and Crisis: Jewish Society at the End of the Middle Ages* (New York: Schocken, 1971), p. 42.

11. Jacob J. Petuchowski, *Prayerbook Reform in Europe* (New York: World Union for Progressive Judaism, 1968), pp. 31–84.

12. Henry L. Feingold, *Zion in America, The Jewish Experience from Colonial Times to the Present,* rev. ed. (New York: Twayne, 1981), pp. 68–81, 96–128.

13. Isaac M. Wise, *Reminiscences* (Cincinnati: Leo Wise, 1901), p. 38; see also Israel Knox, *Rabbi in America: The Story of Isaac M. Wise,* ed. Oscar Handlin (Boston: Little, Brown, 1957). A few of these princes founded retail dynasties: the Strauses of Macy's, the Gimbels, the Bloomingdales, the Bergdorfs, and so on; most, however, remained middle-class.

14. Feingold, *Zion in America,* pp. 68–81.

15. The author has been unable to ascertain any information about her early years, her education, her feelings about compulsory marriage traditions, and the like.

16. Monroe, the youngest, committed suicide in 1923 or 1924. Solomon Sonneschein was a Reform rabbi at Temple Israel in the center of German-speaking America and a stronghold of Reform Judaism (Max Darrish, *Writings on the St. Louis Jewish Community* [St. Louis, Mo.: Jewish Genealogy Society of St. Louis, 1984]; Sherryl Lang, *Fulfilling the American Dream: Jewish Life in St. Louis* [St. Louis: Missouri Historical Society, 1986]).

17. She was assigned to write a history of the club, and she chose a humorous format. The association published it privately.

18. Jack Nusan Porter, "Rosa Sonneschein and *The American Jewess:* New Historical Information of an Early American Zionist and Jewish Feminist," *American Jewish Archives* 32, November 1980, p. 20.

19. Ibid.

20. She met his second wife and advised her how to handle her husband.

21. Solomon H. Sonneschein was born in Hungary in 1839 and earned a Ph.D. in 1864. He served as rabbi in New York, St. Louis, and Des Moines. Also, he contributed

to many German and English periodicals; he wrote sermons, lectures, papers, book reviews, and instruction manuals. He died in 1908.

22. The author is unable to determine why she chose a magazine for expressing herself and for needed income. She mentioned to her grandson that she had been one of the first shareholders of U.S. Steel Corporation, and he had the impression that before World War I she had bought annuity. At the end of her life, she had enough only to maintain herself in a shabby room in an old hotel in St. Louis, according to Loth (Porter, "Rosa Sonneschein and *The American Jewess*," p. 25).

23. Joseph Gutmann, "Watchman on an American Rhine: New Light on Isaac M. Wise," *American Jewish Archives* 10.2, October 1958, pp. 135–144 (article on *Die Deborah*).

24. Moses Rischin, *The Promised City: New York's Jews, 1870–1914* (Cambridge: Harvard University Press, 1977), p. 52.

25. For instance, see Barry Supple, "A Business Elite: German-Jewish Financiers in Nineteenth Century New York," *Business History Review* 31, Summer 1957, pp. 143–178.

26. "Editor's Desk," April 1895, p. 49.

27. Faith Rogow, *Gone to Another Meeting: The National Council of Jewish Women, 1893–1993* (Tuscaloosa: University of Alabama Press, 1993); Ellen Sue Elwell, "The Founding and Early Programs of the National Council of Jewish Women: Study and Practice as Jewish Women's Religious Experience" (diss., Indiana University, 1982).

28. "Report of the Convention: Council of Jewish Women," December 1896, pp. 125–130.

29. April 1895, p. 20.

30. The author has been unable to determine how the editor obtained pieces for her magazine; a guess is she solicited them.

31. May 1895, pp. 82–83; see also "Editor's Desk," pp. 101–102 in the same issue.

32. April 1895, pp. 47–51.

33. Articles on white slavery ran in several issues; see, for example, July 1896, p. 554.

34. "The Woman Who Talks," April 1895, pp. 38–41; "Household Hints," September 1895, p. 311.

35. "The Woman Who Talks," May 1895, pp. 90–92.

36. "Household Hints," June 1895, p. 141.

37. "Household Hints," September 1895, p. 311.

38. "Ehe [The] Woman Who Talks," March 1897, pp. 286–289.

39. "Woman's Part in the Drama of Life," pp. 63–66.

40. Sophie Wolff, "The Woman and the Wheel," August 1895, p. 252; Fanny Rice, "Cycling as an Exercise for Women," April 1897, pp. 7–10.

41. "How Bicycles Are Made," June 1896, pp. 42–46.

42. "Editor's Desk," June 1895, pp. 153–154.

43. "The Jewess at Home and Abroad," June 1895, pp. 114–115.

44. "A Word to Advertisers," April 1898, p. 23; "There Is No Other like It," June 1898, p. 161.

45. April 1898, inside cover.

46. Theodor Herzl, "Anti-Semitism and Zionism," April 1897, pp. 156–157; Max Nordau, "On the General Situation of the Jews," October 1897, pp. 21–28; Nordau,

"The Present Situation of the Jews," August 1899, pp. 5–9; "Dr. Herzl's Address at the Zionist Congress," August 1899, p. 13.

47. "The Pope and Madame Dreyfus," January 1898, pp. 156–157; "Anti-Semitism in France," April 1898, pp. 14–15; "A Word to Our Readers," April 1898, pp. 22–23; "Convention of Zionist [sic]," May 1898, p. 64.

48. A. H. Fromenson, "The Dreyfus Mystery," July–August 1898, p. 3; Jeannette Feingold, "Can We All Be Zionists?" May 1899, pp. 29–30; "Zionism at the Council," May 1899, p. 65; "The Dreyfus Case, as Illustrative of French Justice," August 1899, p. 26 (from *The American Lawyer*).

49. Jennie Wertheimer, "Destruction Fund Association," June 1898, p. 130.

50. "Jews in the Army," November 1898, pp. 38–39.

51. P. 64.

52. Porter, "Rosa Sonneschein and *The American Jewess*," attributed to Loth.

Information Sources

BIBLIOGRAPHY:

Porter, Jack Nusan. "Rosa Sonneschein and *The American Jewess:* New Historical Information of an Early American Zionist and Jewish Feminist." *American Jewish Archives* 32.2, November 1980, p. 20.

Rogow, Faith. *Gone to Another Meeting: The National Council of Jewish Women, 1893–1993.* Tuscaloosa: University of Alabama Press, 1993.

INDEX SOURCES: None.

LOCATION SOURCES: American Jewish Archives, Cincinnati; Cincinnati Public Library; St. Louis Public Library; Jewish Theological Seminary (Microfilm); and other libraries.

Publication History

PERIODICAL TITLE AND TITLE CHANGES: *The American Jewess.*

VOLUME AND ISSUE DATA: Vols. 1–4 (April 1895–August 1899). Monthly (April 1895–May 1899); quarterly (May 1899–August 1899).

PUBLISHER AND PLACE OF PUBLICATION: Rosa Sonneschein (1895–1899). Chicago (1895–1896); New York (1896–1899).

EDITORS: Rosa Sonneschein (1895–1899).

CIRCULATION: 31,000 (unverified).

Barbara Straus Reed

THE ANTI-SUFFRAGIST

The New York State Association Opposed to Woman Suffrage started *The Anti-Suffragist* (quarterly) in July 1908. Continuing through April 1912, the magazine was superseded by *The Woman's Protest* the publication of the newly formed national antisuffrage association.

Antisuffrage organizations of the early twentieth century tended to be "overwhelmingly" female, and their leaders tended to be the socially prominent of the community.[1] The New York State Association Opposed to Woman Suffrage was no exception. It was an organization of women, with the wealthy and prominent as its leaders. The New York group was prominent among state groups opposed to woman suffrage. Its magazine was edited by Mrs. William Winslow Crannell, chairman of the Executive Committee of the New York State Association Opposed to Woman Suffrage. Crannell published the magazine in Albany, where she resided; she had organized the Albany Association Against Woman Suffrage in 1892. She had gained national recognition by addressing both the Republican and Democratic national conventions in 1896, neither of which added a plank endorsing woman suffrage to its platform.[2]

The antisuffrage movement considered itself much more than a reaction to the woman suffrage movement, which was to peak in 1920 with the Nineteenth Amendment, which enfranchised women nationally. Therefore, answering the question, What is an antisuffragist? in a broader framework was central to antisuffrage discourse. "Those who call themselves 'antis' think there is much more included in the term than merely saying no," Estelle R. McVickar, a regular contributor, wrote in a small volume she devoted to answering that question,[3] combining lofty theological and political perspectives.

An anti-suffragist is one who believes that the feminine principle is equally as important as the masculine in the plan of the universe. . . . [W]oman, in return for her services as child-bearer and child-trainer, and in consideration of the disabilities incident thereto, has been allowed immunity from further service; her rights as a citizen being taken care of for her by her male representatives.[4]

Sentiment opposing woman suffrage had a strong cultural foothold in tradition. Woman's proper sphere was the domestic realm of the home. Contravening tradition, the vote would place women squarely in the *public* sphere of politics, properly the male arena. But by the early twentieth century, antis were aware that the cultural climate was shifting, seemingly in the direction of granting woman suffrage. The magazine clarified the antisuffrage stance and crafted definitions of antis in its own terms, often against a public depiction of antis as apathetic, "downtrodden" creatures.[5] Much as the female suffragists were compelled to distinguish themselves from evil women, female antis had to distinguish themselves from "lazy, stay-at-home folk." *The Anti-Suffragist* noted, "[A] lazy Anti-Suffragist is a contradiction in terms. The woman who simply 'doesn't want to vote' doesn't organize either. She stays at home now, and she would continue to take no interest at all in politics, no matter how many votes you gave her."[6]

Definitions usually began with an appeal to the self-explanatory nature of cultural assumptions, often with a dig at suffragists for being so dense on the issue. "What do anti-suffragists stand for?" was often answered in this manner.

[E]ach time the simple answer that our organization stands for women's doing their work in the world *outside* of the political arena, as Suffragists stand for their doing it *within* that arena seems too simple for our Suffragist friend to understand. . . . It seems as though the Suffragists were constitutionally unable to take in . . . that the best way to get results is to stick to the purpose for which you organize—in our case the opposition of the spread of Woman Suffrage . . . which "stands for" the freedom of all women from political affiliations, that exceptional women may the better accomplish those ends.[7]

The Anti-Suffragist charted this sentiment on the local level as well. For instance, at the Albany association's annual meeting, a resolution was passed "restating the well-known fact that though organized to oppose the thrusting of the burden of politics upon all women, our Association . . . stands for the broadest and best civic, intellectual and industrial development of women."[8]

With publications such as *The Anti-Suffragist,* antis voiced their arguments and broadcast their philosophies, which ran from the conservative theological stance that it was unnatural for women to engage in work obviously meant for men, to the more progressive political stance that women would gain the vote when the majority wanted it; but that for now, pro-suffrage sentiment was in such a minority that enfranchising women would damage society. The eight-page magazine proclaimed:

> The aim of this paper is to put before its readers, in concise form, the various arguments against the ballot for women; to disseminate a knowledge of such facts in the case as can be substantiated; to make public such ideas as may seem to the editor to be of weight or worthy of consideration; in short, to be the mouthpiece of a no longer silent majority; and we trust that we are not in error in thinking that interest in this question is widespread enough to make the publication of such a paper desirable.[9]

This first issue carried a reassuring article that calculated registered suffrage supporters as "less than two percent" of the state's population.[10] *The Anti-Suffragist* often bolstered its readers with this type of information designed to show them that they were in the majority. For example, on the local level:

> The Annual Meeting last year, having overflowed the limits of even a commodious private house, it was found best to meet this year in the Albany Historical Society building, on the 20th of January. . . . Nearly 250 people were present at the meeting."[11]

The Anti-Suffragist enthusiastically reported woman suffrage defeats state by state, clucking lament when a state went for suffrage. "Our sympathy goes out to those women, and men too, of the state of Washington, who for lack of active and organized resistance allowed their state to become 'feminized.' "[12] Framing woman suffrage as an immediate legislative issue, the pages were often filled with legislative information, particularly presentations made by antisuffragists, at the local, state, and national levels of government.

For example, the presidents of the Massachusetts, New York, Illinois, Pennsylvania, and Rhode Island associations opposed to woman suffrage sent Congress "their earnest protest against the proposed amendment of the Constitution of the United States which would confer full suffrage upon all the women in this country."[13] They penned their protest for the good of the social order, driving home their argument that their views represented those of the majority of women. They stated they had

> the welfare of the State and the highest possible development for woman herself very much at heart; and a careful study of this question . . . from the point of view of governmental expediency, has convinced us that the State would be weakened by attempting to equalize and identify the functions of the sexes. . . . And finally we believe that woman . . . would, with the ballot in her hand, become but another spoke in the wheel of political machinery and lose in a measure the power which is now hers.[14]

The Anti-Suffragist supported such political theory by citing what women were doing with the vote where they had been granted suffrage. Suffrage states were shown to be no better, and sometimes worse, than the states in which women were not enfranchised. The magazine ran a partial account from the *Ladies' Home Journal* that made disparaging observations on the Western suffrage states with regard to child labor and literacy.[15] *The Anti-Suffragist* editors commented, "This certainly bears out our conviction that no real advance in civilization has followed the 'reform against nature.' "[16]

One of the most dramatic examples of this type of evidence was the coverage of the "wet" vote in Colorado. Although the outlawing of alcohol was a given of the woman vote, *The Anti-Suffragist* reported that this was not being borne out. The story from Denver read, "The 'Wets' and the 'Drys' divided the state almost equally at yesterday's municipal elections. The woman vote was large, and the 'Wet' victory is ascribed to the fact that an unusually large percentage of the women voted against prohibition."[17]

Western states were consciously held up as wrongheaded models. A year before the Colorado vote on alcohol, *The Anti-Suffragist* had run an interesting reprint from the *Fort Collins* (Colorado) *Express*. Contrary to *The Anti-Suffragist*'s stance that voting was a privilege, the article took the view that voting was a right. Even within this liberal framework, the magazine's perspective was clear: one had only to look at the results to reconsider woman suffrage.

> While every one [sic] must concede that women have as much right to vote as do men, yet no one has ever pointed out where woman suffrage

had any influence for good. . . . The women of Colorado are on trial in regard to the suffrage movement. Their failure to benefit Colorado by their suffrage is doing more to retard woman suffrage in other States and nations than anything else."[18]

To lend credence to the antisuffrage platform, *The Anti-Suffragist* quoted prominent people, from editors to heads of state. News accounts were reprinted, as well as editorial opinions. For instance, the *Hartford* (Connecticut) *Courant* rallied "tradition" against the suffrage movement.

The traditions of the paper are all against the revolutionary project, and so are the convictions of those now in charge. . . . There has never been in "The Courant" any purpose to treat woman otherwise than with respect, but if the paper has exhibited "contempt" for "the cause" [woman suffrage], it at least cannot be accused of hypocrisy.[19]

An article with a London dateline read:

Her majesty let it be known through Princess Louise, who, at the opening of the nurses' congress, said:
"Queen Alexandra has the fullest sympathy in your work. She feels it is work women can do. Some women nowadays try to be like men, but nursing is work men cannot do."[20]

A missive from President Theodore Roosevelt read by the Reverend Lyman Abbott at a meeting of the National League for the Civic Education of Women ran on the front of the second issue. Roosevelt's letter stated, "I do not think that giving the women suffrage will bring any marked improvement in the condition of women."[21]

The Anti-Suffragist used its voice to cast aspersions on the woman suffrage movement. In a response to the president's letter, the magazine reported that Carrie Chapman Catt, president of the International Suffrage League, "compared Mr. Roosevelt to a tree-toad that takes on the color of the tree on which it finds itself."[22]

Additionally, woman suffrage was often equated with socialism. "California Socialists forced suffrage upon the women of that State."[23] The president of the Illinois association cited woman suffrage as but the first step of an economically based socialist overthrow.[24]

Another strategy employed by antisuffragists was undermining the logic of well-publicized woman suffrage arguments. One prominent argument had been resurrected from colonial days—that of taxation without representation, with the modern angle stating that women were taxed but, because they did not vote, were not represented. *The Anti-Suffragist* published articles to invalidate the woman-centered interpretation of this argument.

[W]hen men and women are jointly members of the same community: when taxes are laid not upon women for the benefit of men or *vice versa:* when, finally, they are imposed by representatives drawn from the community and not by outsiders, the dictum is absolutely and utterly irrelevant."[25]

Another contradiction cited to the parallel of the vote with representation was, "A man may own taxable property in a dozen different States and yet can vote in only one."[26]

Theological arguments were used against women's gaining the vote, and religious figures were quoted, from local ministers to the pope.

Father Wynne, editor of The Messenger, interprets the Pope's statement as meaning that "the Catholic church has always stood strongly for the domestic position of womanhood; it has looked with disfavor on any movement likely to interfere with their functions as wives and mothers—with their position in the home."[27]

Editor Crannell, who had founded and guided the publication through its four-year existence, was, by 1912, traveling more. She had moved from Albany and was residing in her native Pittsburgh, Pennsylvania. "The life of The Anti-Suffragist was threatened by the continued absence from the State of the senior editor."[28]

The Anti-Suffragist died when Crannell left the operation in the hands of junior editors. A magazine of predominantly editorial commentary and reprints, *The Anti-Suffragist* had never carried advertising. It was, however, able to provide a newly formed national magazine with an established readership eager for information on antisuffrage activity and news of organizations across the nation. The National Association Opposed to Woman Suffrage, which had been formed in November, "proposed publishing a monthly anti-suffrage organ to be known as The Woman's Protest, and . . . we realized that this monthly would cover all our ground, and more."[29] *The Anti-Suffragist* was discontinued after its April 1912 number;[30] the new publishers allowed subscribers of *The Anti-Suffragist* to fill out the year with *The Woman's Protest.*[31]

Notes

1. Susan E. Marshall, "In Defense of Separate Spheres: Class and Status Politics in the Antisuffrage Movement," *Social Forces* 65.2, December 1986, p. 331.

2. "Mrs. Crannell's Burial/Set for Wednesday in Albany—/She Fought Suffrage," *New York Times,* November 2, 1936, p. 21.

3. Estelle R. McVickar, *What Is an Anti-Suffragist?* (Mount Vernon, N.Y., n.d.), p. [3].

4. Ibid, pp. 6, 9.

5. McVickar, *What Is an Anti-Suffragist?,* p. [3].

6. Margaret Doane Gardiner, "What We Stand For," June 1911, pp. 7, 8.

7. Ibid.

8. "The Annual Meeting," March 1910, p. 3.

9. July 1908, p. 1.

10. "New York State Woman Suffrage Statistics as Published in Their Annual Report of 1907," July 1908, p. 8.

11. "The Annual Meeting," March 1910, p. 3.

12. "Suffrage in Washington," December 1910, p. 4.

13. Mrs. G. Howland Shaw, Mrs. Francis M. Scott, Mrs. Caroline F. Corbin, Mrs. J. Gardner, and Mrs. Rowland G. Hazard, "The following *Protest* was sent April, 1910: —*To the Honorable Members of Senate and House in Congress now assembled,*" June 1910, p. 7.

14. Ibid.

15. Richard Barry, quoted in "What Women Have Actually Done Where They Vote," December 1910, p. 6.

16. "What Women Have Actually Done Where They Vote," p. 7.

17. June 1911, p. 5.

18. "Women Vote 'Wet', [*reprinted from the Fort Collins Express, May 17.*]," June 1910, p. 8.

19. "Opposed to Woman Suffrage," January 1912, p. 7.

20. "The Queen Opposed," June 1909, p. 5.

21. Theodore Roosevelt, "President Roosevelt's Letter," December 1908, p. 1.

22. "Mrs. Catt's Comment," December 1908, p. 1.

23. "Socialists' Victories," editorial, January 1912, p. 4.

24. President, Illinois Association Opposed to the Extension of Suffrage to Women, "Socialism and Woman Suffrage," letter to the editor, July 1908, p. 8.

25. Frederick Dwight, "Taxation and Suffrage," September 1909, pp. 1, 2.

26. Ibid, p. 1.

27. *New York Times* cable, "Pope Is against Women in Politics. Only Eccentrics Would Wish to Legislate, He Tells Women," June 1909, p. 4.

28. "The Last Issue of the Anti-Suffragist," editorial, April 1912, p. 4.

29. Ibid.

30. "Anti-Suffrage Papers Merge," *The Woman's Protest,* May 1912, p. 4.

31. Josephine Dodge, "The Woman's Protest," April 1912, pp. 5, 6.

Information Sources

BIBLIOGRAPHY:

"Anti-Suffrage Papers Merge." *The Woman's Protest* 1.1, May 1912, p. 4.

Camhi, Jane Jerome. *Women against Women: American Anti-Suffragism, 1880–1920.* New York: Carlson, 1994.

McVickar, Estelle R. *What Is an Anti-Suffragist?* Mount Vernon, N.Y., n.d. (some sources list this book's publication date as 1910.)

"Mrs. Crannell's Burial/Set for Wednesday in Albany—/She Fought Suffrage." *New York Times,* November 2, 1936, p. 21.

INDEX SOURCES: None.

LOCATION SOURCES: Library of Congress and other libraries.

Publication History

PERIODICAL TITLE AND TITLE CHANGES: *The Anti-Suffragist* (1908–1912). (Superseded by *The Woman's Protest.*)

VOLUME AND ISSUE DATA: Vols. 1–4. (March 1908–April 1912). Quarterly. (Some irregularities in issuance: vol. 1.1, March 1908; vol. 1.2, December 1908; vol. 2.1, September 1909; vol. 3.1, September 1910; vol. 3.5, September 1911; vol. 4.1, January 1912.)

PUBLISHER AND PLACE OF PUBLICATION: New York State Association Opposed to Woman Suffrage (1908–1912). Albany, New York.

EDITOR: Mrs. William Winslow Crannell (1908–1912).

CIRCULATION: Unknown.

Therese L. Lueck

—————————
——— B ———

THE BIRTH CONTROL REVIEW

In an October 1917 *Metropolitan Magazine* column, Theodore Roosevelt alerted the nation to a developing crisis: Harvard and Yale alumni were having children in alarmingly small numbers. With the birthrate of their progeny averaging 2.3 children per family, Roosevelt argued there was a dangerously low future supply of sons for the Ivy League. In Roosevelt's opinion, access to contraception was contributing to the dying out of America's best stock.[1]

The December issue of *Metropolitan Magazine* provided space for a counterargument.[2] Answering the former president with a defense of birth control was a thirty-eight-year-old mother of three who garnered national attention when she and her sister were arrested in that same year for distributing contraception information to women at a New York City clinic.

Margaret Sanger, whose slight build belied her unshakable resolve, had solidified her stature as the leader of the birth control movement in the United States earlier in 1917, when she published the first issue of *The Birth Control Review.*

Roosevelt's complaint of birth control's effectiveness stood in stark contrast to what Sanger knew as the reality of women's lives in the opening decades of the twentieth century, particularly the lives of immigrants and the poor. Trained as a nurse, Sanger witnessed that many women were ruining their health and dying because they lacked information about contraception.[3] They died from childbirth, repeated miscarriages, failed abortions, and diseases they were too weak to fight because they were constantly pregnant. The techniques that dampened the birthrate of Ivy League families (assuming Roosevelt's statistics were correct) were a mystery to most families. Since the 1873 passage of the Comstock Law, which generally made sending "lewd and lascivious" material through the U.S. mail a crime (and specifically listed birth control information as lewd and lascivious), ''no information on contraception had been sent through the mails or by interstate commerce.''[4]

Sanger and her first husband were active in the socialist and anarchist movements. The well-known anarchist Emma Goldman, who had attended the Paris Neo-Malthusian Conference in 1900, had long discussions with Sanger about the emancipation of women. The connection between contraception and women's health and development seemed obvious, as did the societal ills that could result from families' having children they could not support.[5] The ideas of Thomas Malthus, an economist, warned that unchecked human reproduction would quickly outpace the food supply.

Sanger originally developed an interest in information about sex and reproduction by giving a series of talks to mothers and children in Hastings-on-Hudson, a New York suburb where she lived from 1905 to 1912.[6] Asked to substitute for a speaker at a labor meeting in New York City one night in 1912, she turned the lecture's subject to what she knew best: sex and reproduction. The talk's success led to Sanger's taking more speaking engagements and writing a regular column for the socialist newspaper, *The Call.* A planned article on venereal disease prompted the post office to threaten *The Call* with suppression under the Comstock Law; *The Call* ultimately did not run the article.[7]

In October 1913, Sanger traveled with her husband to France to pursue research on birth control methods. Months of searching libraries in the United States, including the Library of Congress, had revealed only one pamphlet on the topic—and that from 1832.[8] When she returned, she set out to publish a new monthly newspaper, *The Woman Rebel.** The first issue, mailed in March 1914, was partially confiscated by the post office in April.[9] She was charged under the Comstock Law, and rather than spending the summer preparing for her trial, she used the time to write *Family Limitation,* a pamphlet that described birth control methods in simple and explicit terms.[10] When Sanger's trial came up in October, she fled to England, leaving her husband and children behind.

As she continued her research on contraception there, she was introduced to Havelock Ellis, a British literary critic who became widely known for writing *Studies on the Psychology of Sex,* in which he defended sexual gratification.

> Ellis's ideas . . . engaged . . . such outspoken feminists of the era as Emma Goldman, Olive Schreiner, and Ellen Key . . . [who] looked to him as inspiration for a philosophy that argued for the recognition of a different voice, and for the accommodation of woman's special needs and values, in the making of social and political policy.[11]

Sanger returned to the United States in October 1915, the charges against her were dropped in February 1916, and she opened a birth control clinic in Brooklyn, the first in the United States, in October 1916. She was soon arrested for dispensing birth control information and treatment. She spent the next months preparing her defense and the first issue of *The Birth Control Review.* When convicted, Sanger chose thirty days in jail rather than agree to obey the Comstock Law or pay a fine.

The Birth Control Review made its debut in February 1917 while Sanger was in jail. Months before, she had met Frederick Blossom, a young socialist, while in Cleveland on a speaking engagement. An experienced fund-raiser, Blossom followed Sanger to New York to raise money and work on the *Review*. Edited by Sanger, Blossom, and Elizabeth Stuyvesant, the first issue declared its purpose in a full-page manifesto signed by all three. In part it said:

> Birth control is the most vital issue before the country to-day. . . . The time has come when those who would cast off the bondage of involuntary parenthood must have a voice, one that shall speak their protest and enforce their demands. . . . This Review comes into being, therefore, not as our creation, but as the herald of a new freedom. It comes into being to render articulate the aspiration of humanity toward conscious and voluntary motherhood.[12]

By the third issue, Sanger and Blossom had incompatible ideas about the tone and content of the *Review*. Sanger's version of the conflict is that she "wrote a pacifist editorial; he refused to run it and resigned."[13] The *Review's* survival was threatened when Blossom informed Sanger as the third issue came out that all the money for the year had been spent. Blossom departed with the *Review*'s files, and Sanger never did receive a full accounting of the publication's funds.

The financial blow was serious. Despite the tenuousness of the *Review,* at this time Sanger chose to affiliate with neither of the competing birth control organizations in New York but instead "tried to maintain her own leadership and autonomy by keeping the *Birth Control Review* afloat on income from its several thousand subscribers, newsstand sales, and generous individual benefactors."[14] Juliet Rublee, a Chicago heiress, helped Sanger establish herself among the wealthy and powerful in New York, Washington, and Chicago, even while paying the rent on the *Review*'s office and helping Sanger with spending money.[15] Rublee helped "incorporate the New York Women's Publishing Company as a parent venture for the magazine. She sold $10,000 worth of stock in shares of $10 each, though it was never likely to be a money-making proposition."[16]

Sanger, working with Walter Roberts, a journalist and close friend, managed to publish a fourth issue in June, but the fifth issue did not come out until December 1917. By 1918, Sanger had assembled a team to work on the *Review*. Eleven issues were published that year. Sanger wrote in her autobiography about the first issues:

> It was not a very good magazine then; it had few contributors and no editorial policy. Anyone—sculptor, spiritualist, cartoonist, poet, free lance—could express himself here; the pages were open to all. In some ways it was reminiscent of the old days of the *Woman Rebel,* when every-

body used to lend a hand—always with this vital difference, that we held strictly to education instead of agitation. I had learned a little editorial knowledge from my previous magazine efforts and now obtained a more professional touch from newspaper men and women who gradually came in, among them William E. Williams, formerly of the Kansas City *Star,* Walter A. Roberts, who later published the few issues of the *American Parade,* and Rob Parker, editor and make-up man. Among the associates were Jessie Ashley, Mary Knoblauch, and Agnes Smedley.[17]

From the beginning, the *Review* attracted several prestigious writers, Havelock Ellis chief among them. Sanger had personal contacts around the world and often enlisted them as contributors, including George Bernard Shaw. Serious examinations of doctrine were commonplace, including a lengthy discussion of Malthusian principles published in several installments.

During the first three years, the *Review* often addressed issues outside the strict realm of birth control. Articles on child labor abuses, the impending world food shortage, and woman suffrage shared space with the more expected fare of reports of activities of the local birth control league, news of international activity and potential changes in laws, and readers letters, usually outlining pathetic circumstances and begging for birth control information. For example, the June 1917 issue contained in its eight pages a two-page article by Havelock Ellis, an article on "Woman and War" by Sanger, an article by Walter Roberts on "Birth Control and the Revolution," and the full text of the June 6, 1917, decision by the New York State Supreme Court, which restrained the New York City commissioner of licenses from revoking a theater's license because it planned to show Sanger's movie, *Birth Control.* Other issues contained plays and poems, including a one-act play on the plight of Negro women in a theme issue on "Negroes."

Readers who bought the *Review* thinking they would get explicit information on contraception must have been disappointed. In February 1920 a statement first appeared that clarified the *Review's* purpose:

> The Birth Control Review cannot publish information as to contraceptives because it is unlawful, in this country, to give such information. One of the objects of this magazine is to show why such laws are obsolete, pernicious, and injurious to the individual, the community, and the race. These laws must be changed. Read *The Birth Control Review* and you will understand why.

In the same issue, Sanger exhorted female readers to join in a five-year birth strike to avert food shortages, a serious concern of the neo-Malthusians. An article in the next issue examined whether the suffrage movement had attained its goals.[18] The militant tone did not appear to please some of the directors on the magazine's board. A formal statement of editorial policy was issued in June

1919, "limiting the magazine's interests to 'Birth Control pure and simple. No other propaganda work of any kind.' "[19]

In November 1921, Sanger organized a conference at the Plaza Hotel in New York that launched the American Birth Control League (ABCL), with herself as president. The December 1921 issue of the *Review* stated the designation of the "Official Organ of the American Birth Control League." After the April 1922 issue, "Owned and Published by the New York Women's Publishing Company, Inc." was omitted. Credit to the American Birth Control League as publisher started in the August 1923 issue. Throughout the 1920s, Sanger had her share of struggles with the ABCL Board, in part due to her absences on long speaking tours and in part due to issues of editorial policy in the *Review*.

The *Review* settled into a more regular publication schedule and quieter rhetoric in the 1920s. The arguments for contraception were more often based on the work of scholars rather than the theories of radicals. The logic often depended on assumptions inherent in the field of eugenics, then studied as an academic subject at many universities. Underlying most eugenics arguments was an assumed benefit from selective breeding that is regarded as an anathema today when applied to humans. Edward Ross, a professor of sociology at the University of Wisconsin, wrote in the March 1920 issue of the *Review:*

> The reduction [in the thirty years prior to World War I] of the mortality [of babies] . . . has, indeed, been sensational. . . . Baby-saving, besides preserving many sound constitutions, enables some of inferior stamina to reach maturity, so that the very success in conserving lives, adds to the difficulty of reducing the mortality of older lives. Moreover, there is no doubt that individuals are enabled to survive and reproduce themselves who transmit to their children a poorer physical inheritance than was found among those who grew up before the art of infant-saving was so advanced.
>
> Compare, for example, America and China in respect to natural selection. Out of ten children born in America at least seven reach maturity. Out of the same number born in China, only two grow up. The Chinese lose the three weakest just as we do but in addition they lose five more who can survive under American conditions but not under Chinese conditions . . . the two Chinese who grow up ought to possess greater strength of constitution than the seven whites who grow up. As parents the latter cannot be expected to transmit as valuable a physical heredity as the former, so that in respect to toughness of physique the people with the less . . . relentless elimination of the weaker infants, is at a disadvantage. The proper moral to draw from this is not to relax our efforts to prolong life, but to apply the principles of eugenics to reproduction.[20]

Although she later objected to eugenics arguments because of their bigotry, Sanger clearly endorsed the basic principles behind eugenics. Typical was the heading in the November 1921 issue: "Birth Control: To Create a Race of

Thoroughbreds.''[21] In the May 1924 issue Sanger answered a question about methods of sterilization by explaining the options of salpingectomies and vasectomies. She added:

> We do not think sterilization advisable for strong, healthy people, for they may change their minds in four or five years' time. However, if there is a taint of insanity or epilepsy in either the husband's or wife's ancestry, sterilization is advisable.[22]

The official Principles and Aims of the American Birth Control League included ''sterilization of the insane and feeble minded and the encouragement of this operation upon those afflicted with inherited or transmissible diseases, with the understanding that sterilization does not deprive the individual of his or her sex expression, but merely renders one incapable of producing children.''[23]

The broad thrust of the *Review,* however, remained its attacks on laws against birth control and reports of progress in striking down those laws. News of local birth control leagues and articles on the status of birth control in countries throughout the world appeared in almost every issue. Reports of activities in France, Germany, England, Japan, China, Mexico, New Zealand, and India, among other countries, were common. Most of all, the *Review* was the only place women could seek information on the birth control movement and, through its notices and advertisements, information about how to prevent unwanted pregnancies. It appears that at the highest point of circulation, between fifteen thousand and thirty thousand copies were printed per issue.[24] The best indication of its effectiveness was the mail it received:

> In 1925 alone, the league's Motherhood Department answered almost 30,000 letters from women who wrote for practical advice on contraception, infertility, and a whole host of sexual problems, referring them to sympathetic local doctors when possible, or just offering words of understanding, since the mailing of practical instruction remained illegal. In some instances, volunteers, including [Sanger] herself, also took letters home and answered them privately, removing the organization from legal liability.[25]

The *Review* sold itself both through subscriptions and street sales (newsstands did not carry it). Street sales were made a success almost single-handedly by Kitty Marion, an Englishwoman who became a staunch feminist. She purposely staked out the most visible corners in New York City, favoring Herald and Times Squares. She was repeatedly arrested, but she relished the conversations she engaged in and felt it was crucial to the success of the movement to expose people to the term ''birth control'' just by having them see the title of the publication. Over the years, her visibility caused people to confuse her with Margaret Sanger.[26]

The form of the *Review* stabilized by 1920 and continued through the decade. The length started as sixteen pages (except for the eight-page June 1917 issue) and gradually grew (usually twenty pages in 1920 and 1921 and twenty-four pages in 1922) until February 1923, when the first thirty-two-page issue was published. That remained the usual length (summer issues were often shorter, and the first five issues of 1926 contained thirty-six pages) with a few exceptions until 1933, when it was generally shortened in the first half of the year. In October 1933, the *Review* shrank to eight pages when it became the newsletter of the American Birth Control League. The price remained very stable. At first subscriptions cost $1.50 a year, then rose to $2.00 in March 1920, with no change until the *Review* ceased publication. Single copies cost fifteen cents, then twenty cents. In 1921 single copies rose to twenty-five cents but later went back down to twenty cents.

The *Review* carried some advertising, most of it informing readers of books, conferences, pamphlets, and other matters relating to birth control. However, the most faithful paid advertisements were for Three-in-One Oil. Sanger's second husband, J. Noah Slee, was the president of the company. Advertising pages reached a high of nine pages in the October 1921 issue, but most of them were probably unpaid, as they concerned the upcoming Birth Control Conference. Ad pages typically numbered from four to seven pages per issue throughout the 1920s and early 1930s.

Even as the *Review*'s effectiveness grew, Sanger's relationship with the ABCL Board of Directors became more difficult. Sanger was traveling a great deal to give speeches and was often at odds with the board over strategic decisions and budgetary constraints. In 1928, Sanger resigned as president of the ABCL, and Mrs. F. Robertson Jones was elected—against Sanger's wishes.

> [Sanger's] official letter of resignation acknowledged a growing interest in birth control research and clinical service, along with a recognition that the league had reached a new stage of "maturity and organization" and was moving forward in its educational and legislative objectives without her. She could afford to be gracious, because the league board had worked out an agreement allowing her to remain as a director and also retain her title as editor-in-chief of the *Birth Control Review*. . . . The final break came when Jones . . . tried to reclaim control of the *Review* by appointing an editorial advisory board. Margaret then angrily resigned altogether.[27]

The March 1929 issue is the first without Sanger listed as editor. Mary Sumner Boyd and Annie G. Porritt, who had been instrumental in helping Sanger publish the *Review* for years, were listed as managing editors. The April issue lists no editors, and the May issue identifies an editorial board, something Jones had been fighting for. For those three issues, Sanger continued to be listed as the founder of the ABCL. By June 1929, the first issue edited by Stella Hanau, even that reference to Sanger was eliminated. Sanger contributed articles to the

October 1929 and October 1931 issues, but her influence had clearly ended by 1929.

The editorial board, which remained in place until the July 1933 issue (the last before the *Review* officially became the ABCL newsletter), was large, usually composed of twenty-one members. Most were academics or otherwise identified by having degrees listed after their names. Annie C. Porritt served as chairman of the editorial board until her death, which is referred to in the October 1932 issue. After that, no chairman is identified.

The *Review* did not publish an August or September issue in 1933. When it resumed publication in October, it was as volume 1, number 1 in a new series, now the newsletter of the ABCL. It shrank to eight pages and stopped listing an editor. Although it carried some articles, most of the content now focused on ABCL activities, board meetings, and announcements. In October 1934 Stella Hanau is identified as publications director under ABCL staff listings. The February 1935 issue fails to list ABCL staff, and the following issue lists staff but does not include a publications director. The April and May issues credit guest editors, Ellsworth Huntington, president of the American Eugenics Society, and Eduard Lindeman, professor of social philosophy. The June issue again lists no editor, and there is no issue for July or August. Mabel Travis Wood is then listed as publications director, and in October 1937 her title is listed as editor. With that issue, the *Review* started to increase its pages, first to twelve, then sixteen pages. The old-volume series was resumed, making volume 5 in the new series volume 22. Twenty-two consulting editors were identified. In November 1939, Mrs. Leopold K. Simon became the editor, continuing to work with the consulting editors. The *Review* ceased publication two months later, with the January 1940 issue.

The demise of the *Review* coincided with the 1939 reorganization of the ABCL into the Birth Control Federation of America, a move created to facilitate a reconciliation with Sanger in order to unify the birth control movement. In 1942, against Sanger's objections, the federation renamed itself the Planned Parenthood Association.[28]

Notes

1. "Birth Control for the Positive Side," *Metropolitan Magazine,* October 1917, p. 5, as cited by Ellen Chesler, *Margaret Sanger: Woman of Valor* (New York: Simon and Schuster, 1992), p. 164.

2. Chesler, *Margaret Sanger,* p. 164.

3. Lawrence Lader, *The Margaret Sanger Story and the Fight for Birth Control* (Westport, Conn.: Greenwood Press, 1955), pp. 43–46.

4. Ibid., p. 48.

5. Madeline Gray, *Margaret Sanger: A Biography of the Champion of Birth Control* (New York: Richard Marek, 1979), p. 40.

6. Ibid., p. 35.

7. Ibid., pp. 41–43.

8. Lader, *The Margaret Sanger Story and the Fight for Birth Control,* pp. 49–50.

9. Ibid., pp. 54–55.

10. Chesler, *Margaret Sanger,* pp. 102–103.

11. Ibid., p. 124.

12. Margaret Sanger, Frederick A. Blossom, and Elizabeth Stuyvesant, ''To the Men and Women of the United States,'' February 1917, p. 3.

13. Margaret Sanger, *Margaret Sanger: An Autobiography* (Elmsford, N.Y.: Maxwell Reprint, 1970), p. 253.

14. Chesler, *Margaret Sanger,* p. 167.

15. Ibid., p. 167.

16. Ibid., p. 168.

17. Sanger, *Margaret Sanger,* p. 252.

18. March 1920, p. 3.

19. Chesler, *Margaret Sanger,* p. 169.

20. Edward Ross, March 1920, p. 5.

21. November 1921, p. 3.

22. Sanger, May 1924, p. 150.

23. September 1924, p. 257.

24. Chesler, *Margaret Sanger,* p. 224.

25. Ibid., p. 224.

26. Sanger, *Margaret Sanger,* pp. 256–257.

27. Chesler, *Margaret Sanger,* pp. 238–239.

28. Ibid., pp. 391–393.

Information Sources

BIBLIOGRAPHY:

Chesler, Ellen. *Woman of Valor: Margaret Sanger and the Birth Control Movement in America.* New York: Simon and Schuster, 1992.

Douglas, Emily Taft. *Margaret Sanger: Pioneer of the Future.* Garrett Park, M.D.: Garrett Park Press, 1975.

Gray, Madeline. *Margaret Sanger: A Biography of the Champion of Birth Control.* New York: Richard Marek, 1979.

Kennedy, David M. *Birth Control in America: The Career of Margaret Sanger.* New Haven: Yale University Press, 1970.

Lader, Lawrence. *The Margaret Sanger Story and the Fight for Birth Control.* Westport, Conn.: Greenwood Press, 1975.

Moore, Gloria, and Ronald Moore. *Margaret Sanger and the Birth Control Movement, A Bibliography, 1911–1984.* Metuchen, N.J.: Scarecrow Press, 1986.

Roosevelt, Theodore. ''Birth Control from the Positive Side.'' *Metropolitan Magazine* 46.5, October 1917, p. 5 (as cited by Chesler, *Woman of Valor,* p. 164).

Sanger, Margaret. *Margaret Sanger: An Autobiography.* Elmsford, N.Y.: Maxwell Reprint, 1970 (originally published in New York by W. W. Norton, 1938).

INDEX SOURCES: New York Times.

LOCATION SOURCES: Sarah Lawrence College Library; William Paterson College, Sarah B. Askew Library; and other libraries.

Publication History

PERIODICAL TITLE AND TITLE CHANGES: *The Birth Control Review.*

VOLUME AND ISSUE DATA: Vols. 1–24 (February 1917–January 1940) (vols. 18–

21 were identified as vols. 1–4 in a new volume series; vols. 22–24 resumed instead of vols. 5–7 in the new series). Monthly with irregular publication in some years; five issues (1917); eleven issues (1918); ten issues (1932); ten issues—seven as vol. 17 and three as vol. 1 in a new series, later counted as vol. 18—(1933); nine issues (1934); ten issues (1935); ten issues (1936); seven issues (1937); nine issues (1938); seven issues (1939); one issue (1940).

PUBLISHER AND PLACE OF PUBLICATION: Margaret Sanger, Frederick A. Blossom, and Elizabeth Stuyvesant (February 1917–April/May 1917); Margaret Sanger (June 1917–April 1918); the New York Women's Publishing Company, Inc. (May 1918–May 1923); the American Birth Control League (June 1923–January 1940). New York.

EDITORS: Margaret Sanger (1917–1929); Mary Sumner Boyd and Annie G. Porritt (1929); Stella Hanau (1929–1935); Mabel Travis Wood (1935–1939); Mrs. Leopold K. Simon (1939–1940). This list of editors extrapolates editorial leadership for *The Birth Control Review* over its years of publication. The title of editor was not always used for these people and was often shared by others; some issues had no editor listed. Detailed editorial listings are as follows (the title given is editor(s) unless otherwise indicated): Margaret Sanger (Vol. I 1.1, 2 1917); Margaret Sanger, Frederick A. Blossom, Elizabeth Stuyvesant, and Walter Roberts (Vol. 33, 1917); Margaret Sanger and Walter Roberts (vol. 1.4 1917); Margaret Sanger, Walter Roberts, and Cornelia Barnes (vol. 1.5, 1917); Margaret Sanger, Walter Roberts, Lily Winner, and Gertrude Williams, literary editors (vol. 2.1, 2, 1918); Margaret Sanger, Walter Roberts, Lily Winner, Gertrude Williams, Maude Edgren, and Jessie Ashley, literary editors (vol. 2.3 1918); Margaret Sanger, Walter Roberts, Lily Winner, Maude Edgren, Jessie Ashley, Lola Ridge, literary editors (vol. 2. 4–8, 1918); Margaret Sanger, Walter Roberts, Lily Winner, Maude Edgren, and Jessie Ashley, literary editors (vol. 2. 9–11, 1918; Vol. 3.1, 1919); Margaret Sanger, Maude Edgren, Lily Winner, Mary Knoblauch [and lists Jessie Ashley, who died in January 1919, among the editors, saying, "And in recognition of a Vital Spirit that Still Animates this Magazine] (vol. 3.2–4, 1919); Margaret Sanger (vol. 3.5–7, 1919); Mary Knoblauch, acting editor, and Margaret Sanger, editor (Vol. 3.8–12, 1919); Margaret Sanger, Mary Knoblauch, Frances M. Bjorkman, Blanche Schrack (vol. 4.1–12, 1920; vol. 5.1, 1921); Margaret Sanger (others listed as associate editors) (vol. 5.2–12, 1921; vol. 6.1, 1922); Margaret Sanger (Annie G. Porritt listed as managing editor) (vol. 6. 2–12, 1922; vol. 7.1–5, 1923); Margaret Sanger (vol. 7.6–12, 1923; vol. 8.1, 1924); Margaret Sanger and Annie Porritt (vol. 8.2, 1924); Margaret Sanger (vol. 8.3, 1924); Margaret Sanger (Annie G. Porritt, managing editor) (vol. 8.4–11, 1924); Margaret Sanger (Mary Sumner Boyd, managing editor) (vol. 8.12, 1924; vols. 9–12, 1925–1928; vol. 13.1, 2, 1929); Mary Sumner Boyd and Annie G. Porritt, managing editors (vol. 13.3, 1929); no editor listed (vol. 13.4, 1929); editorial board (three members and Annie G. Porritt, chairman) and Mary Sumner Boyd, managing editor (vol. 13.5, 1929); Stella Hanau and editorial board (Annie G. Porritt, chairman until her death in October 1932 and usually five other members) (vol. 13.6–12, 1929; vols. 14–17, 1930–1933); no editor listed (vol. 1 [vol. 18 in sequence], 1933–1934); no editor listed but Stella Hanau is identified as publications director (vol. 2 [vol. 19 in sequence]: 1–4, 1934–1935); no editor or staff listed (vol. 2 [vol. 19 in sequence]: 5, 6, 1935); Ellsworth Huntington, guest editor (vol. 2 [vol.

19 in sequence]: 7, 1935); Eduard C. Lindeman, guest editor (vol. 2 [vol. 19 in sequence]: 8, 1935); no editor listed (vol. 2 [vol. 19 in sequence]: 9, 1935); no editor listed but Mabel Travis Wood is identified as publications director in almost alternating issues (vols. 3, 4 [vols 20, 21 in sequence]: 1935–1937; Mabel Travis Wood; lists consulting editors (usually twenty-one members) (vols. 22, 23, 1937–1938); Mrs. Leopold K. Simon; lists consulting editors (usually twenty members) (vol. 24, 1939–1940).

CIRCULATION: 15,000–30,000 (Chesler, *Woman of Valor,* p. 224).

Diana Peck

THE BUSINESS WOMAN'S JOURNAL

As the nation headed into the gay 1890s, Mary Foot Seymour, president of the Union Stenographic Company, began a magazine for the advancement of women in business, "hoping to stimulate others to rise out of frivolity and idleness into the larger and better field of industry and true culture."[1] The magazine was a unique source of information and inspiration for American women employed in a wide variety of fields. Although the publication continued for a few years after Seymour's death in 1893, it foundered in its attempt to redefine itself, becoming less a magazine for businesswomen and, finally, less a magazine for women at all.

Seymour started 1889 with the first issue of *The Business Woman's Journal: Devoted to the Interests of Women.* The thirty-six-page magazine ran its title in decorative script along with the contents on the front cover. The back page advertised "the best Carbon Papers and Ribbons for your writing machines."[2] Although this first issue ran only two and one-half pages of advertising, the typical number of advertising pages in issues thereafter was about ten pages, usually at the back of the magazine. The pages of the issues were consecutively numbered throughout the year.

In the first number, Seymour—herself "one of the best-known business women in the country"[3]—presented her rationale for starting the magazine:

> It must be acknowledged by every one [*sic*] that nothing has so contributed to the advancement of women as their participation in active pursuits. . . . This journal will, therefore, advocate the adoption of some avocation by every woman whose time is not occupied in household duties.[4]

In her definition of businesswoman, she incorporated the homemaker as part of the audience. "Although some one [*sic*] has aptly said, house-wives belong to the great army of unpaid laborers, we still intend to claim them as business-women."[5] Indeed, the greatest number of articles was directed toward women following "their traditional domestic occupations into the workplace [to] office work—the service work for business."[6]

To the women workers, she would offer volumes of advice. For example, Seymour penned the regular feature "Practical Hints to Stenographers and Type-Writers," which was often expanded to include a page of instructive illustrations on skills such as shorthand. She also investigated male-dominated fields. The magazine would "endeavor to suggest new fields of labor, hoping thus to prevent overcrowding and consequent reduction of salaries in others."[7] She noted that telegraphy was a field recently opened to women. But once opened, it was flooded with female laborers, and the salaries fell. Seymour suggested that her readers consider the field of architecture, which was still a male stronghold.[8]

"A Magazine Devoted to the Interests of All Women, Especially Those Engaged in Active Pursuits" was how the subtitle was enhanced on the title page. The magazine was "the organ of no special reform, but of all. . . . In other words, it will look at the woman's side of every question."[9]

> We shall strive to make The Business Woman's Journal a wide-awake magazine, which will keep pace with the spirit of the times. To accomplish this we need the support, not of one class of women, but of all. By their kind cooperation we hope to give our readers tidings from all parts of the world, which shall be an inspiration to them and an irresistible force in hastening on the great wheel of progress.[10]

Although aimed at women, the magazine recognized some male interest: "It will be part of our mission to give men occasional glimpses of the woman's world," particularly so they could see that a woman's involvement in an active sphere did not necessarily rob her of her womanly charm. In the second number she called attention to the magazine's pieces, such as the practical stenography columns—service journalism at its best. She urged male bosses and managers to buy their female employees subscriptions.[11]

Each number profiled—with a frontispiece portrait as well as a profile feature article—a successful woman. "By recording the deeds of the brave we hope to inspire the feeble, and we trust that in our work we shall receive the sympathy and co-operation of the standard bearers of our sex."[12] Temperance leader Frances E. Willard was portrayed in the first issue, although she was "not, strictly speaking, a business woman." Seymour wrote that "as a leader in many reforms," Willard exhibited "an executive ability which if devoted to business would have won her both fame and fortune."[13] Medical doctor Elizabeth Blackwell was also profiled in that first issue. This profile was written by a female physician who used the article as a platform for social commentary.

The early issues carried other features that became mainstays of the magazine: news of improvement societies and clubs, lectures by women of note, news briefs, and reprints called "Gleanings." Seymour ran inspirational, albeit often secular, quotations along with short, humorous pieces as "Leisure Moments." After having petitioned readers in the first issue for information, in the second number Seymour promised a "Mail Box" in future issues.

With the September–October issue that first year, the price was reduced from its original twenty cents an issue to ten cents an issue and from one dollar per year to fifty-five cents per year.

With the first number of the second volume, Seymour had given over sole ownership to become a part owner in the Mary F. Seymour Publishing Company.

> The motives of the former publisher in thus disposing of a portion of her interest in The Business Woman's Journal were threefold; first, that, not being dependent on the life of one individual, its chances of perpetuity may be increased; secondly, that it may be improved through the means of additional capital; and, thirdly, in order to introduce the principle of co-operation, in the efficacy of which, she has a profound belief.[14]

Ironically, this savvy business move and these hopes did not prove enough to sustain the magazine, for when the founding publisher died several years later, it was realized that she had contributed far more than financial backing to the magazine.

The new publishing company's prospectus in the next number showed new departments in keeping with its goal of broadening the scope of women's employment. The magazine continued to emphasize occupations for women, including regular departments on stenography and typewriting and special advice, profiles of successful businesswomen, "sensible" fashions, and club news. In addition, the magazine added editors and news departments to address education, law, journalism, health, and philanthropy and reform. Home-centered departments were added as the "Housekeeper's Guide" and, for children, "The Home Circle." Contents included more illustrations, love stories, and editorials on the "woman question."

Although the magazine had always carried a variety of departments, in order to highlight the diversity of women's work as well as point out opportunities, it broadened its scope further in 1892. The move brought a name change to *The American Woman's Journal.* The "business" designation was dropped from the title. However, each issue of the magazine contained a section labeled "Business Woman's Journal," having a volume and issue number of its own. Seymour was never able to fully flesh out the vision this "journal within a journal" may have signified. The following spring, founder Seymour, who had been acting both as editor and as business manager, died unexpectedly at age thirty-three. "She left her office at night, and before morning was stricken down by a severe attack of pneumonia. She lived only four days, dying on the morning of March 21."[15] As the April issue went to press, another sudden pneumonia death claimed the life of her assistant, Miss M.A.G. Griffin.[16] No editor was listed for the following issue, but it was noted that "an entire change of management became an absolute necessity."[17] Cornelia K. Hood probably assumed the duties of editor when she became president of the Board of Managers upon Seymour's death.[18] Despite the upheaval in management, the reorganized staff committed itself to continuing the magazine's mission and enacting its newer vision. "It will be the aim of the present management to maintain the high character which the Journal has already maintained, to enlarge its scope, and thus increase its sphere."[19]

Despite this pledge, the magazine seemed to lose its focus when it lost its founder. Seeing meaningful labor as key to women's advancement, Seymour had been unapologetic for women's working. However, this pledge to carry on the work came couched in a tone very different from that of Seymour's writing.

Whatever may be one's views of the desirability of such a career for women as compared with a sheltered home life, we must be glad that while so many have no choice, but must work or starve, there are such strong hands to help, and so true a heart to give advice, and to show by a brilliant example that the home is not the only sphere in which genuine courage and true womanliness can be developed, and exert their influence for good.[20]

This shift in tone, coupled with the editorial upheaval, weakened the magazine. With Seymour gone, the magazine's driving force and purposeful motivation were gone as well. The issues following her death noted a new publishing company; and, although apologizing for publishing delays, the magazine went to a monthly publishing schedule in 1894.

Also in 1894, Helen Kendrick Johnson became "working editor," and Hood retained "her connection as consulting editor."[21] In May of that year *Business Woman's Journal* was reinstated as a part of the magazine's title; yet the magazine retained the format of presenting the *Business Woman's Journal* as an insert. On the July–August masthead, both Johnson and Hood were listed as editors, with Johnson emerging as editor in chief by the March–April issue of 1895.

In August 1895, the magazine started volume 10 with another new publisher. The magazine went through a formal split of business- and non-business-oriented pages. The new publisher, R. vH. Schramm, became editor of the business section, and Johnson became the editor of the "literary supplement," to which the remainder of the magazine was referred. Seymour had been an advocate of suffrage; but the magazine—under new ownership—began to sidestep even that stance. The content split that Seymour had initiated became more pronounced but took a decidedly different direction.

The magazine is divided into two separate departments, which will each have their own illustrated frontispiece and heading to mark the division. It is intended to give both departments equal space in the magazine. The literary part will be entitled "The American Woman's Magazine" and the

Business Woman's department, under the heading "Business Journal,"
will be edited by the publisher.

The object of the magazine is to serve as a forum for the debate of
important questions and to be an epitome of literature, current events and
matters of interest to womankind.[22]

More changes were announced in January 1896, although no editors were listed
from this time until the magazine suspended publication. The changes further
eroded Seymour's practices and invalidated the earlier tone of the magazine in
an attempt to further redefine its mission.

The publication was started with the idea that it should supply high grade
original articles on subjects of interest to refined and educated readers,
and also aid women engaged in the more active pursuits by helpful suggestions. The somewhat didactic tendency which very naturally ensued
will in the future be offset by the introduction of lighter reading matter,
and particularly of fiction in the form of short stories.[23]

In September of that year, under a new publishing company, the magazine
dropped its emphasis on women altogether in calling itself *The American Magazine.* Contents, which had begun to rely heavily on illustrations, were stereo-
typically woman-centered. The next issue, published in November, was its last.

Seymour's ambitious magazine garnered its early success from her perspective, which unabashedly addressed the American woman as worker. Far from
apologizing for women's working, Seymour considered work healthy for women
and a means for their self-fulfillment. Through this underutilized perspective,
she alerted women to the opportunities, pitfalls, and politics of the business
world. In sharing knowledge that women were generally not privy to, she opened
the door for workplace reform. It is a sad irony that Seymour relinquished sole
publishership to enable the magazine to carry on beyond her. The reform-based
periodical that she began did indeed rely entirely on her guidance, losing the
mission she had given it as it sank unremarkably into indistinguishable and thus
unsustainable magazine fare.

Notes

1. M. F. DeHart, April 1893, [p. 161].
2. Advertisement, January 1889, back cover.
3. "Miss Mary E. [sic] Seymour," *New York Times,* March 22, 1893, p. 9.
4. Mary Foot Seymour, "Prospectus," editorial, January 1889, p. 4.
5. Mary Foot Seymour, editorial, September/October 1889, p. 163.
6. Gerda Lerner, *The Female Experience: An American Documentary.* (Indianapolis: Bobbs-Merrill, 1977), pp. 257–258.
7. Seymour, January 1889, p. 4.

8. "What Occupation Shall I Choose? Women as Telegraphers, Architects, etc.,"
January 1889, p. 24.

9. Seymour, January 1889, p. 4.

10. Ibid.

11. "To Business Men," February? 1889, p. 59.

12. Seymour, January 1889, p. [3].

13. Ruth Sanford, "Frances E. Willard The Woman Who Leads an Army of 200,000
Women," January 1889, p. 4.

14. "Editorial," February 1890, pp. 30–31.

15. M. F. DeHart, April 1893 [p. 161].

16. "Editorial Comments," April 1893, p. [204].

17. "Editorial Comments," May/June 1893, p. [223].

18. " 'The American Woman's Journal' and Its Founder," April 1894, p. [316].

19. "Editorial Comments," May/June 1893, p. [223].

20. M. F. DeHart, "In Memoriam," April 1893, p. [161].

21. " 'The American Woman's Journal' and Its Founder," April 1894, p. [316].

22. "To the Reader!" August 1895, n.p.

23. A.W.H., "To the Reader!" January 1896, n.p.

Information Sources

BIBLIOGRAPHY:
"Miss Mary E. Seymour [sic] Dead. Her Career as a Business Woman—Widely and
    Favorably Known." *New York Times,* March 22, 1893, p. 9.
INDEX SOURCES: None.
LOCATION SOURCES: Library of Congress and other libraries. Microfilmed in the
    Gerritsen collection, reel P18.

Publication History

PERIODICAL TITLE AND TITLE CHANGES: *The Business Woman's Journal* (Jan-
    uary 1889–July/August 1892); *The American Woman's Journal* (October 1892–
    1894); *The American Woman's Journal and Business Woman's Journal* (1894–
    July 1895); *The American Woman's Magazine and Business Journal* (August
    1895–November/December 1895); *The American Woman's Magazine* (January
    1896–July/August 1896); *The American Magazine* (September 1896–November
    1896).
VOLUME AND ISSUE DATA: Vols. 1–10 (January 1889–November/December 1895);
    vol. 1 (new series), nos. 1–8 (also called vol. 11; January 1896–November 1896).
    Bimonthly (January 1889–January/February 1891); monthly (July 1891–October
    1895, with some months combined or omitted issues); bimonthly (November/
    December 1895–November 1896).
PUBLISHER AND PLACE OF PUBLICATION: Mary F. Seymour (1889); Mary F.
    Seymour Pub. Co. (1890–1893); American Journal Publishing Co. (1893–1895),
    R. vH. Schramm (1895–1896), the American Magazine Pub. Co. (1986). New
    York.
EDITORS: Mary Foot Seymour (1889–1893); Cornelia K. Hood (1893?); Helen Ken-

drick Johnson and Cornelia K. Hood (1894–1895); Helen Kendrick Johnson (1895); Helen Kendrick Johnson and R. vH. Schramm (1895–1896).

CIRCULATION: Publisher's notes, September/October 1889, p. 164: 20,000 (guaranteed circulation for the November/December 1889 number).

Therese L. Lueck

C

THE CATHOLIC WORKER

To a very great extent, the story of *The Catholic Worker* is the story of its founder, Dorothy Day. The flagship newspaper of the Catholic worker movement has been published since May 1933 to give voice to Day's philosophy of social justice, pacifism, and voluntary poverty. In fact, she has been described as "the inspiration behind the creative force of the American Catholic left."[1]

That Day turned to journalism to promote her social philosophy was logical, given her background. She was the daughter of a sportswriter father who had worked at numerous newspapers around the United States. Thus, Day, who was born on November 8, 1897, the third of five children, moved with her family many times throughout her childhood. She began writing while she was a scholarship student at the University of Illinois in Urbana. After she dropped out of school, she moved to New York City and began writing for the *New York Call,* a socialist newspaper. There, she wrote about rent strikes, pacifism, and the birth control movement. She quit the *Call* in 1917 and found work as an assistant editor of *The Masses.* That job, however, fell through when the U.S. Post Office refused to mail it because of its vocal opposition to World War I.

While journalism was a natural path for Day, the road to Catholicism was rockier. Day lived a fast and loose life in New York. She divorced and had several failed relationships—one resulting in an abortion and another in the birth of her daughter in 1927. Searching for a moral compass, Day became interested in Catholicism, and, when her daughter was nine months old, Day was baptized a Catholic.

Day began publishing *The Catholic Worker* in 1933 after she met, and was greatly influenced by, Peter Maurin, a former Christian brother who gave Day "a way of life and instruction."[2] With Maurin's moral support and literally no financial backing, Day put the paper together on a shoestring. It was "planned, written and edited in the kitchen of a tenement on Fifteenth Street, on subway platforms, on the 'L,' the ferry.''[3] She published the first issue of *The Catholic Worker* on May Day of that year, in the height of the Great Depression, and circulated copies among the unemployed who gathered in New York's Union Square. She scraped together the fifty-seven dollars the Paulist Press wanted to publish 2,500 copies of the first issue by delaying payment of her already overdue rent and utility bills. The second edition was funded in part by Day's sale of her typewriter.[4] *The Catholic Worker* explained its circulation strategy in that second issue—workers wanted the communists there to realize there was more to Catholicism than "squeezing money from the people to send to Rome." In fact, according to writer Joe Bennett, an early recruit to Day's project, "We who edit and contribute to this sheet are unemployed ourselves, barely eking out an existence." This editorial asserted that "the Church Militant is interested in man's welfare as well as his soul."[5]

Although Day was clearly influenced and inspired by Maurin, they had fundamental disagreements on what should be part of the newspaper. When the journal's title was debated, Maurin argued in favor of the *Catholic Radical;* Day suggested *The Catholic Worker*—a clear alternative to the *Communist Daily Worker.*[6] Maurin stated that he did not want to be an editor but preferred to submit essays and articles as he pleased. While he was the original visionary of *The Catholic Worker,* Day gave it life. As she put it, "I do admit it takes a woman to put flesh on the bare bones of an idea."[7]

Day saw herself as "journalist and housekeeper" for both *The Catholic Worker* and its movement. Simply put, the concept behind the movement was a philosophy of anarchism, voluntary poverty, personal accountability, pacifism, activism, and advocacy. Day said the "consistent theme" of both the newspaper and its movement had been "that we must work for the common good, that men are responsible for each other, that God has a special love for the poor and the destitute, the insulted and the injured, and that where they are, we must be, too. We have been consistent in our pacifism and our endeavor to portray non-violent means of bringing about a new social order."[8]

For many, Day was a teacher. Through her thoughts and reflections in the newspaper, Day taught others how to embrace her philosophy. "When St. Paul says to pray always, to pray without ceasing, he is also talking about practicing the presence of God."[9] Conservative Roman Catholics have often considered Day a radical and a threat to traditional Catholicism. Yet, she publicly supported Catholic doctrine and always asserted that she was first a Catholic, then a radical. "If the Chancery ordered me to stop publishing the Catholic Worker tomorrow, I would," she said in 1952.[10] Today, it is more difficult to envision her effect on many conservative Catholics; many of her ideas and beliefs actually seem conservative themselves—she opposed abortion and birth control; she disliked the trend in the late 1960s of nuns' abandoning their habits; and she opposed women as priests. "I guess I'm pretty much of a conservative in Church matters," she said.[11] Her position on secular, social matters was more to the left.

When 1960s radical Abbie Hoffman told Day, " 'You were the first hippie,' she was flattered."[12] Now, people committed to the Catholic worker movement have been working toward the eventual canonization of Day.[13] In a recent issue of *The Catholic Worker,* an article by Pope John Paul II was published—a far cry from the radicalism of its beginnings.

That first issue, which explained the purpose of *The Catholic Worker,* was to call attention to the Catholic Church's social program and to the fact that radicalism and Catholicism could indeed work together. "Is it not possible to protest, to espouse, to complain, to point out abuses and demand reforms without desiring the overthrow of religion?"[14] The paper got right down to the business at hand. That first issue exposed the exploitation of black workers by the U.S. War Department. The article claimed the government was paying its black workers ten cents an hour and forcing them to work seven-day weeks. Another article announced a drive against sweatshops; still another article noted that the child labor force had been reduced because there were so many experienced adult workers who were unemployed that there was no longer a market for child labor. Maurin's "Easy Essays" column promoted the need for activism. "Catholic scholars have taken the dynamite of the Church, have wrapped it up in nice phraseology, placed it in an hermetic container, and sat on the lid. It is about time to blow the lid off so the Catholic Church may again become the dominant social dynamic force," Maurin asserted.[15] That same issue printed letters from workers who vividly described their exploitation and their pitiful plight.

Yet, the paper's financial position was obviously precarious. "It is not yet known whether it will be a monthly, a fortnightly, or a weekly. It all depends on the funds collected for the printing and distribution. Those who can subscribe and those who can donate are asked to do so," the editors requested.[16] As it turned out, the paper returned promptly with a June–July 1933 issue. After that, the paper published monthly, with occasional combined issues because of financial difficulties.

Although Day had a sense of journalism and journalistic style, the same could not be said for others in her midst. The Catholic worker movement attracted all sorts of people to its New York headquarters. High school students volunteered; homeless people worked to say thank you for assistance; idealistic young people who had been touched by *The Catholic Worker*'s message came enthusiastically into the fold. "They are not journalists, thank God," Day once said. "They are revolutionists."[17]

From its humble beginnings, the Catholic worker movement grew, and, as it did, so did the importance and influence of its newspaper. The newspaper carefully tracked and reported on important labor movements. Strikes were followed closely, with the *Worker* always supporting the plight of the striker. Day, in fact, said she had been moved by the labor slogan urging: "Workers of the World Unite. You have nothing to lose but your chains." The newspaper always reflected this philosophy. "Feed the poor—Starve the bankers," read one typical front-page headline.[18]

Appealing to underpaid laborers, the homeless, and the unemployed at a time of great hardship throughout the United States, the Catholic worker movement grew. Worker houses opened in cities throughout the United States. The movement suffered a setback in terms of its popularity during World War II, when Day remained completely committed to her philosophy of pacifism. In January 1943, Day promised readers that if conscription was extended to women, she would practice what she preached and disobey the law.[19] By the end of the war, only ten Catholic worker houses remained open in the United States. Those numbers did not increase significantly until the Vietnam War caused many Americans to question the federal government's right to be there. Public draft card burnings prompted the arrest of some Catholic workers and focused publicity once again on the movement's philosophy.[20]

The Catholic Worker mirrored the success of the movement itself. Circulation, according to figures published in the newspaper, peaked at 190,000 in May 1938 and then dropped to about 50,000 by the end of World War II.[21] Day decided to remove herself from the editorship for a year beginning in 1943 so that she could pray and devote herself to less worldly occupations. To fill the void, Arthur Sheehan took over as temporary editor. But Day could not stay away. "A life even of partial solitude was not for her," one friend stated. Day and her followers braced themselves for serious censure during World War II because of their unpopular pacifist beliefs. Day herself was listed by the U.S. government for possible detention in the case of a national emergency because her views were considered so dangerous. When news of the Holocaust became known to her, even Day's steadfast adherence to pacifism was shaken. "If I had know all this, known it while it was happening, would I have been able to maintain my pacifism?" she questioned. But then she added, "But all the violence didn't save the Jews."[22]

When the war ended, former soldiers were attracted to Day's movement, and the movement found renewed vigor in its new recruits. But it took years for the circulation figures of the newspaper to climb significantly. By 1965, the *Ayer Directory of Publications* estimated *The Catholic Worker* circulation at seventy thousand; by 1977, the estimate stood at ninety thousand. *The Catholic Worker*'s own circulation figures always exceeded the Ayer estimate by many thousands, but this discrepancy can be explained by the failure of so many readers to cancel their subscription or alert the newspaper office to an address change. Indeed, the very cost of an annual subscription—still the same twenty-five cents that was asked for in 1933—is less than the cost of a stamp; the cost of a single issue has always been one cent. Obviously, then, the cost of producing the newspaper has always far exceeded the money from incoming subscriptions. *The Catholic Worker* has always relied on the kindness and generosity of its supporters. "When we need money, we pray for it," Day explained.[23]

Day remained involved with *The Catholic Worker* until her death on November 29, 1980, at the age of eighty-three. Although her name remained as editor and publisher in the editorial box until her death, she gradually stepped back from the day-to-day operations of the newspaper. In 1975, she wrote that she was "leaving everything to our generous crowd of young people who do the editing and getting out of *The Catholic Worker*."[24] She continued to make the important editorial decisions and to write a regular column, but she retired from public life in 1976, when she suffered a heart attack and was debilitated by congestive heart failure. When she died, newspapers around the United States acknowledged her influence in shaping an activist program of Catholic social justice. "It was a Christian revolution she was starting," one priest was quoted in the *New York Times* obituary as saying. "She was opening the minds of bishops, priests, seminarians and lay people to the fact that Christianity was not a stuffy sacristy affair. She was a trumpet calling for all of us to find Christ in the bread lines, the jails, a tenant farmer, migratory worker or Negro."[25]

Today, the newspaper holds few surprises, although the number of issues has gradually been reduced to seven times a year. The number of annual issues is a reflection of the high cost of composing, printing, and mailing the newspaper, said editor Jane Sammon. In 1995, the newspaper spent $12,500 per issue on postage and close to $6,000 for printing.[26] Each issue usually numbers eight pages of inspirational prayers, essays, and letters. As always, it prints no paid advertising. It is illustrated with high-quality black-and-white line art. While other newspapers routinely modernize their typeface and layout, *The Catholic Worker* of the 1990s has changed hardly at all. The columns are wider than its original numbers in the 1930s, and the layout uses more white space, but photography, graphics, and other new printing techniques have no place in the newspaper. Even the masthead has changed only slightly since 1933. In the first issue, the masthead art featured two workingmen on either side of the printed title, one with a pick, the other a shovel. Those sketches were amended in the seventh issue to include one black worker and one white one. Then, in May 1935, the masthead illustration was changed to a centered cross with Jesus' bringing together the black man and white man, who are joining hands. The art on the masthead today shows nearly the same drawing, with one change: the white man and his hammer have been replaced with a white woman carrying a child on her back and holding a plate of food.

Technologically, the newspaper entered the world of computers somewhat begrudgingly in 1983, when editors purchased an Apple computer. The purchase had become necessary because it was no longer possible to replace parts on the outdated addressograph machine that was used for mailing labels. Some of the workers were morally opposed to the purchase of the computer equipment.[27] In 1995, the editorial copy of the newspaper was still composed on manual typewriters and then sent to a printer. This reflected a deliberate aversion to technology. "We see computers as yet another level of technology that is a community dissembler," said editor Jane Sammon. "We want to be as close to a form of manual labor as we can."[28]

The newspaper even today relies heavily on the writings of Dorothy Day, who died in 1980, and Peter Maurin, who died in 1949. Their essays, articles, and ideas frequently are reprinted as the newspaper continues to grapple with the same themes of pacifism and activism as it did in its infancy. If *The Catholic Worker* has lost its feeling of revolutionary zeal, it is perhaps because the ideals preached by Day and Maurin no longer seem radical, only sane.

While the message of *The Catholic Worker* has remained constant, the face of poverty has changed in the more than sixty years since the creation of the movement and the newspaper. Today, Catholic workers must cope with the reality of HIV/AIDS and the ramifications this condition has on the people who seek their help. Some of the more than one hundred Catholic worker houses in the 1990s focus all their energies toward ministering to the victims of AIDS. Other houses have a more broad-based social agenda. "Although there may be disagreement over particular actions within the tradition of nonviolence, we are all of one mind that the works of mercy, the works of peace, oppose the works of war," *The Catholic Worker* editors wrote in an anniversary edition.[29] While *The Catholic Worker* is indeed the "flagship" newspaper of the movement, some of the other houses also publish newsletters and newspapers.

The Catholic worker philosophy toward government has put them at odds with federal and state authorities. The workers have performed numerous acts of civil disobedience, including their refusal to participate in mandatory air raids during the 1950s and their highly visible burning of draft cards during the Vietnam War. Day's staunch positions also landed her in prison nearly a dozen times.[30] Once, when she sat in a New York park in front of city hall during an air raid, she was sentenced to a thirty-day sentence in the Women's House of Detention in Manhattan. After her death, veteran social activist Daniel Berrigan reflected that "without Dorothy, . . . the resistance we offered would be unthinkable."[31]

The Catholic workers also have been at odds with the Federal Bureau of Investigation (FBI), which sent investigators to the newspaper's offices on several occasions during the 1950s, and the Internal Revenue Service (IRS). The Catholic worker movement has never officially declared itself a nonprofit organization because the very act of registration with the government violated its philosophy. In 1972, the IRS created a publicity nightmare when it unpopularly demanded Day pay three hundred thousand dollars in back taxes, fines, and penalties. The agency eventually dropped the matter.[32]

Perhaps one of the greatest challenges the newspaper has faced in recent years has been to grapple with its own program of social justice in the face of the Catholic Church's unbending positions on abortion, birth control, and homosexuality. Day herself upheld the Catholic position on these issues and tried to present a "constructive" policy in *The Catholic Worker*. In an article about birth control written in 1934, Day said her newspaper would highlight ways needy women could obtain prenatal and health care for their children.[33]

Today, *The Catholic Worker* mainly leaves such debates to other Catholic newspapers and concentrates instead on its own specific agenda. "We're very interested in social justice—feeding the hungry and clothing the naked," said editor Jane Sammon. "We don't really write about sexuality in general at *The Catholic Worker.*" Sammon said that the newspaper has exhibited a "recognizable silence" about homosexuality, mainly because the movement has attracted committed workers who are also gays and lesbians. She said the workers believe that issues of sexuality, homosexuality especially, are divisive issues that the church will have to deal with, but, she said, *The Catholic Worker* hasn't devoted much editorial space to these issues because they are debated and elaborated on in other Catholic newspapers.[34]

Notes

1. Raymond A. Schroth of George Washington University after Day's death, in Alden Whitman, "Dorothy Day, Catholic Activist, 83, Dies," *New York Times,* December 1, 1980, p. D12.

2. Nancy L. Roberts, *Dorothy Day and the Catholic Worker* (Albany: State University of New York Press, 1984), p. 27.

3. "Filling a Need," May 1933, p. 4.

4. Roberts, *Dorothy Day and the Catholic Worker,* p. 35.

5. Joe Bennett, "First Issue of *Catholic Worker* Distributed May Day in Union Square," June/July 1933, p. 5.

6. Dwight MacDonald, "Introduction" to the reprint edition of *The Catholic Worker* (Westport, Conn.: Greenwood, 1970), p. 6.

7. Ibid., p. 12.

8. Dorothy Day in the Preface to *The Catholic Worker* reprint (Westport, Conn.: Greenwood, 1970), unnumbered page.

9. Dorothy Day, "We Have to Leap into Faith," May 1993, p. 1.

10. MacDonald, "Introduction," p. 9.

11. Ibid., p. 8.

12. Ibid., p. 7.

13. Garry Wills, "The Saint of Mott Street," *New York Review of Books* 41.8, April 21, 1994, p. 36.

14. "Filling a Need," May 1, 1933, p. 4.

15. Peter Maurin, "Easy Essays," May 1, 1933, p. 8.

16. "Filling a Need," May 1, 1933, p. 4.

17. Roberts, *Dorothy Day and the Catholic Worker,* p. 38.

18. Peter Maurin, "Feed the Poor—Starve the Bankers," May 1935, p. 1.

19. Dorothy Day, "If Conscription Comes for Women," January 1943, p. 1.

20. Rosalie Riegle Troester, ed., *Voices from the Catholic Worker* (Philadelphia: Temple, 1993), p. 5.

21. See the appendix in Roberts, *Dorothy Day and the Catholic Worker,* for circulation figures.

22. Eileen Egan, "Dorothy Day: Pilgrim of Peace," in Patrick G. Coy, ed., *A Revolution of the Heart: Essays on the Catholic Worker* (Philadelphia: Temple, 1988), pp. 87–88.

23. MacDonald, "Introduction," p. 11.

24. Dorothy Day, "On Pilgrimage," March–April 1975, quoted in Roberts, *Dorothy Day,* pp. 166–167.

25. Alden Whitman, "Dorothy Day, Catholic Activist, 83, Dies," *New York Times,* December 1, 1980, p. D12.

26. Jane Sammon, telephone interview October 9, 1995.

27. Roberts, *Dorothy Day,* p. 44.

28. Sammon interview.

29. "60th Anniversary Issue," May 1993, p. 1.

30. June O'Connor, *The Moral Vision of Dorothy Day: A Feminist Perspective* (New York: Crossroad, 1991), pp. 68–69.

31. Egan, "Dorothy Day," p. 91.

32. Roberts, *Dorothy Day,* pp. 144, 166.

33. Roberts, *Dorothy Day,* p. 39.

34. Sammon interview.

Information Sources

BIBLIOGRAPHY:

Coy, Patrick G., ed. *A Revolution of the Heart: Essays on the Catholic Worker.* Philadelphia: Temple, 1988.

Day, Dorothy. *The Long Loneliness: The Autobiography of Dorothy Day.* Garden City, N.Y.: Image Books, 1959.

Miller, William D. *A Harsh and Dreadful Love: Dorothy Day and the Catholic Worker Movement.* New York: Liveright, 1973.

————. *Dorothy Day: A Biography.* New York: Harper and Row, 1982.

O'Connor, June. *The Moral Vision of Dorothy Day: A Feminist Perspective.* New York: Crossroad, 1991.

Roberts, Nancy L. *Dorothy Day and the Catholic Worker.* Albany: State University of New York Press, 1984.

Troester, Rosalie Riegle, ed. *Voices from the Catholic Worker.* Philadelphia: Temple, 1993.

Whitman, Alden. "Dorothy Day, Catholic Activist, 83, Dies." *New York Times,* December 1, 1980, p. D12.

Wills, Garry, "The Saint of Mott Street." *New York Review of Books*, April 21, 1994, pp. 36, 45–48.

INDEX SOURCES: Catholic Periodical and Literature Index; Alternative Press Index; Peace Research Abstract Journal.

LOCATION SOURCES: Library of Congress and other libraries. Microfilm available through University Microfilms International.

Publication History

PERIODICAL TITLE AND TITLE CHANGES: *Catholic Worker* (1933–present).

VOLUME AND ISSUE DATA: Vols. 1– (May 1933–present). Monthly (1933–1980); eight times a year (1980–1994); seven times a year (1994–present).

PUBLISHER AND PLACE OF PUBLICATION: Dorothy Day (1933–1980); no publisher is listed in the editorial box (1980–present). New York.

EDITORS: Dorothy Day (1933–1943); Arthur Sheehan (1943–1944); Dorothy Day (1944–1980); Daniel Mauk and Peggy Scherer (1981); Mary Humphrey and Peggy Scherer (1981–1982); Peggy Scherer (1983); Robbie Gamble and Peggy Scherer (1984); Frank Donovan, Jane Sammon, and Katharine Temple (1986–

present). (Other editorial names occasionally appeared for a few months, but the preceding names are the ones that were constant. The *Worker*'s tradition is to rely on the help of editorial volunteers and managing editors.)

CIRCULATION: Ulrich's, 1995: 90,000. (The *Catholic Worker* stated in 1995 that it also sends out 1,200 bundles of two or more papers, requiring 16,000 copies foreign and domestic, while the rest are subscriptions.)

Agnes Hooper Gottlieb

THE CELIBATE WOMAN JOURNAL

The Celibate Woman Journal, begun in 1982, provided a unique and sympathetic forum for women who wanted to explore celibacy. Subtitled "A Journal for Women Who Are Celibate or Considering This Liberating Way of Relating to Others," the periodical acknowledged several reasons—without advocating any single one in particular—women might consider this. At the same time, as the subtitle's adjective suggested, it celebrated nongenital and nonsexual explorations of friendship and love.

The Celibate Woman Journal's inaugural issue explicitly defined its mission. Martha Allen, the editor, saw the journal as a way to open up affirmative discussion of alternatives to a sex-oriented society; it presented another view of self and relationships in opposition to the pornographic, or at least oversexualized and degrading ones, pushed by most mass media.[1] A formal statement of purpose called the journal "a communications network among women who are interested in exploring new and meaningful ways of relating to others—including those with whom we are intimate—rather than taking our affections in a sexual direction. Our sexuality is a part of our being and does not need to be expressed through genital interactions; indeed, we find new levels of creative energies available which can be expressed in a variety of ways when we don't focus on sex."[2] Allen began the periodical after attending a meeting of celibates, where she heard women complaining that they were treated as abnormal if they were not involved in a sexually active relationship; on the other hand, as Allen acknowledged, a sense of media-induced pressure and emotional neediness did not make for satisfying relationships.[3]

As editor, Allen generally preferred the "editorial we," but her opening statement in 1982 was fairly personal. She announced that while she had been celibate for most of her thirty-four years, "it was only when I consciously chose celibacy as the way I wished to live my life and relate to others that I began to experience its full benefits. . . . In fact, I find that when I do not narrow my affection by directing it sexually, I experience more equal and warm relationships with everyone I care about. . . . I believe that the closeness, warmth and sharing that I seek in an intimate relationship can be attained without sexual involvement (when the other person also has a positive attitude and understands my concept of celibacy)."[4] Later, Allen expanded on this. As a single woman living independently, she explained, she "increasingly appreciated being able to go in the directions I wish without the necessity of fitting my life around the needs and interests of another, or of explaining myself."[5] She added, "I have specific ideas of what I want to accomplish in my life and I choose to give the majority of my time to my own determined 'causes.' . . . I do find, though, that celibacy can provide the greatest range of relationships; fewer demands on my time; and the most harmonious continuity in the way I wish to live my life."[6]

Allen went to some pains to point out that celibacy was not for everyone; she simply wished this to be understood as an option. On the other hand, she was determined to offer a positive definition of celibacy that avoided defining that choice in terms of lack, exclusion, or absence. Her vision of celibacy was flexible, but consistently maximized, personal autonomy: it was a path of self-determined vision, context, and duration. Allen wanted to define celibacy as always freely chosen, as opening up additional avenues. Some celibate women would satisfy their own sexual desires; some turned their energies to other activities. Either way, women would define for themselves the kind and extent of physical touching and intimacies with loved ones. In this way, many articles in *The Celibate Woman Journal* underscored a vision and sexual politics of liberation. Candace Watson began an essay, "On Autonomy," by asserting, "Feminism is synonymous with personal autonomy." That claim is controversial, and many cultural and socialist feminists would disagree. Nonetheless, having distinguished celibacy from asexuality, Watson asserted that "celebrating one's own sexuality is radical and political."[7]

The irregularly, but essentially semiyearly, published journal was, in some sense, the production of a family intensively involved in progressive causes and especially in feminist media, although this was not publicly stated. Martha Allen was also responsible for typesetting on the family-owned equipment. Her mother, Donna Allen, was listed on the masthead as paste-up artist and cofounder. Donna Allen, the founder of the Women's Institute for Freedom of the Press and for many years the editor of the *Media Report to Women,** is a heroic figure in efforts to develop a feminist theory of, and for, mass media. Martha's sister Indra Dean Allen provided the cover art and sketches. The July 1982 issue reprinted a 1972 interview with Indra Allen on why she chose to be celibate that had been transcribed by another sister, Dana Densmore, and published ten years before in Densmore's *No More Fun and Games,** a leading women's liberation periodical of the second wave. Densmore had also published *Black Belt Woman* and had founded Artemis Institute, where Martha Allen, who held black-belt rank, taught self-protection through self-empowerment. Indra Allen, a songwriter and guitarist, had, from 1974 to 1977, edited *Musica,* a newsletter about women in music. True to the family tradition, a brother has produced programming for a community radio station dealing with, among other topics, labor history.

The layout was also unvaryingly, if quietly, academic. Nothing was fancy or glitzy; even headlines were plain and inconspicuous. But if the style was essentially formal, contributors often referred to ''I'' and ''me.'' They called ''Martha'' and other contributors by first name, and their letters expressed delight in seeing their alternative lifestyle legitimized and even glorified. The March 1986 issue, for example, included a grateful letter from a seventy-one-year-old Arizona woman who had been celibate for thirty years: ''You gave me great heart for our species.'' Another woman wrote, ''i can't tell you how affirmed i have felt from reading the celibate woman journal.'' She added that even her therapist was reading it. Consistent with the Allens' general approach to feminist publishing, the contributions were individually copyrighted in the name of the writer. Brief autobiographical statements accompanied most essays and articles, although several writers were somewhat cryptic about their sexual and/or career histories. Others, however, adopted a more confessional approach to explaining their marital backgrounds, professional and religious affiliations, and philosophical approaches.

While most of the articles represented fairly stable, if not permanent, thinking, some of the writing had a more conversational tone and seemed to represent ideas in progress. For example, a fifty-four-year-old British feminist, a former chemist and divorcee who regularly contributed to the journal, began a long essay by acknowledging that she had enjoyed an incredible sense of euphoria and freedom once she achieved the ''desired state of celibacy.''[8] On the other hand, Marjorie Calow underscored her continuing desire for physical intimacy with a man. Calow frankly admitted that the only time she felt like masturbating was when she was already ''turned on psychologically by some gorgeous man.'' With no ''real'' man to fantasize about, she added, she would simply save her energy.

The bulk of the journal was devoted to essays, but it also offered drawings and poetry, usually first-person and also having to do with celibacy. Most of the readers/writers were women, although the journal printed a couple of essays and appreciative letters from men, sometimes addressed to men. A few other submissions from men were rejected.[9] It carried a little advertising, mostly for feminist bookstores or periodicals. Since all labor was donated, advertising and the subscription fees (four dollars a copy) allowed the journal to break even.[10]

Few of the writers assumed that celibacy was a permanent state. Instead, celibacy was for the present and foreseeable future. For example, the inaugural issue led with an essay by a writer and martial arts colleague of Martha who had decided to remain celibate for one year. Thus far, Mecca Rylance noted, she had enjoyed more satisfying relationships and more affection than ever before. She attributed this to her newfound ability to send out and receive ''energy that is uncomplicated by any underlying sexual message.'' ''During this year I've become more aware of my sexuality and its uses. I've learned how to tap into it as a renewable energy source. It is a power that I control; it doesn't control me so I'm neither afraid of passion nor of being judged on the form of my sexual expression.''[11] That first issue also quoted a feminist newsletter: ''Celibacy can be a positive, fulfilling, freedom-enhancing choice, not necessarily a reflection of psychological problems, a repressed sexuality or a cold nature. A decision to be celibate does not mean taking 60 year 'vows.' Instead, a celibate period can last a month, a year or several years, however long the individual chooses.''[12]

Regardless of when they anticipated resuming sexual relationships, most of the writers chose not to identify their subjects, audiences, or themselves (present, past, future) in terms of sexual orientation. The writing often referred to relationships with ''someone you love'' or ''intimate friends'' in sex/gender-free language. A few writers did refer to themselves as being, or having been, lesbian or bisexual. Most seemed to imply an essentially heterosexual orientation. Martha Allen, for example, mentioned that married celibates often follow this lifestyle ''for the heightened spirituality and communication, and the potential for deepened love and affection,'' although her own editorial note looked forward ''to the day that our society is less couple oriented and single women can pursue their interests and feel at home in their single lifestyles.''[13]

Several heterosexual contributors referred to unhappy marriages and, especially, divorces. One poet had been married five times. Dorrie Jacobs took seven pages to outline ''Why Some Women Are Choosing Celibacy'': it is a refreshing alternative for those who resent pressure to conform; is a simpler lifestyle; gives women a sense of power and freedom; is a way to ensure that a relationship deepens; avoids sexually transmitted diseases; can be a satisfying way to take care of one's own sexual needs (i.e., masturbation); is preferable to unsatisfying and stressful encounters. Several of Jacobs' reasons explicitly referred to men: there is a shortage of men; some men are celibate; male attitudes and behaviors make some women angry.[14]

Martha Allen grew up in Washington, D.C. After graduating from Oakland University in Rochester, Michigan, she lived in the South, where she volunteered for several civil rights and other political causes. She founded a community bookstore that sponsored a number of progressive activities. She spent four years with a biracial women's media project that was negotiating with media in Memphis to reform their hiring and programming practices and also trying to plan a women's cable channel. She then returned to Washington to help her mother with the projects of the Women's Institute for Freedom of the Press. She became editor of its annual *Index and Directory of Women's Media.* At the time of her work with *The Celibate Woman Journal,* Martha Allen was also a doctoral student in the history department at Howard University. Her dissertation, ''The Development of Communication Networks among Women, 1963–1983,'' was completed in 1988. Now married, Martha is the director of the Women's Institute for Freedom of the Press.

The Celibate Woman Journal reached nearly one thousand subscribers. It even attracted an audience outside the United States. After eight issues, however, Martha Allen concluded that although responses to the periodical were enthusiastic, she could not find enough ''positive material'' on celibacy.[15] She stopped publishing *The Celibate Woman Journal* in 1988.

Notes

1. July 1982, p. 2.
2. February 1984, p. 2.
3. Martha Allen, interview August 17, 1995.
4. July 1982, p. 2.
5. March 1986, p. 3.
6. Ibid.
7. February 1984, p. 23.
8. February 1987, pp. 9–13.
9. Allen interview.
10. Ibid.
11. July 1982, p. 3.
12. "Our Own Write," July 1982, p. 4.
13. March 1986, pp. 5, 6.
14. February 1984, pp. 7–14.
15. Allen Interview.

Information Sources

BIBLIOGRAPHY:
Kranich, Kimberlie A. "Women's Media: By, for, and about." *Press Woman,* November 1988, pp. 6–9.
INDEX SOURCES: None.
LOCATION SOURCES: Northwestern University; the Women's Institute for Freedom of the Press, Washington, D.C.

Publication History

PERIODICAL TITLE AND TITLE CHANGES: *The Celibate Woman Journal.*
VOLUME AND ISSUE DATA: Vols. 1–4 (1982–1988). Irregular, although roughly semiannual.
PUBLISHER AND PLACE OF PUBLICATION: Martha Leslie Allen. Washington, D.C.
EDITOR: Martha Leslie Allen (1982–1988).
CIRCULATION: under 1,000.

Linda Steiner

CHRYSALIS

Taking as its theme the butterfly's emergence from a dark, sheltered, and shrouded state into its perfect form, the appropriately named *Chrysalis* burst into the feminist publishing arena in 1977. As "a vehicle for exploring the radical changes which women are initiating in the realms of theory and praxis," *Chrysalis* took its vision and content from the women's movement of the 1970s.[1] Writing in the second issue of the quarterly, the editors explained:

Last February we introduced *Chrysalis* as a challenge to traditional magazine publishing concepts. We wanted to create a magazine that would be uncompromising (though pluralist) in its feminism: serious, yet without the jargon and tendentiousness of academic journals; entertaining and accessible to a wide audience without the superficiality and chic of commercial glossies. The subscriptions, letters and contributions sent in by thousands of readers across the country have affirmed our approach.[2]

From the start, then, this quarterly "magazine of women's culture" offered a welcome juxtaposition of the practical with the analytical. The result was a creation that was as intellectually satisfying (some articles were scholarly with footnotes) as it was informational (every issue contained a catalog of resources, models, and listings on topics ranging from health, to finance, to feminist publishing outlets and self-publishing tips).

Chrysalis spent four years in the larva stage, growing out of *The New Woman's Survival Catalog* and *The New Woman's Survival Sourcebook,* two volumes dedicated to describing self-help resources for women and to "the documentation of the incredibly exciting and significant emergence of female consciousness."[3] Kirsten Grimstad and Susan Rennie, editors of the two books, wanted to show the diversity and myriad levels of feminist commitment in the United States but quickly discovered that "the women's movement is growing too fast for any single book any longer to encompass or even represent adequately the resources and ideas which feminism generates."[4] So they transformed themselves into *Chrysalis.* As "a new national feminist magazine published, edited, and printed by women," *Chrysalis* could reach a wider audience and "work for the achievement of women's liberation."[5] From two hundred charter subscribers in February 1977, *Chrysalis* would peak at more than thirteen thousand readers across the United States by the summer of 1979.[6]

Although explicitly feminist in orientation, *Chrysalis* wasn't narrow or strident in its approach. Indeed, the content and topics chosen reflected the editors' determination to present a diversity of material that would embrace all the dimensions of women's culture. *Chrysalis,* like many women's journals of the 1970s, took a forum approach to content, serving as a facilitator to a wide range of viewpoints and dialogues. Consequently, *Chrysalis* mixed reviews of art, literature, and film with articles on pornography, Freud, Patricia Hearst, Susan B. Anthony, transsexualism, female friendship, holistic healing, racism, the environment, science fiction, and a feminist/cultural interpretation of *Gone with the Wind.* The tone of the articles was often bold and fearless, breaking "new ground in the feminist analysis of society and the creation of feminist culture."[7] Surprisingly, *Chrysalis* was even amusing, knocking down the popular belief that feminists lacked a sense of humor and were incapable of poking fun at themselves.

Unusually broad in scope, *Chrysalis* did not substitute breadth for quality. A look at the authors, poets, essayists, and researchers contributing to *Chrysalis'* pages reveals a veritable who's who of towering intellects in the feminist movement: black lesbian activist Audre Lorde; the magazine's poetry editor, Robin

Morgan, who later served as editor of *Ms.* from 1990 to 1993; award-winning poet Adrienne Rich; novelist Marge Piercy; artist Judy Chicago; science fiction writer Joanna Russ, plus Mary Dale, Dolores Hayden, Andrea Dworkin, Marilyn Hacker, Arlene Raven, and Elizabeth Janeway. The editors eloquently described the magazine's editorial range in a house advertisement:

> We feature writers who create out of a sense of urgency. They deal with issues no one thought of before and no one else will print. Original. Insightful. Just two reasons to read *Chrysalis.* If you want more, subscribe regularly. *Chrysalis,* where women give birth to issues.[8]

Readers across the country enthusiastically responded to the birth of this publication, based in Los Angeles. Jane Gould of New York wrote to the editors: "*Chrysalis* is a wonderfully sensitive, beautiful magazine and a remarkable addition to feminist literature. I found myself weeping as I concluded with Adrienne Rich and Honor Moore's poems. It's a tribute to you that with all that is pouring from the pens of feminists, that you can make such an important and fresh contribution."[9] Other readers praised the magazine for presenting "the clearest and most thorough female thinking I've encountered" and for being "committed to an undiluted feminism."[10]

Librarians also praised the new publication. Calling *Chrysalis* an "impressive new feminist journal" in his regular column about magazines for *Library Journal,* Bill Katz wrote: "The magazine fills the gap between the more popular feminist magazines such as *Ms.,* the more scholarly such as *Signs,* and the more local. It deserves a place in all libraries."[11] Edi Bjorklund, writing in *Serials Review,* said of *Chrysalis,* "*Chrysalis* is essential for any women's studies collection. I also recommend it for libraries with strengths in contemporary literature, art, feminism, or religion. The resources sections and reviews, not to mention the ads for new publications in each issue, are also very helpful for use in library collection development."[12]

Only ten issues of *Chrysalis* were published from 1977 to 1980, but readers got good value for their ten-dollar yearly subscription. Every *Chrysalis* had at least three major scholarly articles complete with bibliographies, several shorter provocative essays, fiction, poetry, a lengthy (at least twenty pages) resource catalog, first-rate book reviews, a Q&A interview with a significant feminist artist, a feminist double-crostic puzzle, and selections from the "First Wave," original writings by those involved in the nineteenth and early twentieth centuries' woman's rights movement. These "First Wave" articles were intriguing, including letters from Susan B. Anthony and Amelia Bloomer about the tyranny of women's clothes, or contemporary observations about Emma Goldman's political activism versus Jane Addams' support networking.

The writers often challenged conventional assumptions. For example, Kathleen Barry took a feminist theoretical perspective in comparing Patricia Hearst to female sex slaves who were abducted and sold into brothels.[13] Barry argued that Hearst was a victim of patriarchal judgment who was criticized and punished when she should have been praised for her survival skills. The Hearst newspaper heiress stayed alive by cooperating with her captors, yet it became evident during her trial that many Americans thought she should have died rather than collaborate. Janice Raymond's "Transsexualism: The Ultimate Homage to Sex-Role Power" argued that transsexualism was another form of sexual stereotyping that feminists should seek to dissolve.[14] She urged readers to deny the idea that anatomy is destiny and that sex roles are biologically determined. Articles like these outraged some readers, who wrote long, passionate, fiery rebuttals in their letters to the editors. The letters, printed in their entirety, took up as many as eight or nine pages of a single issue at a time when mainstream women's magazines might run a single column devoted to readers' thoughts.

But no article evoked more smoldering comments than did Nancy Sahli's piece about the hidden heritage of women's intensely affectionate friendships during the nineteenth century and the point at which society began to regard female bonding as threatening.[15] Author Joanna Russ criticized Sahli for not acknowledging the erotic intensity of the friendships, writing, "I'm not sure what the taboo really is here. Is 'Lesbian' still so loaded a word that its very presence impugns the innocence, the emotionality, even the human decency of the relationships Sahli describes?"[16] Russ wanted more explicit commentary on lesbian themes, yet Janet Robin canceled her subscription to Chrysalis because of its lesbian material:

> I did not realize that Chrysalis is a Lesbian magazine of feminist arts. While I am vitally interested in feminist arts, I must say that your message, both implicit and explicit, that the only honorable and valuable relationship between human beings is a Lesbian one is disturbing to me, since I am not a Lesbian. It also disturbs me that your articles on lost matriarchal mythologies and history are attempts to strengthen this argument, and not (to my mind) honest efforts to uncover very important and ignored areas of human thoughts and action.[17]

The editors responded to Robin that Chrysalis was not a lesbian magazine, nor was it a heterosexual magazine: "It is a feminist magazine that more truthfully reflects the sexual diversity of women—both in the feminist movement and in the larger society—than those mainstream publications which attempt to deny that diversity through silence, omission, distortion."[18] The editors added that since the start-up of Chrysalis, they had received numerous such letters indicating "an uncomfortable awareness of the homophobia which still pervades our society."[19] Concerned about this phenomenon, the editors asked:

> It is not conceivable that a lesbian might have something of general merit and interest to say? Do people cancel subscriptions to magazines because of an article on black culture, or youth culture, or European culture, or

Asian culture, or the poor, or the rich, or beautiful people, or fat people? Yet when lesbianism comes up in *Chrysalis,* in whatever way, letters come in saying, "Cancel my subscription; I'm not one of them." Sadly, this issue continues to divide us from each other and from our selves on the deepest level."[20]

What seemed to unite readers, however, was the emphasis on poetry, art, and previously invisible artists. Distinctively avant-garde, there was a wealth of "artistic" material here written in many voices on a multitude of topics. The magazine was deluged with unsolicited submissions, making it difficult for the volunteer editorial staff to keep up. Like the majority of its feminist sister magazines, editorial decisions at *Chrysalis* were the result of a collective process involving at least a dozen members of the editorial board and staff. Articles were accepted only if there was consensus.[21]

By the fifth issue, when *Chrysalis* began its second year of publication in 1978, editors wrote, "We wish to apologize to those writers who have waited anxiously for prolonged periods of time for a response from us. Delays imply no disrespect for the work submitted, but rather reflect the limitations imposed by our present overloaded working conditions."[22] Two issues later, the editors told readers that because of the heavy volume of poetry, fiction, and literary criticism received, they wouldn't consider manuscripts in those areas for a year, asking for no more submissions until after January 1, 1980. Editors appeared surprised at the outpouring of creative work:

Clearly, one of the most exciting and dramatic effects of contemporary feminism has been the unleashing of terrific creativity in women, an outpouring which, in the written media, is manifesting itself primarily as poetry—and to a lesser extent, fiction, and criticism of poetry and fiction. . . . We are inundated with poetry, fiction, and literary criticism. Good! But where is the theory? Where is the hard-hitting, muckraking investigative reporting? Where is the scrutiny that helps us think about and transform the issues that shape and dominate our lives?[23]

Interestingly, feminist publications of the 1970s were dominated by poetry and journal writing, another genre grounded in self-discovery to which *Chrysalis* also devoted considerable space. It's obvious that many women writers of this period felt more comfortable with validating the familiar and the emotional rather than aggressively following the objective demands of reportorial, investigative journalism.

But then, *Chrysalis* didn't look remotely journalistic in its presentation. The editors offered a spare, yet dense, layout, with pages set in either three narrow columns or one large, booklike column. Whichever format was used for the 132-page magazine, there were lots of white space at the top and bottom of the page and no color, just black-and-white drawings or line art. The illustrations subtly enhanced the uncluttered text. Articles tended to start on a right-hand page opposite a blank left-hand page. The four-page cover was of extremely heavy paper stock, generally with an illustration of a singular object like a glove or a stocking, wrapping around the front and back. Explained the editors in their first issue, "The design of *Chrysalis* follows the processes we have valued in our own interaction in the feminist movement. Written and graphic material has been designed so as not to compete for your attention, nor to entice, induce, or seduce you, the reader."[24]

The layout struck a responsive chord in readers like Kathleen Cerveny of Cleveland Heights, Ohio, who wrote, "As an artist, I am especially concerned with visual presentation—and *Chrysalis* makes one of the most tasteful and comprehensive visual impressions of any publication I have seen. There is space for each article and poem to breathe. The reader/viewer can consider each entry in a comfortable, untrammeled setting."[25]

Each quarterly issue averaged 132 pages, with advertising, located at the back of the magazine, constituting about 10 pages per issue. Half-page, one-third-page, and one-quarter-page ads grouped together on a single page were primarily for women's books and feminist and women's studies journals, published by small feminist publishing houses. Periodically, mainstream book publishers such as Harper and Row and W. W. Norton took out full-page ads for books targeted to feminist readers. No ads ever competed with the editorial layouts, and only occasionally were there full-page advertisements on the inside front cover, inside back cover, or back page. The classified ads emphasized women's sensibilities and contributions, promoting such obvious offerings as feminist gift items (T-shirts, jewelry, leather patches, vibrators, and decals), lesbian music ("Lavender Jane Loves Women"), and educational retreats for feminists in the mountains of Southern California (where women would "develop feminist political theory by living it"). Obviously, this was a very narrow advertising product range that could not be expected to expand or to offer significant financial support.

That there wasn't enough advertising or capital to support *Chrysalis* became clear by the third issue in 1977. Editorial board member Joanne Parrent wrote "All about Our Own Money" as a companion piece to a resource catalog compilation on money matters. Parent clearly laid out income sources, expenses, average income per copy sold, expenses by category per copy sold, break-even point, and how the magazine had been financed to date. No salaries were paid to any of the editors or staff, nor would they ever be paid during the existence of *Chrysalis*. Parent estimated the break-even point would occur when sales hit thirty-three thousand copies per issue; by this third issue *Chrysalis* was selling five thousand copies per issue. She also estimated that it would be necessary to raise one hundred thousand dollars before the magazine would be fully capitalized.[26]

By the start of its second year, *Chrysalis* had grown to eight thousand subscribers.[27] With the eighth issue in the summer of 1979 and a circulation of thirteen thousand, the editors decided "to stop pretending that *Chrysalis* springs into existence magically and instead let you in on some of the sweat, tears and anxiety that accompany the birth of each issue."[28] Editors bluntly asked for reader support in the form of extended renewals for two or three years or through gift subscriptions to friends. "Never mind that you've only just received your first issue," the editors said. "Only your belief in and support of our future will make that future a reality. This is no joke, friends. Our need is great for cold, hard cash."[29] Pointing out that only about twenty-five hundred copies of *Chrysalis* were available in retail outlets, editors also suggested that readers take a copy of the most recent issue to their favorite bookstore and request that the owner or manager stock the magazine. "Let us know which store(s) you've approached, and when we receive their order we'll give you a free subscription or renewal," editors promised.[30]

By the ninth issue, *Chrysalis* was asking readers to make a loan to the publication, which would be repaid at 8 percent interest, 2.5 percent more than passbook accounts were earning.[31] Other suggestions were for educators to require *Chrysalis* as a text in women's studies classes, for students to become representatives selling subscriptions on college campuses, and for "hardworking, dedicated and responsible" individuals willing to commit to "regular weekly hours" as interns at *Chrysalis'* headquarters in Los Angeles.[32]

The barriers facing *Chrysalis* were not unique. The magazine was struggling against the same publishing problems endemic to the feminist press of the 1970s, primarily lack of nitty-gritty expertise and rising inflation in the form of cost increases for postage and paper. Feminist publications generally started up with a lot of energy and romantic ideals, failing to recognize the work and expenses involved in distribution, marketing, promotion, and advertising sales. Mainstream bookstores were reluctant to stock feminist journals, thus limiting publication availability to small, alternative bookstores that also were understaffed, poorly capitalized, and struggling against the same financial winds. Readers complained about problems in receiving their issues, yet few feminist magazines could afford to use efficient fulfillment agencies. A horrific cycle would begin, with readers reluctant to renew, or even subscribe to, a magazine that wasn't distributed in a timely manner.

Grant money was not available to feminist endeavors, and the nonprofit route was costly to establish. "Choosing self-sufficiency seemed the more solidly feminist approach," *Chrysalis'* editors wrote, "and carried the additional benefit of forcing us to market the magazine aggressively in order to increase our circulation.... Of course, plans that work out perfectly in the untainted realm of pure theory often take very different shape when applied to actual practice— where unexpected variables enter the picture and muck things up."[33]

Despite maintaining a quarterly schedule for its first year, *Chrysalis* published only two issues during 1978 and three during 1979 before folding in 1980 with its tenth issue. In what would be its last editorial, the editors seemed frustrated and demoralized by the bitter realities of publishing a magazine that had to depend on reader support rather than advertising dollars. Wearily, they wrote:

And need we say that the constant worrying and fretting and financial cliffhanging sap energy that we would rather direct into editorial matters? At the risk of sounding sorry for ourselves, we would like our readers to know that there are times when we are just too damned tired and worn out to function with the drive and vigor which we believe characterize our enterprise at its best.[34]

That was the last message from the editors and publishers of *Chrysalis*. Perhaps readers didn't want to hear about the magazine's financial difficulties or to have the publishing process demystified and personalized. More likely, the financial burden became too great for the volunteer editorial staff (all of whom were dependent on other means of earning a living) to bear. One later critic of the magazine, writing in 1983, argued: "As *Chrysalis* ran into deeper trouble, its letters to readers began to sound haranguing, implying that while the editors were flailing away without a salary, readers were taking it all for granted, failing to subscribe or to make donations. There is some doubt in my mind whether readers want to share a publisher's woes, and whether they should be expected to do so."[35]

Yet even its detractors agreed that it was unfortunate that *Chrysalis* folded:

Among nonacademic cultural women's magazines, *Chrysalis* was among the best, and it is unfortunate it did not overcome its problems. Because it was not an academic publication, it could neither make use of academic institutions nor offer advertisers a clearly defined audience. . . . Strongest in this magazine were its informational articles—on women of historical importance, on the history of housework—which were scholarly and thorough and which served to fill in women's missing past. Its essays, on pornography, for example, or on racism, were also intelligently done. At its best, *Chrysalis* served to define the issues women needed to think about and to provide the information with which they might do so.[36]

Chrysalis had the potential for success, and it is sad that the era into which it was born could not be more nourishing. It was the kind of magazine that this author would have shared with her friends, passing it around from woman to woman, then keeping it as an important feminist reference in the home library. *Chrysalis* upheld its promise of being written, produced, and published by women—no male bylines or letters ever appeared, nor were any male artists ever featured. In retrospect, more than fifteen years after its demise, *Chrysalis* remains a treasure that should be read and reread as a powerful women's magazine.

Notes

1. "Announcing *Chrysalis*," in Kirsten Grimstad and Susan Rennie, eds, *The New Woman's Survival Sourcebook* (New York: Knopf, 1975), p. 158.

2. number 2, 1977, p. 3.

3. "Introduction, *The New Woman's Survival Sourcebook,*" no page number.

4. Ibid.

5. Ibid.

6. "Dear Readers," number 8, 1979, p. 3.

7. G. Llewellyn Watson, *Feminism and Women's Issues: An Annotated Bibliography and Research Guide, Volume II* (New York: Garland, 1990), p. 1707.

8. "Our Mothers of Invention," number 8, 1979, inside front cover.

9. "Letters to the Editors," number 2, 1977, p. 6.

10. Ibid.

11. Bill Katz, "Magazines," *Library Journal,* October 15, 1977, p. 2145.

12. Eli Bjorklund, "*Chrysalis,*" in Jean Farrington and Cristine C. Rom, eds., "Feminist Periodicals," *Serials Review,* October/December 1979, p. 15.

13. Kathleen Barry, "Did I Ever Really Have a Chance? Patriarchal Judgment of Patricia Hearst," number 1, 1977, pp. 7–17.

14. Janice Raymond, "Transsexualism: The Ultimate Homage to Sex-Role Power," number 3, 1977, pp. 11–23.

15. Nancy Sahli, "Smashing: Women's Relationships before the Fall," number 8, 1979, pp. 17–27.

16. "Letters," number 9, Fall 1979, p. 6.

17. Ibid., p. 8.

18. Ibid.

19. Ibid., p. 9.

20. Ibid.

21. "Dear Readers," number 10, 1980, p. 4.

22. number 5, 1978, p. 2.

23. "Dear Readers," number 10, 1980, p. 5.

24. number 1, 1977, p. 3.

25. "Letters," number 6, 1978, p. 7.

26. Joanne Parrent, "All about Our Own Money," number 3, 1977, p. 117.

27. number 5, 1978, p. 3.

28. "Dear Readers," number 8, p. 2.

29. Ibid., p. 3.

30. Ibid., p. 2.

31. "Dear Readers," number 9, 1979, p. 3.

32. Ibid.

33. Ibid., p. 2.

34. "Dear Readers," number 10, 1980, p. 4.

35. Gail Pool, "Women's Publications: Some Issues," *The Massachusetts Review,* Summer 1983, p. 471.

36. Ibid.

Information Sources

BIBLIOGRAPHY:

Joan, Polly, and Andrea Chesman. *Guide to Women's Publishing.* Paradise, Calif.: Dustbooks, 1978.

Mather, Anne. "A History of Feminist Periodicals, Part I." *Journalism History* 1.2, Summer 1974, pp. 82–85.

————. "A History of Feminist Periodicals, Part II." *Journalism History* 1.4, Winter
    1974–1975, pp. 108–111.
————. "A History of Feminist Periodicals, Part III." *Journalism History* 2.1, Spring
    1975, pp. 19–31.
INDEX SOURCES: None.
LOCATION SOURCES: Library of Congress; The Woman's Collection, Texas Woman's
    University, Denton, Tex.

Publication History

PERIODICAL TITLE AND TITLE CHANGES: *Chrysalis.*
VOLUME AND ISSUE DATA: Vols. 1–3 (number 1, 1977–number 10, 1980). Quar-
    terly. (Issues are numbered and do not carry monthly dates.)
PUBLISHER AND PLACE OF PUBLICATION: Chrysalis, a Magazine of Women's
    Culture, a California Corporation, Los Angeles (1977–1980). (*Chrysalis* took a
    collective, consensus approach to all magazine operations, not listing individual
    publishers until Number 7, 1979, and Number 8, 1979, when Kirsten Grimstad,
    Ruth Iskin, Joanne Kerr, Elisabeth Kreutz, and Alana Probst are named. Number
    9, 1979, and Number 10, 1980, list Kirsten Grimstad, Joanne Kerr, and Elisabeth
    Reinhardt as publishers.)
EDITORS: Kirsten Grimstad is listed as managing editor for numbers 1–6, 1977–1979.
    Grimstad is listed as executive editor for numbers 7–10, 1979–1980. Because
    Chrysalis took a collective, consensus approach to editorial operations, a large
    editorial board is listed on the masthead, with Grimstad's being the only individ-
    ual to serve as a member of the editorial board as well as managing or executive
    editor.
CIRCULATION: 13,000.

Sammye Johnson

D

DAUGHTERS OF SARAH

The first issue of the Christian feminist publication *Daughters of Sarah,* in November 1974, was an eight-page mimeographed newsletter that grew out of conversations and a weekly Bible study among a group of women who were students or faculty wives at North Park Seminary in Chicago. They chose the title *Daughters of Sarah* to parallel the identification "sons of Abraham" from the Judeo-Christian heritage. The masthead on later issues explained, "Sarah was a strong woman, very human, and equally called by God to a new land of promise."

The first editor was Lucille Sider Dayton (later, Groh). She and the Bible study group pooled funds to send the first issue of *Daughters of Sarah* to a mailing list of about two hundred in November 1994. The new publication was promoted with a classified advertisement in the peace and justice magazine, *The Other Side.* That ad was spotted by Reta Halteman Finger, who sent in her two dollars for the bimonthly newsletter. A year later, when Finger moved to the Chicago area, she joined those monthly meetings to gather material for the new publication and to volunteer for clerical duties. At the end of the first meeting she found herself with the title of book review editor.[1]

Later, Finger's responsibilities included copyediting, and in 1979, when founding editor Groh had begun study for a doctorate in counseling and psychology, Finger took over the management and editorial role, which continued until 1994. Although Finger clearly had the primary editorial responsibilities, the rejection of hierarchical relationships is reflected in the alphabetical listings of all the part-timers and volunteers, without identification of duties, that persisted on the masthead for many years. Most of the editorials from 1979 to fall 1994 were signed by Finger, and she was referred to as editorial coordinator.

In the editorial reflections about the beginnings of *Daughters of Sarah,* several events in the evangelical Protestant culture of 1974 are described as converging to bring about the energizing of the Christian feminist movement. The launching of *Daughters of Sarah* was one of these events.[2] It closely followed the publication of a seminal book, *All We're Meant to Be: A Women's Approach to Biblical Liberation,* by Letha Scanzoni and Nancy Hardesty. In a survey of the periodical's readers in its tenth-anniversary year, that book still was named most influential.[3] *Daughters of Sarah*'s appearance was closely related to the organization of the Evangelical Women's Caucus in Washington, D.C., a nationwide gathering of Protestant women who discovered that others shared their convictions that feminism and biblical faith were compatible.

The magazine as a mouthpiece for Christian feminism described itself in each issue, beginning on page 1 of vol. 1. 1, with the following statement or a slight variation of it:

> Christianity and feminism for us are inseparable.
> DAUGHTERS OF SARAH is our attempt to share our discoveries, our struggles, and our growth as Christian women. We are committed to Scripture and we seek to find in it meaning for our lives. We are rooted in a historical tradition of women who have served God in innumerable ways, and we seek guidance from their example. We are convinced that Christianity is relevant to all areas of women's lives today. We seek ways to act out our faith.

These Christian feminists shared their experiences of put-downs by both feminists and those in the pews and pulpits of their churches. In the best feminist tradition, they related and listened to these personal stories. However, the magazine was not only reflective narrative but also serious exegesis and theologizing. Although many of their secular contemporaries identified the church as a primary oppressor of women, the magazine's creators and contributors sought to begin an intellectual and social dialogue among those who wished to explore Christian faith and feminism. Articles in *Daughters of Sarah* explored alternative theological interpretations of biblical passages that have been used to belittle women's roles and to justify hierarchical power in institutions and family life. For examples, see the May/June 1980 issue with the theme "Violent Hermeneutics" (uses and abuses of the Bible); "Unveiling the Goddess" (September/October 1983); and "Estranged: Women in the Church" (May/June 1983).

By its tenth anniversary the publication had evolved into a thirty-two-page, 5.5 by 8.5-inch format, and it boasted of a circulation between three thousand and four thousand. The articles continued a focus on exegetical-theological issues, like ordination of women in January/February 1979 and July/August 1980; on historical biography of Christian women like Catherine Booth, cofounder of the Salvation Army, in November 1974 and July–August 1978; and on social justice issues, in March/April and May/June 1984 with the theme "Our Sisters in the Third World."

The editorial process involved the group of Chicago women, many of whom were volunteers or who were hired part-time, getting together to brainstorm about the theme, article topics, and the approach to be taken. For many years the conversations sought consensus, but when that become impossible, as it soon did, various points of view were included, and controversial articles were followed by responses and rebuttals.

Each issue contains several features that revolve around a theme or topic; there are usually some poems and book reviews related to justice issues, feminism, theology, and ministry. The frontispiece is an editorial/opinion piece on the theme of the issue. A regular feature, "Grapevine," is a compendium of conference announcements, resources, and reprinted news items. One seminary librarian characterized that content as "chatty."

Often appearing inside the front cover in earlier issues were items called "Journey to Christian Feminism," personal accounts "by readers on how they came to Christian feminism." Beginning in 1971, this kind of material appeared under the standing headline, "Segue." In the spring 1995 "Segue," a Catholic sister, described her work in New York City working with women AIDS patients.

Daughters of Sarah accepts advertising, although minimal effort is made to solicit advertising. Most ads are for religious books. There are some classifieds, often from seminaries or Christian colleges seeking faculty. A one thousand-dollar grant from Church Women United in 1979 paid for a direct-mail campaign that gave the fledgling magazine an early boost. Often supporters are solicited for charitable donations, as the magazine is a nonprofit religious corporation. Readers are generous to other causes, too. Mention of the Sewing Folk Arts Industry in Mississippi resulted in boxes of fabric remnants sent for quilts.

The letters column, "Dear Daughters," reflects a broad readership, from prison inmates to clergy—both male and female, including writers from almost every state and from foreign countries. Letter writers objected when the magazine announced it was seeking donations totaling eight hundred dollars to contract for fulfillment and labeling services formerly done by Threshold, an organization that rehabilitates emotionally disturbed adults. One reader wrote, "Your request left me with a vision of you all hurrying and scurrying, busily abandoning hurting people you'd been helping just to steal a week on eternity." The editor explained how those served by Threshold would not be disadvantaged.[4]

But the controversy caused by that business decision paled next to others that involved the theological doctrine of the Atonement, goddess religious imagery, abortion, and homosexual practice.

One of the most controversial was "Divine Child Abuse," a book excerpt with the thesis that Christianity has been the primary force in shaping acceptance of abuse because Jesus' Crucifixion depicts suffering as redemptive.[5] Several point-counterpoint-type responses followed: theologians argued the centrality of the Atonement to Christian belief, and a clinical counselor, specializing in treating victims of religious abuse, reacted from his experiences.

The September/October 1983 issue, "Unveiling the Goddess," sparked more reader response than any until that time. While some readers advocated listening to new ideas, even those they found repugnant, other readers angrily canceled their subscriptions.[6] Ten years later, when the Re-Imagining Conference that explored the divine feminine caused national denominational controversy, *Daughters of Sarah* explored the fallout by publishing a variety of viewpoints in the fall 1994 issue.

A pro-life advertisement, inadvertently not identified as an ad, also brought reader reaction. Readers were referred to an earlier issue in which the statement on abortion issued by the Church of the Brethren was reprinted with the note that it was a statement that "most of us can also affirm and appreciate."[7] Although in that issue, editor Finger reflected that the magazine had avoided the topic of abortion for years because of the political irrationality and the moral dilemmas surrounding it, the articles presented sensitive and reasoned discussions from a broad spectrum of views. One writer reflected with irony, "I am adamantly anti-abortion and radically prochoice—I have no friends."[8]

Dialogue on abortion continued in the fall 1992 issue with the theme of "Birth, Adoption and Abortion," including articles that discussed experiences of labor, infertility, single-parent adoption, parenting a rebellious teen, and a mother's surrender of her eleven-month-old child when she found mothering impossible. A particular view on abortion will not likely earn the label of either Christian heretic or feminist heretic from this magazine.

The issue of biblical attitudes toward lesbians is also one with which *Daughters of Sarah* has wrestled. Finger recalled that the topic of homosexuality received extensive discussion before continuing feedback from readers identified it as an issue that could no longer be ignored editorially, even if the editorial committee could not agree on biblical interpretation. Articles discussing homosexuality were printed as early as 1977. In 1984 one writer declared her support of homosexual marriage.[9] Two 1988 issues grappled with the "Feminist Straight and Lesbian." As with other topics, various views were printed, as biblical passages were explored and interpreted. One former staff member reportedly left the magazine because of theological disagreement on this issue.

In the spring 1994 issue featuring "Interreligious Dialogue," the editors posed the question, At what point are the religious boundaries stretched so that the magazine no longer has a specific Christian orientation? Although supporting dialogue and publishing material reflecting cultural-racial-religious diversity, the editors emphasized that confessional Christianity is so bound up with exclusive claims that it cannot be relative without losing its essence.[10]

In 1994, longtime editor Finger moved to Virginia to follow her husband in his academic career and sought to devote time to finishing her own doctoral dissertation. Although she attempted to continue some editorial responsibility, the fall 1994 issue was her last. Elizabeth Anderson, an Episcopal seminary graduate, became the new editor. She explained that family reasons kept her in the Chicago area, and she was unable to find employment in any local Episcopal parish. Just as with these two editors, employment, family, and educational life changes have meant that no one of the original North Park Seminary group is left, but others have taken their places, and the Christian feminist voice continues and is reaching a more denominationally and geographically diverse audience.

Although subscribers have declined from a high of about sixty-eight hundred in 1988, founding editor Groh claims that *Daughters,* which had some competition in the beginning, is now the only surviving magazine or journal devoted to exploration of Christian feminism.[11]

As a Chicago reporter concluded after interviews with Finger and several of the other *Daughters* editors, "The God she and the other women of *Daughters* find in the Bible has a much different attitude than the one found by [evangelist] Jerry Falwell and the pope."[12]

Notes

1. Rita Halteman Finger, "Beginnings, Endings, and Middles," Fall 1994, pp. 4–6.
2. Anne Eggebroten, "40 Years to Go," November/December 1984, p. 10.
3. Patricia Broughton, "Survey Results," March/April 1985, pp. 16–19.
4. "Dear Daughters," September/October 1985, p. 32.
5. Joanne Carlson Brown, "Divine Child Abuse?" Summer 1992, pp. 24–28.
6. "Dear Daughters," January/February 1984, pp. 21–22; "Dear Daughters," May/June 1984, pp. 22–23.
7. "Statement on Abortion," September/October 1985, p. 21.
8. Karen Osman, "Sex, Babies, and Other Good Stuff," September/October 1985, p. 18.
9. Eggebroten, "40 Years to Go," p. 10.
10. Cathi Falsani and Reta Finger, "Relativizing Christianity?" Spring 1994, pp. 39–40.
11. Harold Henderson, "Was Christ a Feminist?" (Chicago) *Reader,* August 27, 1993, p. 9.
12. Ibid.

Information Sources

BIBLIOGRAPHY:
Hayes, Kathleen. "Daughters of Sarah." *The Other Side,* November 1985, pp. 10–11.
Henderson, Harold. "Was Christ a Feminist?" (Chicago) *Reader,* August 27, 1993, pp. 8–9, 24–25.
Hulteen, Bob. "A 20th Anniversary and a 20s Comic." *Sojourners,* November 1994, p. 40.
Willett, Dawn. "Christian Feminists Look to Daughters." *Chicago Tribune,* August 1, 1986, sec. 2, p. 7.
INDEX SOURCES: Religion Index One (RIO): periodicals; Index to Book Reviews in Religion (BRR). (Both indexes are published by the American Theological Library Association and are available on-line through BRS, Dialog, Wilsonline, and Wilson Disc CD ROM Information Services.)

LOCATION SOURCES: St. Louis University, St. Louis, Mo.; Jesuit-Krauss-McCormick
    Library, Chicago; Garrett-Evangelical and Seabury-Western Theological Semi-
    naries, Evanston, Ill.

Publication History

PERIODICAL TITLE AND TITLE CHANGES: *Daughters of Sarah* (1974–present).
VOLUME AND ISSUE DATA: Vols. 1– (November 1974–present). Bimonthly (No-
    vember 1974–July/August 1991); quarterly (fall 1991–present).
PUBLISHER AND PLACE OF PUBLICATION: Daughters of Sarah, Inc. Chicago
    (1974–1993); Evanston, Ill. (1993–present).
EDITORS: Lucille Sider Dayton (later, Groh) (1974–1979); Reta Halteman Finger
    (1979–1994); Elizabeth Anderson (1994–present).
CIRCULATION: 4,500.

Anna R. Paddon

E

EQUAL RIGHTS

Equal Rights for thirty years was the mouthpiece of the women who introduced and unsuccessfully struggled decades for an equal rights amendment to the U.S. Constitution. *Equal Rights* was the first, and for many years the only, newspaper to argue that a single constitutional amendment was not only the logical next step in the woman's movement that won the vote in 1920 but the only way to achieve equality between the sexes in all realms of American life. The journal reflected the feminist identity of its publisher, the National Woman's Party (NWP), the only women's group to publicly avow itself feminist in the 1920s.

Equal Rights began publishing on February 17, 1923, as part of the NWP's nascent campaign for an equal rights amendment, which it formally declared on July 20, 1923.[1] Replacing a one-page weekly bulletin of the same name, the eight-page weekly tabloid *Equal Rights* emulated in style and format the NWP's defunct publication, *Suffragist.** Like the suffrage newspaper, *Equal Rights* featured cover illustrations by Nina Allender and continued columns such as "Notes from the Field," "Press Comment," "Feminist Notes," and feminist book reviews. Photographs showcased the theatrical NWP in activities ranging from its lavish pageant at Seneca Falls to a delegation to President Calvin Coolidge. Other recurring themes involved countless tributes to suffragists and notices of Susan B. Anthony's birthday, which the NWP wanted declared a national holiday.[2]

Equal Rights' first editorial also looked to the past by likening the fledgling equal rights movement to NWP protesters who picketed the White House. This fixation upon past glories foreshadowed the difficulties the NWP faced unifying postsuffrage women behind a single ideological vision. Although *Equal Rights* sought to bind "free-souled women together, to hearten them by contact with others of like spirit,'' it failed to rouse them to its campaign for a constitutional amendment.[3]

Equal Rights struggled hard to demonstrate the futility of tackling piecemeal the thousands of state laws, court rulings, and customs that discriminated against women. It amassed a vast amount of research documenting statues restricting women's right to work, earn as much as men, serve on juries, own their wages, keep custody of their children, and even retain their citizenship if they married a foreigner.[4] ''One gets weary of fighting the same fight over and over again,'' said a 1933 editorial arguing that the amendment would, in a single stroke, eradicate all sex discrimination.[5]

Yet virtually all other women's organizations opposed an equal rights amendment. *Equal Rights* found itself invariably on the defensive, answering their charge that a constitutional amendment would actually handicap the nation's eight million women workers, since motherhood and other factors placed women at a disadvantage when competing with men. Critics claimed an equal rights amendment would remove hard-won protective legislation regarding working-women's hours and wages. Between *Equal Rights'* pages, one can trace the origins of the ideological question that continues to perplex the modern women's movement: Beyond their biological functions, are women and men different?

The newspaper defended the unpopular concept of absolute sexual equality, even arguing women should be drafted.[6] As an alternative to protective legislation that it claimed paternalistically restricted women's work, *Equal Rights* called for a family allowance.[7] ''Let the State compensate mothers as it compensates soldiers for their sacrifices,'' an editorial said.[8] Although critics claim the single-minded NWP ignored the needs of working-class women, *Equal Rights* also published many articles and editorials championing women's right to work and decrying job discrimination, especially as it escalated during the depression.

Equal Rights was one of the few publications challenging the view that workingwomen were stealing jobs from family men. Section 213 of the National Economy Act, prohibiting more than one member of the same family from working for the civil service, particularly rankled, and *Equal Rights* vigorously protested it.[9] The NWP's main focus remained on an equal rights amendment, however, as the cure for sex discrimination.

That focus became sharper after the party dismissed *Equal Rights* editor Edith Houghton Hooker. Hooker had served as editor since its inception, and her physician husband's money had kept the publication afloat for a decade from an office near their Baltimore home. Yet her attempts to broaden the agenda of the newspaper and reorganize the NWP to make it more democratic annoyed party leaders.[10] The NWP National Council voted at the end of 1934 to replace Hooker's publication with a biweekly newsletter to be produced at NWP headquarters.[11] Hooker refused to relinquish her publication, which she called *Equal Rights: Independent Feminist Weekly.* Meanwhile, the NWP published *Equal Rights: Official Organ of the National Woman's Party* until the two factions, financially strapped and now faced with advocating an amendment to a public further distracted by billowing European war clouds, merged in January 1937 under a new editor.

The merged publication retrained its focus upon the stalled equal rights amendment in the United States and the international equal rights movement spearheaded by NWP founder Alice Paul. The newspaper had always emphasized international feminist news, juxtaposing lengthy articles on the state of feminism in India, Japan, and elsewhere with briefs about women's accomplishments around the world.[12] The amount of space devoted to women's activities on the other side of the globe unwittingly cast light on the void of woman's rights news back in the United States. Photographs of conventioneering white-haired women likewise revealed that the NWP was failing to attract the younger generation.

Ever optimistic, however, *Equal Rights* kept readers well apprised of Paul's unsuccessful crusade for a treaty guaranteeing equal rights to women citizens in the doomed League of Nations. Articles, editorials, and photographs filled every issue with Paul's quixotic quest, even as Adolph Hitler issued pronouncements relegating women to the home.

In the United States, *Equal Rights* provided copious coverage of the equal rights amendment for fewer than two thousand paid subscribers as the campaign seemed finally to gain a little momentum in the late 1930s and 1940s before foundering in the early 1950s. The newspaper also foundered financially during these years, appearing monthly, then every other month and even more sporadically as a revolving door of editors futilely tried to spark an indifferent public's interest in an equal rights amendment. The final issue appeared in November 1954.

Equal Rights' approach to keeping feminism rolling after suffrage was validated in the 1960s, when the second wave of feminism revived the call for an equal rights amendment. The amendment may have died, but *Equal Rights* helped keep feminism alive in the years between the wars.[13]

Notes

1. Leila Rupp and Vera Taylor, *Survival in the Doldrums: The American Women's Movement, 1945 to the 1960s* (New York: Oxford University Press, 1987), p. 39, "Women Open Campaign for Equal Rights," July 28, 1923, p. 189.

2. "Susan B. Anthony," January 7, 1933, p. 386. Its call to replace Theodore Roosevelt with Anthony on the planned Mount Rushmore sculpture also went unanswered. "Anthony vs. Roosevelt," December 29, 1934, p. 378.

3. "The Picket Line," February 17, 1923, p. 8. Discussions of the early campaign for an equal rights amendment can be found in Susan Becker, *The Origins of the Equal Rights Amendment: American Feminism between the Wars* (Westport, Conn.: Greenwood Press, 1981); William Chafe, *The Paradox of Change: American Women in the twentieth Century* (New York: Oxford University Press, 1991), pp. 47–60; "Equal Rights and Economic Rules," in Nancy Cott, *The Grounding of Modern Feminism* (New Haven, Conn.: Yale University Press, 1987), pp. 115–142; Christine Lunardini, *From Equal*

Suffrage to Equal Rights: Alice Paul and the National Woman's Party, 1910–1928 (New York: New York University Press, 1986), pp. 164–165; Susan Ware, *Holding Their Own: American/Women in the 1930s* (Boston: Twayne, 1982), pp. 107–110.

4. "The Need for a Federal Equal Rights Amendment," July 7, 1923, p. 166; "Legal Discrimination against Women," November 17, 1923, p. 317; "News from the Field," March 17, 1923, p. 36; "Summation of the Woman's Party Legislative Campaign (1921–1023," July 21, 1923, p. 183; "The High Cost of Protection," October 12, 1929, p. 282; "Equal Rights Amendment Is Surest Solution," August 27, 1932, p. 236; "Legal Status of Women," November–December 1951, p. 44.

5. "Advantages of the Equal Rights Amendment," March 25, 1933, p. 58.

6. "Equal Rights and Conscription, January 23, 1926, p. 396.

7. "Why the Argument?" October 6, 1923, p. 268.

8. "The Farce of Restrictive Legislation," August 25, 1931, p. 91.

9. "Section 213 on Trial," May 1, 1935, p. 3; "Is Marriage a Crime?" May 13, 133, p. 14.

10. "Plan of Organization for National Woman's Party by Edith Houghton Hooker," in "Minutes of the Council Meeting," March 5, 1933, Reel 115, National Woman's Party Papers 1913–1974, microfilm edition (Glen Rock, N.J.: Microfilm Corp. of America, 1977–1978) (hereafter referred to as NWP Papers).

11. "Minutes of the National Council Meeting," December 29, 1934, Reel 115, NWP Papers.

12. See, for example, "Women in Korea," August 8, 1931, p. 212; "Jamaican Women Go Forward," June 1939, p. 79; "Notes of the Week," December 15, 1923, which contained articles about equal rights in Australia and China and news of a woman in the Polish senate.

13. "The Challenge of the Ages," January 21, 1933, p. 402.

Information Sources

BIBLIOGRAPHY:

Becker, Susan D. *The Origins of the Equal Rights Amendment: American Feminism between the Wars.* Westport, Conn.: Greenwood Press, 1981.

Chafe, William. *American Women in the 20th Century.* New York: Oxford University Press, 1991.

Cott, Nancy. *The Grounding of Modern Feminism.* New Haven, Conn.: Yale University Press, 1987.

Lunardini, Christine. *From Equal Suffrage to Equal Rights: Alice Paul and the National Woman's Party, 1910–1928.* New York: New York University Press, 1986.

National Woman's Party Papers, 1913–1974, microfilm edition, Glen Rock, N.J.: Microfilm Corp. of America, 1977–1978.

Rupp, Leila, and Verta Taylor. *Survival in the Doldrums, The American Women's Rights Movement, 1945 to the 1960s.* New York: Oxford University Press, 1987.

Ware, Susan. *Holding Their Own: American Women in the 1930s.* Boston: Twayne, 1982.

INDEX SOURCES: None.

LOCATION SOURCES: Library of Congress. *Equal Rights* is available in the microfilm edition of the NWP Papers.

Publication History

PERIODICAL TITLE AND TITLE CHANGES: *Equal Rights: Official Organ of the National Woman's Party.* (A second unauthorized publication, *Equal Rights: In-*

dependent Feminist Weekly was published in Baltimore from January 5, 1935 through December 26, 1936 following editor Edith Houghton Hooker's split with the NWP. It merged into the official publication January 15, 1937.)

VOLUME AND ISSUE DATA: Vols. 1–40 (February 17, 1923–November 1954). Weekly (1923–December 29, 1934); biweekly (February 15, 1935–April 15, 1939); monthly (May 1939–December 1944); bimonthly (January–February 1945–May–April 1948); three times yearly (May–August 1948–September–December 1948); quarterly (January–March 1949–April–June 1949); bimonthly (July–August 1949–May–June 1953); appeared September–December 1953; only two numbers in 1954: October 1954 and November 1954, the final issue.

PUBLISHER AND PLACE OF PUBLICATION: National Woman's Party. Baltimore (1923–1934); Washington, D.C. (1935–1954).

EDITORS: Edith Houghton Hooker (1923–1934); Emily Hooker and others (1935–January 1, 1937); Helen Hunt West (January 15, 1937–May 1940); Anna Kelton Wiley (October 1940–November–December 1945); Alma Lutz and others (January–February 1946 to November–December 1946); Anne Carter (January–February 1947 to March–April 1951); Dorothy Russell (May–June 1951); Virginia Starr Freedom (July–August 1951 to May–June 1953); Florence Armstrong (September–December 1953); Anne Carter (October 1954–November 1954).

CIRCULATION: Paid subscriptions: 2,170 (April 1, 1923); 1,500 of 4,000 printed (February 1951).

Linda Lumsden

F

FAR AND NEAR

Beginning in the mid-1880s and continuing into the early twentieth century, unmarried women working in factories, offices, and stores organized themselves into social and educational clubs sponsored by upper-class women interested in social reform. From 1890 to 1894, a loose-knit national coalition of these "working girls' clubs" had its own journal, *Far and Near*.[1]

The publication grew out of the first national meeting of the clubs in New York City in the spring of 1890, when delegates agreed they needed a forum for the interchange of ideas and club news. That fall, in November 1890, *Far and Near* was founded by the Auxiliary Society of the Association of Working Girls' Societies of New York, with Maria Bowen Chapin of New York City as editor. Chapin would continue as editor throughout *Far and Near*'s four years of existence, aided by associate editors in Hartford, Connecticut, and Boston.[2]

The journal's goal, as the editors explained in the lead article in its inaugural issue, was to represent the Working Girls' Societies of America, the national organization of clubs. Toward that end, the journal's title represented the genesis of the clubs. "They begin with nearness. A few girls who are already near each other in location wish to gain opportunities to grow nearer in sympathy, in mutual comprehension, and in aim, and the first Club is formed. From this the suggestion passes to other girls, who in their turn unite in a Society, and the idea constantly spreads from the near to the far."

"[T]he principal office of this paper," the editors explained, "is to bring those who are far apart near to one another. We are glad to have the circle of Clubs widen indefinitely, but we hope that the twelve yearly issues of *Far and Near* will, like the spokes of a wheel, unite all its parts to a common centre."[3]

The opening paragraphs of the first issue set the tone for the content of the succeeding four years; the journal's editors appealed to readers to "send us news of their doings, their methods, and their hopes.'' Members were urged not only to send in club news but to supply articles on broader topics of interest to wage-earning women. The editors also announced a series of regular features that would prove to be a staple of the journal, including biographical sketches of wage-earning women, household tips, fashion advice, a summary of world news, and feature articles on manners and the social graces.[4]

Far and Near's content, geared as it was to self-improvement, closely reflected the goals of the clubs it served. "Working Girls' Societies are organizations formed among busy women and girls," an 1890 club circular explained, "to secure by co-operation means of self-improvement, opportunities for social intercourse, and the development of higher, nobler aims."[5]

The first issue of the journal contained an article on working girls' responsibilities to their clubs, written by Grace H. Dodge, vice president of the Auxiliary Society at the time of *Far and Near*'s founding and later the society's president. It was appropriate that Dodge write for the first issue. A philanthropist from a prominent, well-to-do New York City family, Dodge had helped to found the clubs in the mid-1880s, presided over its first national convention, and became their most prominent national proponent. She was introduced to the 1894 convention as "[t]he best known working women's club woman in America . . . who set in motion the ball which has assumed such tremendous proportions." She remained active in the working girls' movement until her resignation as president in 1906, after the clubs had become more active in economic struggles that she felt unsuited to lead.[6]

Far and Near was successful from the beginning. Its first issue was greeted with attention, interest, and "hearty applause," according to its editors, and by March 1891 the journal claimed a circulation of ten thousand copies a month, sold by subscription to club members and their acquaintances. Subscription revenues made up most of the journal's revenue, as only one or two pages of each issue were devoted to advertising. Some clubs offered prizes to the member who sold the most subscriptions, which were one dollar a year. Individual copies sold for ten cents. The small journal, published first by *The Critic* magazine of New York and later by Oswald Weber Jr., contained from sixteen to twenty-four pages a month.[7]

In its early years, *Far and Near* concerned itself not at all with organized labor in general or with economic concerns of wage earners in particular, positions in line with the more individualistic concerns of Dodge and the clubs' other well-to-do patrons. When a correspondent opined to the editors that the working girls' clubs should help organize trade unions, the editors politely demurred. "Labor questions, like politics and religion, must be left to each member to settle for herself, and our organizations exist for the improvement of the individual, not to deal with conditions of work and wages."[8]

Far and Near's concerns for the individual woman were addressed in scores of wide-ranging articles intended to improve her practical skills and beauty. Fashion tips offered hints for making skirts and collars. Practical columns suggested ways to improve memory, write better letters, buy life insurance, and live thriftily. An advice column called "Aunt Jane's Talk with the Juniors" offered practical counsel. In one typical column, Aunt Jane warned against the use of slang and counseled young women that the only appropriate response to the telling of unclean jokes was stony silence.[9]

Not all of *Far and Near*'s articles were geared to the practical. The journal also aimed to benefit the mind. Articles appeared regularly explaining great works of literature, art, and music. Poetry, fiction, and short essays were also regular fare. Biographical sketches of famous women authors provided ready role models, as did tidbits about women who were in the news.

In offering such wide-ranging guidance, *Far and Near*'s editors addressed their readers in the manner of a gentle teacher correcting the crudities of an ignorant, but promising, student. Typical of this approach was an 1891 editorial on "The Vulgar Girl." "[T]his underbred girl may have good qualities beneath the rude exterior. She often has good principles, holds her honor sacredly, though in a rough way, and her word is never doubted," the editors wrote. "Her lapses are the result of ignorance, false ideas and low standards." *Far and Near* aimed to reveal the new, higher standards to its women readers and to transform them in the process.[10]

Of course, a staple of each *Far and Near* issue was a lengthy section devoted to club news. Most often, club news was provided by state correspondents who provided news directly to the journal. Most news came from clubs in the Northeast, the stronghold of the working girls' clubs. A typical issue included news from clubs in New York, Massachusetts, Rhode Island, Connecticut, New Jersey, Pennsylvania, Maryland, Illinois, Missouri, and Iowa. News was occasionally printed from clubs in Canada.

In 1893 and 1894, *Far and Near* exhibited a greater sympathy with wage-earning women's economic concerns, which were slowly gaining sway in the clubs, partly due to the nationwide depression of the early 1890s. An 1893 article entitled "Why Not?" sympathetically described some club members' call for greater attention to economic issues. Then, in October 1894, Mary E. Kenney wrote in the magazine's leading article that only organized labor and organized capital, balanced by fair-minded public opinion, could supply the wants of civilization.[11]

The depression was taking its toll on the working girls' clubs and on *Far and Near*. Pressing economic concerns began to replace the previous goal of reforming "the vulgar girl." "The working-girls' clubs are experiencing a loss of buoyancy and a sense of discouragement," the editors wrote in December 1893. "In some places, especially in manufacturing towns, their very existence is threatened. The principles which underlie the clubs will be tested this winter as never before."[12]

It was *Far and Near*'s last winter. The following autumn, in the depths of the depression, *Far and Near* published its forty-eighth, and last, issue. "There is no such thing as absolute failure for any conscientious effort," the editors declared in a farewell editorial in the October 1894 issue, choosing to see the best of their four-year effort. ''Some boundaries we have shown to be impassable, some limitations we have helped to define, some questions we have settled by the things we have eliminated.''[13]

Notes

1. For background on the club movement, see Priscilla Murolo, ''Working Girls' Clubs, 1894–1928: Class and Gender on the 'Common Ground of Womanhood' '' (Ph.D. diss., Yale University, 1992).

2. November 1890, p. 1.

3. Ibid.

4. Ibid.

5. Ibid.

6. ''Grace Dodge Dead; Noted for Charities,'' *New York Times,* December 28, 1914, p. 9; ''Grace Hoadley Dodge,'' *Digest of American Biography,* Vol. 5 (New York: Scribner's, 1930), pp. 346–347; Abbie Graham, *Grace H. Dodge: Merchant of Dreams* (New York: Womans Press, 1926), pp. 103–116. Dodge is perhaps best remembered for her work on behalf of Teachers College in New York and the Young Women's Christian Associations.

7. November 1890, p. 17; March 1891, p. 71.

8. November 1891, p. 16.

9. August 1894, p. 138.

10. November 1891, p. 2.

11. March 1893, p. 93; October 1894, p. 163.

12. December 1893, p. 28.

13. October 1894, p. 166.

Information Sources

BIBLIOGRAPHY:

Graham, Abbie. *Grace H. Dodge: Merchant of Dreams.* New York: Woman's Press, 1926.

''Grace Dodge Dead; Noted for Charities.'' *New York Times,* December 28, 1914, p. 9.

''Grace Hoadley Dodge.'' *Digest of American Biography.* Vol. 5. New York: Scribner's, 1930, pp. 346–347.

Murolo, Priscilla. ''Working Girls' Clubs, 1884–1928: Class and Gender on the 'Common Ground of Womanhood.' '' Ph.D. diss., Yale University, 1992.

INDEX SOURCES: None.

LOCATION SOURCES: Library of Congress; North Carolina State University; University of Virginia, and other libraries.

Publication History

PERIODICAL TITLE AND TITLE CHANGES: *Far and Near* (1890–1894).

VOLUME AND ISSUE DATA: Vols. 1–4 (November 1890–October 1894). Monthly.

PUBLISHER AND PLACE OF PUBLICATION: *The Critic* magazine (1890–1893); Oswald Weber Jr. (1893–1894). New York.

EDITORS: Maria Bowen Chapin (November 1890–October 1894).
CIRCULATION: Magazine reports, 1891: 10,000.

David R. Davies

FARMER'S WIFE

The *Farmer's Wife* was as much a part of the Populist movement[1] as the farmers' alliances. Born in a stronghold of Populism (Kansas) at a time when the movement was at its strongest (the early 1890s), the *Farmer's Wife* was a voice of rural women activists who were committed to alliance policies, politics, and procedures. That meant that the *Farmer's Wife* was not strictly a woman's suffrage organ, although it editorially supported that reform. The monthly newspaper favored a range of Populist positions. The close association between the newspaper and Populism probably explained the *Wife*'s relatively short life. After the People's Party suffered a devastating defeat in 1894 in Kansas (taking the suffrage amendment down with it), the *Farmer's Wife* ceased publication. But for three stormy years, the newspaper illustrated just how important women were to the farmers' alliances and the Populist movement.

The *Farmer's Wife* came by its Populism honestly. The newspaper was the product of the marriage of Ira and Emma Pack. Ira was the publisher[2]; Emma was the editor. Both had ideal backgrounds for publishing a Populist woman's publication. Ira had been associated with the Farmer's Alliance and Industrial Union, a group better known as the strong Southern Alliance.[3] Emma's whole life read as a Populist profile. Born on a dairy farm in Pennsylvania, she graduated in 1869 from the Elmira, New York, Female College. After marrying in 1870, Emma and her husband moved west, first to Iowa, where they worked a small fruit farm, and then to Kansas. While in Iowa, Emma was prominent in the Grange movement. She shifted the focus of her activism to the Farmer's Alliance and Industrial Union and the People's Party once the family moved to Topeka, Kansas.[4]

By then, the couple had shifted its business from farming to publishing. Ira published the *City and Farm Record,* a publication that covered real estate and land sales. Emma edited *Villa Range: Ladies' Home Journal,* which covered the standard fare of fiction, fashion, and domestic life. By 1891, they terminated both papers, pooled their resources, and started the *Farmer's Wife.*[5]

From its first issue, the *Farmer's Wife* was clearly more than just a "suffrage paper." It endorsed a wide range of People's Party tenets:

FREE Coinage for the People.

PROHIBITION for the Nation.

LOWER Rates for Transportation.

SERVICE Pension for the Soldiers.

FIFTY Dollars per Capita.

PROTECTION for Industries.

ONE Flag for North and South.

DEATH for Trusts and Combines.

HOME Dealings for Home Making.

EQUAL Suffrage for All Citizens.

AND Education for all.

FOR the Farmers and all useful Laborers of the country.

SOCIAL Purity and Home Protection. . . .

FAIR Play to all People of every race and both sexes.[6]

The women of Kansas had a role in changing politics and society. "Woman's sphere," the editor contended, "is to be measured not by theories but by her individual capacities and limitations, and these she can discover only by effort."[7]

The monthly always reflected that commitment. The farmer's wife was a thinking, responsible adult with a wide range of interests, responsibilities, and duties; this newspaper aimed at serving its readers, rural women aligned with the Farmers' Alliance and Industrial Union and the Populist cause. Thus, the monthly offered poetry, fiction, updates on the alliance, inspirational tracts, news of suffrage and Prohibition locally and in other states, farm hints, fashion, and editorials. The *Farmer's Wife* offered it all—from news of a "Cheap Clod Crusher," to the qualities of women who lived on the range; from a short story on how a girl saved a bank, to how to make lace curtains; from reading material for the young, to reprinted news from eastern papers.[8]

The newspaper also provided a blueprint for women's involvement in the farmers' alliances and the People's Party. From Pack's perspective, farm women had roles to play in government, in society, and in politics.

WOMEN should organize.

WE must discuss remedies.

WE must fight for our rights.

WE must demand, not request.

WE must not tolerate our enemies.

WE want simple justice, not charity.

WE want representation if we pay taxes.

WHO are the people, men, or men and women?

WE must purify our minds if we would elevate.

WE must express our political ideas from a political standpoint.

IF woman is the better half of man, women are the better half of the
    people.

ALL laws that punish women as men should be made by women, as well
    as men.

WE want a voice in the laws that lock the prison doors against our fallen
    sisters.

WE must be helpmates to our husbands, for when they fail the wife and
    children suffer.[9]

The best way to achieve all this, according to the editor, was through the
National Woman's Alliance, an organization that *Wife*'s editor Pack helped
form. Her newspaper then became the group's voice. The *Farmer's Wife* publicized the women's alliance's formation, outlined its declaration of purposes,
and included its constitution. The newspaper's editor acted as one of the group's
officers, secretary. (The president was Fannie McCormick, a popular Populist
speaker, and treasurer was Bina Otis, wife of the Populist congressman John
Otis.[10] Vice presidents represented most states in the union.)

The National Woman's Alliance was not solely a suffrage or a Prohibition
organization, although both reforms were supported. This alliance was committed to political, economic, and social change by working with the Farmers'
Alliance and Industrial Union and the People's Party. From the editor's point
of view, women and men had to work together for change. Some of the changes
recommended by the *Farmer's Wife* and its readers were radical. They included
government ownership of railroads and telegraphs and the "world wide justice"
of free trade—working through the National Woman's Alliance.[11]

Increasingly, however, suffrage was beginning to dominate the editorial comment of the *Farmer's Wife*. The shift occurred in 1892, when it appeared that
Kansas voters would soon decide the issue. The newspaper editor wanted to
figure in that battle: "This is a fight for humanity, and suffrage should be guaranteed to our women from a non-partisan standpoint."[12] That viewpoint, as well
as Pack's close affiliation with the People's Party, might have hindered the role
that this newspaper would be allowed to play in the state's suffrage campaign.

Many within the state's suffrage association were Republican or hoped for
Republican support to get the state suffrage amendment passed. When Pack and
other Populists linked suffrage to the People's Party, Republican support for the
amendment began to disappear. The head of the state suffrage group warned
Pack and others that the political ties to the People's Party could cause just such
a development.[13] But Pack would not accept that explanation:

The fact is apparent that our Republican friends who profess a change on
this frank pretense [because of People's Party support of suffrage], never
were at heart for woman's suffrage, but have sought this device by which

to paliate the offense it may give to their female friends, thinking they would not be shrewd enough to see the deceit practiced upon them.[14]

From a political perspective, Republican desertions could have made sense, if Pack's perspective on how women would vote was accurate. She predicted that Kansas women who got the vote would follow the People's Party line. "Every woman would vote for the Populist ticket, provided there were good men on the ticket." After all, this party was the "only hope" women had for "saving their homes."[15]

Pack did not keep her support of suffrage to the pages of the *Farmer's Wife*. She, along with a number of others, helped form yet another organization designed to work for suffrage along with a range of other reforms. The Woman's Progressive Political Club of America, an auxiliary to the People's Party, was yet another reform organization committed to suffrage and Prohibition but also opposed to high mortgage rates and railroad monopolies. In her editorial calling readers to the group, Pack explained that women needed such a group "It is in vain we toil from dawn to dark, from youth to old age, if the tax gatherer garners all our savings, and the railroad king demands the lion share of the earnings of a lifetime." This political club stuck to the principle, " 'Honest toil' not the 'gold dollar' ought to be ruler in America."[16]

Although the Packs never seemed to lose their energy or their editorial edge (indeed, their appointments as superintendent and assistant superintendent of the state insane infirmary afforded them a certain measure of financial security), the *Farmer's Wife* seemed to be headed for trouble in 1893. In December of that year, a front-page advertisement urged all to subscribe and promised that all the money would go to support the suffrage amendment campaign. The editor and the publisher were not taking any salaries, the advertisement claimed.[17] Emma Pack, assistant superintendent of the asylum and editor, was increasingly away to lecture on the amendment to suffrage audiences. The editor shifted publication dates from the first part of the month to the last. In the process, the July 1893 issue was not published. September 1894 was also not published. The October 1894 issue was the last, although there was nothing in the newspaper to suggest a farewell. It carried Pack's endorsement of People's Party candidate for governor and hopes that the suffrage amendment would sweep the state. Perhaps the *Farmer's Wife* would have continued if the results of the 1894 election had been different, but the People's Party and the suffrage amendment went down to disastrous defeat. The Populists, who had worked with the Democrats in 1892 to carry the state, split with them in 1894 (in part because of the suffrage issue). The Republicans swept the state, elected their entire state ticket and most of the congressional delegation as well, and soundly defeated suffrage.[18] The Kansas women would have to wait for the new century for suffrage.

The *Farmer's Wife* represented an interesting variation from most suffrage periodicals issued in the late nineteenth and early twentieth centuries. First, it was one of the few designed to appeal specifically to farm women. In general, the suffrage periodicals were aimed primarily at urban, middle-class women. The *Woman's Journal,** the *National Citizen and Ballot Box,** the *Woman Voter,** the *Woman's Advocate,** and so many others were all publications aimed at urban women. The class basis also seemed to set the *Farmer's Wife* apart. Although many farmers were middle-class, this population, as a group, had suffered extensively in the late nineteenth century; and, thus, many of the readers of the *Farmer's Wife* could be seen as having only a tenuous tie to middle-class economic standing. The newspaper also illustrated the importance of women to the farmers' alliances and the People's Party. As a paper committed to radical third-party policies, the *Farmer's Wife* showed how suffrage worked in conjunction with other issues for a united platform for social change.

Notes

1. These ardent Populist ties may explain why neither the *Farmer's Wife* nor its editor Emma Pack is included within Elizabeth Cady Stanton, Susan B. Anthony, and Matilda Gage's *History of Woman Suffrage.* In general, Stanton, Anthony, and Gage failed to fully cover the suffragists of the Populist Party. This may have been a political decision. Anthony, particularly, saw the Republicans as being the greatest ally to suffrage.

2. He was also editor for the first three issues. Marilyn Dell Brady, "Populism and Feminism in a Newspaper by and for Women of Kansas Farmers' Alliance, 1891–1894," *Kansas History* 7.4, Winter 1984/1985, p. 282.

3. Thomas Burkholder, "The *Farmer's Wife,* 1891–1894: Raising a Prairie Consciousness," in Martha Soloman, ed., *A Voice of Their Own: The Woman Suffrage Press, 1840–1910* (Tuscaloosa: University of Alabama Press, 1991), p. 155; John D. Hicks, *The Populist Revolt: A History of the Farmers' Alliance and the People's Party* (Lincoln: University of Nebraska Press, 1961), p. 97.

4. "Publisher's Notice," May 1893, p. 5. Biographical material was provided in a reprint from the *Topeka Daily Capital.* This story was run when Ira and Emma were appointed supervisor and assistant supervisor/matron of the State Insane Asylum.

5. From this arises some confusion with regard to the heritage of the *Farmer's Wife.* In the first issue, July 1891, the *Farmer's Wife* began with new numeration, vol. 1.1, although the publisher noted that the new publication ran the line "Consolidated: City and Farm Record and Ladies' Home Journal." By January 1892, the *Wife* changed its numeration and began the year as vol. 10.7. Thus, the publication went from December 1891 (Vol. 1.6) to January 1892 (vol. 10.7). Vols. 2 through 9 were never issued. After 1892, the editor kept emphasizing that the *Wife* was the continuation of Ira's *City and Farm Record.* See, for example, December 1891, p. 1. See also Brady, "Populism and Feminism," p. 282.

6. "We Stand For," July 1891, p. 4.

7. "Our Readers," July 1891, p. 4.

8. "Real Rural Readings," August 1891, p. 3; Emma Ghent Curtis, "Woman on the Range," August 1891, p. 1; "A Novel Defense," August 1891, p. 5; "Doings of Women Folk," August 1891, p. 5; "For Our Little Folks," August 1891, p. 5; reprinted news, August 1891, p. 6.

9. October 1891, p. 4.

10. Brady, "Populism and Feminism," p. 281; Annie L. Diggs, "The Women in the

Alliance Movement,'' *Arena,* July 1892, pp. 161–179; "The National Woman's Alliance Incorporated,'' October 1891, p. 4; "The 'Farmer's Wife,' '' April 1892, p. 4.

11. Mary M. Clardy, "What Can American Women Do for the People's Party?'' April 1892, p. 4.

12. "Women's War,'' November 1892, p. 1.

13. May 1893, p. 3.

14. August 1894, p. 1.

15. May 1893, p. 3.

16. "To the Women of Kansas,'' May 1893, p. 3.

17. Advertisement, December 1893, p. 1.

18. Hicks, *The Populist Revolt,* pp. 321–333; Burkholder, "The *Farmer's Wife,*'' p. 164.

Information Sources

BIBLIOGRAPHY:

Brady, Marilyn Dell. "Populism and Feminism in a Newspaper by and for Women of the Kansas Farmers' Alliance, 1891–1894.'' *Kansas History* 7.4, Winter 1984/ 1985, pp. 280–290.

Burkholder, Thomas. "The *Farmer's Wife,* 1891–1894: Raising a Prairie Consciousness.'' In Martha Solomon, ed., *A Voice of Their Own: The Woman Suffrage Press, 1840–1910.* Tuscaloosa: University of Alabama Press, 1991, pp. 153–164.

Diggs, Annie L. "The Women in the Alliance Movement.'' *Arena,* July 1892, pp. 161–179.

Hicks, John D. *The Populist Revolt: A History of the Farmers' Alliance and the People's Party.* Lincoln: University of Nebraska Press, 1961.

Smith, Wilma M. "A Half Century of Struggle: Gaining Woman Suffrage in Kansas.'' *Kansas History* 4.2, Summer 1981, pp. 74–95.

Wagner, Mary Jo. "Women in the Farmers' Alliance.'' Paper presented at the Organization of American Historians, Washington, D.C., March 22–25, 1990.

INDEX SOURCES: Not indexed.

LOCATION SOURCES: University of Kansas Library; Kansas Historical Society (Topeka); and other libraries.

Publication History

PERIODICAL TITLE AND TITLE CHANGES: *Farmer's Wife.*

VOLUME AND ISSUE DATA: Vols. 1–12 (July 1891–October 1894. Numeration changes with January 1892 issue; volumes 2 to 9 not issued. July 1893 and September 1894 not issued). Monthly.

PUBLISHER AND PLACE OF PUBLICATION: I. W. Pack. Topeka, Kans.

EDITORS: Ira Pack (July–September 1891); Emma Pack (October 1891–1894).

CIRCULATION: Unknown.

Kathleen L. Endres

FEMINIST TEACHER

From its beginnings, *Feminist Teacher* has striven to make connections between theory and practice in the classroom. The idea for publishing *Feminist Teacher* began during the early 1980s in discussions that took place in a feminist criticism reading group made up of graduate students at Indiana University, most of them from the English Department. The first issue was printed in late 1984 and sent to a small group of subscribers in 1985.

Three members of the reading group who were Ph.D. students in the English Department—Elisabeth Däumer, Paula Krebs, and Sandra Runzo—were earning tuition and a salary by teaching undergraduate students in required English composition and literature courses. The author of this essay was a doctoral student teaching in the School of Journalism, and the other founding collective member, Diane Ledger, who had already earned a master's degree in history, was taking graduate courses in education and counseling.[1] Members of the collective, who were all white women in their twenties and thirties, became intrigued with the possibilities for "subverting" the departmentally mandated syllabi for the courses they were teaching. They also sought to find strategies for incorporating issues of gender, race, and class into the classroom.

In approaching pedagogical issues, *Feminist Teacher* defines teaching as something that takes place not only in traditional classroom settings but also in vocational training programs, prisons, women's centers, and community programs dealing with problems such as sexual assault and other violence against women.

The founders decided early on to act as an editorial collective, with no one individual being in charge of the publication. One of the models for *Feminist Teacher's* nonhierarchical organizational structure was the radical feminist publication *off our backs,** published monthly in Washington, D.C. Along with *Feminist Teacher, off our backs* remains to this day one of the few collectively run periodicals still in operation. *Feminist Teacher* also borrowed from *off our backs* the idea of giving credit to a group of "friends" whose names are listed in each issue.[2] These friends have included women and men who have helped the collective edit and proofread articles, maintain subscription lists, and send out mailings. Another group of volunteers has handled book reviews.

The collective members share a vision of feminism as a political strategy as well as a theoretical position. The work of founding *Feminist Teacher* played an important role in helping collective members grapple with issues concerning the position of feminist scholarship and activism within ideologically mainstream institutions such as universities. The phrase "politics and teaching do mix" is something of an informal motto for the publication, serving not only as a reminder of *Feminist Teacher's* goal of promoting a pedagogy that challenges the dominant ideological, cultural, and political structures but also as an acknowledgment that teaching within the dominant paradigm is also a political act.

Collective members looked at other publications before developing the statement of purpose for the first issue. The group was impressed with Florence Howe's important work with *Women's Studies Quarterly,* for example, but also was aware of the limitations of a publication whose name suggested that it was designed for college teachers in women's studies programs. The founders of *Feminist Teacher* also were influenced by the important work of the Boston-based collective that published *Radical Teacher* but envisioned a publication that would place more emphasis on feminist scholarship written from a variety of perspectives, not just a socialist/Marxist one. *Feminist Teacher* has, from the beginning, been committed to printing articles written from a variety of feminist theoretical perspectives and has not become strongly identified with a specific theoretical or political position within feminist thought, such as cultural feminism, radical feminism, materialist feminism, or liberal feminism.

In developing the format for *Feminist Teacher,* collective members took into account the many feminists who do not have the opportunity to teach in a women's studies program but yet are committed to feminist political and pedagogical strategies. Besides college instructors, the target audience includes feminists in grade schools and high schools who are trying to make their classrooms more equitable. Many of these teachers, particularly those in primary and secondary schools, are isolated from feminist colleagues.

Thus, what the collective started as a project to "subvert" the traditional courses in the curriculum, which often draws upon graduate student labor for staffing, became something the collective envisioned as providing a forum for teachers at all grade levels who were committed to fighting sexism, racism, classism, homophobia, and other forms of social injustice. *Feminist Teacher*'s ambitious mission is outlined in the following copy taken from the collective's first brochure, which was mailed to women's studies programs and individual feminist educators throughout the United States before the first issue was published:[3]

Do you ever feel as if you are the only feminist music/math/preschool teacher in the world? Do you ever wonder whether there really is a feminist way to teach geography/auto mechanics/genetics?

Many of us are trying new ideas in our classrooms, seeking ways to humanize education and to challenge the sexism, racism and other types of oppression that have long been entrenched in our educational systems— from preschools to graduate schools. But none of us should work in a vacuum. We need to know what breakthroughs, however tiny, others like us are making. A computer science teacher in Oregon may have written a nonsexist teaching program that a science teacher in Rhode Island could put to good use. A religion teacher in New Jersey may have compiled a bibliography that a philosophy professor in New Mexico would love to see.

Feminist Teacher . . . examines issues of pedagogy in every discipline and at every grade level. *Feminist Teacher* will serve as a forum for exchanging both practical and theoretical ideas about politics and teaching. . . .

A major goal of *Feminist Teacher* is to give a voice to those who have been excluded from traditional curricula and to make our teaching more accessible and responsive to those who commonly have not found their experiences reflected in the classroom.

Feminist Teacher drew upon the institutional resources of Indiana University to publish its first issue in the autumn of 1984. A mailing address was secured when a collective member put the publication's name on an empty mailbox in the English Department's office, which provided *Feminist Teacher* with a university affiliation that collective members reasoned would appeal to potential authors as well as to those who write the checks when libraries subscribe. In addition, space for an office was appropriated in a house near campus that the English Department used for its teaching assistants.

Financing for the first issues came out of the pockets of collective members and the approximately sixty-five individuals brave enough to send in money to subscribe to a publication that did not yet exist. Eventually, the English Department at Indiana provided money for a half-time graduate assistant who served as an office manager, and as the subscription base stabilized, the publication also hired work-study students to help with the office work.

The first issues of *Feminist Teacher* were typeset during off-hours in the newsroom of the *Bloomington Herald-Telephone,* a daily newspaper for which the author of this essay worked part-time as an editor.[4] This arrangement is one reason the layout of the publication's early issues featured the narrow columns and typefaces commonly seen in newspapers. In addition, with its use of illustrations and photographs, *Feminist Teacher* was purposely designed to look more like a magazine than an academic journal, so, in the words of collective member Paula Krebs, it could "go home with teachers at the end of the day, to be read in the bathtub or on the bus" rather than simply relegated to the journal stacks in the library reading room.[5]

The desire to appeal to educators at various grade levels, in various disciplines, and in various teaching situations also led the collective to include a regular column of news items of interest to feminist educators (entitled "Network News"), as well as a column about teaching resources and another column that announces conferences and calls for papers. Although the collective has never been as successful as it had hoped in reaching elementary and secondary school teachers, it remains committed to publishing articles, news items, and resources that appeal to those educators.

In addition, because the collective wanted to serve educators who find themselves isolated from others who share their commitment to feminism. *Feminist Teacher* published a state-by-state listing of subscribers and their areas of teaching interest, in hopes that these subscribers might contact one another and help relieve their isolation. The publishing of names also followed a practice that collective members had observed in Donna Allen's *Media Report to Women,** a publication that, even under a new editor, continues to name its financial supporters on the second page of each issue.[6]

The collective operated from the beginning with the consciousness that it was part of a much larger social movement dedicated to improving the conditions of women. *Feminist Teacher* has drawn upon local and national networks of feminists that were very well organized by the mid-1980s. In Bloomington, these networks included individuals involved in large-scale cultural projects such as the National Women's Music Festival and Helaine Victoria Press, as well as students, faculty, and staff members at Indiana University.

Also important to *Feminist Teacher's* long-term development was a strong national network of grassroots and academic feminist organizations. For example, mailings of calls for manuscripts as well as solicitations for subscriptions were sent to other feminist periodicals listed in Donna Allen's *Directory of Women's Media,* published annually by the Women's Institute for Freedom of the Press in Washington, D.C. The annual meetings of the National Women's Studies Association proved to be a major recruiting ground for authors and subscribers. Collective members also set up information tables at the National Women's Music Festival and hauled brochures to events such as the Michigan Womyn's Music Festival.

Feminist Teacher has been able to expand its subscription base by drawing upon the important work of the organizers of the National Women's Mailing List, a California-based project that has surveyed thousands of women about their occupational background and their cultural, educational, political, recreational, and health interests. Many feminists have been able to keep informed about feminist events, actions, services, and publications because of the work of the Women's Information Exchange, which publishes the list and makes it available for a nominal fee to feminist organizations and periodicals.

Feminist Teacher has evolved with the lives of the editorial collective members. All of the original collective members have completed their graduate programs: Elisabeth Däumer is on the faculty at Eastern Michigan University in Ypsilanti; Paula Krebs is on the faculty at Wheaton College in Norton, Massachusetts; Diane Ledger recently left the collective to pursue other career goals; Sandra Runzo is on the faculty at Denison University in Granville, Ohio; and the author of this essay is on the faculty at the University of Iowa. A former office manager, Theresa Kemp, recently joined the collective. She holds a faculty position at the University of Alabama-Birmingham. The collective also recently added Gail Cohee, who is a faculty member at Emporia State University in Kansas.

In recent years, *Feminist Teacher* has turned away from printing so many course syllabi and short reflective pieces, concentrating instead on more academically oriented articles about pedagogy. The inclusion of more theoretically grounded articles reflects the intellectual and professional development of collective members as much as it reflects the growing sophistication of scholars writing about feminist and critical pedagogy.

Among the best-selling issues of *Feminist Teacher* has been one devoted to AIDS education and homophobia and another one that included a section that

listed periodicals by and about women of color. *Feminist Teacher* has published
a number of articles about classroom structure and authority issues in the classroom, as well as articles that address feminist approaches to teaching subjects
such as math, literature, political science, psychology, and criminal justice. *Feminist Teacher* has also published articles that have addressed issues of concern
to feminists in administration, outlined strategies for improving the women's
studies holdings of libraries, and helped college teachers plan a women's studies
conference.

   Feminist Teacher continues to struggle with many of the challenges that Marilyn Crafton Smith identifies as contributing to the short lives of many feminist
publications: burnout, financial strain, internal disagreements, and changes.[7]

   The decision in 1993 to have Ablex Publishing Corporation in Norwood, New
Jersey, take over the business end of the publication was a survival strategy
negotiated among collective members who were finding it increasingly difficult
to come together to do the actual hands-on work of production. Because the
collective members were graduate students when the publication started, the
challenges of continuing publication when collective members would move
away from Bloomington had been anticipated. In her 1990 article for the British
journal *Text and ConText,* Krebs noted that a long-term goal of the collective
was "to give over all the layout and paste-up work to paid professionals and to
concentrate strictly on editorial tasks."[8]

   The editorial offices of *Feminist Teacher* moved at the beginning of the 1993
academic year from the English Department house for associate instructors on
Park Street in Bloomington to the English Department at Wheaton College in
Norton, Massachusetts. With the closing of the Bloomington office, the collective added to its ranks a sixth member, former office manager Theresa Kemp.
Collective members continue to maintain regular contact with each other by
taking advantage of electronic mail communication as well as telephone conference calls. In the summer before the move from the Midwest, *Feminist
Teacher* had nearly one thousand subscribers.

   Entering into the agreement with Ablex brought the first price increase ever—
from $12 a year for individual subscriptions and $20 a year for institutional
subscriptions to $18 and $32.50, respectively. However, one of the continuing
goals of the collective is to enable potential subscribers to have access to the
publication rather than to rely on their libraries for subscriptions. Rising costs
that lead to the inaccessibility of many journals to individual teachers are a
major concern to the collective.

   Collective members have made a commitment to work closely with Ablex in
promoting the journal but still maintain complete control of editorial content
and own the copyright to the publication. Despite the affiliation with a commercial academic press, *Feminist Teacher* continues its mission "to encourage
teachers to radically change the face of education, to critique and revise our
own practices and the structures of the institutions in which we work."[9]

Notes

1. Däumer dropped out of the collective before the first issue was published but joined again for vol. 3. in the fall/winter of 1987 and has been on the collective ever since then. Others who have served on the collective are Jane Hilberry (2.2,3) and Gail Rosecrance (3.3, 4.1).

2. In fact, several collective members have written for *off our backs* and served as "friends" of that periodical.

3. Most of these names were taken from the mailing list for the women's studies program at Indiana University and from the membership directory for the National Women's Studies Association. By the time the first issue was published, there were about eighty subscribers.

4. The newspaper is now called the *Bloomington Herald-Times.*

5. Paula Krebs, "Feminist Teaching, Women's Studies and Institutions," *Text and ConText* 4, Autumn 1990, pp. 66–69.

6. The publishing of the Network Names column has been discontinued because the list of subscribers is now being handled by Ablex Publishing Corporation rather than through the editorial offices of *Feminist Teacher.*

7. Marilyn Crafton Smith, "Feminist Media and Cultural Politics." in Pamela J. Creedon, ed., *Women in Mass Communication,* 2d ed. (Newbury Park, Calif.: Sage, 1993), p. 75.

8. Krebs. "Feminist Teaching. Women's Studies and Institutions," p. 69.

9. Ibid.

Information Sources

BIBLIOGRAPHY:
Krebs, Paula. "Feminist Teaching, Women's Studies and Institutions." *Text and ConText* 4, Autumn 1990, pp. 66–69.
Smith, Marilyn Crafton. "Feminist Media and Cultural Politics." In Pamela J. Creedon, ed., *Women in Mass Communication,* 2d ed. Newbury Park, Calif.: Sage, 1993.
INDEX SOURCES: Alternative Press Index; Contents Pages in Education; Studies on Women Abstracts; Women's Studies Abstracts.
LOCATION SOURCES: Indiana University Library and many other, primarily university, libraries.

Publication History

PERIODICAL TITLE AND TITLE CHANGES: *Feminist Teacher.*
VOLUME AND ISSUE DATA: Vols. 1– (1984 to present). Quarterly (1984–1985); Three times a year (1986 to present).
PUBLISHER AND PLACE OF PUBLICATION: Feminist Teacher Editorial Collective, Indiana University, Bloomington (1984–1993); Ablex Publishing Corporation, Norwood, N.J. (1993–present); Editorial Offices: Wheaton College, Norton, Mass. (1993–present).
EDITORS: The Feminist Teacher Editorial Collective.
CIRCULATION: Ablex estimate, 1994: about 800 subscribers.

Sue A. Lafky

FOCUS: A JOURNAL FOR LESBIANS

Focus: A Journal for Lesbians was a pioneer publication in the quest for gay and lesbian rights that occurred in the United States during the 1960s and early 1970s. Following on the heels of more established and more prestigious publications such as *The Ladder,* Focus: A Journal for Lesbians* began in 1971 as the printed mouthpiece for a fledgling lesbian organization in Boston but gained a reputation as an innovative collection of poetry, short stories, and essays by and about lesbians.

Like other gay magazines, *Focus: A Journal for Lesbians* weathered identity crises and financial turmoil during more than a decade of publication. As Clare Potter writes in the *Lesbian Periodicals Index,* "While some themes remain constant, each decade of Lesbian publications reflected the influences of a changing time, a history of a people within a history of a country."[1] In fact, an examination of publications such as *The Ladder, Focus: A Journal for Lesbians,* and *Sinister Wisdom** is especially rewarding for those interested in cultural studies.

Promising in March 1971 to continue "living happily ever after through a multitude of format and staff changes,"[2] *Focus* ceased publication in 1983 because of shaky finances and the exhaustion of its editorial board. Although the Boston-based magazine lasted only twelve years, its editors produced 112 issues from March 1971 to November/December 1983.

Originally called *Focus: A Journal for Gay Women,* the publication began as the monthly magazine of the Boston chapter of Daughters of Bilitis, a group founded in 1969. (The parent gay rights organization was founded in San Francisco in October 1955.) In celebration of the five-year anniversary of the Boston chapter of Daughters of Bilitis, the *Focus* staff in December 1974 compiled a detailed history of the organization, and with great pride the editors and readers of *Focus* recognized their parent organization.

By noting the success of the group, members also were paying tribute to their own courage in the face of public ridicule and hostility. While pushing for social acceptance, lesbian readers had begun to unite and to feel more confident about their own identities.

The national Daughters of Bilitis began as a reaction to a growing cry for gay civil rights in the late 1950s through the 1960s. Its related group, the Mattachine Society, was one of the first gay organizations and was established in 1950–1951 in Los Angeles. All such groups, including the Homophile Action League, used their publications "to work out the goals and needs of their organizations, to inspire membership, to debate issues, to announce demonstrations and dances, to create a network of information in the battle against institutionalized homophobia,"[3] said Potter.

The word "Bilitis" is a Hellenic form of "Ba'alat," the female counterpart of Baal in Semitic mythology. In 1894, Pierre Louys published *Les Chansons de Bilitis.* After Louys' death, *Les Chansons de Bilitis inedites* and *Les Chansons secretes de Bilitis* appeared in 1929 and 1931, respectively. These editions contained explicit lesbian eroticism.

In the novel, the heroine lives in Mytilene on the island of Lesbos and writes elegies to her beloved Mnasidika, having learned to write poetry at the feet of Sappho. This classic of lesbian literature is at the center of the Daughters of Bilitis, the first lesbian political group in America.

Founded in northern California, the Daughters of Bilitis was the brainchild of Del Martin and Phyllis Lyon, who envisioned the group as an extended social organization. Later, they decided the group should dedicate itself to changing cultural attitudes about lesbianism. Wisely, they chose to join forces with the Mattachine Society, a group that took its name from "matachin" or "matachine," meaning "to mask oneself," and with ONE, Inc.

ONE was established in Los Angeles in 1952 and was the publisher of *ONE Magazine,* the first successful gay magazine in America. *ONE Magazine* debuted in 1953 and achieved a circulation of five thousand before it ceased regular publication in 1968. (*ONE Institute Quarterly of Homophile Studies* replaced it and lasted until 1973.)

When the Massachusetts Daughters of Bilitis group was founded in 1969, there was no gay movement in the Boston area. To gain readers, lesbian activists in the area mailed flyers to area subscribers of *The Ladder,* the national Daughters of Bilitis magazine, and they also ran an advertisement in a local underground paper, *Boston after Dark,* and advertised on a talk show on what was then WMEX radio. During this time, according to an issue of *Focus: A Journal for Gay Women,* "virtually everyone involved in the gay movement used pseudonyms," and members were "afraid of getting into trouble if they rented a post office box for the group."[4]

Focus: A Journal for Gay Women actually was preceded by a monthly, eight-page newsletter called *Maiden Voyage.* Appearing in 1969, the mimeographed *Maiden Voyage* was distributed until February 1970. At that time, two Boston Daughters of Bilitis members created *Focus: A Journal for Gay Women* and began to do offset printing on their own press. By March 1971, *Maiden Voyage* had become *Focus.*

When it took over as the official publication of the Boston chapter of Daughters of Bilitis, the group's name appeared under the nameplate in each issue. The new magazine cost fifty cents per issue. Through *Focus: A Journal for Gay Women* and through limited advertising, the chapter became more cohesive and encouraged lesbians to participate in support groups, social events, sports, public education, and political activism.

In December 1973, subscribers could buy the magazine for $3.50 per year, or they could pay $4.50 to get the publication in a brown wrapper. Most of the early covers featured innocuous line drawings. In October 1973, for example, the cover illustration alluded to the popular "Peanuts" cartoon strip by Charles Schulz. It featured Lucy and a friend saying, "Who needs Charlie Brown?"

Other covers featured rather benign photos, such as the gay pride flag in July 1973.

Coverage of timely news and schedules of local gay events was taken over by the *Gay Community News* in 1973, freeing *Focus* to devote itself to encouraging civil rights for gays. In February of that year, the editors reproduced the cover of the December/January 1969–1970 issue of *The Ladder* in order to stress the history and solidarity of the lesbian community. It featured a quotation from Radclyffe Hall's controversial 1928 novel *The Well of Loneliness*. The excerpt supported the group's mission and emphasized the growing numbers of visible lesbians in a culture that "dare not disown"[5] them.

By January 1974, *Focus: A Journal for Gay Women* cost sixty cents per issue, was still published monthly, and featured reviews of emerging lesbian writers and singers, including Judy Grahn, Rita Mae Brown, and Cris Williamson. The staff included reviews, features, poetry, news, a calendar of events, and a crossword puzzle.

Gradually, members of the Boston chapter of Daughters of Bilitis became more involved in advocacy. One woman, quoted in the March 1971 issue of *Focus: A Journal for Gay Women,* said, "We had gotten used to the smell of moth balls, the darkness of that lonely closet somehow seemed more comfortable than putting our jobs and families on the line."[6] By 1974 women were putting their jobs and families, as well as their reputations, firmly on the line.

Having celebrated their anniversary with a party December 8, 1974, the editors began to create covers reflecting the group's growing pride and public visibility. In 1977 a line drawing of women kissing appeared on the cover, and by 1979, a nude woman was featured. With the December 1977 issue, the name of the publication and its emphasis changed. *Focus: A Journal for Lesbians* was born, and the magazine became much more literary in emphasis.

True to its history, *Focus: A Journal for Lesbians* was published in 1978–1979 by five volunteers. They wrote, "We have no office, no equipment, no files . . . no capital, no paid or professional help . . . and precious little experience."[7] They decided to make the publication bimonthly and to increase the number of pages. Editors wrote, "The new *Focus* will be almost twice the size of the old one (32 pages to begin with, 36 if it catches on)."[8]

By the late 1970s, the cost of individual copies rose to $1.30, or subscribers could pay $8 per year. By the time the December/January 1979 issue was released, *Focus: A Journal for Lesbians* had moved its office to nearby Cambridge.

In February 1980, *Focus: A Journal for Lesbians* and the Daughters of Bilitis cut their financial ties. *Focus* became an independent magazine, and subscription was no longer an automatic part of joining the organization. Editors also devoted themselves to particular topics for each issue. In March/April 1981, for example, the publication featured a "Special Sexuality Issue."

Finances remained a constant pressure, however, and in the September/October 1983 issue, editors wrote, "*Focus,* America's oldest literary journal for lesbians—and, therefore, the world's oldest literary journal for lesbians—needs subscribers.'' The ''P.S.'' read: ''Monetary donations in any amount are always appreciated, too.''[9]

Certainly, this plea mirrors those in other centrally important lesbian publications such as *The Ladder* and *Sinister Wisdom,* where requests for financial support from the editors were common. It is not surprising that *Focus: A Journal for Lesbians* disappeared. It is far more surprising that—with their limited resources and editorial experience—its editors persevered for more than a decade and waged a successful war against rising publication prices, competition, dropping circulation, and societal disdain.

However, the editors could not battle the one-two punch of dropping circulation and increasing publication costs forever. In December 1983, the message on the inside front cover of *Focus: A Journal for Lesbians* read: ''To Our Readers: Somewhat to our surprise, we have finally come to grips with our financial situation and, perhaps even more important, with our own fatique [*sic*]. After 12 years in continuous publication, FOCUS is ceasing with this issue . . . thank you AND GOOD-BYE.''[10]

With that note ended one of the most revelatory lesbian publications in the early gay rights movement. Although it remained a low-gloss publication throughout its history, *Focus: A Journal of Lesbians* had become far more than an organizational newsletter.

Notes

1. Clare Potter, *The Lesbian Periodical Index* (Tallahassee, Fla.: Naiad Press, 1986), p. vi.
2. March 1971, p. 6.
3. Potter, *The Lesbian Periodical Index,* p. vi.
4. December 1974, p. 2.
5. February 1973, cover. The full quotation is:

> We are
> coming
> And our name
> is legion
> You dare not
> disown us.

6. March 1971, p. 10.
7. December/January 1979, p. 3.
8. December/January 1979, p. 3.
9. September/October 1983, p. 6.
10. December 1983, inside front cover.

Information Sources

BIBLIOGRAPHY:
Potter, Clare. *The Lesbian Periodical Index.* Tallahassee, Fla.: Naiad Press, 1986.

INDEX SOURCES: *The Lesbian Periodical Index.*
LOCATION SOURCES: Norlin Library, University of Colorado at Boulder; International
    Women's History Archive, Berkeley, Calif.; Women's Collection, Special Col-
    lections Department, Northwestern University Library, Evanston, Ill.

Publication History

PERIODICAL TITLE AND TITLE CHANGES: *Focus: A Journal for Gay Women,*
    (1971–1977); *Focus: A Journal for Lesbians* (1977–1983).
VOLUME AND ISSUE DATA: 112 issues (March 1971–November/December 1983).
    Monthly (1971–1978); bimonthly (1979–1983).
PUBLISHER AND PLACE OF PUBLICATION: Boston chapter of Daughters of Bilitis
    (founded 1969). Boston/Cambridge.
CIRCULATION: Unknown.

Jan Whitt

THE FORERUNNER

Historians chronicling the theoretical underpinnings of today's feminism invariably focus on Charlotte Perkins Gilman.[1] Gilman's sexuoeconomic views and
her insistence on women's genuine equality and autonomy, as well as her theories of "humanness," where both genders achieve perfection, still lie at the
heart of modern feminism.[2] In these analyses, historians and women's studies
scholars have focused on Gilman's fiction, most notably "The Yellow Wallpaper" and *Herland*[3] or her book-length theoretical tracts, especially *Women
and Economics. The Home: Its Work and Influence. Human Work,* and *The Man-
Made World: or, Our Androcentric Culture.*[4] Gilman's journalism—or, more
precisely, her magazine—has been generally lost in these analyses.[5] This represents a peculiar oversight because of the importance this magazine played in
Gilman's career. Between 1909 and 1916, Charlotte Perkins Gilman—at the
peak of her intellectual creativity—devoted herself exclusively to the writing,
editing, and production of her own magazine, *The Forerunner.* In the pages of
this monthly, Gilman worked out her "humanist" theories in fiction, poetry,
essays, and serials. These represented some of her most provocative work. *Herland. The Man-Made World, Humanness, Our Brains and What Ails Them,* and
Social Ethics first appeared in *The Forerunner* in serialized form. Gilman's
poetry in the magazine combined her reformer zeal with the artist's craft. "The
Cripple" and "The Socialist and the Suffragist" still represent important poetic
statements on fashion and suffrage. In *The Forerunner,* too, Gilman continued
her public quarrel with muckraker/antisuffragist Ida Tarbell and German writer
Ellen Karolina Sofia Key. Here was a magazine that went far beyond suffrage
and questioned traditions, institutions, and policies that prevented women from
reaching their "humanness." Here was Charlotte Perkins Gilman uncensored,
free from outside editing, free from restraint.

Charlotte Perkins Gilman had literally been forced into the launch of *The*

Forerunner. Although *Women and Economics* and "The Yellow Wallpaper" had brought her a certain amount of fame, Gilman remained a controversial figure.[6] In the early years of the twentieth century, her reputation did not represent a problem. Her articles appeared in a wide range of publications from the *New York Times* to *Harper's Weekly,* from *Collier's* to *Good Housekeeping,* from *Harper's Bazaar* to the *Delineator,* from *Life* to *Appleton's.*[7] However, by 1909, Gilman realized that she was losing access to an audience. As she explained in her autobiography:

> But as time passed there was less and less market for what I had to say, more and more of my stuff was declined. Think I must and write I must, the manuscripts accumulated far faster than I could sell them, some of the best, almost all.[8]

If she could not sell her work to existing magazines, she vowed to begin her own. But this magazine would be quite different from the others published at the time. This would be the most personal form of journalism. This would be page after page of Charlotte Perkins Gilman. From poetry to advertisements, Gilman wrote it all. *The Forerunner* was very much a personal venture, not only in its editorial content but in its launch, its distribution methods, and its advertising policies.

Gilman never expected *The Forerunner* to be a commercial success. Nothing Gilman did in her business dealings ensured success. The magazine was launched without any financial capital—save her own intellectual "investment."[9] She also expected that her own "name" as well as her network of friends would be enough to bring economic viability to the magazine. She launched it by sending out a tiny leaflet about her publishing venture to all the individuals listed in her address book.[10] Her magazine was distributed through those organizations that she knew and approved of: the Rand School of Social Science, the Women's Political Union, the National Woman Suffrage Association, and the Socialist Literature Co.[11] Not surprisingly, *The Forerunner* never achieved a large circulation. The number of subscribers never probably exceeded fifteen hundred, and that number included the international audience.[12] According to Gilman's estimates, she needed three thousand subscribers to make her magazine economically viable.[13]

Her advertising policy, likewise, prevented the magazine from achieving any measure of financial success. In the first few issues, Gilman did allow advertising. However, the advertising had to be for products that she personally used or could endorse. All other advertising was rejected. Not even friendship could sway Gilman in her selection process. When a friend offered her advertising, she tried the product and disliked it—and rejected that advertising as well.[14]

Even if accepted, advertisers could not be sure that their copy would appear as submitted. Gilman explained in the first issue of *The Forerunner* that she reserved the right to edit any advertisement. "If advertisers prefer to use their own statements, The Forerunner will publish them if it believes them to be true."[15] Gilman preferred to write the advertisements herself and often included personal testimonials. Fels-Naptha Soap, for example, had been a "solid comfort in my kitchen for years," Gilman wrote. Holeproof Hosiery was an ideal product for American homes. Women wasted so much time darning when their time could be better spent reading, Gilman wrote in the advertisement.[16] Few advertisers met Gilman's rigorous standards; and, within a year, The Forerunner discontinued accepting advertising.[17]

The launch, the distribution network, and the advertising policies veered from many of the established publishing practices of the day. However, the editorial content itself set The Forerunner off from most magazines of the time.

This magazine was Gilman's *personal* voice. The only other voices ever heard were from subscribers. (Gilman reprinted testimonials from readers primarily when subscriptions were up for renewal.[18]) Few monthlies, before or since, have been the product of only one writer. Moreover, most of this material was original, not reprinted from other sources.

Gilman's message also set The Forerunner apart. The Forerunner was a suffrage publication in that it editorially supported the franchise. It was a socialist publication in that it endorsed a collective economic system. However, The Forerunner went far beyond suffrage and socialism. Gilman questioned the very fabric of the American social, economic, and political life. She called for fundamental changes in the institutions of the nation, including the family, marriage, and the home. The editor posed many of the same questions still asked in the feminist movement and suggested alternatives that still surface in debates today.

Gilman's editorial approach grew out of her view of women. From her perspective, women were not allowed to fulfill their greatest potential—their "humanness"—because they were chained to archaic traditions, institutions, and sentiments with regard to their sex. Or, as Gilman explained in The Forerunner, "I am not primarily 'a feminist,' but a humanist. My interest in the position of woman, in the child, in the home, is altogether with a view to their influence upon human life, happiness and progress."[19]

In the pages of The Forerunner, Gilman outlined the specific problems that kept women from their "humanness" and recommended changes. The root of the inequality rested on mistaken notions of what women were and were capable of. "That one sex [male] should have monopolized all human activities, called them 'men's work,' and managed them as such, is what is meant by the phase 'Androcentric Culture,' " Gilman wrote.[20] This "androcentric culture" hindered women. Marriage, the home, child care practices, sexual relationships, the educational system, and the economy within this "androcentric culture" isolated women and kept them from reaching the "humanness" stage. Gilman was, perhaps, the first individual to recognize that (in the parlance of today's feminism) the "personal is the political." Accordingly, she focused on the "personal" dimensions of society that hurt women. From her perspective, marriage put women at a disadvantage. However, instead of focusing on the state and national laws that hurt married women, as many of the popular magazines did,[21] she attacked the "personal" relationships within the institution. Gilman saw the isolation within marriage as a major flaw. "Each man wishes his home preserve and seclude his woman, his little harem of one; and in it she is to labor for his comfort or to manifest his ability to maintain her in idleness. The house is the physical expression of the limitations of women; and as such fills the world with a small drab ugliness," she wrote.[22]

The home itself was one of the most insidious creations of the "androcentric culture." Large, ostentatious homes mirrored the husband's success but sapped the wife's energies; better, Gilman argued, to have only two rooms and a bath. The ideal home was a "small, beautiful, simple house, in a fair garden."[23] The kitchen would be eliminated. "There is no more reason why a civilized family should cook its own food in its own kitchen than kill its own pig in its own backyard," she wrote.[24] Instead, Gilman suggested that food be prepared in a central kitchen and delivered to the home; cleaning would become the responsibility of professionals. "Then the woman would have nothing to do at home?" Gilman asked. "She would have as much to do as the man—no more."[25]

Changes in marriage and the home were just the beginning of Gilman's plans as revealed in *The Forerunner.* She also advocated changes in motherhood and child rearing. Her attitudes were more in keeping with the 1990s than the early twentieth century. In Gilman's time, the mother had sole responsibility for child rearing. Gilman advocated a "new motherhood" that was in line with her attitudes on the professionalization of the household. Gilman's mothers should share responsibility for child rearing with experts, specialists in "child culture."

> To give the care that babies and little children ought to have, requires a special gift, a high order of intellect, a real talent. It also requires a full training, long experience and a proper environment.

Freed from constant supervision of children, mothers could go out and do and be all they could. This, in turn, would be beneficial to the child.

> A woman who is something more—who is also a social servant—is a nobler being for a child to love and follow than a mother who is nothing more—except a home servant. She is wiser, stronger, happier, jollier, a better comrade, a more satisfying and contented wife; the whole atmosphere around the child at home is improved by a fully human mother.[26]

These attitudes brought her into direct conflict with most traditional attitudes about child rearing and the writings of the popular feminist Ellen Key. Key argued that only the "all-wise" mother could care for her children. Gilman called such assertions "dangerous" and responded that some women are not capable of such behavior.[27]

Women should also have the right to limit the number of children they bear.

Here, Gilman's attitudes seemed more reminiscent of Victorianism than feminism. Gilman believed in birth control. However, she also argued that sex should be for reproductive purposes only. (Indeed, in "Herland," the women did not experience sexual intercourse. They conceived by "child-longing," the desire for a baby, eventually leading to conception.[28]) Birth control that allowed "safe," unlimited sexual intercourse was against Gilman's principles.

> That for reputable physicians or other competent persons to teach other [birth control] methods . . . is quite right.
>   As for needing a "safe," free and unlimited indulgence on the exercise of the [sexual] function, I hold that to be an abnormal condition.[29]

Gilman preferred restraint and, specifically, restraint on the part of men. (In *The Forerunner,* Gilman never acknowledged that women had any substantial sexual appetite.) Men needed to control themselves in marriage. As Gilman wrote:

> Manhood sufficient to father the necessary number of clean-bred children to the world is manhood enough. If we are to have monogamy, if we are to respect pregnancy, if we are to eliminate prostitution, then we need men who are capable of health and happiness with continence for the greater part of the time.[30]

Although the "personal" aspects of women's lives—the home, marriage, child rearing, birth control—dominated the pages of *The Forerunner,* she also attacked other institutions hurting women. She was especially critical of the American educational system, which stunted women's minds—and fashions that crippled their bodies.

Gilman thought a revision to the educational system would significantly improve women's minds and their status within society. According to Gilman, sound education would be a sort of "mind cleaning," sweeping away harmful old ideas and bringing in progressive ideas. In the process, women could improve and reach that idealized state of "humanness." "Education is a human process and should develop human qualities—not sex qualities."[31] But a sound education was not enough. Women, once fully educated, had to use their brains in their everyday life. Gilman did not believe that women in their domestic, gender-defined sphere used their brainpower. "By denying it [the brain] social use, we have deliberately crippled, stunted, atrophied, 'the female mind'—that is all! It is all there at birth; all there in the keen, eager, questioning child."[32]

Not only had the woman's brain been damaged in this "androcentric culture," but so, too, had the woman's body. Male-defined standards of "beauty" and male-designed "fashion" had destroyed women's health.

Gilman argued that the truly beautiful woman was strong, independent, and athletic, much like the women in "Herland," the serialized novel in *The Forerunner:*[33] In contrast, the women in the "androcentric culture" of America were weak, in large part because of male-defined standards of beauty. As Gilman complained,

> "Slender," "plump," "rounded," "graceful,"—these words suggest beauty in a woman, but "strong" does not. Yet weakness—in a healthy adult,—is incompatible with true beauty—race beauty—the beauty women have lost.[34]

Fashion played a part in the degeneration of women's health. Women dressed to reflect the wealth of their husbands and fathers—not for health, not for weather, not with common sense. Women were ornaments, and fashion was a chief way of showing the man's status in society. Too often fashion robbed women of their dignity as well as their health. As Gilman complained in *The Forerunner*:

> They [fashionable clothes] succeed in changing a dignified, strong, erect, steady, capable, enduring instrument—the human body—into a pitiful, weak, bending, unstable, slow, inefficient, easily exhausted thing, a travesty on the high for which we are built.[35]

Two pieces of clothing especially captured Gilman's wrath—hats and shoes. Gilman classified many hats as just plain silly and came up with a test for judging any hat—put it on a man's head. "If the hat makes the man look like an idiot monkey she may be very sure it is not nobly beautiful, or even a legitimate hat."[36] Hats might be silly, but fashionable shoes were just plain dangerous, crippling women. As Gilman wrote in a poem that has as much pertinence today as in the early twentieth century, when it was written:

> There are such things as hoofs, sub-human hoofs.
> High-heeled, sharp anomalies;
> Small and pinching, hard and black,
> Shining as a beetle's back,
> Cloven, clattering on the track,
> These are hoofs, sub-human hoofs,
> She cares not for true, nor ease—
> Preferring these![37]

Adequately educated and appropriately dressed, women were ready to take their places in the economy of the nation. However, they had few role models within the home or within literature. Men—and women—who wrote most of the books of that time provided few strong workingwomen to emulate. As Gilman complained, women in literature were restricted to their sex roles—"Kuchen, Kinder, Kirche, Kleider"—but "men . . . are not restricted—to them belongs with world's literature!"[38] Thus, it was left to Gilman and her *Fore-*

runner to provide the strong women characters. In both her serialized novels and her short stories, Gilman showed women competing successfully economically and enjoying independent lives. These women ranged from the strong, independent women in the agrarian society of ''Herland'' to the one woman who ventured out of that utopia to ''Ourland'' to view the strange customs and traditions of ''androcentric cultures.''[39] Other serialized novels, including *What Diantha Did* and *Moving the Mountain,* provided a range of female characters that found love and professional success in the ''androcentric culture'' as well as the utopia that Gilman created.[40] Strong female characters were not restricted to the Gilman novels; they also found personal fulfillment in the short stories of *The Forerunner.*[41] Most of Gilman's heroes were middle-class women who found personal fulfillment as workingwomen. A successful businesswoman from Los Angeles was a typical heroine. She declined a marriage proposal from a Montana rancher because she did not want to give up her business, her home, and her family. Just when everything looked hopeless, a friend convinced the suitor to give up his ''prehistoric prejudices'' and his ranch and start a new life in California with the woman he loved.[42] Many of Gilman's heroines turned their backs on social conventions. Some refused to live with their husband, as was the case of Mrs. Elder, who refused to ''retire'' with her husband to a farm. Instead, she started her own business and remained in the city. Her marriage did not end. Her husband spent some of his time on the farm and the remainder with his family in the city.[43] In one of her more controversial short stories, the heroine had a child out of wedlock. Nonetheless, she was not hindered by the action. When her lover left her, she started a successful career. When the lover returned many years later, the woman rejected him, even after he threatened to expose her ''immoral'' past.[44]

Gilman's fiction provided an idealized account of how women could succeed in the labor market. In contrast, her essays offered another perspective. Although her heroines found success, Gilman did not believe that the capitalistic economic system had been kind to women—or to men—workers. Her utopias in fiction were always based on a ''collective'' economic system. Gilman was a socialist and often wrote about the merits of that economic system in *The Forerunner.* Socialism was ''the natural evolution of our economic system,'' one that should not be feared, Gilman argued. The public ownership of public utilities would mean beneficial development for all. Moreover, the labor system under socialism would be humane. Workers of both genders would be decently paid.[45]

According to Gilman, under socialism, the economic system would be stripped of its male-based competitiveness. From Gilman's perspective, socialist principles were more closely aligned with the woman-cultivated collectivism and nurturing. In contrast, capitalism was more in line with the male aggressiveness and assertiveness. Politics and government were similarly crafted. Because men dominated both politics and government, women's input was not welcomed, in large part, because of the male view of the female sex. ''They see the woman only as a female, utterly absorbed in feminine functions, belittled and ignored as her long tutelage has made her; and they see the man as he sees himself, the sole master of human affairs for as long as we have historic record," Gilman wrote.[46] These attitudes had hurt the state and government, Gilman argued. Women's many contributions had been rejected. "As the loving mother, the patient teacher, the tender nurse, the wise provider and care-taker, she can serve the state, and the state needs her service." There was no mystery to voting or to participating in government. "The state is no mystery," Gilman argued, "no taboo place of masculine secrecy; it is simply us."[47] Women should have the vote. However, unlike many other suffragists,[48] Gilman did not see suffrage as the cure for the nation's ills. This did not mean, however, that women should not have the vote. Women, as equal to men, deserved the vote.

For seven long years, *The Forerunner* was Gilman's voice of "human feminism." It was one of the few women's magazines published in the early twentieth century that offered a radical feminist perspective on the nation. It questioned the very social, economic, and political fabric of the nation. It advocated radical reforms. It was perhaps two generations ahead of its time.

In February 1916, Gilman announced plans to fold *The Forerunner*. She could no longer afford—physically or financially—to keep the magazine afloat. Over the seven years, Gilman had written the equal of twenty-eight books. "These twenty-eight books in seven years have relieved the pressure of what I had to say," Gilman admitted. Gilman also could not financially keep the magazine going. The monthly had never been profitable. Gilman had to underwrite her publishing venture with lecture tours. "It is an expensive method of living," Gilman said.[49]

For Gilman, there was a certain joy in producing her own magazine. Finally, she could speak "fully and freely."[50] She did not have to limit herself solely to suffrage, as she did when writing for suffrage periodicals. She did not have to limit her ideas to economic topics, as she did when submitting to socialist publications. She did not have to mince words, as she did when selling to popular, general-circulation magazines. She could cover the breadth of her interests and beliefs—uncensored. This probably explained why *The Forerunner* never developed a large circulation. As Gilman reflected:

> The variety, the breadth, the depth of social alterations suggested in The Forerunner inevitably narrow the circle of readers. Those agreeing on some counts violently disagree on others; fewer and fewer become sufficiently interested in all to enjoy the whole output—or most of it.[51]

Gilman ended *The Forerunner* as she launched it, as she ran it, and as she wrote for it—as her own personal voice. She folded the magazine when she had no more to say.

Notes

1. Nancy Cott saw Charlotte Perkins Gilman's sexuoeconomic theory as a key contribution to current feminist thought. In addition, she points out Gilman's differentiation

between "female" feminists and "human" feminists as an important contribution to the understanding of the feminist movement of today. See Nancy F. Cott, *The Grounding of Modern Feminism* (New Haven, Conn.: Yale University Press, 1987), pp. 41–42, 48–49.

2. Ann J. Lane provides some of the best analysis of Charlotte Perkins Gilman's legacy to today's feminism in *To Herland and Beyond: The Life and Work of Charlotte Perkins Gilman* (New York: Pantheon Books, 1990), pp. 299–302.

3. See, for example, Margaret V. Delashmit, "The Patriarchy and Women: A Study of Charlotte Perkins Gilman's 'The Yellow Wallpaper' " (Ph.D. diss., University of Tennessee, 1990) and Lane, *To Herland and Beyond.*

4. See, for example, Mary A. Hill, *Charlotte Perkins Gilman: The Making of a Radical Feminist, 1860–1898* (Philadelphia: Temple University Press, 1980) and Polly Wynn Allen, *Building Domestic Liberty: Charlotte Perkins Gilman's Architectural Feminism* (Amherst: University of Massachusetts Press, 1988).

5. Few scholarly articles have dealt with *The Forerunner.* One recent exception is Denise D. Knight, "Charlotte Perkins Gilman, William Randolph Hearst and the Practice of Ethical Journalism," *American Journalism* 11.4, Fall 1994, pp. 336–347.

6. Gilman was born in 1860. She was a great-granddaughter of Presbyterian minister Lyman Beecher and grandniece of educator Catherine Beecher, writer Harriet Beecher Stowe, and early suffragist Isabella Beecher Hooker. Gilman (then Charlotte Stetson) made her name initially as a playwright and short story writer. She had been active in the suffrage movement in the United States, often contributing to *The Woman's Journal.* * She was also a socialist. Her economic theories were presented in *Women and Economics.* In this book, published in 1898, Gilman added the sexuoeconomic dimension to the division of labor.

7. Gary Scharnhorst has provided perhaps the most comprehensive listing of Charlotte Perkins Gilman's work. He is one of the few who have attempted to provide her journalistic contributions as well as her fiction and books. This listing of Gilman's work, organized chronologically, clearly shows the reduced popularity of her work in popular magazines (Gary Scharnhorst *Charlotte Perkins Gilman: A Bibliography* [Metuchen, N.J.: Scarecrow Press, 1985].

8. Charlotte Perkins Gilman, *The Living of Charlotte Perkins Gilman: An Autobiography* (New York: D. Appleton-Century, 1935), p. 304.

9. October 1911, p. 282.

10. Gilman, *The Living of Charlotte Perkins Gilman,* p. 308.

11. Madeline B. Stern, "Introduction," to *The Forerunner* reproduction, vol. 1 (New York: Greenwood Reprint, 1968), unnumbered page.

12. Gilman, *The Living of Charlotte Perkins Gilman,* p. 305.

13. Ibid.

14. Ibid.

15. November 1909, p. 32.

16. "Fels-Naptha Soap," November 1909, p. 29, "Holeproof Hosiery," November 1909, p. 29.

17. The magazine continued to carry notices from other reform or women's periodicals as well as advertising for Gilman's own books and lectures.

18. Typically, toward the end of each volume. See, for example, September 1910, pp. 27–29.

19. "On Ellen Key and the Woman Movement," February 1913, p. 35.

20. "Our Androcentric Culture, or the Man-Made World," November 1909, p. 24.

21. See, for example, William Hard's series on state laws in *The Delineator,* October 1911 to November 1912.

22. "Our Androcentric Culture, or the Man-Made World," February 1910, pp. 21–22.

23. "The Model House," December 1913, p. 314.

24. "The Kitchen Fly," August 1910, p. 9.

25. "The Model House," p. 315.

26. "The New Mother," December 1910, p. 17.

27. "Comment and Review," October 1911, p. 280; "On Ellen Key and the Woman Movement," February 1913, p. 37.

28. The strange conception was explained thusly: "When a woman chose to be a mother, she allowed the child-longing to grow with her till it worked its natural miracle" ("Herland," June 1915, p. 154).

29. "Birth Control," July 1915, p. 180.

30. "Humanness," October 1913, p. 276.

31. "Mind Cleaning," January 1912, pp. 5–6; "Our Androcentric Culture," June 1910, p. 19.

32. "Our Brains and What Ails Them," September 1912, p. 247.

33. "Herland," February 1915, pp. 38–44.

34. "The Beauty Women Have Lost," September 1910, p. 23.

35. "The Dress of Women," March 1915, p. 81.

36. "The Dress of Women," June 1915, p. 163.

37. "The Cripple," March 1910, p. 26.

38. "Our Androcentric Culture," March 1910, p. 18.

39. The sequel to "Herland" took one of the heroines into the male-defined culture in "With Her in Ourland." This serialized novel appeared in *The Forerunner* in 1916. "Herland" was serialized the previous year.

40. *What Diantha Did* was serialized from 1909. *Moving the Mountain* was a utopia seen through a man's eyes. There, women were given complete equality. The society incorporated many of Gilman's domestic ideas and provided a peaceful, "human" life for its inhabitants. *Moving the Mountain* was serialized in *The Forerunner* in 1911.

41. Because of the controversial nature of many of these stories, a number of the short stories were not reprinted in books. The serialized novels and theoretical tracts, however, were issued separately after they appeared in *The Forerunner.*

42. "A Cleared Path," October 1912, pp. 253–258.

43. "Mrs. Elder's Idea," February 1912, pp. 29–33.

44. "An Honest Woman," March 1911, pp. 59–66.

45. "For 1911," January 1911, p. 29; "Why We Honestly Fear Socialism," December 1909, pp. 9, 10.

46. "Our Androcentric Culture,", August 1910, p. 20.

47. "Woman and the State," October 1910, pp. 12, 14.

48. Many suffrage magazines emphasized that the vote would mean real changes to society. *The Woman's Column,* The Woman Voter,* The Woman Citizen,** and the *National Citizen and Ballot Box** were just a few of the suffrage publications that argued that woman suffrage would bring lasting social reforms.

49. "Announcement," February 1916, p. 56.

50. Perkins, *The Living of Charlotte Perkins Gilman,* p. 307.
51. "A Summary of Purpose," November 1916, p. 287.

Information Sources

BIBLIOGRAPHY:
Allen, Polly Wynn. *Building Domestic Liberty: Charlotte Perkins Gilman's Architectural Feminism.* Amherst: University of Massachusetts Press, 1988.
"Charlotte Perkins Gilman's Dynamic Social Philosophy." *Current Literature,* July 1911, pp. 67–76.
Cott, Nancy F. *The Grounding of Modern Feminism.* New Haven, Conn.: Yale University Press, 1987.
Hill, Mary A. *Charlotte Perkins Gilman; The Making of a Radical Feminist, 1860–1898.* Philadelphia: Temple University Press, 1980.
Kraditor, Aileen. *The Ideas of the Woman Suffrage Movement, 1890–1920.* New York: Columbia University Press, 1965.
Lane, Ann J. *To Herland and Beyond: The Life and Work of Charlotte Perkins Gilman.* New York: Pantheon Books, 1990.
Scharnhorst, Gary. *Charlotte Perkins Gilman: A Bibliography.* Metuchen, N.J.: Scarecrow Press, 1985.
INDEX SOURCES: Self-indexed (index available with Greenwood Reprint).
LOCATION SOURCES: Library of Congress and many other libraries. (Also available from the Greenwood Reprint Corp.)

Publication History

PERIODICAL TITLE AND TITLE CHANGES: *The Forerunner.*
VOLUME AND ISSUE DATA: Vols. 1–7 (November 1909–December 1916). Monthly.
PUBLISHER AND PLACE OF PUBLICATION: Charlton Publishing. New York City.
EDITORS: Charlotte Perkins Gilman (1909–1916).
CIRCULATION: Gilman, p. 305: less than 1,500.

Kathleen L. Endres

FOUR LIGHTS

During the first few months of 1917, the United States became drawn into the armed conflict raging in Europe. When the U.S. Congress officially declared war on Germany in April, many members of the national Woman's Peace Party (WPP), the first feminist peace organization in U.S. history, supported U.S. intervention and President Wilson's war aim of "making the world safe for democracy."[1] Yet a local branch of the WPP, the New York City Woman's Peace Party (NYC–WPP), broke with its parent organization by standing firmly against U.S. intervention. The New Yorkers' antiwar sentiments appeared in the NYC–WPP's biweekly periodical entitled *Four Lights.* In the first edition of *Four Lights,* the women pledged to "voice the young, uncompromising women's movement for peace and humanity" and to pursue three goals: "to stop the war in Europe, to federate the nations for organized peace . . . [after] the war, and to guard democracy from . . . militarism.''[2] With these goals and objectives, the New York women began their gender-based critique of American society and democracy in *Four Lights*.

The NYC–WPP consisted of a radical contingent of young, educated, working female reformers. Katharine Anthony, Jessie Wallace Hughan, Edna Kenton, Sarah N. Cleghorn, Madeline Z. Doty, Crystal Eastman, Tracy Mygatt, Frances Witherspoon, and Mary White Ovington were all published writers and editors. Hughan taught high school, Lou Rogers drew cartoons, and Crystal Eastman practiced law. Eastman, Ovington, Hughan, and Freda Kirchwey were socialists; Ovington was also a social worker, interested particularly in radical discrimination. Kirchwey, Eastman, Mygatt, and Witherspoon were active in labor issues and organizations. All of these women had attended colleges or universities. Eastman and Hughan had degrees beyond the bachelor's. Eastman, Doty, Kirchwey, Anne Herendeen, Margaret Lane, and Rogers were married; the others remained single. Mary Ware Dennett divorced her husband. Katharine Anthony and Elisabeth Irwin, and Tracy Mygatt and Frances Witherspoon were lesbian couples. Although most had been born into established New York Anglo-American families (Mygatt and Witherspoon were wealthy enough to live frugally on their inheritances), they were relatively free from class allegiances or perspectives.[3]

The U.S. war declaration radicalized the NYC–WPP. Early issues of *Four Lights* urged political involvement on the part of readers, a goal shared by the national WPP. The journal invoked readers to wire their congressmen and urge them to keep the United States out of war. "No compromise with war," pleaded editors Jessie Wallace Hughan, Sarah N. Cleghorn, and Fannie M. Witherspoon, "which is always and everlastingly indefensible!" *Four Lights* communicated the notion of American superiority, also common among members of the national WPP. "May America be true to her destiny, that she may keep forever her place in the sun, the hope of the world."[4] But when Congress voted for war against Germany in April, the NYC–WPP ceased its support of the Wilson administration and continued its gendered interpretations of events, imbuing news about the war with feminist meanings.

In the July 14 issue, for example, *Four Lights* asked in bold letters, "WHAT ARE THE WAR AIMS AND PEACE TERMS OF THE AMERICAN WOMEN? Why have we American women declared war on German women? What do we demand? Upon what terms will we make peace?"[5] With these questions, editors Mary Alden Hopkins and Elisabeth Irwin implored their readers to consider war a gendered issue. The New Yorkers reminded readers that the American democratic government continued to ignore women's participation in matters of foreign policy.

Four Lights rotated its volunteer editorial staff, allowing different styles and views within its pages. (The journal also solicited volunteers from its readership to help with mailing and provide financial support.) Not simply a matter of sharing work, the practice of alternating staff became part of the women's strategy. For example, in the January 27 issue, editors Anne Herendeen, Edna Kenton, and Zoe Beckley noted: " 'Four Lights' will not give any of its lustre to the jewel of consistency. Each fortnightly issue will express the . . . hope of a new Board of three volunteer editors. . . . If you do not like this number, be sure to get the next!"[6] The title of the publication derived from a Magellan poem ("First Voyage 'Round the World"). To the right of the logo was a drawing of a sixteenth-century boat navigating choppy waters.

In addition to complimentary copies for all NYC–WPP members, *Four Lights'* editors announced that they were "sending *Four Lights* free to a large list of newspapers throughout the country in the hope of sounding a new note . . . in the American Press."[7] *Four Lights* offered its readers critiques of militarism, classism, sexism, and racism, themes the NYC–WPP believed were absent from mainstream newspapers.

Four Lights editors adopted a strategy of reprinting news items from the daily press and then topping the story with a mocking headline. Editors Joy Young and Anne Herendeen reprinted a news item about the Red Cross: " 'The American Red Cross is the big brother of the army and the navy.' " The title to this snippet read, in bold letters, **"WE THOUGHT IT WAS A GIRL."**[8] Young's and Herendeen's sense of irony undoubtedly came from their reading of numerous Red Cross recruitment and propaganda posters, which featured women nurses eagerly signing up to join the war effort. By speaking of the organization in male terms, the daily paper overlooked female domination of the Red Cross. *Four Lights'* title suggested that women's work went unrealized by the press and that the Red Cross recruitment posters fooled women into expecting recognition for their work.

Another strategy was to juxtapose two conflicting opinions on the same page. For example, the June 2 issue offered a number of news fragments the editors reprinted alongside each other. Below the headline, "Little Words of Love" (also an ironic title), the editors printed President Wilson's conversation with Representative Thomas Heflin (D–Alabama): " 'There is no hate in our hearts for the German people.' " The editors then described a number of German workers whose U.S. employers had discharged them because of their ethnicity. The next item, under the title, "Still More War Horrors," described Lord Beresford's reaction at London's Savoy Hotel when he discovered he had been eating off plates made in Germany. He and a number of guests hurled their dinnerware to the floor.[9] By placing the stories one right after the other, the editors revealed two different expressions of hatred toward Germans. In the first case, prejudice caused unemployment and hardship for Germans living in belligerent nations. Second, animosity toward the "enemy" resulted in a ridiculous display of childishness, as grown men and women consumed a perfectly fine meal and then rioted when they discovered the origin of the plates. Reading the stories sequentially made *Four Lights'* subscribers aware of the different ways in which hatred manifested itself during war.

Four Lights reported on the 1917 race riots, an event upon which the national

WPP did not comment. In the August 25 issue, Mary White Ovington attacked President Wilson for his indifference toward the atrocities committed against African Americans during the East St. Louis riots of July 1917. "Six weeks have passed since the race riots of July and no public word of rebuke, no demand for the punishment of the offenders, has come from our Chief Executive," charged Ovington. "The American Negroes have died under more horrible conditions than any non-combatants who were sunk by German submarines. But to our President, their deaths do not merit consideration." American military troops instigated the race riots, reported Ovington, making clear connections between racism and militarism. The NYC–WPP was the only peace organization to make such charges.[10]

Four Lights also pointed out the oppressive nature of militarism. In the February 6 issue, for example, editor Sarah N. Cleghorn produced a facsimile of a card and white feather sent to young men who refused to enlist in the army. The card predicted that the men would receive petticoats in the mail if they still refused to obey their nation's call to serve. Below the card, Cleghorn photographed a brooch, explaining that girls who secured the enlistment of ten men were rewarded with jewelry for their efforts. Cleghorn closed the display with the words, "It is of such conditions that the new courage is being born."[11] Advocates of militarism, according to *Four Lights*, maintained their power by ridiculing gender deviance and rewarding gender conformity.

In their most telling feminist critique of militarism, the editors reprinted a commentary from another pacifist journal. *The Nation* described the sexual victimization of young women in Europe by victorious soldiers. "For her own sake she had better in the majority of cases be dead," contended *The Nation*, "From the standpoint of the interests of society, she had much better be dead." In reprinting the article, *Four Lights* revealed the sexism and misogynism underlying the report. Highly critical of the piece, the editors went on to say that "similar 'better dead than dishonor' statements were being constantly made in regard to the unfortunate women outraged by invading armies." This attitude "assumes as self-evident," maintained *Four Lights*, "*that a woman's honor concerns only this one function.* Men seem to be unanimous on this point. It would be enlightening to learn what proportion of women agree that 'From the standpoint of the interests of society she had much better be dead.' "[12]

Some women in the national WPP not only accepted war but also participated in the conflict through war relief work. Government-sponsored programs to conserve food, to enlist as volunteers to roll Red Cross bandages, or to visit soldiers' hospitals involved women in the war effort. Many women of the national WPP heartily endorsed such participation in the war. By contrast, Mary Alden Hopkins offered this mocking "advice" to women in "Woman's Ways in War":

Women have often been accused of being essentially producers and conservers. Now is the time for them to lay forever that slander and prove that they are glad and eager to destroy joyfully all that the ages—and other women—have produced. It takes but a minute to destroy a boy [on a battlefield] into whose making have gone eighteen years of thoughtful care.[13]

Hopkins' article, a radical, hard-hitting, and thorough critique of patriarchy, also mocked the issue of war work. Hopkins addressed women's oppression under patriarchy in two ways. First, she argued against the dominant assumption that women's proper roles as mothers and wives prevented them from participating in politics. Second, she complained that women used their life's work, keeping house and raising children, to perpetuate their own oppression and the destruction of their work—the death of their children on battlefields.

When the U.S. Department of Justice claimed that two issues of *Four Lights* were treasonous, the Post Office refused to deliver the journal. Despite the New York women's protests, a representative from the U.S. Department of Justice interrogated them in August 1917.[14] The women ceased publication after October 1917. A special edition of *Four Lights* came out after the war on June 12, 1919, commemorating the International Congress of Women in Zurich, a meeting that paralleled the Versailles Peace Treaty negotiations. During the Zurich meeting, the Woman's Peace Party became the U.S. section of the Women's International League for Peace and Freedom. The 1919 *Four Lights* issue was the last, until the journal reappeared in 1940.

The NYC–WPP stood on the periphery of mainstream progressive views and interpretations of the war. Unlike other progressives, the New York women did not accept Woodrow Wilson's vision of U.S. intervention in the war as "making the world safe for democracy," because, at that point, they no longer recognized the United States as a democratic nation. The feminist pacifists demonstrated that a society that did not allow women a voice in government and that sent innocent young men to war was not a democracy. Nor was a society that punished innocent African Americans to be trusted with the welfare of its citizens. The NYC–WPP saw that military preparedness and the U.S. belligerency that followed were a government-sponsored form of sexism, classism, and racism. Whereas the national WPP viewed the U.S. government and American society as democratic and basically sound, the NYC–WPP women saw them as undemocratic and flawed. Instead of consenting to the wartime government by aiding the war effort, the NYC–WPP enlightened its readers as to how the system eroded democracy during wartime.

Notes

1. For information on the national WPP, see Marie Louise Degen, *The History of the Woman's Peace Party,* 1939, reprint (New York: Garland, 1972).

2. January 27, 1917, unnumbered page.

3. Complete biographical information on all of the *Four Lights'* editors does not exist. Judith Schwarz's *Heterodoxy: The Radical Feminists of Greenwich Village, 1912–1940* (Norwich Vt.: New Victoria, 1986), pp. 116–128 offers short biographies of many

of these women. Nancy Manahan's article "Future Old Maids and Pacifist Agitators: The Story of Tracy Mygatt and Frances Witherspoon," *Women's Studies Quarterly* 10, Spring 1982, pp. 10–13 is also helpful.

    4. January 27, 1917, unnumbered page.

    5. July 14, 1917, unnumbered page.

    6. January 27, 1917, unnumbered page.

    7. This quote is taken from a letter written by the NYC–WPP, unsigned and undated, Reel 23.1, Woman's Peace Party: Swarthmore College Peace Collection.

    8. See Walton Rawls, *Wake Up America! World War I and the American Poster* (New York: Abbeville Press, 1988), pp. 124–129, 152, 160, for reproductions of Red Cross posters; July 14, 1917, unnumbered page.

    9. June 2, 1917, unnumbered page.

    10. Mary White Ovington, "East St. Louis Riots," August 25, 1917, unnumbered page.

    11. February 6, 1917, unnumbered page.

    12. July 14, 1917, unnumbered page; italics added.

    13. Mary Alden Hopkins, "Women's Ways in War," June 2, 1917, unnumbered page.

    14. For more information on the interrogation, see Harriet Hyman Alonso, *Peace as a Women's Issue: A History of the U.S. Movement for World Peace and Women's Rights* (Syracuse, N.Y.: Syracuse University Press, 1993), pp. 80–81.

Information Sources

BIBLIOGRAPHY:

Alonso, Harriet Hyman. *Peace as a Women's Issue: A History of the U.S. Movement for World Peace and Women's Rights.* Syracuse, N.Y.: Syracuse University Press, 1993.

Degen, Marie Louise. *The History of the Woman's Peace Party.* 1939. Reprint. New York: Garland, 1972.

Kuhlman, Erika A. "The Feminist Pacifist Challenge to Progressive Hegemony: The Debate over U.S. Intervention in World War I." Diss., Washington State University, 1995.

Manahan, Nancy. "Future Old Maids and Pacifist Agitators: The Story of Tracy Mygatt and Francis Witherspoon." *Women's Studies Quarterly* 10, Spring 1982, pp. 10–13.

Schwarz, Judith. *Heterodoxy: The Radical Feminists of Greenwich Village 1912–1940.* Norwich, Vt.: New Victoria, 1986.

Sochen, June. *The New Woman: Feminism in Greenwich Village, 1910–1920.* New York: Quadrangle Books, 1972.

INDEX SOURCES: None.

LOCATION SOURCES: Swarthmore College Peace Collection, Swarthmore College, Swarthmore, Pa., and other libraries.

Publication History

PERIODICAL TITLE AND TITLE CHANGES: *Four Lights.*

VOLUME AND ISSUE DATA: Vols. 1–2 (1917) (January 1917–October 1917 and June 12, 1919). Biweekly.

PUBLISHER AND PLACE OF PUBLICATION: New York City Woman's Peace Party. New York.

EDITORS: New York City Woman's Peace Party members Pauline Knickerbocker An-
gell, Jessie Ashley, Mary Chamberlain, Sarah N. Cleghorn, Dorothy G. Dana,
Mary Ware Dennett, Madeleine Zabriskie Doty, Flora Dunlap, Martha Gruening,
Anne Herendeen, Mary Alden Hopkins, Jessie Wallace Hughan, Elisabeth Irwin,
Mary Johnston, Edna Kenton, Freda Kirchwey, Leonie Knoedler, Margaret John-
son Lane, Tracy Dickinson Mygatt, Mary White Ovington, Mary Katharine Reely,
Neltje T. Shirmer, Miriam Teichner, Florence Guertin Tuttle, Agnes D. Warbasse,
Frannie M. Witherspoon, Joy Young (1917). (Editors rotated).
CIRCULATION: Unknown.

Erika A. Kuhlman

FREE SPEECH AND HEADLIGHT

The story of the *Free Speech and Headlight* is largely the story of Ida B. Wells,
an activist and investigative reporter who used her journalistic skills to enlighten
and ennoble her African American audience; in the process she often enraged
her white contemporaries. In fact, the Memphis-based *Free Speech* died a violent
death in 1892, precipitated by Wells' investigation of the lynchings of three
black Memphis businessmen and by the allegations she leveled in the publication
against the white community.

Wells was only twenty-seven when she became editor of *Free Speech,* but
she had already made her mark as a journalist with fire, integrity, and tenacity.
In her tenure at *Free Speech*—from 1889 until its death—she led the black
community into a discussion of issues such as lynchings, Jim Crow laws, and
the responsibility of blacks to each another. *Free Speech* existed before Wells
became its editor, but little is written about its pre-Wells years; no dates are
given for when it was started or the issues it covered. No copies of the publication remain.

Wells was born a slave in 1862 but was freed at age three at the end of the
Civil War. She attended the State Normal School in Holly Springs, Mississippi,
until age sixteen, when her parents died in a yellow fever epidemic. At eighteen,
she moved to Memphis and took classes at Fisk University and Lemoyne Institute of Memphis.[1] She was qualified to teach by 1884 and was assigned a first-
grade class. With her salary of fifty dollars a month, she joined the Memphis
black elite, became a member of a lyceum, a black literary club, and edited the
group's publication, *The Evening Star.*[2]

She earned her stripes as an activist in 1884, when, at the age of twenty-two,
she was asked to leave the ladies' car of a railroad train, where she sat comfortably reading. The conductor told her to move to the smoking car, where
blacks were required to sit. She refused and was forced off the train, while the
whites who remained stood up and applauded her departure. Indignant and hu-
miliated, she sued the railroad company and was awarded five hundred dollars
in damages.[3] Three years later, though, the Tennessee Supreme Court overturned
the decision.[4]

Almost two hundred black newspapers were published every week in the 1880s, and Wells wrote about her lawsuit for many of them. *The Living Way,* a black church weekly, hired her as a regular contributor. She wrote about civic affairs under the pen name "Iola." By 1886, her articles were appearing in the *Detroit Plaindealer,* the *Indianapolis Freeman,* the *Little Rock Sun,* and *American Baptist.*[5]

A natural next step was her own publication. She found it in *Free Speech and Headlight,* founded by the Reverend Taylor Nightingale, pastor of the Beale Street Baptist Church in Memphis, the largest black congregation in Tennessee. Nightingale aimed the publication at members of his church, and he unabashedly used his sermons to sell copies.

In 1889, Wells purchased a one-third interest in the paper. The third owner was journalist J. L. Fleming. Nightingale was made sales manager, Fleming was business manager, and Wells was editor. Within nine months, the paper's circulation soared from fifteen hundred to thirty-five hundred.[6]

When she bought the paper, Wells was still a teacher, as editing the paper didn't provide a full-time income. Nevertheless, she criticized the public school system for the poor quality of black schools and for the process through which teachers were selected. Not surprisingly, when Wells' contract was due for renewal in 1891, the school system turned her down.[7]

Free Speech earned its place in journalistic history with its campaign against lynchings, largely spearheaded and written by Wells. In 1891, a group of blacks in Georgetown, Kentucky, set fire to the town in retaliation for the lynching of a black man named Dudley. *Free Speech* lauded the action, saying it was the only way to stop lynching:

> Of one thing we may be assured, so long as we permit ourselves to be trampled upon, so long as we will have to endure it. Not until the Negro rises in his might and takes a hand in resenting such cold-blooded murders, if he has to burn up whole towns, will a halt be called in wholesale lynching.[8]

The white community in Memphis reacted with outrage; papers such as the *Weekly Avalanche* and *Public Ledger* supported the lynch mob in cases of rape, saying it was a necessary means of maintaining civil order. The Reverend Nightingale ended up a casualty of the whole issue. Authorities used dissension within his church as justification to level charges of assault and battery against him, which ultimately led to his move from Memphis to Oklahoma. Wells and Fleming bought his portion of *Free Speech,* expanded its audience to Arkansas and Mississippi, and increased circulation to four thousand.[9] Without her teaching job, Wells put all her energies into *Free Speech.* The paper's popularity allowed her to increase her salary and make a living as a journalist.

Free Speech under Wells frequently criticized other blacks for going against what Wells thought was their duty. Isaiah Montgomery learned this the hard way. Montgomery was the only black delegate to the 1890 Mississippi Constitutional Convention and voted for a measure that limited blacks' voting rights. For this, he earned Wells' rebuke. She also wrote critically of a piece in the *Christian Register* written by Booker T. Washington that criticized black ministers. Interestingly, Wells didn't fault Washington for his conclusion—she only thought he should have aired his grievances in the black press, where it would have had more impact.[10]

The incident that led to the death of *Free Speech* was precipitated by the lynching of three prominent Memphis black men. The three were successful shop owners; this, Wells believed, was a threat to white businesses and was the real cause of their lynching. *Free Speech* called for punishment of the murderers of the three men; the white community did not see the act as murder and ignored Wells' calls to justice. Wells refused to be rebuffed. Her response: a suggestion to Memphis blacks that they leave the city:

> The city of Memphis has demonstrated that neither character nor standing avails the Negro if he dares to protect himself against the white man or become his rival. There is nothing we can do about the lynching now, as we are outnumbered and without arms. The white mob could help itself to ammunition without pay, but the order was rigidly enforced against the selling of guns to Negroes. There is therefore only one thing left that we can do: save our money and leave a town which will neither protect our lives and property, nor give us a fair trial in the courts, when accused by white persons.[11]

Wells traveled to Oklahoma and declared it a better place for blacks to live than the prejudice of the South. In two months, six thousand blacks left the city, and businesses that depended on black patronage suffered.

Wells didn't stop there. Rape was given as a reason for the lynching of the three men, as was often the case. Wells did intense investigation, studying more than seven hundred cases. She discovered that the charge of rape was largely an invention to gain white sympathy—in two-thirds of the cases, there was no evidence of rape. In a third of the cases, she discovered a sexual relationship existed, but one that was not forced. Armed with this information, Wells wrote an editorial that angered the white community and initiated the destruction of the newspaper:

> Eight Negroes lynched since last issue of the *Free Speech.* Three were charged with killing white men and five with raping white women. Nobody in this section believes the old thread-bare lie that Negro men assault white women. If Southern men are not careful they will overreach themselves and a conclusion will be reached which will be very damaging to the moral reputation of their women.[12]

The white community saw this as slander against all white women. At the time the editorial appeared, Wells was on a train headed to Philadelphia to the African Methodist Episcopal (AME) General Church Conference. J. L. Fleming had been warned to leave Memphis. A mob ransacked the *Free Speech* offices, destroying the presses and all furnishings. The *Memphis Daily Appeal* ran a front-page story suggesting that the "black wretch who had written that foul lie" be tied to a stake and burned.[13]

It was thirty years before Wells returned to Memphis. Her writing and her activism took her to the eastern United States and Europe. She joined the staff of the *New York Age,* where she continued her antilynching crusade, and she traveled the country as a speaker on the issues she had covered in *Free Speech.* The Women's Loyal Union, a black women's social club, was so impressed by Wells' exile from Memphis that they held a fund-raiser in 1892 at New York's Lyric Hall to restart *Free Speech.* It was a success, bringing black women from Boston, Philadelphia, and New York. Wells, however, used the money to publish the pamphlet *Southern Horrors,* in which she continued her argument against the white defense that lynching protected white women and children. Much of the information in *Southern Horrors* came from her research for *Free Speech.*

Throughout her life, Wells continued the activism that marked her years at *Free Speech.* When she did return to the South, it was to champion the cause of black sharecroppers who had started a union. Many were killed; others were imprisoned and sentenced to death. Wells wrote about the issue and published the pamphlet *The Arkansas Race Riot,* which led to the men's case being heard by the Arkansas Supreme Court; the men were ultimately released.[14]

This activism informed her philosophy as a journalist. She believed that blacks benefited from informed reporting; her emphasis as a writer and editor was on factual reporting and in-depth investigation.

In 1895 Wells married Ferdinand Barnett, publisher of *The Conservator,* a black Chicago weekly, which she eventually bought from him. They had four children. She died in 1931, at the age of sixty-eight.

Notes

1. Darryl M. Trimiew, *Voices of the Silenced: The Responsible Self in a Marginalized Community* (Cleveland, Ohio: Pilgrim Press, 1993), p. 37.

2. Dorothy Sterling, *Black Foremothers: Three Lives* (Old Westbury, N.Y.: Feminist Press, 1979), p. 68.

3. Ibid., p. 72.

4. Mildred Thompson, *Black Women in United States History: Ida B. Wells-Barnett* (Brooklyn, N.Y.: Carson, 1990), pp. 13–14.

5. Sterling, *Black Foremothers,* p. 74.

6. Ibid., p. 76.

7. Henry Lewis Suggs, ed., *The Black Press in the South, 1865–1979* (Westport, Conn.: Greenwood Press, 1983), p. 327.

8. David Tucker, *Black Pastors and Leaders: Memphis, 1819–1972* (Memphis, Tenn.: Memphis State University Press, 1975), p. 47.

9. Suggs, *The Black Press in the South, 1865–1979,* p. 326.
10. Ibid.
11. Thompson, *Black Women in United States History,* p. 28.
12. Ibid., p. 29.
13. Miriam DeCosta-Willis, ed., *The Memphis Diary of Ida B. Wells* (Boston: Beacon Press, 1995), p. 192.
14. Ibid., p. 193.

Information Sources

BIBLIOGRAPHY:
DeCosta-Willis, Miriam, ed. *The Memphis Diary of Ida B. Wells.* Boston: Beacon Press, 1995.
Sterling, Dorothy. *Black Foremothers: Three Lives.* Old Westbury, N.Y.: Feminist Press, 1979.
Suggs, Henry Lewis, ed. *The Black Press in the South, 1865–1979.* Westport, Conn.: Greenwood Press, 1983.
Thompson, Mildred. *Black Women in United States History: Ida B. Wells-Barnett.* Brooklyn, N.Y.: Carson, 1990.
Trimiew, Darryl M. *Voices of the Silenced: The Responsible Self in a Marginalized Community.* Cleveland; Ohio: Pilgrim Press, 1993.
Tucker, David. *Black Pastors and Leaders: Memphis, 1819–1972.* Memphis, Tenn.: Memphis State University Press, 1975.
INDEX SOURCES: None.

Publication History

PERIODICAL TITLE AND TITLE CHANGES: *Free Speech and Headlight* (unknown–May 1892).
VOLUME AND ISSUE DATA: Vols 1–? (1888–May 21, 1892?). Unknown.
PUBLISHER AND PLACE OF PUBLICATION: Taylor Nightingale, Beale Street Baptist Church; J. L. Fleming; Ida B. Wells. Memphis, Tenn.
EDITORS: Taylor Nightingale (Unknown–1889); Ida B. Wells (1889–1892).
CIRCULATION: 4,000.

Patricia Prijatel

THE FRIEND OF VIRTUE

Its masthead was graced with "Blessed are the undefiled in the way that walk in the law of the Lord." Filled with prayers, parables, poems, and platitudes, as well as ministers' tracts, reform society reports, and pragmatic advice on parenting, *The Friend of Virtue* endeavored to guide its audience through the morass of an ever-secular and amoral culture. This magazine of moral reform made it clear that it was "edited exclusively BY A LADY."[1] As a ladies' magazine of moral reform, it was not given to euphemisms but addressed social problems in a straightforward manner.

Published by the New England Female Moral Reform Society, the magazine was begun in 1838, about one year after the society was formed, in order to serve as its messenger.

> The "Friend of Virtue" has been the youthful companion of this society. ... We have high hopes of this young friend, and would gladly do all in our power to assist the Parent Society in sustaining it. It is dear to our hearts ... and an endeared home companion, from its earliest infancy.[2]

The society as well as its magazine was founded during an era known as the Second Great Awakening. This was a time when "a millennial spirit pervaded efforts at transforming United States society," and reformers "sought not merely social change but spiritual transformation, the moral regeneration of the world."[3] The New England Female Moral Reform Society was one of a number of women's reform societies founded during this time. At the time this society started *The Friend of Virtue,* the New York Female Moral Reform Society was reestablishing itself as the national organization, the American Female Moral Reform Society. As a regional society, the New England society could ultimately pull members from the national society and subscribers from its magazine. Although the national organ, *The Advocate of Moral Reform,** recognized *The Friend of Virtue* as competition for subscribers—and its parent organization as competition for members—it tended to view the publication as a comrade in arms in the battle of social reform.

> The formation of the New England Moral Reform Society (a sister enterprise that sustains a periodical—is doing much good, and worthy the encouragement of all friends of Reform) has tended to lessen the number of the New England subscribers and Auxiliaries, but we believe they are still efficient in the cause, and therefore the early bond remains unchanged.[4]

Moral reform was a subject ministers were not addressing from the pulpit. Yet, lay efforts were objected to on the grounds that they were a "promiscuous exhibition of truths or facts relative to a subject. Will those who object to this exhibition forbid their children to read the Bible?" a writer to *The Friend of Virtue* asked.[5] But those who took objection argued that behaviors such as adultery were not appropriate topics for public discussion for anyone, much less women. Reform advocates, impassioned with ridding society of such vices as prostitution and seduction, found themselves consistently called on to rationalize their mission and that of their publications. "Moral Reform we regard as a broad subject. ... Consequently the details of vice, and what is technically called Moral Reform, include but a small portion of the topics presented to our readers."[6]

The mainstay of the magazine's contents centered on the health and education of the future—the children. "[L]et us ask what are you doing to prepare your children ... and what are they doing for themselves?"[7] Training children to become morally upright adults involved far more than feeding, clothing, and educating them.[8] "Allow us to say that you may do much for the promotion of the cause of Moral Reform, by requiring your children to be obedient."[9]

As a small journal of about 9" by 5", the sixteen-page publication carved for itself a large mission:

> The Friend of Virtue: A Semi-Monthly Periodical, Devoted to the Cause of Moral Purity, Namely, By holding out the Light of Divine Truth on the subject, by aiding in the right training of Children and youth, exposing the prevalence of Vice, and the wiles of the Destroyer, by treating the Libertine with merited contempt, extending the hand of sympathy and kindness to the friendless, homeless, unprotected Female, by reclaiming the Wanderers, and respectfully soliciting our Law-makers to defend our sacred rights—our most endearing social privileges.[10]

Rebecca Eaton was listed as editor, although it appeared that she had been acting as editor, or editress as she was often referred, since she had been the corresponding secretary of the New England Female Moral Reform Society. The editor took her mission seriously, acknowledging that the

> responsibility of editing this little work is deeply realized. . . . One circumstance we have regarded as very encouraging; viz.: many who have been opposed to Moral Reform efforts, and especially opposed to Moral Reform publications, having been induced to read our little sheet, have acknowledged that they found it useful themselves as Christians, useful to their families, and that they believed it would be useful to community.[11]

The articles addressed a predominantly female audience, often beginning with "ladies." On occasion, the magazine incorporated men into the household and child-rearing recommendations with its appeals to "parents." In an evenhanded address, the Reverend Tisdale suggested "a few things for the particular consideration of mothers, but which are, by no means, to be disregarded by fathers. I shall, therefore, generally use the term parents."[12] The magazine recognized that parents did not have sole rights over their children. Children were individuals, and rearing them properly was for the betterment of society.

> [T]here are other than parental claims on children. Even children have their rights. And if, when arrived at manhood they perceive that while under parental authority, they were not placed under wholesome restraints, that they did not receive that moral and intellectual instruction which their parents might have given them, they will feel that there is a sense in which injustice has been done them.[13]

The importance of parenting was emphasized throughout each issue: "No relation in which human intelligences are placed towards each other, and towards the world at large, is more important, or more responsible than that of PARENTS."[14] The primary parental goal was to be vigilant against waywardness in children. If parents would not encourage children to be honest, productive, and healthy, they were paving the way for the devil, often referred to as the Libertine. The ways children could be led astray if not under the tutelage of conscientious parents were numerous.

> Some are led away "by their own lusts and enticed," some, in consequence of habits of indolence . . . some by that dangerous familiarity indulged in at fashionable parties . . . some by novel-reading, some by those polluting details told and retold at our common schools . . . some by reading those impure couplets found in sweetmeats bought at the confectionary's, some, when walking the streets, are allured away by the panderers of vice, some by their mothers (those mothers who monsters prove) and some, even by their fathers are encouraged, or even constrained, to walk in the road to death.[15]

Parents were urged to keep the physical as well as the spiritual needs of children's health uppermost. The magazine did not consider it selfish that mothers attend to their own health. "How important an element of domestic order and happiness is the health of the mother! A disordered house, a table alternately extravagant and mean, a group of children with untidy persons and rude manners, too surely indicate the absence of a mother's care."[16] Contrary to conventional wisdom, mothers were urged to encourage the physical education of their daughters, whether it was by getting fresh air[17] or enabling them so they would not become a burden on society.

> The sickliness of our females has become almost a national reproach. . . .
> Its cause may often be traced to improper management in early childhood, and oftener still to that slavery of fashion, in dress and amusements, to which girls are subjected, as they advance in years."[18]

The magazine advocated plain food, exercise, and a good "romp." "Let us give our daughters the training which makes our sons healthy, and they will be so likewise."[19] If mothers neglected these basics, they did so with serious moral consequence.

> Do not mothers, by neglecting important duties in the training of their children, help to swell the dark catalogue of crime? Mothers, I ask you this serious question; are you not educating your daughters so as to make them a burden to their husbands? . . .
> And now, dear mothers, let me give you a little advice, and do not be

shocked at the seeming vulgarity. Instead of consulting half a dozen doctors, . . . give your daughters healthy employment; let them rise early in the morning, clean the parlors. . . . Let them cultivate the flowers."[20]

Mothers were recognized as role models for their daughters. Mothers "can mould and fashion the minds and manners, the habits and feelings of their children, especially those of daughters, into almost any form they please."[21]

The magazine also directly addressed children and young adults. Young women were urged to take up the cause of purity and were given instructive tales of woe featuring girls in the city who cared only for their outward appearance. Young men were urged to have moral courage "that they should control their own impulses, as well as influence others."[22]

Advice also came in the form of reprints from other publications, instructive stories of family adventures and testimonials from readers. One woman wrote that when she was young, a "pretended gentleman" had actually been a stalker. But for the advice of *The Friend of Virtue,* she wondered "what would have become of" her.[23]

Reports of moral reform societies throughout New England and beyond were regularly published and often contained praise for the publication. "We consider the Friend of Virtue, of which a large number is taken among us, an efficient aid in our operations."[24]

The Seventh Commandment was the main subject of the various prose and poetry in the magazine, although it was debated how publicly adultery should be addressed.[25] The society's constitution addressed this mission directly. "This Society shall have for its object the prevention of licentiousness, by diffusing light in regard to the existence and great extent of this sin."[26]

It is objected to Moral Reform Efforts, that by these means, the curiosity of the young is excited, and that they know more about the developments of the seventh commandment than they otherwise would. . . . It is true they would become acquainted with some facts of which, perhaps, they might otherwise have remained ignorant. But these facts are all calculated to show the terrible consequences of the sin of licentiousness.[27]

Adultery was often the subject of lectures, which were chosen for inclusion in the magazine.[28] The magazine also entreated against situations in which amoral behavior was more apt to be tolerated. The theater was considered one such place "productive of general depravity of principles and manners,"[29] as were activities such as horse racing. Not only public pasttimes were debated. "Does the mind need relaxation, and will the reading of fictitious works accomplish this object? This is a controverted question, and one worthy of consideration."[30]

By the mid-1840s, the magazine featured an illustrated masthead of a woman sitting with a lamb. A "Children's Department" was incorporated.

The small magazine contained advertisements, most often for moral tracts for sale at the office. Although the editor on occasion complained of financial difficulties, these seemed to be more generally associated with the moral reform society than the magazine itself.[31] Profits from the magazine went toward sustaining operations that promoted the cause of moral purity, such as temporary shelters. As the magazine was transformed into a monthly called *The Home Guardian* in 1868, advertising was retained, usually at about three pages.

In spite of the society's arguing its mission since its inception, the controversial phrase "moral reform" discouraged contributions and subscribers. Thus, the organization changed the name of its publication to one with the decidedly more popular tone of *The Home Guardian.* Yet not much in the magazine itself changed. Many of the departments and types of articles remained similar: biographies, narratives, essays, and poems. The publication did acknowledge the shift in tone. "The Magazine . . . seeks to enlighten and amuse the social circle, and foster a right love of home and all its tender ties."[32] Fiction became a staple of the magazine, which began running serials. But the fiction was scrutinized. "The reading matter, stories, tales, sketches, poems, etc., original and selected, is of the highest order, and free from anything that can be deemed objectionable in the home circle."[33] The fiction was instructive, and often the author's credentials were reviewed for readers. "To ensure it favorable attention, we need only to say it is from the pen of the author of the interesting and exhaustive paper, entitled 'Woman, her industry and idleness.' "[34] By the 1880s, other periodicals and works of fiction were scoured; if they were found to be of good moral character, they were recommended on the pages of the magazine. For example, the magazine recommended *Scribner's Illustrated Magazine for Girls and Boys* and works by Jules Verne.[35]

The moral reform effort's crusade against immorality branched out to embrace other types of social reform. In the mid-1870s, temperance was strongly embraced. The magazine called liquor licentiousness' "right arm."[36] Support was thrown behind the woman's temperance movement as another strategy to further social reform. The magazine continued broadening its mission in its more popularized format until it folded in 1892.

Notes

1. Publisher's Box, December 15, 1848, p. 327. Although the publication made it clear that it was edited by a "lady," it did not always list *which* lady was editor at the time.

2. H. D. Jones [secretary], "Extract from the Report of the Marlboro N. H. Female Moral Reform Society," February 1, 1840, p. 47.

3. Lori D. Ginzberg, " 'Moral Suasion Is Moral Balderdash': Women, Politics, and Social Activism in the 1850s," *Journal of American History* 73, December 1986, p. 601.

4. "Twelfth Annual Report," *The Advocate of Moral Reform,* June 1, 1846, p. [81].

5. L. W. Wright, "An Address Read before the Maternal Association, Sullivan, N. H.," March 1, 1840, p. [65].

6. "The Friend of Virtue," editorial, July 1, 1851, p. 197.

7. "To Mothers," editorial, April 1, 1840, p. 106.

8. See, for example, editorial, March 1, 1840, p. 72.

9. A member, "For the Friend of Virtue/A Word to Mothers," May 1, 1840, p. 135.

10. January 1, 1849, cover.

11. "The Friend of Virtue," editorial, July 1, 1851, p. 197.

12. The Reverend Mr. Tisdale, "An Address," January 1, 1840, p. 16.

13. Ibid.

14. G., "A Letter to Parents./*Particularly Those Residing in Country Towns and Villages in N. England,*" June 1, 1840, p. [161].

15. "Work of the Destroyer," editorial, October 1, 1849, p. 297.

16. "Health," reprinted from *Mother's Journal,* January 15, 1840, p. 19.

17. "Pure Air and Ventilation," reprinted from *Means and Ends,* February 15, 1840, p. 51.

18. Ibid.

19. Ibid.

20. "For the Friend of Virtue/'For the Mothers,'" January 1, 1850, p. 9.

21. "The Training of Children. No. VI. *As Is the Mother, So Is the Daughter,*" January 1, 1852, p. 10.

22. "Moral Reform—Remarks to Young Men," reprinted from *Oberlin Evangelist,* January 15, 1840, p. 22.

23. "Communicated," July 1, 1851, p. 197.

24. R. Howe [secretary], "Tenth Annual Report of the Charleston Female Moral Reform Society," January 15, 1850, p. 20.

25. See, for example, "For the Friend of Virtue/Conversation between Georiana and Her Aunt," February 1, 1840, p. [33], in which the aunt's dislike of the minister was brought about because he refused to preach on the Seventh Commandment.

26. "Constitution of the New England Female Moral Reform Society," January 1, 1849, p. [2].

27. Unsigned, but attributed to "a venerable lady of this city," "To the Ex[ecutive] Com[mittee] of the N.E.F.M.R.S.," February 15, 1840, p. 55.

28. See, for example, "From the Lectures by the Fireside/By Dr. W. A. Alcott/*Thou Shall Not Commit Adultery,*" December 15, 1852, p. [369].

29. "The Theatre," March 16, 1840, p. 83; see also "Pernicious Influence of the Theatres," reprinted from the *Advocate and Guardian,* February 1, 1849, p. 34.

30. M.S.B., "For the Friend of Virtue/Novel Reading," December 15, 1840, p. 371.

31. "To Our Friends," editorial, February 1, 1849, p. 41.

32. Advertisement, July 1880, inside front cover.

33. Ibid.

34. "Our New Serial," May 1874, p. 234.

35. May 1874, p. 239.

36. "Thirty-Sixth Annual Report of the New England Moral Reform Society," July 1874, p. 330.

Information Sources

BIBLIOGRAPHY:
"Twelfth Annual Report." *The Advocate of Moral Reform.* June 1, 1846, p. [81].

INDEX SOURCES: Union List of Serials.
LOCATION SOURCES: Library of Congress (holdings incomplete) and other libraries.

Publication History

PERIODICAL TITLE AND TITLE CHANGES: *The Friend of Virtue* (1838–1867); *The Home Guardian* (1868–1892).
VOLUME AND ISSUE DATA: Vols. 1–54 (1838–March 1892). Biweekly (1838–1867); monthly (1968–1892).
PUBLISHER AND PLACE OF PUBLICATION: New England Female Moral Reform Society. Boston.
EDITORS: Rebecca Eaton (1838–1874?); Mrs. P. W. Smith (1874?–1880?); M. V. Ball (1880?–1892?).
CIRCULATION: Unknown.

Therese L. Lueck

G

THE GENIUS OF LIBERTY

The Genius of Liberty, a quarto monthly journal edited and published by Elizabeth A. Aldrich in Cincinnati, Ohio, was created in October 1851 to appeal to "the general interests of woman; to whatever will improve her physical, mental, moral, social, and industrial condition."[1] This was extremely optimistic, but it was an optimistic time. The city—then the fourth largest in the United States—was booming,[2] and Aldrich was merely expressing the certitude of many antebellum reformers that, given the appropriate incentive, readers would set about at once to improve their minds and lives.

Details of Aldrich's own life lie hidden behind the persona of her paper, but two things are certain: as the daughter of a local physician, she had the financial resources to launch *The Genius* out of her own pocket, and she had the intellectual stamina to continue the venture through a total of twenty-six monthly issues, from October 1851 to November 1853. *The Genius of Liberty* was professionally typeset and printed by the *Cincinnati Gazette,* a local daily newspaper, and sold at a subscription rate of one dollar per year. By the end of its first year, it was successful enough to expand the original four-page format to eight pages. Although Aldrich included outside material—poetry, sermons, excerpts from exchange papers, and reports from regular correspondents—most of the writing in *The Genius* was her own. In her "forcible, even manly style,"[3] Aldrich focused on the legal and cultural barriers that denied women full participation in the realms of education, professional training, property ownership, salaries, legal protection, and access to business opportunities.

Had Sigmund Freud ever read *The Genius,* he would not have asked his famous question, What do women want? Aldrich spelled it out clearly in an early issue: "They want a mental, moral and business field *equal* to their capacities, and equal to their rights which spring from their capacities."[4] Aldrich saw absolutely no conflict between woman's self-development and her family responsibilities. ''The old dominions of woman—the kitchen and the parlour—she does not wish to give up . . . but she desires the government and labor of them improved, and the boundaries of her territory so much enlarged as to give free scope to her mental and physical abilities.''[5] This melding of the ideal and the practical can be seen in the pages of *The Genius,* where an exhortation for enriching body, soul, and intellect is closely followed by a note on ''How to Make Coffee.''[6] Similarly, ''Useful Hints'' for treating whooping cough and igniting fireplace kindling, shares a column with ''Women in a New Sphere,'' a report of new faculty positions for women at a New York college.[7] To Aldrich, self-development and responsibilities to family were simply complementary aspects of woman's entire nature.

Possibly because of her familiarity with her father's medical library, Aldrich had a deep interest in women's health and published many commonsense articles on diet, exercise, and preventive medicine. She deplored the elaborate and restrictive Victorian dress: ''How unnatural, ungraceful, and antiphysiological those garments are which make the human form a double cone with a common apex. . . . Could each woman look once into her wonderfully constructed body, behold the impacted organs filling every space, and learn their offices . . . and (know) that the least compression stifles and stops their action, curtails life and scatters mischief, then would we all quickly return to a natural healthy costume.''[8] *The Genius* also favored vigorous exercise for women; Aldrich recommended that girls ''who desire rosy cheeks will find them where the roses do—out doors.''[9] This emphasis on comfortable clothing and outdoor exercise was Aldrich's remedy for overcoming helplessness in women. ''Women's principal difficulty is not the opposition of the other sex, but the weakness and imbecility of herself. For we find her in the various walks of life, with no higher aim than to ape the fashions, and to throw off the responsibilities of life . . . in the pursuit of pleasures, which tend to weaken, rather than exalt the mind.''[10] Characteristically, Aldrich offered sensible alternatives; for the mind she favored the rule of eight: ''Eight hours for rest; eight hours for eating, amusement and study; and eight hours for labor.'' For the lungs: ''The perfectly erect position of the head . . . the freedom of the chest and abdomen from compression . . . and pure unadulterated air.'' The stomach can be safeguarded by ''[a] very light supper; a moderate breakfast; a generous dinner; slow eating, and well masticated food.'' The resulting regularity of the bowels would ensure ''[t]he coolness of the brow, the sweetness of the breath, the warmth of the feet, the brilliancy of the eye, the purity of the skin, and the animation of the countenance. . . . These are unalterable teachings of the science of life.''[11]

Above all, Aldrich championed equal education for women, not only to broaden their minds and qualify them for the professions but to free them from ''that *degrading dependence,* so fruitful a source of female misery.''[12] To this end, *The Genius* regularly published news of women's colleges in the United States, tracked the deliberations of state boards of education, and promoted the

German model of primary school education, an eight-year curriculum much favored in midwestern cities like Cincinnati that had large German populations.[13]

The Genius also reported the progress of women in "profitable and honorable" businesses: "Twenty five ladies are now employed in the U. States as telegraphic operators. Fanny Paine is Cashier of the Bank of Chicago. . . . The town of Lynn, Mass., contains 155 shoe factories, which give employment to 10,486 persons of both sexes. . . . The heaviest blow that slavery has received for the last half century, has just been struck by a woman, the writer of Uncle Tom's Cabin.''[14] The development of women writers and editors was a favorite cause: "Every woman that can wield a pen should write and those who cannot should aid those who can. . . . We number about ten millions in this country, and every one should take one or more papers and possess a good library. This would encourage female editors, [in] a new, useful and lucrative field of labor."[15]

Aldrich loved lists. *The Genius* devoted most of the February 1853 issue to an annotated list of occupations denied by law and custom to women. She included medicine, the apothecary trade, art, accounting, banking, the administration of church and social service agencies, retailing, and the ministry. She contrasted them with the "pecuniary avocations," such as needlework, laundering, boarding, and schoolteaching—those jobs women could perform, but at bare survival wages, so low that "no woman can pursue them and accumulate an independence."[16]

Along with progress in the world of work, *The Genius* published news of state and national women's conferences. Aldrich traveled to New York to report on the 1852 national women's conference in Syracuse at which Lucretia Mott, Susan B. Anthony, Lucy Stone, and other stars of the woman's rights movement were gathered. Aldrich wrote: "Our sex everywhere should take courage by these brilliant luminaries; fling away the customary ideas of female inferiority, and feel, claim, and assert the mental equality of the sexes."[17] This was unusually effusive stuff; Aldrich normally preferred "the sledge hammer ring of facts"[18] and scorned writers who were unable to express themselves "in a cool, calm, rational manner. . . . The real design of language is to give expression to thought; that style of writing, therefore, must necessarily be the best which most rapidly and most clearly . . . conveys to the reader's mind what the writer intended."[19] In a notable example of brevity, Aldrich managed to compress thirty-two comparisons of "Legal Differences between Man and Woman in Ohio" into a short column and a half, with plenty of white space left over. Some of the items:

Women are deprived of the right of suffrage.

Men claim and enjoy the right of suffrage.

Women are ineligible to any State or National office, and deprived of all
    its honors and emoluments.

Men are eligible to all State and National offices, and receive all their
honors and awards.

Women are subject to taxation, but deprived of representation.

Men are subject to taxation, but enjoy representation. . . .

Woman, when in common with her husband, accumulates property,
money, etc., and the husband dies, the wife is allowed the *use of
one third* of their common earnings while she lives.

Man . . . retains the whole as his own, and the right to do with it as he
pleases.[20]

In spite of her general preference for simplicity and naturalness, Aldrich welcomed any new technology that would ease women's work. She praised the
development of the sewing machine, even though some of her readers did not
agree. "We shall be careful not again to run into a hornet's nest by speaking
discriminately of Sewing Machines," she wrote. Still, she predicted that in less
than twenty years, "the sewing of a long straight seam otherwise than by machinery . . . would be an anachronism."[21] *The Genius* was equally modern in its
do-it-yourself articles; Aldrich's advice on selecting a homesite, soil drainage,
sanitation, and building ventilation is perfectly appropriate for twentieth-century
readers.[22]

The Genius of Liberty claimed to be nonpolitical, but Aldrich was quick to
chastise members of the U.S. Senate who killed an antislavery amendment, and
she made sure readers knew the names of the supporters of the antislavery clause
in the House. She evaluated the 1852 presidential candidates with a modern
reporter's eye for gossipy detail: Pierce was "a clever lawyer, approachable,
lively and strong in his friendships" (even though he had addressed a women's
meeting in New Hampshire "very patronizingly"), while Winfield Scott, "a
hero in arms," was "punctilious, aristocratic and vain."[23]

True to her Yankee forebears, Aldrich was outspoken on the issue of slavery.
At first she supported the colonization movement that favored transporting free
blacks to Liberia.[24] But in a subsequent issue of *The Genius,* she proposed some
more thoughtful remedies: "(T)he education of free men and women of color
. . . in the departments of science, literature and art" would "demonstrate to the
world, to the foes and friends of Afric's [*sic*] race, that they can become, by
culture, equal to the best specimens of the Caucasians." At the same time, she
also advocated education for poor whites in the South, along with the encouragement of southern manufacturing, schools and books, lectures and discussions,
and other forms of enterprise, which would reduce "high partizan feeling, strife
and denunciation, disunion actions, and the tightening of the bands of bondage."[25]

Letters from readers variously rated *The Genius* as handsome, original, sound,
"a little fire rocket," and an earnest advocate of woman's rights,[26] but, like
most editors of small papers, Aldrich frequently had to remind readers to pay

their subscriptions. Several times she was forced to solicit outright donations, a move that must have wounded her independent spirit, especially since she had a worthy product. *The Genius of Liberty* was "the only paper in the State devoted to the interests of women, and we believe, the only female paper in the Western valley."[27] Many donors responded, but even these did not save the paper in the end. Abruptly and without notice, *The Genius of Liberty* published its last issue in November 1853. Today its twenty-six issues remain as a witness to Elizabeth Aldrich's foresight, intelligence, and courage. Her advice is still good, and many of her battles were so well chosen they are being fought still.

Notes

1. January 15, 1852, p. 13.
2. Stanley Hedeen, *The Mill Creek; An Unnatural History of an Urban Stream* (Cincinnati, Ohio: Blue Heron Press, 1994), p. 87.
3. December 15, 1851, p. 11.
4. September 15, 1852, p. 48.
5. January 15, 1852, p. 15.
6. December 15, 1852, p. 20.
7. February 15, 1853, p. 40.
8. December 15, 1852, p. 20.
9. October 15, 1851, p. 4.
10. Ibid.
11. July 15, 1853, p. 80.
12. January 15, 1853, p. 30.
13. August 15, 1853, p. 87.
14. October 15, 1853, p. 8; March 15, 1853, p. 47.
15. December 15, 1851, p. 11.
16. February 15, 1853, pp. 33–36.
17. September 15, 1852, p. 46.
18. August 15, 1853, p. 11.
19. January 15, 1853, p. 31.
20. September 15, 1852, p. 46.
21. July 15, 1853, p. 78.
22. September 15, 1853, pp. 94–95.
23. May 15, 1852, p. 38.
24. May 15, 1852, p. 32.
25. November 15, 1851, p. 7.
26. December 15, 1851, p. 12; William Coggeshell, "Literary Enterprises in Cincinnati," *The Genius of the West* 5.5, May 1856, p. 133.
27. February 15, 1852, p. 20.

Information Sources

BIBLIOGRAPHY:
Coggeshell, William. "Literary Enterprises in Cincinnati." *The Genius of the West; A Magazine of Western Literature,* 1856, p. 133.
Hedeen, Stanley. *The Mill Creek; An Unnatural History of an Urban Stream.* Cincinnati, Ohio: Blue Heron Press, 1994.

INDEX SOURCES: None.
LOCATION SOURCES: Cincinnati Public Library; Cincinnati Historical Society; Ohio
    State Historical Society.

Publication History

PERIODICAL TITLE AND TITLE CHANGES: *The Genius of Liberty; Devoted to the
    Interests of American Women.*
VOLUME AND ISSUE DATA: Vols. 1–3 (October 15, 1851–November 15, 1853.
    Monthly.
PUBLISHER AND PLACE OF PUBLICATION: Elizabeth A. Aldrich. Cincinnati, Ohio.
EDITOR: Elizabeth A. Aldrich (1851–1853).
CIRCULATION: Unknown.

Jean E. Dye

GFWC CLUBWOMAN

When women's clubs throughout the country joined together in 1889 to plan
the formation of the national General Federation of Women's Clubs (GFWC),
it was only natural that the women establish a magazine to communicate ideas
throughout the association. Considering that the founder and the force behind
the national organization was a journalist, it was only natural that Jane Cunningham Croly serve as the first editor to chronicle the club movement.

The Woman's Cycle, with Croly as editor and Mrs. C. J. Haley as publisher,
was first published on September 19, 1889, six months after the women's clubs
met as a group to discuss the formation of a federation. The goal of the new
magazine was to "represent the life, and particularly the associative life of the
modern woman, its interests and working activities—literary, social, educational
and industrial."[1]

Croly wanted a club magazine to be the medium by which clubs exchanged
ideas. She encouraged readers and clubwomen to send in their ideas and the
accomplishments of their clubs for publication. With telephone communication
still a rarity, especially in some of the remote areas where women's clubs were
being formed, Croly wanted her biweekly magazine to bring together the wide
varieties of women's clubs that were being created.

Croly herself had great aspirations for the club movement as a way for American women to expand their spheres of activities beyond the home. By 1889,
club membership and its related public activity were an accepted and appropriate
way for women (especially those of the middle class) to pass their time. It hadn't
always been that way.

The clubs—which first appeared in the late 1860s—initially had been mocked
by men and also in the press. One of the earliest women's clubs, Sorosis, was
founded by Croly in March 1868 after she had been prohibited from purchasing
a ticket to a Charles Dickens lecture, sponsored by the all-male New York Press

Club. Croly invited a group of women friends, mostly writers, to her home on the first Monday in March 1868 and outlined her plan of a club for women.[2] After the organization of Sorosis (and the New England Woman's Club, which was formed almost simultaneously in Boston), it was only a short time before women's "literary societies" became popular. These clubs principally sought the self-betterment of women but, in time, came to provide a platform for reform work and public involvement by women.[3]

In 1889, sixty-five delegates of women's clubs came together to celebrate Sorosis' twenty-first birthday (or, put another way, to mark the club movement's coming-of-age). Other clubs sent reports of their activities. At this convention, the women discussed club activities, considered future prospects for clubs, and explored the different ways clubs organized.[4] The General Federation of Women's Clubs was born. Croly came away from the meeting with the belief that a magazine for clubwomen was an idea whose time had come.[5]

Unfortunately for Croly, her idea was premature. *The Woman's Cycle* as such lasted only a year and was, during that time, plagued by financial hardships.[6] Despite the acceptance of *The Woman's Cycle* as the official organ for the GFWC, the magazine failed to thrive.[7] Some advertising appeared in *The Woman's Cycle,* but apparently not enough to sustain it. In the inaugural issue, for example, only the first page was devoted to advertisements. Croly's personal finances already had been strained by a ten thousand-dollar investment in *Godey's Lady's Book* in 1887. When that investment turned sour, Croly sold her part-ownership in *Godey's* and turned to other ventures, including *The Woman's Cycle.*

When the biweekly folded, club news began appearing in another of Croly's ventures—this time an existing women's magazine, *The Home-Maker.* Croly took over the editorship of that publication in 1891, when its circulation stood at 53,680.[8] Croly introduced a "Cycle Department" for club members and their activities within this publication. Although some prominent clubwomen were disappointed that their specialty publication had disappeared, they consoled themselves that the increased circulation of *The Home-Maker* provided them with a chance to widen their influence.[9]

Croly, however, was dissatisfied that women's clubs lacked their own publication. Although as many as twenty pages of *The Home-Maker* were devoted to club news, Croly planned for the reintroduction of a monthly publication exclusively devoted to women's clubs. *The New Cycle* premiered in 1892 with Croly as both editor and publisher. Despite continued financial hardships, that publication limped along because the GFWC officers believed they needed a voice to speak to their burgeoning membership. By 1895, *The New Cycle's* circulation stood at three thousand. Readership probably was much higher, however, because individual clubs often purchased a single subscription for their members.

Croly used the magazine to promote women's greater public involvement. She selected articles that highlighted reform possibilities and urged women to involve themselves "in the reforms and philanthropies that advance humanity and help ease the pain of the world."[10] Articles discussed parenting, municipal affairs, public education, public health, and women workers. Despite a laissez-faire attitude toward suffrage by Croly, her publication debated whether the GFWC should support suffrage and temperance—two highly controversial issues facing the women of the 1890s. One article stated, "Undoubtedly the great majority of club members are temperance women and suffragists at heart, although they may not concede that they are panaceas for every evil under the sun."[11] The author, however, urged against GFWC inclusion of these issues on its agenda, so that it could differentiate itself from other organizations.

The New Cycle folded in 1896, when Croly stepped down as editor to write *The History of the Women's Club Movement.* Like its predecessor, *The New Cycle* very simply failed to be a profitable venture, despite the sense that a magazine for clubwomen was an important conduit for networking information in the club. An attempt in 1893 to bolster the publication had also failed. The GFWC voted to underwrite the project by issuing two thousand shares of stock that were to be sold at five dollars a share to clubs and individuals. Every two shares brought a year's subscription to the magazine. *The New Cycle* continued for another thirty months but folded in 1896, when the GFWC assigned Croly the massive task of writing the GFWC history.[12]

Shortly after *The New Cycle*'s demise, club news began appearing in *The Club Woman,* a monthly magazine that was owned and edited by Helen M. Winslow, a Boston writer. The magazine was affiliated with the GFWC from its beginning in 1897 until 1904.[13] Winslow had helped found the New England Woman's Press Association in 1885 and the Boston Author's Club in 1900. A writer who supplied articles in the 1880s to Boston newspapers, Winslow had served as associate editor for the final issues of *The New Cycle* and also had contributed articles to it and *The Home-Maker.*

Never a fancy or polished publication, *The Club Woman* enjoyed greater success in circulation and advertising than Croly's publications. In her first issue, Winslow told readers the magazine, which was based in Boston, was for the "progressive club woman." She said her publication would provide guidance to young clubs that were seeking ways to expand their interests into their communities. She envisioned a publication that served as a vehicle for social reforms, and, basically, the magazine measured up to her lofty goals.

Winslow sent a sample copy of the magazine to presidents and secretaries of women's clubs. She suggested that women in need of money who were reluctant to work outside the home could receive commissions by selling subscriptions to the magazine. She also made the magazine available on newsstands in Brentano's and Wanamakers in Boston, New York, and Philadelphia. Single copies cost ten cents; an annual subscription cost one dollar.

The Club Woman basically relied on the same editorial philosophy as Croly's magazines. Winslow argued for women's increased involvement in municipal affairs and highlighted important reform work that was being accomplished by individual clubs. Through Winslow's efforts, the magazine gained a circulation of ten thousand by 1901.[14] Winslow said later that although the magazine was profitable, it took a toll on her health because she had to "work like a slave" to publish it. She was the magazine's chief writer, editor, manuscript editor, secretary, and advertising manager.[15] Stating that she was exhausted, Winslow sold the magazine after seven years for an unknown price.

The June/July 1903 issue announced that clubwoman Dore Lyon of New York would take over as editor and that the magazine office was being transferred from Boston to New York. Winslow continued as associate editor and wrote her monthly column. The publication, still affiliated loosely with the GFWC, was incorporated as the Club Woman Co., and more department features and artwork were added. Ironically, when the magazine slipped from the hands of a professional journalist to a professional clubwoman, it began looking more slick but lost its zealot flavor. Humor columns, household advice, music, fashion, and theater reviews were added in an attempt to appeal to all women, not just clubwomen. By January 1904, the monthly issue had swelled to 124 pages and also featured fiction. The broad-based appeal failed. The magazine ceased publication in 1904 with a twenty thousand-dollar deficit.

In 1905, the GFWC, seeking to continue its support of a publication, gave its official sanction to a new journal. May Alden Ward had been publishing the *Federation Bulletin* for the Massachusetts State Federation of Women's Clubs for eighteen months when she received the GFWC's official support. She proposed to make her journal a national organ.[16] About this time, the GFWC was the umbrella group for forty-five state federations representing more than one thousand women's clubs and three hundred thousand members.[17] There also were several regional club publications, including *Keystone,** which published from 1899 to 1913 as the journal of the South Carolina State Federation of Women's Clubs: *Club Notes for Club Women,* which published from 1902 to 1912 out of Cleveland; and, the *Courant,* a regional federation journal published in St. Paul from 1899 to 1913.[18]

In 1910, the woman's magazine *The Conquest* purchased the national *Federation Bulletin* and published one joint issue. Then, the name was changed to the *General Federation Bulletin,* which was adopted by the GFWC as the official magazine. In 1914 the title again shifted, this time to *General Federation Magazine,* but it was also referred to as the *General Federation of Women's Clubs Magazine.* Like the club publications that preceded this, the *General Federation Magazine* continued to have financial problems, and it ceased publication in 1920.

The GFWC then began publishing a newsprint tabloid, *The General Federation Bulletin.* The title was changed in 1923 to the *General Federation News.* In 1927, the publication returned to the magazine format, and the editorial offices were established at the GFWC headquarters in Washington.[19]

The *General Federation News* was copyrighted in 1929, but several name changes were yet to occur.[20] In 1930, the magazine was briefly renamed *The*

Clubwoman GFWC, before it was changed to *General Federation News: A Magazine for Club Women.* In 1941, *The General Federation Clubwoman* was published and continued under that name until 1972, when it was reissued as *Clubwoman News,* again in a tabloid format. That change lasted only two years, and in 1978 the magazine emerged under the current name and format, the *GFWC Clubwoman.*[21]

The publication shifted from monthly to a bimonthly basis with the November/December 1982 issue and then from bimonthly to quarterly in 1990. The magazine, however, was scheduled to resume publication as a bimonthly in October 1994.[22] Editor Ellen O'Donnell Kranick said this increased publication schedule was part of an effort to attract more subscribers from among individual clubwomen. The current circulation of twenty thousand includes issues that are sent to the presidents of the eighty-five hundred member clubs that make up the GFWC. A year's individual subscription cost six dollars. The magazine accepted advertising but was constrained by postal regulations that limited advertising to 10 percent of editorial matter while using the nonprofit mail rates.

After more than one hundred years of publications representing the GFWC, the editorial philosophy has varied little. The federation today still sees the magazine as an important tool to communicate information and exchange ideas with members. With issues that range from thirty-two to forty pages, the *GFWC Clubwoman* regularly includes a message from the GFWC president, updates on the volunteer efforts of the federation, information on pending legislation in Washington, D.C., and club news. ''I think the most important part of the magazine is the club news section because you can see what clubs are doing and give other members ideas of what they can do,'' Kranick said.[23] Feature articles in recent issues included the program of the GFWC's 103d annual convention in Atlanta in June 1994; information about United Nations works; an update on legislation to help the disabled; and information on monitoring of water quality by consumers. Thus, after more than one hundred years of publishing a magazine, the GFWC remains committed to fostering volunteer work and involving its members in important reform issues to improve the quality of life.

Notes

1. September 19, 1889, p. 3.

2. Jane Cunningham Croly, *Sorosis: Its Origin and History* (New York: Press of J. J. Little, 1886), p. 7.

3. See, for example, Chapter 5, ''Self-Improvement, Community Improvement,'' in Anne Firor Scott, *Natural Allies: Women's Associations in American History* (Urbana: University of Illinois Press, 1991), pp. 111–140.

4. *Report of the 21st Anniversary of Sorosis* (New York: Styles and Cash, 1890), p. 10.

5. Jane C. Croly, ''The Woman's Club Movement,'' manuscript, p. 117, Sorosis archives, Sophia Smith Collection, Smith College, Northampton, Mass.

6. Circulation for *The Woman's Cycle* was not listed in the 1890 or the 1891 editions of *N. W. Ayer and Son's American Newspaper Annual.*

7. Mary Jean Houde, *Reaching Out: A Story of the General Federation of Women's Clubs* (Chicago: Mobium Press, 1989), p. 39.

8. *N. W. Ayer and Son's American Newspaper Annual* (Philadelphia: N. W. Ayer and Son, 1891), p. 507.

9. Charlotte Emerson Brown, "The Woman's Cycle and the Home—Maker," November 1890, pp. 184–185.

10. May Rogers, "The New Social Force," June 1894, p. 396.

11. Amelia K. Wing, "The Federation Meetings," September 1892, pp. 98–99.

12. Jane Cunningham Croly letter to Mrs. Brush, February 8, 1898, Jane Cunningham Croly letters collection, Schlesinger Library, Radcliffe College, Cambridge.

13. Mildred White Wells, *Unity in Diversity: The History of the General Federation of Women's Clubs* (Washington, D.C.: General Federation of Women's Clubs, 1953), p. 318.

14. *N. W. Ayer and Son's American Newspaper Annual* (Philadelphia: N. W. Ayer and Son, 1901), p. 356.

15. Helen M. Winslow, "Confessions of a Newspaper Woman," *Atlantic Monthly,* February 1905, p. 209.

16. Council Meeting, June 7, 1905, GFWC Records, 1904–1906, p. 135, GFWC Archives, Washington, D.C.

17. Houde, *Reaching Out,* p. 110.

18. Frank L. Mott, *A History of American Magazines,* Vol. 4 (Cambridge, Mass.: Belknap, 1957), p. 356.

19. Name change information provided by the General Federation of Women's Clubs, "History of GFWC Publications."

20. Houde, *Reaching Out,* p. 207.

21. "History of GFWC Publications."

22. Ellen O'Donnell Kranick, telephone interview April 26, 1994.

23. Kranick interview.

Information Sources

BIBLIOGRAPHY:

N. W. Ayer and Son's American Newspaper Annual. Philadelphia: N. W. Ayer and Son, 1891, 1901.

Croly, Jane Cunningham. *Sorosis: Its Origin and History.* New York: Press of J. J. Little, 1886.

Croly, Jane Cunningham Collection, Schlesinger Library, Radcliffe College, Cambridge.

General Federation of Women's Clubs Archives, Publications Record Group, Washington, D.C.

Gottlieb, Agnes Hooper. "Women Journalists and the Municipal Housekeeping Movement: Case Studies of Jane Cunningham Croly, Helen M. Winslow and Rheta Childe Dorr." Diss., University of Maryland, College Park, 1992.

Houde, Mary Jean. *Reaching Out: A Story of the General Federation of Women's Clubs.* Chicago: Mobium Press, 1989.

Mott, Frank L. *A History of American Magazines.* Vol. 4. Cambridge, Mass.: Belknap, 1957.

Report of the 21st Anniversary of Sorosis. New York: Styles and Cash, 1890.

Scott, Anne Firor. *Natural Allies: Women's Associations in American History.* Urbana: University of Illinois Press, 1991.

Sorosis Archives, Sophia Smith Collection, Smith College, Northampton, Mass.
Winslow, Helen M. "Confessions of a Newspaper Woman." *Atlantic Monthly,* February
    1905, pp. 206–211.
INDEX SOURCES: Not indexed.
LOCATION SOURCES: Library of Congress and the General Federation of Women's
    Clubs Headquarters, Washington, D.C.

Publication History

PERIODICAL TITLE AND TITLE CHANGES: *The Woman's Cycle* (1889–1890);
    1891–1892 club news included in *The Homemaker; The New Cycle* (1892–1986);
    The Clubwoman (1897–1904); *Federation Bulletin* (1905–1911); *The General
    Federation Bulletin* (1911–1914); *General Federation of Women's Clubs Maga-
    zine* (1914–1920); *General Federation Bulletin* (1920–1923); *General Federation
    News* (1923–1930); *The Clubwoman GFWC* (1930); *General Federation News:
    A Magazine for Club Women* (1930–1941); *The General Federation Clubwoman*
    (1941–1976); *Clubwoman News* (1976–1978); *GFWC Clubwoman* (1978–pres-
    ent).
VOLUME AND ISSUE DATA: Vols. 1– (current numbering began with vol. 1 in
    August 1920 to present. GFWC historian is unsure why the numbering began
    anew with that issue).
PUBLISHER AND PLACE OF PUBLICATION: General Federation of Women's Clubs.
    New York (1889–1896); Boston (1897–1903); New York (1903 1905); Boston
    (1905 1912); New York (1912–1927); Washington, D.C. (1927–present).
EDITORS: Jane Cunningham Croly (1890–1896); Helen Winslow (1897–1902); Dore
    Lyon (1903); May Alden Ward and Helen Whittier (1905–1911); Harriet Bishop
    Water (1912–1917); Helen Louise Johnson (1918); Lessie Stringfellow Read
    (1920–1926); Mrs. Frederick W. Weitz (1926); Vella Alberta Winner (1927–
    1941); Eleanor Meyer (1941); Sara A. Whitehurst (1941–1943); Mildred White
    Wells (1947–1952); Gerry Sohle (1952–1954); Mary McGinn Taylor (1954–
    1978); Margaret M. Leavitt (1979–1984); Judith Walter Maggrett (1984–1991);
    Deborah Koehle (1992–1993); Ellen O'Donnell Kranick (1993–present).
CIRCULATION: 20,000, including 8,500 subscriptions sent to presidents of individual
    clubs, according to GFWC.

Agnes Hooper Gottlieb

H

HARVARD WOMEN'S LAW JOURNAL

In addressing the issue of how women are more often than not put at a disadvantage to men in the law, Yale sociology professor Rosabeth Moss Kanter argued in 1978:

> From a sociologist's perspective, the goal is not only to get more women into the legal profession in general, but to be very careful where they are placed. We must look at what kinds of women lawyers there are, in what sorts of specialties, with what kinds of colleague support, and with what degree of "unusualness."[1]

This observation on women in the U.S. legal profession explains, in part, why the *Harvard Women's Law Journal* was started in 1978.

Originally, the *Journal* was a project resulting from "Celebration 25: A Generation of Women at Harvard Law School" in the fall of 1978, which was to honor the twenty-fifth anniversary of women at Harvard Law School.

The *Journal,* published annually in spring by the Harvard Law School, finds its raison d'être in the premise that "[w]hen the law first distinguished between men and women, distributing rights and responsibilities on the basis of sex, and provides them with different opportunities for participation in the legal system, the law took on a separate meaning for women."[2]

The *Journal* is aimed at examining the origins and the impact of the differential treatment of women vis-à-vis men in the law. Equally important, the purpose of the *Journal* is to "develop a feminist jurisprudence."[3] Since the first issue of the *Journal* was published in 1978, according to editor in chief Jennifer Middleton, the *Journal* has established itself as "the first exclusively feminist legal journal" in the United States.[4]

Among the more recent articles published in the *Journal* were "Toward a Feminist Internationality: A Critique of U.S. Feminist Legal Scholarship" (1993); "Race, Gender, and Social Class in the Thomas Sexual Harassment Hearings: The Hidden Fault Lines in Political Discourse" (1992); "Progressive Feminist Legal Scholarship: Can We Claim 'A Different Voice'?" (1992); "Contradiction and Revision: Progressive Feminist Legal Scholars Respond to Mary Joe Frug" (1992); and "Defining Feminist Litigation" (1991).

The *Journal* is strongly committed to providing an opportunity for those who are "traditionally underrepresented" in legal scholarship in general and in feminist legal scholarship in particular. For example, volume 12 of the *Journal* illustrates an effort to represent a multiplicity of voices among feminist legal scholars, using both traditional articles and recent developments and less traditional modes such as essays, poetry, and literary analysis.

In 1993, the *Journal* published "Women of Color in Legal Academia: A Biographic and Bibliographic Guide," a seventy-eight-page compilation of law faculty in American law schools. The *Journal* editors hoped that "this guide will advance the struggle to achieve a system of legal education that reflects the realities of a multicultural society."[5]

While the *Journal* is primarily interested in U.S. law from a woman's perspective, it pays attention to the international and comparative approach to women in law. It is especially significant that the first issue of the *Journal* contained an article "International Law and the Status of Women: An Analysis of International Legal Instruments Related to the Treatment of Women," by Natalie Kaufman Heavener.[6] In 1988 the *Journal* analyzed the international maternity leave policies relating to Africa, Chile, and India.[7]

As a premier scholarly journal on women and women's issues in American law, the *Journal* has begun "a trend in feminist legal scholarship as woman- and feminist-oriented law journals have sprung up at law schools around the country."[8]

The current editorial staff of the *Journal* is made up of forty-six students (forty-four women and two men) at Harvard Law School. The editor in chief and executive editors of articles, recent developments, law and literature, and book reviews departments are third-year students, "while primary editors are predominantly second-year students."[9] The editor in chief is selected by the working staff of the *Journal*, including first-year students involved in the journal.

Most of about seven hundred to eight hundred subscribers of the *Journal* are institutional and library.[10] Editor in chief Middleton notes that "our international circulation is rather small."[11] The *Journal* is also available on Westlaw and Lexis.

Most articles published in the *Journal* are scholarly and prepared in conformity with *The Bluebook: A Uniform System of Citation*. But the *Journal* also publishes nontraditional essays and poetry.[12] Most "Recent Developments" articles are solicited from practitioners in the relevant field.

Journal articles are subject to extensive editing prior to final printing. Middleton notes: "Our editing process generally involves two or three substantial rounds of editing with the author, the first for major organizational and substantive changes, the second and third for style and line-editing. In addition, each article goes through exhaustive citation checking by the staff."[13]

Notes

1. Rosabeth Moss Kanter, "Reflections on Women and the Legal Profession: A Sociological Perspective," vol. 1, 1978, p. 17.
2. Editors, "Why a Women's Law Journal?" vol. 1, 1978, p. viii.
3. Ibid.
4. Jennifer Middleton, letter to author, May 11, 1994.
5. "Women of Color in Legal Academia: A Biographic and Bibliographic Guide," vol. 16, 1993, p. 1.
6. See vol. 1, 1978, p. 131.
7. See "International Maternity Leave Policies," vol. 11, 1988, p. 171.
8. Middleton letter.
9. Ibid.
10. Ibid.
11. Ibid.
12. Ibid.
13. Ibid.

Information Sources

BIBLIOGRAPHY:
U.S. Congress. House Select Committee on Aging. *Inequities toward Women in the Social Security System. Hearings before the Task Force on Social Security and Women of the Subcommittee on Retirement Income and Employment and the Select Committee on Aging,* House of Representatives. 98th Congress, First Session, Washington, D.C.
INDEX SOURCES: Abstracts of book reviews in current legal periodicals; Alternative Press Index; Current Law Index; Human Rights Internet Reporter; Legal Resource Index (LegalTrac); Index to Legal Periodicals; Multicultural Education Abstracts; Studies on Women Abstracts.
LOCATION SOURCES: Library of Congress; Harvard Library; New York Public Library; Arizona State University Law Library; and other sources.

Publication History

PERIODICAL TITLE AND TITLE CHANGES: *Harvard Women's Law Journal.*
VOLUME AND ISSUE DATA: Vols. 1– (1978–present). Annual.
PUBLISHER AND PLACE OF PUBLICATION: Harvard Women's Law Journal, Harvard Law School. Cambridge, Mass.
EDITORS: Lisa C. Woods, Beth A. Willensky, and Liz Thomas (1978); Patricia Reilly, Carol A. Schrager, and Beth A. Willensky (1979); Vibiana Andrade (1980); no information available on the 1981 editor in chief; Christine M. Roach (1982); Helen Deiss Irvin (1983); Judith C. Miles (1984); Karen A. Getman (1985); Ruth Borenstein (1986); Catherine Lynn Creech (1987); Paula A. Tuffin (1988); Stacy

Brustin (1989); Suzanne Goldberg (1990); Marie Arnold and Chris Scobey (1991); Kirstin S. Dodge (1992); Peggie R. Smith (1993); Jane E. Willis (1994); Jennifer Middleton (1995).

CIRCULATION: 700–800.

Kyu Ho Youm

K

THE KEYSTONE

In the late nineteenth and early twentieth centuries, clubwomen affiliated with the General Federation of Women's Clubs (GFWC) were likely to leaf through that organization's magazine for news, features, and opinion that had pertinence to them. But, if those clubwomen lived in the South, they were just as likely to spend their time with the regional "club" magazine, *The Keystone*. *The Keystone* had no formal affiliation with the *national* GFWC. It served the "peculiar" needs of the GFWC in five southern states as well as the United Daughters of the Confederacy in two states and the Audubon Society in one. *The Keystone* chronicled the activities of civic-minded women in South Carolina, North Carolina, Mississippi, Virginia, and Florida and remains one of the best sources for historians interested in activist women in those states. Its circulation was not restricted to those five states, however. *Keystone* readers could be found in many states of the union—South and North.[1]

The Keystone started in 1899 as the voice of clubwomen in South Carolina. In its first year, the editor, prominent South Carolina educator Ida Marshall Lining, had no aspirations beyond the state. Indeed, sufficiently covering the "activism" as evidenced in the newly organized South Carolina General Federation of Women's Clubs seemed to be a dauntless task.

> From the mountains to the seaboard the women of South Carolina are banding themselves together in clubs and associations, until to-day there enrolled up on the membership books of the Federation of Women's Clubs upwards of one thousand names, representing the flower and culture of our State.

These women, who formally organized as the Federation of Women's Clubs in 1898, represented a range of clubs from the exclusive Century Club, which was limited to thirty-five members, to the popular Psychology Club, with no such restrictions, which was organized by *Keystone* editor Lining. With such a range of interests, this new federation needed a single voice. That voice, created a year later, was *The Keystone*. The monthly magazine was established to bind together

> the avenues of woman's work, a solid arch of combined effort, upon the Keystone of which shall be engraved the motto, "Unity of Cause.['] To every club, therefore, and to every individual woman, in whatever line of work engaged, the Keystone throws open its door; enter, and give free expression to your thoughts. The Keystone does not mean to be aggressive, excepting where the word is synonymous with progress.[2]

Although the journal was based in Charleston, the editor promised that no part of the state would be ignored. Indeed, the financial underwriting of the publication came from an unidentified woman of the Piedmont. As the editor wrote, "Her interest in its [*The Keystone*'s] behalf is a fair portent that it will be a journal that will endeavor to represent 'Typical South Carolina Womanhood.' " As such, the journal had to be nonpolitical and nonsectarian.[3]

Under Lining, *The Keystone* provided extensive coverage of the South Carolina women's clubs. Each month, the editor provided the news of the activities of such groups as the Society of Colonial Dames, Daughters of the American Revolution, Daughters of the Confederacy of South Carolina, and the King's Daughters. In addition, the magazine kept its readers informed about general benevolent activities in the state, especially the Free Kindergarten Movement, one of Lining's personal causes.[4]

The Keystone was not all news. It was also a journal of comment. In this, Lining had to be mindful of her readership. Topics dealing with racism were ignored. Education of women was a popular topic. As an educator (Lining ran a normal and boarding school for women), the editor was especially interested in this topic. She often pointed out the fact that women in the South failed to take advantage of their educational opportunities. Because of this, women from the North and West had to be brought in to educate southern daughters.[5] She also did not care for how many young southern women frittered away their time and money "in dress, in valueless trifles, in the amusements of the hair" when more important work needed to be done.[6]

But Lining saw her magazine as something more than a periodical of women's benevolent news and comment. She also saw it as a publication of southern literature. From the start, *The Keystone* carried fiction and poetry.[7] Early on, the magazine even sponsored a writing contest for the best short story on women's work. The best story, which was not to exceed one thousand words, received five dollars.

Although *The Keystone* was "liberally supported"[8] by the South Carolina Federation of Women's Clubs and had been adopted as the "official organ" for the South Carolina Audubon Society in February 1900, not all was well at *The Keystone*. In December 1900, the magazine was under new management. Ida M. Lining and Mary Poppenheim, who in July 1900 had assumed the responsibility of coeditor, sold their interests in *The Keystone* to Louisa B. Poppenheim, president of the South Carolina Federation of Women's Clubs. This was a key move, for it opened the way for *The Keystone* to become a regional voice of civic-minded women.

Louisa Poppenheim brought *The Keystone* impeccable credentials Born in Charleston in 1868, Poppenheim came from a family with roots deep in South Carolina history. (Poppenheim was a sixth-generation South Carolinian.) She was well educated, graduating from Vassar in 1889, where she had been president of her senior class. She had helped organize the South Carolina Federation of Women's Clubs and was its first president. But her importance extended beyond the state's boundary. Poppenheim was elected corresponding secretary of the (national) General Federation of Women's Clubs. As corresponding secretary, Poppenheim issued the call for the organization of the North Carolina Federation in 1902 and attended the organizational meeting of the Virginia Federation in 1907.[9] That brought *The Keystone* enormous opportunities. In 1902, the new North Carolina Federation of Women's Clubs voted to make *The Keystone* its official organ, as the Mississippi federation had done earlier in the year. In 1907, the Virginia federation did likewise. In between, the Florida federation voted to make *The Keystone* its official organ as well.

The Keystone was not just the voice of the federation, however. The United Daughters of the Confederacy also saw the benefit of making the monthly its official voice. The South Carolina and Virginia chapters both formally associated with *The Keystone* as well. Indeed, the Daughters of the Confederacy in Virginia affiliated with *The Keystone* two years *before* that state's Federation of Women's Clubs.

Notwithstanding its growing importance within the region, *The Keystone* did not change markedly under Louisa Poppenheim. The monthly continued to provide news coverage of the various organizations that affiliated with it. Poppenheim gently applauded clubs that did their part to improve society and quietly chided women to do more. She also came to the aid of clubwomen who were sometimes under attack by the community. As Poppenheim reminded her readers, clubwomen could be civic-minded and attractive; "can be intellectual and cultured and yet be natural; in fact, can be a promoter of enterprises, causes and philanthropies and yet be charmingly feminine."[10] Poppenheim also continued Lining's commitment to literature. Like her predecessor, she attempted to foster southern literature through *The Keystone:* she was especially committed to cultivating women's literary endeavors. "We are a Southern periodical, aiming for what is highest and best in woman's work in our land."[11]

For more than two years, Louisa Poppenheim worked alone, bringing out *The Keystone*. However, once she was elected the GFWC's corresponding secretary, she could no longer continue putting out *The Keystone* by herself. Mary Poppenheim was brought in as editor in 1903. Louisa Poppenheim retained the title of "proprietor and manager." Although titles changed, Louisa retained many editorial responsibilities. Several editorials emphasized that *The Keystone* had two editors in fact, if not in title.[12] By the time the second Poppeheim had been added to the editorial staff, *The Keystone* represented five organizations in three states. After Mary Poppenheim joined the staff, and as Louisa Poppenheim assumed greater responsibility within the national federation, more southern groups aligned with *The Keystone*. That complicated the production of the periodical itself. Mary Poppenheim had to coordinate the contributions of a number of state managers, who, in turn, worked with club "editors" who were responsible for the news appearing in each individual club's pages. None of the editors were paid. As the editor explained, production of *The Keystone* was a labor of love for everyone but the printers. "There is not a salaried officer on the entire staff of *The Keystone*. The only persons paid for work on this publication are the printers," the editor wrote.[13]

The two Poppenheims agreed on many things with regard to *The Keystone*. Mary retained Louisa's gentle editorial style and her commitment to strengthening the South's literary traditions. She even asserted that the goal of publication was not merely reporting club news. "THE KEYSTONE is a monthly message of culture and suggestion, devoted to the interests of the thinking woman of the day."[14]

When admirers suggested that perhaps *The Keystone* could replace the GFWC's national magazine, the Poppenheims declined, emphasizing that their magazine was regional only. "We know our South, we are part of it, and we claim to represent it. We believe that the outlook here is large enough to support a first-class club publication with literary aspirations, and it is with this plan in view that we expect to continue our field of usefulness in Club Journalism."[15]

The two Poppenheims also shared a view that perhaps a monthly was too much for them to produce and subscribers to read. In 1905, the two merged the August and September issues so they could go to Europe on vacation.[16] Merging issues became a custom as the two Poppenheims vacationed. In 1906, the two formally discontinued the August and September issues. In these months, the editor argued, club activities were disbanded.[17]

By 1907, just as Louisa was about to take over as a director of the national Federation of Women's Clubs, the editorial focus of *The Keystone* shifted. Now club news took precedence. As the editor wrote, *The Keystone* was the meeting ground for the thoughts and experiences of many southern women. "Official club news always took precedence over poetry," she asserted.[18]

By 1908, when Louisa became director of the GFWC, *The Keystone* was increasingly losing its literary edge. More and more the monthly was dominated by club notes and editorials applauding southern benevolence and civic activity and advertising. Poppenheim explained the changes:

The Keystone limits its printing to technical organization news because it cannot afford to print more; it does not enter the field of the general magazine, but is a technical journal intended as a means of communication between women in all their cooperative literary, civic, patriotic and phil-anthropic endeavors; its pages are a meeting ground for many club ex-periences.[19]

This was one of the few times the editor or the publisher referred to any financial problems. Indeed, nothing within the publication suggested financial difficulties. The number of issues had declined, but that had always been ex-plained by lulls in club activities—and the desire of the Poppenheims to travel to Europe. The number of pages in each issue had not been reduced. Nor had advertising declined. *The Keystone* seemed to live a charmed life with regard to advertising. Once Poppenheim took over the publication, the advertising in-creased considerably. Although the largest number of advertisers was South Carolina–based businesses, *The Keystone* also drew in a number of advertisements for nationally marketed products, such as Baker's Cocoa. Nor had the magazine suffered any declines in circulation. Each new organization that affiliated with *The Keystone* brought more readers to the magazine. By 1910, Poppenheim reported that *The Keystone* officially represented twenty-two thousand women.[20] However, that did not represent the magazine's entire cir-culation, because women who were not associated with these groups also subscribed to this periodical.

Although the magazine might have been experiencing a measure of financial difficulty, *The Keystone* continued to publish for another three years. During that time, it extensively covered the activities of the clubs it "officially" rep-resented.

The editorials addressed issues peculiar to the region. Of the growing tuber-culosis in the region, a contributor blamed tourists and "the ever present menace of the carelessness and ignorance of the large negro populations." Women who read *Keystone* had to help improve the situation. " 'Colored' tuberculosis germs in the streets, in the cars and the railway stations are just as apt to infect your child as *'white'* ones, and reducing their volume in your community reduces the risks from the disease for all."[21] The editorials also reflected common concerns that broke through regional boundaries. The editors joined with other women across the nation, applauding the peace movement as one of the "great vital subjects" and urging women to write away (to the North) for reading materials on the subject.[22]

The Keystone died in 1913. Nothing in the June 1913 issue suggested that that would be the last for the magazine. Indeed, the editor was looking forward to a three-month holiday in Europe. *The Keystone* even seemed to be congrat-ulating itself for skirting the politics of the southern club movement.

The Keystone has never been mixed up in organization politics; avoiding scrupulously any expressions which might be construed along such lines, it has endeavored to give honor and praise for all earnest work in the organizations it represents, and has always stood for those into whose hands these organizations had entrusted their welfare and direction, believe that an "official organ" should respect and uphold "those in authority by will of the majority."[23]

For fourteen years, *The Keystone* was a regional voice of the General Federation of Women's Clubs. The magazine chronicled the activities of the southern women, recorded (for a time) the section's literary development, and gently guided the women of the region to improve their communities through their various clubs. Its regional base, while providing a common ground for discussion, restricted the publication. The magazine reflected the racism within the region and the more limited role of women within society.

Although *The Keystone* died, the Poppenheims continued to be active in the Federation of Women's Clubs. In 1926, Louisa was elected an honorary vice president of the national organization.

Notes

1. See, for example, "Editorial," December 1899, p. 3, "Letters to editor," May 1908, p. 3.
2. Editorial, June 1899, p. 3.
3. Ibid.
4. See, for example, Sarah Visanska. "The Free Kindergarten Movement in Charleston, S.C.," June 1899, pp. 8–9.
5. Editorial, October 1899, p. 3.
6. Ida Lining, "A Talk with Southern Women on Their Opportunities," September 1900, p. 4.
7. See, for example, Hulda Leigh, "Modesty," July 1899, p. 5.
8. May 1900, p. 3.
9. Mildred White Wells, *Unity in Diversity: The History of the General Federation of Women's Clubs* (Washington, D.C.: General Federation of Women's Clubs, 1953), pp. 158–159.
10. Editorial, May 1903, p. 3.
11. Editorial, January 1902, p. 3. See also editorial, January 1901, p. 3. The *News and Courier* called *The Keystone* "an excellent representative of the best thought among women of the State, and deserves their liberal support" (Editorial, January 1901, p. 3).
12. See, for example, Editorial, August/September 1905, p. 3.
13. Editorials, December 1905, p. 3.
14. Editorial, June 1904, p. 3.
15. Editorial, July 1904, p. 3. The Lynn, Massachusetts, *News* suggested that *The Keystone* take the place of the *Club Woman,* which had offended some readers by publishing fashion notes and "general frivolity." The *News* observed, "If a change is to be made, the wise course seems to be to substitute the 'Keystone,' which is already a well established official organ of the clubs and organizations in many States, and is conducted on high class lines of thought, and with a noble purpose apparent in every page." This was reprinted in ibid.

16. Editorial, August/September 1905, p. 3.
17. Editorial, July 1906, p. 3.
18. Editorial, February 1907, p. 3.
19. Editorial, June 1909, p. 3.
20. Editorial, June 1910, p. 3. That number role to twenty-five thousand in 1911. See June 1911, p. 3.
21. E. G. Routzahn, March 1912, p. 3. An editorial in 1909 made a similar point. Clubwomen needed to do missionary work among African Americans to protect white children. ''Tuberculosis germs are easily transmitted from gentle black *mammies* to white babies, and so the protection of the black nurse may save its white charge. Let women's clubs look into this matter and take some steps to spread the propaganda of prevention of tuberculosis among the negroes in their communities'' (March 1909, p. 3).
22. April 1912, p. 3.
23. June 1913, p. 3.

Information Sources

BIBLIOGRAPHY:
Wells, Mildred White. *Unity in Diversity: The History of the General Federation of Women's Clubs.* Washington, D.C.: General Federation of Women's Clubs, 1953.
Wood, Mary I. *The History of the General Federation of Women's Clubs for the First Twenty Two Years of Its Organization.* New York: History Department, General Federation of Women's Clubs, 1912.
INDEX SOURCES: Not indexed.
LOCATION SOURCES: Library of Congress and many other libraries, especially in the South. (Reprinted by Greenwood Publishing on microfilm.)

Publication History

PERIODICAL TITLE AND TITLE CHANGES: *The Keystone.*
VOLUME AND ISSUE DATA: Vols. 1–14 (June 1899–June 1913). Monthly (1899–1904); monthly with combined August/September issue (1905); monthly with no August and September issues (1906); monthly with no July, August, September issues (1907–1913).
PUBLISHER AND PLACE OF PUBLICATION: No publisher listed (1899–1900); Louisa B. Poppenheim (1900–1913). Charleston.
EDITORS: Ida Marshall Lining (November 1899–June 1900); Ida Marshall Lining and Mary Poppenheim (July–November 1900); Louisa B. Poppenheim (December 1900–May 1903); Mary Poppenheim (June 1903–1913).
CIRCULATION: Self-reported, June 1911 (p. 3): 25,000.

Kathleen L. Endres

L

LA WISP

Women Strike for Peace spoke in many voices. As a "nonorganization" without an hierarchial structure or a formal national leadership,[1] Women Strike for Peace relied on its chapters for its vitality, its variety, and its voices.[2] Among the best known of those voices was the *La Wisp,* the monthly newsletter of the southern California chapter of Women Strike for Peace (WSP). *La Wisp* was ideally situated to be a major voice in Women Strike for Peace for several reasons. First, it was the voice of an influential, active, and more radical chapter. Second, it had an editor who was also an important leader in the peace movement, both nationally and internationally. Finally, it provided fresh editorial coverage and perspectives on the peace movement.

It was one of the first voices of Women Strike for Peace. Its first issue was dated March 1962, just months after the organization was formed in Washington, D.C., and not long after the southern California chapter was organized. Women Strike for Peace, as a national group, dated to a now-famous 1961 Georgetown cocktail party given by Dagmar Wilson, housewife, mother, and freelance children's book illustrator. That night Lord Bertrand Russell gave a speech over BBC outlining the need for peace. At a time when many Americans feared the "bomb" and what a nuclear war might bring, the women at the Wilson party decided to meet the next day and do "something" about the situation. As Gage-Colby wrote, "They brought their address books, later borrowed some lists of names, and sent out a call to women to 'strike' against the bomb." On November 1, 1961, approximately fifty-thousand women responded to this call and marched on Washington for peace.[3] Dagmar Wilson never took credit for the demonstration, the organization, or the women's peace movement. As she explained, "The Strike was an idea whose time had come and it just happened to be born in my house."[4]

A month later, women in New York and California decided to send a similar call to women in other countries, including the Soviet Union. Women from forty countries responded. Women Strike for Peace had become an international "nonorganization." On January 15, 1962, women marched against nuclear proliferation in Los Angeles, San Francisco, Chicago, Detroit, New York, Washington, D.C., London, Copenhagen, Oslo, Stockholm, Paris, Rome, Cairo, Delhi, Tokyo, and many other cities in the United States and across the world.[5]

By this time the southern California chapter, which included Los Angeles, had been energized and ready to make a permanent mark on WSP. At the June 1962 WSP conference, the Los Angeles coordinating council prepared a statement dealing with communism. At a time when other peace organizations were drumming communists out of their ranks,[6] the Los Angeles coordinating committee pushed for inclusion. Politics, they argued, was a matter of personal conscience.

> If there are communists or former communists working in WSP, what difference does that make? We do not question one another about our religious beliefs or other matters of personal conscience. How can we justify political interrogation?[7]

The women at the WSP conference agreed and adopted a national policy of inclusion. "We are women of all races, creeds and political persuasions who are dedicated to the achievement of general and complete disarmament under effective international control."[8] That position had many implications in light of the fact that many WSP "leaders" were soon called to appear before the House Committee on Un-American Activities (HUAC). As historians have since chronicled, WSP dealt a deadly blow to the HUAC. The WSP hearings represented the beginning of the end for the committee.[9] It was not the beginning of the end of WSP or its southern California chapter, however. Indeed, it was just the beginning. WSP and its southern California chapter were shifting gears—the focus was moving from halting nuclear proliferation to stopping the war in Vietnam.

La Wisp covered it all—the HUAC hearings, the early demonstrations, and the shifting focus. One of the reasons for *La Wisp*'s presence as well as the activism and energy of the southern California chapter was Mary Clarke, one of the most visible leaders of WSP nationally. Clarke initially shared the editorial leadership of *La Wisp,* even as she led the organization and traveled nationally and internationally in pursuit of peace. (Eventually, Clarke became the sole editor of *La Wisp.*) Clarke was also one of the most controversial leaders within WSP and the nation. She and Lorraine Gordon, another WSPer, were the first representatives of the U.S. peace movement to visit Hanoi. In 1967, Clarke (this time with Dagmar Wilson and Ruth Krause) returned to Vietnam. In her various activities internationally, Mary Clarke and other WSPers were jailed in Paris for attempting to deliver a protest to North Atlantic Treaty Organization

(NATO) headquarters there.[10] At home, Clarke was also causing problems. After the 1966 election, WSP initiated an anti-President Lyndon Johnson movement within the Democratic Party. Clarke was one of the few WSP delegates to the 1968 Democratic Convention.[11] Thus, Mary Clarke was a woman of enormous energy. *La Wisp* was only one avenue of her activism.

Clarke was not the only constant in *La Wisp*'s life. From May 1971, Richard Powell, a professional writer, contributed many of the commentaries for which *La Wisp* became known. Other individuals made their contributions to the newsletter and then moved on. For example, between 1967 and 1974, Gail Eaby, Lisa Strada, Varda Ullman, Kathleen McNamara, Kitty Howe, and Roz Levine shared the title of editor with Clarke. In 1971, even Powell was listed as a coeditor. Many others worked on the newsletter, either as writers, associate editors, circulation crews, or "clippers" (those who clipped stories that were reprinted in part in the newsletter). All volunteered their time.

In certain respects, *La Wisp* was like many other WSP newsletters. Like many other chapter newsletters, *La Wisp* reprinted much news from other sources—primarily general-interest newspapers and less-known peace publications. The editors of *La Wisp* were eclectic in their selections. They reprinted information ranging from such publications as *Parade Magazine* to *Newsweek,* from the *Los Angeles Times* to the *Vancouver Sun,* from the *UCLA Daily Bruin* to the *Counterdraft,* from the *Nation* to the *Voice of Woman* (Canada). Like most other WSP newsletters, *La Wisp* reprinted important statements from other chapters. Thus, after the southern California WSP Council adopted the New York WSP statement, *La Wisp* reprinted it in full. A short portion illustrates the tone of the document:

> As you call on our sons, you call on us. We stand as one against the draft, against the war.
>
> For in your failure to stop drafting our boys to be killed for an illegal and immoral war which denies the Vietnamese quest for freedom, you deprive us of our own.
>
> For in your failure to stop wasting our lives and resources for repression of the Vietnamese, you have rendered our country helpless to attack rising dislocations of our unfulfilled society.[12]

Unlike a number of WSP newsletters, however, *La Wisp* offered fresh editorial comment and reporting. Admittedly, such material seldom smacked of objective, journalistic writing. Nonetheless, it captured the passion and commitment of the chapter's opposition to the Vietnam War. After WSP leaders (including Clarke) formed the Jeanette Rankin Brigade, *La Wisp* urged its readers to attend meetings. "THAT HAND THAT ROCKS THE CRADLE IS GOING TO ROCK THE BOAT!! WITH OUR VOTE!" Women, as the majority of the electorate, had to mobilize to change government, to reduce spending on the military.

WE'RE FED UP! THE MAJORITY OF AMERICAN VOTERS ARE WOMEN . . . BUT WE ARE AN UNREPRESENTED MAJORITY! We find our government responding to its military-industrial advisors while *it turns a deaf ear to us*. Oh yes, we have heard and read the stirring speeches against the Vietnam war, made on the floor of Congress. But most of these great orators (men who were put into office with the help of women) proceed to vote for the billion dollar appropriations that make this war possible, while millions of Americans are robbed of their rights to decent housing, health services, education and employment.[13]

Not surprisingly, *La Wisp* editors weren't convinced by President Richard Nixon's peace proposals. In late 1970, the editors called Nixon's latest overture a "peace hoax."

It constitutes a demand for the Vietnamese to stop shooting while US forces would continue to occupy their land for an indefinite period under the threat of resumption of hostilities at any time. The cease-fire without a military or political agreement is really calling for the surrender of the liberation forces in Indochina while the corrupt and repressive govern-ments there continue to be propped up by the U.S.[14]

Passionately, *La Wisp* editorially supported Congresswoman Bella Abzug's resolution to withdraw American troops from Southeast Asia: "To hell with polls and body counts! . . . pious promises from Nixon! . . . Kissinger's Amerika uber alles! TO HELL WITH WAR! LET'S END IT!"[15]

The newsletter also provided information that committed WSPers needed. *La Wisp* told readers when and where the rallies were to be held (an all-day "hap-pening" was planned with Dagmar Wilson "just back from Hanoi" in Santa Monica[16]); when, where, and what to write their representatives (on Mother's Day, 1971, WSP began a nationwide campaign urging members to write the president opposing the war and emphasizing that the writer was a housewife and mother[17]); what boycotts were in effect (the boycott of the May Co. was canceled when the store promised WSP a Peace Booth on an equal-time basis with the naval display[18]); and—perhaps as important—practical advice in civil disobedience. For example, when reporting that Natalie Montgomery had staged an impromptu sitdown strike at an induction center, *La Wisp* editor reminded readers, "We strongly urge anyone planning on committing civil disobedience, regardless of how they intend to plead, to benefit from the advice of an attor-ney—no man is an island."[19] That advice was needed, for WSP members gen-erally were not necessarily experienced in political demonstrations. Most were well-educated, middle-class, married women with children.

The newsletter also offered guidance with regard to draft counseling. The WSP chapter in southern California provided those services, not only on college campuses but in other locales. *La Wisp* reminded readers that all men needed draft counseling—not just the middle-class, white college students. "The emphasis of draft counseling is on *survival*—and the outreach is in search of equity. Draft counseling fails if it serves the advantaged and allows the young men from the ghettos and barrios of our country to serve and die in their place."[20]

The newsletter also served another function. Because of the "nonorganizational" quality of WSP, members often found it difficult to keep up with what friends were doing. Thus, *La Wisp* also served as a medium of personal news. Members read the reason Mary Clarke could not attend the Peace Action Council Rally in 1967; her son had died of cancer. In February 1968, the newsletter had to report that Dina Hoffman had died.

Clarke and *La Wisp* were able to sustain their energy even after the Vietnam War ended. In the 1980s, the so-called "Me" decade, the southern California Women Strike for Peace and *La Wisp* redirected their energies to controlling the arms race[21] and social problems.[22] Clarke, who by then had sole responsibility for the newsletter, supervised the coverage. Richard Powell wrote many of the front-page commentaries. However, the amount of original material produced for *La Wisp* had decreased. More and more of the eight-page newsletters were simply reprints from publications across the nation. This is not to say *La Wisp* did not do innovative stories or provide information not available elsewhere. For example, in 1982 the newsletter recorded the vote of *every* congressman on the nuclear freeze bill in the U.S. House of Representatives. The newsletter devoted two full pages to listing the 406 names (204 against and 202 in favor). The list concluded with a single line, "now that you've checked the vote—throw the rascals out."[23] Readers also continued to contribute letters that were reprinted in *La Wisp*. For example, Karel kept readers informed about the mass demonstrations in Prague:

Me being a "too old" war horse for demonstrations in icy weather, my main "activity" is to support my grandchildren (known to you since your 1983 visit) who are attending all those mass manifestations. Tom is nearing 18; Petra past 18 today, and their generation has achieved here an historically unprecedented victory: They overthrew an establishment that considered itself so strong as to resist Perestroika.[24]

Karel's letter was symptomatic of problems within *La Wisp*, the southern California Women Strike for Peace chapter, and the organization nationally. WSP membership and leadership were getting older. More and more women were joining the labor force and did not have time for WSP. With the nation at peace, the group was having difficulty keeping up its energy, membership, and activism. The March 1990 issue of *La Wisp* was its last. Mary Clarke explained that the Los Angeles chapter of WSP was closing, as was the national headquarters of the organization. " 'The reasons for our closing our office are varied: decline in active membership, the greying of our leadership, the lack of woman power to launch campaigns, diminishing financial support, and a euphoria shared by a majority of our fellow citizens that 'Peace is just around the corner.' ''[25]

WSP and *La Wisp* had become casualties of social, economic, and political changes within the nation. During its lifetime, however, *La Wisp* served its subscribers with a balance of reprinted news, personal notes, reporting, and editorial comment in a special, personal form of protest journalism. At the height of protest against the Vietnam War, *La Wisp* mobilized the middle-class women of southern California. In the 1980s, it returned to the initial focus of WSP: the control of nuclear weapons; but the newsletter expanded that focus and dealt with social issues as well. The newsletter and WSP, however, could not survive or adapt to many of the social, economic, and political changes of the late 1980s and the 1990s. With more women working outside the home and with the nation at peace, WSP could not sustain its membership, its activism, or its newsletters. *La Wisp* was only one of many WSP newsletters[26] that were discontinued during this period. A chapter in the book of peace journalism had closed.

Notes

1. In a short essay in the *New World Review,* Ruth Gage-Colby outlined the group's beginning and evolution. The essay was written just one year after Women Strike for Peace was formed (Ruth Gage-Colby, "Women Strike for Peace," *New World Review* 31.6, June 1963, pp. 5–8.)

2. Women Strike for Peace did issue a *Memo* designed to be sent to certain delegates within each chapter. The *Memo,* however, was not designed to be a national voice of the group. Issued by the National Information Clearing House in Washington, D.C., the *Memo* came out quarterly and provided all proposals and updated information on happenings within the organization to key women in every WSP chapter.

3. Amy Swerdlow, "Ladies' Day at the Capitol: Women Strike for Peace Versus HUAC." *Feminist Studies* 8.3, Fall 1982, p. 493.

4. As quoted in Gage-Colby, "Women Strike for Peace," pp. 5–6.

5. Ibid., p. 6.

6. Swerdlow, "Ladies' Day at the Capitol," p. 498.

7. Los Angeles WISP, Statement 1, Ann Arbor Conference, June 9–10, 1961, as quoted by Swerdlow, "Ladies' Day at the Capitol," pp. 499, 518 fn. 20.

8. "WSP National Policy Statement," *Women Strike for Peace Newsletter,* Summer 1962, pp. 1–2, as reprinted in Swerdlow, "Ladies' Day at the Capitol," pp. 499, 518 fn 21.

9. See, for example, Eric Bentley, *Thirty Years of Treason* (New York: Viking Press, 1971), p. 951.

10. Amy Swerdlow, *Women Strike for Peace: Traditional Motherhood and Radical Politics in the 1960s* (Chicago: University of Chicago Press, 1993), pp. 209, 213, 214–215, 218–219.

11. Ibid., p. 152.

12. "to our government," October 1967, p. 4. This newsletter followed a style that put most headlines in all lowercase. Typographically, this technique gave *La Wisp* a distinctive graphic look.

13. "JEANETTE RANKIN BRIGADE—JANUARY 15TH you cannot have wars without women!!" January 1968, p. 1.

14. "nixon's peace hoax," October 1970, p. 1.

15. "we have made indochina a slaughterhouse," March 1971, p. 1.

16. November 1967, p. 1. See also "dates and details," February 1968, p. 8.

17. "mother's day, 1971," April 1971, p. 1.

18. "uncancel the may company," August 1970, p. 1.

19. "there is a lady fair and kind," November 1967, p. 2.

20. Veronica Sissons, "outreach in search of equity," September 1970, p. 4.

21. See, for example, Richard M. Powell, "an open letter: to 204 members of the house of representatives," September 1982, p. 1.

22. See, for example, Richard M. Powell, " 'the crucifixion of the streets,' " January/February 1988, p. 1.

23. "nuclear freeze roll call vote," September 1982, unnumbered pages.

24. "a letter from prague," March 1990, p. 5.

25. March 1990, p. 3.

26. See entry for *N.Y. Peaceletter,* another WSP newsletter discontinued in 1990.

Information Sources

BIBLIOGRAPHY:
Gage-Colby, Ruth. "Women Strike for Peace." *New World Review* 31.6, June 1963, pp. 5–8.
Swerdlow, Amy. "Ladies' Day at the Capitol: Women Strike for Peace versus HUAC." *Feminist Studies* 8.3, Fall 1982, pp. 493–520.
———. " 'Not My Son, Not Your Son, Not Their Sons': Mothers against the Vietnam Draft." In Melvin Small and William D. Hoover, eds. *Give Peace a Chance: Exploring the Vietnam Antiwar Movement.* Syracuse, N.Y.: Syracuse University Press, 1992, pp. 159–170.
———. *Women Strike for Peace: Traditional Motherhood and Radical Politics in the 1960s.* Chicago: University of Chicago Press, 1993.
INDEX SOURCES: None.
LOCATION SOURCES: Swarthmore College Peace Collection, Swarthmore, Pa.; University of California, Los Angeles; University of Colorado, Denver; Northwestern University Library; and many other (primarily university) libraries. Microfilmed, Herstory, Reel 23.

Publication History

PERIODICAL TITLE AND TITLE CHANGES: *La Wisp.*

VOLUME AND ISSUE DATA: Vols. 1–28? (March 1962 to March 1990) (*La Wisp* never carried volume numbers). Monthly, although many issues were combined.

PUBLISHER AND PLACE OF PUBLICATION: Southern California Women Strike for Peace. Los Angeles.

EDITORS: Mary Clarke, Gail Eaby, and Lisa Strada (1967–1968?); Mary Clarke and Lisa Strada (September–November 1968); Mary Clarke and Varda Ullman (December 1968–March 1971); Mary Clarke, Varda Ullman, and Richard Powell (April 1971); Mary Clark and Varda Ullman (May 1971–May 1972); Mary Clarke, Kitty Howe, and Varda Ullman (June–August 1972); Mary Clarke and

Roz Levine (April–November 1973); Mary Clark (?–1990) (editors were not always listed in the newsletter).
CIRCULATION: Unknown.

Kathleen L. Endres

THE LADDER

On September 25, 1690, the first issue of *Publick Occurrences, Both Forreign and Domestick* appeared. Its editor, Benjamin Harris, had traveled to Boston in 1686, fleeing London because of the hailstorm that followed his opposition to the throne. The newspaper appeared only once. Four days later, the authorities suppressed it because of its controversial articles about a French sex scandal and Indian allies of the British. Subsequently, *The Boston News-Letter* became what historians call the first "successful" or "continuous" newspaper in the colonies. Editor and Boston postmaster John Campbell published the first issue April 24, 1704. As a result, print media scholars debate which of these historic publications is, in fact, the first American newspaper.

In much the same way, two publications often are designated the "first" magazines for lesbians: *Vice Versa* and *The Ladder*. *Vice Versa,* typed and mimeographed by "Lisa Ben" (an anagram of "lesbian"), was printed monthly in Los Angeles from June 1947 to February 1948. According to research by Rodger Streitmatter of American University, the title *Vice Versa* came from the fact that homosexuality was considered a "vice" and from the fact that the lesbian lifestyle was the opposite, or "versa," of the established norm.[1] Neither Lisa Ben's real name nor her address appeared in the publication. *Vice Versa,* which one editor called "an early clandestine effort,"[2] died after only nine issues when its editor, sole reporter, and publisher was given a new job and had less time to work on the newsletter. Also, as Streitmatter reveals, she had accomplished what she had hoped: "I was discovering what the lesbian lifestyle was all about, and I wanted to live it rather than write about it. So that was the end of *Vice Versa.*"[3]

Editors of *The Alyson Almanac: A Treasury of Information for the Gay and Lesbian Community* describe Lisa Ben's early effort by saying:

> She typed each issue manually, making as many carbons as possible, during her lunch break at RKO studios. Copies were then circulated clandestinely from one reader to another. *Vice Versa* was remarkably open for its time: The subtitle read "America's gayest magazine," and an editorial in the first issue stated that the magazine was dedicated "'to those of us who will never quite be able to adapt ourselves to the iron-bound rules of Convention."[4]

In an interview with Kate Brandt in *Visibilities,* Lisa Ben, who lives in southern California and still uses her pseudonym, said:

I had an awful lot of fun putting it together. I would use carbon paper, because in those days we didn't have such things as a Xerox or even a ditto machine. And I would put in the original and then seven copies, and that's all the typewriter would take legibly.

And I would type it out during working hours. I never had enough work—I was a fast typist. And my boss would say, "Well, I don't care what you do if your work is done. But I don't want you to sit there and knit or read a magazine. I want you to look busy."[5]

When she finished printing sixteen copies, she gave them to friends and asked them to pass the copies along: "I never sold it," she said. "I just gave it to my friends, because I felt that it was a labor from the heart, and I shouldn't get any money for it."[6]

Several years later, the women of San Francisco's Daughters of Bilitis chapter created *The Ladder*, which was published continuously for sixteen years. Founded in October 1955, the group produced the first issue in October 1956. Leaders of the organization, which was established as a social club, were Del Martin and Phyllis Lyon. Although the American gay rights movement had begun in Los Angeles, it spread quickly to San Francisco, and Martin and Lyon decided their group should dedicate itself to changing public attitudes toward lesbians. The two remained significant figures in the lesbian movement well into the 1980s.

The group printed only two hundred copies of the first issue of *The Ladder;* the mailing list consisted only of lesbians whom the members knew personally. Lyon served as the first editor. In 1960 Martin was appointed editor by the governing board of the Daughters of Bilitis.

The October 1961 issue celebrated the sixth anniversary of the organization, which had begun in 1955 with eight women. By 1961 Daughters of Bilitis had chapters in San Francisco, Los Angeles, New York, and New Jersey.

The Daughters of Bilitis took their name from "Bilitis," the Hellenic form of "Ba'alat," the female counterpart of Baal in Semitic mythology, and from Pierre Louys' *Les Chansons de Bilitis* (1894). After Louys' death, *Les Chansons de Bilitis inedites* and *Las Chansons secretes de Bilitis* appeared in 1929 and 1931, respectively. Unlike the first novel, they contained explicit lesbian eroticism. Having learned to write poetry at the feet of Sappho, the heroine of the novels lived in Mytilene on the island of Lesbos and wrote elegies to her beloved Mnasidika.

One of the stated purposes of the Daughters of Bilitis—made up predominantly of white, educated, middle-class women—was to promote "the integration of the homosexual into society by . . . advocating a mode of behaviour and dress acceptable to society." This integrationist statement appeared as part of four goals of the organization in all early issues of *The Ladder*. To better accomplish its objectives, the Daughters of Bilitis joined forces with the Mattachine Society, which took its name from "matachin" or "matachine," meaning "to mask oneself," and with ONE, Inc.

All of the organizations sponsored publications. In January 1955 the San Francisco chapter of the Mattachine Society began a journal, *Mattachine Review.* It lasted from 1955 to 1966. ONE, Inc., was established in Los Angeles in 1952 and published *ONE Magazine,* the first successful gay magazine in America (1953–1972). *ONE Magazine* debuted in 1953 and achieved a circulation of five thousand before it ceased regular publication in 1968. *ONE Institute Quarterly of Homophile Studies* replaced it, although the quarterly ceased publication in 1973.

According to the *Encyclopedia of Homosexuality,* the three organizations worked together in the face of the "indifference and hostility of the Eisenhower years, in which 'deviation' and nonconformity were relentlessly decried."[7] Among other things, the Daughters of Bilitis picketed the State Department in 1965, calling for gay rights at the Pentagon, White House, and other federal institutions. The group also picketed the federal building in San Francisco July 3, 1968, demanding an end to governmental employment discrimination against gays and lesbians.

Although *The Ladder* clearly was the more successful of the two publications, both *The Ladder* and *Vice Versa* were important for quite different reasons. *Vice Versa* was the signature of one woman's search for connection with others like her, while *The Ladder* served as an information source for a growing lesbian audience. In her first issue Lisa Ben explained the purpose behind her effort. She wrote:

Have you ever stopped to enumerate the many different publications to be found on the average news stands? There are publications for a variety of races and creeds. A wide selection of fiction is available for those who like mysteries, westerns, science fiction or romantic stories. For those who prefer fact to fiction, a variety of publications on politics, world affairs, economics and sports are available. And news stands fairly groan with the weight of hobby and miscellaneous publications devoted to subjects ranging from radio, engineering, gardening, home improvements and sailing, to travel, fashion and health.

Yet, there is one kind of publication which would, I am sure, have a great appeal to a definite group. Such a publication has never appeared on the stands. News stands carrying the crudest kind of magazines or pictorial pamphlets appealing to the vulgar would find themselves severely censured were they to display this other type of publication. Why? Because *Society* decreed it thus.

Hence, the appearance of VICE VERSA, a magazine dedicated, in all seriousness, to those of us who will never quite be able to adapt ourselves to the iron-bound rules of Convention.[8]

The Ladder was the mouthpiece not of one woman but of a group united by conviction. Still, *The Ladder* did not set out to be a trailblazer as much as it did to be a service publication for lesbians. Historian Evelyn Gettone writes:

> The pages of *The Ladder* reflected the priority that DOB [Daughters of Bilitis] attached to personal problems of the individual lesbian, especially the one living in isolation far from the subculture of the large cities. The magazine reported political news, but was never meant to be a political journal, and so the publishers shunned advocacy, devoting space instead to poetry, fiction, history and biography.[9]

Writers in *The Ladder* did, however, debate issues such as lesbians with children, lesbians married to men, and lesbians dealing with job and salary concerns; clearly, in these cases the political could not be separated easily from the personal.

In fact, the newsletters of the Daughters of Bilitis, the Mattachine Society (the first gay organization established in 1950 in Los Angeles), and the Homophile Action League all became instruments of gay civil rights in the late 1950s and 1960s. All three organizations used their newsletters to support the organizations as well as to debate issues and "create a network of information in the battle against institutionalized homophobia,"[10] writes Clare Potter in her index of gay organizations.

Although designed to serve the need of groups, the publications never lost sight of the individual gay man or woman who struggled daily with institutionalized prejudice. One *Ladder* article by Doris Lyles, entitled "My Daughter Is a Lesbian" (July 1958), symbolizes that goal. Proud of her daughter, whom she describes as intelligent, strong, and determined, Lyles writes, "There are no two more normal persons alive than my daughter and her charming associate."[11]

At the same time, the magazines pushed for collective equality in a climate that treated homosexuality as an aberration. As Potter writes:

> Lesbian journals have always been political as well as cultural acts. Their editors created community with every word put on paper; each mailed edition was an attack on isolation and the social judgement of deviancy. . . . And from these very early pages of *Vice Versa* another theme was clear: we were lovers of each other. The voice of desire was always part of our conversation.[12]

The final issue of *The Ladder* (Vol. 16. 11/12) appeared in August/September 1972. Since then, Barbara Grier and Donna J. McBride have produced *The Index to the Ladder* and have made the publication more accessible to scholars of history, culture, literature, and theory. In 1976, Grier, who had written for, and edited, *The Ladder* under the name "Gene Damon," also published a volume entitled *Lesbiana: Book Reviews from the Ladder, 1966–1972*. With Lee Stuart, she produced the first edition of *The Lesbian in Literature: A Bibliography* in 1967, a book reprinted in 1981.

By the time *The Ladder* ceased publication, it had been transformed from a chapter newsletter to a forty-five-page publication with a national and international circulation of approximately thirty-eight hundred. The publication ran reviews, news, a calendar, short stories, and letters. It was mailed in a plain envelope to members of the Daughters of Bilitis. Early covers were line drawings with typed copy.

In 1963, the Daughters of Bilitis called for a change, saying *The Ladder* should stop being a " 'house organ' for an in-group circulation." Barbara Gittings, founder of the New York chapter of the Daughters of Bilitis, became editor of *The Ladder* from 1963 to 1966. Under Gittings the publication allied itself with more militant gay civil rights groups and began to challenge prevalent views among psychiatrists, ministers, and other professionals that homosexuality was an illness or a sin that needed to be cured or eradicated. Kristin Gay Esterberg writes in *The Journal of Sex Research:*

> The period 1956 to 1965 showed enormous changes in *The Ladder* and the women who wrote for it. From its earliest years, when proclamations that lesbians were mentally ill or unnatural went virtually unchallenged, *The Ladder* grew into a forum for lesbians who wished to replace those conceptions with more positive images. From its earliest years, *The Ladder* shows the power of the psychiatric and medical professions to control the terms of the debate around homosexuality and their ability to cause enormous harm to many lesbian women.[13]

As a result of Gittings' work, the publication also began to feature more provocative covers, including a photo of two women holding hands (October 1964).

After disagreement over editorial emphasis and other issues, Phyllis Lyon and Del Martin once again took the reins of *The Ladder* in September 1966, serving until Helen Sanders took over in December 1966. In August 1967 editors began to typeset the publication, and in November of the same year they began to print every two months.

In October/November 1968, Gene Damon became editor of the publication, which now featured articles, short stories, reviews, editorials, and columns. Sanders stayed with the publication as production manager. By 1971, topics included butch-femme issues, reasons women's liberation needed lesbian activists, Angela Davis, and ethnic issues. The publication averaged fifty pages per issue and featured art by Georgia O'Keeffe and others.

Damon issued her first plea for financial and editorial support ("Bluntly, we must have money")[14] in October/November 1968. In August/September 1969, she wrote, "Don't wait until there is no LADDER to help."[15] The plea continues in December/January 1970–1971:

THE LADDER, though written, edited, and circulated by volunteer labor cannot survive without money. . . . [We need to keep alive] the only
real Lesbian magazine in the world.

Therefore THE LADDER will no longer be sold at newsstands. We will
survive only if there are enough of you sufficiently concerned with the
rights and the liberation of ALL women to spend $7.50 a year to sub-
scribe.[16]

In April/May 1971 on behalf of the staff, Damon requested editorial help and
financial support:

It's true, WE CAN'T stop publishing in terms of need—but we will
have to if we run out of money. We are the only magazine in the country
that deals honestly with the needs of the Lesbian, and the only women's
liberation publication that deals honestly with all women.[17]

Citing a small circulation that made advertising difficult to solicit, Damon added:
"We have no expense of any kind except the actual cost of the printing and
binding and mailing of the magazine. Everything else is a labor or an expense
given out of love. . . . We are also at the point where we can be forced to stop
existing at all."[18]

But the war was to no avail. The final issue of *The Ladder* (August/September
1972) included an angry message from Damon:

After 16 complete continuous years of publication, there are to be no
more issues. Many women reading this editorial will be upset, many will
be sorry. None of you will be as sorry as we are to have to take this step.

To those of you who have supported us . . . we simply wish the best in
the future. For those of you who have casually read us through the years,
indeed sometimes intending to subscribe, but not ever quite getting around
to it, we wish you whatever you deserve and leave it to your own con-
sciences to decide just what that might be.[19]

Even the critical words cannot dim the significance of *The Ladder*. It and its
short-term predecessor, *Vice Versa,* inspired and united a group of women who
desperately needed a social and political center.

Notes

1. Rodger Streitmatter, "*Vice Versa:* America's First Lesbian Magazine," paper delivered at the Association for Educators in Journalism and Mass Communication, August
9, 1995, p. 5.

2. Wayne R. Dynes, *Encyclopedia of Homosexuality* (New York: Garland, 1990), p.
1034.

3. Streitmatter, "*Vice Versa,*" p. 8.

4. *The Alyson Almanac: A Treasury of Information for the Gay and Lesbian Community* (Boston: Alyson, 1990), p. 21.

5. Kate Brandt, "Lisa Ben: A Lesbian Pioneer," *Visibilities,* January/February 1990, p. 8.

6. Brandt, "Lisa Ben," p. 9.

7. Dynes, *Encyclopedia,* p. 840.

8. Lisa Ben, "In Explanation," *Vice Versa,* June 1947, p. 1.

9. Dynes, *Encyclopedia,* p. 137.

10. Clare Potter, *The Lesbian Periodical Index* (Tallahassee, Fla.: Naiad Press, 1986), p. vi.

11. Doris Lyles, "My Daughter Is a Lesbian," Vol. 2, 10 July 1958, p. 4.

12. Potter, *The Lesbian Periodical Index,* p. vi.

13. Kristin Gay Esterberg, "From Illness to Action: Conceptions of Homosexuality in *The Ladder,* 1956–1965," *The Journal of Sex Research* 27.1, February 1990, p. 78.

14. Vol. 13.1–2 (October/November 1968), p. 33.

15. Vol. 13.11–12 (August/September 1969), inside back cover.

16. Vol. 15.3–4 (December/January 1970–1971), inside front cover.

17. Vol. 15.7–8 (April/May 1971), p. 4.

18. Vol. 15.7–8 (April/May 1971), p. 4.

19. Vol. 16.11–12 (August/September 1972), p. 3.

Information Sources

BIBLIOGRAPHY:

Alyson Publications. *The Alyson Almanac: A Treasury of Information for the Gay and Lesbian Community.* Boston: Alyson, 1990.

Brandt, Kate. "Lisa Ben: A Lesbian Pioneer." *Visibilities,* January/February 1990, pp. 8–10.

Dynes, Wayne R. *Encyclopedia of Homosexuality.* 2 vols. New York: Garland, 1990.

Esterberg, Kristin Gay. "From Illness to Action: Conceptions of Homosexuality in *The Ladder,* 1956–1965." *The Journal of Sex Research* 27, February 1990, pp. 65–80.

Potter, Clare. *The Lesbian Periodical Index.* Tallahassee, Fla.: Naiad Press, 1986.

Streitmatter, Rodger. "*Vice Versa:* America's First Lesbian Magazine." Paper presented at the Association for Educators in Journalism and Mass Communication, August 9, 1995.

INDEX SOURCES: Grier, Barbara, and Donna J. McBride. *Index to "The Ladder."* Reno, Nev.: *The Ladder,* 1974; *The Lesbian Periodical Index.*

LOCATION SOURCES: Norlin Library, University of Colorado at Boulder.

Publication History

PERIODICAL TITLE AND TITLE CHANGES: *The Ladder.*

VOLUME AND ISSUE DATA: Vols. 1–16 (October 1956–August/September 1972). Monthly (1956–1967); bimonthly (1967–1972).

PUBLISHER AND PLACE OF PUBLICATION: National Daughters of Bilitis. San Francisco (1956–1970); Reno, Nev. (1970–1972).

EDITORS: Phyllis Lyon and Del Martin (1956–1963); Barbara Gittings (1963–1966);

Phyllis Lyon and Del Martin (September to November 1966); Helen Sanders (December 1966–1968); Gene Damon (1968–1972).
CIRCULATION: 3,800.

Jan Whitt

LIFE AND LABOR

The national Women's Trade Union League (WTUL) launched *Life and Labor* in January 1911 after two and a half years of trying to serve the needs of the Chicago and, later, national WTUL through the pages of Chicago's *Union Labor Advocate*. Under that arrangement, the league had paid the salary of veteran Australian journalist Alice Henry to edit the *Advocate*'s women's section and the publisher $1,225 per year to carry the monthly section. The WTUL also endorsed the paper as its official organ and encouraged supporters to subscribe. The WTUL was not alone. The Chicago Federation of Labor (CFL) and several local unions had similar arrangements until a dispute over advertising policy led them to sever relations in 1910.[1]

The arrangement with the *Union Labor Advocate*, while far more economical than publishing *Life and Labor* would prove, did not meet the league's communication needs. The *Advocate* was primarily read by Chicago union men; as such it could not effectively reach the league's growing national membership or reach out to the unorganized women workers the league hoped to reach. To continue with the *Advocate* after the Chicago Federation of Labor had denounced it would have endangered the league's close relations with the CFL, one of its strongest supporters in the labor movement, upsetting the league's lifelong balancing act among the American Federation of Labor (AFL) and its affiliates, the needs of the women workers it sought to serve, and the women reformers who paid the league's bills.

The Women's Trade Union League was founded as a reform organization that attempted to unite the efforts of progressive reformers and unionists for unionization of women workers, woman suffrage, protective legislation for women workers, and education and other uplift programs. Founded in 1903, in conjunction with the AFL's convention, the league brought together prominent social reformers, women unionists (many of them socialists), and middle- (and upper-) class women, "allies," in league parlance. Although local leagues were set up around the country, the strongest were in Chicago and New York, where the league reached out to workers in the burgeoning garment industries, which employed tens of thousands of women under abysmal conditions and starvation wages.

The Women's Trade Union League initially focused its efforts on organizing women into trade unions, gradually increasing its emphasis on securing protective legislation for women workers after 1913 as the league became convinced that this was the only way to protect the lives and welfare of the tens of thousands of women workers laboring in small, often unorganizable shops.

The Chicago league took charge of the *Union Labor Advocate*'s women's department in December 1904. The section became the league's official national organ in 1908, and veteran movement journalist Alice Henry was appointed to edit the expanded section. Henry was already internationally known for her work in the Australian women's movement when she emigrated to the United States in 1906 in search of an opportunity to earn a living doing serious writing. Henry's reputation as an author and lecturer quickly landed her work first with the settlement house movement and then, in 1907, with the Women's Trade Union League. While editing *Life and Labor,* Henry continued to lecture under league and suffrage auspices, write for socialist newspapers, and argue for closer cooperation between the suffrage and socialist movements.[2]

In *Life and Labor*'s first issue, Henry said the magazine was launched ''in response to the request of the organized women workers as well as students of sociology.'' Only a cross-class movement to place industry ''on a basis just and fair to the worker'' could avoid ''the crude and primitive method of revolution,'' Henry wrote.[3] That first issue reflected Henry's eclectic vision; there was an illustrated history of the recent Chicago garment workers strike, short fiction, poetry, and an article by prominent reformer Louis Post. Later issues offered a series of profiles of male and female labor leaders and working women, reports on industrial conditions, helpful hints, mediocre fiction (tending toward rural romances and fables), league and suffrage news, and editorials promoting the league's reform agenda.

Life and Labor was an uneven publication under Henry's editorship, reflecting the tensions between its efforts to appeal to women workers and to its (relatively) wealthy backers and to speak to women's issues and needs while reassuring male union leaders of the league's loyalty to the labor movement, and the contradictions between conducting a reform journal and a popular magazine. Articles on the struggles of the Lake Seamen's Union (January 1912) or AFL president Sam Gomper's stuffed rabbit (February 1912) seem unlikely to have reached either audience, while its fiction could not compete with popular magazines for literary appeal and was politically at least as incoherent as the serialized fiction running in mainstream union organs.[4] But while Henry sought, unsuccessfully, to simultaneously serve these divergent demands, she did not stifle her voice. In 1912, Henry published an article castigating suffrage leaders for undemocratic factional politics that were paralyzing the movement; league president Margaret Dreier Robins forwarded a letter of complaint, adding her comment that such ''unfortunate controvers[ies]'' ought not be aired in the magazine without prior approval by the WTUL board.[5]

Henry's efforts to reduce *Life and Labor*'s substantial deficits to manageable proportions were similarly unsuccessful, however, undercutting her efforts to maintain editorial independence. In 1915 the financial situation reached a crisis when Robins and other league ''allies'' decided they would no longer continue their financial support. (Robins alone provided $2,500 a year in support.) The league spent more than $11,000 a year publishing the magazine, which brought in only $4,117.19 in income in 1914, mostly from subscriptions and single-copy sales. (Although *Life and Labor* carried advertising throughout its lifetime, it rarely carried more than a few pages of advertisements, typically promoting union-label goods but also for products such as Kellogg's cereal.) The effort to appeal to both middle- and working-class women was failing, and one of Robins' advisers concluded that the effort to reach the latter's "tired out and underdeveloped minds" required an entirely new editorial approach emulating "the educational method used with little children." There were 2,646 subscribers, up substantially over the previous year. (The subscription list never topped 3,000 out of a 4,000 to 5,000 copy press run and was much smaller in the magazine's final years.) The league considered a proposal to suspend publication for three months for a sustained fund-raising campaign, but negotiations for a section in *The Survey* fell through, and the league decided to continue publication of a scaled-back magazine.[6]

Henry was eased out as editor in the reorganization and replaced by her assistant, Stella Miles Franklin (remembered primarily for her novel *My Brilliant Career*). The magazine was cut to sixteen pages from thirty-two, and again to eight pages for a few months when the deficits continued to mount. The subscription price was cut from one dollar to fifty cents in an attempt to broaden circulation beyond a handful of league activists. But losses continued to mount, and Robins, who paid most of the bills, became increasingly heavy-handed in her oversight. Franklin resigned in 1916, referring to herself as the "sole survivor" of a brutal purge. As Franklin later explained, Robins "having expressed her desire to exterminate me, among others, . . . there was nothing else to do."[7] After a brief period when Amy Walker Field held the title of editor, Robins then took the title. Field, the wife of a University of Chicago economist, continued as associate editor and seems to have run the magazine on a day-to-day basis. As editor, Robins sought to transform the magazine from Henry's and Franklin's conception of an uplifting, feminist working women's journal into a lighter, more entertaining magazine ostensibly more accessible to working women.[8]

However, the contradictions had by no means been resolved. Historian Susan Kennedy noted that "*Life and Labor* supported the essential conservatism of the Women's Trade Union League under Mrs. Robins, returning to themes of gradualism, acculturation, and AFL-style unionism."[9] The first issue (December 1916) to appear under Robins' editorship, for example, opened with a five-page commentary on war and democracy, followed by articles on the first Christmas tree, a report on the International Ladies Garment Workers Union convention, a poem by socialist Louis Untermeyer, a report on Jeannette Rankin's election, and league and suffrage news. In September 1917, Robins gave space to a Labor Day message from International Seamen's Union president Andrew Furuseth, in which the aging union leader deplored the evolution from the "natural" division of labor ("Man provided the home; woman kept it") to the modern factory system, which forced women to work instead of rearing children ("We cannot persistently compel woman to live an unnatural life and have a healthy people'').[10]

Journalist Sarah Cory Rippey replaced Field as associate editor with that issue, gradually focusing the magazine more tightly on women workers. Despite Robins' gradualism, Rippey's *Life and Labor* gradually adopted a more demanding tone, challenging union officials to pay more attention to the needs of women workers and to give women positions as union organizers and officers and pressing government officials and employers to extend the range of occupations open to women workers. The magazine was sometimes harshly critical of AFL officials, particularly when they came into conflict with the progressive unionists with whom the WTUL was allied.[11]

In January 1919, *Life and Labor* featured an article on the plight of African-American workers who were in danger of losing their jobs with the end of the war. (The magazine warned that if black women were not given greater opportunities, they might turn to Bolshevism.) This article was strikingly different from earlier *Life and Labor* coverage. In May 1914, for example, a special issue on African-American women workers was distributed through black women's associations as part of a league effort to draw blacks into unions.[12] But by 1919 the magazine—which had always had a strong impulse to a social work orientation—rarely treated women workers as subjects making their own history; rather, they were the objects of study, concern, and the beneficial attentions of reformers. Under Rippey, *Life and Labor* published articles on venereal disease,[13] a series of in-depth articles on the situation of women workers in various industries (including day-in-the-life articles by "college girl" Dorothy Walton about her experiences working undercover in a series of low-status, unorganized jobs),[14] and an appeal to housewives to recognize the advantages of a union for their domestic servants (the union would screen out incompetents).[15] As the war drew to a close, the Women's Trade Union League advanced an ambitious reform agenda: to guarantee for all children the right to complete high school; to abolish night work for women; to secure equal pay for equal work, equal access to trade and technical training, social insurance, maternity benefits, and the forty-four-hour week; to restore free speech rights; to achieve the release of political prisoners; and to work for workers' right to self-government in industry, public ownership of natural resources, and "a standard of life which shall ensure to all citizens, both men and women, free opportunity to work with hand and brain, and secure to them a full measure of health, education, recreation and fruitful leisure."[16]

In 1918 Robins had returned *Life and Labor* to a thirty-two-page, ten-cent magazine, a move that only aggravated the deficit. While the magazine appeared successful on the surface (so much so that one reader wrote in to congratulate the editors on their growing subscription list at a time when subscription income was actually declining), the expansion failed to attract new readers or to resolve the long-standing dispute over its purpose and mission.[17] Only ten issues were published in 1920. The next year founding editor Alice Henry served on a

WTUL committee looking into the perennial problem of *Life and Labor* finances, concluding that the problems arose from the fact that the magazine was called upon to "fulfill different and inconsistent functions" as a movement organ and a popular magazine and was therefore unable to accomplish either effectively.[18] By then the subscription list was down to 1,271, and the magazine was costing the league seventy-five hundred dollars a year. In July 1921 the WTUL Executive Board decided to suspend publication with the October 1921 issue (the August and September issues never appeared), explaining that league income had shrunk while production costs continued to increase.[19] The magazine was succeeded by *Life and Labor Bulletin,* a four-page newsletter published irregularly in its first years and then as a monthly through February 1932, when publication was suspended and later resumed as an irregular mimeographed bulletin. Monthly (more or less) publication resumed in October 1939. The *Bulletin* contained a mix of general labor news, reports on WTUL activities, and information on the situation of women workers. It continued until the June 1950 issue, which announced the national league's dissolution. (Some local leagues continued for several years.) The WTUL's demise had been accelerated by the split between the AFL and the Congress of Industrial Organizations (CIO). The WTUL, which remained tied to the AFL, was increasingly cut off from a new generation of labor activists who had affiliated with the CIO.

Historian Robin Jacoby concluded, "At best, *Life and Labor* was a financial drain on the WTUL."[20] *Life and Labor* never reached a mass audience or projected a clear editorial focus while navigating the conflicts intrinsic to the WTUL's structure as a cross-class alliance obliged to simultaneously speak to its middle-class financial backers and the workingwomen the league was set up to serve. Its relationship with the male bureaucrats who ran the unions into which the league sought to organize women was similarly difficult. While *Life and Labor* did publish criticisms of these unions and of the labor movement more generally, it was always careful to protect its ties to the American Federation of Labor, even when this forced it in one instance to actively undermine a strike by women textile workers organized into the more radical Industrial Workers of the World.

Life and Labor never succeeded in finding an audience for the magazine. Yet the magazine offers rich materials on often little known working conditions and struggles of women workers (particularly on the eastern seaboard and in the Midwest) during its lifetime. Where else could one learn of the struggle of 175 Boston newsgirls selling newspapers from newsstands at subway and elevated stops to unionize or of attempts to fire women streetcar conductors in the aftermath of World War I or the Cleveland cloakmakers' strike of 1911?[21] While the league's opposition to the equal rights amendment (which it feared would reverse decades of struggles to win protective wages, hours, and safety legislation) is well known, its pioneering demands for comparable-worth laws are largely forgotten.[22] The Women's Trade Union League played a key role in organizing women workers at a time when few American Federation of Labor unions evidenced more than a rhetorical concern with women workers' welfare. The WTUL forged mutually beneficial links between those women workers and the feminist movement of the day, and it laid the groundwork for a later generation of women labor activists to fight for their rightful place in the labor movement.

Notes

1. Minutes, Women's Trade Union League National Executive Board Meeting, May 19, 1920, p. 7; Margaret Dreier Robins Papers, Papers of the Women's Trade Union League and Its Principal Leaders (Research Publications Inc. microfilm), reel 8, frame 306. The minutes note that the financial report does not include office rent, the editor's salary (unreported; according to Diane Kirkby in *Alice Henry: The Power of Pen and Voice* [Melbourne: Cambridge University Press, 1991], p. 78. Henry was paid twenty-five dollars weekly), or other miscellaneous expenses, all of which were borne by WTUL president Margaret Robins.

2. Kirkby, *Alice Henry*.

3. January 1911, p. 3.

4. Anne Schofield, ed., *Seal Skin and Shoddy: Working Women in American Labor Press Fiction, 1870–1920* (Westport, Conn.: Greenwood Press, 1988). Also, Schofield, "The Rise of the Pig-Headed Girl: An Analysis of the American Labor Press for Their Attitudes toward Women, 1877–1920" (Ph.D. diss., State University of New York, 1980). Kennedy offered a more sympathetic analysis of *Life and Labor* under Henry's editorship, arguing that the magazine was targeted to working-class women, with direct, simple language and articles calling for "self-improvement through trade unionism and feminism." The biographical sketches (fourteen in the first year of publication) reinforced this message, as did the inspirational literature. After 1914, Kennedy saw this emphasis on inspirational and self-improvement articles gradually supplanted by news reporting and analysis (Susan Kennedy, " 'The Want It Satisfies Demonstrates the Need of It': A Study of Life and Labor of the Women's Trade Union League," *International Journal of Women's Studies* 3.4, July/August 1980, p. 393).

5. Robins to Henry, February 18, 1912. WTUL Papers, reel 1, frame 31.

6. James Mollenbach, quoted in Kirkby, *Alice Henry*, p. 109. Minutes of Meeting of WTUL National Executive Board, February 5 1915. WTUL Papers, reel 8, frames 417–421.

7. Kirkby, *Alice Henry*, pp. 117–118.

8. Although Robins was listed as editor for the remainder of the magazine's life (and had been listed as associate editor before then), she was often away from the offices for months at a time and could not have performed the day-to-day editing responsibilities. However, as WTUL president, titular editor, and primary source of funds, Robins set overall editorial policy and reshaped *Life and Labor* in accordance with her vision.

9. Kennedy, " 'The Want It Satisfies Demonstrates the Need of It,' " p. 398.

10. Andrew Furuseth, "Evolving Bantams from Men," September 1917, pp. 140–141. He was a frequent contributor to the magazine's pages (though few of his articles had much to do with women workers), perhaps reflecting his own orientation toward lobbying and protective legislation. For a sympathetic treatment of his career, see Hyman Weintraub, *Andrew Furuseth: Emancipator of the Seamen* (Berkeley: University of California Press, 1959).

11. See, for example, "More about Labor Parties," March 1919, p. 69, criticizing an American Federation of Labor denunciation of the labor party movement initiated by the Chicago Federation of Labor: "Reaction from without the labor movement is thus comforted by reaction from within."

12. While the league rarely explicitly tackled issues of race, preferring class- and sex-based appeals, league cofounder Leonora O'Reilly was an active member of the National Association for the Advancement of Colored People, and league activists helped African-American women get jobs in the unionized garment trades (Annelise Orleck, *Common Sense and a Little Fire: Women and Working-Class Politics in the United States, 1900–1965* [Chapel Hill: University of North Carolina Press, 1995], pp. 90–91).

13. January 1919, pp. 14–16.

14. For example, "The Cost of Your Sweets to the Candy Worker," February 1919, pp. 29–30; "Negro Women and the Tobacco Industry," May 1921, 142–144; the Pilgrim, "Pilgrim's Progress in a Laundry," April 1920, pp. 115–119, and May 1920, 142–146, 158. Other "Pilgrim's Progress" articles ran in June 1920, pp. 179–182; January 1921, pp. 11–14; February 1921, pp. 48–52; and March 1921, pp. 86–89, 92. "Pilgrim" Dorothy Walton was a journalist on the staff of the Chicago Federation of Labor's weekly *The New Majority* at the time; she also wrote for charity, reform, and religious periodicals. Her papers are included among the Carroll Binder Papers at the Newberry Library in Chicago.

15. Marguerite Mooers Marshall, "Why a Housewife Wants a Household Workers' Union," May 1920, pp. 135–136. The March 1920 issue featured a debate between Marshall and Robins on protective legislation, in which Marshall argued that such laws limited women's work opportunities and undermined struggles for equal treatment ("Newspaper Woman Protests against Maternal Legislation," pp. 84–87). WTUL activists Rose Schneiderman and Pauline Newman wrote indignant rebuttals for the May 1920 *Life and Labor* (pp. 152–154), insisting that while journalists might not need or want protective legislation, it was absolutely essential to protect the lives and health of women working in manufacturing industries.

16. "Program of the Committee on Social and Industrial Reconstruction of the National Women's Trade Union League of America," March 1919, pp. 51–53.

17. Lydia Trowbridge, "What Do You Think of It?" April 1920, p. 126. Trowbridge, president of the Chicago Federation of High School Teachers, referred to suggestions at the WTUL's Philadelphia convention that *Life and Labor* should adopt a new editorial policy. The specific proposals were not presented either in the magazine or in the WTUL minutes. She suggested that women in industry did not supply sufficient news for the magazine to function as a "trade journal" and that the magazine should function as an outreach and education tool for the masses of unorganized women workers. "One test of a magazine's success is its subscription list. The fact that Life and Labor grows in bulk is proof that it has more money to spend, presumably through having more subscribers."

18. Kirkby, *Alice Henry,* p. 123.

19. Auditor's report for two years ending April 30, 1921, Executive Board Minutes, June 6–12, 1921, WTUL Papers, Reel 8, frames 580–601. "Will Suspend Publication," October 1921, p. 244. This short note appears in the middle of the magazine, in a column of miscellaneous short articles. There is no other mention of the suspension in that final issue. The WTUL secretary-treasurer's report covering the last six months of publication showed subscription income of $58.30; $3,915 of the magazine's $4,402.56 in expenses

was covered from WTUL coffers (*Proceedings. Eighth Biennial Convention* [deferred from 1921], June 5–10 1922, WTUL Papers Series IX, reel 1).

20. Robin Miller Jacoby, "The Women's Trade Union League," in Edward T. James, ed., *Papers of the Women's Trade Union League and Its Principal Leaders* (Guide to the microfilm edition) (Woodbridge, Conn.: Research, 1981), p. 280.

21. In the January 1921; January, March, and April 1919; and October 1911 issues, respectively.

22. Orleck, *Common Sense and a Little Fire,* pp. 167, 139–140. In 1919, *Life and Labor* published an article on efforts to organize women employed as machinists. The president of the International Association of Machinists' (IAM) Ladies' Auxiliary (which the IAM placed in charge of organizing the women) stressed that women are not suited to work as all-round machinists but were quite capable of performing specialized small parts work. However, most did not receive pay equal to that of their male counterparts, prompting the IAM's organizing efforts. Forty women were fired in Springfield, Massachusetts, for demanding equal pay (May Peake, "The Woman Machinist: Her Accomplishments and Her Possibilities," December 1919, pp. 326–329).

Information Sources

BIBLIOGRAPHY:
James, Edward T., ed. *Papers of the Women's Trade Union League and Its Principal Leaders.* Woodbridge, Conn.: Research, 1981 (microfilm).
Kennedy, Susan. " 'The Want It Satisfies Demonstrated the Need of It': A Study of Life and Labor of the Women's Trade Union League." *International Journal of Women's Studies* 3.4, July/August 1980, pp. 391–406.
Kirkby, Diane. *Alice Henry: The Power of Pen and Voice.* Melbourne: Cambridge University Press, 1991.
Payne, Elizabeth Anne. *Reform, Labor and Feminism.* Urbana: University of Illinois Press, 1988.
INDEX SOURCES: Published annual index.
LOCATION SOURCES: Library of Congress; Schlesinger Library (Radcliffe College); and other libraries.

Publication History

PERIODICAL TITLE AND TITLE CHANGES: *Life and Labor* (1911–1921).
VOLUME AND ISSUE DATA: Vols. 1–10 (1911–1921). Monthly, except no July 1920, August 1920, August 1921, or September 1921 issues were published.
PUBLISHER AND PLACE OF PUBLICATION: Women's Trade Union League. Chicago.
EDITORS: Alice Henry (1911–1913); Alice Henry and Stella Miles Franklin (1913–1914); Amy Walker Field (1915–1916); Margaret Dreier Robins (1916–1921) (Field initially continued as managing editor; Sarah Cory Rippey was managing editor from 1917).
CIRCULATION: 4,000–5,000 copies.

Jon Bekken

LILITH

Lilith magazine appeared in the fall of 1976 and continues today as a publication for and by Jewish women. It had a publishing goal to appear quarterly, and, indeed, it did so early on. A group of women spearheaded the publishing effort, Susan Weidman Schneider, Amy Stone, and Aviva Cantor Zuckoff. Respectively, they were the executive editor, the senior editor, and the acquisitions editor. They called on experienced women publishers and leaders to share their expertise; among them, the staff of *Women, a Journal of Liberation;* Pat Carbine, cofounder of *Ms.* magazine; Judith Daniels, publisher of *Savvy* magazine; Letty Cottin Pogrebin of *Ms;* and Sally Priesand, the first female rabbi in the United States.

As women, the magazine's founders became attracted to much of the ideology of the women's movement; as Jews, they recognized their particular concerns were not always shared by other groups. Thus, they asked, How do we reconcile our sense of ourselves as worthy individuals while identifying with a religious and social structure that has limited woman's options in the synagogue, the home, and the community at large? No other ongoing forum existed to explore their concerns and conflicts. They needed to know, to learn, what Judaism could offer feminism and how the women's movement could change them as Jews. They asked, Why has Jewish history been the history of Jewish men? Surely that kind of question has been addressed by other feminist groups.

Lilith is named for Adam's legendary first companion and his equal; she predated Eve and originally embodied independent womanhood, the magazine noted in its first issue.[1]

The founders obtained funding for the premier issue from the May and Anna Levinson Foundation and thirty-nine individuals, some of whom became contributors. The foundation gave generously, the magazine noted, and provided "funding for high-risk, innovative projects addressing themselves to social change."[2] Editor Schneider said this was the only "significant money." Individuals contributed between one hundred dollars and five hundred dollars each.

Advertising in the initial issue and those that followed remained scant. Because of lack of funds, *Lilith* slowed publication from quarterly to semiannually and then annually. Ads appeared for *Response* magazine, "an alternative voice in American Jewry"; *Ms* magazine; *The Feminist Art Journal;* Schocken Books; and classifieds. Clearly, these were fringe advertisers, at best. By volume 6, an issue contained a 1 × 4-inch ad for Empire poultry, the nationally distributed, kosher-only poultry company. An ad appeared in the seventh issue for the international edition of the *Jerusalem Post.*[3]

From the first, the magazine has been exceptional in terms of its editorial orientation and thrust. An interview with feminist Betty Friedan reported on a woman who grew up with triple burdens, in Peoria, Illinois: she was intelligent, unattractive, and Jewish. Another article pertained to Jewish liberation and Jewish law, by Blu Greenberg, perhaps the most important Orthodox feminist in America and a noted author and speaker. There was poetry by Muriel Rukeyser and Diane Levenberg, both major names in their field.[4]

A double-page spread was entitled "OY Vey!" and concerned articles and ads that poked fun at Jewish women or at whom the magazine's editors poked fun. For example, an advertisement for J(ewish) A(merican) P(rincess) T-shirts, sunglasses, and shoulder bag; an item for *Hadassah* magazine, the hugely successful Zionist women's association publication, about why women did not drive tour buses in Israel; an advertisement from *Conservative Judaism,* the journal of the largest branch of Judaism, addressing the young leadership—male only— of the United Jewish Appeal, the major fund-raising arm in America; and a snippet of an article about the synagogue in society, again for men only, that stated that "the new aggressiveness of women and their readiness to make demands in sexual relations has distinctly increased the frequency of impotence"[5]—all made their way into the "OY Vey" column.

From the first there was mention of a *Lilith* Speakers Bureau for conferences, meetings, and seminars. Topics included "Jewish and Female: Beyond the Stereotype of the JAP," "The Israeli Woman," "Alternatives to Serving Tea for the Jewish Establishment," "World of Our Mothers," and "Is Judaism Possible without the Jewish Family?"

By the spring/summer issue of 1977, a profile of the *Lilith* reader emerged: Readers were located in every state and province and in Israel, Australia, South America, and Western Europe. Nevertheless, 34 percent of readers reside in the New York area, and another 12.5 percent came from California. Nearly 47 percent had graduate degrees, and another 20.4 percent had done graduate work. A whopping 84 percent had some Jewish education, and many were dissatisfied with its quality. More than half the readers had been to Israel, 57 percent belonged to Jewish organizations, and 48 percent went to synagogues. The readership was "clearly concerned about Jewish life and eager for changes to enable all of us to participate in it fully and equally."[6]

Importantly, *Lilith* has chronicled the fight to have women rabbis in the Conservative movement—Judaism's largest in America. The magazine has written about the politics of ordination and the debate in the movements about the issue. Moreover, after the first woman was ordained, the magazine ran a profile of her and an in-depth interview. Later, the magazine carried a listing of ordained women rabbis and cantors. (While the rabbi or teacher leads the service in a synagogue, the cantor chants or sings prayers and other liturgical music.)[7]

Lilith carried an extraordinary story of Jewish women in prison, which brought letters of praise from such persons as Nat Hentoff of the *Village Voice.* The magazine asked that subscriptions be taken in the names of jailed women and received sixteen such responses right away.[8]

A standard section called "No Longer among Us" consisted of obituaries. The column was added with the fifth issue in 1978. Another new department congratulated women making it in arts, letters, sciences, synagogues, fund-raising activities, community organizations, labor unions, and as students. The magazine noted women's programs all over the world, from San Diego, to Ethiopia, to Siberia.

The first issue carried the name *Lilith,* a quarterly magazine; the second, a new subhead, the *Jewish Women's Quarterly,* and then *The Jewish Women's Magazine.* With the seventh issue, in 1980, came another subtitle: *The Prepared Table,* referring to the *Shulchan Aruch,* the authoritative code of Jewish behavior according to Jewish law. As feminists continued to rediscover and rework Jewish practice, the magazine noted, "the contents of *Lilith* may serve an evolving Prepared Table for a new code of behavior."[9] The new subhead remained. Also in the seventh issue were items about the first kosher day-care center in Toronto about Israeli feminists telling it like it is and another survey.

The next year, the next issue, a new column called "Bima" was added, with an article by Peggy Tishman about the need to end the exploitation of women in the Jewish establishment. The name "bima" means a platform for opinion "by Jewish women on issues of the day," *Lilith* noted.[10] Articles followed about the Jewish stake in abortion rights, women in the Israeli army, and history, titled "Voices from the Sweatshops."[11]

The magazine also inaugurated a lasting practice, a listing of books by *Lilith* authors/contributors. Other issues addressed important subjects: Nobel laureate Isaac Bashevis Singer's misogyny, women aging, Jewish career women. With volume 20.1, spring 1995, came two new names, (Rabbi) Susan Schnur, editor, and Naomi Danis, managing editor.

Lilith attempts to look at Jewish life through a feminine voice, to learn about the lives of Jewish women by listening to them. It trusts in women's own stories.[12] The magazine tries to go beyond the stereotypes, to see how women are responding to their own lives.

First-person writing is requested; the magazine feels strengthened by such writing. Articles, for example, recalling Holocaust memories are remarkable. The magazine prints ten thousand copies, six thousand subscriptions plus single-copy sales. However, the magazine has a readership of twenty-five thousand.[13]

The magazine has expanded the universe of information about Jewish women. It is a resource for college students and faculty members alike, who turn to it for background information and to find issues to write about. The editors are accessible by phone, FAX, or e-mail. They are called on by media in general as well, for their expertise on Middle East politics, AIDS, and other Jewish and general questions.

Notes

1. Fall 1976, p. 3.
2. Ibid., p. 45.
3. Susan Schneider, interview, October 1995.
4. Fall 1976.
5. Fall 1976, p. 5.

  6. Spring/Summer 1977, p. 2.
  7. Number 6, 1979, pp. 9–15, and number 7, 1980, pp. 6–7.
  8. Number 5, 1978, pp. 10–15, and number 6, 1979.
  9. Number 7, 1980, p. 1.
 10. Number 8, 1981, p. 48.
 11. Number 8, 1981.
 12. Schneider interview.
 13. Schneider interview.

Information Sources

BIBLIOGRAPHY:
The Joseph Jacobs Organization, ed. *The Joseph Jacobs Directory of the Jewish Press in America.* 3rd ed. New York: Joseph Jacobs Organization, 1990.
INDEX SOURCES: Index to Jewish Periodicals; Middle East: Abstracts and Index; Women Studies Abstracts.
LOCATION SOURCES: University of Connecticut library; Library of Congress; and other libraries.

Publication History

PERIODICAL TITLE AND TITLE CHANGES: *Lilith* (1976–present).
VOLUME AND ISSUE DATA: Vols. 1– (Fall 1976–present). Quarterly (1976–1977); annual (1978); quarterly (1988–present).
PUBLISHER AND PLACE OF PUBLICATION: Lilith Publications Inc. New York.
EDITORS: Susan Weidman Schneider (1976–1995); Susan Schnur (1995–present).
CIRCULATION: Ulrich's, 1995: 10,000.

Barbara Straus Reed

THE LILY

Amelia Bloomer was living a relatively quiet existence in Seneca Falls, New York, when she became interested in the temperance cause and the war against demon alcohol. She held strong beliefs and opinions on this issue, going so far as to refuse her husband's celebratory toast on their wedding night in 1840.[1] Her husband, Dexter, who was one of the editors and proprietors of the *Seneca County Courier,* convinced Amelia that she would help the temperance cause immensely if she committed her ideas to paper; and while hesitant at first, Amelia Bloomer soon began to make frequent contributions about the moral state of the nation to several local papers, both anonymously and under pseudonyms.[2]

Bloomer's attendance of the first woman's rights convention in 1848 had spurred her to become active in reform; and although she did not agree with all of the principles advocated by the convention attendees, she did agree that women were capable of making significant contributions to the various reform movements. Shortly after the convention, Bloomer and a group of Seneca Falls women organized the Ladies' Temperance Society.[3] The formation of, and initial funding from, this group eventually led to the creation of *The Lily*. As Bloomer recalled, "It was at a meeting of this kind . . . that the matter of publishing a little temperance paper . . . was introduced."[4]

When the first issue of *The Lily* was published on January 1, 1849, it debuted as the official organ of the women's temperance movement, but Amelia Bloomer was the driving force behind its publication. In that first issue, the magazine's flag announced that it was "[p]ublished by a Committee of Ladies."[5] However, in the first issue and all following issues, Amelia Bloomer crossed out the phrase and wrote in her name underneath, saying, "As editor of the paper, I threw myself into the work, assumed the entire responsibility, took the entire charge editorially and financially, and carried it successfully through."[6] After starting out with a coeditor, Anna Mattison, who resigned after only the second issue of *The Lily*, Bloomer took sole responsibility for publishing the journal.[7] Even when faced with incredible obstacles, when the work was left entirely on her shoulders, she continued, saying of *The Lily*, "It was a needed instrumentality to spread abroad the truth of the new gospel to woman, and I could not withhold my hand to stay the work I had begun."[8]

From the beginning, Bloomer boldly acknowledged the purpose of her journal: to advance the temperance movement and womankind. She took her responsibility to her magazine, her women readers, and the temperance cause seriously, saying in her first editorial in *The Lily*:

> It is Woman that speaks through the *Lily*. It is upon an important subject, too, that she comes before the public to be heard. Intemperance is the great foe to her peace and happiness. Surely she has the right to wield the pen for its suppression. Surely she may, without throwing aside the modest retirement, which so becomes her sex, use her influence to lead her fellow mortals away from the destroyer's path. Like the beautiful flower from which it derives its name, we shall strive to make the *Lily* the emblem of "sweetness and purity"—and may Heaven smile upon this our attempt to advance the great cause of Temperance Reform.[9]

The Lily contained opinions and ideas that had never before been publicly addressed by a woman in print, and some of these opinions proved upsetting to the public. It was also, Bloomer claimed, "the first paper devoted to the interests of women and, so far as I know, the first one owned, edited, and published by a woman."[10] Bloomer's claim held some merit in that *The Lily* was the first publication for which a woman served in all major capacities. While other women, such as Jane Swisshelm, had worked as editors and publishers, usually for their husband's papers, Amelia Bloomer was the first to serve as owner, publisher, editor, writer, and business manager of a publication.[11]

From the start, *The Lily* reflected Bloomer's political ideas and was more of a mouthpiece than a magazine intended for a mass audience. Bloomer knew that her readers were women who were interested in reform movements and targeted her messages accordingly. With a meager circulation of only a few hundred for the first printing, *The Lily* drew a quick following, and the circulation rapidly grew into the thousands.[12] Subscriptions cost fifty cents for each copy, with the journal published monthly. The new magazine quickly became a means of communication that banded members of the growing temperance movement together.

The first columns of *The Lily* were a mixture of poetry, literature, and condemnation of intemperance. Bloomer frequently placed the blame for the trafficking of liquor on the people of ''wealth and standing in society''[13] and included horror stories about women and men who had fallen victim to the evil beverage. Bloomer often recounted stories she received from newspaper reports and even neighborhood gossip about men who lost their jobs and ended up being murdered in the streets for bottles of liquor and about women who turned to alcohol and left their families for the streets and prostitution. Articles with titles like ''Shun the Wine Cup'' appeared regularly and launched harsh attacks against those who participated, even slightly, in the drinking of alcohol. She even wrote articles condemning women who used alcohol in their cooking and blamed them for holding back the cause of temperance reform.[14]

Among the more dramatic warnings Bloomer published was this one, aimed at young men, in the first issue of *The Lily:*

> We would extend to you a word of warning, and beseech you by the affections of fond parents, and kind friends, who are watching your steps with anxious solicitude, to shun the wine cup as you would a deadly foe who was thirsting for your blood. If you have any regard for your reputation—if you have any love for your friends—if you have any wish to become useful members of society, and worthy of the respect of the virtuous and good—shun the wine cup![15]

Bloomer also recognized the importance of women's becoming involved in the temperance movement when she wrote this emotional editorial:

> That woman has reason to feel deeply on the subject of Intemperance all must admit. It strikes directly at her happiness, and peace of mind. How often is her heart made to bleed over the ruin of her fondest hopes! She sees those whom she loves more than life itself, ruined in body and soul— their peace destroyed—their hopes blasted, and their bodies consigned to a drunkards grave. And can she—shall she sit idle, and permit this terrible evil thus to inflict upon her its cruel visitings, and she do nothing to stay its progress? No! she cannot—she should not. She is called upon as she loves her own peace of mind—as she loves the happiness of these with whom she is connected in life, to come forth and do what she may to banish the evils of intemperance from the land. We have long felt this to

be her duty. We have long felt that woman was called upon to act, and act efficiently in the work of advancing the great temperance cause.[16]

At this time, Bloomer was being praised by both women and men for her devoted campaign against intemperance, as is evidenced by this extract from a private letter printed in *The Lily* on May 1, 1849:

> We are much pleased with the enterprise in which you are engaged, and although an arduous undertaking, hope you will be encouraged to persevere, for those who enlist in a good cause seldom fail to success. We must need something of the kind, and let me say I do believe there is sufficient talent and influence among those of our own sex if it be called into action, to sustain a paper like yours, and that abundant success will attend the enterprise. Woman has done much, and it is in her power to accomplish much more, by raising the degraded of her own sex, and bringing from obscurity talents that would do honor to the literary world.[17]

Soon, however, Bloomer began to publish articles that discussed more controversial topics than temperance. At that point, a magazine that had been viewed as somewhat moderate became contentious. Bloomer began writing about topics such as mental and physical education for women and girls, legal protection for women who were married to drunkards, and the expansion of women's employment opportunities.

Despite the fact, however, that many of Bloomer's fellow women reformers had begun to speak out publicly in favor of woman's right to legal representation, Bloomer herself had not quite accepted the idea, as she revealed in the following editorial, entitled "Woman's Rights":

> It is not our right to hold office or to rule our country, that we would now advocate. Much, very much, must be done to elevate and improve the character and minds of our sex, before we are capable of ruling our own households as we ought, to say nothing of holding in our hands the reins of government.[18]

By the end of her first year as an editor, the woman who had claimed that she had "engaged in this enterprise without experience, or other qualifications,"[19] was becoming more comfortable with her powerful role as a groundbreaking pioneer and also began to be swayed by the more radical propositions of her sister reformers. Part of the reason for this was her budding relationship with Elizabeth Cady Stanton, who became a regular contributor to *The Lily* at the end of 1849 under the name "Sun Flower."[20]

Stanton's columns on women's enfranchisement and the legal injustices against women brought back painful memories from Amelia Bloomer's childhood that caused her to rethink her position on woman suffrage. Bloomer recalled that when she was fifteen, a dear family friend whose husband had died was left penniless when the bulk of the couple's estate reverted to the only living male relative, a distant cousin who was a virtual stranger to the family, because of laws that did not allow women to legally own property.[21]

Due to Bloomer's change in attitude, *The Lily* also saw changes in its second year. Gone was the majority of the poetry that had predominated during the first year. Also, the "Published by a Committee of Ladies" line was permanently eradicated, and Amelia Bloomer's name appeared alone at the top of each issue as editor and publisher. While the journal remained devoted to the temperance cause, the affiliation with the Ladies' Temperance Society ended in the second year. Most significant, though, was *The Lily*'s shift from purely a temperance journal to one that espoused the ideas and opinions of the controversial woman's rights movement.

In the first issue of the new year, Bloomer published an article by Stanton that said, "Among the many important questions of the day, there is none that more vitally affects the whole human family, than that which is technically termed woman rights."[22] This article demonstrated Bloomer's and the magazine's move away from the sole cause of temperance, and although Bloomer never strayed from her avid support of the temperance movement, she worked with equal enthusiasm for woman's rights. A series of articles by Stanton that examined and denigrated man's claim to intellectual and moral superiority over woman followed this one.[23]

Through her continued and more active participation in the woman's rights movement, Bloomer became convinced that American lawmakers were blind to the concerns of their female constituents and continued to enact legislation that was unfair and even detrimental to them. At the time, Bloomer was not an advocate for woman suffrage, but an event in 1850 changed Bloomer forever into a pioneer for woman's right to vote.

In February 1850, the Tennessee legislature, in debating women's right to own property, came to the conclusion that "women have no souls" and therefore "no right to hold property."[24] This bold pronouncement invoked the wrath of many outspoken women reformers, but none more than Amelia Bloomer, who wrote this biting editorial about the Tennessee lawmakers:

> Although it may be an easy matter for them [men] to arrive at such a conclusion [that women have no souls], it will be quite another thing to make women believe it. We are not so blind to the weakness and imperfections of man as to set his word above that of our Maker, or so ready to yield obedience to his laws as to place them before the laws of God. However blindly we may be led by him—however much we may yield to his acquired power over us, we cannot yet fall down and worship him as our superior.
>
> We have not deigned saying much ourself on the subject of "woman's rights," but we see and hear so much that is calculated to keep our sex

down, and impress us with a conviction of our inferiority and helplessness, that we feel compelled to act on the defensive, and stand for what we consider our just rights. . . . [W]e think it high time that women should open their eyes and look where they stand.[25]

With this forceful editorial, Bloomer started her journey as one of the most outspoken critics of the legislative process in America and one of the most vocal supporters of woman suffrage. From this point on, Bloomer used the pages of *The Lily* to crusade for woman's right to vote and even to run for political office if she so desired, saying in one forceful speech, "Woman has a right to vote for civil officers, to hold office, and so rule over men. If any law against it exists in the *Bible,* it has been overruled by divine sanction."[26]

These ideas were neither common nor popular and with the slightest mention touched off heated debates between supporters and detractors. Bloomer defied the conventional role of woman as seen and not heard and, although involved in an uphill battle, remained determined to show women that they were "worthy of receiving and capable of exercising the right to vote."[27] Although many people, even other women, stepped forward to oppose her, Bloomer remained steadfast in her beliefs and never failed to express them in the pages of her magazine.

Bloomer felt compelled to justify herself and refute her critics when she penned this column:

[T]he *Lily* is a woman's paper and one of its objects . . . is to open a medium through which woman's thoughts and aspirations might be developed. Gentlemen have no reason to complain if women avail themselves of this medium, and here dare utter aloud their thoughts, and protest against the wrongs and grievances which have been so long heaped upon their sex.[28]

For the remainder of the year 1850, Bloomer devoted herself to the work of promoting woman's rights and its various callings. Columns began to appear in *The Lily* that expressed Elizabeth Cady Stanton's opinion on divorce that because "all can freely and thoughtlessly enter into the married state, they should be allowed to come as freely and thoughtlessly out again."[29] While controversial sentiments like these drew much criticism for Bloomer, they were nothing compared to the furor she caused in 1851 when she took up the cause of dress reform.

It is perhaps the year 1851 for which Bloomer and *The Lily* are best remembered. In 1851 she was introduced to a new mode of female dress by Elizabeth Smith Miller, the daughter of abolitionist Gerrit Smith, who was spending the winter in Seneca Falls. During her honeymoon trip to Europe, Miller had taken to wearing an outfit that consisted of full "Turkish" pants underneath a dress that fell below the knees.[30] While absolutely tame by modern standards, the outfit in its time was considered scandalous, due to the short skirt and manly trousers. In the mid-nineteenth century, dresses were expected to sweep the floor in order to protect women's ankles, a particularly well-protected body part, from being seen, and trousers were worn only by men.

Women's attire in the 1800s was anything but comfortable. The long skirts, heavy petticoats, and binding corsets were cumbersome, at the least, and unhealthy, at the worst. Bloomer, inspired by Miller and a small group of radical individualists, became the outspoken champion of dress reform and began publicizing the new outfit through articles and illustrations in *The Lily*.

The topic of dress reform first graced the pages of *The Lily* in February 1851, when Bloomer published an announcement of the impending World's Fair, which was to be held in London and was to include a demonstration on improvements in women's attire. She included a written description of the outfit and suggested that for comfort and health's sake, women should throw aside their corsets and petticoats to adopt the new outfit.[31] In addition to Bloomer and Miller, several other prominent leaders of the woman's rights movement, such as Elizabeth Cady Stanton, Susan B. Anthony, Lucy Stone, and Sarah Grimke, adopted the new style, which was named the "bloomer costume" because, as one columnist put it, "Mrs. Bloomer, if not its inventor, has done more than any other to secure its adoption."[32]

The new mode of dress, which broke every rule of conventional femininity, caused controversy among both males and females, and women who chose to wear the outfit were often subjected to ridicule and scorn. Bloomer, aware of the widespread criticism of the dress reform movement, invited people to "give free vent to your feelings on the subject—praise or blame, approve or condemn. . . ."[33]

Vent their feelings they did. Never before had the mainstream press agreed so heartily on an issue. The *New York Herald* lashed out against the new outfit, saying that "women who throw off the delicacy of their sex are of no reputable stamp," and claimed that "this dress has been for twenty years worn in disreputable houses as a lure to the imagination."[34] The *New York Tribune* remarked, "We have never seen a female thus attired without an emotion of aversion."[35] Sarah Josepha Hale, the respected editor of *Godey's Lady's Book,* a leading fashion magazine, voiced her dislike for the Bloomer costume when she wrote:

> Let no criminal indolence or selfish indifference divert her from making the necessary exertions. Let her not weary of taking the trouble to look as agreeable as possible in her own house. . . . The true lady at home is the real lady elsewhere.[36]

The *New York Herald* pronounced that the leaders of the movement would "very likely soon end their career in the lunatic asylum, or, perchance, in the State Prison."[37]

The controversy raged on throughout the year as Bloomer began including engravings of herself and others wearing the outfit.[38] Eventually, however, despite Bloomer's attempts, interest in the dress reform movement began to die, and many of the women who had once donned the offending garments returned to wearing the acceptable fashions of the day. With the introduction of hoop skirts, a cooler and more comfortable type of undergarment, women were able to put aside their corsets and still wear the stylish fashions from Paris. Stanton and Anthony both gave up wearing the bloomer costume, and eventually even Bloomer herself put aside the outfit for her long skirts, although she would be spotted occasionally wearing the outfit while traveling.[39] Late in life, Bloomer explained her reasons for abandoning the dress reform movement:

> We all felt that the dress was drawing attention from what we thought to be of far greater importance—the question of woman's right to better education, to a wider field of employment, to better remuneration for her labour, and to the ballot for protection of her rights. In the minds of some people the short dress and woman's rights were inseparably connected. With us, the dress was but an incident, and we were not willing to sacrifice greater questions to it.[40]

Although the movement proved ultimately unsuccessful, bloomers, bloomer girls, and the dress reform movement of the 1800s put Amelia Bloomer's name in every modern dictionary and history book. As one writer acknowledged, "If ever a lady waked up one morning and found herself famous, that woman is Mrs. Bloomer; she has immortalized her name."[41] The movement also represented the first time that women had openly rebelled against accepted convention.

While Bloomer continued in her steadfast devotion to both her magazine and the cause of woman's rights, her personal life was undergoing significant change due to her husband's sudden announcement that they would be moving west. In 1854, Dexter purchased a newspaper, *The Western Home Visitor,* located in Mount Vernon, Ohio. Ever the dutiful wife and an equally dutiful editor, Bloomer packed her bags and assured her readers, "*The Lily* will continue to be published and its character will be in no wise changed."[42]

Things did not change, and once again Amelia Bloomer found herself in the midst of controversy. On moving to Ohio, Bloomer not only continued her duties on *The Lily* but also assumed the role of her husband's assistant editor. In March 1854, she hired a woman typesetter to work in the paper's office and help with *The Lily*. The male employees did not find this situation to their liking and declared a strike.[43] The walkout by the male printers prompted Amelia Bloomer to do something that she had always wanted to do and "resulted in the employment of women to set the type for the Visitor."[44]

Soon after this incident took place, Dexter Bloomer, who was increasingly interested in the novelty of westward expansion, sold his share in the newspaper and commenced on a tour of several western states, during which he decided to relocate to Council Bluffs, Iowa. Realizing that with "no facilities for printing and mailing a paper with so large a circulation . . . except a hand press and a stagecoach," Amelia Bloomer decided "it was best . . . to part with the *Lily*."[45]

After six years of hard work on her magazine, Bloomer found herself in the position of having to give up her work. She was not content, however, just to let *The Lily* die without a fight; so she made arrangements for Mary A. Birdsall of Richmond, Indiana, to take possession of the magazine for an undisclosed sum, in exchange for a promise that it would continue to "be published in the same form, and with the same general character."[46] Bloomer also retained the title of contributing editor and continued for a time to contribute columns on the progress of woman suffrage in the West.

In the last issue of *The Lily* published before Bloomer's leave-taking, she wrote of the magazine, of which she admitted she "never liked the name."[47]

> We have deeply cherished *The Lily*, and we have been greatly cheered by the daily evidence we have had of the good it was doing. This has encouraged us to go forward, even when we were nearly fainting over our self-imposed task. Home and husband being dearer to us than all beside, we cannot hesitate to sacrifice all for them. . . . For six years we have devoted the most of our time to *The Lily*—taking upon ourself the whole charge of the business, and doing most of the labor except presswork and composition. We need rest and relaxation—or at least a change of occupation. We have no good-byes to utter, inasmuch as we are still to have a part in *The Lily*—still to aid in preparing, and share in enjoying the intellectual feast which it will furnish to all who see fit to partake of it.[48]

With that, *The Lily* passed from Bloomer's hands and her significant influence. She wrote in one of her later columns: "Woman, after taking long years of inactivity and obscurity, is taking her place on the stage of action. Her part is yet to be performed—her history is not yet written."[49]

Bloomer's history, however, had already begun to be written. Even after her sale of *The Lily*, Bloomer continued her vocal support of woman's rights. Without Bloomer's leadership, however, the journal took on a more literary style.[50] Even at the time of *The Lily*'s discontinuance, Bloomer defended it:

> It had long outlived fun and ridicule and was highly respected and appreciated by its thousands of readers. It had done its work, it had scattered the seed that had sprung up and borne fruit a thousandfold. Its works can never die.[51]

Bloomer continued writing columns for various publications and making speeches throughout the country; and for almost forty years after the death of her beloved magazine, she continued to make herself heard as one of the most outspoken advocates of women's advancement until her death in 1894.[52]

Much has been written about Bloomer's enormous contribution to the women's movement, but very little has been said of her contribution to journalism. In truth, Bloomer, who, recalling her early days as an editor, said that she had "no experience, no education for business" and was "in no way fitted for such work,"[53] was a talented writer and editor with a head for running a successful publication.

Bloomer could be recognized as the pioneer behind the development of a new genre of magazine, known as women's advocacy magazines. While for years before *The Lily* there were publications run by women, never before had one been so solely devoted to the unique concerns of the female sex. Her magazine showed the possibility of success for smaller, more specialized publications, which led to a proliferation of advocacy magazines, such as the *Agitator,* * *The Revolution,* * *Sibyl,* * *Una,* * and others.

Bloomer also opened her pages to young women writers who were just beginning their careers as writers and reformers. While *The Lily* published contributions from many well-known reformers, it also served as a training ground for inexperienced female writers. Bloomer felt it her personal duty to help these aspiring authors and editors. Therefore, she explained, "The contents [of *The Lily*] are mostly original, and from the pens of women."[54]

Bloomer proved herself a courageous editor by tackling unpopular topics that other mainstream papers and magazines could only ridicule. However controversial the issue, though, Bloomer always used a tact and intelligence that even her staunchest enemies could not ignore, as the editor of the *Seneca County Courier* acknowledged in this editorial written at the time of the Bloomers' move from Seneca Falls:

Although we disapprove of some of the measures advocated in the *Lily*, we part with it and its worthy editor with sincere regret. It is now five years since its publication was commenced, and during the whole Mrs. Bloomer has had the entire direction of it, both editorially and financially, displaying talents and business qualifications possessed by few of the gentler sex and which but few of her friends were prepared to see her exhibit.[55]

Perhaps Bloomer's success at the business of journalism represents her most significant contribution. By carrying out her duties as writer, editor, and proprietor so successfully for so long, Bloomer exploded the myth that women could not handle work outside the home and proved that women could compete with men on equal ground. At its peak, *The Lily* boasted a circulation rate of six thousand, higher than that of some popular magazines for both men and women and any other advocacy magazine that followed in the nineteenth century.[56]

Notes

1. D. C. Bloomer, *Life and Writings of Amelia Bloomer* (Boston: Arena, 1895), p. 16. On this occasion, Dexter Bloomer offered his new bride a toast of champagne, to which Amelia Bloomer replied, "I cannot—I must not."

2. Ibid., pp. 19, 20. "Gloriana" and "Eugene" were just two of the names under which Amelia Bloomer wrote.

3. Ibid., pp. 34, 35, 36.

4. Ibid., p. 40.

5. January 1, 1849.

6. Bloomer, *Life and Writings,* p. 42.

7. Leon Stein, ed., *Lives to Remember* (New York: Arno Press, 1974), p. 362.

8. Ibid., p. 45.

9. January 1, 1849.

10. Bloomer, *Life and Writings,* p. 45.

11. Frank Luther Mott, *A History of American Magazines,* vol. 2. (Cambridge: Harvard University Press, 1938), p. 50.

12. Ibid., pp. 43, 44.

13. February 1, 1849.

14. April 2, 1849.

15. January 1, 1849.

16. March 1, 1849.

17. May 1, 1849.

18. October 1, 1849.

19. Ibid.

20. Bloomer, *Life and Writings,* p. 50. Amelia Bloomer acknowledged the presence of the, at that time, unknown Sun Flower in the December 1849 issue: "We publish today the first of a series of articles, which are promised us, over the above signature. We welcome the Sun Flower to our pages, and so long as it will act in concert with the *Lily,* for the promotion of good objects, we shall consider it a valuable auxiliary."

21. Bloomer, *Life and Writings,* pp. 47, 48.

22. January 1, 1850.

23. February 1, 1850. The series of articles, entitled "Man Superiority—Intellectually—Morally—Physically," began in this issue and continued for several months. Each article took an argument for man's superiority and countered it.

24. March 1, 1850.

25. Ibid.

26. Portion of a suffrage speech quoted in Bloomer, *Life and Writings,* p. 158.

27. Ibid., p. 59.

28. April 1, 1850.

29. Ibid.

30. Charles Neilson Gattey, *The Bloomer Girls* (London: Femina Books, 1967), pp. 55–57.

31. February 1, 1851.

32. *The Carpet Bag,* June 21, 1851, quoted in Stein, *Lives to Remember,* p. 365.

33. April 1, 1851.

34. *New York Herald,* June 11, 1851.

35. *New York Tribune,* June 12, 1851, quoted in Stein, *Lives to Remember,* p. 367.

36. *Godey's Lady's Book,* April 1875, p. 370.

37. *New York Herald,* May 21, 1851.

38. The first illustration of the outfit appeared in *The Lily* in September 1851. Soon, illustrations of women wearing the outfit began showing up in publications around the world.

39. Stein, *Lives to Remember,* pp. 371, 372.

40. Gattey, *The Bloomer Girls,* p. 113.

41. *New York Journal,* quoted in ibid., p. 82.

42. Bloomer, *Life and Writings,* pp. 142–145.

43. Ibid., pp. 149, 175, 176.

44. Ibid.

45. Bloomer, *Life and Writings,* p. 187.

46. December 15, 1854.

47. Bloomer, *Life and Writings,* p. 49.

48. December 15, 1854.

49. February 15, 1855 and December 15, 1854.

50. Marion Marzolf, *Up from the Footnote: A History of Women Journalists* (New York: Hastings House, 1977), p. 224.

51. Bloomer, *Life and Writings,* p. 188.

52. Ibid., p. 322.

53. Private letter quoted in Mott, *A History of American Magazines,* vol. 2, p. 52.

54. December 1, 1852.

55. *Seneca County Courier,* December 1853, quoted in Bloomer, *Life and Writings,* p. 145.

56. Marzolf, *Up from the Footnote,* p. 221.

Information Sources

BIBLIOGRAPHY:
Bloomer, D. C. *Life and Writings of Amelia Bloomer.* Boston: Arena, 1895.
Gattey, Charles Nelson. *The Bloomer Girls.* London: Femina Books, 1967.
Marzolf, Marion. *Up from the Footnote: A History of Women Journalists.* New York: Hastings House, 1977.
Mott, Frank Luther. *A History of American Magazines.* Vol. 2. Cambridge: Harvard University Press, 1938.
Stein, Leon, ed. *Lives to Remember.* New York: Arno Press, 1974.
INDEX SOURCES: None.
LOCATION SOURCES: New York Historical Society; Minnesota Historical Society; Columbia University (New York) library and other libraries.

Publication History

PERIODICAL TITLE AND TITLE CHANGES: *The Lily.*
VOLUME AND ISSUE DATA: Vols. 1–8 (January 1, 1849–1859?). Monthly (1849–1853); semimonthly (1853–1856); frequency unknown 1956–1959.
PUBLISHER AND PLACE OF PUBLICATION: Amelia Bloomer (1849–1854); Mary B. Birdsall (1855–1856). Seneca Falls, N.Y. (1849–1853); Mt. Vernon, Ohio (1854); Richmond, Ind. (1855–1859?).

EDITORS: Amelia Bloomer with Anna C. Mattison (January and February 1849); Amelia Bloomer (March 1849–1854); Mary B. Birdsall (1855–1856).
CIRCULATION: Marzolf, p. 221: 6,000 (at its peak).

Barry Wise Smith

THE LOWELL OFFERING

When a sixteen-page magazine of stories, poetry, sketches, recollections, and vignettes appeared in an inexpensive yellow cover in October 1840, the journal's authors never expected that their literary endeavor would attract both national and international attention. It was not the magazine's contents that attracted attention, but rather the authors themselves—female textile workers from the mills of Lowell, Massachusetts.

The Lowell Offering was initially an experimental product of the city's so-called improvement circles—literary clubs where factory women penned stories, poems, loose philosophical tracts, autobiographical sketches, and various essays. As historian Philip Foner noted: "The circles were fostered and encouraged by the clergymen of Lowell and by the mill owners, who looked with favor upon their employees devoting themselves to culture rather than to complaining about their conditions in the mills and acting together to remedy them."[1]

Harriot F. Curtis, later an editor of *The Lowell Offering,* proposed the first improvement circle in 1837. A second, larger circle was formed and supervised by the Reverend A. Charles Thomas, the pastor of Lowell's Second Universalist Church. The magazine emerged from this group.[2] Thomas served as *The Offering*'s editor for its first two years of publication. The first volume of four issues appeared irregularly between October 1840 and March 1841 but afterward began appearing monthly. Issues cost six and one-quarter cents per copy. *Offering* contributor Harriet Robinson noted that the initial experiment was so successful that a regular monthly series began in earnest in 1841.[3] The magazine averaged thirty-two pages per issue. Besides the fiction and editorial commentary, each issue featured numerous essays such as "The Death of My Mother," "A Visit in the Country," "A Picnic Party," "Recollections of My Childhood," "Seasons," "Forgiveness," and "The Sleigh Ride." A number of serialized novels and songs, complete with music scores, also appeared. Fine engravings of Lowell's churches illustrated the volumes.

The little journal and Lowell's female operatives rose to international fame after English visitors, particularly author Charles Dickens and the Reverend William Scoresby, marveled that factory operatives, particularly females, were not only highly literate but capable of producing works of fiction and nonfiction. Dickens, in his *American Notes,* said, "Of the merits of *The Lowell Offering,* as a literary production, I will only observe—putting out of sight the fact of the articles having been written by these girls after the arduous hours of the day— that it will compare advantageously with a great many English annuals."[4] Scoresby proclaimed the magazine "the ninth wonder of the world, considering the source from which it comes.''[5] A book of selections edited from the first two volumes was issued in London in 1844 and republished in Boston the following year, under the title *Mind among the Spindles.*

Only a small number of the city's factory women actually wrote for *The Lowell Offering* and a few subsequent factory publications, however, as historian Thomas Bender noted: ''[T]he contrast with [workers in] Manchester, England, apparently was so sharp that the New England mill girls were celebrated throughout Europe and America for their intelligence and virtue.''[6]

The Lowell Offering existed because so many of the city's female factory workers—mostly American-born farm women—were literate.[7] Lowell's international fame came not so much from its model factories as from the literacy of its workers. Visitors marveled that female millworkers could usually be seen with books in hand. Many of the women tacked pages from the Bible to their looms in order to read them throughout the day. Other women, *Offering* contributor Harriet Robinson recalled, would write in their spare moments. ''The literary girls among us would often be seen writing on scraps of paper which we hid between whiles in the waste-boxes upon which we sat while waiting for the looms or frames to need attention,'' Robinson said.[8]

Lowell factory owners purposely hired women more than they did children or men because they believed young farm women were a reliable source of labor. Until the power loom was invented in 1827 by Samuel Slater in Rhode Island, cloth mills were small and required few workers. Slater and other mill owners did not even do the weaving at their mills, preferring instead to send yarn to farms for women to weave on their own. The power loom was a complex piece of equipment, which mill owners initially thought was too complicated for children to run. Owners turned instead to farm women as a source of labor, believing that women would complain less than men and would stay longer at their jobs. Men were more likely to leave quickly, often for the frontier.[9]

In order to attract the women to Lowell's factories, however, mill owners had to convince farmers that their daughters would be safe. The solution was to make millwork appear a respectable occupation. As such, mill owners initially paid good wages and established a series of boardinghouses and a strict moral code. Most mills required female operatives to live in boardinghouses owned and operated by the factories. Widows served as matrons, and the houses were run by strict rules: all workers had to attend church on Sundays, only those assigned to the boardinghouses could live in them, doors were locked at 10 P.M., no coarse language or immoral behavior was tolerated, and rooms—which were shared—were to be kept clean.[10]

Lowell offered the women a chance to experience something that many had never experienced before—city life. Women could get away from small towns and discover a world of newly emerging libraries, lectures, adult education classes, concerts, and city fashions. Although many of the women needed the wages factories offered to help their families, the lure of the city and of having their own money for the first time drew women.

Lowell Offering writer Lucy Larcom recalled: ''We had all been fairly educated at public or private schools, and many of us were resolutely bent upon obtaining a better education. Very few were among us without some distinct plan for bettering the condition of themselves and those they loved."[11]

The Lowell Offering provided more than just a literary outlet for factory women striving to improve themselves. It also served as a vehicle from which factory operatives could defend their work and station in life. A Boston magazine editor, Orestes Brownson, attacked factory women's virtue in his magazine, the *Boston Quarterly Review,* by stating that factory girls could not "ever return to their native places with reputations unimpaired. 'She has worked in a factory,' is sufficient to damn to infamy the most worthy and virtuous girl," he said. Similarly, other members of the public looked down upon female operatives, calling them "cotton bugs."

The Lowell Offering's writers used the pages of their magazine to set the record straight. Millworkers, according to the magazine, were virtuous, moral, literate, and almost always seeking to improve themselves intellectually. Harriet Farley responded to Brownson's attack in the December 1840 issue of the magazine by stating that Brownson had slandered the workers. "No virtuous girl of common sense would choose for an occupation one that would consign her to infamy."[12] Similarly, editor Thomas noted in the October 1840 editorial: "Confessedly, wherever there exists any depravity or ignorance, there is too much of it. We have this to testify, however, that they who know least of the people of Lowell, including the Factory Operatives, entertain the most unworthy and unjust opinions of them. Close personal observation has satisfied us, that in respect of morality and intelligence, they will not suffer in comparison with the inhabitants of any part of moral and enlightened New England." Other articles that defended workers' virtue and a serialized novel, *Prejudice against Labor,* appeared throughout the first few volumes of the magazine.[13]

The Offering's writers regularly presented and promoted factory work as a dignified means of making one's living. For example, an 1842 article noted:

> To be able to earn one's own living by laboring with the hands, should be reckoned among female accomplishments; and I hope the time is not far distant when none of my countrywomen will be ashamed to have it known that they are better versed in useful, then they are in ornamental accomplishments.[14]

Although many factory women contributed articles, poems, and various sketches to the magazine, *The Lowell Offering* was not a labor magazine, nor did it pretend to be. The magazine gave a rosy picture of factory life, calling millwork pleasurable and presenting Lowell as an extension of bucolic, pastoral life, rather than a humming company town. One author noted:

> In the mills, we are not so far from God and nature, as many persons might suppose. We cultivate, and enjoy much pleasure in cultivating flow-

ers and plants. A large and beautiful variety of plants is placed around the walls of the rooms, giving them more the appearance of a flower garden than a workshop. It is there we inhale the sweet perfume of the rose, the lily, and geranium; and, with them, send the sweet incense of sincere gratitude to the bountiful Giver of these rich blessings.

The article added that "another great source of pleasure" for workers was to send money home to their parents.[15] The article paints a far different picture from that seen by inspectors—humid factories filled with cotton dust because windows were nailed shut.

The women who wrote for *The Offering* were undoubtedly sincere in their views of factory life. Indeed, Harriet Farley genuinely appeared to have believed factory rules were not too strict: "Neither have I ever discovered that any restraints were imposed upon us, but those which were necessary for the peace and comfort of the whole, and for the promotion of the designs for which we are collected, namely, to get money, as much of it and as fast as we can."[16]

Both factory workers of the time and modern-day scholars have criticized the journal for failing to support laborers' interests, particularly the fight for a ten-hour workday. A competing Lowell publication, *The Voice of Industry,* better represented laborers' needs and exposed the "model" mill system's shortcomings. Indeed, a Lowell labor leader, John Quincy Adams Thayer, said of *The Offering:*

This unfortunate publication roves over the country, even to other lands, bearing on its deceptive bosom a continual repetition of notes, less valuable to the reader than to the writer, but destructive to both; leaving behind the abuses and downward progress of the operatives, the very part which becomes their life, liberty, and greatness to give to the world, even if they were compelled to write the record with blood from their own veins.[17]

This first generation of factory labor had many legitimate grievances—twelve-hour days, poor ventilation in mills and boardinghouses, short meal breaks, and wage reductions coupled with boardinghouse rent increases, to name but a few. Millworkers' lives were far from the picture presented by *The Lowell Offering.* Many workers suffered serious illnesses, including hundreds of cases of typhoid in the 1840s, varicose veins, muscular conditions, and other illnesses.[18] Many textile workers in the United States died in fires as well, since it was common practice to literally lock workers into mills during their shifts.

Because *The Lowell Offering* was funded by Lowell textile magnate Amos Lawrence, the magazine was rarely critical of conditions in the city's mills and boardinghouses. What criticisms did appear were relatively mild in tone. Thomas' final editorial, for example, called for shorter working hours, the creation of a hospital fund to pay sick workers' bills, better ventilation in boardinghouses (although he said nothing of the mills), and the creation of libraries in the mills for workers.[19] But Thomas laid no blame; he merely requested the changes. Similarly, Harriet Farley stated in an October 1843 editorial that ''it is much easier to instill a feeling of self-respect, of desire for excellence, among a well-paid, than an ill-paid class of operatives. There is a feeling of independence, a desire to form and retain a good character, a wish to do something for others.''[20] She did not take the argument any further, however, or blame any specific factory owners.

Most discussions of work or living conditions were found on the editorial pages. The magazine's editors did not lobby hard for changes, because they were convinced that working conditions in the mills were no worse than at any other job. Furthermore, they believed themselves powerless to change any wrongs. In the November 1842 issue, for example, the editors stated, ''With wages, board, etc., we have nothing to do—these depend upon circumstances over which we can have no control.''[21] Similarly, the May 1843 editorial denied that factories were unhealthy. ''We believe there is as much good health here as in any place with the same population. True, there are causes existing here unfavorable to constant and perfect health. There is confinement for twelve hours a day . . . and this confinement in a room without a free circulation of air—sometimes a room warmed with steam, giving each laborer . . . 'a moist unpleasant body.' There is hurried eating, and sometimes in rooms at a far lower temperature than that of the mills.'' Yet, the editorial added that workers were no less healthy than other workers in New England, ''[b]ecause those physical laws which are violated in the mills, are almost equally violated throughout New England.''[22] Sometimes *The Lowell Offering*'s editors told readers that factory work was actually better than other labor. ''We are better and more regularly paid than most other female operatives. Our factory life is not often our all of life—it is but an episode in the grand drama and one which often has its attractions as well as its repulsions,'' Farley noted in an 1844 editorial.[23]

One of *The Lowell Offering*'s strongest criticisms was not directed at the mills or boardinghouses, but at street peddlers. A December 1843 editorial noted that newsboys, candy salesmen, shoe salesmen, book peddlers, and others came to the boardinghouses in the evenings, ''breaking in upon the only hours of leisure we can call our own, and proffering their articles with a pertinacity which will admit of no denial. That these evening salesmen are always unwelcome, we will not assert, but they are too often inclined to remain where they know they are considered a nuisance.''[24]

When the magazine's editors placed blame, often operatives, not employers, were targets—particularly those workers who supported the emerging labor reform movements. For example, in the August 1843 issue, Harriet Farley wrote:

We do not think the employers perfect; neither do we think the operatives so. Both parties have their faults, and to stand between them as an umpire is no easy task. The operatives would have us continually ring the changes upon the selfishness, avarice, pride, and tyranny of their employers. We do not believe they possess these faults in the degree they would have us represent them; we believe they are as just, generous, and kind as other businessmen in their business transactions.

Later in the article Farley chastised workers who supported labor reform:

What can we think of those who wish to make the *Offering* a medium for their avarice and ill will? We could do nothing to regulate the price of wages if we would; we would not if we could—at least we would not make that a prominent subject in our pages, for we believe there are things of even more importance.[25]

The editors expressed such views because they did not see themselves as permanent members of the working class. Many of the women spent only a few years in the mills, then were married, moved west, or pursued some other occupation, such as teaching. Lucy Larcom wrote, "For what were we? Girls who were working in a factory for the time, to be sure; but none of us had the least idea of continuing at the kind of work permanently."[26]

Not surprisingly, *The Lowell Offering*'s biggest supporters were upper-class readers outside Lowell. Although the magazine's editors rarely made mention of this fact, Harriet Farley acknowledged, despairingly, in an August 1845 editorial, that the workers she so hoped to reach did not support the journal. Speaking of herself, Farley said:

[T]o hear herself spoken of as a vile tool for aristocratic tyrants, or an absolute imposter—her magazine represented as a hoax; and the support of that class, whom she has most wished to serve, almost entirely withdrawn all this has been trial enough for one to contend with.[27]

The magazine's editors occasionally acknowledged that at least some operatives disagreed with *The Offering*'s views on factory life, yet the editors steadfastly maintained they were not wrong. For example, the December 1841 editorial stated that objections had been launched against the magazine:

We have been accused by those who seem to wish us no ill, of disingenuousness, and unfaithfulness to ourselves, as exponents of the general character and state of feeling among the female population of this city. They say the *Offering,* if indeed it be the organ of the factory girls, is not a true organ. It does not expose all the evils, and miseries, and mortifications, attendant upon a factory life. It speaks, they say, on only one side of the question. . . . We however challenge anyone to prove that we have made false assertions.[28]

Similarly, the June 1843 editorial noted that some readers disagreed with a previous editorial on workers' health:

> Some of the remarks in our last number upon health have been thought, by a few, to be incorrect. We have listened to their objections, and hearing nothing to cause us to change our opinion. And, moreover, some of the operatives themselves, and very intelligent and judicious girls too, have come to us, to express their entire concurrence in our statements.[29]

The Lowell Offering ceased after five volumes in December 1845. In the closing editorial, Harriet Farley stayed her genteel course. She reiterated that the purpose of the magazine was to place female operatives "upon a level with other New England females." Farley also again stated that the mill system need not be denounced nor apologized for. Labor was not excessive, ventilation was adequate, and overseers were generally like brothers or fathers to their workers.

> And where an absolute quarrel arises between an overseer and one of his help—a quarrel in which the girl is not favored by the superintendent, we believe herself to be in fault. Girls with unregulated feelings are more common here than men who would be unjust and unkind to females under their care.

Yet, Farley acknowledged that the magazine was ending because the very workers she wrote for failed to support *The Lowell Offering*. In a rebuff to critics, Farley stated: "Had the number of our mill subscribers been greater, we might have treated these subjects [i.e., labor problems] more frequently and minutely. But those who were our patrons needed not our advice or counsel. And those who might have profited, were the class who would not heed us."[30]

Despite its genteel and, some would say, incorrect presentation of factory life, *The Lowell Offering* is worthy of its place in history. Not only did it demonstrate that factory operatives could rise above society's expectations of them, but the magazine also spawned a host of other factory operative publications in New England in the 1840s, most of which did focus on inequalities, including a Lowell competitor, *The Operatives' Magazine* (later known as the *Operatives' Magazine and Lowell Album*), *The Olive Leaf, Factory Girl's Repository* of Cabotville, Massachusetts, *The Wampanoag and Operatives' Journal* of Fall River, Massachusetts, the New Market, New Hampshire-based publication, *The Factory Girl, The Factory Girls' Garland* of Exeter, New Hampshire, and the *Factory Girl's Album and Operative's Advocate*, also of Exeter.

Furthermore, a number of *The Offering*'s contributors went on to later fame as writers, editors, novelists, teachers, artists, and other creative professionals.[31]

Harriet Farley reestablished the magazine under the title *The New England Offering* in September 1847. She resumed publication again under the same name in April 1848. It lasted until March 1850. However, Farley seemed to encounter the same lack of support for her new *Offering* as she did with the earlier publication. She later married, raised a family, and in 1880 published a volume of Christmas stories.

Notes

1. Philip S. Foner, *The Factory Girls* (Urbana: University of Illinois Press, 1977), p. 26.

2. A. Charles Thomas, "Editor's Preface," March 1841, pp. iii–iv; Maria Currier, "Improvement Circle," January 1845, p. 11; Harriet H. Robinson, *Loom and Spindle* (Kailua, Hawaii: Press Pacifica, 1976), p. 61. Robinson noted that by 1843 at least five improvement circles existed for both men and women to read and criticize each other's work.

3. Robinson, *Loom and Spindle,* p. 63.

4. Reprinted in ibid., p. 67.

5. Quoted in Foner, *The Factory Girls,* p. 27.

6. Thomas Bender, *Toward an Urban Vision* (Baltimore: Johns Hopkins University Press, 1975, p. 35.

7. Helen L. Sumner, *History of Women in Industry in the United States* (New York: Arno Press, 1974), pp. 88–89.

8. Robinson, *Loom and Spindle,* p. 59.

9. Bender, *Toward an Urban Vision,* p. 38.

10. Sumner, *History of Women in Industry in the United States,* pp. 88–89; Bender, *Toward an Urban Vision,* p. 35.

11. "The Editor's Table," *The New England Magazine,* December 1889, p. 471.

12. "Factory Girls," December 1940, p. 17.

13. "Editorial Corner," October 1840, p. 32. In vol. 1, see "Prejudice against Labor," Chapter 1, pp. 136–145, and "Aristocracy of Employment," pp. 268–273.

14. C. B., "Dignity of Labor," June 1842, p. 192.

15. S.G.B., "Pleasures of Factory Life," October 1840, p. 26. In the same issue, see Abigail, "A Merrimack Reverie," pp. 29–30, and "Editorial Corner: Plants and Flowers in the Mills," p. 32.

16. "Factory Girls," December 1840, p. 17.

17. Quoted in Sumner, *A History of Women in Industry,* p. 90.

18. Ibid, p. 103.

19. "Editor's Valedictory," December 1842, p. 380. See also "Plan for Mutual Relief," February 1841, p. 48.

20. Editorial, October 1843, p. 48.

21. Editorial, November 1842, p. 48.

22. Editorial, May 1845, p. 191.

23. Editorial, September 1844, p. 262.

24. Editorial, December 1843, p. 69.

25. Harriet Farley, Editorial, August 1843, p. 284.

26. "The Editors Table," *New England Magazine,* December 1889, p. 471.

27. Harriet Farley, Editorial, August 1845, p. 190.

28. "Conclusion of the Volume," December 1841, pp. 375–376.

29. Editorial, June 1843, p. 215.

30. Editorial, December 1845, pp. 279–282.
31. Robinson, *Loom and Spindle,* pp. 79–119.

Information Sources

BIBLIOGRAPHY:
"The Editors' Table." *New England Magazine,* December 1889, pp. 470–472.
"The Editors' Table." *New England Magazine,* February 1890, pp. 711–712.
Bender, Thomas. *Toward an Urban Vision.* Baltimore: Johns Hopkins University Press, 1975.
Foner, Philip S. ed. *The Factory Girls.* Urbana: University of Illinois Press, 1977.
Robinson, Harriet H. *Loom and Spindle.* Kailua, Hawaii: Press Pacifica, 1976.
Sumner, Helen L. *History of Women in Industry in the United States.* Washington, D.C.: Government Printing Office, 1910 (reprinted New York: Arno Press, 1974).
INDEX SOURCES: None.
LOCATION SOURCES: Library of Congress and other libraries. Microfilm available from Library of Congress and in American Periodical Series.

Publication History

PERIODICAL TITLE AND TITLE CHANGES: *The Lowell Offering* (October 1840–December 1845); *The New England Offering* (September 1847, April 1848–March 1850).
VOLUME AND ISSUE DATA: Vols. 1–7 (October 1841–March 1850). Monthly but irregular (October 1840–March 1841); (new series) monthly (April 1841–December 1845, September 1847, April 1848–March 1850, No publication was issued January 1846 to August 1847).
PUBLISHER AND PLACE OF PUBLICATION: A. Watson (1840–March 1841); Powers and Bagley (1841–1842); W. Schouler (1843); Curtis and Farley (1844–1845); Harriet Farley (1847–1850). Lowell, Mass.
EDITORS: A. Charles Thomas (1840–1842); Harriet Farley (1842–1845, 1847–1850); Harriot F. Curtis (coeditor) (1843–1845); Harriet Farley (1847–1850).
CIRCULATION: Unknown.

Mary M. Cronin

M

MAJORITY REPORT

The New York–based feminist periodical *Majority Report* spanned the 1970s. It reflected a multiplicity of feminist groups and informed many independent feminists in greater New York City and beyond on the issues and events that were central to the progress of women's liberation. From a "mimeographed newsletter"[1] to a twenty-page tabloid, *Majority Report* was published as the product of a collective. Launched by the Women's Strike Coalition, a woman's rights group, the publication soon loosed its socialist ties and formed a publishing group called FOCAS. Later it was independently, but still collectively, published.

The Women's Strike Coalition (WSC) was a women's liberation movement organization made up of diverse New York-area groups and individuals drawn together by their agreement on three major goals: "(1) [f]ree abortion on demand, no forced sterilization, (2) [f]ree, 24-hour child care centers, community controlled, (3) [e]qual job and education opportunities for women."[2] The coalition was formed in order to organize the Women's Strike of August 26, 1970, a nationwide march for woman's rights. Nine months later the coalition established *Majority Report* to "dispense information, encourage participation, and provide support. We intend to arm our sisters with the consciousness and the unity to fight our oppression."[3]

Although the coalition started *Majority Report* with the intention of publishing regularly, the second issue was late, and there was evidence of transition within the organization.

> [W]e are only now beginning to form a true alliance of feminist groups in the NY area. Demands, actions, even our name—all are subject to revitalization and drastic change so that WSC can serve as a unifying

force. What we become is up to you. Consult your group about joining
with us for political effectiveness.[4]

This politically motivated plea for membership was coupled with the group's
admission of financial strain and a call for newsletter volunteers. Although recognizing that the newsletter filled a "long-needed communication link among
feminist groups in the New York area," lack of finances nearly forced the group
"to put off a second issue indefinitely." But motivated by "widespread response, especially to the calendar and factual reports on the movement," the
group came out with the second number. "We have given up the idea of giving
up. After all, if things get worse, we can always go to print with a kiddy rubber
stamp set on the backs of Right-to-Life leaflets."[5]

The coalition also faced other challenges from within. Many of the feminists
united through this organization had come by way of leftist political activism,
specifically the Socialist Workers' Party (SWP). The coalition was realizing the
sexism of the Left and that the stigma of the SWP was hindering both the
coalition's feminist policy making and its recruitment of more feminists.

From the start, an editorial collective ran the newsletter. "The staff consists
of 12 women, all equally owners, and all sharing the work of the paper. Editorial
decisions are made democratically."[6] Nevertheless, Nancy Borman, who had
been involved editorially with the publication since its inception, seemed to
provide guidance and consistency throughout the magazine's decade of transi-
tions with its publishing groups and editorial office locations. Borman was an
outspoken member of the New York chapter of the National Organization for
Women.[7] It was to her in Jamaica, New York, that correspondence was forwarded when the collective was in transition. Her name appears on the cover
of the first issue as one of the "sisters who contributed to and helped produce
Majority Report,"[8] the mainstream press identified her as editor when she represented the publication,[9] and she is listed as the publisher during the last year
of its operation.[10]

It was recognized early at *Majority Report* that publishing a newsletter could
be "a financial burden and a frustration," and the editorial collective sought to
have the publication's pages more fully reflect the editorial approach. *Majority
Report* proposed a truly "*collective* newsletter," offering itself as a vehicle for
disseminating feminist groups' newsletters—for a mailing list and printing costs.
In exchange, each feminist group would receive "quality printing," "a huge
circulation," "an organized staff," and "publication every two weeks." *Majority Report* also offered inexpensive advertising, prompt distribution, and the
promise that "all materials will be printed *intact,* free from editing." The offer
also included "a full-page dedicated to the problems of consciousness-raising
including on-going communication on this subject."[11]

Majority Report was envisioned as an organized format in which a diversity
of feminist views could be presented and a forum through which feminist groups
could communicate with each other. "We would like to see one issue dedicated

to each group's statement of purpose, identity, structure, etc. In this way we can have an understanding of each group involved in the Women's Liberation Movement." *Majority Report* saw its offer of an affordable and accessible feminist medium as a vehicle for the subversion of mainstream patriarchal media. The magazine made

> more than just an offer of services; it is a *plea* for the solidarity and support of *all* women towards the creation of *our own* medium! We must get our heads and actions together to counter-attack the male-chauvinist backlash pervading the mass media today. We welcome and encourage all ideas and inquiries regarding this new and very important venture. So much is happening so quickly that we *must* communicate rapidly to make this idea *reality*.[12]

The publication's fourth issue emerged under a reorganized publishing group that evolved from the Women's Strike Coalition and called itself FOCAS, an acronym for Feminist Organization for Communication, Action and Service. FOCAS charged that the Socialist Workers' Party had abandoned the coalition near the end of May, leaving the coalition with the burden of over three thousand dollars in unpaid bills. So, the coalition

> decided to abandon the albatross and to start FOCAS in order to carry on the intended goals of the new WSC
>
> Since June the WSC changed tactics from mass women's actions to strategic feminist actions. . . . [W]e sustained the coalition newsletter, *Majority Report,* beyond its first issue.[13]

Majority Report was central to the mission of the reorganized group, which offered its support to any women's liberation movement actions by groups in the region. "Our newsletter, *Majority Report,* will be turned into a collective newsletter by inviting all feminist and women's groups in the . . . area to use it as their own newsletter," FOCAS articulated.[14] With "Sisters: let's fight our newsletter problems together," *Majority Report* reaffirmed its commitment to the idea of its being a collective newsletter as "an important step for the basic unification of our movement through a communications link. Let's beat the media by creating our own."[15]

Dissatisfaction with their association with the Socialist Workers' Party escalated as FOCAS pulled support from SWP-supported actions. The fight was taken up by a group sharing the newsletter, Gay-Women's Liberation Front (G-WLF). G-WLF denounced an abortion march as a conspiratorial attempt by the Socialist Workers Party to "gain a better stronghold in the Women's Movement."[16] It pulled support from the Women's National Abortion Action Coalition march in November 1971. "It was no surprise to us, who have been fighting the stigma of 'THE LESBIAN ISSUE' in and out of the women's movement that lesbian rights were the first to be written off."[17]

Other groups shared their uncensored views in their pages within *Majority Report* over the years, many coming and going in the span of just a few issues. *Majority Report* generally sympathized editorially with each of the groups that inserted newsletters of their own; the publication did not fill itself with disclaimers for others' information or opinions. One of the only long-running newsletter inserts in this collective newsletter was provided by the National Organization for Women (NOW), which began its NOW York Woman Section in *Majority Report* in 1972. That this was not a perfect marriage can be charted through the issues, with biting back-and-forth comments between the *Majority Report* pages and the NOW pages. At the center of the conflict were often the differences between radical and liberal feminist perspectives, resulting in rejoinders such as NOW's sardonic, "We apologize to our members for assuming a sisterliness where only a yellow hue exists."[18] Headlining this issue of *Majority Report* was "equal time" allotted to radical respondent Ti-Grace Atkison, who was not allowed equal mainstream media time to counter accusations made by NOW activist Betty Friedan.[19]

Issues were full of topics near and dear to feminists' hearts. In particular, the publication retained its focus on consciousness-raising groups; debates raged on whether to allow use of the slang phrasing "women's lib" and what to do with the Miss America pageants. Abortion legislation remained a primary focus; lesbian rights were a constant push, as was the equal rights amendment; rape was an issue often explored; self-defense techniques and classes, particularly karate, were regularly covered; prostitution was often given the investigative spotlight. The publication ran feminist cartoons, such as "Greta the Greeze Monkey," and comic strips on occasion, including the political cartoon "Doonesbury" because of its character, Ms. Caucus.

Majority Report showed its concern with mainstream media, particularly by exploding the cultural myths patriarchal media propagated. For example, the publication cited a *Redbook* study that revealed that women generally held empathy with the women's movement, contrary to the mass media myth that the movement's goals and sentiments represented a fractional minority of the population.[20] *Majority Report* pointed the finger when women's mainstream media bought into negative and divisive myths, such as when *Cosmopolitan* advised Aquarians, "Treat any female as a rival."[21]

The newsletter issued a popular monthly calendar of feminist events that included events such as woman's rights marches, art openings and performances, alternative media schedules, classes, conferences, and, of course, potluck dinners and consciousness-raising sessions. It ran a feminist business directory that was eventually expanded into an international directory of services.

Majority Report had accepted advertising from the beginning. Its initial issue posed an answer to the alternative question, "Need to reach the most possible Women's Liberation organizations & individual feminists in the NY area? Advertise in MAJORITY REPORT.''[22] Primarily because of its modest rates, it accumulated a healthy feminist advertising base over the years, which featured a variety of services and goods, from truck driving to day care. Advertising was consistently drawn from other feminist publications, whether or not they used *Majority Report* as the vehicle for their pages.

Although it was reported that ''America's Least Ladylike Newspaper''[23] published twenty-six issues in 1979 and planned the same publishing schedule for 1980,[24] it appears that the last number of this publication that provided feminists a collective alternative for nearly a decade came out on April 20, 1979.

Notes

1. Cynthia Ellen Harrison, *Women's Movement Media: A Source Guide* (New York: R. R. Bowker, 1975), p. 20.
2. ''About Us,'' May 10, 1971, p. 2.
3. Ibid.
4. Women's Strike Coalition, ''Looking Inward,'' June 2, 1971, front.
5. ''Please Forgive Us,'' June 2, 1971, front.
6. Harrison, *Women's Movement Media,* p. 20.
7. See, for example, Francis X. Clines, ''Equalizing of State Pensions Urged for Male and Female Teachers,'' *New York Times.* March 3, 1972, p. 27.
8. May 10, 1971, front.
9. See, for example, Joseph B. Treaster, ''U.S. Journals Have Printed Atom Bomb Directions,'' *New York Times,* March 11, 1979, p. 21.
10. January 1–February 20, 1979, publisher's box, p. 2.
11. ''Feminist Groups: *Majority Report* Can Be Your Newsletter,'' June 28, 1971, p. [8].
12. Ibid.
13. ''FOCAS,'' August 26, 1971, p. [1].
14. Ibid.
15. ''Collective Newsletter,'' August 26, 1971, p. [10].
16. ''Hell No We Won't Go!!'' ''G-WLF,'' November 1971, p. 16.
17. Ibid.
18. ''. . . an apology,'' editorial, ''The NOW York Woman Section,'' April 1973, p. 9.
19. Ti-Grace Atkison, ''Betty Friedan, the C. I. A. & Me,'' April 1973, p. [1].
20. ''What Women Think of Feminism,'' May 1972, p. 4.
21. ''Feminist News Briefs,'' June 2, 1971, p. 6.
22. May 10, 1971, p. 4.
23. Subhead, publisher's box, January 1–February 20, 1979, p. 2.
24. Len Fulton and Ellen Ferber, eds., *The International Directory of Little Magazines and Small Presses, 1980–1981,* 16th ed. (Paradise, Calif.: Dustbooks, 1980) p. 238.

Information Sources

BIBLIOGRAPHY:

Fulton, Len, and Ellen Ferber, eds. *The International Directory of Little Magazines and Small Presses 1980–1981.* 16th ed. Paradise, Calif.: Dustbooks, 1980, p. 238.

Harrison, Cynthia Ellen. *Women's Movement Media: A Source Guide.* New York: R. R.
    Bowker, 1975.
Treaster, Joseph B. "U.S. Journals Have Printed Atom Bomb Directions." *New York
    Times,* March 11, 1979, p. 21.
INDEX SOURCES: Women Studies Abstracts.
LOCATION SOURCES: Schlesinger Library on the History of Women in America.
    Microfilmed in the Herstory and Underground Newspaper collections.

Publication History

PERIODICAL TITLE AND TITLE CHANGES: *Majority Report.*
VOLUME AND ISSUE DATA: Vols. 1–8 (May 10, 1971–April 20, 1979). Biweekly
    (May–June 1971); monthly (October 1971–1974); biweekly (1974–1979). (Some
    irregularities.)
PUBLISHER AND PLACE OF PUBLICATION: Women's Strike Coalition (May 10,
    1971–June 28, 1971); FOCAS (Feminist Organization for Communication, Action
    and Service) (1971–1972); New York Area Feminists (1972–1973); The Majority
    Report Co. (1973–1979). New York.
EDITORS: Editorial collective, probably guided by Nancy Borman (1971–1979).
CIRCULATION: Harrison, 1975: over 11,500.

Therese L. Lueck

MEDIA REPORT TO WOMEN

Media Report to Women (MRTW) first appeared June 12, 1972, as a free, mimeographed newsletter that became monthly in 1974, published by the Women's Institute for Freedom of the Press in Washington, D.C. Donna Allen, an economist, civil rights activist, and former university teacher, originated this first feminist media monitor and edited it for its first fifteen years. From the beginning this publication was a vital source of media content about women and information about the status and working conditions of women in the mass media professions. The newsletter serves as an information network among its readers.

   The newsletter introduced paid subscriptions, ten dollars for women and fifteen dollars for men (until the equal rights amendment [ERA] passed), in January 1974, and in 1974 converted to printed form. In just six months hundreds of readers had written to request the publication, which published the facts, actions, ideas, and philosophy reflecting what women were doing and thinking to change the communications media. Allen hoped to reach thousands of readers at a time when the feminist movement was increasingly visible, and people inside and outside the media professions recognized the cultural significance of the mass media in contemporary society. (The circulation remains under five thousand.)

   Also in 1974, with the shift to paid subscriptions, the institute was split off from the newsletter in order to continue its nonprofit work in research and education. *Media Report to Women* was placed on a self-sustaining basis, with

Donna Allen continuing as editor. *MRTW* became bimonthly in 1983 (quarterly in 1992) and in 1987 had new owners, Communication Research Associates, Inc., in Silver Spring, Maryland, with editor Sheila Gibbons and publisher Ray E. Hiebert, both professors at the University of Maryland.[1]

The institute announced its media philosophy in 1973:

According to the First Amendment, freedom of the press belongs to everyone, not just those who own the media. We must find ways for all Americans to have equal access to their fellow citizens—so people can get to know each other as they really are, not as interpreted by others, and so the public can hear and benefit from the contributions of all of us.[2]

MRTW promised it would "continue to provide excerpts from original sources, such as the text of negotiated agreements with broadcast, print or other media, and to quote the actual words of the women who are themselves doing the action and thinking, rather than our opinion . . . report on major communication progress by all people, of any sex, race, creed, color, national origin, or eocnomic level, in addition to our principal reporting of what women are doing and thinking about the communications media and other media events and information of concern to women."[3]

Readers and researchers can turn to this publication to track all significant developments regarding the employment of women in the mass media, women's caucuses, and affirmative action plans and legal challenges in print and broadcast media, research reports of mass media content on feminist issues, stereotyping, sexist language and image, reports on new feminist groups, minority groups and publications, books and media, and the status of women in academic journalism. Reports from Canada and other countries are regularly included. *MRTW* often presents material not published in any other source and culls items from an impressive range of published sources that are impossible to monitor on an individual basis.

The files of *MRTW*, therefore, now provide one of the richest sources for research on the changing conditions for women in the mass media and the perceptions about women in mass media content.[4]

Not only does this newsletter digest the ongoing events and issues, but it also provides names and addresses and contacts, so readers can obtain complete copies of articles, books, and reports or contact the interested organizations or publishers. In 1975 *MRTW* began publishing a regular index to its issues, as well as an extensive directory of women's media.

The indexes also include the institute's seven assumptions for a new philosophy of communication:

1. People make their judgments on the basis of information they have at a given time.

2. Each person is the best judge of her or his own best interest.

3. Media owners give us the information they think it is important for us to know.

4. Media do not mirror society. They represent the owner's views.

5. For the public to obtain the information of the majority, people must be able to speak for themselves.

6. Power is based on the number of people you can reach with your information.

7. Equalizing power among us would require that we all have equal means of reaching the public to communicate our information when we wish, in the way most suitable to our message.[5]

The first three years of *MRTW* covered in detail such important issues as the equal rights amendment and license renewal challenges at WABC-TV in New York City and at WRC-TV (NBC) in Washington, D. C. The newsletter gave explanations of the laws and regulations and samples of how to petition the Federal Communications Commission (FCC) about content, examples of sexist on-air put-downs of women by television reporters and of sexism in language of textbooks and advertising. It announced new femnist publications and the first *MORE* magazine national media conference on women in the media in New York City in 1975.[6]

MRTW continued to cover the important sexual discrimination complaints and Equal Employment Opportunity Commission (EEOC) actions brought by groups of media women in the early 1970s, including those against the *Washington Post, Newsday, New York Times,* the Associated Press, United Press International, *St. Louis Post Dispatch,* the *Detroit News, Readers' Digest, Time,* and *Newsweek,* and complaints settled in the late 1970s and early 1980s are reported in *MRTW.* The *New York Times* women's caucus also supplied tips on how to organize and gather information on hiring, promotion, and salary practices.[7] A special issue covering the *New York Times* settlement was published in December 1978.[8]

National and international meetings pertaining to women and media were regularly announced and reported in *MRTW,* including the World Conference of Women in Copenhagen, July 1980, in Narobi in 1985, and in Mexico in 1990, where women journalists and editors not only covered the events for the international media but also published a daily news report for the conference.[9]

Employment figures, salary, and status comparisons for women in most fields of mass media work have been important, continuing features in the newsletter, including studies of women in newspaper policy-making jobs, 1981–1987, by Dorothy Jurney, former women's editor at the *Detroit Free Press* and *Philadelphia Inquirer,* and regular comparisons of women and men in news employment by Jean Gaddy Wilson, director of New Directions for News at the

University of Missouri, and the status and pay surveys of women at the top by the National Federation of Presswomen.[10]

The pages of *MRTW* record the gradual increase in numbers of women in mass media employment, the continuing pay disparities, and slow encroachment into management ranks. There are similar studies of women educators in journalism and communication departments, where faculty progress is painfully slow, even as women students are now in the majority. In general, the numbers of women in media grew during the 1970s as the doors were opened but began to level off in the 1980s. The Radio and Television News Directors Association (RTNDA) survey in 1990 reports little change for women in broadcast newsrooms during the past decade.[11] Weaver and Wilhoit's 1993 national study finds more women and better pay in the newsrooms but notes that women are still 34 percent of the total, as they were in 1982–1983.[12]

Research reports from scholarly conventions and individually published studies are highlighted in every newsletter, and these indicate the vast range of topics and vitality of this new field of study. The first courses on women in journalism began in 1972, and *MRTW* began offering prizes for the best course outlines in 1979. Later these were compiled in a *Syllabus Sourcebook on Media and Women,* a project continued by the Commission on the Status of Women in the Association for Education in Journalism and Mass Communication.[13]

Several newsletters document the distorted and incomplete media reporting of the equal rights amendment (ERA), rape, and abortion issues by leading newspapers and television news. The ERA study showed that leading newspapers failed to provide the basic facts about the amendment, its wording, its status as states began to ratify, and where to obtain more information. Moreover, there was little difference in reporting of the ERA in 1977 and 1981.[14]

The backlash against feminism and stories heralding a "postfeminist era" (suggesting the women's movement was dead) are reported in recent years, along with continuing information about new women's media organizations like JAWS (Journalism and Women Seminar), founded in 1987, activities of African-American and Hispanic women in media, the Gannett Foundation's endowment of the Women, Men, and Media Center in 1990 (recently moved to New York University) to monitor media progress, discussions on reporting rape and pornography, announcements about dozens of books and research on women and media, new courses, film studies, and *Ms.* magazine's reappearance without ads and dedicated to worldwide coverage of women.[15]

In 1990 *MRTW* noted a new concern from publishers worried about the loss of women readers of the daily newspapers. Newspaper leaders still did not know what women wanted to read in the daily newspapers and sought advice from women media consultants. The new weekly tabloid section, WOMANEWS at the *Chicago Tribune,* was successful enough to spark interest and encourage other new sections for women at several newspapers.[16] As some experienced editors pointed out, women lost a voice when old sections were converted to lifestyle/entertainment sections.[17]

The recent issues of *MRTW,* now a quarterly, follow the newsletter's original philosophy. But with only eight or twelve pages four times a year, it's impossible to cover as much as Allen and her staff did in sixteen or twenty-four monthly pages. The price has risen over the years for individual subscribers, to fifteen dollars in 1978, twenty-five dollars in 1987, and thirty dollars in 1991. A group of around a hundred sustaining subscribers, whose names were first published in 1979 when they paid twenty-five dollars, now pays forty dollars a year to express their support.[18]

Allen announced that the newsletter was for sale at the end of 1986, and a new buyer was found in 1987. By 1988 the current editor, Sheila J. Gibbons, was in place, and Donna Allen writes a regular column. The institute celebrated twenty years of activism in April 1992 and continues to publish reports and books. Allen has given her *MRTW* and institute archives to the National Women and Media Collection at the University of Missouri. She was awarded the Outstanding Women in Journalism Education Award in 1988.[19] Donna Allen was first attracted to journalism in high school, and although she worked as a reporter while she was in college, she majored in history and economics and developed a lifelong interest in the labor movement and political democracy. She worked with union movement and civil rights groups in Chicago and in Washington, D.C., before founding her newsletter. Since 1968, she has been working to change the media images and stereotypes of women and to allow them to speak for themselves.[20]

During its lifetime, *Media Report to Women* has announced the beginnings of hundreds of organizations, magazines, and newsletters, radio, television, and cable programs, and special women's sections or feminist newspapers. It has published hundreds of academic job openings in an effort to attract more women to college and university teaching of journalism and mass media. *MRTW* reflects the vitality and dynamism of hundreds of women who have been engaged with these issues during the contemporary women's movement and continues to do so for a new generation that is finding its own issues and forming new caucuses and associations. It still provides the most reliable and continuing source of this specialized information and feminist research and serves a network of readers, including professional journalists, scholars, and activists.

Notes

1. May/June 1988.
2. "Notice to Readers," undated, author's personal copy.
3. "Notice to Readers," undated, author's personal copy.
4. Files of the *MRTW* archives and a complete run of the newsletter are located at the University of Missouri–Columbia National Women and Media Collection.
5. *Index/Directory of Women's Media* (Washington, D.C.: Women's Institute for Freedom of the Press, 1979), p. 55.
6. June 1972 and December 1975.

7. December 1974.

8. December 31, 1978.

9. September/October 1985. The papers of Marjorie B. Paxson, who edited the United Nations (UN) daily publication, are located in the National Women and Media Collection. University of Missouri–Columbia.

10. November 1981, p. 1; March/April 1986, p. 7; January/April 1987, p. 10; March/April 1989, p. 3; July/August 1990, p. 1.

11. September/October 1990, p. 1.

12. Winter 1993, p. 1.

13. Contact the Association for Education in Journalism and Mass Communication (AEJMC) national headquarters at the University of South Carolina for information on later syllabi compiled by Marion Marzolf.

14. September 1982, p. 1.

15. May/June 1990, p. 1.

16. May/June 1990, p. 3.

17. January/February 1991, p. 1.

18. Based on the author's collection of *MRTW*.

19. Association for Education and Mass Communication, *Women's Words,* March 1994, p. 5.

20. Donna Allen Papers, National Women and Media Collection, University of Missouri-Columbia. See "A Life of Communication as Political Participation in Democracy through People Speaking for Themselves," her biography essay, first installment.

Information Sources

BIBLIOGRAPHY:

Allen, Martha-Leslie, ed. *1986 Index/Directory of Women's Media.* Washington, D.C.: Women's Institute for Freedom of the Press, 1986.

Beasley, Maurine. "Donna Allen and the Women's Institute: A Feminist Perspective on the First Amendment." Paper presented at American Journalism Historians Association, annual meeting, Philadelphia, October 3–5, 1991.

Busby, Linda. "Broadcast Education: Courses on Women, Minorities and the Mass Media." Paper presented at National Association of Educational Broadcasters, national meeting, Washington, D.C., November 13–17, 1977.

Donna Allen Papers, National Women and Media Collection, University of Missouri–Columbia.

Mikutowicz, Sharon. "Women in the Media." *Publishers' Auxiliary,* July 25, 1975, p. 2.

INDEX SOURCES: Chicana Index: Film Literature Index; Human Rights Internet Reporter; Women's Studies Abstracts.

LOCATION SOURCES: National Women and Media Collection, University of Missouri–Columbia Library, and many other libraries.

Publication History

PERIODICAL TITLE AND TITLE CHANGES: *Media Report to Women.*

VOLUME AND ISSUE DATA: Vols. 1– (June 12, 1972–present). Monthly with some combined issues (1972–1983); bimonthly (1983–1991); quarterly (1992–present).

PUBLISHER AND PLACE OF PUBLICATION: Women's Institute for Freedom on the
    Press (1972–1987); Communication Research Associates Inc. (1987–present).
    Washington, D.C. (1972–1987); Silver Spring, Md. (1987–present).
EDITORS: Donna Allen (1972–1987); Sheila Gibbons (1987–present).
CIRCULATION: Under 5,000.

Marion Marzolf

N

NATIONAL BUSINESS WOMAN

Out of the fervor of a national gathering of women in St. Louis in 1919, a publication sprang, seemingly spontaneously. *The Bulletin,* informally dubbed *Can Happen,* was formalized and renamed *The Independent Woman* the next year. It carried a subhead for the organization that also sprang from that convention: *Official Bulletin of the National Federation of Business and Professional Women's Clubs.* Published continuously until 1956, when it was renamed *National Business Woman,* the magazine remains the official organ for the federation, which now refers to itself as Business and Professional Women/USA (BPW/USA).

The Independent Woman emerged in 1920, glistening from the glow of that 1919 excitement. The first issue of *The Independent Woman* in January 1920 carried the number "2" to acknowledge the conference bulletin as the magazine's official start. The periodical characterized its beginning as a type of birthing experience; "conceived in the enthusiasm of the convention, nurtured by the kindly interest of our club women everywhere, the little magazine has come into being."[1] The bulletin was evidence that women from forty-three states gathered[2] and formed a national organization, uniting isolated local business and professional women's clubs.

Published in New York, the magazine was national in scope from its beginning. The first issue carried news from many cities on the East Coast and from the Midwest and from as far west as Boise, Idaho.[3]

To extend an inviting welcome to *The Independent Woman*'s editor, the federation's eloquent executive secretary, Lena Madeson Phillips, graciously downplayed the earlier production of *The Bulletin,* characterizing it as makeshift. A "spasmodic and intermittent career, it was without editor, copy, subscription list or advertisement."[4]

The January 1920 issue came out bearing a look that would characterize the magazine well into the decade and a mission to keep businesswomen informed. On its cover, a silhouette captured Judge Jean Norris in "her most judicial attitude." The caption proudly read, "The First and Only Woman Judge of a New York Court."[5] The cover portrait served more than a decorative purpose; it illustrated the intent of the magazine. "It is suggestive of the high honors to which women may now aspire, and also, in its dignity and feminine grace, we think it typifies the best that woman has to contribute to public life."[6]

The sixteen-page magazine found form, strength, and a voice through its editor, Ida Clyde Clarke, book author and magazine contributor. In her first editorial, she stated, "We believe that there is a distinct need for a medium of expression for the ideals upon which our federation was founded, as well as for an interchange of ideas among the widely separated clubs."[7] From matters of production to editorial content, she proclaimed an open-minded stance. Noting the magazine's new form, she hoped that it would please the readership but invited readers' comments because the staff was not "wedded to any set of ideas as to how *The Independent Woman* should appear or what it should contain. It belongs to *you,* and you may make it what you will."[8] She also demurred, "We have no editorial views to air, no theories to expound, no startling facts to record. Rather we would be the mirror to reflect what others think and say and do."[9] Yet, on that same page she could not help but express editorial views:

> At last we may have discovered why our Government pays men more than it pays women. With marvelous psychological understanding of the deeper currents of a woman's being, some statistician has discovered "that single women, as a rule, living in boarding houses, will feel the necessity for a reasonable amount of amusement. Assuming that some of these expenses will be met by young men, the amount allowed in this budget need not be very large."
>
> Yes, this statement is solemnly given in one of the recent bulletins from the United States Department of Labor. . . . [H]aving figured out how many petticoats, union suits, and rubber heels a woman needs a year, this statistician generously allows the woman Government worker the munificent sum of about 39 cents a week for recreation![10]

Clarke brought with her Floy Pascal Cowan, who was "experienced in the preparation and writing of material."[11] But Clarke laid editorial responsibilities on the readership. "We do not expect you to be satisfied with *The Independent Woman*. . . . [R]emember, it is not altogether an editorial job. . . . Send in your suggestions and see how quickly we will act upon them."[12] Clarke railed against reader apathy, particularly when displayed by women in business. At the same time, she touched on financial considerations:

> While there was at the St. Louis convention a strong sentiment for some kind of an official organ, the magazine can not be considered an organic activity of the Federation. There is no specific fund provided for it in the first year's budget.[13]

Although carrying the flag of official organ, the magazine was nevertheless on its own as the association organized. Not having a budget, the editor realized the importance of a strong advertising base.[14] From its first issue in 1920, *The Independent Woman* carried advertising, the bulk of which was women's business cards. The advertising base soon expanded as the publication got a foothold in the business and professional women's community, a community it was helping to create. Circulation grew quickly, and *The Independent Woman* recorded the gains.[15]

The magazine highlighted women and their achievements in business and the professions, eschewing narrow definitions of "profession" to embrace secretaries, bookkeepers, physicians, civil servants, educators, and lawyers.[16] It ran announcements from clubs across the nation and occasional international pieces. It kept a focus on the women's lack of equity in wages and resources, issues often sardonically decried in editorials. For instance, a profession was mentioned in which a man named "Babe" had a contract for $125,000: "There is a certain very lucrative field—diamond shaped . . . women have not entered. It is a clean, wholesome, all-American field, too, though essentially and probably forever masculine. . . . Wish we had some nice little 'fields' like that."[17] Relevant legislation, particularly with regard to the workplace, was covered, as well as what action women could take to help a measure. The magazine treated suffrage as a given, although it was not national until August 1920. Candidates who curried the female vote with "Let the women vote," were mocked. "Isn't it kind of them! They might say with just as much generosity, 'Let the water run downhill.' "[18] After enfranchisement, the publication ran articles to keep women informed of their rights and duties.

> Inside the front cover of the magazine ran the federation's OBJECTS: To promote the interests of business and professional women; to secure combined action by them; to gather and distribute information relative to vocational opportunity; to stimulate local and state organizations and cooperation among business and professional women of the several states of the United States.[19]

The magazine's mission was integrally tied to that of the organization, recording and paralleling the growth of the federation. From the beginning, though, this connection between the publication and the organization often confounded editorial considerations. For instance, the staff dubbed the magazine *The Independent Woman,*[20] but going into the 1920 convention, the editor warned, "*The Independent Woman* may have an entirely new name; it may have new policies, a new form, a new kind of content."[21] However, the organization retained the name of the publication and officially adopted it as the federation's bulletin. At that time, the federation numbered at least 225 clubs.[22] The magazine benefited from the organization's growth. Circulation went from five hundred to five thousand, with two thousand of these paid subscribers.[23]

The editor soon saw editing a magazine as more than she had bargained for, especially with its being a representative of a fledgling organization. Clarke planned to leave as editor after the 1920 convention. She proposed that the magazine have a paid staff and that a committee be formed to establish a budget and business plan.[24] Clearly, the new magazine—in spite of the circulation growth and advertising revenue—needed the consistent support of the organization. *The Independent Woman* had cost the federation nearly $3,000 its first year; $1,978 was received from subscriptions, and $904.46 from advertising.[25]

After the convention, Clarke left the country. No editor's name ran on the mast from July through January 1921. Clarke resumed the editorship when she returned to the country, no doubt with some urging from the ever-eloquent Phillips.[26] But Clarke did not stay long in that position. From May through July 1921, again, no editor was listed. Nevertheless, the magazine retained its form. It also continued editorials, in all probability thanks to Phillips, who remained the constant through editorial gaps until August 1922, when a new federation executive secretary was elected.

In August 1921, a new editor was culled from federation ranks, but when her tenure was finished in February 1923, there was again no editor listed, although Georgia Emery may have been acting as editor. She was listed as chairman of the standing "Official Bulletin" Committee, which had been formed upon Clarke's recommendation. This confusion of editorial titles persists to the present. Over most of its history editors have come and gone without comment. Titles have also changed: editor in chief was used on occasion; in the 1970s, it was magazine director; and in the 1990s, the titles publications director and senior editor have been used. Indeed, in some of the modern issues, the federation–bulletin linkage has often fused the voice of the federation president with that of the magazine editor. There is no longer an editorial, but always a presidential message; the sporadically run "letters" department is not always answered with an editorial voice.

The magazine has gone through several graphic personalities. Covers and contents have gone through numerous shifts since the mid-1920s, when occasional halftones were used on covers. One color was introduced on the cover and sometimes brought inside, which became fairly characteristic until recent years. The 1930s saw several bold design changes in the prevailing art deco style of the period.

By the late 1920s, issues were paginated consecutively for the year, a practice that was to continue until the mid-1950s. The subhead became *A Magazine for Business and Professional Women,* with the federation an acronym at the bottom of the cover. Design and editorial changes have not always coincided with a change of editors or for any perceivable editorial enhancement. At times, the magazine seems to have lost its identity to serve as merely an information mouthpiece of the federation.

An updated mission statement ran on the editorial pages beginning in the mid-1930s:

> The Independent Woman will serve as a forum for women in the new social order. In line with the Ten Year Objective of the National Federation of Business and Professional Women's Clubs, it will present constructive ideas aiming toward social justice, as well as news of women's contribution in many fields. Widely varying viewpoints will be published upon which readers' comment is invited.[27]

By the 1940s, departments became more regular. Of course, federation news was always the major focus of coverage. Prominent also were stories keeping women abreast of national and international affairs. Women's achievements were still highlighted. More personal columns were introduced, along with poetry and more book reviews.

In the fall of 1956, The Independent Woman became history as the magazine changed its name to National Business Woman, which it remains today. Some objected to the name change, particularly because it left out a portion of the membership—professional women.[28] By then a magazine of over thirty pages, the publication initiated the name change with a serialized salute to the regions and a section called "Careers Unlimited." Contents included articles by women and men on topics from public relations to electronics. An international focus became a staple through articles on the United Nations, particularly its human rights campaigns. In 1959, "The U.N. Corner" became a department.

In 1956, the federation secured a Victorian home in Washington, D.C., which became its headquarters in 1957. With this move came an increase in political coverage, not only legislation but Capitol personalities as well. The national organization's president, Hazel Palmer, was visible in Washington circles as well as on the pages of the magazine. For instance, Palmer discussed women in business with First Lady Mamie Eisenhower and India's Indira Gandhi at a White House luncheon and covered it for the magazine.[29] Despite the changeover in editors that the move to Washington occasioned, the magazine adapted to its the new environment. The move rejuvenated the push for "equal rights, equal pay" during the latter 1950s, reflecting the sentiment of the national organization, which had adopted an equal rights platform at its 1956 biennial convention.[30] Palmer proclaimed the importance of the equal rights amendment to business and professional women, calling it "our number one legislative item."[31]

The 1960s brought several editorial mixes and format revisions. More articles ran with bylines, and in 1965 the masthead proclaimed the magazine "Winner of Three Freedoms Foundation Awards."[32] Although generally on a monthly publication schedule, the summers still ran a combined August–September convention issue. In 1968, the magazine adjusted its volume numbering so it would coincide with the association's fiftieth anniversary in 1969.[33] Throughout 1969, articles excerpted moments from the organization's initiation.

By the 1970s, the editor was called the magazine director, and the updated federation objectives, which retained much of the organization's original aims, with an added emphasis on education, ran on the contents page.

To elevate the standards for women in business and in the professions.

To promote the interests of business and professional women.

To bring about a spirit of cooperation among business and professional women of the United States.

To extend opportunities to business and professional women through education along lines of industrial, scientific, and vocational activities.[34]

In the 1970s, a newspaper insert, "BPW ACTION," was included in the issues, which focused on legislative action. A rallying cry in the early 1970s was for passage and ratification of the equal rights amendment (ERA). "ERA: IT HAS TO BE IN '73," was the call from every level of the federation. The second vice president reminded readers, "State ratification of ERA is a top priority item!"[35] *National Business Woman* did not abandon its press for the failed amendment, reviving the call throughout the 1980s; in the 1990s, the text of the ERA runs in a box below the editorial box. Political action and women's achievements at every level of legislature remain a focus of the magazine.

The look of the magazine remained fairly consistent and unimaginative from the 1970s through the 1990s, with the notable exception of a dramatic shift in format for nearly two years in the late 1980s, which corresponded to the editorship of Karen Suchenski. The "magtab" was a cross between a magazine and a tabloid.[36] After Suchenski's departure as editor, the magazine returned to the same basic format it had had prior to the "magtab."

In the mid-1990s, the thirty-four-page magazine comes out quarterly, usually running a full-color front and a full-page color advertisement on the back cover. Issues regularly carry legislative updates and critiques, as well as address BPW actions and membership. BPW foundation news primarily focuses on educational sponsorship, such as scholarships for workingwomen.

The magazine has chronicled—and continues to chronicle—the BPW organization and to track issues of importance to women who work outside the home, especially in professional life. Over the years, the publication rallied support for movements to advance women in public life, particularly supporting woman suffrage and, later, the ERA.

Notes

1. Ida Clyde Clarke, "Please Page This Woman," February 1920, p. 4.

2. Ida Clyde Clarke, "We Greet You and Entreat You," January 1920, p. 4.

3. "Chips from the Woodshop," January 1920, p. 11.

4. Lena Madeson Phillips, "Our New Editor," January 1920, p. 3.

5. Ida Clyde Clarke, "This Month's Cover," January 1920, p. 5. The cutout was supplied by Sarah E. Cowan, who did much of the early cover art (caption, January 1920, cover).

6. Clarke, "This Month's Cover."

7. Ida Clyde Clarke, "A Little Shop Talk," January 1920, p. 4.

8. Ibid.

9. Ibid.

10. Ida Clyde Clarke, "It Is to Laugh," January 1920, p. 5.

11. Phillips, "Our New Editor."

12. Ida Clyde Clarke, "Just a Minute, Please!" February 1920, p. 4.

13. Clarke, "Please Page This Woman."

14. Ida Clyde Clarke, "Eliminate the Vacuum," February 1920, p. 4.

15. For example, a Cowan silhouette showed a woman receiving mail. "A letter from the Altrusa Club of Louisville, Ky., containing thirty-eight subscriptions—Flora M. Smith, Office Executive, National Headquarters, registers, 'expectancy,' " April 1920, cover.

16. "The Convention's Professional Roll Call," August 1920, p. 11.

17. Ida Clyde Clarke, "A Womanless Field," editorial, May 1920, p. 5.

18. Ida Clyde Clarke, "*Let the Women Vote,*" February 1920, p. 5.

19. January 1920, p. [2].

20. Ida Clyde Clarke, "Born an Orphan," February 1920, p. 4.

21. Ida Clyde Clarke, "Is Your Light under a Bushel?" July 1920, p. 5.

22. Ida Clyde Clarke, "It Has Been Done," June 1920, p. 4.

23. Ibid.

24. " 'We Pledge Allegiance—' " August 1920, p. 5.

25. "Report of the Independent Woman," October 1920, p. 9.

26. Lena Madeson Phillips, box, January 1921, p. 6.

27. January 1935, p. 4?

28. Florence E. Loose, letter, November 1956, p. 23.

29. "White House Luncheon," February 1957, p. 15.

30. See, for example, March 1957, pp. 6, 8, 30; Hazel Palmer, "Work for Equal Legal Rights," April 1957, p. 2; July 1957, cover (and focus of the issue's contents).

31. Hazel Palmer, "A Year of Achievement," August 1957, p. 17.

32. November 1965, contents page; awards from the Freedoms Foundation at Valley Forge "For Outstanding Achievement in Bringing about a Better Understanding of the American Way of Life," 1954, 1960, 1961, and 1973 (quoted from the awards, in a communication with Julianne O'Gara, public relations, BPW/USA, November 3, 1995).

33. "NBW Owns Up to Its Age," January 1968, p. 2.

34. January 1973, p. [3].

35. Maxine Hays, "Plus Two," January 1973, p. [2].

36. Karen Suchenski, "Welcome to the New *National Business Woman:* Letter from the Editor," August/September 1986, p. 3.

Information Sources

BIBLIOGRAPHY:
A History of the National Federation of Business and Professional Women's Clubs, Inc.
Washington, D.C.: National Federation of Business and Professional Women's
Clubs, 1994.
INDEX SOURCES: Self-indexed; Magazine Index, Personnel Literature, Work Related
Abstract.
LOCATION SOURCES: Cleveland Public, University of Akron (Ohio), and other li-
braries.

Publication History

MAGAZINE TITLE AND TITLE CHANGES: *The Bulletin* (also called *Can Happen*)
(July 1919); *The Independent Woman* (1920–1956); *National Business Woman*
(1956–present).
VOLUME AND ISSUE DATA: Vols. 1– (1919–present). (No volume 47 or 48 due to
a volume-numbering adjustment made in 1968.) Monthly (January 1920–1980);
bimonthly (1981–1989); quarterly (1989–present).
PUBLISHER AND PLACE OF PUBLICATION: National Federation of Business and
Professional Women's Clubs, Inc. St. Louis (1919); New York (1920–1956);
Washington, D.C. (1957–present).
EDITORS: Lillian Carr and Louise Dooley? (1919); Ida Clyde Clarke (1920–1921);
Elizabeth Sears (1921–1923); Ruth Rich (1924–1926); Alice P. N. Waller (1926–
1927); Helen Havener (1927–1932); Winifred Willson (1932–1943); Frances
Maule (1943–1955); Faye Marley (1956); Bonnie Crenshaw Kowall (1956–1957);
Sue Timberlake (1957); Marian K. Stocker (1957); Lucy Rogers Baggett (1958–
1970); Lola S. Tilden (1971–1976); Louise G. Wheeler (1976–1980); Bonnie L.
Shelton (1980–1983); Leah K. Glasheen (1983–1986); Karen Suchenski (1986–
1987); Jan Stevens (1987–1988); Maryanne Sugarman Costa (1989–1993); Marcia Eldridge (1993–present).
CIRCULATION: Ulrich's, 1994–1995: 75,000 (paid).

Therese L. Lueck

THE NATIONAL CITIZEN AND BALLOT BOX

Although *The Ballot Box* (renamed later *The National Citizen and Ballot Box*)
had been launched by the Toledo (Ohio) Woman Suffrage Association, it was
not solely the voice of that group. From its launch, it had a broader mission—
and circulation. The editor reported on suffrage activities throughout the nation
and regularly updated readers about activities within the National Woman Suffrage Association (NWSA). That type of coverage brought in subscribers from
all over the nation. Thus, it was natural that Matilda Gage of the NWSA would
formally purchase the monthly, move it to Syracuse, New York, and transform
it *officially* into the organ of the NWSA. What was surprising was its death.
The *National Citizen* became a victim of Gage's involvement in the preparation

of what became *History of Woman Suffrage.* Unable to do both projects, Gage gave up the newspaper.

The Ballot Box premiered in April 1876 in Toledo, Ohio. However, its roots date back to 1869, when woman's rights activists Susan B. Anthony and Elizabeth Cady Stanton stopped in the city during a lecture tour. A Toledo suffrage group was born at that time. By 1871, a local newspaper, the *Sunday Journal,* offered the association a half-column; Sarah Langdon Williams was picked to write it. The half-column quickly grew to a full page. When the newspaper was sold in 1875, the association began work to start its own newspaper. With the financial support of some unidentified Toledoans, *The Ballot Box* became a reality.[1] Williams, at the time president of the Toledo suffrage group, was named managing editor and continued in that position until the newspaper was sold.

Williams' *Ballot Box* was a lively monthly newspaper that was financially self-supporting. Its financial success was based on both a strong, growing national circulation and a sound, primarily local advertising base.

Toledo merchants and manufacturers began advertising in the newspaper from the very beginning. The advertisers ranged from bankers to dry goods merchants, from druggists to importers.[2] However, Williams never drew national advertisers to her periodical, even though the newspaper soon attracted a national following.

Williams credited Anthony for the newspaper's growing national circulation. Once Anthony's own newspaper, *The Revolution,** died, the activist began soliciting subscriptions for Williams' publication.[3] The relatively low price to subscribe (one dollar per year) and the "radical" (by nineteenth-century standards) content, no doubt, were the reasons Anthony urged those who attended her lectures to subscribe.

That "radical" content had been guaranteed from the first issue. An "old friend" applauded the newspaper's launch because clearly the suffrage movement needed a voice:

> Certainly a movement, which like the aggressive advocacy of Woman Suffrage, directly antagonizes the narrow views and senseless prejudices of moss-grown, self-sufficent foggyism, needs a channel through which unremittingly to pour truth into the popular mind.[4]

The small monthly (only four pages in length) carried out its pledge. In both its news and its editorials, *The Ballot Box* never seemed to lose its vision. The newspaper gave the NWSA as much, or more, news coverage than the Toledo group. Certainly, *The Ballot Box* announced local meetings and updated readers on local activities. However, the managing editor also covered extensively national conventions as well as news from suffrage groups in other states.[5] Indeed, in its coverage of the NWSA's "Declaration of Rights of Women of the United States," *The Ballot Box* not only carried the full declaration but also the responses from many states.[6]

Similarly, Williams did not limit editorials to local issues and events. Although the newspaper sometimes directed its comments against local personalities who held antisuffrage points of view (a sermon by the Reverend Charles Cravens at one of the Toledo Unitarian churches was called one of the "corruptions of the period"[7]), the largest number of editorials dealt with national issues and events. The political parties that refused to endorse woman suffrage especially riled Williams. In 1876, when the Democratic Party ignored the topic, and the Republican Party skirted the issue, Williams applauded the National Prohibition Party for its courage in adopting "an unmistakable woman suffrage plank." In contrast, the Democrats ignored the issue "with silent contempt," and the Republicans approached it "with an insipid and meaningless sop of flattery."[8]

Although these stands caused a certain measure of controversy, *The Ballot Box*'s comments on religion and certain ministers seemed to get the newspaper the greatest amount of criticism. From its first year, Williams offered a certain measure of criticism about elements of Christian doctrine that said women were inferior to their husbands.[9] When certain readers opposed the newspaper's positive comments on revivalists who supported suffrage, Williams wrote she welcomed any supporters—whatever their denomination.

> The BALLOT BOX does not aim to sit in judgment upon the advocates of any religious faith. Its sole purpose is the advancement of women's civil and political enfranchisement, and to further this it welcomes aid from all who believe that woman should no longer occupy the civil and political position of the felon, the fool and the life-long minor.[10]

Although suffrage remained the primary focus of the periodical, *The Ballot Box* also editorially addressed other issues affecting women. The monthly editorially supported equal pay for equal work (especially for teachers) and workingwomen who feared for their livelihood.[11]

The Ballot Box soon caught the attention of many leaders in the NWSA. Both Stanton and Anthony wrote to *The Ballot Box,* and their letters were reprinted. In one, Stanton even urged women to leave in the middle of the sermon if the minister preached women's subjugation.

> The point of offense in the woman suffrage movement is just this, we demand complete equality of rights everywhere; in the halls of legislation, in the courts, in the pulpit, at the fireside.[12]

This tenor, this content, this approach seemed to bring the newspaper notoriety, subscribers, advertisers,[13] and financial stability. However, it did not bring Williams peace. In 1877, the November issue was delayed because of the death of Williams' daughter. Five months later, Williams sold the newspaper to Matilda Gage, a leader in the NWSA. Gage changed the name of the publication to *The National Citizen and Ballot Box* and moved it to a new location, Syracuse, New York, not far from her home in Fayetteville. Stanton and Anthony became "corresponding editors," and the newspaper was formally associated with the NWSA. Williams explained the sale by noting that she needed to rest "an overtaxed nervous system."[14] Gage shifted the newspaper's mission somewhat. The name change explained the shift.

> The NATIONAL CITIZEN will advocate the principle that Suffrage is the Citizen's right and should be protected by National law, and that while States may regulate the suffrage, they should have no power to abolish it.
>
> Its [The Citizen's] especial object will be to secure national protection to women citizens in the exercise of their rights to vote; but it will also touch upon the woman question in all its various aspects; it proposes a general criticism of men and things.

Gage, like Williams, promised to support no political party until one was "based upon the exact and permanent political equality of man and woman." The renamed publication "will, in as far as possible, revolutionize the country, striving to make it live up to its own fundamental principles and become in reality what it is but in name—a genuine Republic."[15]

The move to Syracuse did, however, bring some changes to the monthly. Like Williams, Gage's paper had to rely, primarily, on local advertisers. These Syracuse advertisers included photographers, clothiers, insurance agencies, grocers, plasterers, milliners, and even a patent medicine (Indian Syrup).

Although the editorial mission had shifted, the content did not change substantially from the Toledo product. Like Williams, Gage did not appreciate ministers who used biblical passages to subjugate women. Gage wrote, "[W]e know the present degraded condition of woman to-day is due to that interpretation of Scripture which holds . . . that she has no rights to live for herself, to act for herself, to think for herself."[16] Gage also shared Williams' disgust with both political parties. "There can be no peace while one half the citizens are political slaves. There can be no peace while Democrat and Republican alike hold the ballot . . . to be a privilege, under control of the separate states."[17]

Upon one thing, however, Gage and Williams differed. When Williams sold the publication to Gage, the monthly was economically viable. That viability did not last long under Gage. Several things explained why the *National Citizen* faced uncertain times. First, Gage increased the size of the publication, without any apparent advertising base to warrant the expansion. The newspaper often ran eight pages, yet there was no noticeable increase in advertising. Second, Gage "acquired" the unexpired list of *The Woman's Tribune*.* That proved to be a mistake because the *National Citizen* got no revenue for these readers. As Gage complained in the newspaper, "I am carrying the *Woman's Tribune* subscribers at a loss, for although Mrs. Haggart [the publisher of the *Tribune*] announced that she had 'sold' the *Woman's Tribune* to the NATIONAL CITIZEN, that word 'sold' was a figure of speech, meaning less than nothing."[18]

Haggart, however, did promise to work for subscribers when she was on the lecture circuit. Third, Anthony retired from the lecture circuit to write the *History of Woman Suffrage*. That proved to be a devastating blow to the *Citizen*. In 1879, for example, Anthony had brought in four-hundred new subscribers. That revenue was not available in 1880. Throughout that year, Gage was complaining about the financing of the *Citizen*. In April 1880 she even suggested that some prominent suffragists put the newspaper on a permanent base by forming a stock company—just as the *Woman's Journal** was financially supported.[19] That, however, never occurred. Without Anthony's soliciting subscriptions, the *Citizen* faced a dismal future.[20] Finally, with the October 1881 issue, Gage suspended the publication. She expected that this would be only a temporary measure—just long enough for her to complete work on the *History of Woman Suffrage*.[21] Gage never revived the *Citizen*.

    The National Citizen and Ballot Box, under Williams and Gage, gave a voice to the NWSA. Unfortunately, it suffered from some of the ills afflicting its sponsoring organization. Like the NWSA, it lacked sufficient financial resources. While Gage pleaded with readers to renew, she sometimes complained that NWSA's treasury suffered from similar problems. The *Citizen,* like the NWSA, relied too heavily on the services of Gage, Anthony, and Stanton for survival. When Anthony retired from the lecture circuit, and the three prepared the *History of Woman Suffrage,* Gage had no choice but to suspend the publication, apparently because no one was willing or able to assume the responsibility of editor. Unfortunately, that meant that a vibrant, radical voice for the suffrage movement was silenced.

Notes

    1. Elizabeth Cady Stanton, Susan B. Anthony, and Matilda J. Gage, eds., *History of Woman Suffrage,* vol. 3, 1876–1885 (Rochester: Susan B. Anthony, 1886), p. 504.

    2. See, for example, April 1876.

    3. January 1878, p. 2; Stanton, Anthony, and Gage, *History of Woman Suffrage,* p. 504.

    4. "Congratulatory," April 1876, p. 1.

    5. See, for example, "Illinois State Woman Suffrage Association" and "New York State Woman Suffrage Convention." June 1876, pp. 1, 2.

    6. "Declaration of Rights of Women of the United States by the National Women Suffrage Association, July 4, 1876" and "How Women Received the Declaration of Rights," August 1876, pp. 1–4. This particular issue ran eight pages.

    7. "Corruptions of the Period," June 1876, p. 3.

    8. "No Uncertain Sound," September 1876, p. 2.

    9. See, for example, "Rights Not Privileges," July 1876, p. 2.

    10. "Counter-Currents," May 1877, p. 2.

    11. "Our Schools," July 1877, p. 2; "The Petition," February 1877, p. 2.

    12. Elizabeth Cady Stanton, letter to *Ballot Box,* October 1876, p. 1.

    13. The primarily local advertising, however, seemed inconsistent with the national readership.

14. "Mrs. Williams' Farewell," May 1878, p. 1.

15. "Prospectus," May 1878, p. 1.

16. "Theological Christianity, August 1878, p. 2. See also "Men's Translation of the Bible, September 1880, p. 2.

17. "The Present Outlook," June 1879, p. 4.

18. "To Woman's Tribune Subscribers," November 1879, p. 2.

19. "The National Citizen—An Appeal," April 1880, p. 2.

20. "Renew! Renew!" December 1880, p. 2.

21. Readers who still had time on their subscriptions received Caroline B. Winlow's *Alpha*.

Information Sources

BIBLIOGRAPHY:

Stanton, Elizabeth Cady, Susan B. Anthony, and Matilda J. Gage, eds. *History of Woman Suffrage*. Vol. 3 (1876–1885). Rochester, N.Y.: Susan B. Anthony, 1886.

Steiner, Linda. "The Woman's Suffrage Press 1850–1900: A Cultural Analysis." PhD diss., University of Illinois, 1979.

Wagner, Sally Marie Roesch. "That Word Is Liberty: A Biography of Matilda Joslyn Gage." PhD diss., University of California, Santa Cruz, 1978.

Warbasse, Elizabeth B. "Matilda Joslyn Gage." In Edward T. James, Janet Wilson James, and Paul S. Boyer, eds., *Notable American Women 1607–1950*, vol. 2. Cambridge: Belknap Press of Harvard University Press, 1971, pp. 4–6.

INDEX SOURCES: Oess, Mara Ann Pinto *An Index to the National Citizen and Ballot Box*. Toledo, Ohio: Lucas County Public Library, 1976.

LOCATION SOURCES: Library of Congress; Kent State University (Ohio) Library; and many other libraries.

Publication History

PERIODICAL TITLE AND TITLE CHANGES: *The Ballot Box* (1876–1878); *The National Citizen and Ballot Box* (1878–1881).

VOLUME AND ISSUE DATA: Vols. 1–6 (April 1876–October 1881). Monthly.

PUBLISHER AND PLACE OF PUBLICATION: Toledo Woman Suffrage Association (1876–1878); Matilda Joslyn Gage (1878–1881). Toledo, Ohio (1876–1878); Syracuse, N.Y. (1878–1881).

EDITORS: Sarah R. L. Williams (1876–1878); Matilda Joslyn Gage (1878–1881).

CIRCULATION: Unknown.

Kathleen L. Endres

NETWORK NEWS

By 1970, the women's movement was flourishing again in the United States. Within that context, women sociologists began actively to protest discrimination within their profession. At the 1970 American Sociological Association (ASA) meetings, several hundred women sociologists held a counterconvention and formed a Women's Caucus. Led by Alice Rossi, a founding member of the

National Organization for Women (NOW) and the National Abortion Rights Action League (NARAL), they presented a list of resolutions to the ASA business meeting. The events caught most of the members of the ASA by surprise. To the women's surprise, ASA Council agreed to create a Committee on the Status of Women in the Profession, to declare the sociology of sex roles as an area of competence, and to establish a section on sex roles.[1]

In February 1971, twenty members of the Women's Caucus met at Yale to create a permanent organization to represent their interests.[2] The women differed greatly in age, interests, ideology, and commitment, yet no one's voice was silenced as they wrestled with the issues before them. The overriding issue was the fundamental nature of the organization. Would it be radical or liberal, that is, would it empower women as a group or empower individual women in sociology? It was to be both. The radicals got committees on social issues, jobs, and discrimination. The liberals got a constitution, a clear-cut organization with responsibilities assigned. In other words, "The radicals got enough to be able to sell the organization to their peers. The liberals salvaged enough to bear [sic]."[3] They agreed to support a quarterly newsletter and to name their organization Sociologists for Women in Society (SWS). The statement of purposes read:

> SWS is dedicated to maximizing the effectiveness of and professional opportunities for women in sociology; exploring the contributions which sociology can, does and should make to the investigation and humanization of current sex roles; and improving the quality of human life.[4]

A second issue at the Yale meeting concerned the relations of SWS to the ASA. The consensus was that SWS was both inside and outside ASA. SWS members wanted to work with other professional women's groups to aid the cause of women in society, but they did not want to relieve the ASA of its responsibility for protecting women sociologists in the job market and against discrimination in tenure and promotion on the job. This "outsider within" stance would be reflected in all SWS publications.[5]

The first issue of the *Newsletter* was published in March 1971, a month after the Yale meeting. Arlene Kaplan Daniels, the first editor of the *Newsletter,* had founded Scientific Analysis Corporation in San Francisco in the 1960s to provide an organizational affiliation for independent scholars like herself. In the 1970s, her goal was to create a newsletter to give all SWS members an opportunity to participate in the emergent organization. In addition to listing the standing committee of SWS, the *Newsletter* would have regular departments to disseminate information about the activities of the committees and regional women's societies; letters from members on any related topics; and news of general interest or announcements of other organizations and activities.[6]

The first issues of the *Newsletter* gave strong evidence of the extent to which women sociologists were fomenting change in the profession. On the national level, SWS president pro-tem Alice Rossi chaired the first panel session on sociology of sex roles at the 1971 ASA meetings.[7] As national chair of the American Association of University Professors (AAUP) Committee W on the Status of Women in Academia, Rossi reported to the readership on policy revisions concerning nepotism rules and affirmative action guidelines.[8] On the regional level, members reported they were organizing SWS chapters and petitioning regional sociological organizations to offer panel sessions on sex roles.[9]

The *Newsletter* reflected Arlene Kaplan Daniel's commitment to inclusion, regardless of rank or institutional prestige. In addition to Jessie Bernard's insightful report on the Yale meeting,[10] the Job Committee had quickly established a job bureau and solicited vitae from members to facilitate their search for employment.[11] The Publications Committee collected both course syllabi on sex roles and reprints of articles or papers about research on women. The Discrimination Committee was in the process of developing policies and procedures for dealing with individual cases of discrimination that came to SWS's attention. To facilitate networking, the full membership list of over two hundred was listed; the names and contact people in other social science disciplines and organizations were also listed.

Having established the network of communication, Rachel Kahn-Hut and Marcia Millman urged members to use the *Newsletter* for "the exchange of information about the treatment of women in society and how this affects the quality of life for everyone as it is affected by this treatment."[12] Despite their urging, the *Newsletter* remained focused on the treatment of women in sociology. Members, however, were impatient with the rate of change in the profession.

Capitalizing on their "outsider within" status, SWS sent a questionnaire to all nominees for office in the ASA, asking their opinion on issues of concern to SWS members. The issues in 1972 included preferential hiring of women in sociology departments and efforts to end sex and racial discrimination in sociology departments, to develop campus day-care centers for students, staff, and faculty, and to permit part-time graduate work and the appointment of part-time tenured faculty. Candidates' responses to these issues were published verbatim in the *Newsletter* prior to the ASA elections.[13] In this way, SWS hoped to influence the election of candidates who would promote professional opportunities for women in sociology.

In 1973, the editorship of the *Newsletter* moved from the West to the East Coast. Upon becoming editor, Helen McGill Hughes established a board of associate editors to produce the *Newsletter* in Cambridge, Massachusetts.[14] Thus began a practice of collaborative production of the *Newsletter* that continued for more than ten years as the editorial office moved from one university setting to another on the East Coast.

The editorial policy of the *Newsletter* was not clearly articulated until 1977, when a committee headed by Muriel Cantor in Washington, D.C., took over editorial responsibility. Their editorial policy was explicitly liberal.

Ideally, we would like the *Newsletter* to be a journal of ideas, news and opinions addressed to those women and men in sociology who are concerned with the position of women within and without the discipline. The reality, however, is that we have time, space and money problems. Therefore news and opinions will be concerned primarily, through not entirely, with the special interests of women as teachers, researchers and students in the field of sociology.[15]

The fifth editor, Janet Hunt at the University of Maryland, and her committee saw the primary function of the *Newsletter* "to report on the activities of SWS and events and issues affecting our membership."[16] At their urging, the *Newsletter* was renamed *Network* in 1979 to reflect the strength, connectedness, and purpose of SWS.[17]

Reflecting this policy, the regular features of the newsletter included minutes of national meetings, committee reports and job offerings, regional news, and book reviews. Two features, "Women on the Move" and "Announcements," helped members keep up with their friends and colleagues as well as prospects for research, funding, publishing, and professional meetings. The president's column became an important vehicle for the incumbents to present their agenda for SWS.

The newsletter was increasingly used for professional development. In 1978, Muriel Cantor and her editorial committee introduced the special insert. It included twelve essays on "Teaching Sociology: For Women, about Women, to Women."[18] This was the first forum for SWS members to share their experiences about teaching courses on women, teaching women's studies, teaching reentry women, and expanding the concepts of sex and gender. In 1979, Janet Hunt and her editorial committee included an insert of six essays on "Sociologists at Work: Women in Research, Administration, Government and Community Service."[19] Given the constricting job market for academic sociologists, these six essays suggested the range of possible employment opportunities for women and weighed the advantages and disadvantages of the various options.

The ASA candidates questionnaire resounded through SWS over the years. In 1979, Joan Huber, a founding member and former president, questioned the practice.

By 1975 many candidates had learned to make motherhood-and-apple pie statements about women's issues in the discipline, hence judging among candidates became difficult. In 1977, 1978, and 1979, therefore, the Steering Committee has endorsed or denied endorsement to all ASA candidates. . . . (yet) endorsement is counterproductive for several reasons.[20]

Despite Huber's opposition and increasing uneasiness among other members, SWS continued to endorse candidates. Three years later, in 1982, *Network* devoted seven pages to the issue, including the report of the Ad Hoc Committee on Endorsement.[21] The Steering Committee voted to continue the policy of endorsement, but, rather than print candidates' verbatim responses, *Network* printed a brief rationale for each candidate based on his or her responses.[22] By 1985, SWS returned to the practice of printing candidates' verbatim responses in *Network*, but without endorsement.[23]

Another long-term, potentially divisive issue played out on the pages of the newsletter was the charge that SWS was elitist in its focus on the interests of women in sociology. Sheryl Ruzek addressed this issue in an opinion column:

I have not attended an annual or midyear SWS meeting where someone did not accusingly ask at least once, "Are we really for women in society?" The implication is that we are not (in the judgement of the speaker) really for women except ourselves. I take strong issue with the accusation because it devalues the myriad of ways many of us are involved in working with and for women—teaching and counseling women students, writing on women's issues, working with community groups, serving as expert witnesses, and creating personal and professional relationships which go beyond the bounds of traditional expectations for women in society.[24]

Seen through Ruzek's lens, both the *Newsletter* and *Network* reported many activities that indicated SWSers really were for women in society. In 1977, a report from the SWS Task Force on Working Class Women and Their Families called for a nationwide boycott of products manufactured in J. P. Stevens textile plants.[25] Not only did SWS adopt ERA resolutions, but *Network* reported that SWS was successful in getting the ASA to boycott non-ERA states in selecting convention cites for the ASA meetings.[26]

SWS also broadened its focus beyond the United States. Special inserts in 1981 reported on delegations of SWS members who went to China and Cuba to meet and observe women in socialist societies.[27] Another delegation of SWSers reported on their 1982 trip to Bulgaria for a joint conference on Women and Work in Bulgaria and the United States.[28]

These reports reflected a shift in emphasis in the activities of SWS. As SWS grew, as women established careers in the profession, and as sex and gender became a legitimate area of study, the membership expanded the scope of its activities. The liberal agenda was increasingly paired with a more radical, activist agenda. The quarterly *Network* could not be timely enough to keep abreast of an activist agenda. Thus, a second newsletter was initiated in 1984 to convey information of immediate concern to members. *Network News,* edited by Judith Levy, would be a brief, inexpensive, bimonthly newsletter representing a more activist agenda.[29] *Network,* edited by Beth Hess, would continue to report quarterly on SWS business and matters of professional interest.

Judith Levy continued the tradition of the editorial committee at *Network News.* She and her committee created features to satisfy political and professional agendas. The "Action Alert" column of the Social Issues Committee focused on items requiring immediate pressure on members of Congress, such as the Civil Rights Restoration Act, the Non-Discrimination in Insurance Act, the Reproductive Health Equity Act, and funding Title III of the Child Abuse Prevention and Treatment Act.[30] The Social Issues Committee also provided resources on "comparable worth" and "pay equity."[31] In 1987, they were able to announce that SWS had been granted status as a nongovernmental organization (NGO) associated with the United Nations.[32] The Discrimination Committee kept readers informed about SWS members' "tenure grievances" against universities, including Harvard, Clark, Northwestern, Wayne State, and the University of California–Santa Cruz.[33]

Professional interests were addressed in several columns. "Between the Lines" focused on the "how to" of getting published. "At the Cinema" provided feminist reviews of movies, television programs, and videos. "Ms. Manners" gave advice on issues of professional etiquette.

Ms. Manners (aka Arlene Kaplan Daniels) advised junior members how to approach senior members for advice, recommendations, or editorial comments on manuscripts and how to survive the annual ASA meeting. She advised senior members on the etiquette of writing letters of support for colleagues being considered for tenure. Other delicate issues included sexual harassment, discrimination on search committees, and women colleagues who lack a feminist consciousness. On generosity and gratitude in the network, Ms. Manners wrote:

> Seniors who are trusted and respected enough to offer advice develop their reputation through generosity in assistance: they read manuscripts, advise about dissertations, give career counseling. But juniors should learn how to use these favors with discretion. . . . Large projects like the revision of a dissertation into articles or a book or a judgement about the publishability of a research report require delicate negotiation. . . . In return for any help offered them, how might juniors best show appreciation? Some obvious responses come quickly to mind: acknowledgements, dedications, citations in published work can show both appreciation and respect for the work of seniors.[34]

In 1986, the Publications Committee announced that SWS would launch a scholarly journal to advance the study of gender and feminist scholarship.[35] Given the cost of publishing a journal, SWS could no longer afford to publish two newsletters. *Network* went out of business when *Gender & Society* made its debut. *Network News* then took on the responsibility for the collective memory of the organization, but it was reduced from a bimonthly to a quarterly publication.

Emphasizing theory and research from a social structural perspective, *Gender & Society* would contain scholarly articles, book reviews, review essays, and commentary on current feminist issues. According to founding editor Judith Lorber, each major article was to be framed by a theoretical perspective or policy issue and illuminate or advance critical thinking in its area.[36] Special issues have focused on violence against women, women and development in the Third World, Marxist feminist theory, sexual identities, and interlocking systems of race, class, and gender. By advancing feminist scholarship, *Gender & Society* advances the possibility that doing sociology can make a difference for women in society.[37]

Network News continued to be a vital channel of communication for SWS. The change from a bimonthly to a quarterly publication, however, meant that the newsletter was again unable to convey information of immediate concern to members. In 1992, the Social Concerns Committee created an electronic bulletin board for "Action Alerts."[38] In 1993, a subtle name change from *Network News* to *Network news* reflected the latest shift in the activities of SWS.

SWS celebrated its twenty-fifth anniversary in 1995. Both the name and scope of the newsletter have changed through the years, reflecting changes in the organization. Regardless of the name, the newsletter has reflected the tensions between liberal and activist feminists, as well as SWS's "outsider within" status in the ASA. Although it is now supplemented by an electronic bulletin board, *Network news* is the primary medium of communication among the membership of SWS.

Notes

The author thanks Beth Hess, a former SWS president and the last editor of *Network,* for helpful suggestions.

1. Alice Rossi, "The Formation of SWS: An Historical Account by a Founding Mother," November 1985, pp. 2–4.

2. Sociologists for Women in Society, "Formation," March 1971, p. 10.

3. Jessie Bernard, "Report on the Yale Meeting," March 1971, pp. 5–7.

4. Sociologists for Women in Society, "Purposes," March 1971, p. 10.

5. Patricia Hill Collins, *Black Feminist Thought: Knowledge, Consciousness, and the Politics of Empowerment* (New York: Routledge, Chapman and Hall, 1991), pp. 10–13.

6. Arlene Kaplan Daniels, Editorial, March 1971, p. 1.

7. Alice Rossi, "Section Panel Session: Sociology of Sex Roles," March 1971, p. 3.

8. Alice Rossi, "AAUP Committee W Formed and Takes First Actions," March 1971, pp. 1–2.

9. "Eastern Sociological Society," May 1971, p. 11.

10. Barnard, "Report on Yale Meeting."

11. "Job Committee Report," August 1971, p. 6.

12. Rachel Kahn-Hut and Marcia Millman, Editorial, August 1971, p. 2.

13. "Election of ASA Officers," January 1972, pp. 7–10.

14. "Editorial Board 1973," Winter 1973, p. 22.

15. Muriel Cantor, Editorial, June 1977, p. 1.

16. Janet Hunt, Editorial, October 1978, p. 2.

17. Janet Hunt, "Editorial," July 1979, p. 2.

18. Muriel Cantor, Barbara Hetrick, and Bobbi Spalter-Roth, eds., "Teaching Sociology: For Women, about Women, to Women," July 1978, pp. 1–12.

19. Janet Hunt, ed., "Sociologists at Work: Women in Research, Administration, Government and Community Service," July 1979, pp. 1–8.

20. Joan Huber, "In My Opinion," April 1979, pp. 3, 5.

21. "ASA Candidates: To Endorse or Not to Endorse," July 1982, pp. 8–14.

22. "SWS Endorses ASA Candidates," July 1982, p. 14.

23. "Candidates for ASA Office," April 1985, pp. 1–10.

24. Sheryl Ruzek, "Some Thoughts on SWS and Social Action," January 1980, p. 4.

25. Shirley Nuss, "Task Force Votes J. P. Stevens Boycott," October 1977, p. 5.

26. Janet Hunt, "SWS Takes Action," October 1978, p. 1.

27. Barbara Hetrick, ed., "Special Issue: SWS Goes to China and Cuba," October 1981, pp. 1–14.

28. Joan Mandle, "SWSers Travel to Bulgaria," January 1981, pp. 11–12.

29. Beth Hess, "Passing the Torch," November 1984, p. 2.

30. See, for example, SOCIAL ISSUES ALERT, February 1985, p. 12.

31. Barrie Thorne, "Key Readings for Teaching about Pay Equity," January, 1987, p. 13.

32. "NGO Status Approved," May 1987, p. 25.

33. See, for example, "Ah . . . Justice!!" June 1986, p. 13.

34. Ms. Manners, "On Generosity and Gratitude in the Network," July 1985, p. 6.

35. "Between the Lines," April 1986, pp. 4–5.

36. Judith Lorber, "Between the Lines," April 1986, p. 4.

37. Margaret Anderson, Editorial, *Gender & Society,* April 1994, p. 149.

38. Joey Sprague, "Social Policy Committee Report," March 1992, p. 1.

Information Sources

BIBLIOGRAPHY:
Collins, Patricia Hill. *Black Feminist Thought: Knowledge, Consciousness, and the Politics of Empowerment.* New York: Routledge, Chapman, and Hall, 1991.
INDEX SOURCES: None.
LOCATION SOURCES: Schlesinger Library, Radcliffe College.

Publication History

PERIODICAL TITLE AND TITLE CHANGES: *Newsletter* (1971–1978); *Network* (1979–1986); *Network News* (1984–1993); *Network news* (1993–present).
VOLUME AND ISSUE DATA: Vols. 1– (current numeration begins with January 1984 to present). Quarterly (*Newsletter,* 1971–1986); bimonthly (*Network News,* (1984–1986); quarterly (*Network News,* 1986–present).
PUBLISHER AND PLACE OF PUBLICATION: Sociologists for Women in Society. Akron, Ohio.
EDITORS: Arlene Kaplan Daniels (1971–1972); Helen McGill Hughes (1973–1974); Helen McGill Hughes and Evelyn Glenn (1975–1976); Muriel Cantor (1977); Janet Hunt (1978–1980); Barbara Hetrick (1981–1984); Beth Hess (1984–1986); Judith Levy (1984–1988; Barbara Mori (1988–1989); Betty Morrow (1989–1993); Kathryn M. Feltey (1993–present).
CIRCULATION: SWS membership: 1,000+.

Patricia M. Ulbrich

NEW DIRECTIONS FOR WOMEN

For more than two decades, from 1972 to 1993, *New Directions for Women,* a feminist news publication that had a national audience, brought an alternative approach to the coverage of women's issues.

According to its statement of purpose, the publication, initially titled *New Directions for Women in New Jersey,* began as "a quarterly newspaper to inform the women of New Jersey about equal rights—in legislation, employment, abortion, advertising, education, the arts, the family, child care, religion—in everything." The aim was to reach all women, not only feminists, "with hard news and detailed information about every aspect of the movement—statewide, national and international."

Designed for consciousness-raising, "[i]t is written to energize women to take action to advance their position," the statement of purpose continued. "New Directions is convinced that when women understand sex discrimination, they will reach for the tools to combat it."[1]

Receipts of $240 from a 1971 conference of the same name funded the first issue. This conference was sponsored by a coalition of all the woman's rights groups then in New Jersey. The founder, editor, and publisher, Paula Kassell, who formerly had been a social worker and a technical editor, launched the publication with a volunteer staff in her Dover, New Jersey, home. Work was done in two bedrooms furnished as offices, and the paper was pasted up on her dining room table.

The first issue appeared in January 1972, making *New Directions for Women in New Jersey* the first statewide feminist periodical in the United States. It began as a fourteen-page mimeographed newspaper with a press run of two thousand. It was distributed free to feminist groups and as many different types of women's clubs in New Jersey as could be located. An editorial in the spring 1977 issue pointed out: "The first issue was very well received and highly praised. And we thought we would just have to sit back and the subscriptions would come rolling in—that anybody reading it would be inspired to sit down and write us a check for $3 for a year's subscription."[2] Unfortunately for the publication, only eighty-five did so. Although the 4.25 percent response rate was considered a respectable return for a mail solicitation, the second issue did not appear until August 1972.

This time Kassell concentrated on nonsexist education and distributed the issue free at the state teachers' convention in Atlantic City, publishing an eight-page tabloid with a press run of fifty-three thousand and trucking it down to Atlantic City in addition to mailing copies. Promoting its distribution to teachers and librarians, the publication sold several hundred dollars' worth of advertising to book publishers and a few feminist businesses, an initial effort to gather the book advertising that became its most sustaining commercial force. That issue wound up with a deficit of only $140.

A similar plan of offering advertisers circulation targeted for a specific message financed the next issue, which came out in the winter of 1973. Emphasizing employment and child care, the issue was distributed to all members of the American Association of University Women and Business and Professional Women within the state and to the personnel managers of 350 New Jersey companies—all those employing five hundred or more. This issue produced enough revenue to launch the publication on a quarterly basis.

In its first few years *New Directions for Women* expanded both in size and in content, changing focus from a state to a national publication. It dropped New Jersey from its title with its spring 1975 issue and initiated a classified advertising section. Cartoons and verses tended to be angry or sarcastic, but occasionally humor surfaced, such as in this excerpt:

Recipe

1 c. crushed ego

1 teaspoon job discrimination

¼ teaspoon chauvinism

1 well-beaten path to the washing machine

one-half teaspoon grated nerves

1 pencil from a man on the street

1 punch from a man on the street

1 dash from the dentist to the babysitter

Mix all ingredients, one on top of the other and stir violently. Cook until you feel a slow burn and then add one last straw. Serves 51 percent of the population.

Brenda Turner[3]

Subjects continued to range through all the feminist issues and personal statements of experience. In November 1975 the publication reached twenty pages. The following year it ran series on assertiveness, menopause, and feminist psychological counseling. It also served to bring women together at conferences, sponsoring a gathering of feminist business owners in 1973 and, in 1976, a conference, "New Directions for Women in the Media: How to Market Your Executive Talents and Your Writings in Books, Newspapers and Magazines." Other projects included essay contests for high school students on equal rights for women.

In February 1977 *New Directions for Women,* which had about eight thousand paid subscribers, moved from Dover to offices in Westwood, New Jersey, and went to bimonthly publication with the winter 1979–1980 issue. At the time, its readership was divided roughly into thirds: one-third on the East Coast, one-third on the West Coast, and the rest scattered across the country. An editorial board was established as well as a Board of Trustees for the nonprofit enterprise. Vivian J. Scheinmann, a librarian, was named managing editor, working closely with a small group of other women, including Marjorie Lipstyte, book review editor. Kassell remained associate editor and a member of both boards. Six federal grants under the Comprehensive Employment and Training Act (CETA) from 1975 to 1980 provided for on-the-job training of minority women and displaced homemakers in the business side of publishing. All subsequently found jobs in the private sector, and two became paid employees of *New Directions for Women.*

According to Scheinmann, the subscription base and readership grew as the CETA staff learned the publishing business. Contents during this period included a series on the leading national organizations working for women's equality.[4] In a 1979 anniversary issue, the publication, which featured artwork and photographs as well as news stories and reviews, described itself as "a national feminist newspaper reaching tens of thousands of women outside the activist core of the women's movement."[5] It had a varied list of contributors and volunteers, some of whom moved on to write novels, teach in women's studies programs, and take responsible jobs in mainstream publishing for which their work on the paper gave them credentials.

In 1981 *New Directions for Women* received a three-year Ford Foundation grant totaling about sixty thousand dollars for a subscription campaign to broaden its readership among minority women and to strengthen its financial position. Utilizing the grant, the editors sent the publication free to women in prisons and mental institutions as well as to university women's centers and women's clinics.

For the January/February 1982 issue, the trustees revised the statement of purpose to reflect the coming-of-age of the "Second Wave" of the women's movement: "*New Directions for Women* is committed to publishing the many voices of feminism. We believe the diversity of the women's movement must be seen as one of its strengths. *New Directions for Women* is a national feminist periodical written for feminists and committed to reaching out to those not yet dedicated to a feminist future. *New Directions for Women* believes when we understand the pervasive force of sexism, we will act to effect change."[6]

In addition to a strong book review section and broad coverage of the arts, *New Directions for Women,* which was sold at feminist bookstores as well as by subscription, covered subjects such as child abuse, domestic violence, prostitution, rape, homophobia, and sexuality. Columns took up legal and tax issues affecting women. Although it always provided a feminist perspective, the paper was not allied with any particular group within the women's movement and sought to offer a broad spectrum of opinion. A ten-year cumulative index was published in 1981, making the publication more accessible for reference purposes.

In 1983 Phyllis Kriegel, a graduate of the women's history program at Sarah

Lawrence College, became managing editor, and the publication moved to a women's center in Englewood, New Jersey. According to Kriegel, when she took over, the publication had a $43,000 annual budget compared to an annual budget of $157,000 in its final year of publication.[7] The increase reflected Kriegel's decisions to compensate staff members and contributors.

"We started to pay the staff in the mid-1980s and in the late 1980s we started to pay writers (who got two cents a word), artists and photographers," she said. Although no one was ever employed more than part-time, "we were paying out an added cost of $1,000 per issue," she said. "We felt we could no longer ask women to be volunteers on a continuing basis. The times had changed. A lot of good writers wanted a token that they were professionals and we honored that," she continued.

Articles were written by professionals; "[w]e were careful to make the copy tight and lively," Kriegel commented. Unlike some other feminist newspapers that run submissions word for word, "[w]e felt we had a literary and grammatical standard [to uphold]. We cared passionately about writing and how it sounded," she explained.[8]

By 1993 New Directions for Women had a readership of some sixty-five thousand and was a nationally and internationally recognized and respected agent of social change. Its size had grown to between forty-four and forty-eight pages, with up-to-date style and professional design and layout by computer. This was accomplished, in part, by grants from such foundations as the Ms. Foundation for Education and Communication; the Funding Exchange; ADCO Foundation; the Sophia Fund; North Star, the Foundation for a Compassionate Society; and the Harbach Foundation. But grants were sporadic and small. "A $2,000 to $3,000 grant for us was handsome," Kriegel said. She explained that each year she contributed her own funds to hire a staff and to "help leverage other funds" with limited success. "It was my life and I was delighted that I could do it."[9]

One gift was substantial. Kreigel said New Directions for Women was distributed internationally starting in 1989–1990 due to a thirty thousand-dollar grant for two years from Genevieve Vaughan, a philanthropist. The grant financed an international pull-out section called "Country of Women." This section, which ran for three years, highlighted a quotation from Virginia Woolf: "As a woman I have no country. As a woman I want no country. As a woman my country is the whole world."

"Country of Women" carried a variety of material on worldwide women's issues, including reports from a women's newspaper in Italy on feminist conferences in Europe. Due to the grant at the time of the collapse of communism, New Directions for Women had a correspondent, Jill Benderley, in Eastern Europe, reporting the effects of the end of the cold war on women.

Beset by rising production costs and falling subscriptions, which had declined to about thirty-five hundred, New Directions for Women was forced to fold with the September/October 1993 issue. The subscription price, held at ten dollars for most of Kriegel's tenure, was eighteen dollars a year at the time the publication ceased. Kriegel, who had prepared a business plan at the request of a woman's foundation, decided to end the operation, which advertised a total circulation of sixty-five thousand because of free distribution, after she failed to get expected funding. "We were disheartened and knew that we would live a hand-to-mouth existence [that couldn't continue]."

Under Kriegel's leadership, the paper stressed more investigative journalism. "We were far ahead of other publications. We had a wonderful issue on women in prisons in the early 1990s," she said. "We were the ones telling the story of the grassroots women's movement at a time when people said it was dead. We tackled what feminist think tanks say about feminists. We wrote about women's funding sources, social change, women's health, women losing their children. That was part of the problem—people said reading it [*New Directions*] was a downer. We were bringing a lot of bad news." Under Kriegel the paper regularly covered the environment, activism, and spirituality. A New York metro area supplement was added in 1989, and news from the Women's Action Coalition was carried regularly starting early in 1993.

According to Kriegel, lack of promotion led to the demise. "We never had enough money or talent to get on radio programs and be visible. I couldn't do it and run the paper," she said. "Book advertising was the largest source of advertising [and] we went up to $5,000 an issue on advertising." Tying into editorial themes, the publication solicited advertising for issues on special topics like women's history, black history, and women's spirituality. Yet *New Directions for Women* lacked local circulation and, consequently, failed to attract local advertising.

Another problem was its newspaper-type format. Even though its bimonthly publication schedule made it hard to cover news events, "[w]e attempted to be timely," Kriegel said. "We were a news magazine." She thinks a gap has been left in the media since *New Directions for Women* went under.[10]

But, in the opinion of its former editors, *New Directions for Women* had a lasting influence on its staff and helped change the lives and minds of its readers. Under Kriegel's leadership, *New Directions for Women* operated a valuable intern/co-op program, drawing students of diverse backgrounds from different colleges and universities who were then trained and supervised by staff. Many of the interns went on to work for social changes in such areas as the Peace Corps, politics, religious organizations, city government, and hospitals and clinics, as well as in journalism with mainstream magazines, newspapers, and publishing houses.

Notes

1. "Statement of Purpose," January 1972, p. 1.
2. "Looking Back—Moving Ahead," Spring 1977, p. 2.
3. Spring 1973, p. 3.
4. Excerpt from "Chronicle of New Directions for Women" prepared by Vivian

Scheinmann in 1995 on her period as managing editor (1978–1983) for twelve-year cumulative index of *New Directions for Women.*

5. "Women's Alternative Press," January (Anniversary Issue) 1979, p. 1.
6. "Statement of Purpose," January/February 1982, p. 1.
7. Phyllis Kriegel, telephone interview, January 21, 1995.
8. Ibid.
9. Ibid.
10. Ibid.

Information Sources

BIBLIOGRAPHY:
Allen, Martha L. *The Development of Communication Networks among Women, 1963–1983.* Ann Arbor, Mich.: University Microfilms International, 1989.
INDEX SOURCES: Alternative Press Index; Book Review Index; Children's Book Review Index; Human Rights Internet Reporter; Studies on Women Abstracts; Women Studies Abstracts. (Cumulative index issued by *New Directions for Women* in 1981 and 1995.)
LOCATION SOURCES: New York Public Library; National Women and Media Collection, University of Missouri; and other university and community libraries. Microfilm available through University Microfilms Inc.

Publication History

PERIODICAL TITLE AND TITLE CHANGES: *New Directions for Women in New Jersey* (1972–1975); *New Directions for Women* (1975–1993).
VOLUME AND ISSUE DATA: Vols. 1–22 (January 1972–September/October 1993). Quarterly (1972–1977); bimonthly (1979–1993).
PUBLISHER AND PLACE OF PUBLICATION: New Directions for Women, Inc. Dover, N.J. (1973–1977); Westwood, N.J. (1977–1983); Englewood, N.J. (1983–1993).
EDITORS: Paula Kassell (1972–1977); Vivian J. Scheinmann (1977–1983); Phyllis Kriegel (1983–1993).
CIRCULATION: Self-reported, 1993: 65,000 (3,500 paid).

Paula Kassell and Maurine Beasley

THE NEW NORTHWEST

In introducing a reprint of Abigail Duniway's 1914 autobiography, Eleanor Flexner described Duniway as a highly talented, witty suffrage worker. Nonetheless, the historian added, "Her belief in her own powers and judgment eventually turned into unbridled vanity."[1] If it is true that the record number of unsuccessful suffrage campaigns in Oregon resulted from Duniway's prickly, even irascible nature, the major woman's rights periodical of the Northwest was certainly the product of the indefatigable Duniway, who published *The New Northwest* for sixteen years, beginning in 1871, with the help of only her family.

Duniway was a fan of Elizabeth Cady Stanton and Susan B. Anthony, among the more radical of the suffragists. Duniway once served as Anthony's business manager during a West Coast tour; Duniway also used the tour to promote her paper and solicit subscribers. The vehement language she had read in the *Revolution** also appeared in the *New Northwest*. An editorial reprinted each week announced that *The New Northwest* would be "a Human Rights organ, devoted to whatever policy may be necessary to seduce the greatest good to the greatest number." Duniway added: "It knows no sex, no politics, no religions, no party, no color, no creed. Its foundation is fastened upon the rock of Eternal Liberty, Universal Emancipation and Untrammeled Progression." Later the masthead described the Portland weekly as "A Journal for the People Devoted to the Interests of Humanity Independent in Politics and Religion, Alive to all Live Issues and Thoroughly Radical in Opposing and Exposing the Wrongs of the Masses."

Abigail was born in 1834 in an Illinois log cabin to Ann Roelofson and John Tucker Scott, the third of their twelve children. "Jenny" Scott was a wild and difficult child who hated her assigned chores on the family farm.[2] In 1852 the Scott family joined a large-scale, but arduous, westward migration. Abigail's mother died of cholera en route. Penniless by the time they reached Oregon, the father became an innkeeper at a "temperance house" and quickly remarried. Although she had less than a year's worth of formal education, Abigail Jane Scott earned a teaching certificate and in 1853 married Benjamin C. Duniway, who had also recently come to Oregon from Illinois. She later told *New Northwest* readers she had omitted the word "obey" from her wedding vow.

Abigail Duniway had a hard, tough, exhausting life. Her first daughter was born ten months after the wedding; she suffered from several physical maladies as a result of having had six children by 1869. Her autobiography notes bitterly how Ben loved to entertain his friends at their cabin while she prepared meals— when she was not washing, scrubbing, churning, or nursing. "[T]o be, in short, a general pioneer drudge, with never a penny of my own, was not a pleasant business," Duniway said, believing that, having already been worn to a frazzle by her mother, she was poorly fitted to this work.[3] Certainly, the Duniways had significant financial problems. Against her advice, Benjamin signed some notes that ultimately resulted in the loss of all their savings; as a result of a farm accident, he also became depressed and unable to work much. So Abigail opened a private boarding school in their home. She later opened a millinery store, apparently highly successful.

Duniway, an early reader of Amelia Bloomer's *Lily,** was friendly with several women involved with suffrage papers. While attending an 1871 suffrage convention in California, she met Emily Pitts Stevens, publisher of *The San Francisco Pioneer,** who named Duniway her Oregon editor and whom Duniway long defended in her own pages; and Myra Bradwell, the pro-suffrage editor of *Chicago Legal News*.[4] Already in 1870 Duniway had discussed with friends the possibility of publishing a paper. Her friends expressed doubt about the feasibility of such a project, although they were eager to help found a new suffrage organization in Oregon. On her own, therefore, Duniway purchased tiny secondhand type and found someone to set type and to teach her sons printing. In her first issue, on May 5, 1871, she told readers she was "naturally acquisitive, calculating, and fond of active business life."

Several of Duniway's children earned money by helping to produce the paper, which did not appear during their yearly vacation. For a few years her sister Catherine Coburn, whom Duniway called "a lady of rare journalistic ability," helped out.[5] After Duniway took on her three oldest sons as partners, Coburn accepted editorial positions elsewhere, including the *Oregonian,* an influential Republican paper that one of their brothers, Harvey Scott, edited.

The four-page folio *New Northwest* ranged from the mundane to the serious, from reporting local personalities and accidents to exposing Oregon's own Tammany Ring and problems at local prisons and asylums. It covered agricultural, business and cultural events, and meetings. In tight, neat columns, it reported on various injustices, such as one woman's trial for murder without jury of peers; the refusal of Pacific University to admit an illegitimate child of a prostitute; and the problems of President Grant. She filled its pages with editorials, reprints, serialized novels, and her editorial correspondence, including sarcastic comments to other editors across the country with whom she "exchanged" and defenses of her position and character. Her advice to readers covered exercise and dress, marriage and morals, child rearing, and business and work opportunities.

She also published the creative efforts of others, both known authors like John Ruskin, Bret Harte, Mark Twain, and Fanny Fern as well as unknowns. She also printed her often critical evaluations and warned that poetry was never well paying. Duniway herself published occasional poems, including some suffrage-themed odes. But she apparently took to heart the suggestion from a newspaper publisher who had published some of her early poetry that she switch to prose. She wrote some twenty novels, many of which can be seen as highly autobiographical (especially in their heroines, who were often overworked, had too many children in too few years, and whose husbands made any number of bad decisions). A couple of these novels were commercially published; the rest appeared serially in *The New Northwest.*

Duniway had a clear view of the heroine of *The New Northwest:* "Our idea of a perfect woman is that she would be piquant, sprightly, agreeable, energetic, ambitious, affectionate; that her domestic world is in her home and household, loving her husband and looking upon him as an equal; loving, caring for and judiciously governing her children." Moreover, the ideal woman would be educated, working for pay in some profession or trade, and "in no way should she allow herself to become a clog or hindrance to her husband."[6] Duniway counted on "intelligent" women wanting to look fashionable; she ran regular fashion columns as well as advertising and promotion of her millinery business in the *New Northwest,* along with carrying advertising for other Portland businesses.

Of course, *The New Northwest* called attention to suffrage workers, suffrage arguments, and suffrage activities. It extensively detailed conventions and meetings, especially those of the newly emerging suffrage organizations of the western territories, thus bringing into the fold women who were too poor, overworked, or geographically isolated to attend. Duniway used her caustic wit to burn holes into antisuffragists and their cause. Rhetorically exemplifying her own argument that enfranchisement was a matter of rights—not women's tendency to sweetness and to reform—she attacked one opponent as "this woman slanderer, this flippant tongue simpleton, this brazen-faced sham . . . making frantic efforts to induce all men to believe that all women were as bad as herself."[7] She was no gentler on men, saying once she knew "many rum-soaked 'sturdy oaks' whose pestiferous rottenness can support no 'clinging vine.' "[8] She demolished the logic of the antisuffragists and outlined the theory of East Coast suffragists that the Fourteenth and Fifteenth Amendments enfranchised women. Like Susan B. Anthony, Duniway herself tried to vote in Portland in 1872.

Duniway took on some very thorny problems then plaguing the cause of the new woman, although the long-term effectiveness of her support is unclear. For example, Duniway initially supported the two sisters who published *Woodhull and Claflin's Weekly,* and at one point she even offered free subscriptions to that "valuable, stirring, and wide-awake paper" to her own new subscribers. Once she realized their advocacy of "free love," she backed off. On the other hand, Duniway did not mask or modify her admiration of Victoria Woodhull's cleverness and daring and specifically her political clout. Furthermore, Duniway argued, men were publishing hundreds of immoral journals.[9] Her complex reasoning on, and distancing from, the Prohibition movement raised even more suspicions among suffragists.

Duniway, who apparently was the primary wage earner of the family, faced constant financial problems and never stopped pleading for paying subscriptions, which topped one thousand by 1880.[10] In 1883, in preparation for a public referendum on suffrage, local antisuffragists established a *Northwest News,* apparently aiming to bankrupt Duniway. Duniway sued against its use of her paper's name. But after the case languished in court for nine months (until after the referendum), the judge ruled against Duniway, who had to pay substantial court costs, at which point the competitor folded. Ultimately, in 1887, given censure even within the suffrage movement over Duniway's strong-minded style (but using the excuse she was anti-Prohibition), she sold her paper to a Portland businessman and friend of her brother Harvey Scott. The buyer promised to advocate equal rights and justice and planned to add articles on history, science, and culture; but he went out of business after two months.[11]

Duniway apparently hoped to use money from the sale of the paper to develop land she owned in Idaho with her sons to set up an institution for cooperative housekeeping, but her family opposed the idea.[12] In 1892 Duniway tried to established a monthly journal devoted to literature and liberty. *The Coming*

Century soon failed for financial reasons, however. In 1895 she became editor of a suffrage and temperance weekly, *Pacific Empire,* but she chafed under the authority of her publisher Frances Gotshall.[13] In 1899, as president of the Oregon Equal Suffrage Association, Duniway established a monthly bulletin, *The Campaign Leaflet.*[14]

Duniway's autobiography appeared in 1914, two years after, at the request of the governor, she was able to sign the equal suffrage proclamation that had finally passed in Oregon and the year that, despite Duniway's best efforts, Prohibition also passed. Duniway died in 1915, after several years of health problems (perhaps undiagnosed diabetes), including lingering infections and the amputation of two toes.[15] Again, the real impact of Duniway's vehemence, passion, and refusal to mince words is unclear. Nonetheless, *The New Northwest* provided a model of, and for, the strong-minded pioneer woman. It dramatized at least one important line of reasoning among suffragists, namely, that women should enjoy the same political, cultural, and economic rights as men.

Notes

1. Eleanor Flexner, "Introduction," in Abigail Scott Duniway, *Path Breaking. An Autobiographical History of the Equal Suffrage Movement in Pacific Coast States* (New York: Schocken Books, 1971, 2d ed.; reprinted from the James, Kerns and Abbott edition of 1914), p. xi.
2. Ruth Barnes Moynihan, *Rebel for Rights* (New Haven, Conn.: Yale University Press, 1983), pp. 1–3.
3. Duniway, *Path Breaking,* p. 10.
4. Ibid., p. 85.
5. Ibid., p. 51.
6. June 30, 1871, p. 2.
7. April 5, 1872, p. 2.
8. July 14, 1871, p. 2.
9. July 14, 1871, p. 1; January 10, 1873, p. 2; January 17, 1873, p. 2.
10. *Amercian Newspaper Directory* (New York: George P. Rowell, 1880), p. 971.
11. *The Woman's Journal,* January 25, 1887, p. 36.
12. Moynihan, *Rebel for Rights,* pp. 187–189.
13. *The Woman's Journal,* September 7, 1895, p. 281.
14. *The Woman's Journal,* November 11, 1899, p. 301.
15. Moynihan, *Rebel for Rights,* p. 218.

Information Sources

BIBLIOGRAPHY:

Duniway, Abigail Scott. *Path Breaking. An Autobiographical History of the Equal Suffrage Movement in Pacific Coast States.* 2d ed. New York: Schocken Books, 1971; reprinted from the James, Kerns, and Abbott edition of 1914.

Moynihan, Ruth Barnes. *Rebel for Rights.* New Haven, Conn.: Yale University Press, 1983.

Steiner, Linda. "The Woman's Suffrage Press, 1850–1900: A Cultural Analysis." Diss., University of Illinois at Urbana–Champaign, 1979.

INDEX SOURCES: None.
LOCATION SOURCES: Rutgers University; Stanford University; University of California at Berkeley; Library of Congress.

Publication History

PERIODICAL TITLE AND TITLE CHANGES: *The New Northwest.*
VOLUME AND ISSUE DATA: Vols. 1–16 (1881–1887). Weekly.
PUBLISHER AND PLACE OF PUBLICATION: Abigail Scott Duniway (1871–1887). Portland, Ore.
EDITOR: Abigail Scott Duniway (1871–1887).
CIRCULATION: 1,000–2,000.

Linda Steiner

NEW WOMEN'S TIMES

During its ten years of life, *New Women's Times* often invoked the name of woman's rights activist Susan B. Anthony. It was a natural name for the newspaper to use. *New Women's Times* and its editorial collective admired Anthony's radical perspectives on the role of women in society and shared her suspicion of the patriarchal media system in the country. The connection was not just ideological. They were also linked geographically *New Women's Times* and Susan B. Anthony shared the same hometown, Rochester, New York.[1]

Throughout its life, the *New Women's Times* editorial collective seemed mindful of Anthony's caution, which the newspaper often reprinted:

Just as long as newspapers and magazines are controlled by men, every woman upon them must write articles which are reflections of men's ideas. As long as that continues, women's ideas and deepest convictions will never go before the public.[2]

New Women's Times was founded in January 1975, at a time when the feminist press was flourishing. *off our backs** was already five years old; *Big Mama Rag* was energizing the feminists of the West; *Union Wage** offered a labor point of view; *La Wisp** and other women's peace publications reminded readers of the need for peace at a time of war; and *Prime Time** provided perspectives of the "mature" woman. When it was founded, *New Women's Times* did not fit comfortably into this group, however. When it was launched, this newspaper was designed to serve the informational needs of the feminists in Rochester. While it always offered much news from the New York State area, the periodical gradually expanded its editorial vision and its circulation.[3]

Although the newspaper began in 1975, the planning for it dated back to 1974. Maxine Sobel, a Rochester feminist, called an open meeting to discuss the possibility of starting a feminist newspaper. Unlike the early days of many other feminist newspapers (including *off our backs,** *No more fun and games,** and *Voice of the Women's Liberation Movement**), Sobel drew professional journalists to the project from the beginning. At that first open meeting, an editor, a photographer, an artist, and a writer all came. Like other feminist newspapers, however, *New Women's Times* was underfinanced. The initial capital investment was just fifty dollars, the amount that Sobel earned selling bagels. Fund-raising followed. Nearly six thousand dollars was donated the first year to make the planned newspaper a reality.[4] *New Women's Times* never outgrew its underfinancing. The newspaper often commented on its financial problems.

The early focus on Rochester, New York, soon shifted. By the late 1970s, the newspaper was attempting to carry news and features that touched on the high points of feminist life throughout America. Religion became a special focus. The pope's trip to America was covered extensively, albeit from a feminist perspective: "The Pontiff repeated the same, tired old dogma as reason why women should continue to be second-class members of the Church."[5] When feminist Sonia Johnson was excommunicated from the Mormon Church for her role in the equal rights amendment (ERA) campaign, the *New Women's Times* applauded her courage: "[W]e should always remind ourselves that all feminists are 'excommunicated' from the patriarchal mainstream to one degree or another." The collective continued, "Our wish for the New Year is that we all have the courage to risk exclusion from a society we know is predicated on our oppression."[6]

Social and political issues always received extensive coverage, oftentimes from an international perspective. For example, the *New Women's Times* covered the failure of marriage reform in Kenya, the missing children in Argentina, and Iranian men who threatened women demonstrators.[7] (Although it was facing an uncertain financial future, the newspaper even sent a correspondent to the International Women's Year Conference in Copenhagen.[8])

The greatest amount of coverage of social and political issues dealt with the United States and, more specifically, the Great Lakes area. Thus, the newspaper kept its readers up-to-date on threats to abortion rights,[9] the women's campaigns against pornography,[10] government oppression of women's groups,[11] and health threats facing women.[12]

Like many radical feminist newspapers, *New Women's Times* covered the campaign for the ERA only halfheartedly. The *New Women's Times* editorial collective found the *philosophical base* of the amendment faulty. The ERA failed to question the appropriateness of the laws or who had the power to make the laws. As two women wrote in their editorial: "Laws won't equalize our lives. We as women must create and demand what we need and want."[13] Instead, the *New Women's Times* editorial collective suggested new goals, new ways of looking at society, and new strategies for change. "Our power must not come from the oppression of others. It is born of a collective struggle, fueled by the need to end male supremacy, and guided by our spirits and creative approach to go on beyond that which we know." For real change, one collective member suggested:

> We need to go beyond the inadequate; the question is not how do we comfortably place ourselves in the present society, but what kind of a society do women need, and what kind of movement will it take to bring us there. The rejection of power doled out from the hands of men will force us to imagine a society free from patriarchal hierarchy.[14]

Politics, however, never excluded other topics from the newspaper. From the beginning, the newspaper had a special commitment to improving the coverage of the arts and, more specifically, the art of feminists. Thus, *New Women's Times* extensively covered such feminist artists as singer Holly Near, such women-centered arts festivals as Michigan's Womyn's Music Festival,[15] and feminist cinema in a department entitled "Film Review." This commitment to literature and the arts explained the launch of the "Feminist Review," a special insert into the *New Women's Times* that was issued six times a year. Launched in 1978,[16] the "Feminist Review" had its own editorial collective (many of whom were also involved in the production of the *New Women's Times*), its own nameplate, and its own numeration system. Here was a showcase for feminist art, literature, and reviews. The "Feminist Review" was an extremely popular addition to the *New Women's Times* editorial package.[17] Praise for the section came from within the feminist community and outside it as well. Even standard reference works praised the new section. Bill Katz and Linda Sternberg Katz endorsed it in their *Magazines for Libraries;* they called the section a "laudable publication by itself."[18]

In spite of the popularity of the "Feminist Review," *New Women's Times* was having serious financial difficulties. The problems dated back to the undercapitalized launch. Things did not improve as time passed, even though circulation in 1981 had reached twenty-five thousand.[19] Part of the reason for this might have been a circulation policy that allowed complimentary issues to be sent to women in mental hospitals and in prison as well as to women who could not otherwise afford to subscribe.[20] This circulation policy, however, failed to explain *New Women's Times'* ongoing financial problems. The newspaper failed to draw an adequate advertising base.[21] Although the newspaper had a national and international circulation,[22] the newspaper had to rely on an advertising base of primarily small businesses in the Rochester, New York, area. The (Wo)Managerial Collective that ran the *New Women's Times* business operations simply could not attract a large, national advertising base. Likewise, the collective had difficulty dealing with continually mounting production and legal expenses. Repeatedly, the newspaper had to rely on fund-raising and donations.

Summer 1980, just after the newspaper celebrated its fifth anniversary, brought extensive financial and legal problems. In part, these were due to conditions outside the newspaper's control. *New Women's Times* was sued by a new consumer women's magazine called *New Woman*. Although the lawsuit was eventually settled in the newspaper's favor,[23] the legal expenses left *New Women's Times* two thousand dollars in debt.[24] By the end of the year, the newspaper started a campaign to raise ten thousand dollars to place it on a stronger financial footing. The newspaper established female-focused contribution categories: ten dollars for a "spinster"; twenty-five dollars for a "hag"; fifty dollars for an "amazon"; and seventy-five dollars or more for a "great goddess." However, the campaign met with only limited success. By 1981, the newspaper had to increase its newsstand price (to eighty cents per issue). By the middle of the year, *New Women's Times* continued to lament its problems with "Money, Money, Money."[25] By 1983, *New Women's Times* was still in debt and kept publishing only because of short-term loans from "friends" and fund-raising. As a cost-cutting measure, no August edition was issued.

In January 1984, *New Women's Times* celebrated its tenth anniversary. But the year did not bring any better financial news to the newspaper. The collective could not put out an October issue. The combined October/November issue was small. The newspaper remained heavily in debt. The prospects for improvement seemed remote. The newspaper had been losing subscribers by the "hundreds." Advertising never generated the revenue that the newspaper needed. As the newspaper explained:

> The women at NWT find themselves at a crossroads. After our first decade of publication, we wonder is there a mandate to carry on. We lack money, readership, and energy (read staff members), but if we knew that what we do is wanted, is supported, then perhaps we could find ways of resolving our financial disaster and get more readers.

The newspaper asked readers to send a ten-dollar birthday gift[26] as a gesture of support. The newspaper heard little in response. Only eight or nine readers sent the ten-dollar check. The December 1984 issue was *New Women's Times'* last. *off our backs* continued all *New Women's Times* subscriptions and also ran some of the essays and reviews that had been scheduled for publication. A chapter in feminist news, features, and the arts had ended.

Notes

1. The connection was not lost on others as well. Kirsten Grimstad and Susan Rennie in their *New Women's Survival Sourcebook* observed that the *New Women's Times* was a "feminist newspaper that Susan B. Anthony would be proud of" (Kirsten Grimstad and Susan Rennie, *New Women's Survival Sourcebook* New York: Knopf, 1975), p. 153.

2. "The Need for Women's Publishing," January 4–17, 1980, p. 2.

3. Bill Katz and Linda Sternberg Katz, *Magazines for Libraries,* 4th ed. (New York: R. R. Bowker, 1982), p. 911.

4. Karen Hagberg, "New Women's Times," March 1981, p. 27.

5. Beverly LaBelle, "John Paul II on Abortion, Woman's Place," October 26–

November 8, 1979, p. 1. See also Maxine Sobel, "More on the Pope," editorial, November 23–December 6, 1979, p. 2.

6. "Bravo Sonia," December 21, 1979–January 3, 1980, p. 2. See also news report, p. 1.

7. "Marriage Reform Fails—Wife Beating Upheld in Kenya," September 14–27, 1979, p. 4; "International News," January 4–17, 1980, p. 4.

8. See August 29–September 25, 1980, p. 2.

9. See, for example, "Supreme Court Upholds Paternalism," "Bishop Files Suit," "Abortion Clinic Invaded," all September 14–27, 1979, p. 7.

10. Karen Hagberg, "Hello Broadway, Goodbye Porn" and "A Call for Unity," September 28–October 11, 1979, pp. 2, 4–5; Maxine Sobel, "Working Out Strategies: East Coast Pornography Conference," October 12–24, 1979.

11. "New FBI Guidelines—Women among Targeted," April 1983, p. 1.

12. See, for example, "Warning: Preganancy and Aspirin May Not Mix" and "The State Vs. DES," October 12–25, 1979, p. 4. The newspaper had a department entitled "Health," which focused on women's health issues.

13. "B.R. . . . A.R.," November 1982, p. 2.

14. Lynn Breslawski, "Feminism vs. the Women's Movement," January 1981, p. 2.

15. Leah Warnick, "Holly Near: Growing Up," October 26–November 8, 1979, p. 3; "Music as Cultural Work: The Power to Change," October 12–25, 1979, p. 6; Karen Hagberg, "Controversy at Women's Hall of Fame," September 14–27, 1979, p. 1.

16. The first issue appeared in November 1978. The "Feminist Review" had its own nameplate and its own numeration. Thirty-six issues of the "Feminist Review" were published. This section included a number of well-known, well-regarded feminist writers and artists as contributors. For example, E. M. Broner, author of *A Weave of Women;* Jan Clausen, editor of *Condition;* Mary Sojourner, a columnist for *off our backs;* and Susan Carter, a sculptor and illustrator, all contributed to the September "Feminist Review."

17. Karen Hagberg has been generally credited with the idea and founding of the "Feminist Review." Hagberg, a leader in both the feminist and gay rights movements in Rochester, had a Ph.D. in music and a commitment to feminist arts. Besides writing and editing the "Feminist Review," she also did typesetting and taught piano (Lucy Owen, "Karen: 'I'm Lucky. I'm a Born Dyke,' " February 1981, p. 12).

18. Katz and Katz, *Magazines for Libraries* p. 911.

19. Karen Hagberg, "New Women's Times," March 1981, p. 27.

20. Advertisement, December 1984, p. 16.

21. *New Women's Times* had an advertising policy that prevented them from accepting advertising from liquor and cosmetic firms and companies that objectified women, such as the Playboy Press. See advertisement, December 1980, p. 3.

22. In 1981, Hagberg noted that the newspaper had readers from Florida to Alaska and fifteen foreign countries (Hagberg, "New Women's Times," p. 27).

23. "Resources," *Communities,* July 1978, pp. 57–60; "New Women's Times Sued," *Gay News,* January 20, 1979, p. 2; "New Woman Sues New Women's Times and Loses," *WIN Magazine,* September 27, 1979, p. 17.

24. "Money," June 20–July 3, 1980, p. 2.

25. "Money, Money, Money," June 1981, p. 2.

26. Lynn Breslawski, Editorial, October/November 1984.

Information Sources

BIBLIOGRAPHY:
Grimstad, Kirsten, and Susan Rennie, eds. *The New Woman's Survival Sourcebook.* New York: Knopf, 1975.
Katz, Bill, and Linda Sternberg Katz. *Magazines for Libraries.* 4th ed. New York: R. R. Bowker, 1982.
"One Voice Less for Women." *off our backs* June 1985, p. 17.
INDEX SOURCES: Alternative Press Index.
LOCATION SOURCES: University of Illinois Library; Historical Society of Wisconsin; Harvard University Library; and other libraries.

Publication History

PERIODICAL TITLE AND TITLE CHANGES: *New Women's Times* (1975–1984).
VOLUME AND ISSUE DATA: Vols. 1–10 (January 1975–December 1984). Monthly (1975–1978); semimonthly (1979–1980); monthly (1981–1984).
PUBLISHER AND PLACE OF PUBLICATION: New Women's Times Inc. Rochester, N.Y.
EDITORS: New Women's Times Editorial Collection (membership changes over time) (1975–1984).
CIRCULATION: Self-reported, 1981: 25,000.

Kathleen L. Endres

9T05 NEWSLINE

It was inevitable that 9to5, National Association of Working Women would eventually get around to starting a newsletter. After all, the founders and the leaders of the group had always been committed to communicating their concerns and working for change. What is surprising is that it took so long to get a newsletter started.

9to5 started in Boston in 1973 as an organization of clerical workers at Harvard who objected to the salary inequities and limited advancement opportunities at that college. One of the first things the members did was start a newsletter. It is unclear what became of that newsletter.[1] However, it was not until 1982 that 9to5, by then a national association, began its own newsletter and distributed it to its membership.[2]

By the time the *9to5 Newsletter* debuted, the Boston group had gone through myriad changes. In 1978, the group had convened its first Convention for Working Women. In 1979, it joined with other cities to create the Working Women Organizing Project, based in Cleveland, Ohio. In 1980, the Cleveland organization, by then called 9to5, National Association of Working Women, enjoyed the publicity surrounding the hit movie, *9to5,* starring actresses Jane Fonda, Lily Tomlin, and Dolly Parton. The film had been inspired by the National Association of Working Women and its executive director, Karen Nussbaum, a friend of Jane Fonda. Two years later, the national group developed the Bill of Rights for Office Workers, which covered pay equity, flextime, job sharing, maternity leave, and medical benefits.[3] The next year, the *9to5 Newsletter,* debuted under editor Ellen Cassedy, one of the founding members of the group.[4] It is difficult to chronicle the first years of the newsletter; few copies are extant.[5] However, this much is known: from its beginning, the newsletter apparently followed a consistent format: four pages of organization news, issued five times a year.

By 1987,[6] the newsletter (then edited by Deborah Meyer) reflected the energy and vitality of the national association—although in an unimaginative layout and design. Nonetheless, the newsletter had a friendly, inviting tone. The writing was clear; even complex issues were presented in an easy-to-understand manner. For example, in March/April 1987, Meyer outlined "parental leave" and 9to5's support of national legislation to achieve those leaves.[7] The January/February 1988 issue dealt with "VDT syndrome" in the same clear, concise manner.[8] Meyer encouraged a certain familiarity with the leadership of 9to5 through her use of language. For instance, Executive Director Karen Nussbaum was simply "Karen" in the second reference. Although page 1 was always reserved for just one story of top importance, page 2 tended to be the "editorial page," with letters from Nussbaum, summaries of important issues surfacing on the organization's telephone hot line,[9] updates on how to contact representatives in Congress to lobby for measures endorsed by 9to5,[10] and news on national issues affecting women.[11] Page 3 featured "9to5@work," short news stories about specific chapters across the United States. Page 4, "backspace," offered news updates on developments that could affect workingwomen.

Under Meyer the newsletter introduced advertising. In the March/April 1987 issue, the newsletter ran a special advertising insert. Most of the products advertised were designed for use in the office. One notable exception was an advertisement for *New Directions for Women,** a feminist publication. The newsletter also carried this disclaimer: "We want you to know that 9to5 has not tested any of the products, nor does 9to5 endorse or recommend any of the products that have advertised with us. But we do appreciate their patronage!"[12] Three years would pass before another advertising insert would appear in the newsletter. This time it would be an advertisement for *Working Woman* magazine.[13]

Cindia Cameron replaced Meyer in 1989, but she stayed only a brief time. Less than a year later, the newsletter had a new editor, a new design, a new name, a new color, and a new excitement. Barbara Otto was the individual responsible for the changes. Under Meyer and Cameron, the newsletter had a certain comfortable appeal. Under Otto, the newsletter seemed to graphically reflect the dynamism within the organization. The newsletter was renamed *9to5 Newsline* with a redesigned logo that suggested movement. New subheads intensified the immediacy. Updates from the hot line were now called "HOT-NEWS from the Hotline." A second color was also added—purple (later changed to orange). A vertical stripe on the front page (with a purple screen) highlighted news inside.

In spite of the "graphic" changes, the newsletter had not changed significantly. Page 1 continued to emphasize the single, top story the organization wanted highlighted. The range varied from results of the "National Boss Contest: The Good, the Bad & the Downright Unbelievable,"[14] to stories of members who successfully sued their employers,[15] from updates on privacy issues affecting office workers,[16] to legislation that would help women and their families.[17] Page 2 continued to be the editorial page. Page 3 continued to offer news on the local chapters. Page 4 offered other news updates.

Major changes came to the group and its newsletter in 1993 after President Bill Clinton nominated 9to5 executive director Karen Nussbaum to be head of the Labor Department's Women's Bureau. Ellen Bravo was picked to succeed Nussbaum; but this was not a simple move. With it came changes that shook the whole organization. Ellen Bravo was from the active Milwaukee chapter of 9to5. When she was elected the new executive director of the association, the national headquarters—and the newsletter—moved to Milwaukee to be with her.

Since 1993, there have been three different editors of the *Newsline:* Regina Stoltzfus, Sherri Jones, and Maripat Blankenheim, who also acts as director of public relations for the organization. The move to Milwaukee meant a number of changes to the newsletter. The second color became orange, instead of the familiar purple; the typeface was switched to a smaller, condensed, more difficult-to-read font; the layout changed from its clean design to a more cluttered look.

Since Maripat Blankenheim took over as editor with the September/October 1994 issue, there have been some changes in the format. The condensed, difficult-to-read typeface has been replaced by one that is easier to read. This is in keeping with the "subtle changes" she plans.[18] However, the editorial content and the mission of the newsletter should not change much. She sees her newsletter accomplishing three things: (1) "to keep members informed on 9to5's role in national events affecting working women"; (2) "to use the *Newsline* as our means of advertising" for such 9to5 activities as the summer school program or the boss contest; and (3) "to let members know what their fellow members are up to." Those things, she insists, will make the newsletter more pertinent to the membership.[19]

Notes

1. "The History of 9to5," Cleveland *Plain Dealer,* June 12, 1993, p. 8A.

2. Current editor Maripat Blankenheim said that the circulation of this newsletter is limited to the 9to5 membership and a few "friends." The newsletter is not sent to the press or government officials, unless, of course, they are members of the association. A limited number of libraries subscribe to the newsletter. The newsletter is included in the cost of membership.

3. Ibid.

4. Cassedy went on to write with Ellen Bravo *The 9to5 Guide to Combatting Sexual Harassment: Candid Advice from 9to5, the National Association of Working Women,* New York: Wiley, 1992.

5. The author was unable to locate a complete collection of this periodical at any of the libraries consulted. The national headquarters of 9to5, National Association of Working Women in Milwaukee also does not have a complete run of the publication.

6. Cleveland Public Library's holdings of *9to5 Newsline* begin in 1987.

7. "Parental Leave: 9to5 Supports a National Bill to Help Working Families," March/April 1987, p. 1.

8. "VDT Syndrome: The Physical and Mental Trauma of Computer Work," January/February 1988, p. 1.

9. 9to5, National Association of Working Women introduced its Job Problem Hotline in 1989.

10. See, for example, March/April 1987, p. 2.

11. See, for example, January/February 1989, p. 2.

12. "Important Notice," March/April 1987, p. 4.

13. October/November 1990, insert.

14. The contest was introduced in 1990. "The History of 9to5," p. 8A. The *Newsline* first covered the contest in May/June 1990, p. 1.

15. See, for example, "Teresa Fischette: One Woman Can Make a Difference," August/September 1991, p. 1.

16. See, for example, "Watch Out Big Brother," November/December 1991, p. 1.

17. See, for example, "Paid Leave Is Possible, Says 9to5 Report," August/September 1992.

18. Maripat Blankenheim, interview, November 30, 1994, Milwaukee, Wis.

19. Blankenheim interview.

Information Sources

BIBLIOGRAPHY:

Baker, Bob. "Workplace Horror Stories." *Los Angeles Times,* April 30, 1990, sec. E, p. 1.

Beyette, Beverly. "Still Hot under the Pink Collar." *Los Angeles Times,* April 24, 1991, sec. E, p. 1.

"The Future According to 9 to 5." *New York Times,* July 11, 1993, sec. 3, p. 23.

Haber, Lynn. "Survey by 9 to 5 Links VDTs, Health Problems." *Computerworld,* February 27, 1984, p. 12.

"The History of 9to5." *Cleveland Plain Dealer,* June 12, 1993, p. 8A.

Noble, Barbara Presley. "Speaking for the Working Woman." *New York Times,* July 11, 1993, sec. 3, p. 23.

Washington, Roxanne. "9to5 Rally Celebrates 20th year." *Cleveland Plain Dealer,* June 12, 1993, p. 1.

"What Employees Need to Know." *New York Times,* August 1, 1993, sec. 3, p. 23.

INDEX SOURCES: Not indexed.

LOCATION SOURCES: Cleveland Public Library; New York Public Library; and other libraries (holdings are often incomplete).

Publication History

PERIODICAL TITLE AND TITLE CHANGES: *9to5 Newsletter* (1982–1990); *9to5 Newsline* (1990–present).
VOLUME AND ISSUE DATA: Vols. 1– (May/June 1982–present). Five times a year.
PUBLISHER AND PLACE OF PUBLICATION: 9to5, National Association of Working Women. Cleveland, Ohio (1982–1993); Milwaukee, Wis. (1993–present).
EDITORS: Ellen Cassedy (1982–?); Deborah Meyer (?–1989); Cindia Cameron (1989–1990); Barbara Otto (1990–1992); Regina Stoltzfus (1993); Sherri Jones (1993–1994); Maripat Blankenheim (1994–present).
CIRCULATION: 9to5, 1994: approximately 20,000.

Kathleen L. Endres

NO MORE FUN AND GAMES

The women of Cell 16 of Boston were the ''movement heavies,'' at least that is how feminist Susan Brownmiller characterized them.[1] A small, well-organized ''vanguard cadre,'' Cell 16 was involved with many projects, including self-defense training for women and the production of one of the earliest radical feminist periodicals, *No More Fun and Games.* The periodical was a reflection of Cell 16. Editorially committed to celibacy, self-defense training for women, and separatism, *No More Fun and Games* illustrated Cell 16's vision of where *female* liberation should be heading.

To understand *No More Fun and Games,* one must understand Cell 16. Cell 16 was organized in the summer of 1968 by Roxanne Dunbar, who had moved to Boston from the West Coast, where she had been active in the New Left.[2] She organized the group by taking out an advertisement in an underground newspaper. The ad announced the formation of a ''Female Liberation Front. . . . To question: all phallic social structures. . . . To demand: free abortion and birth control on demand—communal raising of children by both sexes and by people of all ages.''[3] The original membership of Cell 16 cut across educational and socioeconomic boundaries. The original members were Dunbar; Dana Densmore, daughter of Donna Allen, one of the founders of the Women Strike for Peace and founder of *Media Report to Women**; Jeanne Lafferty; Lisa Leghorn; Abby Rockefeller, of the New York Rockefeller family; Betsy Warrior, a welfare mother; and Jayne West. Dunbar, Densmore, Leghorn, and Warrior were the most active in the writing and production of *No More Fun and Games.*

Although most female collectives preferred an equality, avoiding a hierarchical organization, Dunbar was the obvious leader and theoretician of Cell 16. Meredith Tax, who had been denied membership to Cell 16 prior to forming the socialist feminist group Bread and Roses, observed that Dunbar wanted to be the leader—''to be a charismatic leader in that very male style of charismatic leaders. She basically believed that she was Lenin. And she was certainly very good.''[4]

Dunbar was devoted to Valerie Solanas' thinking on male inferiority, and the women of Cell 16 read her radical "[Society for Cutting Up Men] S.C.U.M. Manifesto" early.[5] Indeed, many of Solanas' attitudes can be seen in much of the writing of *No More Fun and Games*.

When the journal first appeared in October 1968, it carried no name, no date, and no page numbers. Nonetheless, that first journal outlined the current thinking of Cell 16. While many radical feminist groups of the time (especially the Redstockings) blamed men for the position women were in, Cell 16—and particularly Dunbar—felt there was blame to go around. Men were the enemy—all men. "Yes, all men who identify with the Master class is [*sic*] our enemy." But women carried a heavy share of responsibility for their position in society. Women had to liberate themselves; they could not depend on men to do so. Women had to shake off their sex-role conditioning. "The ONLY way any human being can approach another on the basis of equality, or work for an egalitarian society, is if he or she is a WHOLE, and not seeking a body to leach off of."[6]

Dana Densmore articulated Cell 16's thinking on celibacy:

> Until we accept it [celibacy] completely, until we say "I control my own body and I don't need any insolent male with an overbearing presumptuous prick to come and clean out my pipes" they will always have over us the devastating threat of withdrawing their sexual attentions and worse, the threat of our ceasing even to be sexually attractive.[7]

Another writer emphasized that women must work for liberation separately. The currently existing radical organizations were not the forum for female liberation. "Radical politics is a man's business because politics is traditionally a man's business." Moreover, the men of the movement had a "vested interest in women's enslavement."

> It is up to the women to stand independently, to demand a society not based on an enslaving family unit with its male/female dependency, but based on the liberated individual, a sexless society where there is no distinction between the roles of male and female.[8]

This first issue was chock-full of essays, poetry, and polemics. Not surprisingly, there was no advertising. *No More Fun and Games* (under any of its various titles) never carried advertising. It relied on nontraditional methods to underwrite the expense of publishing. The group sponsored a showing of a film at a Boston theater to fund the first issue. Women without experience in journalism, layout, or production put the journal together. Distribution did not appear to be systematic. Betsy Warrior, a member of Cell 16, recalled selling the publication on Harvard Square.[9]

The second issue came out about five months later. (Cell 16 never promised a specific frequency, and the publication did not come out on any obvious schedule.) The name *No More Fun and Games* formally debuted in that February 1969 issue. Not only did the journal have a name, but it also had a date and page numbers.

This issue called for a revolution in woman's personal life. She should give up the nuclear family as one of the most oppressive institutions; women should remain single, avoiding pregnancy; women should stop buying and wearing cosmetics and wear only comfortable clothes. They should confront men who follow or bait them. In other words, *No More Fun and Games* urged its readers to take control of their own lives.[10]

In this analysis, men—no matter what their politics—stood in the way of real progress. Betsy Warrior saw men as an "Obsolete Life Form." "Like the tyrannosaurus, man is blocking evolution and sustaining his life at the expense of other better life forms."[11] Another writer took issue with "Mr. Smug Liberal," who was willing to push for woman's rights as long as they don't infringe on family life. The men of the radical movement were little better; they were chauvinistic, competitive, and elite—as diseased as the society that they protested.[12]

The journal also provided a radical analysis of the mass media, especially women's magazines; discussed articles appearing in general-interest periodicals; urged women to enroll in self-defense training, especially karate and judo; provided quotes and comments on women's role in society by Marx and Engels; and offered social commentary on the similarity of roles that women and African Americans played in society.[13]

The first real threat to the future of Cell 16 and its publication came in early 1970, when Roxanne Dunbar moved to New Orleans to organize southern women into the movement.[14] The group survived the move. However, the periodical did change. The April issue carried a new name, *The Female State: A Journal of Female Liberation*. The journal also shifted many of its editorial positions. The heavy leftist/Marxist orientation had shifted to a more clearly radical feminist stance. The periodical retained its viewpoint on celibacy as an alternative, self-defense for women, and separatism. However, the writers began to explore other issues that affected women in society. More and more the journal was dealing with issues and topics that influenced the personal lives of women. Dana Densmore looked at "androcentric language"; Lisa Leghorn wrote about child-care centers; Hilary Langhorst offered a look at women under Christianity.[15] Many of the essays seemed to harken back more to American feminist philosopher Charlotte Perkins Gilman[16] than to Marx.

Although Cell 16 had weathered Dunbar's departure, it had yet another, more serious crisis to face. In the fall 1970, Cell 16—and, by implication, its journal—faced the threat of co-optation by the Socialist Workers Party/Young Socialist Alliance (YSA). It all began innocently. The YSA women started attending Cell 16's karate classes. By the summer of 1970 several Cell 16 members were helping organize a YSA lecture series. In the process, the YSA women gained access to Cell 16 offices. Gradually, the YSA began the co-operation.

One offered to run Cell 16's office; others offered to store back issues of the journal and copies of Cell 16's posters that the group sold for revenue. When it became apparent that there was a deep division within the group between the YSA women and the others, the cell voted to disband. By mid-November 1970, the YSA tried to appropriate journal funds, cell files, and mailing lists. Betsy Warrior, a non-YSA cell member, sent out a three-page newsletter to subscribers, friends, and groups across the nation, informing them of the attempted takeover by the YSA.[17]

By the time the journal (now called *The First Revolution: A Journal of Female Liberation*) came out in July 1971, the crisis had passed. Cell 16 was reformed by the non-YSA women. This issue introduced a new practice. The periodical itself was not copyrighted; instead, each individual article was copyrighted by the author. Warrior and Densmore seemed to be the leading figures in this issue as well as the one that followed; this one reverted back to the original title, *No More Fun and Games: A Journal of Female Liberation*. But this issue, dated May 1973, was the last. Cell 16 ceased to function in 1973; its periodical died with it.

In all, the women of Cell 16 published only six issues in six years. However, those six issues contained one version of what radical feminism meant. As one of the first radical feminist periodicals published in the United States, it opened the discussion on the future of female liberation. That discussion was left to others to continue.

Notes

1. She was not alone in that characterization. After meeting some members in 1968, Carinne Coleman recalled thinking the women of Cell 16 were "very strong" (Alice Echols, *Daring to Be Bad: Radical Feminism Is America, 1967–1975* [Minneapolis: University of Minnesota Press, 1989], p. 158).

2. Ibid.

3. Flora Davis, *Moving the Mountain: The Women's Movement in America since 1960* (New York: Simon and Schuster, 1991), p. 83.

4. Echols, *Daring to Be Bad,* p. 159.

5. Ibid.

6. Roxanne Dunbar, "Slavery," [October 1968], unnumbered page.

7. Dana Densmore, "On Celibacy," [October 1968], unnumbered page.

8. Maureen Davidica, "Women and the Radical Movement," [October 1968], unnumbered pages.

9. Davis, *Moving the Mountain,* p. 83.

10. "What Do You Women Want?" February 1969, pp. 7–11.

11. Betsy Warrior, "Man as an Obsolete Life Form," February 1969, p. 78.

12. Dana Densmore, "Against Liberals," February 1969, pp. 60–63; Betsy Warrior, "American Radicalism: A Diseased Product of a Diseased Society?" February 1969, pp. 97–101.

13. See, for example, Dana Densmore, "Women's Magazines and Womanhood, 1969," November 1969, pp. 30–39; Roxanne Dunbar, "The Man & Woman Thing," February 1969, pp. 32–37; "What Do You Women Want?" pp. 4–13; February 1969,

pp. 64–65; Helen Hacker, "Castelike Status of Women and Negroes," November 1969, pp. 10–11.

14. Echols, *Daring to Be BAD*, p. 166.

15. Dana Densmore, "Speech Is the Form of Thought," April 1970, pp. 9–15; Lisa Leghorn, "Child-Care for the Child," pp. 26–29; Hilary Langhorst, "Eve's Sex Under God's Law," pp. 73–85.

16. See *Forerunner.**

17. Davis, *Moving the Mountain*, pp. 139–140; Judith Hole and Ellen Levine, *Rebirth of Feminism* (New York: Quadrangle Books, 1971), pp. 164–165; Echols, *Daring to Be BAD*, p. 166.

Information Sources

BIBLIOGRAPHY:

Davis, Flora. *Moving the Mountain: The Women's Movement in America since 1960.* New York: Simon and Schuster, 1991.

Echols, Alice. *Daring to Be BAD: Radical Feminism in America, 1967–1975.* Minneapolis: University of Minnesota Press, 1989.

Hole, Judith, and Ellen Levine. *Rebirth of Feminism.* New York: Quadrangle Books, 1971.

INDEX SOURCES: None.

LOCATION SOURCES: Microfilm available in the Herstory Series Reel 10 and Update 1, Reel 12.

Publication History

PERIODICAL TITLE AND TITLE CHANGES: Untitled (October 1968); *No More Fun and Games: A Journal of Female Liberation* (February 1969–November 1969); *The Female State: A Journal of Female Liberation* (April 1970); *The First Revolution: A Journal of Female Liberation* (July 1971); *No More Fun and Games: A Journal of Female Liberation* (May 1973).

VOLUME AND ISSUE DATA: Vol. 1 (six issues, October 1968–May 1973). Irregular frequency.

PUBLISHER AND PLACE OF PUBLICATION: Publisher not named (1968–1970); Cell 16 (1971); Female Liberation (1973). Somerville, Mass. (1968–1970); Cambridge, Mass. (1971–1973).

EDITORS: Not named.

CIRCULATION: Unknown.

Kathleen L. Endres

NOTES FROM THE FIRST YEAR

Initially a conversational summation of a year's worth of discussions and position papers by an early group of radical feminists, *Notes*[1] provided the conceptual and chronological link between the New York Radical Women and the New York Radical Feminists. In its rapid progression from conversations, to theories, to actions and an early demise, the publication mirrored the movement it recorded, laying social and theoretical foundations for the nationwide women's liberation movement.

Spurred by the New Left movement's denial that women's issues had relevance, radical feminist Shulamith Firestone came to New York from Chicago in October 1967, a month after trying to have women's issues heard at the National Conference for a New Politics.[2] Along with Pam Allen,[3] she formed New York's first women's group, Radical Women, which was soon called New York Radical Women. They culled members primarily from political activist groups, finding feminists disillusioned with the New Left's hostility toward women's issues and civil rights workers already sensitized to the devastating effects of oppression. Early meetings drew fifteen to thirty women.[4] Collectively, New York Radical Women was responsible for publishing the first issue of *Notes*.

The mimeographed journal was distributed as *Notes from the First Year* in June 1968.[5] As "the first feminist journal put out by the new Women's Liberation Movement,"[6] its lack of page numbering and copyediting reflected its lack of centralized editorial control. This resistance to editorial leadership was in keeping with the radical tenet to resist hierarchal organization leadership. A list of the twenty New York Radical Women "involved in producing the NOTES"[7] ran in lieu of an editor's name. The list included the name of a woman to whom correspondence could be sent; however, the publication asked that "[r]equests for reprints, or letters concerning the opinions stated, should be addressed to [the] authors."[8]

Primarily distributed in New York, copies of *Notes* nevertheless "managed to make their way across the country."[9] Despite the crude appearance of the thirty-seven-page journal, the second year's editorial stated that the effort had been so successful that even within the movement, copies were so hard to find that "one dare not leave one's tattered copy unguarded."[10] This second issue was published by a new group composed of some of the same members, the New York Radical Feminists.

Radical feminists had first gotten together to talk, or "rap" in small "rap groups" or "rap sessions," which allowed the women not only to gather but to talk among themselves on political as well as personal issues. These group sessions were "structures created specifically for the purpose of altering the participants' perceptions and conceptions of themselves and society at large."[11] The technique that enabled this attitudinal change was "consciousness-raising," which evolved out of the New York Radical Women's meetings and was more fully developed by the Redstockings group.[12] "The goal of consciousness-raising is to relate fragmented and seemingly unrelated problems in the lives of individual women and to construct a politic from the issues discovered in the process."[13] Radical feminists who gathered in these small groups began their sessions by each woman's stating her response to a question, such as whether she would prefer to have a boy, a girl, or no children. After each woman had stated her thoughts, time was spent on analysis, with the women often finding deep-seated sexism within themselves. Recognition of internalized sexism and self-hatred, along with the newfound knowledge of its pervasive nature, was self-actualizing and socially motivating. An early proponent of consciousness-raising wrote:

> I believe at this point, and maybe for a long time to come, that these analytical sessions are a form of political action. . . . One of the first things we discover in these groups is that personal problems are political problems. There are no personal solutions at this time. There is only collective action for a collective solution.[14]

However, the third year's issue published a newcomer's frustration with such groups. While she admitted that they had some usefulness, she wondered where feminists, having now achieved a presumably higher consciousness, should go from here.[15] This opinion symbolized the rift that developed among radical feminists on this issue.

With its constructed conversations from yearlong dialogues and its four-page "Women Rap about Sex," *Notes from the First Year* was the first publicly issued journal to use "rap" as a written technique, which became a popular form of the movement's literary expression.[16] The women rapped about the predominance of white, middle-class females in the movement, analogies to the black liberation movement, the "plastic sword" of feminine wiles, and sex-role definitions. The first issue also ran thought-provoking articles on sex, notably Anne Koedt's "Myth of the Vaginal Orgasm," which she ran more fully developed in the second issue. The first issue reprinted speeches on the right to abortion, an issue central to radical feminism. It also recounted the New York Radical Women's symbolic burial of traditional womanhood during the Jeannette Rankin Brigade's Washington march protesting the Vietnam War, which brought the group media coverage.

Also during 1968, however, divisions became apparent within the group. A few of the New York Radical Women formed a separate activist group called WITCH,[17] which specialized in ad hoc, or "zap," actions. At a Thanksgiving conference that year, the papers "The Myth of the Vaginal Orgasm" and "A Program for Feminist 'Consciousness Raising' " were read. Divided particularly on the issue of consciousness-raising, the New York Radical Women split into three groups after this conference.[18] New York Radical Women's Group I carried out counterinaugural demonstrations in January 1969 after Richard Nixon's election. Returning from these activities and "unable to convince other NEW YORK RADICAL WOMEN how badly they had been treated," Group I members Firestone and Ellen Willis formed Redstockings as a radical group within the New York Radical Women;[19] New York Radical Women who advocated consciousness-raising soon joined them.[20] Some of the New York Radical Women joined The Feminists, originally The October 17th Movement founded by radicalized New York National Organization for Women (NOW) founding member Ti-Grace Atkinson.[21]

In November 1969, New York City was host to a regional conference, the Congress to Unite Women, "the first large-scale structured meeting of the various women's groups."[22] With New York Radical Women in demise, Redstockings, as well as the Stanton–Anthony Brigade, which would soon become the nucleus of the New York Radical Feminists, was in attendance. After this conference, Firestone and former Feminists member Anne Koedt, both of the Stanton–Anthony Brigade, formed the New York Radical Feminists. On December 5, 1969, Firestone and Koedt presented a draft of the manifesto "Politics of the Ego," primarily written by Koedt, and the organizing principles, penned by Firestone, to about forty women.[23] The earlier group, New York Radical Women, was dissolved in the winter of 1969.[24] Firestone and Koedt brought their unit or "brigade" organizational structure to the formation of the New York Radical Feminists, formalizing it in the organizing principles and in adherence to their manifesto, which has been characterized as "a highly psychological analysis of male supremacy."[25]

Whereas New York Radical Women had opened the discussion of radical feminism with *Notes from the First Year,* Firestone and Koedt sounded out theories in editing *Notes from the Second Year.* Although the women were "cautioned that to present our ideas undiluted to the public might be a mistake," *Notes from the Second Year* was made available outside the movement because "we are sick and tired of having our views presented for us to other women by (usually distorting) intermediaries."[26] The second issue boasted a healthy 128 typeset pages, complete with photographs. Based far less on discussions, or "raps," than the first number, the second annual issue ran numerous reflective pieces and theoretical articles that analyzed and explained radical feminist stances. The journal proclaimed itself "the first overground publication *by* radical feminists rather than *about* them."[27] Manifestos and position papers were presented in this second issue by Atkinson, founder of The Feminists; Joreen [Jo Freeman], editor of *Voice of the Women's Liberation Movement**; Roxanne Dunbar, founder of Cell 16 and one of the founders of *No More Fun and Games**; Ellen Willis, journalist and cofounder of Redstockings; and author Kate Millet. New York Radical Feminist cofounders Firestone and Koedt published their manifesto "Politics of the Ego," along with the group's organizing principles. Also included were the manifesto of The Feminists, Jo Freeman's "Bitch Manifesto," and the "Redstockings Manifesto," which had first been published in July 1969.

As these manifestos were acted upon, tensions mounted within the New York Radical Feminists, particularly with regard to the Stanton–Anthony Brigade's being recognized as the leader in a professed leaderless group. About six months after the group's founding, these tensions worsened. In the summer of 1970 the Stanton–Anthony Brigade disbanded and left the New York Radical Feminists. Another brigade, which included activist Susan Brownmiller, assumed unofficial leadership as the New York Radical Feminists continued militant actions, and it counted about four hundred members by early 1971. But without the founding brigade, the group lacked cohesion and direction.[28] Although Koedt distanced herself from the group, she edited *Notes from the Third Year*.

In its "yearly collection of radical feminist writing,"[29] *Notes from the Third Year* followed up the discussions and theorizing with "fewer manifestoes and more work on specific issues such as prostitution, women's literature, rape, and lesbianism," characterizing the progression as "a period of intensive rather than extensive analysis."[30] This 142-page volume liberated history by tracing the work of early feminists, examined woman's place through articles on home-making, violence, children's books, and the arts, analyzed women's sex and power relationships, and questioned whether consciousness-raising had served its purpose. Reprints and original work included articles by Brownmiller, Jo Freeman, authors Mary Daly and Elaine Showalter, and Radicalesbians, a group of women-identified feminists.

Emanating from New York, the radical feminists traced their heritage to the rich nineteenth- and early twentieth-century feminist history of the area and the nation. Along with achieving a higher awareness of sisterhood, they ventured to globalize their perspective. The "Fourth World Manifesto" stated:

> There have been a great deal of comparisons of women's position with the position of minority groups in feminist literature. . . . to prove that females are in fact an oppressed group.
>
> But really the analogy should go the other way around. One should compare the stereotypes of blacks and other minority groups and sup-pressed cultures to the female stereotypes.
>
> Woman was the first group to be oppressed and subordinated as a caste to another group—men.[31]

Radical Feminists consciously recovered women's work that history had bur-ied, reconstructing the boldness of its nature for a modern generation desensi-tized by the civil upheavals of the 1960s. "Remember that to attack the Family, the Church, and the Law was no small thing in the Victorian Era."[32] After having distinguished themselves from the liberal feminists, who pushed for leg-islative reform, and instituting manifestos that stressed the need for social rev-olution and reconstruction, radical feminists recognized the need for a solidarity among feminists and the potential for a "cross-fertilization" with other feminist groups that was not possible with any other reform group.

> Each sector [liberal and radical] makes important contributions to the larger feminist struggle; the "rights" sector's strong emphasis on legal changes, for example, must be united with the "liberation" sector's stress on internal changes. Together, we can win important victories, always with

the understanding . . . that the final victory lies both in destroying the institutions of sexism and in the changed consciousness of all women.[33]

As the movement progressed, radical feminists called for a dismantling of society's insidious sex-role stereotype casting as a necessary vehicle for change. *Notes* emphasized that one's sexual preference did not make a radical; traditional marriage, however, was considered a fundamentally oppressive institution. Yet the transgression of social sex roles was more than a liberating personal choice.

[W]omen's liberation challenges the very nature of the sex role system, not just whether one may be allowed to make transfers within it. On the other hand, the gay movement has helped open up the question of women loving other women.[34]

Consciousness-raising was their most publicized technique. In recognizing that the way a woman lived her personal life was indeed a political statement, rap sessions and consciousness-raising groups situated women within the larger sociopolitical structure. This technique was subsequently adopted and mainstreamed by the liberal feminists.

In publishing the first "conversations," revolutionary foundational documents, and an analysis of the specific experiences that detailed the growth of the radical feminist movement, *Notes* cataloged the blossoming of the women's liberation branch of the new women's movement of the late 1960s and early 1970s. The publication's increased professionalism and thickness reflected the maturation of the modern feminist movement. The publication did not bow to commercial interests by running advertising, but it ran occasional "classifieds" for jobs or information. Although later issues cost $1.50, its first issue sold at fifty cents for women and $1 for men. One reason for the price differential

was that the authors wanted to reach women, thus preferring to keep the price low, but felt men ought to be charged for the privilege of reading the magazine if they insisted on it. They fully realized that a man could get a woman to buy a copy for him at the lower price. This was the second purpose. It was a form of political education to demonstrate to men and women the discomforts of having to go through someone else to fulfill one's desires or needs. It illustrated the true nature of the female role by reverse example as well as the high price of independence.[35]

New York Radical Feminists continued to function until 1972,[36] having evolved in ways "their founders never intended."[37] By 1972, the women's movement had become factionalized. The year 1973 saw the radical feminist movement give way to cultural feminism and liberal feminism.[39]

Notes was a publication that existed in what Stanton–Anthony Brigade member and one of the few black women involved in the women's liberation movement, Cellestine Ware, termed "feminist time":

> Feminist time is not like standard time in America. Liaisons are formed, educations are acquired, philosophies are discarded, and groups form, reconstitute themselves and dissolve all in a matter of seasons. Feminists move from city to city, often to meet other women known from their last location. And all the time there is the excitement of knowing that women are making history.[39]

Notes

1. Unless a specific issue is particularly being addressed, the publication will be referred to as *Notes,* as each title varied with the year; parentheses were occasionally used. For example, *Notes (From the Second Year).*

2. Judith Hole and Ellen Levine, *Rebirth of Feminism* (New York: Quadrangle, 1971); both Firestone and Jo Freeman, members of the ad hoc radical women's caucus at the conference, formed the first women's groups of the movement after this episode, with Freeman's group based in Chicago.

3. Cellestine Ware implies the other cofounder was Ellen Willis, in *Woman Power* (New York: Tower, 1970), p. 38.

4. Hole and Levine, *Rebirth of Feminism,* p. 115.

5. This first volume was the only one to run with a date. The others had copyright years and were published after the preceding year's discussions and writings. (The publication date of *Notes from the Second Year* was listed as April 1970 in Hole and Levine, *Rebirth of Feminism,* p. 416.)

6. Editorial, 1970, p. [2]; this assertion is substantiated by Hole and Levine, who more specifically call it the "first radical feminist journal," ibid., p. 407.

7. June 1968, p. [2]. The list included Kathy Amatniek (Kathie Sarachild) (Redstockings, cofounder of the New York feminist newspaper *Woman's World*); Rosalyn Baxandall (Ros), the woman to whom correspondence could be sent (Redstockings); Cindy Cisler (abortion activist and author); Corinne Coleman (Redstockings, editor of the short-lived women's liberation magazine *Feelings*); Judith Duffett (author); Shulamith Firestone, cofounder of New York Radical Women (cofounder of New York Radical Feminists, author); Ann Forer (member of the New Left); Jennifer Gardner (worked for the Bay Area women's liberation newspaper *The Woman's Page*); Carol Hanisch (civil rights worker, author); Anne Koedt (cofounder of the New York Radical Feminists).

8. June 1968, p. [2].

9. Hole and Levine, *Rebirth of Feminism,* p. 119.

10. Editorial, 1970, p. [2].

11. Jo Freeman, *The Politics of Women's Liberation* (New York: David McKay, 1975), p. 118.

12. Hole and Levine, *Rebirth of Feminism,* p. 137.

13. Ware, *Woman Power,* p. 110.

14. Carol Hanisch, "The Personal Is Political," 1970, p. 76.

15. Carol Payne, "Consciousness-Raising: A Dead End?" 1971, p. 99.

16. Hole and Levine, *Rebirth of Feminism,* p. 119.

17. Hole and Levine stated that the acronym WITCH at first stood for Women's

International Terrorist Conspiracy from Hell, but it tended to change with an action undertaken; for instance, "telephone company workers protesting conditions became Women Incensed at Telephone Company Harassment." (Hole and Levine, *Rebirth of Feminism,* p. 127.)

18. Ibid., pp. 132–133.

19. Ware, *Woman Power,* p. 38. For the account of the January 1968 protest in Washington, D.C., at which the women's liberation presentation was met by jeers and threats from the radical men, see Ellen Willis, "Women and the Left," 1970, pp. 55–56.

20. Hole and Levine, *Rebirth of Feminism,* pp. 133, 136.

21. Ibid., p. 143.

22. Ibid., p. 150. Over five hundred women represented organizations from the entire eastern seaboard at the congress, November 21–23.

23. Ibid., p. 152.

24. Alice Echols, *Daring to Be BAD* (Minneapolis: University of Minnesota Press, 1989), p. 388.

25. Ibid., p. 187.

26. Editorial, 1970, p. [2].

27. Ibid.

28. Echols, *Daring to Be BAD,* pp. 191–194.

29. Editorial box, 1971, p. [2].

30. Editorial, 1971, p. [2].

31. Barbara Burris, "The Fourth World Manifesto," 1971, p. 117.

32. Shulamith Firestone, "The Women's Rights Movement in the U.S.: A New View," June 1968, p. [3].

33. Editorial, 1971, p. [2].

34. Interviewee, "Loving Another Woman: Interview by Anne Koedt," 1971, p. 25.

35. Freeman, *The Politics of Women's Liberation,* p. 116.

36. Echols, *Daring to Be BAD,* p. 388.

37. Ibid., p. 198.

38. Ibid., pp. 198–199.

39. Ware, *Woman Power,* p. 121.

Information Sources

BIBLIOGRAPHY:

Freeman, Jo. *The Politics of Women's Liberation: A Case Study of an Emerging Social Movement and Its Relation to the Policy Process.* New York: David McKay, 1975.

Hole, Judith, and Ellen Levine. *Rebirth of Feminism.* New York: Quadrangle, 1971.

Yates, Gayle Graham. *What Women Want: The Ideas of the Movement.* Cambridge: Harvard University Press, 1975.

Ware, Cellestine. *Woman Power: The Movement for Women's Liberation.* New York: Tower, 1970.

INDEX SOURCES: Not indexed.

LOCATION SOURCES: Microfilmed in Herstory.

Publication History

PERIODICAL TITLE AND TITLE CHANGES: *Notes from the First Year* (1968); *Notes from the Second Year: Radical Feminism* (1970); *Notes from the Third Year: Women's Liberation* (1971).

VOLUME AND ISSUE DATA: Vols. 1–3. (No volume or issue numbers.) Yearly.
PUBLISHER AND PLACE OF PUBLICATION: New York Radical Women (1968);
    Shulamith Firestone and Anne Koedt (1970); Notes from the Second Year, Inc.
    (1971). New York.
EDITORS: Members of the New York Radical Feminists (1968); Shulamith Firestone
    and Anne Koedt (1970); Anne Koedt (1971).
CIRCULATION: Unknown.

Therese L. Lueck

N.Y. PEACELETTER

The *N.Y. Peaceletter* (then simply called the *Women Strike for Peace Newsletter*) was one of the first publications of any chapter of Women Strike for Peace (WSP), a nationwide association with no leaders, no members, and no hierarchical organization. Serving the women in the New York, New Jersey, and Connecticut region, the newsletter—when it premiered—reflected well upon the group it served: it read well, it looked good, and it articulated clearly the problems associated with nuclear proliferation. Ten years later, the *Peaceletter* served only the New York WSP chapter but still read well and looked good; by then, the editors of the monthly were arguing for the end of the Vietnam War. Ten years later, the nation at peace, the *Peaceletter* had returned to its roots, debating and denouncing a new generation of nuclear weapons, the so-called Star Wars arsenal. The newsletter, its editors, and WSP seemed to have come full circle.

Women Strike for Peace had started modestly enough at a cocktail party in Georgetown in 1961. Dagmar Wilson, an affluent wife, mother, and freelance illustrator, gave the party. That night Lord Bertrand Russell gave a speech over the BBC outlining the need for peace. At a time when many Americans feared the "bomb" and what nuclear war might bring, the women at the Wilson party decided to meet the next day and do "something" about the situation. Ruth Gage-Colby explained what happened next: "They [the women] brought their address books, later borrowed some lists of names, and sent out a call to women to 'strike' against the bomb."[1] What followed made headlines around the country. On November 1, 1961, approximately fifty thousand women responded to this call and marched on Washington for peace.[2] A month later, women in New York and California decided to send a similar call to women in other countries, including the Soviet Union. Women from forty countries responded. Women Strike for Peace had become an international "nonorganization." On January 15, 1962, women marched against nuclear proliferation in New York, Los Angeles, Washington, D.C., Detroit, Chicago, London, Copenhagen, Oslo, Paris, Stockholm, Cairo, Tokyo, and many other places across the United States and the world.[3]

The *Women Strike for Peace Newsletter* (New York, New Jersey, Connecticut) debuted in the summer of that year. Amy Swerdlow, an affluent, well-educated, married mother of three from Great Neck, New York, acted as editor. (With her educational, marital, and economic background, Swerdlow fitted comfortably into the profile of the typical WSP member.[4]) Swerdlow, just thirty-nine at the time, had no background in journalism.[5] Nonetheless, she took on the responsibility of launching and then continuing the New York WSP newsletter. The publication reflected her talents well. The new publication had a professional feel to it. The nameplate was graphically appealing; the type was clear; the layout was clean and uncluttered. Although it was designed to be a New York/New Jersey/Connecticut regional publication, it had a national tone. Besides announcing the United Nations Plaza demonstration against atmospheric nuclear tests, the publication also explained WSP's "loose, national structure," highlighted the WSP tour of the Soviet Union (only two of the twelve women were from New York), announced WSP's national goal of one million voters for peace, and urged all readers to pressure Congress on the test ban question.[6]

By the next year, Swerdlow teamed up with Miriam (Mimi) Kelber to produce the newsletter. Nonetheless, the tone and the content of the publication had not changed markedly. Although this newsletter still served the New York, New Jersey, and Connecticut region, it maintained its "national" news base. In October 1963, the editors explained how WSP celebrated the Nuclear Test Ban Treaty ratification. However, Swerdlow and Kelber reminded readers that President John F. Kennedy had agreed to continue underground nuclear testing. "This means a change of locale for the arms race, rather than a major reversal. It also means a continuing threat of radioactive contamination."[7]

Since 1964 was a presidential election year, the newsletter mobilized for defeating Goldwater, which is not to say that WSP approved of Lyndon Johnson's administration. From WSP's perspective, the election was one of a lesser of two evils. The newsletter came out against Goldwater—in a statement that made this regional WSP publication seem as if it was speaking for the whole organization. "Indeed, we in WSP *cannot* be quiet. We must summon all our energies in these next fateful weeks to defeat Goldwater." Nor did that mean that the group would endorse Johnson:

> The Democratic national platform statement relies too heavily on talk of armed might and is weak on specific commitments to world peace. It's up to us to press for stronger commitments by the individual candidates as the election debate develops. It is our job to prove to all candidates that there is a deep desire on the part of the electorate for affirmative peace action and that such action will bring out votes.[8]

By 1965, Women Strike for Peace had shifted its focus from nuclear proliferation to ending the war in Vietnam. The New York WSP *Newsletter* reflected that changing focus[9]; and, again writing with what sounded like the authority of the national organization, the editor (Swerdlow alone by this time) emphasized the need to end the war to protect children. With the shift of focus, the tone of the publication changed. No longer was the approach a well-reasoned, argued one. The arguments now had more immediacy, emotion, tension. In an "Emergency Issue," April 1965, the editor asked, "[H]ow can you be silent?"

CARING IS NOT ENOUGH—YOUR VOICE MUST BE HEARD! Vietnamese children are dying. When a crime is being committed—it is not enough to deplore it, One must be willing to bear witness against it.

The women of WSP had to work against the war and save the children.[10]

Women Strike for Peace had always framed its arguments in feminine, as opposed to feminist, terms. The protest against the Vietnam War emphasized this appeal. The war should end to stop the killing of children. The newsletter used sensational, sentimental appeals to make its point. The newsletter carried pictures of Vietnamese parents or women attempting to protect their children.[11] The newsletter carried appeals designed to bring the war home to all readers. As one appeal implored, "save the children—save our sons—save our souls— STOP THE BARBAROUS WAR."[12] The newsletter reprinted letters from servicemen, outlining the conditions they faced in Vietnam. A letter from Corp. Wilson related how he had killed a Vietnamese mother and baby.[13]

The newsletter also illustrated shifts in WSP tactics. The abysmal showing of WSP at the polls caused the group to rethink its nonpartisan stances. The New York newsletter—almost as the singular voice of the national WSP—called for a change in tactics. "We must make the political machinery reflect our views by participating in it on every level."

Let us never again wait until the eve of elections. Let us start now to organize Woman Power to help build the broadest coalition within and without the political parties to guarantee that in '68 the American electoral process will afford a choice.[14]

Up until 1968, the New York/New Jersey/Connecticut newsletter read as if it were speaking for the entire WSP. In January 1968, the newsletter changed dramatically. It seemed to turn its back on the national focus and become a truly regional publication. The change in editorial direction was accompanied by a slight variation in name, to *W.S.P. Women Strike for Peace New York Newsletter,* a renumeration of the periodical (back to vol. 1.1 with the January 1968 issue), and a graphic redesign. (The redesign gave the newsletter an amateurish look.) The new publication remained committed to ending the war in Vietnam: "As mothers, sweethearts, and wives, we have cried out against the wanton destruction of lives, and our cry has been consistent: End the war in Vietnam. Bring our boys home now." The editors also emphasized the need for greater political involvement.[15] However, in a dramatic departure from the earlier publication, the "new" newsletter began extensively covering the activities of the *local* groups. The newsletter started carrying the news under the department heading of "Local Group Activities—N.Y. WSP." The column was divided into geographic regions, like Queens, Five Towns, Northeast Bronx, Upper East Side, Chelsea. The publication also covered draft counseling being offered in specific boroughs.[16] That approach continued through much of 1968.[17] In 1970, however, the New York chapter had a new publication.

This time the publication was called the *N.Y. WSP Peaceletter*. It restarted its numeration with vol. 1.1 with the May 1970 issue. The publication was redesigned again, but this time it donned a graphically more appealing nameplate with a child, a dove, and the skyline of New York. The periodical, however, had not deserted its local mission. The publication still concentrated on local issues and local matters.

But that approach had special energy in 1970, for one of New York's WSPs was running for Congress. Bella Abzug, a WSP founder in New York, was running for the nineteenth congressional seat. Abzug's run for Congress soon came to dominate the publication. The *Peaceletter* editorially endorsed Abzug and called on all WSPers to work for the campaign and donate financially.[18]

The *Peaceletter* also came to address more of the national issues than it had in its previous form. The *Peaceletter* reminded readers that letters were still needed to get "peace" legislation passed. The newsletter called on readers to support the repeal of the Selective Service Act and to oppose authorizing the ABM system and the Washington, D.C., Omnibus Crime Bill.[19] Late 1970 found the *Peaceletter* reaching out to allied groups, some of which were male-run and had little to do with the peace movement. The *Peaceletter* urged women to financially support Black Panthers,[20] boycott "scab lettuce,"[21] and work in favor of New York abortion laws.[22]

However, the expanded war in Indochina made the publication reaffirm its "peace" orientation with graphically dominant pleas to end the war: "WAR EXPANDED! Scream Bloody Murder!"[23] The newsletter also publicized the many demonstrations that the New York WSP chapter sponsored or participated in. For example, the newsletter carried calls for the Duffy Square demonstration in August under the headline "Hiroshima—Nagasaki—Vietnam."[24] The *Peaceletter* also carried information on special, peace-related programs, such as the "SUMMER TRAINING IN NON VIOLENCE."[25] This is not to say that the newsletter turned its back on other reforms that benefited women. Throughout 1971, the *Peaceletter* continued to cover new developments in the abortion movement as well as the racism within the nation.

Jump ahead ten years; the nation is at peace. Women seem more interested in equal rights, reproductive rights, and economic rights than in peace. Nonetheless, *Peaceletter* continues to remind readers of the issues that threaten their safety and the safety of their families. Or, as the *Peaceletter* emphasized: "[T]he nuclear danger that faces us leads to the conclusion that it's time for peace women to come together to plan joint action. Our issue must be up there as part of the main thrust—that PEACE *IS* A WOMEN'S [*sic*] ISSUE!"[26] But clearly, editors Martha Baker and Jean Shulman were facing some difficulty. The newsletter of the 1980s lacked the polished look and editorial energy of the decade before. Much of the December 1980/January 1981 issue was personal notes or reprints from daily newspapers on WSP demonstrators who had been arrested at the Pentagon.

The Star Wars weapons issue added some energy to the WSP crusade and the *Peaceletter*. When President Ronald Reagan endorsed a concept of Strategic Defense Initiative (Star Wars) with technologically advanced weaponry, New York Women Strike for Peace reached out to form new alliances to defeat the new threat. Dusting off its old slogan, "End the Arms Race—Not the Human Race," the *Peaceletter* outlined the old campaign that had worked so well in the 1960s: write your congressperson or senator; write the president; and distribute literature designed to educate and activate.[27] As in the protests against the Vietnam War, the N.Y. WSP was ready to work with other groups—this time, a whole new generation of mothers, MOM (Mothers Opposed to Militarism).

Nuclear weapons, however, were not the only threat. The *Peaceletter* reprinted in full the New York chapter's position on the Chernobyl nuclear reactor accident. The chapter saw a link between the nuclear reactors and nuclear testing: "To prevent future accidents and victims of nuclear technology we call upon the leaders of the U.S. and the USSR to convene an urgent meeting on the twin nuclear dangers: nuclear testing and nuclear reactors. It is time to negotiate a Comprehensive Test Ban Treaty to stop nuclear weapons development and to consider international plans for the eventual elimination of nuclear reactors." Almost twenty-five years before, the New York WSP newsletter reported in the flurry of excitement the partial nuclear test ban treaty and looked forward to a complete nuclear test ban treaty. In 1986, the newsletter was still waiting and still urging its readers to push for a comprehensive test ban treaty to "End the Arms Race, Not the Human Race."[28]

The 1990s brought the end to the *N.Y. Peaceletter*. Still hammering away at the need for a comprehensive test ban (this time from President George Bush), the newsletter was still dedicated to peace, but in terms that the 1990s could understand. The term was now "economic conversion" from weapons facilities to civilian use. The newsletter brought plans for a Fifth Avenue march "For Jobs with Peace."[29] Somehow the new vocabulary seemed inconsistent with Women Strike for Peace. The organization and the *N.Y. Peaceletter* seemed out of step with the decade. In 1990, the national office of Women Strike for Peace in Philadelphia closed. In 1990, the *N.Y. Peaceletter*, also, apparently died.[30]

The *Peaceletter*—under its various names—underwent four distinct stages. In the first stage, from 1962 to 1967, the newsletter served the large New York/ New Jersey/Connecticut contingent. As such, the *Newsletter* had a reasoned, well-presented look. Once the focus shifted to protest of the Vietnam War, the tone of the periodical became more immediate and emotional, with the graphics reflecting that shift. Stage two began in 1968, when the periodical assumed a new name, a new look, perhaps new editors (the editorial staff was never identified in this period), and a new, regionally based editorial philosophy. Of all the stages in the newsletter's development, this was the least graphically attractive and the most amateurish. In the third stage, the *Peaceletter* returned to its higher editorial and graphic quality. Although the periodical remained regional in its orientation, it was not parochial in the issues it addressed. It dealt with abortion, racism, and labor policies as well as the Vietnam War and peace. During its final stage, the *Peaceletter* adjusted to life after the Vietnam War. Editors found that the arms race, Star Wars, and "economic conversion" failed to evoke the emotional response of the Vietnam War.

Notes

1. Ruth Gage-Colby, "Women Strike for Peace," *New World Review* 31.6 (June 1963), p. 6.

2. Amy Swerdlow, *Women Strike for Peace: Traditional Motherhood and Radical Politics in the 1960s* (Chicago: University of Chicago Press, 1993), p. 236.

3. Gage-Colby, "Women Strike for Peace," p. 6.

4. Swerdlow, *Women Strike for Peace,* p. 66.

5. *Who's Who of American Women,* 10th ed., 1977–1978 (Chicago: Marquis Who's Who, 1977), p. 868.

6. Summer 1962, pp. 1, 2, 4. The first issue had only four pages.

7. "WE WERE THERE on RATIFICATION DAY," October 1963, p. 1; "The Arms Race Continues," October 1963, pp. 1–2.

8. "The 'Quiet Woman'—and Goldwaterism," October 1964, p. 1.

9. Amy Swerdlow discusses this shift in her essay " 'Not My Son, Not Your Son, Not Their Sons.' " She suggests that part of the reason for the shift in focus from nuclear proliferation to the Vietnam War might have been related to the ages of the sons of WSP leaders. By 1965, many WSP leaders had sons of draft age (Swerdlow, " 'Not My Son, Not Your Son, Not Their Sons': Mothers against the Vietnam Draft," in Melvin Small and William D. Hoover, eds. *Give Peace a Chance: Exploring the Vietnam Antiwar Movement* (Syracuse, N.Y.: Syracuse University Press, 1992), p. 160.

10. "how can you be silent?" April 1965, p. 1.

11. See, for example, April 1965, p. 1.

12. February 1967, p. 3.

13. October 1965, p. 1.

14. Bella Abzug, "Woman Power Means Political Power," November 1966, p. 1.

15. January 1968, p. 1.

16. "WSP and Draft Counseling Services, January 1968, p. 6.

17. The publication may have, for a time been discontinued. In the revived *Peaceletter* the editor did not note that it replaced a previous periodical. Instead it took the place of the minutes of the central coordinating committee.

18. "A Real Peace Candidate," May 1970, p. 1; "Abzug for Congress!" June 1970, p. 2; "Hurricane Bella Heads to Washington," July/August 1970, p. 1.

19. "On the Draft," May 1970, p. 1.

20. "Repression," July/August 1970, p. 4.

21. "Boycott Scab Lettuce," November 1970, p. 3.

22. "2 ABORTION LAWS TO SUPPORT," February 1971, p. 5.

23. February 1971, p. 1.

24. July/August 1971, p. 1.

25. June 1971, p. 4.

26. "EMERGENCY MEETING FOR WOMEN'S PEACE ACTION PLANNING," December 1980/January 1981, p. 1.

27. "A ONE-TRILLION DOLLAR LEAKY UMBRELLA" and "WHAT YOU CAN DO," May 1986, p. 1.

28. "WOMEN STRIKE FOR PEACE *STATEMENT ON THE SOVIET REACTOR ACCIDENT,*" May 1986, p. 3.

29. "WSP ANNUAL LUNCHEON HONORS CONGRESSMAN TED WEISS" and "ON FIFTH AVENUE—FOR JOBS WITH PEACE," January 1990, p. 1.

30. The last issue of the *N.Y. Peaceletter* received by Swarthmore College's Peace Collection is dated August 1990.

Information Sources

BIBLIOGRAPHY:

Gage-Colby, Ruth. "Women Strike for Peace." *New World Review* 31.6, June 1963, pp. 5–8.

Swerdlow, Amy. " 'Not My Son, Not Your Son, Not Their Sons': Mothers against the Vietnam Draft." In Melvin Small and William D. Hoover, eds. *Give Peace a Chance: Exploring the Vietnam Antiwar Movement.* Syracuse, N.Y.: Syracuse University Press, 1992.

———. *Women Strike for Peace: Traditional Motherhood and Radical Politics in the 1960s.* Chicago: University of Chicago Press, 1993.

INDEX SOURCES. None.

LOCATION SOURCES: Swarthmore College Peace Collection, Swarthmore, Pa.; State Historical Society of Wisconsin; and many college libraries. Microfilmed in Herstory, Reel 23.

Publication History

PERIODICAL NAME AND NAME CHANGES: *Women Strike for Peace Newsletter* (1962–1967); *Women Strike for Peace New York Newsletter* (1968–1969?); *N.Y. WSP Peaceletter* (WSP dropped from title by 1980) (1970–1990).

VOLUME AND ISSUE DATA: Vols. 1–6 (Summer 1962–1967); Vols. 1–2? (January 1968–1969?); Vols. 1–20 (May 1970–August 1990?). Bimonthly, but many months not issued.

PUBLISHER AND PLACE OF PUBLICATION: Women Strike for Peace. New York.

EDITORS: Amy Swerdlow (1962); Amy Swerdlow and Mimi Kelber (1963–1964); Amy Swerdlow (1965–1967); Alice Mehling, Amy Swerdlow, and Jean Shulman (July/August 1970); Jean Barnes, Jean Shulman, and Norma Spector (November 1970); Martha Baker and Jean Shulman. (Editors were not always identified.)

CIRCULATION: Unknown.

Kathleen L. Endres

$$ O $$

OFF OUR BACKS

off our backs (*oob*) is the longest published, probably the most widely circulated, and the best-known newspaper of the radical feminist "family." Members of the *oob* collective, who run the monthly newspaper, would probably blanch at those comparisons. The collective has always been committed to nonhierarchical, noncompetitive principles. Nonetheless, *off our backs* (at this writing well into its third decade of publication) has survived when many of its radical feminist "sister" publications have faltered and folded.[1] The longevity of *oob* can be traced to editorial content supported by a small but loyal readership, a collective whose membership has changed but remains committed to the newspaper, and adherence to conservative financial policies that have enabled the newspaper to survive a number of business catastrophes.

off our backs was born in 1970, but its roots and its philosophy date to the 1960s. As Marilyn Webb, cofounder of *off our backs,* recalled, the newspaper was the "quintessential child of the sixties—born of naive enthusiasm, a pinch of planning and a little bit of dope."[2] The money used to launch the publication—four hundred dollars—had been raised to open a coffee shop where Vietnam War–era servicemen could meet with peace activists. The money had been raised by Webb and her friend Margie Stamberg, both of whom were "loosely connected" with the Students for a Democratic Society (SDS),[3] a radical student group of the 1960s and 1970s. After Stamberg moved to California, the money was tucked in a bank, gathering interest until late 1969, when the time seemed right to launch a radical feminist newspaper. As a reporter with the New York *Guardian,* Webb had seen firsthand the handling of news about women; the newspaper had a consistent "black out of feminist news."[4] With Stamberg's permission, Webb, working with Marlene Wicks, decided to start a radical feminist newspaper.[5] By December 1969, Wicks and Webb were working with Heidi and Nan Steffens, Norma Lesser, and Nancy Ferro to develop *off our backs*. Although men were never allowed to join the collective, at least one man was involved in the early history of the publication, Jim True, designed the paper, picked the typefaces, developed the grid/page layout, and designed the logo.[6] But male input—throughout the history of *off our backs*—has been minimal. This newspaper has always been an enterprise by, for, and about women. It was named by the original six women—the two Steffens, Lesser, Ferro, Webb, and Wicks. The name had special meaning. As the collective explained in the first issue, the name

> reflects our understanding of the dual nature of the women's movement. Women need to be free of men's domination to find their real identities, redefine their lives, and fight for the creation of a society in which they can lead decent lives as human beings. At the same time, women must become aware that there would be no oppressor without the oppressed, that we carry the responsibility for withdrawing the consent to be oppressed. We must strive to get off our backs, and with the help of our sisters to oppose and destroy that system which fortifies the supremacy of men while exploiting the mass for the profit of the few. Our position is not anti-men but pro-women. We seek, through the liberation of women, the liberation of all peoples.[7]

The launch was timed to coincide with International Women's Day. As the collective called on women to celebrate the occasion, the women also explained the reasoning behind the new periodical: existing periodicals failed to meet the needs of women.

> Women who have worked in the media are well acquainted with the patterns of discrimination which define and confine their news within the "Style" and "Fashion" sections. Serious and competent women journalists soon learn that they can expect to remain research assistants or be satisfied with the dullest and least important assignments. So-called radical and movement periodicals usually retain token articles while vital issues wind up on back pages or in waste baskets.

off our backs would deal with all the vital issues—not just the ones that were politically based and not just the ones of interest to the middle class. "*off our backs* is a paper for *all* women who are fighting for the liberation of their lives and we hope it will grow and expand to meet the needs of women from all backgrounds and classes." Nor was the periodical necessarily dedicated to accepted journalistic maxims of objectivity and impartiality. "We intend to be just; but we do not intend to be impartial. Our paper is part of a movement; we ourselves are committed to a struggle and we will take stands to further the cause of that struggle," the collective promised in the first issue.[8]

Commitment to a cause alone could not keep the newspaper going. The collective was also guided by some sound business principles and journalistic understanding. Wicks took over the business side. The four hundred dollars was enough to put out the first issue. The plan called for the second issue to be underwritten by new subscriptions. To do this, the collective needed mailing lists. Few list brokers offered radical feminist mailing lists. So the collective drew on Webb's connections with Vietnam Summer, a national antiwar group, for the initial mailing list. This was supplemented with lists of women from other antiwar groups in Chicago, San Francisco, and other cities. This initial mailing achieved a response rate of almost 100 percent[9]; such a response rate is virtually unheard of in publishing. The new subscriptions allowed the collective to put out a second issue three weeks later and plan for a twenty-four-issue-a-year frequency cycle. The collective was frugal. Indeed, conservative business practices have helped explain the long life of *off our backs.* The first office was in the basement of Heidi and Nan Steffens' home; then the periodical moved to the Lesser household. None of the staff was paid. Today only one staff member, the individual who runs the office, is paid.

In the earliest periodicals, Wicks and Webb were the most heavily involved in the periodical, although neither had a title. Wicks supervised the business end; Webb did much of the writing and editing. The first year, although the periodical billed itself as a biweekly, it did not always achieve that frequency and settled for a cycle that was approximately triweekly. Many of the issues in the first year were dedicated to specific themes. March 19, 1970, was dedicated to working women; April 19, 1970, looked at women and ecology; April 25, 1970, dealt with women and the media; July 10, 1970, was the Emma Goldman issue; and July 31, 1970, was devoted to child care. The first year offered a combination of practical information, articles, viewpoints covering topics of interest to radical feminists (much of it written by women outside the collective), and controversial humor.

off our backs provided updates on conferences and demonstrations from across the United States. (The newspaper was never designed to be circulated only in the Washington, D.C., area, although much of its "bulk" distribution appeared to be based there.[10]) Even the first issue offered information on Durham, North Carolina, women's liberation groups; a women's conference in Lexington, Kentucky; and a strike of clerical workers in Detroit. All were grouped in the periodical's department entitled "struggle."[11]

In its first year the newspaper offered practical, how-to advice in a department called "survival." In this department, the newspaper dealt with a wide range of topics from how to use spermicide contraceptives, to illustrated directions for changing a tire, from explanations on examining a breast for lumps, to a guide to abortion.[12]

Features also covered a wide range of topics. The newspaper used a chart to show how few women and how many men were employed in editorial positions at ABC, CBS, National Educational Television, the *New York Times,* and many

other newspapers and news services. The radical press did no better; those newspapers did not carry news about women and did carry sexist advertising. Following its promise to be just (although not impartial), the newspaper urged
women to reconsider their service to the male-run underground press and start
their own news service.[13]

Personal journalism was a key aspect of the first year, and in the years that
followed, Charlotte Bunch-Weeks wrote about her trip to Southeast Asia, including Laos and North Vietnam.[14] Sue Tod wrote about the weakness of
"Jane" in "Tarzan" movies; Jessica Finney talked about girls in her junior
high school who dressed and acted to attract boys; and Roxanne Dunbar, who
had been affiliated with another radical feminist periodical, *No More Fun and
Games,** and Martha Atkins offered a southern female list of demands.[15]

Humor was also a part of the *oob* editorial package. In April 1970, *oob* ran
a nude centerfold of a man in a *Playboy* magazine–type pose. The newspaper
lost its printer when the collective delivered an issue with two male centerfolds
with daisies strategically covering genitalia. "Butter Balls by House of Penis"
was a satire on female hygiene sprays. The printer refused to print the controversial issue, claiming the centerfold was obscene. A number of other printers
refused as well, sometimes because of the radical nature of the publication.
Eventually, the collective found a printer in New York.[16]

Although the editorial content was dynamic and energizing, there was trouble
brewing beneath the surface. Two events threatened the future of *oob:* the withdrawal of Webb from the collective and the departure of the lesbian members
from the group.

By 1970, Webb, the only collective member with journalism experience, had
taken over the editorial side as de facto editor and leader of the collective. That
did not go over well with some members of the collective. As Marlene Wicks
recalled,

> I really welcomed her [Marilyn's] direction and her thoughts. She was a
> great asset to *oob*. People like Onka [Dekkers] and Norma [Lesser], how-
> ever, were really turned off and there were other people in the women's
> movement in D.C.—not particularly on the paper, who encouraged cen-
> suring Marilyn and telling her that things would be decided collectively.
> Their ultimatum was that the direction of the paper would be more col-
> lective or they weren't going to work on it. Marilyn was absolutely dev-
> astated.[17]

The remaining collective members carried on, but there was a split developing. In 1971, the lesbian members left *oob* to form their own newspaper, *Furies.*
These women felt that they had to suppress their lesbian activities. The heterosexual women reported that they felt abandoned when the others left.[18]

Over the long history of *oob,* the editorial content has reflected the interests
and employment status of the ever-changing collective. It has also reflected the

thinking of the radical feminist community as well as events and activities of the women's movement in the nation.

In the 1970s, for example, there was considerable investigative and in-depth reporting in the newspaper because a number of collective members were semi-employed or collecting unemployment.[19] That probably helped explain the lengthy investigation of the women in Cuba, the look at child care that was "child"-based, the "children's liberation supplement," and a question-and-answer interview with writer Lillian Shirley that focused on women who left the convent.[20]

The newspaper published documents that represented a range of positions within the women's movement. It reprinted the "C.L.I.T. [Collective Lesbian International Terrorists] papers" unedited; ran the Redstockings' charges that women's liberation leader Gloria Steinem had ties to the Central Intelligence Agency (C.I.A) and included Steinem's response as well; printed Weather Underground communiqués and then offered testimonials from women who quit (or were fired) in protest over the hierarchical structure in the Feminist Women's Health Centers in California. The newspaper also covered the splits and problems within specific women's groups. Reporters covered the problems within the Women's National Abortion Action Coalition.[21]

These types of stories brought the newspaper a certain notoriety. *The New Woman's Survival Sourcebook* criticized the newspaper for its critical coverage of women's groups. The book blamed changes within the collective for the new editorial emphasis that "switched its [*oob*'s] emphasis from national news reporting with a radical feminist slant to focusing on intra-movement factionalism, from what appears to be a predominantly male left perspective."[22] The sourcebook's comments notwithstanding, *oob* remained well regarded within the feminist community generally. In 1974, a survey of feminist editors revealed that *oob* was regarded as the best-produced publication in the feminist movement.[23] The radical coverage also brought clandestine activities by the government. As early collective members Carol Ann Douglas and Fran Moira recalled, "After we published a Weather Underground communiqué, we found that our offices had been broken into and our paperwork had been gone through, but no money had been taken." The two explained that for a while the collective members thought *oob*'s telephone had been tapped: "At one time we went so far as to discuss designating ourselves by code names when we talked on the telephone because we assumed that our telephone was tapped. However, we never actually used the code names."[24]

Editorials provided a glimpse into the inner workings of the collective and revealed the tensions within the collective as well as the difficulty in living the nonhierarchical principles.[25] Getting the collective to agree on all the points in an editorial proved to be difficult. Increasingly, in the 1970s, the newspaper turned to signed commentaries by collective members rather than editorials. These commentaries revealed the thinking of specific members. Often these commentaries were signed only by the first name of the collective member. Thus, "Frances" wrote about lesbianism and the radical feminist movement:

> The essence of the radicalesbian challenge to the rest of the women's movement is that men fuck women over, yet women continue to live with them, screw them and pick up after them. Women, tell men to fuck off and be with women.[26]

An editorial, however, was needed to explain *oob*'s controversial decision not to move into the D.C. Women's Center. The collective had to be concerned about the newspaper's existence and did not have time to deal with the internal structure of the Women's Center. Likewise, the newspaper had to retain its independence, even though the collective supported the Women's Center itself.[27]

The 1980s brought a different—political, economic, and social—climate to the newspaper. The decade also almost brought the demise of *off our backs*.

The end was threatened as early as 1980 when a collective member embezzled five thousand dollars from the newspaper. Four other collective members lent the newspaper the money to continue. Perhaps even more dangerous was the situation in 1988, when the number of "active" collective members had dwindled to only two or three. Soon additional collective members were found, and the newspaper was again charged with new energy.

Although the newspaper was facing these challenges behind the scenes, it—by now a monthly—retained its activism and strong editorial content throughout the decade. The newspaper continued to cover important academic, political, and activist conferences concerning women. These ranged from the National Women's Studies Association, to the Barnard Conference on the politics of sexuality, from the United Nations' woman's conference in Nairobi and the first African-American lesbian conference, to the Republican and Democratic Conventions. The newspaper also kept tabs on the increasingly hostile government in Washington, D.C. At least once, an *oob* reporter made news as well as covered it by disrupting the Senate Judiciary Subcommittee hearing on "when life begins."[28] Government news coverage highlighted how "Reaganomics" and government cutbacks especially hurt women and children.[29]

International news continued to be an important part of the *off our backs'* editorial mix. Ever since the founding of the newspaper, the collective has extensively covered news that included not only European developments but so-called Third World countries as well. Thus, the newspaper has covered everything from the women freedom fighters in Zimbabwe and Nicaragua, to updates on the Spanish feminist movement. That emphasis continues even into the 1990s with the newspaper's coverage of women of Bosnia, Serbia, and Croatia. Indeed, *off our backs* was the first newspaper to report that Croatian women's groups had retained an attorney to seek relief for Croatian Muslim women raped by Serbian soldiers in "ethnic-cleansing" actions.[30]

The 1990s found a reenergized *off our backs* collective. Since 1988, when the collective faced extinction, new women have come into the group. This "new generation" of women (guided by Carol Ann Douglas, who has been with the collective for more than twenty years) has brought new perspectives to the newspaper. The newspaper carried updates on the "Riot Grrls," a collective of women in their late teens and early twenties organizing in Washington, D.C. Conference coverage now includes the Young Women's Project conference as well as the more traditional National Women's Studies Association convention. International news remains an important dimension to the newspaper. In the mid-1990s, the newspaper carried updates on Sakhi, a lesbian collective in New Delhi, and stories about Haitian feminists.[31] The newspaper continues to provide news of hostile government action and updates on important health trends. *off our backs* has been one of the few newspapers to consistently cover how AIDS affects women—not only heterosexual women but lesbians as well.[32]

From a small, cramped basement office in Washington, D.C., collective members continue to meet, eat, and work on the newspaper on "layout" weekends. They edit submissions from radical feminists from across the world. They lay out the newspaper; they share a sense of community. Those "layout" weekends have gone on for many years.

In February 1995, *off our backs* celebrated its twenty-fifth anniversary. That longevity has made the newspaper an "institution" of sorts in the alternative press. Nonetheless, *off our backs* seems to keep its freshness and energy, in large part, because of changes within the collective. New women bring in fresh perspectives—and dynamism to the paper. Yet the concept of radical feminism remains the link that binds the original collective (Marlene Wicks, Marilyn Webb, Heidi and Nan Steffens, Norma Lesser, and Nancy Ferro) to the 1995 collective (Laura Butterbaugh, Carol Ann Douglas, Gina Ebner, Farar Elliott, Dawn Gifford, Alice Henry, Amy Hummel, April Jackson, Barbara Kraus, Julia Kyles, Tricia Lootens, Karla Mantilla, Jennie Ruby, and Suzanne Sullivan).

Notes

1. Many of these periodicals are profiled elsewhere is this volume, including *New Women's Times, No More Fun and Games,* and *Notes from the First Year.*
2. Marilyn Webb, "marilyn webb, co-founder of oob," February 1980, p. 5.
3. Jennie Ruby, "Off our backs," in Cynthia M. Lont, ed. *Women and Media: Content, Careers and Criticism* (Belmont, Calif.: Wadsworth, 1995), p. 44.
4. Webb, "marilyn webb, co-founder of oob," p. 5.
5. "marlene wicks, co-founder of oob," February 1980, p. 4.
6. Webb, "marilyn webb, co-founder of oob," p. 5.
7. "dear sisters," February 27, 1970, p. 2.
8. Ibid.
9. Webb, "marilyn webb, co-founder of oob," p. 5; Ruby, "Off our backs," p. 44.
10. The newspaper provided a list of where the periodical was sold within the Washington, D.C., area. Early on, the newspaper, apparently, was not sold on the newsstand in other cities. Newsstand distribution (through feminist bookstores) continues.
11. Paula Goldsmid, "north carolina"; Charlotte Bunch-Weeks, "conference in lex-

ington''; Bonnie McFadden, ''strike!'' February 27, 1970, p. 10. Throughout much of its history, *off our backs* used a lowercase headline style.

12. ''spermicide contraceptives,'' April 19, 1970, p. 16; ''on the road,'' March 19, 1970, p. 12; ''a poke in time . . . ,'' June 26, 1970, p. 16; ''abortion do's'' and ''and don'ts'', July 31, 1970, p. 20.

13. ''newsroom bias: establishment style,'' April 25, 1970, p. 4; ''seize the press, sisters,'' April 25, 1970, p. 5.

14. Charlotte Bunch-Weeks, ''back from hanoi,'' June 26, 1970, pp. 2–4.

15. Sue Tod, ''forever june,'' and Jessica Finney, ''junior high,'' p. 9; Roxanne Dunbar and Martha Atkins, ''southern female rights,'' p. 10. All in the February 27, 1970, issue.

16. ''Butter Balls by House of Penis,'' November 8, 1970, pp. 8–9; ''Flash! Read This,'' November 8, 1970, p. 11.

17. ''marlene wicks, co-founder of oob,'' February 1980, p. 4.

18. An account of the event can be found in ''goodbye ruby tuesday,'' May 16, 1971, p. 18. When the four lesbian members left, the writer recounted that the rest felt ''angry, upset, frightened and generally depressed.'' The departure must not have been totally unexpected. The writer related how editorial meetings had become disasters. The split in *oob* had been between ''those who wanted to put out a women's paper and get involved with other things including men, and the 'heavies,' '' who wanted to relate to women exclusively. ''Each side was afraid of the other. Staff meetings were a disaster with side comments and dirty looks'' (''goodbye ruby tuesday,'' May 16, 1971, p. 18). See also Carol Ann Douglas, ''Looking back on the last 20 years,'' February 1990, p. 15. In hindsight, the exodus of the lesbians seemed ill timed. As Carol Ann Douglas explained, more lesbians joined the collective in the 1970s, and in the latter part of the 1980s the collective was made up entirely of lesbians (Carol Ann Douglas, p. 15).

19. Douglas, ''Looking back on the last 20 years,'' p. 15.

20. ''Cuba, que linda us cuba,'' January 24, 1971, pp. 2–5; Lisa Leghorn, ''child care for the child,'' July 31, 1970, p. 9; ''children's liberation supplement,'' October 25, 1970; ''a nun's story (revised),'' March 25, 1971, p. 18.

21. ''ten years of off our backs,'' February 1980, p. 2; Carol Anne Douglas and Fran Moira, *''off our backs:* the First Decade, 1970–1980,'' in Ken Wachsberger, ed. *Insider Histories of the Vietnam Era Underground Press,* vol. 1 of *Voices from the Underground* (Tempe, Ariz.: Mica Press, 1993), p. 122.

22. Kirsten Grimstad and Susan Rennie, eds., *The New Woman's Survival Sourcebook* (New York: Knopf, 1975), p. 139.

23. Maurine H. Beasley and Sheila J. Gibbons, *Taking Their Place: A Documentary History of Women and Journalism* (Washington, D.C.: American University Press, 1993), p. 193.

24. Douglas and Moira, *''off our backs:* The First Decade, 1970–1980,'' p. 122.

25. See, for example, ''us,'' January 21, 1971, p. 2; ''good-by ruby tuesday,'' May 6, 1971, p. 18; editorial, September 1972, p. 2; ''ten years of off our backs,'' February 1980, p. 2.

26. Frances, ''the soul selects a new separate way,'' January 1972, p. 7.

27. editorial, September 1972, p. 2.

28. Carol Ann Douglas, ''from our pages: the first half of the eighties,'' February 1980, pp. 8–10; Carol Ann Douglas, ''Looking back on the last 20 years,'' pp. 15–16.

29. See, for example, April 1981, pp. 6–7.

30. Jennie Ruby, "Off our backs," in Lont, *Women and Media,* pp. 43–44.

31. See February 1994, pp. 20–21.

32. See, for example, Beth Elliott, "Does Lesbian Sex Transmit Aids? Get Real!" November 1991, p. 6.

Information Sources

BIBLIOGRAPHY:

Beasley, Maurine H., and Sheila J. Gibbons. *Taking Their Place: A Documentary History of Women and Journalism.* Washington, D.C.: American University Press, 1993.

Douglas, Carol Ann, and Fran Moira. *"off our backs:* The First Decade, 1970–1980." In Ken Wachsberger, ed., *Voices from the Underground,* vol. 1. Tempe, Ariz.: Mica's Press, 1993, pp. 107–123.

Grimstad, Kirsten, and Susan Rennie, eds. *The New Woman's Survival Sourcebook.* New York: Knopf, 1975.

Kelly, Janis. "The Life and Times of *off our backs:* A Women's News Journal." *New Women's Times,* March 1981, pp. 25–26.

Ruby, Jennie. "Off our backs." In Cynthia M. Lont, ed. *Women and Media: Content Careers and Criticism.* Belmont, Calif.: Wadsworth, 1995, pp. 41–53.

Searing, Susan. "Feminist Publications." *Utne Reader,* November/December 1989, pp. 134–139.

"Ten Years as Women's News Source—Venerable 'off our backs' Sets Record." *Media Report to Women,* April 1, 1980, pp. 1, 6, 7.

INDEX SOURCES: Alternative Press Index; New Periodicals Index; Studies on Women Abstracts; Women Studies Abstracts.

LOCATION SOURCES: Wisconsin Historical Society; Kent State University Library (Ohio); and other (primarily university) libraries. Microfilm available in Underground Press Collection (1970–1985).

Publication History

PERIODICAL TITLE AND TITLE CHANGES: *off our backs.*

VOLUME AND ISSUE DATA: Vols. 1– (February 27, 1970–present). Twenty-four issues a year (approximately triweekly) (1970–1971); monthly (no August issue) (1971–present).

PUBLISHER AND PLACE OF PUBLICATION: off our backs, inc. Washington, D.C.

EDITORS: off our backs collective.

CIRCULATION: Ulrich's 1995: 29,000 (7,000 paid; 22,000 nonpaid).

Kathleen L. Endres

P

PEACE AND FREEDOM

In May 1919, six months after the end of World War I, the International Congress of Women met in Zurich, Switzerland, to discuss the postwar situation in Europe. The meeting brought forth two significant results: first, the pacifists formed the Women's International League of Peace and Freedom (WILPF), an organization that later admitted the Woman's Peace Party as the U.S. section of WILPF. Second, the women condemned the Treaty of Versailles, marking the end of the world war, as a violation of "the principles upon which alone a just and lasting peace can be secured." The treaty, according to WILPF, sanctioned secret diplomacy, denied self-determination for people, and "created all over Europe discords and animosities which *can lead only to future wars.*"[1]

In 1939, only twenty years after the Zurich convention, the women's predictions proved correct. When overzealous nationalism again erupted in armed aggression, the U.S. WILPF resurrected *Four Lights,** a publication initiated by the New York City branch of the Woman's Peace Party during World War I. The women resumed the journal (referred to here as *Peace and Freedom,* as the women renamed the periodical in 1970) "with the hope that in another period of stress it can again serve a useful purpose . . . of bringing peace and goodwill back to a war-torn world."[2] WILPF's National Literature Department published *Peace and Freedom* monthly except August and September. The women sold subscriptions to the journal until March 1942, when membership dues included a year's subscription to the periodical.

From 1941 until 1970, *Peace and Freedom* reflected WILPF members' perception of women as primarily homemakers responsible for the bearing and nurturing of children. Emily Cooper Johnson, editor of *Peace and Freedom* until May 1947, embodied many of the characteristics typical of WILPF leadership during the 1940s, 1950s, and 1960s. Johnson, born in 1891 to an established

Quaker family living in New Jersey, was educated at Bryn Mawr, married, and was in her fifties during World War II.[3] To help her illustrate the connection between pacifism and womanhood, Johnson excerpted part of Pearl S. Buck's book *Of Women and War,* in which Buck stated that "women must determine . . . that they will not go on having their work of bearing and rearing [children] wasted by war or even the fear of war." Women were ready to enter national and international affairs, wrote Buck, where they could use their "creative natures" to bring about peace. Buck's article set the tone for subsequent issues of *Peace and Freedom,* which, although dealing with a variety of political and social issues, viewed those issues from the standpoint of women's domestic niche. For although excessive nationalism during the war, the paranoia of McCarthyism during the 1950s, and the militant feminism of the late 1960s caused declining membership, WILPF owed much of its success and endurance to its conceptualization of conventional roles for women.[4]

Peace and Freedom represented a group of pacifists generally satisfied with women's status in American society but dissatisfied with the politics of international relations. To prevent repetition of World War II atrocities, WILPF advocated the limitation of national sovereignties in the interest of an international organization (WILPF steadfastly backed the United Nations), supported measures that would allow fair and orderly procedures for access to raw materials and markets as a substitute for those competitive and monopolistic methods that invited conflict, and advocated the internationalization of waterways, minimum standards for working conditions, and basic human rights, "without regard to sex, race, color, class or nationality"[5] (only the last item in WILPF's program dealt directly with woman's rights). The members also objected to the U.S. government's perpetuation of social injustices suffered by minority groups and labor, but they often perceived domestic turmoil as jeopardizing women's fundamental prerogative: a safe, stable, orderly home and family environment. WILPF stood ready to protect conventional womanhood from any interferences.

For example, the 1943 WILPF committee studying minority groups living in the United States summed up their activity by declaring that

> the race issue lies ready to shatter all established order and all possibility for lasting peace unless we are strong enough as individuals, communities, states, and nations to face realistically the unfair practices and attitudes which affect this group. If we do not face [this] we are doomed to witness another conflict which will be a racial war.

The committee supported an antilynching bill and efforts to make the poll tax illegal.[6] The women saw injustices in discriminatory practices aimed at African Americans, but their motive in ameliorating the situation was primarily to maintain domestic order, in addition to correcting a wrong.

In "Labor and the War," Alice Hanson noted the coincidence of "flag-waving and coining of defense slogans" with "serious attack on labor rights"

in the form of antistrike legislation and the repudiation of unionism by management and government. Hanson supported union activity as a way to boost
production and consumption of goods, thereby averting a peacetime depression.
Peace and Freedom writers tied the status of labor directly to "economic security," a goal they saw as fundamental to the stability of the home.[7]

In fact, WILPF objected vociferously to any measure designed to disconnect
women from their roles as homemakers. When the United States declared war
in December 1941, the women did not obstruct prosecution of the war,[8] but
they did denounce the 1943 Austin–Wadsworth National War Service Act,
which proposed the conscription of women. Many WILPFers belonged to a
newly formed group, the National Committee to Oppose the Conscription of
Women, which opposed the bill on the grounds that it would disrupt the family,
resulting in "juvenile delinquency, the loss of family morale, and the dislocation
of the foundations of the home." Instead, countered members, the government
should encourage women's traditional role as mothers, teachers, and social
workers, thereby ensuring domestic stability while so many men fought over-
seas.[9]

In the aftermath of World War II, WILPF faced the possibility of interference
by the U.S. government. The cold war began with the U.S. bombings of Hiroshima and Nagasaki (events WILPF unreservedly condemned[10]) and the Soviet
deployment of its own atomic bomb in 1949. Fears of national security threats
posed by perceived communist infiltrations permeated all aspects of American
society, including the pages of *Peace and Freedom*. The term "national security" took on dual meaning: it referred to the loyalty of bureaucrats and officials
to the U.S. government and also to the home and family as a secure fortress
behind which families strengthened their moral fiber against communist pene-
tration.[11] Originally designed to cleanse the American government of disloyal
officials, the House Un-American Activities Committee (HUAC) began censor-
ing filmmakers, other media, and educators. WILPF perceived HUAC as a menace to the homemaker and the American family.

Meta Riseman wrote an article definitive of WILPF's political position relative to the "second red scare" in 1951. In "Mrs. Everybody and Civil Liberties," Riseman established a connection between *Peace and Freedom* readers
and the political paranoia surrounding them. Riseman defined WILPFers as
"Mrs. Everybody, busy with daily chores of keeping the home clean, meals
cooked, the children comforted, and the atmosphere secure," going about her
business without much thought to political issues. But under the 1950 Internal
Security Act, the fear of communist infiltration had intensified to the point where
even Quakers were suspect, according to Riseman. This affected homemakers
because "the house is the center of existence," where all books, magazines,
radio—including all the ideas within them—were the housewife's responsibility.
Should housewives hide suspect books because her children's friends might
"turn her in" to authorities? Could she be sure the friends she herself invited

home had never been to a public meeting where communism was discussed? wondered Riseman.

Children were "Mrs. Everybody's" main concern. Women must examine their friends, schools, and teachers—anyone influencing them. Riseman instructed mothers to familiarize themselves with the Feinberg Law, passed in New York State, which obstructed the presentation of controversial issues in classrooms. Free speech, warned Riseman, was central to a strong democratic educational system.

After performing her child-care duties, "Mrs. Everybody" took time for herself to develop her hobbies and join clubs and organizations. But in Bartlesville, Oklahoma, warned Riseman, Mrs. Ruth Brown was not free to join an interracial club without losing her job as a librarian. Women in Texas could not see certain films because they had been censored, one in particular because it showed children of different races playing together. Government censorship of films thus prevented women from developing interests outside the home.

But the ultimate worry, according to Riseman, was for the job held by "Mr. Everybody." How could women be sure their husbands would not be labeled a "poor security risk?" How could she provide a safe atmosphere in the face of such intrusions? Riseman concluded, "[W]ith these threats levelled at her mind, the minds of her children and friends, as well as at her husband's job—*the very economic foundation of her existence*—Mrs. Everybody may well begin to ask herself: 'how will I be able to keep the home secure in the face of these serious threats to my way of life?' " Riseman thus rejected governmental "red-baiting" on principle, but even more so because it jeopardized women's primary social role as homemaker.[12]

The cold war heated up considerably with the conflict between the United States and Vietnam, and, according to historian Harriet Hyman Alonso, opposition to the war fostered a resurgence of feminism in the United States. But while newer, younger women's pacifist organizations attracted feminists who challenged women to rethink their traditional roles as wife and mother, WILPF generally maintained its traditional focus on motherhood as the cornerstone of its pacifist agenda. While most of the new groups ultimately disbanded after the Vietnam War ended, WILPF remained intact.[13]

WILPF began criticizing the U.S. government's presence in Vietnam as early as 1952.[14] The women contended that the Vietnamese fought a civil war, and the U.S. presence had served only to escalate the conflict. In addition to leveling criticism, WILPF used demonstrations and theatrics designed to promote U.S. withdrawal from Vietnam. Continuing their time-honored tradition of linking peace with motherhood, the women began a "Stop the Killing" campaign on Tuesday, August 12, 1969, and each Tuesday thereafter. Members dressed in black and carried a coffin labeled "America's sons." On the steps of the Capitol, the mourners opened the coffin, which contained thirty-five thousand cards embossed with the name of an American killed in the war.[15]

The education of their children during wartime alarmed the pacifists. After investigating classroom materials, Ann Berthoff concluded that schoolchildren were mindlessly indoctrinated with "official foreign policy" regarding the Vietnam War. In another article, Libby Frank charged that corporations, such as Xerox, sent school districts specialized kits that instructed teachers to present the Vietnam War according to State Department foreign policy, while omitting news about antiwar dissension at home. Berthoff suggested that peace workers tactfully counter teachers by presenting them with alternative views. In addition, parents must protest against "extracurricular activities," such as military recruitment in high schools and civil defense procedures in all schools. Later, in July 1969, WILPF resolved to document supposed "guidance counseling" in high schools that, in truth, funneled boys with mediocre scholastic records into the army.[16]

During World War II and the cold war era, WILPF members consistently opposed armed conflict, the arms race between the United States and the Soviet Union, and the war in Vietnam. Concomitantly, the pacifists weakened animosities between the two superpowers by opening up avenues of dialogue between U.S. and Soviet women. Although some of its members were virulently anticommunist, WILPF nevertheless recognized the weaknesses within American society, particularly discriminatory policies toward racial minorities. Despite their critical posture, WILPF's advocacy of traditional roles for women in American society safeguarded the pacifist organization from direct attack by McCarthyites and supporters of the Vietnam War. The U.S. section of WILPF continues to represent many American women pacifists today.[17]

Today, the magazine of the International League of Peace and Freedom has another name, *Peace and Freedom*. The name was adopted in 1970 to more closely reflect the organization's identity. However, little in the magazine itself changed. The periodical continued to reflect the organization's commitment to peace. In the 1990s, however, the focus of the magazine shifted somewhat. Wendy Rosenfield, editor of *Peace and Freedom* until 1995, attempted to expand the periodical beyond the "peace mode to the justice mode." The periodical, thus, began dealing with the "isms" of American life, specifically with issues such as racism and feminism.[18]

At this writing, *Peace and Freedom* is without an editor but continues its role within the Women's International League for Peace and Freedom.

Notes

1. June 12, 1919, unnumbered (emphasis added).
2. June 1941, unnumbered.
3. See biography of Emily Cooper Johnson in November 1947 issue. The women made their marital status clear in brief biographies that appeared in *Peace and Freedom* when they held annual elections. Catherine Foster, *Women of All Seasons: The Story of the Women's International League for Peace and Freedom* (Athens: University of Georgia Press, 1989), pp. 118–203, includes brief biographies of some U.S. WILPF leaders. Harriet Hyman Alonso, *Peace as a Women's Issue: A History of the U.S. Movement for*

World Peace and Women's Rights (Syracuse, N.Y.: Syracuse University Press, 1993), p. 204, states that most WILPFers were over the age of fifty.

4. Pearl S. Buck, "Women and War," September 1941, unnumbered. The first volume of *Peace and Freedom* included a September issue.

5. "Programs and Policies, Annual Meeting May 1941" July 1941, unnumbered.

6. "The Negro," January 1943, unnumbered.

7. Alice Hanson, "Labor and the War," September 1941, unnumbered; "Domestic Policies," July 1953, unnumbered.

8. Dorothy Detzer, "The Task Ahead," February 1943, unnumbered.

9. See "Manpower Draft," November 1942, unnumbered; Dorothy Detzer, "Registration for Women," June 1942, unnumbered; Alonso, *Peace as a Women's Issue*, pp. 149–150.

10. Dorothy Detzer, "The Spectacular and the Significant," October 1945, unnumbered; "Statement of the National Board on the Atomic Bomb," November 1945, unnumbered.

11. Elaine Tyler May, *Homeward Bound: American Families in the Cold War Era* (New York: Basic Books, 1988).

12. Meta Riseman, "Mrs. Everybody and Civil Liberties," November 1951, unnumbered (emphasis added).

13. Alonso, *Peace as a Women's Issue*, pp. 220–225.

14. See Joan V. Bondurant, "Indo-China—A Second Korea," April 1952, unnumbered; Alonso, *Peace as a Women's Issue*, p. 197.

15. "WILPF Action," July 1969, unnumbered.

16. Ann Berthoff, "The Cold War in the Classroom," April 1968, unnumbered; Libby Frank, " 'My Weekly Reader' Learns a Lesson," April, 1968, unnumbered; "Resolutions at Annual Meeting," July 1969, unnumbered.

17. Alonso, *Peace as a Women's Issue*, pp. 195–196; 206–207.

18. Wendy Rosenfield, telephone interview, October 31, 1995.

Information Sources

BIBLIOGRAPHY:

Alonso, Harriet Hyman. *Peace as a Women's Issue: A History of the U.S. Movement for World Peace and Women's Rights.* Syracuse, N.Y.: Syracuse University Press, 1993.

Bacon, Margaret Hope. *One Woman's Passion for Peace and Freedom: The Life of Mildread Scott Olmsted.* Syracuse, N.Y.: Syracuse University Press, 1992.

Bussey, Gertrude, and Margaret Tims. *Pioneers for Peace: Women's International League for Peace and Freedom, 1915–1965.* 1965. Reprint. Oxford: Alden Press, 1980.

Foster, Catherine. *Women for All Seasons: The Story of the Women's International League for Peace and Freedom.* Athens: University of Georgia Press, 1989.

May, Elaine Tyler. *Homeward Bound: American Families in the Cold War Era.* New York: Basic Books, 1988.

INDEX SOURCES: 1961/1962, reel 23.03, Women's International League of Peace and Freedom, Swarthmore College Peace Collection.

LOCATION SOURCES: Swarthmore College Peace Collection, Swarthmore College, Swarthmore, Pa., and other libraries.

Publication History

PERIODICAL TITLE AND TITLE CHANGES: *Four Lights* (1941–1970); *Peace and Freedom* (1970–1984); *Peace & Freedom* (1985–1987); *Peace and Freedom* (1988–present).

VOLUME AND ISSUE DATA: Vols. 1– (June 1941–present). Monthly (except August and September) (1941–1977); nine issues (1978–1985); eight issues (1986–1988); six issues (1989–present).

PUBLISHER AND PLACE OF PUBLICATION: Women's International League for Peace and Freedom. Philadelphia.

EDITORS: Emily Cooper Johnson (1941–1947); Mercedes Randall (1947); Elizabeth Tolles (1948); Josephine Lifton (1950–1956); Celia Daldy (1956–1966); Martha Molarsky (1967); Elizabeth Weideman (1967–1969); Gladys P. Thomas (1969); Angela Hoffman (1970); Elizabeth Weideman (1971–1972); Naomi Marcus (1975–1976); Barbara Armentrout (1979?–1985); Roberta Spivek (1985–1992); Wendy Rosenfield (1992–1995).

CIRCULATION: Ulrich's 1995: 10,000.

Erika A. Kuhlman

THE PIONEER

When Emily A. Pitts bought a half interest in the *California Weekly Mercury* of San Francisco in January 1869 and became coeditor, the paper was, according to its subtitle, ''A Journal of American Literature.'' Its contents consisted of articles on literary and historical topics, personal essays, a few news reports, miscellaneous notes, reviews of cultural events, serial romances, biographical sketches, answers to queries from readers, and advertisements. Pitts continued to use most of these but gave the paper a new focus. As her ''Salutatory'' said,

> With this issue, a new field has been laid out for the *Mercury*. The wrongs of woman, the many abuses she has suffered, have at last aroused from their lethargic sleep not alone the oppressed, but those who have for all time been the oppressors.
>
> We defend the rights of women fearlessly and to the best of our ability. We shall insist upon woman's independence—her elevation, socially and politically, to the platform now solely occupied by man. We shall claim for her each privilege now given to every male citizen of the United States. In short, we shall claim for her the right of suffrage—believing that by this she will gain the position for which God intended her—equality with man.[1]

From her native New York, Pitts had come to San Francisco in 1865 at the age of twenty-one to help establish and then teach in the Miel Institute, a female seminary. Teaching occupied her until, as she put it, ''the value and importance of woman's industrial enlargements and political enfranchisement, so filled our entire mind, heart and soul, that we were constrained to abandon all other interests and to consecrate ourselves to the promotion of that great movement that held within its sacred embrace, the destinies of half the human race."[2] She intended her paper not only to champion women's causes but also to employ them as typesetters and printers.

Until she sold the paper in 1873, Pitts devoted a substantial portion of each issue to the suffrage cause. In editorials, in articles, and in reports of suffrage meetings at the local, state, and national levels, she supported equal rights—and particularly voting rights—for women. Hers seems to have been the first paper in the West with this as its principal aim.

Her paper did not remain the *Mercury* for long. Pitts explained in September 1869, when she assumed complete control: "The old name did not please us. It symbolized neither our thought nor our object . . . Mercury, the classic divinity, typefies more the character of the modern financier than that of the sincere and earnest reformer of the last half of the nineteenth century. . . . We have selected for the name of our paper *The Pioneer*." As subtitle Pitts chose "Devoted to the Promotion of Human Rights" and as motto, "Liberty, Justice, Fraternity." She explained that she used "fraternity" only because "the paucity of our language . . . has no word to express the brotherhood and sisterhood of the race."[3]

Not long after she changed the name of the paper, the editor changed her own name, as well. She married August K. Stevens and soon began referring to herself in the paper as Mrs. Pitts Stevens, often with a hyphen.

At the same time Pitts Stevens worked to establish her paper as a voice of the suffrage cause, she attempted to help organize women in California and Nevada into suffrage associations. As vice president of the San Francisco society, she supported efforts to establish affiliates of the Woman's State Suffrage Association of California in every county seat and insisted in her paper not only that justice demanded voting rights for women but also that women would uplift the political sphere by their participation—two common themes of the suffrage movement.

Pitts Stevens held that association in political activities would benefit women and men personally, as well as politically, because "the habit of free, graceful, contented conversation with the other sex" would make them superior to those who restricted their dealings to their own sex. As for fears that political participation might make women less feminine or less devoted to their husbands and children, Pitts Stevens dismissed them. An ardent champion of happy families in happy homes, she agreed with an 1872 suffrage convention speaker that "there is nothing so beautiful as home life" and saw suffrage as a means of making it even more satisfying.[4]

Not averse to proclaiming her own success as a homemaker, she published Abigail Scott Duniway's report of a day spent with her and her husband. Duniway served as Oregon editor of *The Pioneer* and later published a woman's rights paper in Portland, *The New Northwest.** She found the Stevens' lodging "dainty" and "cozy," peopled by "the twin sisters, love and harmony," and called August Stevens "a genial, happy, whole-souled gentleman, with love-light in his eyes, and a pardonable pride of his gifted wife in his heart."[5]

The Pioneer reported regularly and at length upon the meetings of the local, state, and national suffrage associations and, sometimes obliquely, upon the quarrels that arose within and among them. While claiming that California stood aloof from the dissension in the national groups, Pitts Stevens admitted that she supported the liberal views of Susan B. Anthony and Elizabeth Cady Stanton, rather than the conservative position of Lucy Stone and her Boston followers.

Certainly, she found herself in the middle of the squabbles among California suffrage supporters. After announcing the formation of a state association in *The Pioneer,* she conducted its first meeting, held in January 1870 in San Francisco, and won election to its board of control. However, a splinter group condemned the state organization for usurping power and urged county associations to withdraw. In *The Pioneer,* Pitts Stevens lamented "that the men and women friendly to our movement cannot see through the cunning and craft of those who would make the woman-suffrage cause a stepping stone for their individual advancement."[6]

Opponents of the state association also resorted to attacks on Pitts Stevens' character. Without specifying the exact nature of their charges, she defended her respectability in *The Pioneer.* The *San Francisco Chronicle,* always ready to ridicule suffragists, proved less reticent, naming her in 1872 as a member of the Radical Club, an institution "composed exclusively of Socialists, Spiritualists, Free Lovers, Woman Suffragists and all who by reason of their sentiments are ostracised from the society which they so much condemn."[7]

Also in 1872 Pitts Stevens organized the Woman Suffrage Party of the Pacific Coast, which elected her its president. As November approached, she filled the pages of *The Pioneer* with articles supporting presidential candidate George Francis Train, the eccentric reformer who had helped finance the national woman's rights paper, *The Revolution.**

At the 1873 meeting of the state association the free-love accusation caused another split. Officers adjourned the convention two days early, and Pitts Stevens and her supporters reconvened to hold sessions at which they elected their own slate of leaders. Even there, the free-love issue caused trouble, and Pitts Stevens made a speech "with tears in her eyes" disclaiming any belief in free-love heresies and denouncing the *Chronicle* reporter who put her in the free-love camp.[8]

The Pioneer reported none of this. Only after the *Chronicle* published a statement from the deposed officers of the state association calling Pitts Stevens an instrument of conspirators who would capture the organization for "the Woodhull phase of woman suffrage" and vaccinate it with the virus of free love, did she respond. Without defending herself directly, she published a statement signed by ten prominent women that denounced the "vile and scurrilous attack" upon her. It pronounced "many of the charges, particularly that relating to Free Love, UNFOUNDED AND UNTRUE."[9] She also reprinted editorials from San Francisco daily newspapers other than the *Chronicle* testifying that she had led a life beyond reproach.

The controversy occupied relatively little space in *The Pioneer,* and Pitts Stevens continued to devote much space to woman's rights. At the same time, she published a variety of content dealing with other topics. Articles supporting reforms like temperance ran alongside serial fiction, poetry, household and gardening hints, theatrical notes, humor columns, and informative pieces about scientific and historical topics. A column titled "Chow Chow" offered miscellaneous tidbits of local and national news. As she put it, "We give entertaining stories, choice selections of poetry, a great deal of news about the suffrage cause, men and women personals, facts, fun and philosophy and miscellaneous news, historical and biographical sketches, etc."[10]

Advertising filled at least one of the paper's pages, more during its early years, and included notices for tailors, insurance agents, clothing and shoe stores, educational courses, tea and candy shops, patent medicines, windmills, and a clairvoyant. Barlow J. Smith sought customers for his Hygeian Home Water Cure and boasted that he could determine by an examination of the head, even while blindfolded, diseases to which a person might be constitutionally subject.[11]

Like many other periodicals of the time, *The Pioneer* offered premiums to those who recruited new subscribers. For forty-eight subscriptions at the regular three-dollar rate, an enterprising reader could claim a sewing machine—silver-plated, with elegant cabinet and lock. *The Pioneer* also offered "club rates" to readers who also subscribed to one of several other periodicals, among them *Godey's Lady's Book* and *American Stock Journal.*

George P. Rowell's *American Newspaper Directory* reported circulation estimates for *The Pioneer* of 3,000 in 1870, 1,800 in 1871 and 1872, and 1,250 in 1873. While submitted, unverified, by the publisher and thus not completely reliable, these figures reflect a decline in circulation over the paper's life that may have contributed to Pitts Stevens' decision to sell. Along with the strain of defending her character, she also may have wearied of the tasks involved in its production, for, as she reported, in addition to her editorial labors, she solicited for readers and advertisers, made collections, assisted in mailing, and devoted any proceeds from teaching or lecturing to the paper's advancement.[12]

Pitts Stevens gave neither an explanation nor a farewell message to her readers before Mrs. C. C. Calhoun took over the paper in September 1873, promising that it would continue to promote suffrage but adding, "Its columns will be tainted with none of the impure chimeras of the day, and it will not be obscured in any degree in the pestilential atmosphere of FREE LOVE, so called."[13] The paper apparently survived for only two months under the new management, and California's woman suffrage movement was left without an editorial voice.

Notes

1. January 24, 1869, p. 2.
2. October 15, 1870, p. 1.
3. September 13, 1869, p. 1.
4. March 31, 1869, p. 2; June 27, 1872, p. 8.
5. January 5, 1871, p. 1.
6. February 12, 1870, p. 2.
7. *San Francisco Chronicle,* June 2, 1872, p. 1.
8. *San Francisco Chronicle,* April 11, 1873, p. 3.
9. *San Francisco Chronicle,* April 27, 1873, p. 5; *The Pioneer,* May 8, 1873, p. 2.
10. February 6, 1873, p. 4.
11. June 4, 1870, p. 3.
12. November 13, 1869, p. 1.
13. September 1, 1873, p. 1.

Information Sources

BIBLIOGRAPHY:
Bennion, Sherilyn Cox. "*The Pioneer:* The First Voice for Women's Suffrage in the West." *The Pacific Historian* 25. 4, Winter 1981, pp. 15–21.
———. *Equal to the Occasion: Women Editors of the Nineteenth-Century West.* Reno: University of Nevada Press, 1990.
INDEX SOURCES: None.
LOCATION SOURCES: Bancroft.

Publication History

PERIODICAL TITLE AND TITLE CHANGES: *The Pioneer* (continues *Saturday Evening Mercury*).
VOLUME AND ISSUE DATA: Vols. 1–4 (November 13, 1869–October 1873). Weekly (1869–June 27, 1872); semimonthly (July 4, 1872–October 1873).
PUBLISHER AND PLACE OF PUBLICATION: Emily Pitts Stevens (1869–August 1873); Mrs. C. C. Calhoun (September–October 1873). San Francisco.
EDITORS: Emily Pitts Stevens (1869–August 1873); Mrs. C. C. Calhoun (September–October 1873).
CIRCULATION: *Rowell* directory, 1870, 1871, 1872, 1873: 1,250–3,000.

Sherilyn Cox Bennion

PITTSBURGH SATURDAY VISITER

Although she had to share the title of editor with her husband at one time and with a male business associate at another, Jane Grey Swisshelm was the heart and soul of the *Pittsburgh Saturday Visiter,* a weekly newspaper devoted to abolitionism, woman's rights, and general social reform in the mid-nineteenth century. She founded the newspaper, and she funded it through its most precarious days. She wrote most of the editorials; edited the copy; bore the brunt of the criticism; and relished in the notoriety the newspaper brought. Jane Grey Swisshelm affectionately called the weekly her "baby."[1] Ironically, the birth of her child, Nettie, and her ill health afterward eventually led to the merging of the *Visiter* into the *Family Journal*.[2]

Even before the launch of the *Pittsburgh Saturday Visiter,* Jane Grey Swisshelm was well known in the city's abolitionist circles. She had written for *The Spirit of Liberty,* the *Albatross,* and a variety of other abolitionist newspapers. In addition, she had presented her decidedly radical views in general newspapers, including the *Pittsburgh Commercial Journal.* After the *Albatross* folded, Pittsburgh had no abolitionist newspaper. Upon the prodding of Charles Sumner, later a Republican senator from Massachusetts, George W. Julian, later a Republican senator from Indiana, and Charles Shiras, brother of well-known Pittsburgh judge George Shiras,[3] Swisshelm decided to launch the *Saturday Visiter* to fill the gap. Although Sumner, Julian, and Shiras provided moral support, they offered little by way of financial support (apart from a promise to subscribe). Swisshelm used her inheritance to underwrite the venture. As she wrote in her autobiography, "I said my husband approved [of the venture], the matter was all arranged, I would use my own estate, and if I lost it, it was nobody's affair."[4] Some predicted that the editor would lose her money. Although Robert M. Riddle, editor of the *Pittsburgh Commercial Journal,* was one of those naysayers, he agreed to print the paper anyway. On December 20, 1847, the *Pittsburgh Saturday Visiter* premiered.

Its appearance was not necessarily greeted with enthusiasm. Many editors from Maine to Georgia were taken aback by the fact that a woman was editing a political paper, for the *Saturday Visiter* was the Liberty Party's organ in Allegheny County. However, Horace Greeley of the *New York Tribune* and Nathaniel P. Willis of the *Home Journal* expressed confidence in her ability.[5]

The confidence was well placed. The newspaper, which provided a combination of poetry, short stories, news, and biting editorials, quickly grew in circulation. The newspaper, however, was never able to attract much advertising; and frequently the editor had to remind readers to renew their subscriptions.

The newspaper went through three phases during its short life. Launched as a political paper in preparation for the campaign of 1848, the *Pittsburgh Saturday Visiter* proved to be a strident antislavery organ. In everything from poetry[6] to editorials, Swisshelm and her *Saturday Visiter* badgered the slaveholders and their supporters. Perhaps most important in more immediate terms were her endorsements. She supported the Liberty Party slate: John P. Hale of New Hampshire for president and Leicester King of Ohio for vice president.

After the election, the newspaper became independent, and Swisshelm converted her weekly into a "family newspaper—devoted to literature, truth, general news, arts and sciences, history, biography, agriculture, mechanics, education, morality, amusements &c."[7] Yet little changed in the tone of the periodical; she remained stridently abolitionist. As she wrote of the Constitution,

We repeat without hesitation that if the Constitution guarantees any man's right to his neighbor's wife and children, it is a mean cowardly libel on itself—an insolent attempt to annul the laws of Jehovah and not worth as much of an honest man's breath as would give it one good, hearty curse. Any if it fixes the curse of slavery upon one human being—makes merchandise of one creature made in the image of God, it is not worth straw enough to burn it.[8]

The newspaper was not strictly devoted to one reform. Swisshelm was writing more and more about woman's rights. Indeed, the largest number of editorials after the 1848 election dealt with woman's rights. She supported suffrage, equal education, and woman's right to own her own property, even after marriage.[9] She did not support dress reform or the so-called Bloomer garb.[10] Swisshelm's newspaper could be seen allied with the more conservative arm of the woman's rights movement. She explained her position to her readers:

We agree with the old conservative party that the performance of the duties of "wife, mother, daughter, sister and friend" are woman's highest glory, and her "proper sphere," and we believe the exercise of the political franchise is necessary to the proper performance of these duties.[11]

Although neither she nor her newspaper formally affiliated with any woman's rights organization, Swisshelm was considered a leader of sorts in the movement. She sometimes attended the various conventions held in Pennsylvania or Ohio, and her newspaper covered the conventions taking place elsewhere. However, she seriously questioned the need for such gatherings.

We never saw any necessity for, or propriety in her imitating man in getting up those great, unwieldy cabals called conventions, contrived like firecrackers, and a cartridge without ball, for producing *reports* and nothing else.[12]

Although she questioned the need for conventions, Swisshelm never once questioned the need for reform. Women had to have their legal and economic rights. She often consoled woman's rights leaders on tactical matters, urging them not to combine reforms. Abolitionism and woman's rights should remain separate, even though Swisshelm personally supported both. As she explained, mixing the two would only weaken both:

The women of this glorious Republic are sufficiently oppressed without linking their course to that of the slave. The slave is sufficiently oppressed without binding him to the stake which has ever held woman in a state of bondage. There is no kind of reason why the American prejudice against color should be invoked to sink woman into a lower degradation than that she already *enjoys*—no kind of reason why the car of emancipation, for the slave, should have been clogged by tying to its wheels the most unpopular reform that ever was broached, by having all the women in the world fastened to the axle as a drag.[13]

During this period, she transferred her views on woman's rights into action. She went to Washington, D.C., in 1850 and opened the congressional press gallery to women. However, she did not stay long in the city—politics got in the way. As might be expected, she abided no compromise with slavery. Senators Henry Clay and Daniel Webster promised just that. Swisshelm reported that "their drivelling arguments about compromises, and fear for the safety of our glorious Union, just sounded like twaddle."[14] However, those comments did not get her in trouble; another news dispatch threatened to. In the dispatch that appeared in the *Saturday Visiter,* Swisshelm accused Webster of fathering eight mulatto children; that dispatch—only a paragraph long—was eventually reprinted as many as one hundred times in anti-Webster and anti-Whig papers.[15]

Although her woman's rights and antislavery editorials dominated the *Saturday Visiter,* she also supported a number of other causes. Especially dear to her was the temperance crusade. Readers often complained about the "extreme" solutions she advocated. Swisshelm saw two solutions to the widespread problem with drunkenness· the horsewhip and woman suffrage. The horsewhip would "reform" individual drunkards; woman suffrage would end the sale of liquor in the country. Those solutions alone would end the problem: "To us, no object on earth is so loathsome, so hateful, so abominable as a drunkard."[16]

Although reform represented an important component of the *Saturday Visiter*'s editorial package, there was another, softer part of the weekly during this period of its life. Swisshelm began her series "Letters to Country Girls" in 1849. The enormously popular letters, which were eventually collected and published in book form in 1853,[17] revealed Swisshelm's attitudes on everyday life. She counseled the "country girls" to eat healthy diets, cultivate beauty, and appreciate their surroundings. These uplifting letters were often cited in other newspapers.[18] The style, the tone, the content of these letters stood in stark contrast to the reform component of the rest of the newspaper.

Yet that blending of the two approaches seemed to strike a responsive chord among the readers of the *Saturday Visiter.* Circulation increased considerably during this period. Its strength, however, was not necessarily in Pennsylvania or Pittsburgh. As Swisshelm emphasized, the largest number of subscribers were outside Pennsylvania.[19] That fact helped explain Swisshelm's next move. She tried to sell her newspaper to "some woman who could have kept up with the age, and made it an organ of the accredited woman's rights party." Swisshelm had found that she could not manage a baby and her "baby" *Visiter.* She complained, "Baby Visiter has been sadly neglected." Unable to sell, Swisshelm settled for a renewed partnership with Riddle, who would take over the business end of publishing, while she would continue the editorial side. This seemed to be the best solution.[20] However, it was only a temporary one; 1852 was an election year, and the *Visiter* entered a new stage of development. In a sense, it was returning to its political roots. Swisshelm and her husband offered the Free Democrats the newspaper. As she explained, "We were anxious they should engage some one to take precedence as senior editor, and let us take some secondary place; but they voted, unanimously, to leave the Visiter in our hands and give it their most cordial support."[21] Of course, that meant that husband William and Jane would alone run the paper—without the business advice and help from Riddle. During that campaign, the *Visiter* supported the Free Democrats, continued antislavery agitation, and focused attention on the need for woman's rights. Although the Swisshelms kept to their part of the agreement, the Free Democrats were remiss in theirs. The party paid for few of the political advertisements published in the newspaper and provided few new *paid* subscribers. From Swisshelm's perspective, the party benefited, and she was left to "hunt exchanges and documents while darning stockings and making dresses."[22] The Free Democrats never came through with the needed financial support, and Swisshelm made good on her threat to go independent—again. But it was a short-lived independence. A month later, Swisshelm announced that the *Visiter* would merge with Riddle's *Family Journal.* She continued to contribute to that periodical until 1857.

The *Pittsburgh Saturday Visiter* represented an interesting chapter in reform journalism. In a time when women lacked the vote, property rights, or even the right to the children in the event of a divorce, Jane Grey Swisshelm ran her reform newspaper and worked for social betterment. The newspaper gained its share of notoriety. However, it took a terrible toll on Swisshelm. The newspaper never achieved much of a profit, and thus it represented a drain on Swisshelm's finances. It required an enormous commitment of time and energy, a commitment that Swisshelm's health could not afford. All this, no doubt, added to pressures already existing in the Swisshelm household. In the end, it may have cost Swisshelm her marriage. In 1857, Swisshelm deserted her husband, took her small child, and headed west.

Notes

1. "A Change," May 15, 1852, p. 66.
2. Arthur Larsen, *Crusader and Feminist: Letters of Jane Grey Swisshelm 1858–1865* (St. Paul: Minnesota Historical Society, 1934), p. 8.
3. Details vary with regard to the launch of the newspaper. The Sumner, Julian, and Shiras account is in Kathleen L. Endres, "Jane Grey Swisshelm: 19th Century Journalist and Feminist," *Journalism History* 2.4, Winter 1975–1976, p. 129. Swisshelm is vague on the details in her autobiography, *Half a Century* (Chicago: Jansen, McClurg, 1880), pp. 106–107.
4. Swisshelm, *Half a Century,* p. 107.
5. Ibid., pp. 113–115.

6. See, for example, one stanza from "The Slave Mother's Petition," February 26, 1848, p. 1:

> "Oh God—and is there no redress
> For me in my despair?
> Must I then toil from year to year,
> Beneath the tyrant overseer?
> Oh, Father! hear my prayer.

7. January 20, 1849, p. 1.

8. "Mrs. Swisshelm and the Constitution," February 17, 1849, p. 18.

9. See, for example, "Schools, April 14, 1849, p. 50; "Woman's Rights and Duties, August 4, 1849, p. 114; "The Masculine Qualification for the Rights of Citizenship," November 30, 1850, p. 182.

10. "A Lady in Pantaloons," September 22, 1849, p. 142.

11. June 21, 1851, p. 82.

12. "Our Past and Our Future," January 24, 1852, p. 2.

13. "Woman's Rights and the Color Question," November 23, 1850, p. 178.

14. "Editor's Correspondence," April 27, 1850, p. 58.

15. Swisshelm, *Half a Century,* p. 138; Kathleen L. Endres, "Jane Grey Swisshelm," in Perry Ashley, ed., *Dictionary of Literary Biography, Vol. 43: American Newspaper Journalists* (Detroit: Gale Research, 1985), p. 431.

16. "Horsewhip," April 28, 1849, p. 58.

17. Jane Grey Swisshelm, *Letters to Country Girls* (New York: J. C. Riker, 1853).

18. See, for example, "Letters to Country Girls," March 24, 1849, p. 38; April 7, 1849, p. 46; April 28, 1849, p. 58.

19. "To Free Democrats of Pennsylvania," December 31, 1853, p. 193.

20. "A Change," May 15, 1852, p. 66.

21. "Explanatory," August 21, 152, p. 122.

22. "To Free Democrats of Pennsylvania," December 31, 1853, p. 193.

Information Sources

BIBLIOGRAPHY:

Burleigh, Celia. "People Worth Knowing: Jane Grey Swisshelm." *Woman's Journal,* August 20, 1870, p. 257; August 27, 1870, p. 265; September 3, 1870, p. 274.

Endres, Kathleen. "Jane Grey Swisshelm: 19th Century Journalist and Feminist." *Journalism History* 2.4, Winter 1975–1976, pp. 128–131.

———. "Jane Grey Swisshelm." In Perry J. Ashley, ed., *Dictionary of Literary Biography, Vol. 43: American Newspaper Journalists, 1690–1872.* Detroit: Gale Research, 1985, pp. 430–435.

Fisher, S. J. "Reminiscences of Jane Grey Swisshelm." *Western Pennsylvania Historical Magazine* 4, July 1921, pp. 165–274.

Klement, Frank. "Jane Grey Swisshelm and Lincoln: A Feminist Fusses and Frets." *Abraham Lincoln Quarterly,* December 1950, pp. 227–238.

Larsen, Arthur J. *Crusader and Feminist: Letters of Jane Grey Swisshelm.* St. Paul: Minnesota Historical Society, 1934.

Stearns, Bertha-Monica. "Reform Periodicals and Female Reformers, 1830–1860." *American Historical Review* 37, July 1932, pp. 678–699.

Swisshelm, Jane Grey. *Half a Century.* Chicago: Jansen, McClurg, 1880.
INDEX SOURCES: None.
LOCATION SOURCES: Carnegie Library, Pittsburgh; Western Reserve Historical So-
    ciety, Cleveland; and other, primarily scattered holdings.

Publication History

PERIODICAL TITLE AND TITLE CHANGES: *Pittsburgh Saturday Visiter* (1847–
    1851); *Saturday Visiter* (1851–1854) (merges with *Family Journal* under the title
    Family Journal and Visiter).
VOLUME AND ISSUE DATA: Vols. 1–6 (December 20, 1847–January 28, 1854, when
    it merges with *Family Journal*). Weekly (1847–1854).
PUBLISHER AND PLACE OF PUBLICATION: Jane G. Swisshelm (1847–1849); Jane
    G. Swisshelm and Robert M. Riddle (1849); Jane G. Swisshelm and William
    Swisshelm (1850–1852); Jane G. Swisshelm (1852); Jane G. Swisshelm and Rob-
    ert M. Riddle (1852); Jane G. Swisshelm and William Swisshelm (1852–1854).
    Pittsburgh.
EDITORS: Jane G. Swisshelm (1847–1849); Jane G. Swisshelm and Robert M. Riddle
    (1849); Jane G. Swisshelm and William Swisshelm (1850–1852); Jane G. Swis-
    shelm (1852); Jane G. Swisshelm and Robert M. Riddle (1852); Jane G. Swis-
    shelm and William Swisshelm (1852–1854).
CIRCULATION: Larsen, p. 8: 6,000; Endres, p. 431: 7,000.

Kathleen L. Endres

PLAINSWOMAN

The "Perils of Pauline" could describe the struggles to publish the *Plainswoman,* a feminist periodical of the northern Great Plains. *Plainswoman* was
published through the perseverance of pioneering editors who, with a little
money and a lot of imagination, managed to put it out month after month for
twelve years.

The first pioneering editor, Jean Butenhoff Lee, had been publishing a newsletter for the Women's Center at the University of North Dakota, (UND) when
she decided, "We can do more than this." She convened a group of feminists
from the university's intellectual community who longed to get to know one
another better. According to Kathryn Sweney, who later became associate editor
of *Plainswoman,* the women of the group were "driven by a sense of cause,"
writers and readers wanting to connect with others. The group decided on March
17, 1977, to extend the newsletter to four pages. The first issue was projected
for June.[1]

Their first problem to solve was the name. The board wanted something that
was feminist but not threatening, according to Lillian Elsinga, who later became
UND dean of students. One of the board members came up with the title *Plainswoman.* Elsinga managed to find some university-dedicated money to launch

the publication. Everything the board did was designed to give the *Plainswoman* permanence—even the paper stock.[2] Kathryn Sweney, former associate editor, said Lee—as an archivist—made sure *Plainswoman* was published on quality paper that would not disintegrate over time. First editor Lee said, "In the Dakotas I saw a lot of recent history that needed to be preserved, that needed recording. I wanted *Plainswoman* to be a permanent and accurate record of women's history for libraries and schools, and we were careful in choosing paper stock that would hold up on library shelves."[3]

Women were involved in every phase of the development of this periodical. The board held a logo contest. A graphic artist at the local office of the Cooperative Extension Office at the university provided the winning entry.[4]

Lee's enthusiasm for the project put *Plainswoman* on the literary agenda, and the project caught the imagination of feminists and decision makers statewide. As early as April 1977, Lee had met with UND president Thomas Clifford about the need for such a publication. Her plans included a statewide advisory board and university space for an office. Clifford was agreeable, and he committed office space, equipment, and a telephone. Even though the first steering committee comprised residents from Grand Forks, soon a statewide group of women and men got involved. Sweney said the board included clergy, farmers, ranchers, educators, administrators, journalists, and legislators.[5]

However, some way had to be found to fund the project in the long term. In May 1977, *Plainswoman* was incorporated as a nonprofit organization, thereby making it eligible for government support. Funds were obtained through the Comprehensive Employment and Training Act (CETA), administered through the U.S. Department of Labor. The funds allowed the organization to obtain a full-time editorial and administrative assistant, Charlotte West. Later, funds from Community Development allowed for the purchase of better equipment. By July 1977 Lee and West worked on the publication in an office at UND's Robertson Hall.[6]

By October, the first issue was ready to go. Lee said in the first editorial:

Valuing the past . . . enhancing the present . . . expanding the future. These are the purposes to which *Plainswoman* is dedicated. Published monthly, its pages will carry brief sketches of the contributions that women have made to the development of the United States, with emphasis on the northern Great Plains. There will also be extracts from letters, journals, diaries and other personal writings, In these ways *Plainswoman* intends to contribute to the collection and preservation of the history of women in America.[7]

The early articles were thought-provoking; a representative example of articles included sexist stereotyping in textbooks, how to get and keep a good credit rating, a comparison of American and Soviet women, descriptions of Project Equal, and the displaced homemaker program. *Plainswoman* also became a forum for creative writers of poetry, stories, essays, and book reviews.

In that first issue, also, the *Plainswoman* published first impressions of the prairie drawn from oral histories of pioneer women of the late nineteenth century. The interviews had been conducted during the 1930s by Works Progress Administration (WPA) workers. Readers learned, for instance, that Mrs. James Crider traveled alone in 1890 with her twins, aged two, to join her husband in North Dakota: "She rode out to the homestead on the running gears of the wagon. There was nothing to see for miles and miles but prairie and hills. She noticed that the ground was cracked here and there, and thought to herself, 'It must be so dry here.' "[8]

Readers were told that "[c]oming in November" there would be more of the same: diaries, letters, and reminiscences of Dakota pioneering women, featuring an interview with Vonda Kay Redman, who researched the material at the State Historical Archives in Bismarck. The readers were also promised news on the Women's Education Equity Act, an article about group credit life insurance, and a poem about the prairie.[9] This mixture of articles providing practical information and cultural stimulation set the standard for future issues.

Lee envisioned a publication paid for by memberships. A plan was developed but was repeatedly shelved by the first advisory board. The initial subscription rate for the magazine was four dollars for twelve eight-page issues. For two years, *Plainswoman* continued to publish monthly. The issue of midsummer 1979 became a combined July–August publication.[10]

Bigger changes were still ahead. Sweney said things were in an uproar that critical summer of 1979. The driving force behind the publication was leaving. Lee had received a Woodrow Wilson Scholarship and was planning to pursue graduate studies at the University of Virginia. CETA funding had become uncertain. West quit, and the office had been abandoned. All the files had been moved to storage areas at UND's Plant Services. Only the telephone remained in what once was the office of a vital publication.[11]

The publication then went through a period of retrenchment, with little or no funding sources. A master's student named Karla Spitzer agreed to work mostly on a volunteer status. She served as editor for several months. Sweney said the organizational expense and cost of mailings to keep the statewide advisory board active became a hindrance.[12] But the publication still had its strong supporters. Elsinga said, "People were donating what they could in terms of time and money toward this newsletter as well as to other feminist and social issues."[13]

As CETA moneys materialized and a development director was hired, problems did not disappear—they seemed to multiply. The publication lost its office space, its typesetting equipment, its telephone. Subscriptions dropped from one thousand to five hundred. Still the periodical struggled on. Three bimonthly issues were produced the first half of 1980, but subscriptions continued to drop. The publication was suspended.[14]

Six months later, in January 1981, the board met once again, this time to dissolve the corporation and settle debts. One board member, Elizabeth Hampsten, would not go along with the idea. She convinced the board to try again, and the publication's office was moved once again to the Women's Center on campus.

In March 1981, an issue was published, this time with the financial backing of the North Dakota Humanities Council. Subscriptions were raised to eight dollars, and less expensive paper stock was used. Twenty women were asked to provide one hundred-dollar lifetime subscriptions. By September, a new cover design featured the artwork of artist John Vleck. A fiction contest was soon initiated. All this was only the beginning.

By 1983, a grant from the Bremer Foundation for subscription development came through.[15] Hampsten planned to use the grant to send sample copies to libraries, historical societies, Bremer banks, women's studies programs, and other likely readers. She also planned to make a slide show about *Plainswoman* to market the publication.[16]

Plainswoman became a monthly publication, with the exception of February and August. Publication size ran from sixteen pages for single issues to twenty-eight for the double issues. By 1987, subscription price had gone up to fifteen dollars a year, but actual cost of publishing was closer to twenty dollars per year. Considering a lower rate of ten dollars was offered to low-income subscribers,[17] *Plainswoman*'s subscriptions did not completely cover publication costs.

Hampsten, of the UND English Department, continued to be active in the publication. The *Plainswoman* editor is known for talking plain, as in her well-reasoned argument and her vision of the publication's mission. That was reflected in the content of the periodical. She devoted the fall issues to women's involvement in agriculture and the December issue to the theme of the Indian woman. This latter editorial decision brought some complaints. In December 1984, Hampsten editorially defended devoting still a third issue to Indian women in as many years.[18] The December 1986 issue included three short stories by Native American writers Ann Dunn of Case Lake, Minnesota; Joanie Whitebird of Houston, Texas; and Denise Panek of Eau Claire, Wisconsin. Hampsten was not apologetic. She said on behalf of the editorial committee, "We cannot explain . . . why so much good fiction by and about Indian women is coming our way, but readers may have noticed that it has been for some time."[19]

In the tenth year of publication, Hampsten noted there was cause for celebration because the publication had taken on a life of its own. The editor wrote: "Each issue is a wonder to us that it was accomplished, and certainly we are always thankful for continued support."[20]

Plainswoman continued to publish two more years, until the June–July issue of 1989. Elizabeth Hampsten wrote the last editorial for an issue devoted entirely to fiction. She wrote from French Creek, West Virginia, saying that she had given in entirely to the pastoral setting, where she was visiting her daughter and grandchildren. Hampsten said, "I read a little, write a few letters, and otherwise cook and clean, hang out laundry, plant beans (they miraculously came up in a week), go for walks and dandle babies."[21]

In the editorial, Hampsten bemoaned the loss of computer disks for an extended fictional work for which she labored:

> [W]e know stories work when we can't help giving ourselves into them; they happily make us leave our baggage behind for residence in another country, an experience we hope our readers will have with stories here.[22]

Hampsten found the disks for her fictional work at the end of summer, too late to do any writing. In the same way, by 1989, she apparently felt *Plainswoman*—to use an expression of the Great Plains—was a day late and a dollar short. And, it was too late to do anything about it. She was clearly frustrated that she could not find editorial help to meet the monthly deadlines. In the last several years of the publication, she had struggled to continue publishing with only one other staff member. Hampsten, the final driving editorial force of *Plainswoman,* just simply decided she could not continue to do all the work. She decided to pioneer a country of other interests, even as she continued to serve in the English Department at North Dakota University.

Even then, she did not give up hope entirely. Like a woman who watches beans come up in the garden, she was hoping for a miracle. She announced in that last issue that she planned to suspend publication for only a year, to return with a January 1991 issue. Correspondence was directed to "an interim editor."[23] However, as noted, her efforts were not fruitful in the new season, and no further issues were published.

The last issue still carried this legend in the masthead, in deference to the first driving force behind the *Plainswoman:* "Jean Lee, Founding Editor, 1977."

Notes

1. Kathryn Sweney, "*Plainswoman*'s Ten Years," November 1986, pp. 17, 19.
2. Ibid.
3. Ibid., p. 18.
4. Ibid; "The *Plainswoman* Letterhead," October 1977, p. 6.
5. Sweney, "*Plainswoman*'s Ten Years," p. 17.
6. Ibid.
7. Jean Butenhoff Lee, editorial, October 1977, p. 2.
8. Vonda Kay Redman. Interview with Mrs. James Crider, Historical Data Project, State Historical Society, Bismark, 1930.
9. "First Impressions," October 1977, p. 6.
10. Sweeney, "*Plainswoman*'s Ten Years," p. 18.
11. Ibid.
12. Ibid.
13. Ibid.
14. Ibid.

15. Ibid.
16. Ibid.
17. Subscription Box, in various issues in the mid 1980s.
18. Elizabeth Hampsten, "From the Editors," December 1984, p. 2.
19. Elizabeth Hampsten, "From the Editors," December 1986, p. 2.
20. Elizabeth Hampsten, "From the Editors," November 1986, p. 2.
21. Elizabeth Hampsten, "From the Editors," June–July 1989, p. 2.
22. Ibid.
23. Editorial announcement of suspension, June–July 1989, p. 2.

Information Sources

BIBLIOGRAPHY:
Sweney, Kathryn. "*Plainswoman*'s Ten Years." *Plainswoman,* November 1986, pp. 17–19.
INDEX SOURCES: North Dakota Periodicals Index.
LOCATION SOURCES: North Dakota: Public Library, Grand Forks; University of North Dakota Library Special Collections; Bismarck State College Library, Bismarck; North Dakota State Library, Bismarck; Jamestown College Library, Jamestown; Fargo Public Library, Fargo.

Publication History

PERIODICAL TITLES AND TITLE CHANGES: *Plainswoman* (1977–1987).
VOLUME AND ISSUE DATA: Vols. 1–10 (October 1977–June/July 1989) Monthly (1977–1979); bimonthly (1979–June–July 1989) (with several months missed intermittently).
PUBLISHER AND PLACE OF PUBLICATION: Plainswoman Inc. Grand Forks, N. Dak.
EDITORS: Jean Butenhoff Lee (October 1977–August 1979); Karla Spitzer (September 1979–June 1980); Lee Hudson (April 1981–January 1982); Editorial Committee (February 1982–September 1982); Jeanne Anderegg (October 1982–July 1983); Elizabeth Hampsten and Editorial Committee (September 1983–June/July 1989).
CIRCULATION: 500–1,000.

Beverly G. Merrick

PRIME TIME

Today's media-savvy consumers associate the words "prime time" with television—either the best evening time slots or the network news magazine show with Sam Donaldson and Diane Sawyer. But a generation ago, "prime time" had a different meaning, serving as a cultural and social barometer for a small, but significant, group within American society during the 1970s. Then, *Prime Time* referred to the magazine founded by an angry fifty-nine-year-old woman who had been "phased out of my job when my company relocated—along with all the other women over 35" and who subsequently had to go on welfare in order to have an operation.[1]

A freelance photographer during and after World War II, Marjory Collins also had been a reporter during the civil rights marches of the 1960s. "Collins found that a childhood of affluence and her many adult years as a freewheeling, independent professional did not prepare her for the crunch meted out to the older woman."[2] She was shocked to lose her job in 1971 as a researcher and associate with the Center for the Study of Democratic Institutions, where she organized seminars on the impact of technology on warfare, race relations, and employment. She quickly found that no one would give her a job because of her age, and she was "overqualified" for the paltry salaries that some companies were willing to pay older women.[3]

"But it was good to get angry," Collins said, "because anger either destroys you, or drives you to *do* something about the situation. It was anger that motivated me to start *Prime Time*."[4]

Marjory Collins' *Prime Time,* premiering in September 1971, was frighteningly factual. Six of the newsletter's eight pages consisted of grim statistics that underscored the economic and social plight of 21.8 million women over forty-five years of age in the United States. Many of these women were single—widowed, divorced, separated, or never married. Most were stuck in dead-end jobs, the lowest paid members of the workforce who were the last hired, the first fired, and the first to be tossed on the economic scrap heap.

Among Collins' many figures (gathered from the 1970 U.S. Census, the Bureau of Labor Statistics, and the Department of Health, Education and Welfare) were these: 47 percent of men ages forty-five to sixty-four had incomes between ten thousand dollars and fifteen thousand dollars per year. Yet women in this age range had incomes that were downright pathetic: the largest percentage of them, 28.6 percent, had annual incomes between three thousand dollars and five thousand dollars. Only 8.4 percent of older women were in the ten thousand-dollar to fifteen thousand-dollar bracket.[5]

Pointing out that the forty-five to sixty-four age bracket was said to be "the prime of life," Collins wrote that *Prime Time*

> is addressed to all women who have suffered from age discrimination in their economic or personal lives. There are millions of us who would be living through our most rewarding years were it not for the shadow of age prejudice that haunts us daily—in the carefully worded rejection of a potential employer, in the scornful look of a young person accusing us of a "dated" remark, in our own unhealthy resentment that no one whistles at us any more. For a long time we were silent, considering our problems to be private, individual matters. We have done our best to be invisible as a group because a youth-oriented culture has subtle ways to make us feel ashamed of our age, to devalue our experience and make us feel unneeded.[6]

This was a group not to be found on the covers of the major women's magazines or addressed in the articles or fiction of the 1970s. "Although magazines are frequently directed toward specific age groups—children, teenagers, young homemakers—the elderly have been overlooked. In part, the pattern relates to a national unwillingness to confront the reality of aging, either on a practical or a psychological level."[7]

Collins argued that "the key to winning the fight for economic survival as an older woman is through knowledge of facts as they are now, and woman to woman communication and self-help."[8] She was determined to make older women visible through *Prime Time*, which was subtitled "for the liberation of women in the prime of life." Collins was the sole writer, editor, designer, publisher, and distributor of that first issue—and all subsequent ones—from her New York apartment.

In 1970 Collins had joined an older women's consciousness-raising group in New York City that called itself the Older Women's Liberation, or OWL.[9] This would become *Prime Time*'s main audience. The National Organization for Women (NOW) did not even name a Task Force on Older Women until February 1973, and "the OWLs soon discovered that other NOW women weren't ready to cope with ageism, a word not yet in use," wrote Collins in the third anniversary issue of *Prime Time*.[10] She was an early member of NOW, although that group and the women's liberation movement were dominated by young women under forty who burned their bras and wanted sexual equality as much as they wanted economic equality with men. Older women of the period, in contrast, had different agenda concerns.[11]

Collins gave *Prime Time* a strong feminist agenda, with hard-hitting, fact-filled articles exploring the health (physical and mental), employment, and financial, social, and legal problems facing older women. There also were book reviews, position papers, and condensations of significant speeches made by women like radical feminist Ti-Grace Atkinson and Congresswoman Bella Abzug (D-NY), and interviews with prominent international feminists like writer Simone de Beauvoir and Selma James, founder of the Wages for Housework movement in Italy. Special services included a speakers bureau, a readers service to research questions about divorce, employment, and social Security laws, and a telecommunications department to produce audiotapes and videotapes for and about older women. Like many feminist periodicals of the 1970s, *Prime Time* wanted to be a clearinghouse for information and news to its specific audience. Yet it distinguished itself from its fellow feminists in publishing by including little poetry, no fiction, and few diary excerpts.

Averaging sixteen pages per month, the early *Prime Time* initially looked and felt like a newsletter. There were at least two pages of "news and views" in every issue; these short paragraphs included political and financial items of interest to older women from around the world. But for the most part, the approach was clearly magazine-like in depth and detail, and by 1974, the look of the book matched the content. Here, and only here, could women over forty-five years of age find frank, forthright articles about cosmetic surgery, depression, divorce, survival skills, and finding a job. Mainstream women's magazines of the 1970s avoided those topics, content to discuss fads, fashion, and food for the middle-class stay-at-home mom in suburbia.

Health topics were often discussed in the first person, as in "Menopause Speak-Out," where five women shared their experiences.[12] That particular article generated more than a dozen letters, including one that filled two pages of the May 1974 issue. Wrote Lynn Laredo of New York City:

> I'd like to suggest that we keep a section constantly open as a regular feature of *Prime Time* for women to continually write about menopause. To date, there's no such women's movement reference, and we need it. . . . Who ever talks about it unless they have to? Unless they are actually in it? It's almost as untalked about as death, and far more mystified with *real* mystery.[13]

Male chauvinism in physicians, breast cancer, and mental health treatments were equally hot topics for *Prime Time* readers, who responded immediately in writing to articles. Generally, one-fourth to one-third of each issue was filled with mostly positive letters from readers commenting on the preceding one. Typical were comments like this one from Patricia Carney of Milton, Massachusetts: "Your paper helps. In attacking the problems of older women, in even acknowledging them, I feel not quite so alone. And if older women can face the situation they are in, perhaps we can—some of us—get it together enough to find solutions."[14]

Prime Time tried hardest to offer solutions to the question of ageism in America, publishing thirteen articles on the topic over a six-year period. Initially, ageism was defined broadly as "the negative attitudes and/or oppressive actions of an individual directed at a person or people of another age group, younger or older, *because of age*.[15] But in article after article, the focus understandably was on society's negative attitudes toward older women—attitudes that resulted in institutionalized ageist policies in employment, in the granting of scholarships, and in insurance rates, to name just a few of the areas *Prime Time* would discuss. Perhaps the sharpest example of ageism was provided by psychologist Dorothy Tennov, who wrote of being identified by a New York newspaper as an "elderly woman" at a conference. Exclaimed an irate Tennov, "Elderly at 43! When John Kennedy was assassinated at my age, we lost our 'youthful' leader."[16]

A research project with the New Hampshire Institute for the Study of Women in Transition was *Prime Time*'s greatest undertaking. A pilot questionnaire, with twenty-six open-ended questions, ran in the November 1975 issue of the magazine. Readers were asked to take as much space as they needed to answer the questions, with the assurance that all responses were confidential. As early as March 1976, Collins shared some of the responses:

> Most destructive of all is the ageism a woman expresses toward herself. For instance, in answer to the question: "As an adult, before you consid-

ered yourself an older woman, what thoughts, if any, did you have about growing older?'' one woman wrote "I remember thinking that I would not want to get fat or let myself go. I knew people wouldn't love me if I was not pretty." Another respondent, taken in by the diminishing sexuality myth, said: "I dreaded the thought of being over 40 and losing my sex appeal."[17]

In a later issue, condensed responses from three women, who were thirty-six, fifty-two, and seventy-one years old, were published.[18] The three narratives were powerful documents because of their first-person honesty about growing old. The eloquent words of these anonymous women had a far greater impact than a "standard" investigative article about ageism would have.

Some issues were built around a theme. The October 1975 international issue included a report about concerns affecting older women on nearly every continent on the planet. Other issues revolved around money matters, the education gap experienced by older women, women-owned businesses, and whether older women were pressured into being volunteers. Connie Calvert of Seattle, Washington, best summed up readers' attitudes toward the topics covered: "You're doing a terrific job with *Prime Time*. It's stimulating, supportive and argument-producing. I sit around reading it and yelling 'yes' and 'no' and 'right on.' "[19]

But not all issues were warmly and gratefully received. Hotly criticized was the September 1973 periodical, featuring several articles about chauvinism written by men, and others about male sexuality, double standards, and Watergate and its male games. Readers complained about the number of male-dominated articles (both in topic and author): "The September issue of *Prime Time* really upset me. . . . I want a publication that speaks to me, my age, my needs, my questions. . . . In what way do these articles speak to me as an older woman?"[20]

Editor Collins responded that the September issue

> was deliberately planned as a deviation from its usual stance as a forum where older women speak for themselves. It had occurred to the editor that readers might be interested, from time to time, to hear the thoughts and feelings of the opposite sex vis-a-vis ourselves. . . . To be sure, we committed an editorial boo-boo in springing this issue on readers without warning, without an editorial note explaining its *raison d'être.*[21]

No male bylines ever appeared again in *Prime Time,* nor were there any more articles from a masculine point of view.

Obviously, *Prime Time* was responsive to its audience. Indeed, the letters became the nerve center of the publication, a forum where readers communicated with each other throughout the United States and as far away as Saudi Arabia, Japan, England, and Germany. Letters were seldom shortened; some ran more than two pages in length, often resulting in more than half of the magazine devoted to reader comments. Many missives happily applauded the publication of *Prime Time,* but others were poignant, even sad in their relaying of the painful circumstances of older women's lives and why they needed this magazine.

Prime Time opened its pages without charge for space to women wanting to find or start OWL support groups in their towns or needing a job. This resulted in an extensive and breezy classifieds section that was likely one of the most read portions of the periodical. One of the most interesting free listings was from thirty-five-year-old Jubal Sky, who was trying to form a rural feminist OWL community near Santa Fe, New Mexico.[22] Over a six-year period, there would be listings for older women to return to the land in Oregon, Arizona, and Canada.

Unfortunately, paid advertisements were few and far between in *Prime Time,* with occasional paid classifieds offering handmade items like quilts or shawls for sale or a feminist taxi service. Classified ads were charged a mere ten cents a word for many years. A *Prime Time* mail order department was established in late 1973 to support subscribers who wanted to sell or distribute products made by women or of particular interest for women. There was no charge to run the ad; *Prime Time* just asked for a small commission on orders placed through its mail order department. The service lasted only a year. There were no full-page, one-third-page, or one-fourth-page ads during the publication's existence. Only a single one-half-page ad ever ran, in June 1976: a feminist book-publishing house promoted five novels by and about older women. The lack of advertising explains why *Prime Time* had difficulty sustaining itself over six years. This was a problem many feminist publications had during the 1970s, since they were justifiably picky about the kinds of product advertising they would accept. Of course, it didn't help matters that Madison Avenue really wasn't interested in the feminist consumer.

Exacerbating the nonexistent advertising revenue base was *Prime Time*'s enormous success with readers. The first issue consisted of a mere one hundred copies distributed in Manhattan and financed with Collins' unemployment insurance check. Only fifty-six women in the New York area made up the subscription list of the second issue. Just six issues later, *Prime Time* found itself reaching women in forty-four states, Canada, Italy, and Japan.[23] By September 1973, *Prime Time* had a circulation of more than twelve hundred readers, growing at an average rate of one hundred subscriptions a month.[24] Subscription rates were low, too, at $5 for eleven issues ($3.50 if unemployed or living on Social Security benefits).

Prime Time had no outside capital backing it and therefore no start-up funds. Writers were paid in blocks of subscriptions, which they could then sell.[25] Given the lack of money, it's not surprising to find that the early issues were typed on plain white bond using an elite typewriter, then printed back to back, stapled twice along the left-hand side of the front page, folded in the center and stapled, then mailed first class (an Eisenhower stamp cost eight cents in 1971). Occasionally, issues had a colored first and second page of pale blue, yellow, or green. Headlines were typed in all capital letters; asterisks were used to highlight interesting items; articles began on the first page immediately below the name-plate; and hand-drawn rules separated some of the copy. Wide margins on the sides made the periodical appear uncluttered and easy to read. Though there were no photographs, the use of line art and whimsical cartoons resulted in a low-key and pleasant effect.

Prime Time initiated a magazine format with the January 1974 issue: a sep-arate cover with story lines; a masthead listing editors, advisory board, and contributing writers; more attention paid to two-page spread design principles; photos on the cover and inside; saddle stitched binding; and the use of bulk mail. But *Prime Time* never adopted the slick, glossy format of its sisters at the larger consumer women's magazines like *McCall's, Ladies' Home Journal,* or *Vogue.* What *Prime Time* readers got in every issue was a no-nonsense layout and a formidable aggressiveness in approach to traditionally undiscussed topics.

The lack of malarkey is probably why Collins felt comfortable writing about *Prime Time*'s financial problems and growing pains. Initially, Collins hoped that readers alone would be able to support the magazine through regular contribu-tions in addition to a small subscription rate—as benefited an independent fem-inist journal. She simply didn't foresee the rate of growth the magazine would experience, nor did she anticipate the expenses involved in overhead, collating, and mailing as a staff of one.[26] After a year, Collins realized that she was investing much more than she was receiving, since she did not include a salary for herself in *Prime Time*'s budget.

In an effort to reach a larger audience and increase the periodical's revenue base, Collins tried a number of routes. In February 1973, she asked readers to consider becoming promoters or distributors of *Prime Time* on a commission plus expenses basis. This would involve getting *Prime Time* "sold in local stores, placed in libraries and schools, distributed and sold at all kinds of wom-en's meetings; selling group subscriptions; perhaps placing ads in local papers and magazines."[27] There must not have been many takers, since *Prime Time* wasn't available in bookstores until 1976.[28]

By September 1973, subscription revenue was insufficient to cover all bills for the first time. In publishing the magazine's negative financial statement, Collins explained that incorporation would be necessary before *Prime Time* could apply for a loan or grant. Funds were needed for a lawyer and a pro-spectus, so Collins exhorted readers to contribute money ("no amount is too small"), recruit new subscribers among friends or acquaintances, raise funds at a party or event, and help find a lawyer who would handle *Prime Time*'s busi-ness for free or a reasonable fee.[29] A progress report the next month noted that twenty-seven readers contributed $430.13, another twenty-two had agreed to serve on a newly established advisory board, and a "male feminist" had donated his services for the incorporation paperwork.[30]

But *Prime Time* was not out of the woods yet. Although incorporated as a nonprofit corporation in the state of New York by the January 1974 issue, *Prime Time* still lacked money and staff. Wrote Collins, "We have learned the hard way that a publication cannot live by subscriptions and contributions alone. The editor must spend more time looking for seed money and soliciting advertising. Until we have achieved some measure of success in these endeavors, it will be necessary to make a definite decision: to clearly state that *Prime Time* will appear irregularly."[31] But she was quick to add that readers would receive the number of issues paid for—no matter how long a period it took to receive them.

Rather than bombarding readers with coy reminders that their subscriptions were running out, *Prime Time* began publishing monthly "banns" naming those who needed to renew before another issue would be mailed. Collins bluntly called this decision "liberating ourselves from shitwork usually relegated to underpaid women."[32]

In May 1974, Collins and *Prime Time* even moved to the country to live in a house in Piermont, New York, owned by the Underwater Women of the Twentieth Century Renaissance Collective.[33] The group contributed typesetting as well as space in support of the continued publication of *Prime Time*. But within six months, Collins and her magazine were back in New York City, with no explanation for the return. Because *Prime Time* was Collins' "baby" and always based in her apartment, its editorial and distribution offices moved when she did. There would be six moves between 1971 and 1977, mostly within New York City.

No magazine came out in July, August, or October 1974 despite a new circulation high of more than two thousand readers. The November and December 1974 issues were combined. Dismayed by the publication's irregularity, Collins even considered making *Prime Time* a business corporation with shareholders rather than continue with its nonprofit, tax-exempt status.[34] She thought ownership would be more satisfying to readers, and more than seventy readers from twenty states wrote that they would like to be shareholders in *Prime Time*. But Collins soon learned that the cost to change status was prohibitive. Up to twenty thousand dollars would be necessary just to register with the Securities and Exchange Commission; even a limited partnership would involve a six-figure amount.[35]

There were no issues published in January, February, March, June, or July 1975. Then in August 1975, Collins wrote to readers: "Your generosity has again made it possible to continue publishing. We are writing a personal letter of thanks and appreciation to the sixty-six women who sent in money—*Prime Time*'s life blood."[36] Contributions ranged from one dollar to one thousand dollars and made it possible for Collins to attend the first International Year of the Woman Conference launched by the United Nations in Mexico City in June 1975. While there, she distributed one thousand copies of *Prime Time*.

Collins acknowledged the problems facing feminist publications in general in September 1975: "Feminist publications are folding right and left. *Prime Time* may totter, space out, but not fold. One reason for this is a strange, stubborn resurgence of optimism on the part of the editor."[37] Quite simply, Collins would continue to publish *Prime Time* even if it was never able to pay an equitable salary to its editor or to any publication staff. In addition to Collins as editor/ publisher, *Prime Time* listed a staff artist, speakers bureau coordinator, and a dozen contributing editors.

Collins continued to publish *Prime Time* sporadically, finally stating in the June 1976 issue that the magazine would begin bimonthly publication. Still concerned with making sure readers got value for their money, Collins had increased *Prime Time* in size from sixteen pages to twenty-four pages beginning in March 1976. Not only would that allow for longer, more in-depth articles, but it was in lieu of raising rates. Collins explained that "henceforth new subscribers will receive six (fatter) issues instead of eleven for $7. However, all subscribers paid up by July 1 will receive their eleven issues as originally contracted."[38] Then Collins once again asked for readers' help, saying, "We only have enough money in the bank to publish one more issue. Please contribute as much as you can. No amount is too large or too small, and *all contributions are tax deductible.*"[39]

There would be just three more issues of *Prime Time,* and discerning readers probably noticed that the fourteen-member advisory board appeared to have disbanded with the August/September 1976 issue. Additionally, no contributing writers were listed, and the masthead named only "people who helped on this issue." Collins remained the only full-time (still nonpaid) staff member, helped by seven volunteer part-timers and a cat called Graypower. It obviously was the beginning of the end.

In August/September 1976, Collins made a depression analogy by asking, "Sister, can you spare a dollar? . . . If every *Prime Time* reader contributed one dollar six times a year, we'd never have to ask you for anything more."[40] With this issue, the subtitle changed to "by and for older women." No October/ November issue appeared, yet neither the December 1976/January 1977 nor the subsequent April/May 1977 issue mentioned financial concerns. Instead, amid the usual mix of news items, letters, and articles, Collins reminded readers:

It is my opinion that we women—in our 40s, 50s, and 60s—are pioneers. For we are exploring new territory. We are the first generations of women with such long life expectancy—up from 47 years at the turn of the century to 74 today. We are the first women to face several decades of living after our traditional roles of wives and mothers have been completed, decades in which we *should* have the opportunity to forge a new and fulfilling life for ourselves.[41]

June/July 1977 was the last issue of *Prime Time,* which died during its sixth year of operation. The masthead now listed only Collins and two helpers. There was no farewell message inside. Only in retrospect is it clear that Collins' editorial letter was the final one:

We are proud to have survived 1976 and the first half of 1977. These are difficult times for many of us, including *Prime Time*. Scarcely a day passes that we don't receive word that a reader has lost her job. And if she can afford to renew her subscription at all, it is at the half rate for those who are unemployed or subsisting on Social Security. This means that even though our rate of new subscriptions and renewals has remained constant, our income has fallen while prices rise. We had to get a loan from the New York Feminist Credit Union to get through last year, and one printer's bill was paid out of the editor's Social Security income.[42]

She thankfully observed that since 1972, readers had contributed one-third to one-half of the magazine's expenses, above and beyond subscriptions and renewals. One issue of *Prime Time* costs fifteen hundred dollars to produce, or about sixty-one cents a copy, she said, while income per issue ranged between seven hundred dollars and one thousand dollars.[43]

Eventually, Collins chose not to count on the more than three thousand readers for support in her publication struggle. The financial problems seemed insurmountable, and she needed to save all her strength for her battle against cancer. When readers next heard from Collins, it was in a different publication. Writing in the spring 1978 issue of *New Directions for Women,** Collins explained that *Prime Time* had shut down. She added that she had agreed to write a "Prime Time" column for older women in forthcoming issues of *New Directions for Women.*[44] Then she commented:

> Despite my sadness in terminating *Prime Time,* I feel a healthy optimism about the future of older women. Judging from the mail I receive, older women are growing progressively stronger. They are attempting to change their lifestyles in positive ways, and learning to defy the ageist attitudes of the world around them. Although I may be rationalizing to some degree, it would seem that the inevitable time has come for us to desegregate. The experience of segregating ourselves as we did in *Prime Time* was historically necessary in our process of self-discovery. While remaining fully aware of our special problems and concerns, are we not strong enough now to hold our own among women of all ages?[45]

Collins wrote just three more "Prime Time" columns in *New Directions for Women.* With the summer 1979 issue, authorship of the "Prime Time" column was rotated among a variety of writers.

Collins' magazine tried to make sense of the aging process, of the dilemmas and difficulties of growing old as a woman in a youth-oriented American society. In her roles as primary writer, editor, and publisher, Collins didn't attempt to dictate a packaged image of the older woman, nor did she wistfully and futilely long for different circumstances. Instead, she firmly, sensibly, and creatively confronted the public's treatment of older women. She told her readers they could do something about their lives if they were willing to be assertive and to learn from one another.

Essentially, *Prime Time* presented grim and discouraging details about the lives of older women. To Collins' credit, the magazine developed a good-natured, provocative tone, rather than a badgering and accusatory one. For example, even though she discussed the magazine's financial woes, Collins never whined about the lack of advertiser support or seed money from venture capitalists.

Ironically, a later *Prime Time* launched in January 1980 for older men *and* women would last only two years despite a 325,000 circulation and a nest egg of four million dollars.[46] Madison Avenue still wasn't ready to support a magazine for the mature reader—of whatever sex.

Today's Americans are just now waking up to the needs of an aging population. Current large-circulation magazines for older men and women, such as *Modern Maturity, Mature Outlook,* and *New Choices,* simply don't generate the passionate reader response found in Collins' *Prime Time.* Even the beautifully designed and written *Lear's* did not resonate with older women quite the way *Prime Time* did.

Following Collins' death in May 1985, Betty Dewing, who had been one of *Prime Time*'s contributing writers through most of its existence, provided an epitaph for that determined editor and publisher. Dewing's closing words in *New Directions for Women* sum up the impact of *Prime Time,* then and now:

Marjory Collins left a rich legacy in the issues of *Prime Time.* It was the prime publication for older women and its contents need to be read and reread. Her important work must be remembered by all thoughtful older women and by their younger sisters as well.[47]

Notes

1. Marjory Collins, "Ageism, Anger, and 'Oh, to Be a Lovedu?' " October 1973, p. 7.

2. Ann Keiper Needham, "Prime Time: A Newsletter by and for Older Women," *Home Reporter and Sunset News,* August 4, 1972, p. 3.

3. Ibid.

4. Collins, "Ageism, Anger."

5. Marjory Collins, "On Becoming Visible and Vocal," September 1971, p. 5.

6. Ibid., p. 1.

7. Gail Pool, "Magazines," *Wilson Library Bulletin,* November 1983, p. 220.

8. Needham, "Prime Time."

9. Marjory Collins, "Older Women's Liberation Takes New Steps toward Becoming a National Movement," Spring 1972, p. 1.

10. Betty Dewing, "Prime Time: Prime Mover Dies," *New Directions for Women,* March/April 1986, p. 8.

11. Recognizing its importance and impact for older women, Collins placed every

issue of *Prime Time* on file at the Women's History Research Center in Berkeley, California. In June 1974, *Prime Time* was made available to the National Organization for Women Task Force on Older Women as an official publication.

12. "Menopause Speak-Out," April 1974, pp. 7–10.

13. Lynn Laredo, "Garbage Pail Syndrome," May 1974, p. 5.

14. "Letters," February 1973, p. 4.

15. "What Does Ageism Mean to You?" November 1975, p. 7.

16. Dorothy Tennov, "Dorothy Tennov Makes a Strong Plea to Exorcise This Latest Ism," August 1972, p. 1.

17. Marjory Collins, "What Does Ageism Mean to You?" March 1976, p. 2.

18. "Experience with Ageism," August/September 1976, pp. 10–14.

19. "Letters," July/August 1973, p. 8.

20. "Castigation," October 1973, pp. 10–11.

21. Marjory Collins, "Explanation," October 1973, pp. 11, 13.

22. "Pioneers Wanted in New Mexico," November/December 1973, pp. 6, 10.

23. Marjory Collins, "Concerning the Future of Prime Time," October 1972, p. 12.

24. Marjory Collins, "Prime Time Has Reached a Crucial Turning Point," September 1973, p. 9.

25. Marjory Collins, "A Message from the Editor," July 1972, p. 8.

26. Collins, October 1972, p. 12.

27. Marjory Collins, "Would You Like to Be an Associate of Prime Time?" February 1973, p. 7.

28. "You Can Buy Prime Time in the Following Bookstores," August/September 1976, p. 22.

29. Collins, September 1973, p. 9.

30. Marjory Collins, "Prime Time Progress Report," October 1973, p. 14.

31. Marjory Collins, "The Suffering of Success," April 1974, p. 2.

32. "Breaking the $$$ Barrier," May 1974, p. 2.

33. Ibid.

34. Marjory Collins, "You Can Help Prime Time Take That Great Leap Forward," November/December 1974, p. 7.

35. Marjory Collins, "An International Collective," April 1975, p. 13.

36. Marjory Collins, "Readers, You've Done It Again!" August 1975, p. 2.

37. Marjory Collins, "Confessions of an Optimist," September 1975, p. 2.

38. Marjory Collins, "Prime Time Marches on Thanks to You," June 1976, p. 23.

39. Ibid.

40. Marjory Collins, "Sister, Can You Spare a Dollar?" August/September 1976, p. 23.

41. Marjory Collins, "Pioneering the Future," December 1976/January 1977, p. 4.

42. Marjory Collins, "Into Our Sixth Year," June/July 1977, p. 2.

43. Ibid., pp. 2, 24.

44. Marjory Collins, "Introducing Prime Time," *New Directions for Women,* Spring 1978, p. 11.

45. Ibid.

46. Barbara V. Hertz, "Dreaming the Big Dream: Prime Time," *Folio: The Magazine for Magazine Management,* February 1982, pp. 65–66, 109. The 1980–1982 *Prime Time*

made no acknowledgment of the earlier Collins publication with the same name. This later *Prime Time* identified itself as "the first magazine devoted to the opportunities, pleasures and problems of men and women in their mid-life years," defined as ages forty-five to sixty-four. Though its fifty-eight-year-old editor, Barbara Hertz, had considerable magazine experience (eleven years as managing editor of *Parents*) and fund-raising savvy (nine as director of development for Barnard College), she came up against the same financial problems Marjory Collins had faced.

    47. Dewing, "Prime Time."

Information Sources

BIBLIOGRAPHY:

Cooper, Nancy. "Feminist Periodicals." *Mass Comm Review* 3.3, Summer 1976, pp. 15–23.

Marzolf, Marion. *Up from the Footnote: A History of Women Journalists.* New York: Hastings House, 1977.

Mather, Anne. "A History of Feminist Periodicals, Part I." *Journalism History* 1.2, Summer 1974, pp. 82–85.

———. "A History of Feminist Periodicals, Part II." *Journalism History* 1.4, Winter 1974–1975, pp. 108–111.

———. "A History of Feminist Periodicals, Part III." *Journalism History* 2.1, Spring 1975, pp. 19–31.

INDEX SOURCES: None.

LOCATION SOURCES: The Woman's Collection, Texas Woman's University, Blagg-Huey Library, Denton, Texas. (The Herstory microfilm collection includes *Prime Time* issues from September 1971 through June 1974. The additional *Prime Time* issues, through June/July 1977, can be found in their original form in the Woman's Collection vault. To the best of this author's knowledge, this is the only library holding all copies of *Prime Time*. The author wishes to thank the Texas Woman's University library for its generous access to the original issues of *Prime Time* and for its archival support of this project.)

Publication History

PERIODICAL TITLE AND TITLE CHANGES: *Prime Time: For the Liberation of Women in the Prime of Life* (September 1971–June 1976); *Prime Time: By and for Older Women* (August/September 1976–June/July 1977).

VOLUME AND ISSUE DATA: Vols. 1–5 (September 1971–June/July 1977). Monthly (issues are numbered consecutively by volume, even though the magazine published irregularly after June 1974).

PUBLISHER AND PLACE OF PUBLICATION: Marjory Collins (1971–1977). Brooklyn, N.Y. (September 1971–October 1972); New York (November 1972–April 1974); Piermont, N.Y. (May 1974–June 1974); New York (September 1974–June/July 1977).

EDITOR: Marjory Collins (1971–1977).

CIRCULATION: 3,000.

Sammye Johnson

THE PROGRESSIVE WOMAN

The rise and fall of the *The Progressive Woman* were linked to the U.S. Socialist Party and its policies with regard to women. Although this magazine was never an "official" Socialist Party periodical, its success hinged on continuing good relations with the group. When those relations soured, the monthly died.

The Socialist Woman, the original name of *The Progressive Woman,* was born in Chicago in June 1907. These were tumultuous times for the party. The female members, who numbered only about two thousand at the time of the magazine's launch,[1] increasingly resented the antiwoman attitude within the U.S. party organization. This resentment, along with a need for women to educate themselves, led to a separatist push. Women organized their own socialist organizations.[2] Thus, at the time of the launch of *The Socialist Woman,* there was considerable tension between the socialist sexes.[3]

The Socialist Woman grew out of an impulse to educate women about socialism. As the editor explained in the first issue,

> It is essential, then, that the truths, the beauty, the fairness, and the scientific possibilities of the Socialist movement be made into a propaganda, with a special appeal to the women of our land, which will brush away the cobwebs of ignorance, and break down the bars of prejudice that have been so skillfully wrought and engrained in the minds of womankind by teachers of the capitalist regime.[4]

From the perspective of *The Socialist Woman,* women were absolutely essential to the success of any socialist movement, even if the men within the party failed to recognize that fact. There could be no socialism without "the aid and consent of women," the editor argued. Thus, a publication designed to appeal to, and educate, women was essential to the future of socialism in America. "The Socialist Woman exists for the sole purpose of bringing women into touch with the Socialist idea. We intend to make this paper a forum for the discussion of problems that lie closest to women's lives, from the Socialist standpoint."[5]

Socialist women, some of them from this separatist movement, were behind the push for this periodical. However, only one woman made this publication a reality, Josephine Conger-Kaneko. Conger-Kaneko had already made a name for herself as a socialist journalist before she launched her monthly magazine. Born in Centralia, Missouri, Josephine Conger went to college at Columbia, Missouri, and learned the printing trade and publishing business from her brother, who ran a country newspaper. She then spent two years at Rushkin College, Trenton, Missouri, where she was apparently "radicalized." She left the campus a socialist journalist. Given the attitudes of socialists and the status of women in journalism in general in the day,[6] Conger was relegated to reporting "women's" news, even on socialist newspapers. She worked in the "women's" department of Walter Vrooman's *The Multitude.* The seeds of *The Socialist Woman* can be seen in her work on the enormously popular *Appeal to Reason.* Conger wrote a "women's" column for that national newspaper. Initially called "Hints to the *Appeal*'s Wise Woman," the column showed Conger's understanding of her audience. Conger reported on the contemporary suffrage movement as well as socialism. By linking the two issues, Conger seemed to strike a responsive chord among her readers. When she designed a coupon with the sentence, "I am interested in Socialism and the Emancipation of Women," and invited readers to make personal comments, she received a thousand letters from across the middle and far West, which she edited and printed in her column.[7]

By 1907, when she launched *The Socialist Woman,* Conger had married (the prominent Japanese socialist Kiichi Kaneko) and moved to Chicago, where the national headquarters of the Socialist Party was located. However, the Socialist Party provided no financial assistance for the launch. A small group of socialist women was behind the project. This group of twenty-six represented the subscription base and subscription solicitors; many also wrote for the new publication. These included some of the biggest female names in American socialism: Lena Morrow Lewis, May Woods-Simons, Gertrude Bresleau Hunt, Anna Maley, Luella Twining, Theresa Malkiel, and others.[8] Conger-Kaneko was editor, but her name always appeared below her husband's in the staff box. He was given the title of managing editor.[9] Both wrote for the publication. Kiichi Kaneko wrote essays, often covering women's issues from an international perspective.[10] Josephine Conger-Kaneko wrote essays, editorials, and poetry for the publication. But this new periodical was not just the voice of the Kanekos. It was for, and of, many socialist women. In a return to some of the successful methods from her days at the *Appeal.* Conger-Kaneko printed many of the letters from socialist women across the country. Some were well-known names, such as Meta L. Stern and Elizabeth Gurley Flynn of New York City and E. H. Thomas of Milwaukee; others were not famous, such as Jennie Potter of Conneaut, Ohio, and Louise Kumme of Philadelphia; many were from the separatist socialist women's organizations that were popular at the time: Anna B. Touroff of the Organization of Socialist Women in New York and Grace Merritt of the Woman's Socialist Club of Oakland, California.[11]

These women and others all looked to *The Socialist Woman* for news, information, advice, encouragement, and a sense of belonging, a sense that had been sorely missing in the male-dominated Socialist Party at the time. Conger-Kaneko attempted to do all this in an interesting editorial mix of poetry and editorials, essays and reporting, how-tos and letters to the editor—in an appealing graphics package. Almost everything in the magazine gave the female reader a sense of worth, from front covers that almost always pictured prominent socialist women, to editorials that argued that socialism would not bring the end to marriage,[12] from how-tos on organizing socialist Sunday schools,[13] to news about socialist women's separatist groups and information on how to contact them.[14] In its earliest days, *The Socialist Woman* seemed especially aligned with the women's separatist movement.

The new magazine never skirted controversy; one of the most controversial issues, at least with regard to the Socialist Party, was woman suffrage. Conger-Kaneko believed in suffrage, as did many female socialists. Many were outraged when the International Socialist Congress passed a resolution saying that socialist women should not work for suffrage in an alliance with middle-class women.[15] Josephine Cole, a longtime socialist, wrote in Conger-Kaneko's magazine that "the Congress cannot dictate to the Socialist women the particular time when they shall break off their struggle for political power in alliance with the bourgeois women or any other class who will help them to get the ballot."[16] Conger-Kaneko shared that opinion. *The Socialist Woman* often carried stories in favor of the franchise by suffragists, socialist or not.[17] This reaching out beyond the party was bringing encouraging circulation news to the magazine. In November 1907, the publisher reported that the magazine was distributed everywhere in the country—except the South. Nonetheless, the actual circulation figures must have been disappointing. Although Conger-Kaneko hoped for a circulation of ten thousand by the end of 1907, that figure apparently was never reached, because the editor wrote that the magazine needed money to survive.[18]

The year 1908 was a pivotal one for *The Socialist Woman*—politically and financially. Indeed, the year represented a turning point for the Socialist Party with regard to women. Two factions jockeyed for dominance: women who wanted to continue with their separatist organizations and those who favored assimilation into the male-dominated party. Conger-Kaneko preferred separation. As she wrote in *The Socialist Woman,* the party had too long catered solely to men, meeting in places where few women dared venture and crafting appeals solely to men's concerns and problems. The concerns of women had to be addressed, "or will we treat it to a 'conspiracy of silence' and leave it to solve itself as an included part of a man's movement?"[19]

In spite of this point of view, Conger-Kaneko retained good relations with the "assimilation" faction, a fortunate situation, because at the May 1908 socialist convention, delegates approved the creation of the "Woman's National Committee." The move showed the strength of the assimilationists.[20] This committee would have much to do with the continuing success and the eventual demise of the publication.

Financially, also, 1908 was a turning point. That year, Conger-Kaneko took *The Socialist Woman* and her ailing husband to Girard, Kansas. This represented a kind of "coming home" for Conger-Kaneko and an ideal solution for any production problems that *The Socialist Woman* might have been experiencing. Girard was the home of the *Appeal to Reason,* where Conger-Kaneko had edited a "women's" column. The *Appeal to Reason*'s publishing house assumed responsibility for the production of *The Socialist Woman.*[21]

Freed from production problems, Conger-Kaneko could now concentrate on editorial content, thus starting one of the most creative periods in the publication's life. In late 1908, fiction was added to the editorial mix; then came a series of "special issues": in November 1908, a teacher's edition; in December 1908, a temperance number; in February 1909, a child labor number. These special issues with their wide appeal as well as the fiction should have brought more readers to the magazine. Yet the circulation stalled. Had Conger-Kaneko wanted only socialist readers, there would have been no reason for change. However, by 1909, Conger-Kaneko wanted to reach beyond the "believers" to an audience not yet familiar with socialist ideas, doctrines, and principles. There was another—capitalistic—reason some change had to be made: Conger-Kaneko wanted to bring in more advertising, and this was difficult to do with a publication named *The Socialist Woman*. So with the March 1909 issue, the monthly's name was changed to *The Progressive Woman*.

Conger-Kaneko promised that the name change would bring no shift in the editorial message: "It [*The Progressive Woman*] will reach out for the oppressed among womankind—the underpaid wage earner, the political and sex slave— with the message and hope of Socialism."[22] The March 1909 issue illustrated the way that Conger-Kaneko was going to "reach out for the oppressed among womankind." That special suffrage edition blended socialist essays with stories that appealed to a wider audience. The issue included a story on Mary Wollstonecraft and reprinted a speech by Bryn Mawr's M. Carey Thomas, along with a new essay on the future of America's family by Conger-Kaneko, Clara Brown's "Evolution of a Socialist Woman," as well as news of the Chicago socialist women holding suffrage meetings.[23] The press run was substantially increased to accommodate the additional readers this special issue would attract. Certain special issues with such wide appeal as suffrage, temperance, and child labor had large press runs, far in excess of the actual circulation of *The Progressive Woman*.[24]

The name change did have the desired effect. Circulation did increase. By 1910, the circulation ranged from twelve thousand to fifteen thousand.[25] However, advertising remained disappointing. For the most part, *The Progressive Woman* had to rely on circulation to survive. However, the monthly was making its way, paying its bills with a "small surplus" for "a rainy day."[26]

The editorial quality remained high. The special issues, including one appealing to children,[27] innovative new departments, short stories, and poetry (some by Upton Sinclair and Charlotte Perkins Gilman[28]), as well as essays by the leading socialist women in the nation and a few socialist men (including Eugene V. Debs[29]) and nonsocialist suffrage leaders like Abigail Scott Duniway,[30] meant good reading for women of liberal-to-radical politics.

But problems were on the horizon. In late 1908, Kiichi Kaneko, who had returned to his native Japan to recover his health, died. In 1910, *The Progressive Woman* almost lost its mailing privileges for its "candid" "White Slave" issue.[31] In 1911, the *Appeal to Reason* management regrouped; the newspaper's printers would no longer publish any periodicals not owned by the *Appeal*. Conger-Kaneko and *The Progressive Woman* were left to their own devices.

Conger-Kaneko returned to Chicago, the national office of the Socialist Party and the headquarters of the Woman's National Committee. That proved to be a fatal mistake. The printing rates were high, astronomically high. ("Our experience with printers is that they are not on the job for the mere love of it," she observed.) No one was around to take care of the details. Expenses were so much higher. The solution turned out to be advertising; yet few advertisers were interested. So *The Progressive Woman* came to rely on the notorious patent medicine advertising to survive. Conger-Kaneko explained, "[W]e find on the whole, deplorable as we have been taught to consider it, the 'patent medicine ad' pays the best on the whole. So the medicine ad is being used *purely as a business proposition.*"[32]

Conger-Kaneko came to see that no matter how good *The Progressive Woman* was, no matter what an important role it played in educating women, no matter how valuable it was as an organizational voice, she could no longer handle all the aspects of publishing this monthly. At the national convention of the Socialist Party of 1912, Conger-Kaneko tried to convince the party to take over the paper as the "official propaganda and educational medium of the Woman's National Committee [WNC]." The WNC was willing, but the Executive Committee rejected the plan as "incompatible with party principles." Instead, the paper would remain hers, but the Woman's National Committee would enter into a "loose cooperation" with *The Progressive Woman.* The WNC would solicit circulation, help raise funds through a stock company, and contribute small amounts of money to the publication.[33] Conger-Kaneko took this to be a goodwill gesture toward eventually taking over the publication. She moved *The Progressive Woman* into the national party office as part of the Woman's Department. The name Winnie Branstetter appeared in *The Progressive Woman*'s staff box as the individual responsible for the WNC department. That was ironic, for Branstetter would be the woman who was most largely responsible for the demise of *The Progressive Woman.* The WNC support of *The Progressive Woman* had been the result of Caroline Lowe and her supporters. When Lowe resigned, Branstetter was appointed to replace her. Although Branstetter attempted to undercut WNC support of *The Progressive Woman,* she was unable to do so. Soon, Branstetter turned to less formal—but still damaging—methods. She argued that the magazine was on the verge of bankruptcy. After those charges, sales in the stock company plummeted.

In October 1913, Conger-Kaneko announced plans to reposition the magazine and rename it *The Coming Nation,* after an enormously popular, although defunct, magazine. The new publication would no longer be aimed at a distinctly female audience. "We believe the time has come when the separate magazine of progressive appeal is growing superfluous." The new publication would appeal to both women and men.

> The coming nation should be a national of human beings equal in opportunities and sharing all the blessings of government equally. There should

be no discrimination because of sex, and there should be no upper and lower classes. There should be only the HUMAN RACE, strong, splendid, intellectual to the highest degree of an advanced civilization."[34]

However, *The Coming Nation* was very much a continuation of *The Progressive Woman*. Features from the old publication continued. (The serialization of "A Little Sister of the Poor" even continued uninterrupted from *The Progressive Woman* to *The Coming Nation*.) Many of the women who had made *The Progressive Woman* so successful continued to write for the new publication. Although Conger-Kaneko now held the title of publisher, and Barnet Braverman took over as editor, she was very much a part of the new publication, writing many of the essays and editorials. But even this move opened Conger-Kaneko to criticism. Branstetter, not just content with hurting *The Progressive Woman*, seemed out to destroy or, at least, irreparably harm the new publication as well. She claimed that Braverman, the new editor, was a "red" sympathizer and had ties to the International Workers of the World, serious charges within the Socialist Party at the time.[35] She then dropped the new publication from the WNC literature list. Historian Mari Jo Buhle called the action the "closest approximation to personal expulsion from the party that a privately owned Socialist magazine could receive."[36] After issuing a bitter denunciation of party actions, Conger-Kaneko ended *The Coming Nation* with the July 1914 issue.

It was a bitter ending for *The Socialist Woman/The Progressive Woman/The Coming Nation,* for Conger-Kaneko and, especially, for the women of the Socialist Party. They no longer had a "voice of protest"[37] or even a place to turn for news of their activities.

However, socialist May Wood-Simons best explained the publication's importance when she urged women to subscribe to it. The monthly was the "bond to hold women together when they have once come into the organization, to give them a glimpse into what women are doing in other parts of the country, to suggest new lines of activity."[38]

Notes

1. Ira Kipnis, *The American Socialist Movement 1897–1912* (New York: Columbia University Press, 1952), p. 262.

2. Ibid, pp. 262–263; Mari Jo Buhle, *Women and American Socialism, 1870–1920,* (Urbana: University of Illinois Press, 1981), pp. 119–121.

3. The tension never seemed to go away. In 1908, 1909, and 1912, the *International Socialist Review,* a socialist left journal, carried articles by John Spargo, Lida Parce, and Theresa Malkiel, pointing out the problems within the party. Spargo, Parce, and Malkiel also wrote for the *Progressive Woman* (Kipnis, *The American Socialist Movement,* pp. 262–263).

4. "Why 'The Socialist Woman' Comes into Existence," June 1907, p. 4.

5. "To Our Readers," August 1907, p. 2.

6. In this period, women reporters were often relegated to the "women's pages" on newspapers.

7. Buhle, *Women and American Socialism,* pp. 114–115.

8. Josephine Conger-Kaneko, "A Party-Owned Press," p. 4; Buhle, *Women and American Socialism,* p. 148.

9. In most newspapers and magazines, the job of managing editor is under the editor. Thus, it is unclear why Kiichi Kaneko was listed first. It may have been due to his prominence within the Socialist Party.

10. *The Socialist Woman* often covered news of socialist women's activities in England, Europe, and Japan.

11. "Some Letters," July 1907, p. 7.

12. "Woman and Socialism," October 1907, p. 6.

13. This was one of the few activities perceived especially as socialist "women's work" ("Plan Socialist Sunday School," July 1907, p. 8).

14. "Progressive Societies," July 1907, p. 8.

15. This was a long-standing controversy in the U.S. Socialist Party. In general, separatist groups did cooperate with middle-class women for the vote, even though many in the Socialist Party (primarily men) did not want party women to work for the franchise until the party was in power (Josephine R. Cole, "The International And Woman Suffrage," November 1907, p. 3).

16. Ibid.

17. See, for example, Corinne Brown, "Votes for Women," February 1908, p. 4; B. Borrman Wells, "The Militant Woman Suffrage Movement in England," February 1908, p. 5. The February 1908 issue was the special suffrage number.

18. "Publisher's Column," November 1907, p. 12; "Publisher's Column," September 1907, p. 11; "What Will You Do with the Socialist Woman?" December 1907, p. 6.

19. Josephine Conger-Kaneko, "Are the Interests of Men and Women Identical?" May 1908, p. 3.

20. Buhle, *Women and American Socialism,* p. 150.

21. The name of the publishing company itself did not change (Josephine Conger-Kaneko, "A Party Owned Press," July 1914, p. 4).

22. "Our New Name," February 1909, p. 2.

23. March 1909.

24. Buhle, *Women and American Socialism,* p. 156.

25. "Three Years Old This Month," June 1910, p. 8.

26. Josephine Conger-Kaneko, "A Party-Owned Press," July 1914, p. 4.

27. December 1909.

28. Upton Sinclair, "The Red Flag," July 1909, p. 6; Charlotte Perkins Gilman, "Mother," November 1909, p. 6.

29. See, for example, Eugene V. Debs, "Enfranchisement of Womanhood," March 1909, p. 5 and "Why We Have Outgrown the U.S. Constitution," August 1911, p. 5.

30. See, for example, Abigail Scott Duniway, "The Women Suffrage Movement and Political Parties," July 1910, p. 7.

31. Details available in Buhle, *Women and American Socialism,* p. 255.

32. "Our Advertising," February 1912, p. 8.

33. "A Journalistic Tragedy," June/July 1913, p. 3. See, for example, the appeal for circulation by May Wood-Simons. Wood-Simons, a member of the WNC, said that the committee had pledged to do everything it could do further the paper and urged all to

subscribe (May Wood-Simons, "The Progressive Woman: Our Paper," February 1913, p. 16).

34. "Announcement," October 1913, p. 5.

35. Mari Jo Buhle, "Socialist Woman/Progressive Woman/Coming Nation," in Joseph R. Conlin, ed., *The American Radical Press, 1880–1920,* vol. 2 (Westport, Conn.: Greenwood Press, 1974), p. 447.

36. Ibid.

37. Ibid.

38. May Wood-Simons, "The Progressive Woman: Our Paper," February 1913, p. 16.

Information Sources

BIBLIOGRAPHY:

Buhle, Mari Jo. "Women and the Socialist Party, 1901–1914." *Radical America* 4.2, February 1970, pp. 36–47, 50–54.

———. "Socialist Woman/Progressive Woman/Coming Nation." In Joseph R. Conlin, ed., *The American Radical Press, 1880–1920,* vol. 2. Westport, Conn.: Greenwood Press, 1974, pp. 442–449.

———. *Women and American Socialism, 1870–1920.* Urbana: University of Illinois Press, 1981.

Kipnis, Ira. *The American Socialist Movement, 1897–1912.* New York: Columbia University Press, 1952.

Kraditor, Aileen S. *The Radical Persuasion 1890–1917: Aspects of the Intellectual History and the Historiography of Three American Radical Organizations.* Baton Route, La.: State University Press, 1981.

Leonard, John William, ed. *Woman's Who's Who of America 1914–1915.* New York: American Commonwealth, 1914.

Spargo, John, "Women and the Socialist Movement." *International Socialist Review* 8, February 1908, pp. 449–455.

INDEX SOURCES: None.

LOCATION SOURCES: Library of Congress; New York Public Library; and other libraries.

Publication History

PERIODICAL TITLE AND TITLE CHANGES: *The Socialist Woman* (1907–1909); *The Progressive Woman* (1909–1913); *The Coming Nation* (1913–1914).

VOLUME AND ISSUE DATA: Vols. 1–7 (June 1907–October 1913), new series Vol. 1 (November 1913–July 1914). Monthly (combined issues June/July 1913).

PUBLISHER AND PLACE OF PUBLICATION: The Socialist Woman Publishing Co. (1907–1909); The Progressive Woman Publishing Co. (1909–1913); Josephine Conger-Kaneko (1913–1914). Chicago (1907–1909); Girard, Kans. (1909–1911); Chicago (1911–1914).

EDITORS: Josephine Conger-Kaneko (1907–1913); Barnet Braverman (1913–1914).

CIRCULATION: Self-reported, April 1910: 12,000 to 15,000.

Kathleen L. Endres

Q

THE QUEEN BEE

The *Queen Bee* and its predecessor, *The Colorado Antelope,* spread the ideas and idiosyncrasies of their editor, Caroline Nichols Churchill, through Colorado and other western states between 1879 and 1895. Churchill claimed that with her papers she had "performed a wonderful work under most difficult circumstances," adding, "It is not at all likely that another woman on the continent could under the same conditions accomplish as much."[1]

Born in Canada of American parents, the future editor attended school briefly in the United States and then, like many other women involved in the woman's rights movement, taught school for a time. She married a man named Churchill, who died after eleven or twelve years of marriage, leaving her with a young daughter. By that time she had moved to Minnesota and found a role model in Jane Grey Swisshelm, the crusading feminist and former Washington correspondent who had edited the *Pittsburgh Saturday Visiter** and a paper in St. Cloud since 1857.

By 1869 Churchill had developed ideas of her own and felt free to carry out her plans for advancing the new ways of thinking she saw "ripening and materializing all over the civilized world."[2] She left her daughter in the care of a married sister and set out for California to begin what she always referred to as "a traveling business."

This consisted of touring, writing about her experiences, publishing what she had written, traveling to sell her books, and gathering material for new sketches in the process. In California for several years, she contributed sketches to San Francisco and eastern newspapers and wrote two books, *Little Sheaves Gathered While Gleaning after Reapers* in 1875 and *Over the Purple Hills* in 1877, but eventually decided that the climate did not suit her.

In 1876 Churchill moved east. She found a publisher for *Over the Purple*

Hills in Chicago, then traveled through Texas, Missouri, Kansas, and Indian Territory until 1879, when she visited Denver. She liked its climate and, at the age of forty-six, decided to settle there and start a paper, a project she had contemplated for several years. She assessed the social and business climates, as well as the weather, writing that she chose a newly settled region because "all reforms take root in new countries sooner than in older communities, and in inaccessible places there is not the same means at hand for getting rid of money. There is more money in the community and less competition."[3]

The first number of her monthly, *The Colorado Antelope,* appeared in October 1879. She explained its name in the following month's issue:

> In the first place we wanted a name never before given to any paper under the sun; we wanted something that had the least feminine suggestion; something graceful and beautiful, and above all something that was alive and has some "git up" to it.

Also, she concluded, "the *Antelope* is a little deer, and is so difficult to overtake."[4]

As for her purpose in founding the paper, she believed that "every State in the Union should have a live feminine paper published at the Capital" and that "as the acquisition of women to the educational department has raised the standard of education and general cultivation, so acquisition of women to the journalistic department will advance the standard of journalism. It is not good for man to be alone in journalism any more than in any other enterprise."[5] The motto appearing under the *Antelope*'s title read "A paper devoted to the interests of humanity, woman's political equality and individuality."

In a list of the advantages of the *Antelope* over all other papers, Churchill included:

> Its editor is the oldest and handsomest in the United States.
>
> It has the only lady editor who wears a seven by nine boot and dares tell her own age.
>
> It has the only lady editor who dares so far defy underlying principles of political subjection as to write and publish a joke perpetrated upon herself.
>
> It is the most original paper published in the United States. . . . it is the wittiest, spiciest, most radical little sheet published in the United States.[6]

Along with considerable editorial comment, the four-page *Antelope* contained travel sketches, news notes from near and far, essays, columns, fiction, correspondence, recipes, household hints, and advertising. In a column titled "Laconic Sermons," Churchill gave advice to readers on topics ranging from the necessity of women's involvement in community affairs to the importance of tempering hard work with recreation.

She credited her travel sketches with "doing more to advertise the state than is done by any local paper in the country; or for that matter any dozen local papers." They sometimes combined fiction with fact. "The Way the Future Historian Will Write up Leadville" continued for more than a year and featured characters named Romeo and Juliet. Romeo, having lost his way, wandered into the mining community and discovered such oddities as "men wearing night shifts and men wearing day shifts who worked for the most part in holes in the ground." In another episode Romeo, having observed the quantity of successful saloons in town, encouraged his father, the merchant of Venice, to set up shop there.[7]

Churchill used humor in supporting woman's rights and other causes, as well as in her travel sketches. In reply to someone who asked the politics of her paper, she wrote:

> We are a Democratic-Republican, a Greenback-Know-Nothing, Pro-China-Woman Suffragist. We are also Anti-Polygamist. . . . They say that people "talk about us," we should feel dreadful if they did not; let them talk, we have lived in the world long enough to realize that the pathway of life is literally lined with snarling *curs,* and we should remember that the same Creator made the cur as made the thorough-bred, and if they can stand being a cur and behave like one, we can stand being snarled at, because we are a thorough-bred.[8]

In a more serious vein, she described her view of woman's sphere: "to seek every good place and good thing in life and to shun the evil and the bad." A man's sphere was no more and no less, she added, "and all acknowledge these facts except the bigot and the individual, whether man or woman, not capable of comprehending the situation." Even her opinions about proper spheres for the sexes she laced with humor, as when she admitted that "there is no one who thinks more of a man than the '*Queen Bee*' does, but we want him to keep his proper sphere, and we propose to decide what that sphere is."

Although she considered her paper the voice of the Colorado suffrage movement, participated in state suffrage conventions, and wrote a woman's column for *The Denver Republican* in 1881, Churchill never became part of the suffrage establishment. Neither did she win popularity with the Woman's Christian Temperance Union, although she supported its aims. In explanation she wrote that "popularity was not what she was looking for." Her methods were her own, and "she made no effort to curry favor."[9]

By selling out each number of the paper before printing the next, Churchill managed to make a profit and increase the number of pages. She set up an office in her home and hired a printer, the first of many to whom she entrusted production of the paper during her absences. Some proved to be unreliable or dishonest or both, and a portion of her autobiography devoted to the vicissitudes of running the paper from a distance described some who caused her grief. Over the years she also employed several women, both as printers and as editorial assistants. At one point she reported that ladies did all the mechanical work, thus learning skills that would keep them from being "obliged to wash or keep boarders when they are called upon to support their families."[10] From 1892 to 1894 *The Queen Bee* listed Hattie Nichols, undoubtedly a relative, as publisher, with Churchill as editor and proprietor.

By mid-1882 the *Antelope* had eighteen pages, about four of them full of advertising for such products as shoes, books, pianos, groceries, and Sawyer's blueing and for such services as assaying, medical assistance of many varieties, architectural design, and train travel. However, Churchill decided that the paper's book format made it too expensive to produce and transformed it into a four-page weekly, *The Queen Bee,* a name she also used to refer to herself.

The new paper continued the numbering of the *Antelope* and carried the same sort of content. From news notes to serial fiction, it bore the stamp of the editor's personality. She continued the regular feature titled "What Our Editor Encounters" and tried columns like "Young Folks," "Fonetik," and "Woman Suffrage," the latter contributed by the president of the Nebraska Woman Suffrage Association. She also offered recipes and household hints and used "Locals" to boost businesses that advertised in the paper. A considerable number of illustrations brightened *The Queen Bee*'s appearance.

Churchill published many favorable comments on the new paper from both individual readers and editors of other papers. Sometimes they referred more to the editor than to the paper, like one from the Las Vegas, New Mexico, *Daily Optic:* "With all her crankisms and vagaries, Sister Churchill is a brainy woman, and the tongue of scandal has never assailed her, although she has been snubbed and insulted by men thousands of times all over the West."[11] The Colorado Press Association also snubbed her, refusing to admit her to membership in 1881.

In a plea for subscribers, Churchill claimed to have done "as much to amuse and stir up the Western men as any ten journalists in the country" and suggested they show their appreciation by buying the paper. She also characterized *The Queen Bee* in 1884 as the only real family paper published in the Rocky Mountain region and boasted that it had more than twice the circulation of any paper in Colorado or the five surrounding territories.[12] The 1885 Rowell's *American Newspaper Directory* listed its circulation in the three thousand to five thousand range, although Churchill usually reported lower figures, generally around two thousand and dropping to a low of less than one thousand just before its demise.

In spite of its generally healthy circulation and good advertising support, the paper never allowed its editor to live extravagantly. In 1893 she complained that, although she had given the world's fair about a thousand dollars worth of advertising, she lacked the funds to travel to it, then suggested that society operated on the assumption that "woman is expected to work for every body and every thing and get no compensation."[13] Approval of woman suffrage by Colorado voters later that year cheered her, however, and she kept the paper going until just before she turned sixty-two, although with less energy and regularity.

In the issue for September 4, 1895, she announced that *The Queen Bee* would not appear for some weeks, the office having been shut down for "repairs and different arrangements," because "the introduction of machinery in printing and the general cheapening of literature has made some changes imperatively necessary." That issue is the last that survives in complete form. Two torn pages of a later, undated issue survive, with a letter "To Our Readers" on page 1 referring to a lapse in publication of several months and indicating that the paper would in the future serve as an educator upon various subjects and not be a regular newspaper with dates and volume numbers. It concluded with an appropriate epitaph, "The paper is here to help straighten up a defective civilization."

Notes

1. Caroline Nichols Churchill, *Active Footsteps* (Colorado Springs: Mrs. C. N. Churchill, 1909), p. 81.
2. June 18, 1890, p. 1.
3. Churchill, *Active Footsteps,* pp. 146–147.
4. November 1879, p. 2.
5. October 1879, p. 2.
6. January 1880, p. 4.
7. August 31, 1887, p. 1; October 1879, p. 1; December 1879, p. 2.
8. February 1880, p. 4.
9. Churchill, *Active Footsteps,* pp. 213–214.
10. July 2, 1884, p. 1.
11. May 19, 1886, p. 1.
12. July 2, 1884, p. 1.
13. March 22, 1893, p. 1.

Information Sources

BIBLIOGRAPHY:
Bennion, Sherilyn Cox. *Equal to the Occasion: Women Editors of the Nineteenth-Century West.* Reno: University of Nevada Press, 1990.
Churchill, Caroline Nichols. *Little Sheaves Gathered While Gleaning after Reapers.* San Francisco: Woman's Publishing, 1875.
———. *Over the Purple Hills.* Chicago: Hazlitt and Reed, 1877.
———. *Active Footsteps.* Colorado Springs: Mrs. C. N. Churchill, 1909.
INDEX SOURCES: None.
LOCATION SOURCES: Colorado State Historical Society.

Publication History

PERIODICAL TITLE AND TITLE CHANGES: *The Colorado Antelope* (1879–June 15, 1882); *The Queen Bee* (July 5, 1882–September 4, 1895).
VOLUME AND ISSUE DATA: Vols. 1–17 (October 1879–September 4, 1897; first two years of *The Queen Bee* numbered Vols. 1 and 2, third year Vol. 5). Monthly (1879–June 1882); weekly (July 5, 1882–September 4, 1895).

PUBLISHER AND PLACE OF PUBLICATION: Caroline Nichols Churchill (1879–
    September 7, 1892; October 3, 1894–September 4, 1895); Hattie Nichols (Sep-
    tember 14, 1892–September 26, 1894). Denver.
EDITORS: Caroline Nichols Churchill (1879–1895).
CIRCULATION: *Rowell* directory, 1885: 1,000–5,000.

Sherilyn Cox Bennion

R

RED STAR

Red Star was a periodical for the communist feminist. More precisely, it was the newsletter of the Red Women's Detachment of the Marxist–Leninist Party, a group that followed the teaching of Chairman Mao Tse Tung and was committed to the violent overthrow of the U.S. government. *Red Star* reflected that revolutionary commitment. While many other feminists rejected the Marxist interpretation and organized separate women's liberation groups,[1] *Red Star* and the Red Women's Detachment remained true to the classic communist principles of working with men to overthrow U.S. capitalism first and expected that women's liberation would follow.

Feminists of the day would have called the *Red Star* and its founding organization, the Red Women's Detachment, "politicos" because both the newsletter and the group emphasized that capitalism and "Soviet social imperialists"[2] were the enemies. Feminists, in contrast, viewed male-dominated institutions as the problem.[3] *Red Star*'s position was not uncommon. As women's studies scholar Jo Freeman emphasized, many women who came from a New Left background opted to work within the radical fold for liberation, while those from civil rights and related pasts preferred independence.[4]

The *Red Star* premiered in March 1970 under the title *Hammer Sickle Rifle*. The original newsletter was published by the Workers and Defense Group, a group not specifically committed to women's liberation or to improving the female status within the revolution. Indeed, this group and its newsletter spoke little of women at all. According to the Workers and Defense Group, women were just another oppressed class, along with the Puerto Ricans, African Americans, and Native Americans. Together, all the oppressed classes must work for the violent overthrow of the U.S. government.[5]

The next month, this newsletter had changed dramatically. The name had been changed to *Red Star*; the name of the sponsoring organization had become the Red Women's Detachment; the editorial appeal had switched to communist women or women with communist sympathies; the editorial content remained essays, but the subject matter dealt almost entirely with women. The Red Women's Detachment and its newsletter illustrated the classic "politico" interpretation. The Red Women's Detachment was a "women's liberation group" of working-class and welfare women working together for revolution. Women's liberation could come only through revolution bringing socialism and communism. "It will never be done by begging the imperialist government to repeal the work laws concerning women or the abortion laws or begging for an increase in our checks," *Red Star* emphasized. Men and women had to work together. "We are not a separatist group hating men. We realize that workingclass men are not our enemies; instead, armed workingwomen and armed workingmen are uniting to fight for Communism."[6] In contrast, the Red Women's Detachment had little in common with middle-class women's groups. "The workingwomen's movement has nothing in common with 'oppression' of bourgeois-coquettes. We realize that the emancipation of women is achieved by violent proletarian revolution," the *Red Star* observed.[7]

Unlike many "politicos," *Red Star* and the Red Women's Detachment were not committed to any party committed to the Soviet brand of communism. "For many years, we have been fooled and tricked by the phony Welfare Rights groups completely controlled by the Communist Party revisionist clique." Instead, the Red Women's Detachment emphasized improvements designed to help women directly. Welfare and working-class women needed day care, to teach children politics, physical education, and self-defense to make them "revolutionary fighters." "Genocide" programs would be eliminated. Birth control and abortion would be the decision of the welfare women, not the "quack doctors," *Red Star* argued.[8]

The Red Women's Detachment was a New York City–based organization that practiced "democratic-centralism." Unlike many feminist groups that followed a nonhierarchical leadership and relished a type of structurelessness, the Red Women's Detachment was highly structured, run by a central committee, the members of which were never identified in the *Red Star*. The organization had three levels: the "Mao Tse Tung Study Groups," testing grounds for the prospective cadre; "Martial Arts Collectives," self-defense training clubs; and the clandestine "Women's Armed Defense Groups." The central committee of the Red Women's Detachment reported directly to the central committee of the Marxist–Leninist Party. *Red Star* was a product of the central committee of the Red Women's Detachment. Thus, *Red Star*'s editorial material had to be in keeping with the thinking and philosophy of the central committee of the Red Women's Detachment. The central committee was responsible not only for the editorial content but also for the distribution of the newsletter.[9] The newsletter was distributed through a "network of cadres and contacts at various levels." Exact circulation figures were never disclosed. However, certain policies of the central committee probably kept the circulation small. The central committee decided not to send the periodical to libraries, even those that requested subscriptions. "It [*Red Star*] is not produced for profit nor for the perusal of bourgeois-academicians who pay libraries for CIA [Central Intelligence Agency] data-banks."[10] The newsletter was sent, however, to groups within the women's liberation movement that were perceived as sympathetic to their goals. Thus, the newsletter was sent to Cell 16, publishers of *No More Fun and Games,** Bread and Roses, a socialist-feminist group in Cambridge; Radical Women in Seattle, and Joreen, publisher of *Voice of Women's Liberation** in Chicago.[11]

Red Star retained close ties with certain other women's groups as well. The New Orleans Female Workers Union reprinted a collection of articles from the *Red Star*. The White Panther Party kept the *Red Star* informed of its activities in Ann Arbor, Michigan.[12]

However, *Red Star* was highly critical of others in the women's movement. Much of the criticism was based on perceived class differences. As the periodical observed:

> The line which demarcates the revolutionary women's movement from the reformist trot[sky]-dominated 'women's liberation movement' is the class line which can only be carried through by the armed authority of proletarian women.[13]

The National Organization for Women (NOW) was "bourgeois-feminist."[14] Others were dismissed because of their naiveté. Perhaps in reaction to the Redstocking's emphasis on consciousness-raising and disavowal of Marxist predictions of equality after revolution, *Red Star* warned, "Naivete and unsophistication characterizes [*sic*] the psycho-therapeutic consciousness-raising sessions which dwell on intimate personal trivia are often conducted as open meetings in rooms with undoubtedly bugged telephones."[15] After meeting with the New York Feminists, a radical splinter group from NOW, the Red Women's Detachment dismissed the other group's philosophy and strategy. As the *Red Star* emphasized:

> The task now is to overthrow the bourgeoisie to bring about the dictatorship of the proletariat, not fight the male supremacy *by itself* as if it were not a component of bourgeois class rule.[16]

Comment on the contemporary women's liberation movement was only a part of *Red Star*'s editorial package. The newsletter carried a variety of essays, many of them reprinted from communist periodicals across the world. Many of those newspapers and news services were based in China. News reported the oppression of women across the world, including Albania and India.[17] News dealing with domestic issues tended to be interpretive and often reprinted from other periodicals. A reprint from the *People's Paper* on New York's attempt to control prostitution ended with a call, "DEATH TO PIMPERIALISM AND SEX-PLOITATION."[18]

The newsletter carried occasional profiles of prominent communist female leaders, including Mrs. Kang Ban Sok, "Mother of the Great Leader of Korea."[19] Few stories carried bylines, unless they were reprinted from other sources. Thus, it is difficult to determine who was writing for this publication.

The newsletter often carried photographs, although the reproduction quality was not always good. Printing tended to be uneven, as did the quality of the proofreading. Often words were misspelled. Articles were not always clearly written, and essays were sometimes illogical and pedantic.

Whether in domestic or international news, criticism of contemporary feminist groups, or essays on unrelated topics, the *Red Star* continued to hammer away at the same idea: only revolution (violent revolution) would lead to true liberation for women. Its revolutionary commitment was most clearly evidenced in the March 1971 issue, in which the *Red Star* provided diagrams of the male body with "targets of pain and severe pain" noted. The newsletter also provided instructions on how to injure each target.[20]

The Red Women's Detachment published only six issues of *Red Star* from 1970 to 1971. The newsletter was never issued on a discernible schedule. The October 1971 issue appeared to be the last. Nothing within that issue suggested that the newsletter might be suspended.

The *Red Star* could be dismissed as a typical communist polemic. However, that would overlook the role played during its brief lifetime. *Red Star* offered a voice to the radical feminist "politicos" who held the Marxist–Leninist principles (as interpreted by Mao Tse Tung) dear.

Notes

1. The New York Redstockings, for example, issued a manifesto rejecting the classic Marxist prediction that women would be liberated once capitalism was overthrown. In their manifesto, the group said that women are an oppressed class, and the agents of oppression were men (Roberta Salper, "The Development of the American Women's Liberation Movement, 1967–1971," in Roberta Salper, ed., *Female Liberation: History and Current Politics* [Old Westbury: State University of New York, 1972], p. 176).

2. "Long Live the Victory of Class War," March 1970, unnumbered page.

3. Jo Freeman provides one of the best discussions of the differences between politicos and feminists in *The Politics of Women's Liberation: A Case Study of an Emerging Social Movement and Its Relation to the Policy Process* (New York: David McKay, 1975).

4. Ibid., p. 107.

5. "Long Live the Victory of Class War."

6. "Open Letter to Welfare Women," April 1970, pp. 1–2.

7. "To NUC Women's Caucus," April 1970, p. 4.

8. "Open Letter to Welfare Women."

9. "Draft Constitution of the Red Women's Detachment," insert into April 1970 issue.

10. August 1970, p. 3.

11. April 1970, p. 3. Joreen was Jo Freeman.

12. "Communications Report from the Central Organization," August 1970, p. 4.

13. Ibid.

14. August 1970, p. 3.

15. Ibid, p. 2.

16. "To the Feminists," March 1971, p. 5.

17. "Indian Heroines in Peasant Armed Revolutionary Struggle," August 1970, pp. 4–5; "On Some Aspects of the Problem of the Albanian Women," December 1970, p. 2.

18. " 'Fun City' A Hellhole for Women," October 1971, p. 3.

19. "Mrs. Kang Ban Sok, Mother of the Great Leader of Korea," December 1970, p. 3.

20. March 1971, p. 5.

Information Sources

BIBLIOGRAPHY:

Freeman, Jo. *The Politics of Women's Liberation: A Case Study of an Emerging Social Movement and Its Relation to the Policy Program.* New York: David McKay, 1975.

Salper, Roberta. "The Development of the American Women's Liberation Movement, 1967–1971." In Roberta Salper, ed., *Female Liberation: History and Current Politics.* Old Westbury: State University of New York, 1972, pp. 169–184.

INDEX SOURCES: None.

LOCATION SOURCES: University of Connecticut library and other libraries. Also available in Herstory, Reel 20.

Publication History

PERIODICAL TITLE AND TITLE CHANGES: *Hammer Sickle Rifle* (March 1970); *Red Star* (April 1970–October 1971).

VOLUME AND ISSUE DATA: Vols. 1–2? (periodical carried no volume data) (March 1970–October 1971). Irregular.

PUBLISHER AND PLACE OF PUBLICATION: Workers and Defense Group (March 1970); Red Women's Detachment (April 1970–October 1971). New York City.

EDITORS: Unknown.

CIRCULATION: Unknown.

Kathleen L. Endres

THE REMONSTRANCE

Established in 1890, *The Remonstrance* served as a major voice for the anti-suffrage movement until the federal amendment allowing women to vote was enacted in 1920, and all hope of repealing the amendment was lost. In many ways the publication was a reflection of the character and ideologies of those in support of the antisuffrage movement: it was principally reactive; it closely followed the ideology of separate spheres for men and women, and it was presented as an expression of the majority belief rather than the views of a few individuals in prominent positions.

The publication was reactive in that the topics it published were almost exclusively in response to developments in the suffrage movement. The majority of its stories, for example, were devoted to reports on the outcome of suffrage campaigns and refutations of suffrage claims. The frequency of its publication was also influenced by the intensity and number of suffrage campaigns, and when in 1907 the suffrage movement began to collect political as well as popular impetus, the annual publication converted to a quarterly.[1] Even the number of copies printed, which varied from two thousand to ten thousand per issue, was determined by the number of states considering suffrage at any given time.[2]

The Remonstrance supported the concept of separate spheres (woman's sphere was in the home, while it was the man's place to go out into the world of commerce and politics) not only in its stories but also in its editorial organization. Although a woman's association published the paper, the members typically sought anonymity, preferring to defer to the counsel of a male editor and male advisers.[3] The association, in fact, did not even adopt its name—the Massachusetts Association Opposed to the Further Extension of Suffrage to Women (MAOFESW)—until 1895 and did not publish it in the paper until 1896.[4]

Finally, *The Remonstrance* eschewed any appearance that the views expressed in its pages represented those of a few well-spoken leaders. Instead, such views were attributed to the "average woman,"[5] the "voice of the majority,"[6] and "the great majority of women."[7] Thus, the publication, much like the association that published it, maintained a veil of anonymity, especially in its earlier years, and appeared to well up from a groundswell of public opinion rather than from the actions and organization of a few well-placed individuals opposed to change.

The Remonstrance first appeared in February 1890 as a four-page paper distributed to Massachusetts legislators who were considering a bill to extend the vote to women. The paper, which indicated only that it had been published in Boston, carried neither the name of a publisher nor the name of an editor and gave no attribution whatsoever to any of its dozen articles. These addressed a number of topics that would be often repeated in the next thirty years—the failures of woman suffrage in those places where it existed, the defeat of suffrage campaigns in a number of states and cities, contradictory statements by suffrage leaders, and antisuffrage statements by prominent men, usually professors, judges, or doctors.[8]

The Remonstrance, in fact, was published through the efforts of a handful of Boston women who, since 1882, had been delivering antisuffrage petitions— "remonstrances"—to the Massachusetts legislature. These women had first organized at the suggestion of state Senate president George G. Crocker, an antisuffragist, and continued to meet regularly in the homes of members of the group. Here they had teas and ladylike "parlor meetings" in which they discussed the suffrage question and prepared their petitions. At first they had no formal organization and relied greatly on the advice of male friends and relatives such as Crocker, many of whom belonged to the Man Suffrage Association.[9] In 1890, the group hired forty-year-old journalist Frank Foxcroft to edit a paper for them.[10]

Foxcroft acted as the editor of *The Remonstrance,* as well as the publicist, literary adviser, and speaker for the women's association, until Mrs. James M. Codman took over the position sometime after 1916.[11] An assistant editor at the *Boston Journal* until 1904 and an editor at *Living Age* and *Youth's Companion,* Foxcroft was an ardent antisuffragist but preferred to keep his connection with the antisuffragist women and *The Remonstrance* private. Thus, although he frequently spoke against suffrage at legislative hearings and public meetings at the request of the association, he did so as an unaffiliated antisuffragist. Although he received a regular salary for these as well as his editorial services, his official connection to the association was never publicly acknowledged, and in all the years he worked on *The Remonstrance* his title as editor was never printed in the paper.[12]

Although Foxcroft was the editor, much of the work on *The Remonstrance* was done by committee. The women antisuffragists suggested topics and articles to Foxcroft, reviewed material he suggested, and had the final say on what he would print. Thus, a portion of every meeting was devoted to discussion of what would go into the paper.[13] The system generally worked smoothly, albeit slowly, partly because the association's leaders were concerned almost obsessively with accuracy and went to extremes to correct mistakes that became public. In 1901, for example, when Foxcroft underreported the number of women who had voted in the 1895 Massachusetts school elections, *The Remonstrance* was brought to task by Elizabeth Stone Blackwell in the suffragist *Woman's Journal,** and the story was reprinted in the general press. The association immediately suffered emotional and organizational upheaval. Foxcroft not only offered a correction of the article and a reprint of the paper at his own expense but also wrote a letter of immediate resignation. After considerable discussion at several meetings, the association solved the problem by writing a letter of apology to Blackwell and reprinting and redistributing the erroneous edition of the publication. As for Foxcroft's resignation, this was turned down, and he instead received a full vote of confidence from the group.[14] The publication of *The Remonstrance* continued in this unwieldy fashion until 1908, when a permanent committee was appointed to serve as liaison with Foxcroft.[15]

At first a simple four-page paper laid out in three-column pages and identified only by its name and place and date of publication, *The Remonstrance* gradually took on a more substantial aspect as it became the established voice of the antisuffrage association and as the association became more organized. Part of this process was to identify who was responsible for the publication and its purpose. Thus, in its 1891 issue, the paper published a prospectus on its front page. This message, which remained essentially the same over the next three decades, aptly summarized the basic arguments of antisuffrage:

The Remonstrance is addressed to the Legislatures of the several States by Women Remonstrants against the extension of suffrage to women. It expresses the views of such Remonstrants in Massachusetts, Maine, Illinois, and other States who believe that the great majority of their sex do not want the ballot, and that to force it upon them would not only be an injustice to women, but would lessen their influence for good and would imperil the community. The Remonstrants ask a thoughtful consideration of their views in the interest of fair discussion.[16]

The next substantive change occurred in 1896, one year after the Boston women formally organized under the name Massachusetts Association Opposed to the Further Extension of Suffrage to Women. In that year, the prospectus was changed to state that *The Remonstrance* was published by the organization, and the names of the members of the association's executive committee were listed in alphabetical order. In keeping with the group's discomfort with singling out individuals, no officers had been selected, although Mrs. Charles Eliot (Mary) Guild, who had called for the formal organization, was elected secretary. In addition, a man, Laurence Minot, was identified as treasurer.[17]

In 1898, MAOFESW took a further step toward defining itself by publishing on its front page a paragraph describing the association. This brief description included the date of its organization, the number of its branch committees, the number of communities in which members lived, and a description of the membership. In an apparent effort to deflect suffrage criticism that antisuffragists came from the privileged elite, *The Remonstrance* stated that the association's membership included "professional women, wage-earners, and home-keeping wives and mothers."[18] With these words the antisuffragists also attempted to appear more representative of the general population than they actually were and to attract professional and workingwomen to their cause.[19]

MAOFESW elected its first officers in 1897, but it wasn't until 1899 that their names were published in *The Remonstrance*. Despite antisuffrage arguments that the place of the woman was in the home, all of these women, all of them affluent members of the upper and upper-middle classes, had been active in civic and philanthropic activities for years. Mrs. J. Eliot Cabot, for example, who was elected president, had held an elective position as overseer of the poor in Boston for several years and had been a member of the Brookline School Committee as well as chair of the Volunteer Aid Association.[20]

About this time, MAOFESW began to actively campaign throughout the state. It expanded the number of branch committees and held frequent parlor meetings where it distributed antisuffrage literature and copies of *The Remonstrance* to recruit new members and influence voters. For the antisuffragists, both the paper and the pamphlets were vital tools in their campaign to convince women to convince their menfolk to oppose suffrage. "We hope," Guild told a meeting of women in Suffolk County in 1897, "that every woman interested will persuade others, both men and women, to read these papers, and to make up their minds only after a fair examination of the subject." Like many reformers of the time, suffragists included, Guild was convinced that people had only to read her side of the story to be convinced.[21]

The Remonstrance was also distributed to women's colleges, libraries, and the increasing number of state legislatures that addressed suffrage bills each year. When suffrage was defeated in those states, as it was almost inevitably in these early years, Foxcroft attributed the defeat to *The Remonstrance*'s power of persuasion.[22]

As MAOFESW expanded its activities, financial pressures, which had always been a problem, became acute. The financial situation directly affected *The Remonstrance,* and many editorial decisions—the number of pages per issue, the number of copies per issue, the number of issues per year—were determined by the amount of money the association had in its treasury. The executive committee, however, was severely hampered in fund-raising attempts since it was reluctant to solicit funds directly and depended heavily on "the gentlemen" of the Man Suffrage Association and a few independently wealthy female members to come up with the needed cash.[23] Certainly, money was a distasteful subject to these women, and it was only after considerable debate that it was decided in 1902 that "there would be no harm" in sending regular subscribers and donors an appeal for additional funds, explaining the obvious—that the "Association needs[s] money to carry out its work."[24] Four years later, the executive committee had become either so accustomed to appealing for money or so desperate for it that it sent a circular to men throughout the state asking for a contribution of twenty-five dollars to allow a wider distribution of the association's views on suffrage.[25]

Only a fraction of the money brought in by these methods went toward publication of *The Remonstrance,* but when in 1906 Foxcroft first suggested the paper become a quarterly, much of the ensuing debate focused on whether the association could afford the additional cost.[26] The executive committee voted to support the project, and the first quarterly edition appeared in 1907, but when Foxcroft proposed in 1913 to make the paper a monthly at a cost of one thousand dollars per year, "the cost was considered prohibitive," and the proposal was rejected.[27]

The association never did, in fact, devise a way to make *The Remonstrance* self-supporting. Although it began soliciting twenty-five cents per year for annual subscriptions in 1908, the majority of copies were given away free to state legislatures, organizational committees, newspaper editors, women's colleges, libraries, members of the standing and executive committees, and donors.[28] The possibility of soliciting paid advertisements was brought up in 1913 but was quickly rejected as either too impractical (circulation was thought to be too small to attract advertisers) or too distasteful.[29]

Although the Massachusetts association was the first women's antisuffrage group to organize in the country and eventually claimed more than forty-one thousand members, it was soon overtaken in both numbers and influence by the New York Association Opposed to the Woman Suffrage, which organized in 1895 and published a newspaper, *The Anti-Suffragist,** from 1909 to 1912.[30] Both groups eventually became part of the National Association Opposed to Woman Suffrage (NAOWS), established in New York City in 1911. NAOWS became an umbrella organization for a number of state associations, providing them with speakers and antisuffrage literature, and published a national organ, the *Woman's Protest,* in New York from 1912 to 1918. In 1918, NAOWS moved to Washington, D.C., where it joined forces with the Man Suffrage Association to publish the *Woman Patriot.*[31]

Both the Massachusetts women's association and *The Remonstrance* survived until 1920, when the suffrage amendment became the law of the land.[32] In its last year, the association tried desperately to continue its mission, but as the number of ratifying states had begun to add up after Congress approved the amendment in June 1919, support of antisuffrage evaporated. Even veteran members of the executive committee began to withdraw their support, and on July 26, 1919, for the first time since its official organization in 1895, the executive committee had to cancel a meeting because it lacked the required quorum.[33] During these last months, a frequent question at meetings was whether *The Remonstrance* should be continued, but not until September 3, 1920, did the committee vote to discontinue the paper after the October edition and to render a "vote of appreciation to the editor."[34]

The final eight-page issue of the paper gave absolutely no indication that this was to be its last appearance. It published the names of the officers of the association in its usual manner and "earnestly requested" members to "keep headquarters advised of changes of address." It refused to concede defeat and argued as adamantly as ever that "the majority" of men and women truly did not want woman suffrage. It recognized the current state of affairs but argued that the federal amendment was a violation of states' rights, that the ratification by the last state, Tennessee, had been bogus and illegal, that a repeal would be sought before the Supreme Court before the November election, and that, despite the recent events, the majority of women still did not want the vote and would not benefit by their new access to politics.[35]

The Remonstrance had, for thirty years, represented the conservative belief held by a considerable percent of the population that woman's place was in the home. Although both the Massachusetts association and *The Remonstrance* ceased to exist after the passage of the suffrage amendment, this conservative view persisted well into the century and resurfaced some fifty years later in the movement to stop the equal rights amendment. That women's road to complete equality would be a long and rocky one was eerily forecast in the last edition of *The Remonstrance* when it printed the words of National Woman's Party

Chairman Alice Paul: "It is incredible to me that any woman should consider the fight for equality won. It has just begun."[36]

Notes

1. Massachusetts Association Opposed to the Further Extension of Suffrage to Women (hereafter, MAOFESW) Executive Committee Minutes, December 30, 1904, MAOFESW Papers, reel 1A, Massachusetts Historical Society, Boston.

2. MAOFESW Executive Minutes, February 14, 1902, MAOFESW Papers, reel 1A; MAOFESW Executive Minutes, MAOFESW Papers, March 27, 1908, reel 2.

3. Although publication began in 1890, not until 1896 was *The Remonstrance* issued under the name of the MAOFESW and the names of the officers of the organization published (1896, p. 1).

4. Mrs. Charles Eliot Guild, "The Early Days of the Remonstrants against Woman Suffrage: A Memory Sketch by Their First President," MAOFESW Papers, reel 2. MAOFESW changed its name to the Women's Anti-Suffrage Association of Massachusetts in 1916.

5. "Average Women," 1892, p. 2.

6. "The Voice of the Majority," 1899, p. 3.

7. "Anti-Suffragists in Vermont," 1897, p. 1.

8. "Wyoming as an Example," "A Bad Year for Suffrage," "A Fatal Admission," "Goldwin Smith on Suffrage," all in 1890.

9. Some of the men were Judge Francis Lowell, Massachusetts Institute of Technology (MIT) professor William T. Sedgewick, and state representative Charles R. Saunders, who was later hired to act as counsel to the women's association (Guild, "The Early Days of the Remonstrants against Woman Suffrage," p. 10.) In 1912, the men's organization was renamed the Men's Association against Extension of Woman Suffrage ("A New Men's Association," October 1912, p. 8.)

10. Guild, "The Early Days of the Remonstrants against Woman Suffrage," p. 2.

11. Ida Husted Harper, "Associations Opposed to Woman Suffrage," *History of Woman Suffrage,* Vol. 5 (Rochester, N.Y.: Charles Mann, 1889), pp. 678–679.

12. "Frank Foxcroft," *Who Was Who in America, 1897–1942* (Chicago: A. N. Marquis, 1943), p. 420; MAOFESW Executive Committee Minutes, April 12, 1900, MAOFESW Papers, reel 1A; MAOFESW Executive Committee Minutes, Treasurer's Report, October 9, 1903, MAOFESW Papers, reel 1A; MAOFESW Executive Committee Minutes, August 15, 1913, MAOFESW Papers, reel 2.

13. MAOFESW Executive Committee Minutes, December 22, 1899, MAOFESW Papers, reel 1A; MAOFESW Executive Committee Minutes, November 3, 1904, MAOFESW Papers, reel 1A.

14. MAOFESW Executive Committee Minutes, February 8, 1901, MAOFESW Papers, reel 2; MAOFESW Executive Committee Minutes, February 12, 1901, MAOFESW Papers, reel 1A; MAOFESW Executive Committee Minutes, February 22, 1901, MAOFESW Papers, reel 2.

15. MAOFESW Executive Committee Minutes, March 27, 1908, MAOFESW Papers, reel 1A.

16. 1891, p. 1. Over the years this prospectus was lengthened to include the names of the states in which antisuffragists had organized.

17. 1896, p. 1; Guild, "The Early Days of the Remonstrants against Woman Suffrage," p. 3.

18. 1898, p. 1. At this time the association claimed eighteen branch committees and members in 141 Massachusetts communities.

19. For an excellent summary of antisuffrage arguments and strategies, see Eleanor Flexner, *Century of Struggle*, rev. ed. (Cambridge, Mass.: Belknap Press of Harvard University Press, 1975), pp. 304–318.

20. 1902, p. 1.

21. "An Early Statement of Mrs. Guild's", 1897, p. 4, MAOFESW Papers, reel 3.

22. MAOFESW Executive Committee Minutes, February 14, 1908, MAOFESW Papers, reel 1A.

23. "Report of Special Meeting of Executive Committee with the Gentlemen," MAOFESW Executive Committee Minutes, December 15, 1899, MAOFESW Papers, reel 1A; MAOFESW Executive Committee Minutes, April 18, 1909, MAOFESW Papers, reel 1A; MAOFESW Executive Committee Minutes, May 8, 1914, MAOFESW Papers, reel 2. Mary S. Ames, MAOFESW president from 1910 to 1912, donated substantial sums to the association.

24. MAOFESW Executive Committee Minutes, March 14, 1902, MAOFESW Papers, reel 2.

25. "Dear Sir," November 15, 1906, MAOFESW Papers, reel 3. This appeal, however, was signed by the three male members of the association's finance committee, George G. Crocker, Laurence Minot, and Charles Warren. The names of the officers of the MAOFESW were placed after these at the bottom of the letter.

26. MAOFESW Executive Committee Minutes, December 12, 1906, March 12, 1907, MAOFESW Papers, reel 1A.

27. MAOFESW Executive Committee Minutes, August 15, 1913, MAOFESW Papers, reel 2.

28. MAOFESW Executive Committee Minutes, October 8, 1908, February 14, 1908, MAOFESW Papers, reel 1A.

29. MAOFESW Executive Committee Minutes, August 15, 1913, MAOFESW Papers, reel 2.

30. October 1919, p. 1; Harper, "Associations Opposed to Woman Suffrage," p. 679.

31. Harper, "Associations Opposed to Woman Suffrage," pp. 678–680.

32. In 1916, MAOFESW changed its name to the Women's Anti-Suffrage Association of Massachusetts, and in 1917, the name of its publication was lengthened to *The Remonstrance against Woman Suffrage*. The executive committee, greatly reduced, continued to meet until 1921 (MAOFESW Executive Committee Minutes, April 1, 1921, MAOFESW Papers, reel 2).

33. MAOFESW Executive Committee Minutes, July 26, 1919, MAOFESW Papers, reel 2.

34. MAOFESW Executive Committee Minutes, September 3, 1920, MAOFESW Papers, reel 2.

35. "An Outrageous Invasion of State Rights," p. 7; "Every Step Illegal," p. 1; "To The Supreme Court," p. 6; "What Suffrage Means in the Cities, p. 8—all in October 1920.

36. "What the Suffragists Want Now," October 1920, p. 8.

Information Sources

BIBLIOGRAPHY:
Flexner, Eleanor. *Century of Struggle.* Rev. ed. Cambridge: Belknap Press of Harvard
    University Press, 1975.
"Frank Foxcroft." *Who Was Who in America, 1897–1942.* Chicago: A. N. Marquis,
    1943, p. 420.
Harper, Ida Husted, ed. "Associations Opposed to Woman Suffrage." *History of Woman
    Suffrage.* Vol. 5. Rochester, N.Y.: Charles Mass, 1889, pp. 678–680.
Massachusetts Association Opposed to the Further Extension of Suffrage to Women
    Papers. Massachusetts Historical Society, Boston.
INDEX SOURCES: None.
LOCATION SOURCES: University of Wisconsin Memorial Library, Madison; State
    Historical Society of Wisconsin, Madison; and other libraries.

Publication History

PERIODICAL TITLE AND TITLE CHANGES: *The Remonstrance* (1890–1916); *The
    Remonstrance against Woman Suffrage* (1916–1920).
VOLUME AND ISSUE DATA: Vols. 1–30 (1890–October 1920). Annual (1890–1906);
    quarterly (April 1907–October 1920).
PUBLISHER AND PLACE OF PUBLICATION: Massachusetts Association Opposed to
    the Further Extension of Suffrage to Women (1890–1916); Women's Anti-
    Suffrage Association of Massachusetts (1916–1920). Boston.
EDITORS: Frank Foxcroft (1890–1916?); Mrs. James Codman (1916?–1920).
CIRCULATION: 2,000–10,000 (determined by the number of suffrage campaigns).

Elizabeth V. Burt

THE REPLY

The Reply's name emulated the question-response mode of argument of the
times that treated the phrase "woman suffrage" as a question. *The Reply: An
Anti-Suffrage Magazine* was launched as a response to the threat of militancy
in the suffrage movement. The antisuffrage movement itself has been characterized as "one of reaction, expanding and contracting as the suffrage movement
did."[1] Particularly as the magazine viewed militancy as inseparable from woman
suffrage, its name also reflected the reactive dynamics of the larger movement.

The magazine had one editor throughout its two-year existence, its founder,
Helen S. Harman-Brown, who was secretary of the New Canaan Branch of the
Connecticut Association Opposed to Woman Suffrage and member of the local
branch's organization committee. With the second issue, Harman-Brown was
listed as both editor and publisher. An ardent antisuffragist, Harman-Brown
continued her efforts past the cessation of *The Reply*, although by then her
activities were based in New York, where she had moved *The Reply* after its
first year of publication.[2] Along with Harman-Brown, officers of the various
antisuffrage associations provided much of the magazine's copy.

Harman-Brown lent the publication its initial Connecticut focus, and the magazine's Connecticut antisuffrage affiliation was through her as well. The Connecticut Association Opposed to Woman Suffrage had been started in November 1911, the same month as the National Association Opposed to Woman Suffrage,[3] as was the New Canaan branch, the state's first local antisuffrage organization. Having female officers and being a predominantly female group, the New Canaan branch claimed a membership of over three hundred women by May 1913.[4]

Harman-Brown began the monthly in May 1913 as a response to the threat of militancy by U.S. suffragists.[5] Placed prominently at the front of each issue, editorial comment often railed against militant tactics. The first issue began:

> The Reply has come into existence in response to a distinct demand.
> . . . Woman Suffrage has, until very lately, been looked upon by men with amusement and by women, with indifference. England is responsible for the changed attitude of both towards this question . . . [although] the "Militancy fad" has not yet crossed the sea. Faint echoes are beginning to be audible in the speeches. . . . It is in response . . . that the demand arises for an expression by Anti-Suffragists of Connecticut, as well as the country, of their reasons for opposing this movement for Woman Suffrage. The Reply has undertaken this task.[6]

Militancy remained a theme throughout the run of this magazine, in both editorials and stories. For example, an August 1913 editorial asked, "[D]o we in America look forward with pleasure to these imported methods of Suffrage work?"[7] while a feature proclaimed:

> We are constantly surprised at the failure of the Suffragists to come out squarely in favor of militancy. From the Anti-Suffrage point of view, the militants are perfectly justified in fighting. It is the only logical thing to do. That is why we are opposed to Woman Suffrage.[8]

The magazine also took to task the major arguments of the day, attempting to dispel the notions that woman suffrage was good, necessary, or imminent. For example, the conventional wisdom that the woman vote would duplicate or cancel the male vote was elaborated upon.

> [I]f women had the franchise, and if fathers and mothers agreed, the mothers' votes would merely double the number cast without in any way altering the result.
> The only sane ground on which women can demand the ballot is that their vote will change conditions and legislation for the better. That means that there must be a good way of voting and a bad way, of which women must choose the good and men the bad. . . . [I]f men choose the good way,

women have no need to vote, and if women choose the bad way, they cannot bring about reforms.

[M]others must vote one way and fathers the other, thus practically cancelling the vote of each family and leaving the power entirely in the hands of the unmarried. Logically the situation is a little difficult to fit into the Suffrage arguments.[9]

Abundant Christian viewpoints supported arguments that woman suffrage would upset the God-given balance. For example, an article cited equal suffrage as a petition for change not only of social custom but of the "Creator's law," characterizing the danger of the action as "monkeying with the buzz-saw."[10] A priest's three-part article elaborated on views against suffrage in "a plain Catholic treatment of a semi-religious subject."[11] He reasoned that although women's voting was not inherently evil, a woman should not enter "the public arena of political strife if she wishes to maintain her womanly dignity and the sweet fragrance of reserve."[12]

Like other antisuffrage publications, the magazine charted suffrage defeats state by state. The first number highlighted the Michigan defeat as doubly important, for not only was Michigan considered a legislatively "progressive" state, but "[i]t would have been the first State east of the Mississippi River, and psychologically would have meant much to the Suffrage movement."[13]

In addition to original articles, the magazine regularly ran reprints from general-circulation magazines, women's magazines, and daily newspapers that supported its stance. Book reviews were common editorial fare as well as a mainstay of the advertising. Later issues often carried recommended reading lists, which included other antisuffrage magazines. The magazine recognized the importance of its advertising base. In the first issue's editorial and then, from the second issue forward, reprinted below the table of contents, the magazine urged the readership not only to read the magazine's advertisements "but patronize its carefully selected advertisers."[14]

Through advertisements and editorial content, the magazine promoted an antisuffrage organization called the Guidon Club. The reactive nature of this club was in line with the publication's own stance. The first number ran a letter from the president of the club endorsing the publication and introducing the club to the readership: "Its founding marked the hour when the Suffrage movement began openly to merge with the Socialist movement from which it really originally sprang."[15] The club was an independent organization with female officers that admitted men in 1912, when the New York State legislature endorsed suffrage.[16]

One rallying cry against suffrage that *The Reply* relied on was an assumed alliance with socialism. The first issue's editorial stated that antisuffragists had seen no need to mobilize opposition until the "national danger" was posed by "the formation of the following quartette—Fashion, Militancy, Socialism and Woman Suffrage."[17] With militancy the catalyst for the formation of the association's organ, the theme was later modified. Socialism and woman suffrage were allied with feminism and referred to as a triple threat. The explanation ran that suffrage was part of feminism, which was part of socialism, which wanted a social revolution.[18] An editorial at the end of the first year of publication stated, "Standing, as it does, for but one purpose—to help the Majority—THE REPLY wishes to 'lend a hand' wherever the 'hand of fellowship' can become the means of striking at the triple alliance of Suffrage, Socialism, and Feminism.'"[19]

With its second issue, the masthead announced that *The Reply* was available in New York; by the end of the first year the magazine was also available at newsstands in Washington, D.C. Despite its editorial claim, "[s]tarting in a little Connecticut town, with no expectation of growing beyond the limits of the State,'"[20] the magazine was envisioned as a publication that would not be confined by its state, much less its local bounds. For instance, the Guidon letter of support in the first number stated that to "the men and women of New England farms, the journal will go with a message and inspiration.'"[21] From its first issue, the magazine noted national and state, along with local, antisuffrage organizations and updated lists of their officers.

The editorial at the end of *The Reply*'s first year boasted a 400 percent increase in circulation in the preceding three months, a circulation that included a subscription list that had five hundred farmers on it, "which means that the purpose of the magazine to reach those who are too far from any center to attend Anti-suffrage meetings, is being accomplished.'"[22] In addition, the editorial noted that *The Reply* was circulated in twenty-five states, Canada, and several countries in Europe.[23]

Following an increased reliance on New York–based advertising, in May 1914 Harman-Brown moved the magazine's publishing to New York City with the start of the second volume. The move seemed to generate more New York-centered news than ever. The magazine still covered Connecticut news, such as that state's legislative vote against suffrage in 1915. Although the magazine maintained an editorial office in New Canaan, Connecticut, until at least June 1914, it quit running lists of the local associations and their officers. By dropping local Connecticut antisuffrage news in favor of news with a national focus, by pursuing New York-based advertising, and by relocating its operation to New York City, Harman-Brown positioned *The Reply* against the national organization's publication, *The Woman's Protest*. The national organ had begun publication a year earlier than had *The Reply,* and it had come on board by superseding the established New York publication, *The Anti-Suffragist.**

Despite advertising and a call for reports from state, national, and international antisuffrage organizations in its last number, *The Reply* ceased publication a year after its move to New York, in May 1915.

Notes

1. Jeanne Howard, quoted in Janet Saltzman Chafetz and Anthony Gary Dworkin, "In the Face of Threat: Organized Antifeminism in Comparative Perspective," *Gender and Society* 1.1, March 1987, p. 50.

2. See, for example, Helen S. Harman-Brown, "The Suffrage Amendment," letter, *New York Times,* June 27, 1918, p. 10.

3. "Anti-Suffrage Organizations," May 1913, p. 23.

4. Ibid.

5. Jane Jerome Camhi, ed., *Women against Women: American Anti-Suffragism, 1880–1920* (New York: Carlson, 1994), p. 91.

6. May 1913, editorial, p. [1].

7. Editorial, August 1913, p. [73]; see also, for example, editorial, February 1914, p. [221].

8. Mrs. William Forse Scott, "Militancy Perfectly Logical," August 1913, p. 81.

9. Olive Reamy, "The Suffragist's 'Mothers [*sic*] Helper,' " May 1913, p. 8.

10. Kate C. Towle, " 'Monkeying with the Buzz-Saw': A Quarrel with the Laws of Creation," May 1913, p. 11.

11. A. J. Wolfgarten, "Shall Women Vote?—An Attempt to Cut a Gordian Knot," March 1914, p. 253.

12. Ibid., p. 255.

13. Elizabeth R. Burnell, "Suffrage Defeated in Michigan," May 1913, p. 4.

14. Editorial, May 1913, p. 2.

15. Helen K. Johnson, "The Guidon Club: Opposed to Woman Suffrage," May 1913, p. 13.

16. Ibid.

17. Editorial, May 1913, p. [1].

18. See, for example, Everett P. Wheeler, "The Feminist Movement," October 1913, p. 125.

19. Editorial, April 1914, p. 270.

20. Editorial, April 1914, p. [269].

21. Johnson, "The Guidon Club," p. 13.

22. Editorial, April 1914, p. [269].

23. Ibid.

Information Sources

BIBLIOGRAPHY:
Camhi, Jane Jerome, ed. *Women against Women: American Anti-Suffragism, 1880–1920,* New York: Carlson, 1994.
INDEX SOURCES: None.
LOCATION SOURCES: Library of Congress and other (academic) libraries.

Publication History

PERIODICAL TITLE AND TITLE CHANGES: *The Reply: An Anti-Suffrage Magazine.*
VOLUME AND ISSUE DATA: Vols. 1–2 (May 1913–May 1915). Monthly. (Some inconsistency in issuance, but numbering consistent.)
PUBLISHER AND PLACE OF PUBLICATION: Helen S. Harman-Brown. New Canaan, Conn. (1913–1914); New York (1914–1915).
EDITORS: Helen S. Harman-Brown (1913–1915).
CIRCULATION: Unknown.

Therese L. Lueck

THE REVOLUTION

The Revolution's name outlined loud and clear its editorial position. While other fledgling woman's rights publications had evoked floral images like *The Lily** or mythical images like *The Una,** there was no room for such sympathetic representations in the call to arms that was *The Revolution*. First published in 1868 by the founders of the woman's rights movement, Elizabeth Cady Stanton and Susan B. Anthony, *The Revolution* was designed to ignite a fire of indignation and reform in the hearts of its readers. The journal, published as a weekly, made clear that nothing short of a revolution on behalf of the plight of women was acceptable. As Stanton explained, "A journal called the *Rosebud* might answer for those who come with kid gloves and perfumes to lay immortal wreaths on the monuments which in sweat and tears others have hewn and built; but for us . . . there is no name like the *Revolution*."[1] Their motto reinforced that belief: "The true republic.—Men, their rights and nothing more; women, their rights and nothing less." Anthony underscored that philosophy in one of her few signed editorials, in which she said their plan was for "new constructions, not reconstructions. Old foundations as well as old fabrics must be removed. Down with politicians, up with the people, has been our cry from the beginning."[2] That their message of revolution was about fifty years premature and that Stanton and Anthony's liberal platform was simply too radical for many in the reading public did nothing to dim their editorial fervor.

For Anthony and Stanton, *The Revolution* represented just one strategy in a life-consuming campaign to win equal rights for women. While they had been writing for both mainstream newspapers and earlier suffrage publications, this weekly journal represented their one official foray into the field of newspaper publishing. Stanton believed strongly in the power of newspaper publicity, arguing that it would "start women thinking, and men, too."[3] By the time she and Anthony entered the world of publishing, they had endured years of ridicule and mirth at their own expense in mainstream newspapers. Even Horace Greeley's *New York Tribune*, the one newspaper that had been sympathetic to their cause and also provided a forum for the writing of Stanton, severed its relationship with them after the cantankerous Stanton locked horns with an equally eccentric Greeley in 1867.[4] With little or no positive press coverage and lacking a national suffrage publication to promote their goals, Anthony and Stanton themselves naturally turned to publishing.

Yet, from the very first issue, *The Revolution* caused upheaval and dissension. Rather than inform and woo women interested in their goals, the newspaper served to alienate potential advocates and anger lukewarm supporters. In addition to its deliberately belligerent tone, *The Revolution* generated controversy swiftly when readers became aware of the publication's financial backing. Anthony and Stanton had accepted monetary support from George F. Train, a millionaire with political aspirations. Train was a Democrat (one strike against him) with an ambivalent track record concerning treatment of blacks (strike two for the many abolitionists who were attracted to the woman's rights movement). In exchange for Train's financial support, the women agreed to allow him to express his political opinions in the journal and also provided a forum for his friend, David Meliss, financial editor of the *New York World,* to write about business.[5] Despite the quid pro quo, Stanton's fervor was such that she believed "it would be right and wise to accept aid from the devil himself"; other potential advocates felt differently.[6] In the second edition of *The Revolution,* Stanton felt obligated to defend her association with Train and argued that although many prominent Americans supported woman suffrage *intellectually,* very few lent *monetary* support.

The mainstream newspapers used the inauguration of a new journal as an opportunity to continue their relentless joking at the suffragists' expense. The *New York Times* called *The Revolution*'s motto "meaningless" and "foolish."[7] The *Sunday Times* resorted to personal attack on both of the women:

> If Mrs. Stanton would attend a little more to her domestic duties and a little less to those of the great public, perhaps she would exalt her sex quite as much as she does by Quixotically fighting windmills in their gratuitous behalf, and she might possibly set a notable example of domestic felicity. . . . As for the spinsters, we have often said that every woman has a natural and inalienable right to a good husband and a pretty baby. When, by proper "agitation," she has secured this right, she best honors herself and her sex by leaving public affairs behind her and by endeavoring to show how happy she can make the little world of which she has just become the brilliant centre.[8]

While other, more prudent souls might have followed the New Testament admonition to turn the other cheek, no one ever accused Stanton of being prudent. She printed the reactions of the general newspapers to her publication and then, point by point, attacked their positions in print. She told the *Sunday Times* that she was a paragon of domesticity and that she was an expert in "how to take care of a child, make good bread, and keep a home clean." In fact, she turned the argument in her favor and advised, "Now let every man who wants his wife to know how to do likewise take *The Revolution,* in which not only the ballot, but bread and babies will be discussed."[9]

True to her word, Stanton presented an eclectic mix of editorial matter in *The Revolution.* Early issues of the weekly covered such topics as women workers, divorce reform, the status of suffrage in various states and territories, international feminist activities, wife abuse, and other topics naturally of interest to women. While the general focus of the publication always was equal rights and suffrage for women, *The Revolution* sought a broad-based editorial approach. A financial department covered business news and political affairs, including reports of President Andrew Johnson's impeachment hearings and the political conventions. Poetry and short fiction rounded out the editorial offering. The editors also made an appeal to subscribers to send in publishable material but noted that the writers needed to understand space constraints. They asked that submissions be "sharp, short and spicy."[10]

The Revolution first appeared on January 8, 1868, with Stanton's sharing the editorial duties with Parker Pillsbury, a reformer who had been working on the *Antislavery Standard*.[11] Pillsbury was editor only until mid-1869 but continued his association as a writer for a while longer. Anthony was named proprietor, which meant she ran the office, paid bills, and hired printers, using funds from Train. In January 1870, Paulina Wright Davis, former editor of the premier suffrage publication, *The Una,* joined the newspaper as a corresponding editor. Yet, throughout the changes in leadership, Stanton supplied the bulk of the editorial copy.

The editorial offices were first located at the New York headquarters of the American Equal Rights Association, but when that group withdrew, the editorial and business offices were moved to the home of the Woman's Bureau, a townhouse on East 23d Street. The building was owned by Elizabeth B. Phelps, who wanted to establish a meeting place for women, but other women's groups refused to meet there in protest of the editorial space allotted to *The Revolution*.[12]

The trio had ten thousand copies of the first edition published and distributed around the United States, using the franking privilege of New York representative James Brooks, who apparently was criticized in Congress for assisting the suffragists.[13] Despite the wide dissemination, *The Revolution*—which usually numbered sixteen pages—attracted only about three thousand subscriptions at its peak, including one sent to the White House.[14] Anthony told readers that they had set a goal of one hundred thousand subscribers. "Nothing short of this ensures our complete success," she wrote.[15] The subscription price of two dollars lasted until mid-1869, when it was raised to three dollars. Initially, it was the organ of the National Party of New America; but when a wrenching split factionalized the suffragists, *The Revolution* remained closely affiliated with Stanton and Anthony's National Woman Suffrage Association.

The newspaper's subscriptions, however, never reflected the numbers of women interested or even active in suffrage. It simply could never get past the fact that the financial backing of a man like Train had served to alienate the very people who were potential subscribers. Stanton lamented in print that "old friends" had complained about their affiliation and that "subscriptions would pour in" if Train's association ended.[16]

In fact, Train went to England shortly after the paper's debut and was sent to prison for his own highly publicized backing of Irish rebels there. His financing of the operation slipped away, and for a time David Meliss helped defray expenses, but he also stepped aside. The prominent Beecher family also backed down from its offer of financial support because the women refused to change the name of the publication to *The True Republic*.[17]

Until its last issue under the guidance of Stanton and Anthony, they made it clear that they could never compromise the profound editorial message they were disseminating. They boasted some of the most prominent women writers of the day, including Harriet Beecher Stowe and Alice and Phebe Cary, but said they tried to avoid men's opinions on their pages. Noting that "masculine ideas have ruled the race for six thousand years," the women said they wanted *The Revolution* to be a "mouth-piece of women."[18] Thus, while Parker Pillsbury shared the title of editor for a time, it was always clear that Stanton and Anthony were in control. In fact, by early 1870, Pillsbury's name had been replaced on the masthead by woman's rights activist Pauline Wright Davis.

Given the editorial message, it is not surprising that the magazine had trouble securing backers and never made a profit. This was also due, in part, to the strict advertising policy overseen by Stanton. For even after the failure of *The Revolution,* Stanton was proud that, despite constant financial woes, she and Anthony never stooped to accept any "advertisements of quack remedies." While other magazines of the day thrived on advertisements promoting home remedies and patent medicines, *The Revolution* under Stanton remained committed to a policy of accepting advertisements for "nothing that we did not believe in." In fact, Stanton reminisced years later that she was upset to see that a clerk had placed an advertisement for bread powder in the magazine. In the following issue, Stanton told her readers just what she thought of this particular brand of bread powder and then defended her position when the man who had placed the ad came to question her. Bowing to his concerns, she did not charge him for the advertisement because, she told him, "the editorial probably did you more injury than the advertisement did you good." The bread powder man warned ominously, "I prophesy a short life for this paper."[19] Stanton's proud advertising policy fell by the wayside, however, after the journal was sold in 1870. Toward the end of its publishing days, more than five pages of the sixteen-page magazine were devoted to advertisements, including some for the patent medicines that Stanton abhorred.

Stanton, however, had little to lose in the publishing venture. The money that was being invested and depleted belonged to Anthony. After she sold the journal for a token one dollar, Anthony assumed sole responsibility for the ten thousand-dollar debt the venture had accrued. The journal went to the hands of Laura Curtis Bullard, whose fortune ironically had been made by the sale of Dr. Winslow's Soothing Syrup.[20] While Anthony mourned the death of her "firstborn," Stanton refused to help dissolve the debt.[21]

Not only did *The Revolution* fail in its mission to attract women to equal rights and suffrage, but its radical editorial policy also contributed to the splintering of the suffrage movement into rival factions. At the May 1868 meeting of the American Equal Rights Association, opposition factions accused *The Revolution*'s editors of using the group's funds to finance the publication. Although Anthony was able to account for all of the expenditures, the rift deepened. The matter came to a head over Stanton and Anthony's adamant refusal to support both the Fourteenth and Fifteenth Amendments in editorials in the newspaper.

Stanton and Anthony steadfastly refused to support suffrage for black men only, futilely insisting that the wording be changed to include black and white women.

After the icy reception for her ideas at the convention, Stanton realized that she could not rely on support from the American Equal Rights Association. She and Anthony organized a meeting of the Woman Suffrage Association of America and received support from prominent suffragists, except Lucy Stone. The following year, at the May 1869 meeting of the American Equal Rights Association, Stanton again met opposition to her platform and realized finally that woman suffrage would never be the main priority of that organization. She invited the woman delegates at that meeting to *The Revolution* offices for a reception and then reorganized the group into the National Woman Suffrage Association because she so fervently believed that woman suffrage needed to be the primary goal of some organization. She also barred men from membership.

For some reformers, this bold strategy provided the breaking point. Stanton and her ideas were seen as too unbending and too liberal to hold weight with a more moderate populace. Lucy Stone refused to join any organization that barred her husband, Henry Blackwell, from voting.[22] Stone and her husband banded together with other, more conservative reformers to organize the American Woman Suffrage Association. That group voted to publish its own newspaper, *The Woman's Journal,** which first appeared in January 1870. The rift lasted twenty years.

The constitution and platform for Anthony and Stanton's National Woman's Suffrage Association were published in *The Revolution,* along with a request that new members of the group should subscribe to *The Revolution.* When the rival faction began printing *The Woman's Journal, The Revolution* welcomed it as a "new and valiant auxiliary to the field of conflict." *The Revolution* article asserted that because it had paved the way in a hostile environment, *The Woman's Journal* could anticipate a warmer reception.[23] Yet, the creation of *The Woman's Journal* symbolized how deep and uncompromising the rift between the rival factions was. If the women had been able to work together and compromise their positions, surely the already established *Revolution* should have been a sufficient national journal to disseminate and publicize their ideals and goals.

But the head-to-head competition that pitted Anthony and Stanton against editors Lucy Stone, Henry Blackwell, and Mary Livermore of *The Woman's Journal* lasted as such only a few months. During that time, *The Revolution* noted that despite the presence of a "rival . . . absolutely hostile body," it would stay on its course seeking "woman's elevation and enfranchisement."[24] Then, in the May 26, 1870, issue, Stanton announced that she, Anthony, and Davis would hand over editorial control of *The Revolution* to Bullard. Anthony was planning an extensive lecture tour that would prohibit her involvement in the newspaper, while Stanton asserted that she no longer wanted the pressure of deadlines that a weekly newspaper required. The ownership as such was reorganized to include Stanton, Bullard, and others in a stock company, but the reality was that Anthony handed over ownership to Bullard for one dollar.[25]

After Bullard took over as editor in chief, she maintained the newspaper's name and described it as "a weekly newspaper devoted to the welfare of Women," but it lost its belligerent, strident tone, as evidenced by the change in the motto on the masthead: "What, therefore God hath joined together, let no man put asunder." Certainly, the new editorial policy was a long stretch from Stanton's support of divorce. Bullard continued to support suffrage but backed away from other of Stanton's more liberal beliefs. "We have one sharp issue to present to the American people. Everything else that is involved in our cause—education, fair wages, justice before the law, social equality with men— is centered in and represented by the one word suffrage."[26] Stanton continued to supply editorial copy for the journal, but its revolutionary flavor had been diluted. New columns called "Gossip" and "About Women" were introduced, and more advertising was accepted.

Bullard continued as editor until October 1871, when she stepped aside because she was spending so much time abroad. J. N. Hallock, the New York publisher of the *Liberal Christian,* acquired the journal and handed the editorial duties over to the Reverend W. T. Clarke, who was a former editor of Hallock's paper. Clarke wanted to make *The Revolution* into a home journal that emphasized women's duties as opposed to their rights.[27] That move sounded the death knell to any possible connection to the revolutionary ideas of its founders, but the journal itself quietly merged into the *Liberal Christian* in February 1872.

Notes

1. Letter from Elizabeth Cady Stanton to Susan B. Anthony as quoted in Elisabeth Griffith, *In Her Own Right: The Life of Elizabeth Cady Stanton* (New York: Oxford, 1984), p. 131.

2. Susan B. Anthony, "The Work of the Hour," August 6, 1868, p. 72.

3. Griffith, *In Her Own Right,* p. 58.

4. Lois W. Banner, *Elizabeth Cady Stanton: A Radical for Woman's Rights* (Boston: Little, Brown, 1980), pp. 98–99.

5. Lynne Masel-Walters, "To Hustle with the Rowdies: The Organization and Functions of the American Woman Suffrage Press,"*Journal of American Culture* 3.1, Spring 1980, p. 169.

6. Banner, *Elizabeth Cady Stanton,* p. 101.

7. "The New York Times on the Revolution," January 15, 1868, p. 24.

8. "What the Press Says of the Revolution," January 22, 1868, p. 33.

9. "What the Press Says of The Revolution," January 22, 1868, p. 33.

10. "Condense," June 4, 1868, p. 346.

11. Lynne Masel-Walters, "Their Rights and Nothing More: A History of *The Revolution,* 1868–70," *Journalism Quarterly* 53, 1976, p. 244.

12. Griffith, *In Her Own Right,* p. 132.

13. "James Brooks," June 4, 1868, p. 347.

14. Griffith, *In Her Own Right,* p. 132.

15. S.B.A., "One Hundred Thousand Subscribers," April 9, 1868, p. 1.

16. E.C.S., "To Our Radical Friends," May 14, 1868, p. 296.

17. Masel-Walters, "To Hustle with the Rowdies," p. 170.

18. "The Revolution for 1870," January 6, 1870, p. 1.

19. Elizabeth Cady Stanton, *Eighty Years and More: Reminiscences, 1815–1897* (Boston: Northeastern University Press, 1993, first published in 1898), pp. 257–258.

20. Griffith, *In Her Own Right,* p. 133.

21. Ibid.

22. Griffith, *In Her Own Right,* p. 138.

23. "The Woman's Journal," January 13, 1870, p. 26.

24. P. P., "The Two Associations," March 24, 1870, p. 185.

25. Griffith, *In Her Own Right,* p. 133.

26. August 24, 1871, p. 1.

27. Frank L. Mott, *A History of American Magazines, 1865–1885,* vol. 3 (Cambridge, Mass.: Belknap, 1957), p. 395.

Information Sources

BIBLIOGRAPHY:

Banner, Lois W. *Elizabeth Cady Stanton: A Radical for Woman's Rights.* Boston: Little, Brown, 1980.

Griffith, Elisabeth. *In Her Own Right: The Life of Elizabeth Cady Stanton.* New York: Oxford, 1984.

Masel-Walters, Lynne. "Their Rights and Nothing More: A History of *The Revolution, 1868–1872.*" *Journalism Quarterly* 53, 1976, pp. 242–251.

———. "To Hustle with the Rowdies: The Organization and Functions of the American Woman Suffrage Press." *Journal of American Culture* 3.1, Spring 1980, pp. 167–183.

Mott, Frank L. *A History of American Magazines, 1865–1885.* Vol. 3. Cambridge, Mass.: Belknap, 1957.

Stanton, Elizabeth Cady. *Eighty Years and More: Reminiscences, 1815–1897.* Boston: Northeastern University Press, 1993 (originally published 1898).

INDEX SOURCES: None.

LOCATION SOURCES: Library of Congress and many other libraries. Microfilm is available through Greenwood Publishing.

Publication History

PERIODICAL TITLE AND TITLE CHANGES: *The Revolution* (1868–1872).

VOLUME AND ISSUE DATA: Vols. 1–4 (January 8, 1968–February 17, 1872). Weekly.

PUBLISHER AND PLACE OF PUBLICATION: R. J. Johnston (Susan B. Anthony, proprietor) (1868–1870); Revolution Association (1870–1871); J. N. Hallock (1871–1872). New York.

EDITORS: Elizabeth Cady Stanton and Parker Pillsbury (1868–1869); Elizabeth Cady Stanton (1869–1870); Laura Curtis Bullard (1870–1871; W. T. Clarke (1871–1872).

CIRCULATION: Griffith, p. 132: 3,000.

Agnes Hooper Gottlieb

S

THE SIBYL

During the Civil War, Lydia Sayer Hasbrouck was a voice crying in the wilderness. The conflict had silenced much of the debate on woman's rights. Hasbrouck, however, would never allow anything as insignificant as a "civil war" deter her from putting out her reform newspaper, *The Sibyl,* or continuing to push for woman's rights. That independence, that singularity of purpose did not surprise anyone familiar with Hasbrouck or her newspaper.

Lydia Sayer Hasbrouck never fitted comfortably among the woman's rights leadership. Perhaps her training set her apart. As a hydropathic physician, she approached woman's rights from a distinct perspective, often framing her support in health arguments. Perhaps it was the way she dressed. Both before—and long after—the so-called bloomer garb gained and fell from popularity among woman's rights leaders, Hasbrouck sported the Turkish pantaloons and insisted this was the *only* healthy way for women to dress. Perhaps it was the way she criticized the leadership of the woman's rights organizations. She often took them to task for failing to stand firm for justice, woman's rights, and dress reform. Of course, that was just Lydia Sayer Hasbrouck's way—and *The Sibyl* reflected the editor's temperament.

Hasbrouck did not begin as a woman's rights reformer, although her background, education, temperament, and experiences would inevitably lead her in that direction. She was the daughter of an affluent, politically active Orange County, New York, farmer, landowner, and distiller of apple brandy. She was well educated for the time, attending high school and college. She was an independent spirit. In 1849, well before Amelia Bloomer "discovered" the garb that would carry her name, Lydia Sayer, only twenty-two, began wearing the knee-length skirt and pantaloons. She was denied admission into one school because of her unconventional dress, but she could not be denied her "medical" training because of it. She attended a three-month course at the Hygeio-Therapeautic College, a water-cure medical school in New York City, from which derived her title of physician and her right to practice medicine.[1] Shortly after, she moved to Washington, D.C., to practice medicine. There she joined the lecture circuit and wrote for various dailies in the city, including the *Washington Star.*[2]

The year 1856 was an eventful one for her. She returned to her native New York on a lecture tour, started her *Sibyl,* and soon after married John Whitbeck Hasbrouck, the editor of the Middletown, New York, *Press,* a Whig, and an abolitionist. Lydia Sayer launched her reform publication, *The Sibyl: A Review of the Tastes, Errors and Fashions of Society* on July 1, 1856. *The Sibyl* was a reform publication in its truest sense. The biweekly opposed a number of ills—from tobacco to liquor[3]—but clearly its major push was for woman's rights. Like many other reformers of the day, Hasbrouck saw abolitionism and woman's rights as vitally linked. As she wrote in the first issue,

> The bonds of the southern slaves are not riveted more strongly than are the bonds of custom upon society; for let one but seek a change, and the "border ruffians" send forth their bloodhounds eager for the chase, and goad those who dare defy these time-honored principles, sanctified by folly and every conceivable absurdity.[4]

However, she was never willing to give up woman's rights to push solely for abolitionism. As she saw it, both women and slaves were victims, so she could not afford to devote her newspaper to that solitary reform. As she explained later in 1856,

> We [*The Sibyl*] have another mission. It is with white slaves both of the north and south. The mass are as servilely bound as are the black slaves of the south. Many are content with their bonds; yet, as maybe seen by our columns, others are writhing beneath the burthen, and would fain cast them off. For these and all others we labor; for every slave bound on this broad earth we toil; yet wholly and solely refuse to devote *all* our energies to one particular branch of slavery. Our mission . . . is too broad for this.[5]

Indeed, it was. Until the newspaper was folded in 1864, it remained a voice for woman's rights and abolitionism.

Hasbrouck's editorial stance for abolitionism was simple: everything should be done to eliminate the evil. Hasbrouck believed in the immediate abolition of slavery without compensation.[6]

Her vision with regard to the abolition of woman's slavery was more complex. Women should dress to free themselves from the bondage of society. They should wear the lighter weight bloomer garb, which allowed them freedom from the constriction of the corset and nineteenth-century fashion. When others in the woman's rights organizations abandoned the reform, Hasbrouck labeled them "conservatives." "Short dresses were, in their estimation, too *weighty* a question to sustain," she argued.[7]

In her woman's rights vision, married women should be given full rights to property. In the antebellum period, few states accorded such rights. In most states, the husband assumed ownership of his wife's property. Women should also have the vote. Neither Hasbrouck nor readers would accept the argument that the husband represented the wife at the ballot box. As Hasbrouck wrote, "Every woman vote with her husband? That is a base subterfuge and bare-faced *lie,* as they know."[8] Moreover, women should be paid the same amount as the men. One subscriber complained about the money paid female clerks compared to men doing the same job. Women made only six hundred dollars a year, compared to twelve hundred to eighteen hundred dollars a year for men. The writer asked, "Is that justice?"[9]

That subscriber illustrated an important function that *The Sibyl* played within the woman's rights movement, especially during the Civil War. Like other reform publications, *The Sibyl* welcomed letters from readers. In so doing, Hasbrouck and her *Sibyl* accomplished two things: first, the news coverage expanded, and, second, feminist editorial comment increased. In their letters to Hasbrouck and *The Sibyl,* subscribers offered news from their various communities (especially in the Midwest). Letters from readers also offered feminist perspectives. *The Sibyl* was one of the few forums for such "radical" thoughts. Hasbrouck welcomed the controversial letters from woman's rights advocates. Women from Wisconsin, Illinois, and Indiana, especially, shared their perspectives on dress reform, equal pay for equal work, and national politics and policies. Hasbrouck had no objection to publishing critical comments on the president, the personalities, and the policies during the Civil War. After all, those were sentiments that she regularly expressed on *The Sibyl*'s editorial pages.

Hasbrouck was no admirer of Abraham Lincoln. Her disappointment grew as Lincoln delayed a vigorous pursuit of the war and the abolition of slavery. "Our President may be an honest man," she wrote in 1862, "but we cannot reverence the principles of any man who will sacrifice the substance and lives of his friends to strengthen the hands of his deadly foes. Whatever may be said to the contrary, this has been the policy of our Administration from the beginning of the war to the present."[10] She also didn't think much of the generals that Lincoln appointed. She dismissed General George B. McClellan, then general in chief of the Union troops, as a "do-nothing, mud-stuck, stubborn imbecile."[11] Her hero, and the hero of many Civil War radicals, was General John C. Fremont, who had freed slaves of rebel Missourians in his jurisdiction and was later removed from command because of his actions. As she wrote,

We say, let both Jessie [Fremont] have a chance to free the slaves of Southern Nabobs, catch Davis & Co., set them up at public auction to the highest bidder, who will promise to drive them through the cotton fields under whip and spur the rest of their natural lives.[12]

Women had a special role to play in this conflict, Hasbrouck argued in *The Sibyl.* They should turn their back on fashion, wear the bloomer garb, and do their part on farms and in businesses.[13] Women should also work in the hospitals, caring for the sick and wounded, one reader suggested.[14] Here was something that Hasbrouck could wholeheartedly support. However, she was ill at ease with Dorothea Dix's handling of women nurses during the war, especially after Mrs. F. R. Harris Reid of Berlin, Wisconsin, reported that female nurses had been instructed to leave their bloomer outfits at home. Reid wrote, "If men cannot be nursed by women in comfortable but unfashionable attire, they may die for all my going in long skirts to nurse them."[15] Soon Hasbrouck was editorially questioning Dix's other rulings. She wrote that Dix "seems to be particularly *hard* on young women, pretty women, and we were about to add women of common sense."[16]

Although the war increasingly dominated the editorial columns of *The Sibyl,* Hasbrouck never gave up the woman's rights cause. She was dismayed to no end that the established woman's rights groups languished during the Civil War.

They have money at their disposal, and should combat these wrongs to women when they are accruing, instead of waiting until they become laws and fixtures, harder to set aside than now.

Why, when every interest is represented before our Legislators at Washington, this Association is so remiss, and sends no protestants to try at least to arouse men to acts of justice, is most singular.[17]

Although established woman's rights activities languished, Hasbrouck and her *Sibyl* did not. She frequently editorially supported dress reform. (In 1863–1864, she also served as president of the National Dress Reform Association.) Even though the nation was at war, she urged women not to pay taxes until they had the vote.

That so long as men held women as inferiors, and unworthy of citizenship, and of no account politically, save when the tax-roll was called, we should demand, as Jeff. Davis does, to be "let alone," and let men pay the fiddler who gives all the golden music to them.[18]

Hasbrouck followed her own advice. She refused to pay taxes for a number of years. Finally, in 1863, she was ordered to work on the road crew to cover her taxes—and she worked there for several days. As she reported to her readers, "Remember we did not go there to do a man's day's works or to work out a man's tax."[19]

The war did take a toll on both Hasbrouck and *The Sibyl.* At the start of the

THE SIBYL

war, the frequency of the newspaper had to be cut, from biweekly to monthly, and its subscription price slashed from four dollars to fifty cents a year. While her husband published the newspaper at his shop, Hasbrouck did all the writing and editing of *The Sibyl*. Although the newspaper's editorial quality never slipped, its popularity did begin to wane.[20] Meanwhile, Hasbrouck became more heavily involved in her medical work, converting her home to the Sibyl Ridge Hygienic Retreat, a financially unsuccessful venture.[21] In 1863, as mentioned, she was also elected president of the National Dress Reform Organization. A growing family put additional demands on her time. Clearly, something had to be sacrificed, and that "something" was *The Sibyl*. Faced with raising the price of subscriptions to cover expenses, Hasbrouck opted to suspend the publication. She thought it would be only a temporary respite. As she explained, "Friends, we must rest, if we eve[r] hope to do any good in this sphere of action."[22] She took her leave on an optimistic note and predicted that soon at least some women would win the vote:

> In the political world, we miss our guess if men do not in self defence grant the elective franchise to tax-paying women, if no others. The foreign imigration is so great, and our losses so enormous in the war, unless this is resorted to, the foreign vote will overwhelm and carry all before it.[23]

Hasbrouck was wrong on both counts. The women of the nation had to wait decades before the Nineteenth Amendment was finally ratified, and *The Sibyl* was never again revived. The June 1864 issue was its last. Hasbrouck, a dress reformer and a hydropathic physician to the last, recommended the *Laws of Life,* the organ of the Jackson Sanatorium in Danville, New York, to her readers.

The Sibyl never had a large, national circulation. Yet, it is still played an important role, especially during the Civil War, when most woman's rights voices were silenced. For women committed to woman's rights and dress reform, *The Sibyl* was a constant reminder that there were other like-minded women in the nation. Moreover, it was a forum for an exchange of news and views that was needed during this lag in the woman's rights movement.

Notes

1. Paul S. Boyer, "Lydia Sayer Hasbrouck," in Edward T. James, Janet Wilson James, and Paul S. Boyer, eds., *Notable American Women 1607–1950: A Biographical Dictionary,* vol. 2 (Cambridge: Belknap Press of Harvard University Press, 1971), p. 151; E. M. Ruttenber and L. H. Clark, *History of Orange County, New York, with Illustrations and Biographical Sketches of Many of Its Pioneers and Prominent Men* (Philadelphia: Everts and Peck, 1881), p. 197.
2. Ruttenber and Clark, *History of Orange County,* p. 197.
3. See, for example, August 1, 1856.
4. July 1, 1856.
5. November 1, 1856.
6. See, for example, "Women and the Crisis," March 15, 1861.
7. February 1, 1861.

8. January 1862.
9. April 1864.
10. "The Situation of Affairs," July 1862.
11. "President Lincoln's Message," March 1862.
12. March 1862.
13. "Women and the Crisis," March 15, 1861.
14. April 15, 1861. See, also May 1, 1861.
15. June 1, 1861.
16. August 1861.
17. April 1862.
18. February 1862.
19. September 1863.
20. Boyer, "Lydia Sayer Hasbrouck," p. 152.
21. Ibid.
22. April 1864.
23. May 1864.

Information Sources

BIBLIOGRAPHY:
Boyer, Paul S. "Lydia Sayer Hasbrouck." In Edward T. James, Janet Wilson James, and Paul S. Boyer, eds., *Notable American Women 1607 1950: A Biographical Dictionary.* Vol. 2. Cambridge: Belknap Press of Harvard University Press, 1971, pp. 151–152.
Mott, Frank Luther. *A History of American Magazines 1850–1865.* Vol. 2. Cambridge: Harvard University Press, 1938.
Ruttenber, E. M., and L. H. Clark. *History of Orange County, New York, with Illustrations and Biographical Sketches of Many of Its Pioneers and Prominent Men.* Philadelphia: Everts and Peck, 1881.
INDEX SOURCES: None.
LOCATION SOURCES: Denver Public Library; Radcliffe; University of Minnesota.

Publication History

PERIODICAL TITLE AND TITLE CHANGES: *The Sibyl: A Review of the Tastes, Errors and Fashions of Society.*
VOLUME AND ISSUE DATA: Vols. 1–7. (July 1, 1856–June 1864). Biweekly (1856–1861); monthly (1861–1864).
PUBLISHER AND PLACE OF PUBLICATION: John Whitbeck Hasbrouck (1856–1864). Middletown, N.Y.
EDITORS: Lydia Sayer Hasbrouck (1856–1864).
CIRCULATION: Unknown.

Kathleen L. Endres

SINISTER WISDOM

By the mid-1970s, *Focus: A Journal for Lesbians** and *The Ladder** had made the idea of lesbian publications far more familiar. The lesbian community had become more connected and more politically aware. What would be the next challenge? What about a lesbian magazine designed, written, and published in the Deep South? The possibility, as one of the founding editors later said, was like "raising pineapples on the North Pole."

Sinister Wisdom began in February 1976, when Harriet Desmoines and Catherine Nicholson received a phone call inviting them to a lesbian writer's workshop in Knoxville, Tennessee. As Desmoines wrote in one issue of the publication, "Catherine and I brazenly announced that we were starting a magazine. The women appeared to believe us, and we taped ideas for the first issue."[1]

Neither Desmoines nor Nicholson knew much about publishing, and they questioned the wisdom of starting a publication in Charlotte, North Carolina. In an editor's note, Desmoines wrote:

> Earlier this year it dawned on us that we were publishing a journal of Lesbian writing in the hometown of the "Praise the Lord" television network and that this was somewhat akin to raising pineapples on the North Pole. Our solution? Move to New York, move to Boston, move to L.A., move to San Francisco! Finally, we decided to just stay where we were. For one thing, it freaks out people in the Bay area. For another, most Lesbians live, love, work and politic outside the metropolitan centers.[2]

So, in July 1976 the editors committed themselves to three issues per year at a subscription rate of $4.50. They decided on *Sinister Wisdom* as the title, borrowing it from the publication *The Female Man* by Joanna Russ. Then they acknowledged the support of the women of the Charlotte Lesbian Center, and the first lesbian publication in the land of magnolias and mint juleps was born.

In vol. 1, issue 1, Desmoines and Nicholson wrote their "Notes for a Magazine":

> We're lesbians living in the South. We're white; sometimes unemployed, sometimes working part-time. We're a generation apart. . . . *Sinister Wisdom* is also our political action. We believe that writing of a certain consciousness has greater impact when it's collected, when several voices give weight, harmony, and counter melody to the individual message.[3]

Introducing the next issue, the editors dedicated the publication to "lesbians, who have been without faces, without voices, without a validating herstory."[4] The masthead promised essays, fiction, poetry, drama, reviews, and graphics and stated as its mission the development of the lesbian imagination in politics and art.

Touting itself as *Sinister Wisdom: A Journal of Words and Pictures for the Lesbian Imagination in All Women,* the publication began to enlist artists and writers such as Audre Lorde, Rita Mae Brown, and Adrienne Rich, with editing assistance provided by Mab Segrest. The fall 1976 issue was dedicated to Barbara Grier, who wrote sixteen years for *The Ladder* and was editor for four years. She later became the editor of Naiad Press, the largest U.S. feminist-lesbian press.

Sinister Wisdom survived its first year, and in the spring 1977 issue, Desmoines wrote that the publication had begun "at point zero: isolation and ignorance. We decided to make a magazine because we wanted more Lesbian writing, we wanted more friends, and we wanted to express the power we felt building up inside ourselves, that was both us and not-us. (We didn't want much, just everything.)"[5] Defying lack of experience and geography, the group had not only survived but prevailed.

With the summer 1978 issue, the publication broke one hundred pages and moved from Charlotte to Lincoln, Nebraska. By this time, *Sinister Wisdom* was printing the work of reputable writers such as Judy Grahn, Jane Rule, Carol Seajay, Andrea Dworkin, and Gloria Anzaldua. That fall, *Sinister Wisdom* became a quarterly publication costing $7.50. The editors included the following note along with the plea for subscriptions: "Without [you], *Sinister Wisdom* dies of a broken pocket book."[6]

In the spring of 1980, *Sinister Wisdom* announced its new editors, Michelle Cliff and Adrienne Rich, and a new place of publication, Amherst, Massachusetts. That same year, subscription costs rose to ten dollars for four issues. Through its sixteenth issue (1981), *Sinister Wisdom* was written by its former editors, printed in Lincoln, and distributed by the new editors in Massachusetts.

By issue 17, *Sinister Wisdom* had developed a sense of its own history, listing Desmoines and Nicholson as "founding editors" (with issue 18, they dropped the "founding editors" designation), and Cliff and Rich were "editors and publishers." In issue 17, Cliff wrote the "Notes for a Magazine" and promised a sustained commitment to social revolution.[7] Rich echoed her, saying, "In their first issue, in 1976, Harriet and Catherine described the founding of *Sinister Wisdom* as a political action. We reaffirm that purpose here."[8]

In a new emphasis on the seriously disfranchised in the lesbian community, the editors began to focus on specific issues. For example, a combined issue (22/23) was entitled "A Gathering of Spirit" and dealt with Native Americans. Melanie Kaye/Kantrowitz continued that tradition through the 29/30 issues with the "Jewish Women's Anthology," a 336-page effort.

In the fall of 1983, Cliff and Rich, who had devoted two years to the publication, resigned. Rich said that having suffered for thirty-three years with rheumatoid arthritis, she was in too much pain to continue her editorial responsibilities: "I have been slowed down by physical pain and its impact on the spirit."[9] Kaye/Kantrowitz and Michaele Uccella took over as editors of a four thousand-circulation publication that cost fifteen dollars per year. Desmoines and Nicholson reappeared on the masthead as "founding editors."

New editors Kaye/Kantrowitz and Uccella wrote in the next issue, "We will try, during our time with *Sinister Wisdom,* to make her—like a good dyke—

both tough and sensitive.''[10] At the end of that year, the publication cost fourteen dollars per year, and by 1985, Kaye/Kantrowitz was the sole editor and publisher. When she left the publication in the winter of 1987, Kaye/Kantrowitz said she had brought a ''greater emphasis on class issues and on the experience of working class women.''[11] Cost of the publication had risen to seventeen dollars per year.

When Kaye/Kantrowitz left her editorial position, she wrote ''Notes from the Editor: A Letter to Elana'' for issue 32 (Summer 1987). Now subtitled *A Journal for the Lesbian Imagination in the Arts and Politics, Sinister Wisdom* was to be headed by Elana Dykewomon, who published in the thirty-third issue what she called ''Notes for a Magazine: A Dyke Geography.'' Taking over in the fall of 1987, Dykewomon wrote, ''*Sinister Wisdom* is a place. A country. To which lesbians add their own villages, their own geography, issue by issue.''[12]

Dykewomon began producing topical collections dealing with friendship, the disabled, Italian-American women, class, lesbians of color, lesbian relationships, and other topics. Berkeley became the place of publication for *Sinister Wisdom,* now touted as a ''political journal for radical lesbian feminists,''[13] although it continued to be called a ''feminist and lesbian literary journal''[14] in most indexes and by most reviewers.

In the summer of 1991, issues 43–44 celebrated the history of the publication from 1976 to 1991 with ''The 15th Anniversary Retrospective.'' Dykewomon wrote, ''This issue is a marker of our movement: small and bright, bobbing in a difficult channel, sometimes obscured by waves and weather, showing direction.''[15]

By this time, the publication had been through seven editors, six address changes, and what the editor often called ''all those Republican years.'' Its 368-page issue was testimony to the survival of the community it represented. In a letter for that issue, Harriet (Desmoines) Ellenberger wrote:

> We began it in Charlotte, North Carolina (a more unlikely place you could not pick) in utter (and I do mean utter) isolation. . . . It was an act of love. . . . For me, *Sinister Wisdom* was never really about lesbian community. It was never really about art or politics either (since, for starters, the distinction between the two is not clear to me). It was about transformation, nothing less. It was about releasing the power of passionate love between women through language and image, words and pictures, with the intent of saving the earth and her creatures, including ourselves, from destruction.[16]

With issue 46 (Spring 1992), *Sinister Wisdom* became a tax-exempt corporation and seemed financially solvent. By 1993–1994, however, the warnings began: ''This place, *Sinister Wisdom,* is in danger of closing down.''[17] Like *Focus: A Journal for Lesbians* and *The Ladder, Sinister Wisdom* could not withstand falling subscription rates and rising publication costs, and it, too, disappeared, but not without having made a substantial contribution to the history of the gay press in America.

Notes

1. Spring 1977, p. 99.
2. Spring 1977, p. 100.
3. July 1976, pp. 3–4.
4. July 1976, p. 72.
5. Spring 1977, p. 99.
6. Summer 1978, p. 2.
7. Issue 17, 1981, pp. 2–4.
8. Issue 17, 1981, p. 4.
9. Issue 24, 1983, p. 3.
10. Issue 25, Winter 1984, p. 3.
11. Issue 31, Winter 1987, p. 3.
12. Issue 33, Fall 1987, p. 3.
13. Alyson Publications, *The Alyson Almanac: A Treasury of Information for the Gay and Lesbian Community* (Boston: Alyson, 1990), p. 241.
14. H. Robert Malinowsky, *International Directory of Gay and Lesbian Periodicals* (Phoenix: Oryx Press, 1987), p. 115.
15. Issues, 43–44, Summer 1991, p. 5.
16. Issues 43–44, Summer 1991, pp. 8–9.
17. Issue 51, 1993–1994, p. 5.

Information Sources

BIBLIOGRAPHY:
Alyson Publications. *The Alyson Almanac: A Treasury of Information for the Gay and Lesbian Community.* Boston: Alyson, 1990.
Malinowsky, H. Robert. *International Directory of Gay and Lesbian Periodicals.* Phoenix: Oryx Press, 1987.
INDEX SOURCES: *Alternative Press Index; International Directory of Gay and Lesbian Periodicals; Feminist Periodicals.*
LOCATION SOURCES: Norlin Library, University of Colorado at Boulder.

Publication History

PERIODICAL TITLE AND TITLE CHANGES: *Sinister Wisdom.*
VOLUME AND ISSUE DATA: 53 issues published (July 1976–Summer/Fall 1994). Three times a year (July 1976–Fall 1978); four times a year (Fall 1978–Summer/Fall 1994).
PUBLISHER AND PLACE OF PUBLICATION: Charlotte, N.C. (1976–1978); Lincoln, Nebr. (1978–1980); Amherst, Mass. (1980–1985); Rockland, Maine, and Montpelier, Vt. (1985–1987); Berkeley, Calif. (1987–1994).
EDITORS: Harriet Desmoines and Catherine Nicholson (1976–1980); C. Colette, Harriet Desmoines, Catherine Nicholson, and Carolyn Shafer (winter 1980); C. Colette, Harriet Desmoines, and Catherine Nicholson (spring 1980–1981); Michelle Cliff and Adrienne Rich (1981–1983); Melanie Kay/Kantrowitz and Michaele Uccella

(1983–1984); Melanie Kaye/Kantrowitz (1985–1986); Elana Dykewomon (1987–1994).
CIRCULATION: 4,000.

Jan Whitt

SKIRTING THE CAPITOL

The first legislative publication in the nation written specifically for women, *Skirting the Capitol with Marian Ash* was a newsletter based in Sacramento, California, and covered that state's legislature. Its focus was on news that directly affected women's lives, particularly California's Advisory Commission on the Status of Women, which was first created in 1965. The newsletter also addressed the impact general legislation had on women's issues.

Skirting the Capitol was intended as a weekly during the legislative session and a biweekly during legislative recess. But the nominal fifteen-dollar yearly subscription rate could not sustain this frequency, so shortly after its 1967 debut it became a biweekly publication. As a one-woman operation,[1] it was often irregularly published. The four-page, legal-size[2] bulletin intended to educate women about the legislative process as well as inform them on legislation's effect on their lives.

> It is based on the premise that most women in California are not as well informed as they would like to be, and should be, on their legal rights, protections and disabilities. It is written in the belief that women generally tend to accept things as inevitable that they could easily change if they were better informed and encouraged to do so.[3]

Marian Ash, who founded the publication and served throughout as its editor and publisher, launched her newsletter, in great part, to watchdog California's new Commission on the Status of Women. She had been the secretary for the commission when it was first constituted by Governor Jerry Brown in 1965. Ash noted, as political weaknesses, that that commission "was a predominantly 'labor' oriented group, with a politically 'liberal' image." When the governor left office, the committee was disbanded.[4] A second commission had been constituted in 1967 by the next governor, Ronald Reagan. Ash noted with dismay that the new commission was

> a predominantly conservative group made up of affluent, socially prominent women with a "home and family is the place for women" image who had even less idea than had the original members about the purpose of the Commission. . . .
> Worse! Governor Reagan tactfully cautioned the members, at their first meeting, NOT to get into Legislative matters but to confine their studies

to "family and children" problems—leaving a distinct impression that he did not consider women qualified to study other issues.[5]

An active liberal feminist, Ash often represented her region at the national level. In 1969, she became president of the Sacramento Valley Chapter of the National Organization for Women.[6]

She articulated the mission of the newsletter: "STC is a newsletter designed to promote political, economic and social equality for women (and to foment unrest by informing them they don't have it).''[7] She encouraged women to be knowledgeable about politics and active in the political process, through voting as well as lobbying: "It is designed to stimulate more effective participation by women in governmental affairs." The newsletter clearly saw women's proper realm of activism as a ladylike endeavor, relying on the notion of women as the standard-bearer of social morals. "It will reflect the view that women can exert a beneficial and positive influence in politics and government and that it is essential for them to be more active participants.''[8] Women were seen as a varied lot and not as a homogeneous voting mass, but the newsletter espoused a notion that an essential coordination would be possible among them when these differences were recognized and negotiated.

UNANIMITY will be possible when women all realize their circumstances are NOT static—and that sooner or later they may find themselves in a different situation, requiring different attitudes. It will also help when they compromise on method and approach, and agree on effective, persistent but LADYLIKE tactics.[9]

Ash critically analyzed pertinent political issues and actions, from the Status of Women Commission, to protective labor laws and the national equal rights amendment. She provided readers with detailed accounts on the introduction of legislation and its debates on the floors of the California Assembly and the Senate, along with interviews and informal discussions with legislators and lobbyists. Ongoing accounts of pending legislation kept readers anticipating the next issue much as serial fiction might. She enlivened accounts with emotional as well as physical descriptions of the legislators. Her powers of observation were particularly honed on the first day of each session. She noted that the "three lady legislators certainly brighten up any Chamber." She commented that Assemblywoman March Fong, a woman of Asian descent, "sported a chic new hairstyle and a mossy green pants-suit. And on her, it looked fine. March is tiny, saucy and slim." Along with her description of the other two assemblywomen Ash added that the three "set a high standard for women by *being* ladies—involved, conscientious, courageous and intelligent." She also commented on a few male legislators' "sartorial elegance.''[10]

Although Ash was liberal in her politics and her feminism, the newsletter presented nonpartisan consideration of many issues. Information on bills and resolutions was thoroughly researched; and, although it came from an articulated liberal Democratic perspective, arguments for and against each measure were usually presented. In addition to writing from a formal political stance, Ash overlaid it with her personal politics, generally defined by a right-leaning liberal feminist perspective but interspersed with radical notions, such as advocating the repeal of all abortion laws. Some of the newsletter's copy was labeled "one woman's opinion," but it all was punctuated with her personal blend of women's advocacy.

Compelled to create a newsletter by the lack of adequate representation that women and women's issues received in the California legislature, she was driven to disseminate an actual account of how women's interests were routinely trivialized and ridiculed. She commented in her first issue that the legislature's renewal (albeit belated) of the Commission on the Status of Women was "encouraging—unless you have been sitting in Senate and Assembly hearing rooms listening to various legislators DISCUSS the status of women."[11] Despite such observations on the lack of seriousness that permeated consideration of women's issues, Ash addressed her endeavor with enduring optimism and humor. She believed in the inherent goodness of the political system, yet she did not believe in its sanctity. A prominent example of her sardonic vein was a mock "help wanted ad" in which she advertised for legislators. "NO EXPERIENCE NECESSARY," the headline teased, touting the job as an "UN-EQUAL opportunity."[12] She did not shrink from naming names; indeed, personalities were as much a part of the story as the legislation. This approach, of course, incurred criticism, to which she replied, "[The newsletter] is intended to be personal because women like to know about people as well as issues, and because legislation can seem a very dry, boring subject to women unless the human element is brought to them."[13] As editor of the newsletter, she had press credentials, and she used them, often as the sole media representative at meetings—since she was concerned with women's issues, which were not the stuff of real news.[14]

Ash recorded debate and uncovered gamesmanship bent on keeping women in their second-class status, from the procrastination that prevailed when the Commission on the Status of Women came up for renewal to the open hostility used to prevent women's equal employment opportunities and wages. She implored women to get involved in the political process, trying to convince them that the political arena was where the true power of society resided—and it was distinctly mysogynist. "Legislators, by and large, treat the whole subject of women—and their status—as a slightly off-color joke with which they have gotten bored."[15]

As Ash tracked the progress of California's Commission on the Status of Women, she often found herself justifying its existence amid attacks by legislators.

EVERY SERVICE we have ever had in this country has been established, primarily, to serve "white MEN". At last, we are attempting to *equalize*

services through help to minority people and a study of the unique problems of women. . . . Are they suggesting that Governor Ronald Reagan is
a ''wild spender'' because he supported the continuation of a Status of
Women Commission?[16]

Since commission meetings were open to the public, she ran advance notices,
as well as membership profiles and meeting notes. As an advisory commission,
it had no actual authority; however, it did make recommendations. These recommendations—which dealt with removing archaic provisions from older laws,
conforming California law to national ones such as the Civil Rights Act, and
creating new laws—were then brought to the floor by friendly legislators. For
instance, a commission recommendation to create women's counseling centers
was introduced in the Assembly by March Fong, an often-covered favorite of
Ash.[17] In a typical move, although the legislature had just renewed the commission for a second two-year term, it did not give the commission's proposal
serious consideration. Fong castigated the membership for this contradiction:

I appreciate a good joke as much as anyone . . . but I doubt if many women
would understand the levity with which some members of the Legislature
have treated this bill—and others relating to women—any more than I do,
because raising children alone, for example, is not amusing.[18]

At the beginning of each legislative session, Ash would summarize each action that concerned women and note hurdles in its path. Ash kept score, publishing each legislator's voting record on women's issues. Prior to elections, she
would run a table of voting records, evaluating each legislator with adjectives
that ranged from ''perfect'' to ''terrible,'' and she grouped legislators according
to their voting records. ''Some male legislators are hopeless, but the largest
percentage are worth educating and are educable.'' She advocated voting out
the hopeless.[19] She did remind her readers that hers was not an assessment of
a legislator's entire record. ''PLEASE REMEMBER that SKIRTING THE
CAPITOL cannot assess a legislator's overall political view or activity—only
that which concerns women directly.''[20] At the end of 1971 she identified the
key women's issues under national consideration as the equal rights amendment,
Title VII of the Civil Rights Act of 1964, higher education, and child development programs. She found that her record keeping was paying off on the
national level as well.

For perhaps the very first time in history it is possible for women to
identify those members of Congress who are sympathetic to the cause of
women as well as those who are its enemies. There have been enough
key issues affecting women directly during the First Session of the 92nd
Congress to make evaluation of voting records not only possible, but significant.[21]

Protective legislation was hotly debated, with women and women's groups coming to bear on both sides of the issue. The debate was also fueled by confusion. It was not clear to anyone what women in what industries the law applied to, which left it open for abuse. Ash ran full coverage. For example, women were protected from working more than eight hours a day; the other side of the coin was that they were not allowed overtime, which was a disadvantage in hiring. Restrictions on how much weight women could lift at the workplace also cut both ways. Debates on protective legislation and commission recommendations pointed out to Ash the class division of women. Opinions of legislators and appointments of the governor were drawn from the upper classes, whose situations did not often reflect the lives those laws directly impacted. "Some politicians appear to evaluate the status of women by looking at their own wives."[22] As much as having a Commission on the Status of Women pleased her, Ash recognized that women appointed by Governor Ronald Reagan were of the leisure class. She pondered if this commission were truly able to represent the women of California, and she made it clear that the commission must represent *all* women.[23]

Ash also favored revising California employment to include nondiscrimination by sex, repealing any existing abortion legislation (on the grounds that the state had no compelling interest), and although finding arguments on both sides of the equal rights amendment (ERA) debate "profound and rational,"[24] advocating conformity of California's laws with the ERA.

She was hard on legislators, media, unions, and big business when they did not seem to have the interests of women uppermost, but she was equally hard on the voting population of women when they displayed little or no interest in working toward measures that would benefit themselves. For instance, when an attempt to make it unlawful to discriminate in employment on the basis of sex was defeated, she exhorted, "Women did not put enough pressure on to make much impression! They have plenty of pressure, but didn't apply it OR didn't apply it properly."[25] Her optimism would sometimes fail her as she viewed the disunity and inactivity of her intended public. "STC [*Skirting the Capitol*] has, on occasion, become fretful and frustrated (as only a newsletter which is written, edited, published and designed by one woman can be) over the lack of *dynamic group effort* on the part of women to influence 'what goes on in the world.' "[26] She would also fault California's Commission on the Status of Women when it did not do its job, which she defined as educating and orienting legislators "where the problems of women are concerned."[27]

Interspersed with these issues, Ash would insert diatribes on tenuously related material that tended to reveal the philosophy behind her perspective.

Since STC is becoming known as a newsletter concerned with women's rights, it may conceivably be referred to as a "feminist publication" one

of these days, and the editor must decide whether to be offended or not.
. . . Given such alternatives [as *Roget's Thesaurus'* synonyms for "feminine" and "lady"], "feminist" becomes less objectionable and STC accepts it![28]

Along with the development of the newsletter, its mission was refined, occasionally with the late-night, one-woman operation strain getting the better of
her keyboard.

STC originally started out as a liberal Democratic newsletter that was
determined to be fair and nice and nonpartisan to those bad Republicans.
You might as well know that the whole situation has gotten out of hand
. . . what with a lot of Democrats . . . consistently voting against all kinds
of good bills for women . . . and some Republicans supporting [these
bills.] Why don't you become a REPOCRAT, which is the new "liberal-
conservative" party . . . dedicated to the advancement of women, naturally![29]

The newsletter ran profiles of women's organizations, such as Business and
Professional Women and the National Organization for Women. (Ash belonged
to both organizations.) She ran occasional illustrations, such as holly leaves on
Christmas issues, or a cartoon, such as one reprinted from *McCall's* magazine
depicting a harried wife at the stove with children, a dog, and a mess while the
husband sat at the kitchen table nonchalantly waving his evening drink at her,
saying, "I don't understand you, Helen. You used to be a fun person."[30] The
newsletter did not run photographs, but in a special section in the April 29,
1974, issue endorsing Fong for secretary of state, Ash ran a head shot of the
congresswoman. Although the newsletter was not a literary publication, Ash
could not resist recommending an occasional read, which included the book
Born Female by Caroline Bird and premier task force reports by state and national status of women commissions.[31]

Ash maintained the publication as a one-woman operation with a subscription
base for revenue. She accepted speaking engagements and consultant fees to
supplement subscriptions, always mindful of avoiding conflicts of interest. In an
open letter to subscribers in 1974, she stated that she was resigning as analyst
for the Assembly Standing Committee on Employment chaired by Fong. After
accepting the position, she had found out that publishing her newsletter constituted a conflict of interest, and she stated that she did not intend to sacrifice the
newsletter. The letter was also to inform subscribers that the next issue would
be out late because she had to extricate herself from the position before publishing another number.[32] Although the newsletter was still considered a biweekly, there were continual gaps in the publication cycle until it ceased later
that year.

Notes

1. "Since Skirting the Capitol is a one-woman operation—quite literally—typing and proofing errors may occur" ("Editors [sic] Note," August 14, 1967, p. 5); Ash noted obtaining Maureen Schauss as associate editor, research assistant, and lecture consultant and Mrs. Laine Pirie as a volunteer staff assistant ("Skirting the Capitol Developments. . . ." October 16, 1967, p. 4), but they are not mentioned when she moved the operation into her home, "which will be more economical of time and money" ("Skirting the Capitol Has Moved," August 5, 1968, p. 4). With rare exceptions, all articles were written by Ash, as she noted in a response to criticism: Skirting the Capitol "isn't too editorial, its [sic] ALL editorial" ("An Editorial—On Feminism and Other Things," December 9, 1968, p. [1]).

2. The newsletter went to 8½" × 11" with the January 11, 1971, issue. "Most readers suggested that the 8½ × 11 size would be easier to file and keep" ("Skirting the Capitol Changes it's [sic] Skirt!" December 14, 1970, p. 4). Some issues had more than four pages, commonly prior to an election. Periodically—usually during a legislative recess—she ran informational issues, which at first were not numbered but considered "bonus publications for subscribers." The first of these was September 26, 1967.

3. "A Newsletter for Women," July 24, 1967, p. [1].
4. "You've Come a Long Way, Ladies!" December 23, 1968, p. [1].
5. Ibid.
6. "It's a Long, Long Way from Los Angeles to Atlanta!" December 23, 1968, p. 4.
7. "A Feminist?? Heaven Forbid!!" February 5, 1968, p. [1].
8. "A Newsletter for Women," July 24, 1967, p. [1].
9. "What Do Women Want? Well . . ." February 5, 1968, p. 2.
10. "High and Low Lights . . ." January 12, 1970, p. 2.
11. Ash, "The Status of Women," July 24, 1967, p. [1].
12. "Help Wanted: No Experience Necessary," September 9, 1968, p. [1].
13. "An Editorial—On Feminism and Other Things," December 9, 1968, p. [1].
14. "Absent: Members of the news media . . . with the above exception [Ash]!" box on Status of Women Commission meeting notes, September 11, 1967, p. 4.
15. "The Status of Women," p. 2.
16. "Is a Status of Women Commission Discriminatory?" October 13, 1967, p. 2.
17. There were three women in the California Assembly in 1967. The Senate had no women in it. There were favorable senators, such as Alan Short, who had introduced more bills to implement Status of Women recommendations than "any other legislator" ("The Status of Women Commission," July 31, 1967, p. [1]). Ash described the Senate as a hostile environment for women's issues: "The prevailing attitude in the California State Senate is that women should leave politics and government alone" ("A Crisis for Women/The State Senate and the Status of Women," October 2, 1967, p. [1]).
18. March Fong, as quoted in "Information and Guidance Centers for Women," July 24, 1967, p. 4.
19. "A Male Backlash." April 1, 1968, p. [1].
20. "Editors [sic] Note," p. 5.
21. "Voting Records—California Congressmen . . . ," December 6, 1971, p. [1].
22. "The 'New Look' in Politics . . . ," November 18, 1968, p. [1].
23. "The Commission," August 28, 1967, p. 3.

24. *"Do We Really Want Equality? . . . / . . .* AND what's the best way to get it!'' February 12, 1968, p. 4.

25. "Analysis," March 25, 1968, p. 2.

26. Ibid.

27. *"A Great Disappointment!''* April 1, 1968, p. 2.

28. "A Feminist?? Heaven Forbid!!''

29. "The Good Guys and the Bad Guys," February 26, 1968, p. 2.

30. December 11, 1967, p. 4.

31. "Highly Recommended Reading," November 18, 1968, p. 4.

32. Ash, "To my Subscribers," February 18, 1974.

Information Sources

BIBLIOGRAPHY:

Danky, James P., ed. *Women's Periodicals and Newspapers from the 18th Century to 1981.* Boston: G. K. Hall, 1982.

INDEX SOURCES: None.

LOCATION SOURCES: Library of Congress and other libraries.

Herstory microfilm collection.

Publication History

PERIODICAL TITLE AND TITLE CHANGES: *Skirting the Capitol with Marian Ash.*

VOLUME AND ISSUE DATA: Vols. 1–8 (July 24, 1967–May 1974). Irregularly published.

PUBLISHER AND PLACE OF PUBLICATION: Marian Ash. Sacramento, Calif.

EDITOR: Marian Ash (1967–1974).

CIRCULATION: Unknown.

Therese L. Lueck

SOJOURNER

Inspired by the example of Sojourner Truth, a publication called *Sojourner* has traveled far into a land of strangers to become a national feminist newspaper.

Sojourner was founded In September 1975 to overcome the isolation of the women attending and working at the Massachusetts Institute of Technology (MIT). "Voices from the women's community" read the line right below the title of the newly launched publication. Women faculty, staff, and students of the MIT Women's Forum announced to their new readers that they had started *Sojourner* because those with many voices felt isolated in the "very much male-dominated institution."[1]

The original target market for such a publication was very much in evidence. In addition to the Women's Forum, many of the eleven hundred women students and twenty-five hundred employees had formed a wide network of women's organizations on campus: the Association of Women's Students; the Technology Matrons (for women staff and faculty wives); the Technology Wives (open to wives of students and faculty); the Lesbian Caucus; the Women's Athletic Council; the IPS Women's Group (Office of Administrative Information Services); the Department of Urban Studies and Planning Women's Group; the Women Faculty and Staff Steering Committee; the MIT Women of Tech Square; and the Women's Advisory Group.[2]

One of those women, administrative assistant Martha Taylor, said of the first issue: "*Sojourner* has the potential to bring us closer together than perhaps anything else could. I hope that the paper will be a voice for all women on campus, and that in time it will address itself to issues broader than those specifically affecting MIT women."[3] As it turns out, her hopes for the publication were on target.

The front page of the premier edition featured a memorial tribute to Diana Gay Lawford Warner, twenty-nine, who had been an active member of the steering committee for *Sojourner* before she was hit and killed by a car near campus. The administrative assistant in the Psychology Department had become active in women's politics at MIT after hearing feminist Gloria Steinem speak. Friend Camille Motta said of Warner, "Her death, though our loss, is our inspiration."

The first staff was inspired by the journeys of Sojourner Truth, the former slave who found herself in such company as suffragists Elisabeth Cady Stanton, Susan B. Anthony, Lucretia Mott, and Lucy Stone. The edition carried a story on the first Sojourner, citing her extemporaneous "Ain't I a woman" speech at the 1851 woman suffrage convention in Akron, Ohio.[4]

Another article in the first edition presented a case for a women's center on campus.[5] A writer complained about the open display of *Playboy* and *Penthouse* at the Tech Coop.[6] Opinion pieces addressed abortion and the concerns of midwives.[7]

The monthly tabloid ventured further afield with each issue. By the end of the first year, the newspaper staff was calling *Sojourner* a feminist publication, and the staff expanded its market to address the needs of women in the greater Cambridge and Boston areas.[8] Circulation ran around five thousand.[9] The line under the title now read "A feminist journal of news, opinions and the arts."[10]

The main feature article of the anniversary edition was the coverage of "The First International Hookers' Film Festival and Feminist Party Convention" at Washington, D.C., which had occurred during the summer. The convention had been organized by Margo St. James, head of Coyote (Call Off Your Old Tired Ethics), a San Francisco-based prostitutes organization whose gained goal was to decriminalize prostitution.[11]

By the third year, the newspaper staff announced coverage would be expanded to the New England region. The staff had closed the campus office and moved nearby, to Cambridge.[12] The publication was suffering from the hazards of volunteerism: lack of continuity, too little money, and overextended energies. The editorial board wanted *Sojourner* to become self-sustaining.[13]

The inside story was much more troubling. Lindsey Van Gelder of *Ms.* reported that staff schisms, hassles over hierarchy, and burnout had been as "pervasive as printer's ink."[14] However, the founding editor, Allison Pratt, had weathered it all, and she was still working for *Sojourner*. "We made the structure of the paper real clear. The more you work, the more input you have," Pratt said. "Volunteers want to do the editing, but they're never around when someone has to take out the garbage. It was time for us to start thinking differently—not that we were going to do this someday, but *now*."[15]

More problems arose because the original newspaper had been incorporated as a nonprofit organization. The staff found they were unable to obtain tax-exempt status, which was key to attracting grants and donations. In July 1977, Sojourner Inc. became a regular Massachusetts business corporation, developed a long-range business plan and a prospectus, and began to raise funds through the sale of stock.[16]

The magazine reportedly sold nearly twenty thousand dollars in stock and invested the proceeds in new equipment and salaries for the staff, including an advertising manager. The ad income is said to have doubled by the next issue.[17] At the time, there were plans to move *Sojourner* to a biweekly format within a year, with more pages.[18]

Joining Pratt on the editorial board were Kathryn Lombardi and Mary Rowe, both of MIT, and Martha Thurber, former executive director for the Latimer Foundation. Among their expertise were backgrounds in law, economics, fundraising, writing, editing, design, typesetting, market research, and computer science.[19] Thurber would become editor within the year, in December 1979.[20]

The wider distribution effectively transmogrified into a much wider audience. The current target audience comprises feminists nationwide. Editions have varied in size from twenty-eight pages to fifty-four pages, of which about 55 to 65 percent is advertising. Estimated national readership is forty thousand.[21]

Karen Kahn, who became editor in 1987, said that *Sojourner* has become a national forum for women. Kahn said, "*Sojourner* provides what's often the earliest forum for significant new feminist thinking. From the politics of breast cancer to the backlash against incest survivors—fresh ideas and movements unfold and develop here on our pages."[22]

Kahn said that the publication helps thoughtful feminists stay connected with their counterparts "next door, across the Rockies and around the globe."[23] However, the editorial mission statement says the goal of the publication is "to present a space in which *all* women can speak freely about their concerns."[24]

The publisher's statement made by *Sojourner* today notes that the staff is committed to the elimination of sexism, racism, homophobia, classism, ageism, ableism, anti-Semitism, and other issues that oppress and divide women and society in general.[25] Subscribers are invited to "discover women's news that's often ignored by the mainstream press" and to get "a feminist take on more familiar headlines."[26]

These goals do not preclude the publication of unpopular ideas. The mission statement says: "*Sojourner* as *Sojourner* does not take an editorial stand on any subject, even if everyone on the editorial board agrees with a viewpoint. And, if someone on the staff writes a viewpoint article, it too will be labeled as such. We do this because we want all women to feel that their opinions are welcome in our pages, even if they disagree with some (or many) of the articles we print.''

The editorial content continues to be rather eclectic, including news, features, interviews, poetry, fiction, artwork, humor, and coverage on health, politics, film, books, theater, and events. *Sojourner* often publishes unsolicited articles and thereby features the work of well-known women as well as the work of first-time writers.

Recent issues have, for instance, featured conversations with, and commentaries by, Pat Gowens, welfare rights activist and editor of *Welfare Mother's Voice;* a report by Susan Lowe, breast cancer specialist; Marj Schneider, publisher of Womyn's Braille Press; JoAnn Tall, Lakota environmental activist; poet Kate Rushin, author of *The Black Back-Ups;* film critic Kathi Maio, author of *Popcorn and Sexual Politics;* and Barbara Mcdonald, coauthor of *Look Me in the Eye: Old Women Aging and Ageism.*

Kahn said *Sojourner* makes being "a living breathing feminist may not be as tough as it used to be, but it's still hard work. *It's easier in good company.*"[27]

Notes

1. Martha Taylor, quoted by Cynthia Helsel, "Why a Woman's Newspaper?" September 1975, p. 1.

2. Publisher's advertisement, September 1975, pp. 4, 8.

3. Taylor, quoted by Helsel, "Why a Woman's Newspaper?"

4. Mimsi Dorwat, " 'I Want Women to Have Their Rights'—Sojourner Truth, 1867," September 1975, p. 2.

5. "Needed: A Women's Center," September 1975, p. 2.

6. Cynthia Mutti, "Nudie Magazines," September 1975, p. 2.

7. Maggie Popkin, "Report on the Abortion Business," and Cynthia Mutti, "Female-Oriented Health Care," September 1975, pp. 4, 2.

8. Catherine Corliss, letter to Beverly Merrick, August 1995.

9. Lindsey Van Gelder, "Can Feminists Sell Out . . . on the Newsstand?" *Ms.*, July 1979, p. 23.

10. September 1976, p. 1.

11. "Hookers Converge on Washington, D.C.," September 1976, p. 1.

12. Corliss, letter.

13. "The Best of *Sojourner*," January 1982, p. 2.

14. Van Gelder, "Can Feminist Sell Out . . . ?"

15. Ibid.

16. "The Best of *Sojourner*," p. 2.

17. Van Gelder, "Can Feminists Sell Out . . . ?"

18. Ibid.

19. Ibid.

20. Ibid.

21. Corliss letter.

22. Karen Kahn, subscription letter, 1995.

23. Ibid.
24. "Open Editorial Policy," cited in masthead, 1995.
25. Corliss letter.
26. Kahn, subscription letter, 1995.
27. Kahn, subscription letter, 1995.

Information Sources

BIBLIOGRAPHY:
Van Gelder, Lindsey. "Can Feminists Sell Out . . . on the Newsstand?" *Ms.,* July 1979,
    p. 23.
INDEX SOURCES: Alternative Press Index; Popular Magazine Review.
LOCATION SOURCES: Leslie College Library, Cambridge, Mass.; New York Public
    Library; University of Cincinnati library; and other libraries. Also held at the
    National Registry of Microfilm Masters, Washington, D.C.

Publication History

PERIODICAL TITLES AND TITLE CHANGES: *Sojourner* (subtitle varies) (1975–present).
VOLUME AND ISSUE DATA: Vols. 1–   (September 1, 1975–present). Monthly.
PUBLISHER AND PLACE OF PUBLICATION: Sojourner Inc. Boston.
EDITORS: Alison Pratt (September 1975–November 1979); Martha Thurber (December
    1979–January 1983); Molly Lovelock (February 1983–May 1983); Shane Snow-
    don (August 1983–December 1986); Karen Kahn (October 1987–present).
CIRCULATION: Ulrich's, 1995: 40,000.

Beverly G. Merrick

SUFFRAGIST

Beginning in 1913, the *Suffragist* newspaper challenged the federal government
and hence American patriarchal authority with a militancy matched only by
Susan B. Anthony thirty years earlier and women's liberationists five decades
later.[1] *Suffragist* provided a much-needed voice for its publisher, the National
Woman's Party (NWP), which launched unprecedented picketing of the White
House on January 10, 1917, to protest for votes for women. Over the next two
years, about half of 1,000 women involved in peaceful NWP picketing and
related protests were arrested, and 168 were jailed.[2] *Suffragist* served as the
forum for the women to sound the battle cry for what, in effect, served as
American women's Boston Tea Party, since the pickets' eventual legal and
moral victories proved that the Bill of Rights spoke to women, too.

That's because before women won the vote in 1920, sex was the most salient
political division in America. While men controlled the public, political sphere,
women had expanded the private, domestic sphere until they wielded considerable influence in public affairs through massive organizing into women's clubs
and reform associations. The suffrage movement represented the convergence

of these two powerful and parallel, yet separate, strands of American political life. The college-educated, professional women who ran *Suffragist* typified the emerging public woman. *Suffragist* was unique, as it billed itself, as "the only political newspaper published in the United States by and for women."[3]

The first issue of *Suffragist* rolled off the presses in Washington, D.C., on November 15, 1913, with well-known journalist Rheta Childe Dorr at its helm. Its publisher was the NWP's predecessor, the Congressional Union (CU), a scrappy affiliate of the National American Woman Suffrage Association (NAWSA). CU chair Alice Paul and Vice Chair Lucy Burns had served sentences in London jails for their roles in British suffragette demonstrations. Back in the United States, the messianic Paul believed it essential to publish a national suffrage publication to secure a federal suffrage amendment. She and the brash CU soon parted from the conservative NAWSA, and the CU became the NWP in 1917.

Suffragist gave the women a voice to counter negative interpretations of NWP protests in the mainstream, male-dominated media.[4] When the press chided as bothersome early CU deputations to President Woodrow Wilson, the *Suffragist* argued that as disfranchised citizens, women had no recourse but to petition the White House for redress.[5] Editorials also explained why the NWP made the controversial decision to picket Wilson during wartime.[6]

The White House had tolerated the pickets until after the United States entered World War I on April 6. Crowds attacked the women. District police started to charge them in June with blocking the sidewalk. Dozens of women that summer and fall were sentenced for as long as seven months at Occoquan workhouse, although they always remained peaceful in the face of the violence directed at them by mobs and the police. Paul, secretly locked up in a District prison psychiatric ward, launched a hunger strike. Occoquan inmates followed, and officials began force-feeding them through tubes rammed down their throats. A court ruled the women's incarceration illegal, and at the end of November District officials released all of the suffragists rather than endure the barrage of criticism stirred by their maltreatment.[7] Wilson finally came out for the amendment a year to the day after the picketing began, and the House narrowly approved the amendment on January 10, 1918.[8] Dozens more women were arrested over the next year in more flamboyant demonstrations to prod Wilson to push the Senate to approve suffrage, which it finally did on June 4, 1919.[9]

Suffragist refused to be intimidated as the confrontation escalated. An editorial entitled "Kaiser Wilson" castigated the president, and a news article held him personally responsible for the mob attacks upon the women.[10] "An Arraignment of the Police" and "The United States Convicts Eleven More Women for Demanding Democracy" underscored the newspaper's defiant stance.[11] One editorial charged that authorities had plotted to "terrorize" the pickets.[12] An account of a particularly rough Occoquan incident described as a "revolution" sixteen suffrage prisoners' decision to hunger-strike.[13]

Such language linked *Suffragist* to the *Revolution,** the radical newspaper published in the late 1860s by Susan B. Anthony and Elizabeth Cady Stanton. *Suffragist*'s publishers consciously emulated *Revolution*'s righteous, combative tone but did not adopt its broad agenda for woman's rights. *Suffragist* limited itself to a single issue: obtaining a federal suffrage amendment.

Since the newspaper expected its subscribers to be activists, it provided forms and advice for readers to send resolutions, letters, petitions, and telegrams to representatives or to lobby their local press for supportive editorials.[14] Its staff's activism gave *Suffragist* moral authority to make demands on its readership— even advertising manager Betty Gram dropped nineteen pounds on a prison hunger strike, and Paul proofread *Suffragist* pages on the picket line.[15] The paper would have folded without sizable subsidies from donors.[16] Volunteers also sold the paper on the street.[17] "Selling the paper was a significant ritual of initiation for new [NWP] members," sociologist Marjory Nelson observed.[18]

Initially, *Suffragist* resisted the label "militant" bestowed upon the NWP by the mainstream press, since the women believed that their protests were legal and that their cause was in keeping with the democratic principles upon which the nation was founded. Further, suffragists had been called militant every time one of their new campaign techniques transgressed the bounds of acceptable female public behavior—gathering at conventions, speaking on soapboxes, and parading. But as the suppression intensified, the newspaper became more defiant; finally, by December 15, 1917, the cover featured an illustration of a pretty young woman entitled, "The Militant."

The cover subverted the popular image of the suffrage pickets. *Suffragist* cartoons enabled the Woman's Party to define itself rather than succumb to denigrating stereotypes. Clever cover illustrations by Nina Allender helped alter the image of the dour suffragist. *Suffragist*'s description of Allender also fitted its ideal of the "new woman" to whom the no-nonsense organization appealed: "a young, a very young, person—cool, efficient, unsentimental; with a feminine fondness for pretty clothes, and a fine new logical ruthlessness."[19] Yet Allender's work is better characterized as bemused rather than belligerent.

Early Allender cartoons played off traditional gender roles. In one, a woman labeled "East" sitting alone at a dance looks enviously at the men surrounding another woman labeled "West"—who flutters a fan labeled "Voter."[20] Allender became more confrontational as picketing arrests multiplied. "Celebrating Independence Day in the National Capital," for instance, shows police and a mob threatening a lone, banner-wielding woman.[21] One reader canceled her subscription over a cartoon satirizing Wilson.[22]

The weekly tabloid also marshaled photographs to make its case, publishing 173 photographs during the fiscal year 1917–1918.[23] Large, dramatic photos of police and hecklers harassing respectable-looking pickets vividly emphasized the lopsided confrontation between peaceful, middle-class women and federal authorities.[24]

News articles further exploited the David-versus-Goliath aspects of the saga. *Suffragist* claimed, for instance, that the officers who arrested Katharine Morey were four times her size.[25] The newspaper favored diminutives when describing its campaign: the NWP's was a "little protest," and the pickets "little" women.[26] One article referred five times to the "young" pickets.[27] Picket organizer Mabel Vernon decades later shrewdly analyzed the picketing strategy as "pursuing peaceful means to achieve a violent reaction."[28] The strategy gradually won some mainstream-press support as the administration's assault upon the pickets' constitutional rights became more extreme.[29]

The hunger strikers proved perfect propaganda fodder. "I am afraid this letter is not well written," concluded an articulate, smuggled note from inmate Mary Winsor printed in the *Suffragist,* "as I am rather light headed from hunger."[30] According to its imprisoned leader's orders, the *Suffragist,* now doubled to sixteen pages, missed no opportunity to highlight the women's martyrdom. Paul wrote to an executive committee member that force-feeding provided "excellent ammunition." "The more harsh we can make the Administration seem . . . the better," she wrote.[31]

Suffragist traced a direct line between the suffrage pickets and patriots of the Revolutionary War. Articles brimmed with quotes reiterating the women's irrefutable argument that the United States was hypocritical to fight for democracy abroad when it denied its female citizens the vote. The paper argued its case for votes for women on the natural rights philosophy that had electrified patriots during the Revolutionary War. One passionate editorial explained: "Physical discomfort, jail, humiliation, mob violence, terror, and torture cannot break spirits with a vision of freedom or silence a demand for justice."[32] Unlawful assembly charges like those facing the pickets had been used to "throttle free expression for more than a century," stated another of many articles that framed the standoff as a showdown over fundamental democratic principles.[33]

Free speech was at stake in 1917. More than one thousand dissidents during World War I were convicted under federal espionage and sedition acts, many sentenced to ten to twenty years in prison. More than fifteen publications were banned because they criticized the war effort.[34]

Suffragist also risked suppression. Individuals and publications had been charged under the sedition acts for messages less provocative than those carried by the banner bearers and reprinted in *Suffragist* alongside its harsh criticism of governmental repression. Editor Pauline Clarke was aware of the dangers, worrying that the paper sounded "contemptuous" of women's war work.[35] The *Suffragist,* in fact, ran virtually no news about women's war work, the tack taken by NAWSA to earn the vote.[36]

Yet *Suffragist* never was banned as seditious. The newspaper probably was insulated partly by the women's elite status and partly by a sense of male chivalry. Most important, the administration probably did not tamper with *Suffragist* because the NWP restricted its criticism to the nation's lack of progress in obtaining its reformist goal of attaining votes for women. The newspaper never specifically criticized the war or draft. Its message was less threatening to the administration than those delivered by banned socialist, anarchist, and foreign-language publications.

Still, the fifty thousand members of the NWP were viewed as traitors by many Americans. Boosting morale and forging a sense of solidarity among readers were among the *Suffragist*'s most important functions. Journalism historian Linda Steiner has analyzed how nineteenth-century suffrage publications identified, legitimized, and sustained a community of "new women" who challenged restrictive gender roles. "[S]uffrage papers . . . brought suffragists into a new and exhilarating world in which their lives had special purpose and meaning," she wrote.[37] *Suffragist* offered readers that same soaring sense of possibilities and sorority.

That sorority did not extend to African-American women, however, and the newspaper's casual racism remains the largest blot on its record of fighting for equal rights. Black faces never appeared in *Suffragist* photographs, and its columns contained neither news of numerous black suffrage clubs nor commentary on the double burden borne by African-American women seeking equal rights.[38] Several articles argued that women suffrage would uphold white supremacy in the South.[39] The pervasive racism of the era was captured in a cover illustration of Occoquan inmates captioned, "Refined, Intelligent Society Women act as Pickets and Are—Thrown into the Workhouse with Negroes and Criminals."[40]

Suffragist suffered an identity crisis not unlike its publishers' confusion about their postsuffrage role after the struggle shifted from the capital to the ratification battle in the states in mid-1919. The paper suspended publication in October 1919, reappearing as a monthly in February 1920.[41] Yet the revamped publication fell short of its goal of becoming a wide-ranging feminist publication.[42] A series entitled "What Next?" summed up the NWP's lack of direction.[43] Women's priorities changed during the postsuffrage decade, when feminism moved from the collective struggle for suffrage to individual struggles for careers. At the same time, powerful forces were at work to drive women back into the home.[44] After thirty-six states ratified the Nineteenth Amendment on August 26, 1920, even *Suffragist*'s title became an anachronism. It ceased publication in January 1921.

The publication had mirrored both the strengths and weaknesses of the NWP. It was passionate, idealistic, intelligent, articulate and courageous, and possessed great style. Yet the newspaper also was elitist, racist, and narrowly focused. Although some NWP members were working-class or socialists, most were like Paul, who held a doctoral degree in economics, or Vassar alumna Burns, making them part of what historian Nancy Woloch called a female "new elite."[45] The women's privilege helped explain their blindness to concerns of working-class women and others when the NWP trained all of its energy upon an equal rights amendment in the postsuffrage years.[46]

During its short life span, however, *Suffragist* served the CU and NWP well on many fronts. It legitimated the demand for a federal suffrage amendment. It kept women informed about the NWP campaign and educated women about politics. It created unity among its diverse and far-flung membership. It sustained the morale of beleaguered NWP workers. It kept suffrage in the public eye during wartime. It served as a voice for the NWP viewpoint. Perhaps most important, it served as the nation's conscience about the disparity between democratic rhetoric and voteless women.

Notes

1. "The right of citizens of the United States to vote shall not be denied or abridged by the United States or by any State on account of sex" (U.S. Constitution, Amendment 19).

2. Doris Stevens, *Jailed for Freedom* (New York: Boni and Liveright, 1920), p. 177.

3. Advertisement, February 21, 1914, p. 7.

4. See, for example "Silly, Silent and Offensive," *New York Times,* January 11, 1917, p. 14. NAWSA's newspaper also criticized the pickets. See "Pickets Are behind the Times," *Woman Citizen,* November 17, 1917, pp. 470–471.

5. "Heckling the President," June 11, 1914, p. 2; May 22, 1915, p. 4.

6. "Why We Keep on Picketing," September 1, 1917, p. 6.

7. "Miss Paul on Hunger Strike," *New York Times,* November 7, 1917, p. 13; "Hunger Striker Is Forcibly Fed," *New York Times,* November 9, 1917, p. 13; "Government Forced to Release Suffrage Prisoners from Occoquan," November 30, 1917, pp. 4–5.

8. "Susan B. Anthony Amendment Passes House," January 12, 1918, p. 5.

9. Most women served sentences only a few days long. See "Summation of Facts about the Demonstrations," August 31, 1918, p. 9; "President's Words Burn at Suffrage Protest in Front of White House," September 28, 1918, pp. 6–7; "American Women Burn President Wilson's Meaningless Words on Democracy," December 21, 1918, pp. 6–7.

10. August 18, 1917, p. 6; "President Onlooker at Mob Attack," August 18, 1917, p. 7.

11. July 14, 1917, 4; June 30, 1917, p. 5.

12. "Opposition, Direct and Indirect," July 13, 1918, p. 4.

13. December 15, 1917, p. 1; "A Week of the Women's Revolution," November 23, 1917, p. 4.

14. "Help Win Suffrage This Session," December 29 1917, p. 6; "The Vote in the House of Representatives/Telegraph Your Representative!" January 2, 1915, p. 6.

15. "Suffrage Picket Weds after Hunger Strike," *New York Tribune,* no date, Reel 95, National Woman's Party Papers: The Suffrage Years 1913–1920, microfilm edition, Thomas Pardo, ed. Sanford, N.C.: Microfilm Corp. of America, 1979; "Suffrage Paper Editor at Gates of White House," unidentified newspaper clipping, Reel 33, National American Woman Suffrage Association Papers, microfilm edition, Sanford, N.C.: Microfilm Corp. of America, 1979.

16. The CU and the NWP were great fund-raisers, raising three-quarters of a million dollars from 1913 through 1920 (Inez Haynes Irwin, *The Story of the Woman's Party* [New York: Harcourt, Brace, 1921], p. 4).

17. "Paper Sellers," December 6, 1913, p. 32; "Learning How to Be a Successful Suffragist," December 13, 1913, p. 45.

18. Marjory Nelson, "Ladies in the Street: A Sociological Analysis of the National

Woman's Party, 1910–1930'' (Ph.D. diss., State University of New York at Buffalo, 1976), pp. 156–157.

19. "Cartooning for the *Suffragist,*" July 29, 1916, p. 4. Allender had studied at the Pennsylvania Academy of Fine Arts and worked in studios in New York City and England, where an acrimonious divorce may have informed her feminist sensibilities. Past president of the District of Columbia suffrage associations, she had helped organize the CU's open-air meetings and picketed the White House (Official Program of the Woman Suffrage Procession, Reel 49, NAWSA Papers; "The Women Who Are 'Guarding' the White House Portals," *Washington Post,* February 4, 1917, p. 1).

20. January 22, 1916.

21. July 14, 1917, p. 1.

22. Alice Sheppard, *Cartooning for Suffrage* (Albuquerque: University of New Mexico Press, 1994), pp. 23–24.

23. Annual Report of the *Suffragist* Editorial Department, Reel 87, NWP Papers: The Suffrage Years.

24. See, for example, July 7, 1917, p. 7; August 10, 1918, p. 9.

25. "Six Suffragists Are Tried by the United States Courts," July 7, 1917, p. 5.

26. "The Fight Must Go On," July 7, 1917, p. 4.

27. "The Seventh Week of the Suffrage Picket," March 3, 1917, p. 5.

28. Sidney Bland, "Techniques of Persuasion: The National Woman's Party and Woman Suffrage, 1913–1919" (Ph.D. diss., George Washington University, 1972), pp. 113–114.

29. Linda Lumsden, " 'Rampant Women': The Role of the Right to Peaceably Assemble in the Woman Suffrage Movement, 1908–1919" (Ph.D. diss., University of North Carolina at Chapel Hill, 1994), p. 292 and notes.

30. "Notes from the Prisoners," August 24, 1918, p. 8.

31. Alice Paul to Dora Lewis, November 1917 (?), Reel 53, NWP Papers.

32. "Free Will," November 30, 1917, p. 8.

33. "An Arraignment of the Police," June 30, 1917, p. 5.

34. Margaret Blanchard, *Revolutionary Sparks: Freedom of Expression in Modern America* (New York: Oxford University Press, 1992), pp. 49, 76, 94.

35. Pauline Clarke to Clara Wolfe, November 5, 1917, Reel 51, NWP Papers: The Suffrage Years.

36. This absence contrasted to the expansive publicity accorded women's war work in NAWSA's newspaper, *Woman Citizen.* See, for example, "The Clearing House for Women's War Service," *Woman Citizen,* June 30, 1917, p. 87; "National Woman Suffrage and Congress," *Woman Citizen,* September 15, 1917, p. 292; "An Appeal to All Suffragists," October 19, 1918, *Woman Citizen,* p. 409.

37. Linda Steiner, "Finding Community in Nineteenth Century Suffrage Periodicals," *American Journalism,* Vol 1, 1983, pp. 2, 12.

38. At least thirty African-American suffrage groups or women's clubs that focused on gaining the vote existed in the 1910s (Rosalyn Terborg-Penn, "Afro-Americans in the Struggle for Woman Suffrage" (Ph.D. diss., Howard University, 1977), p. 313.

39. "National Suffrage and the Race Problem," November 14, 1914, p. 3; Helena Hill Weed, "The Federal Amendment and the Race Problem," February 6, 1915, p. 4.

40. September 15, 1917, p. 1. For other examples of racism, see "Justice," August 11, 1917, p. 9; "The Prison Note of Rose Winslow," December 1, 1917, p. 6.

41. Report of the *Suffragist* Circulation Department, February 1, 1918, Reel 87, NWP

Papers: The Suffrage Years; Report of the Executive Secretary, October 1917, Reel 87, NWP Papers: the Suffrage Years; Minutes of the Executive Committee of the Woman's Party, December 14, 1919, Reel 87, NWP Papers: the Suffrage Years.

42. *"The Suffragist*—A Feminist Magazine,'' undated, Reel 149, NWP Papers.

43. October 20, 1920, p. 235.

44. For an insightful analysis of how feminism changed in the 1920s, see Nancy Cott, *The Grounding of Modern Feminism* (New Haven, Conn.: Yale University Press, 1987).

45. Nancy Woloch, *Women and the American Experience* (New York: Knopf, 1984), p. 282.

46. The NWP in 1923 launched a new publication entitled *Equal Rights** to publicize its ill-fated campaign for that amendment.

Information Sources

BIBLIOGRAPHY:

Blanchard, Margaret. *Revolutionary Sparks: Freedom of Expression in Modern America.* New York: Oxford University Press, 1992.

Bland, Sidney. "Techniques of Persuasion: The National Woman's Party and Woman Suffrage, 1913–1919." Ph.D. diss., George Washington University, 1972.

Irwin, Inez Haynes. *The Story of the Woman's Party.* New York: Harcourt, Brace, 1921.

Lumsden, Linda. " 'Rampant Women': The Role of the Right to Peaceably Assemble in the Woman Suffrage Movement, 1908–1919." Ph.D. diss., University of North Carolina at Chapel Hill, 1994.

Nelson, Marjory. "Ladies in the Street: A Sociological Analysis of the National Woman's Party, 1910–1930." Ph.D. diss., State University of New York at Buffalo, 1976.

Sheppard, Alice. *Cartooning for Suffrage.* Albuquerque: University of New Mexico Press, 1994.

Steiner, Linda. "Finding Community in Nineteenth Century Suffrage Periodicals." *American Journalism* 1, 1983, pp. 1–15.

Stevens, Doris. *Jailed for Freedom.* New York: Boni and Liveright, 1920.

Terborg-Penn, Rosalyn. "Afro-Americans in the Struggle for Woman Suffrage." Ph.D. diss., Howard University, 1977.

Woloch, Nancy. *Women and the American Experience.* New York: Knopf, 1984.

INDEX SOURCES: National Woman's Party Papers: The Suffrage Years 1913–1920. Microfilm edition, Thomas Pardo, ed. Sanford, N.C.: Microfilm Corp. of America, 1979; National American Woman Suffrage Association Papers. Microfilm edition, Sanford, N.C.: Microfilm Corp. of America, 1979.

LOCATION SOURCES: Library of Congress; University of North Carolina—Chapel Hill library; and other libraries.

Publication History

PERIODICAL TITLE AND TITLE CHANGES: *Suffragist: Official Organ of the National Woman's Party.*

VOLUME AND ISSUE DATA: Vols. 1–9 (November 15, 1913–January–February 1921). Weekly (1913–October 1919); monthly (February 1920–January–February 1921, suspended publication October 1919–January 1920 inclusive).

PUBLISHER AND PLACE OF PUBLICATION: Congressional Union for Woman Suffrage (1913–March 3, 1917); National Woman's Party (March 3, 1917–January–February 1921). Washington, D.C.

EDITORS: Rheta Childe Dorr (1913–May 1914); Lucy Burns (May 1914–December 30, 1916); Vivian Pierce and others (January 24, 1917–1918); Sue S. White (May 24, 1918–September 1919): Florence B. Boeckel (1920–1921).

CIRCULATION: NWP, 1918: 5,599 paid circulation with some 15,000 free copies circulated to members of Congress, daily newspapers, and others.

Linda Lumsden

THESMOPHORIA

Thesmophoria was the voice of the "feminist witch." The term is not used disparagingly. It merely acknowledges the newsletter's roots, editorial philosophy, and many of its readers. Published by the Susan B. Anthony Coven # 1 in Los Angeles, the newsletter was designed to serve the informational needs of "Goddess-minded wimmin." The terms "Goddess-minded wimmin" and "feminist witch" were also applied to the periodical's founder, Zsuzsanna Budapest.

Z. Budapest, as she was usually called, came to journalism and American witchcraft in a roundabout way. Witchcraft, however, did run in her family in Hungary. Her mother and her aunt were both witches. "Mother talked to the ancestors if she wanted something, and she prayed on the winds. She had names for the winds. To her, every wind was a different entity," Budapest recalled.[1] Budapest shared some of her mother's "witch's" senses. They probably saved her life as she demonstrated against the Russian occupation of Hungary. As the demonstration marched toward the Parliament, she saw helmets in the grass, "and my witch sense told me that these were soldiers," Budapest recalled. "I thought, my god, they are coming to kill us." This time her witch's "sense" was accurate. Thousands died, including four of her classmates.[2] She then emigrated, first to Vienna and eventually to the United States, where she married, had two children, and lived a typical suburban existence until 1967, when she left her home and family, hitchhiked to Los Angeles, and began a new part of her life.[3] This part of her life was marked with activism, feminism, and journalism.

When she arrived in Los Angeles, she got involved in the women's liberation movement, as feminism was called in the late 1960s. She became a staffer at the Women's Center and quickly displayed her organizational skills, running the speaker's bureau and starting a clinic, the women's liberation school, the antirape squad (which became the Rape Hotline). She also dabbled in journalism as editor of *Sister* magazine. In 1971, Budapest "came out" as a witch and held her first Sabbat in December with six close friends, all members of the first women's center in Los Angeles.[4]

Eight years passed between that first Sabbat and the launch of the newsletter initially called *Themis* (later renamed *Thesmophoria*). In those years, Budapest developed a feminist witchcraft following, established the Susan B. Anthony Coven # 1, and created the Feminist Wicca, a religious group committed to the worship of the "Goddess."[5] Budapest had actually planned to start her newsletter much earlier, but she was arrested on a charge of fortune-telling for reading tarot cards, a conviction that was upheld on appeal.[6]

When the newsletter finally appeared in midsummer 1979, the periodical— and the coven as publisher and Budapest as editor—challenged the principles of many institutions. Contrary to many modern religions, the newsletter carried the gospel of American witchcraft and a spiritual tenet that called for no established temples, no centralized leadership, and no male gods. Contrary to some of the principles of journalism and business, the newsletter debuted without a substantial readership base, advertising contracts, or a regular editorial staff. Like many newsletters, this one was founded on a commitment to a cause— in this case, a religious/social one. Or, as the newsletter explained in its second issue:

> We chose THEMIS for the communication between ourselves because we need a unified voice, a visible articulation in the chaos of birthings, and to show that religious instinct and social instinct are mother-daughter to each other.[7]

Themis offered an intriguing combination of religious principles ("Learn the Aspects of the Goddess"), practical advice ("Ideas on Spellcasting" by Janet Roslund, "Menstruation Ritual" by Lady Medea Ostara), departments appropriate to the readership ("Herb of the Month"), news ("Report from Halloween"), editorials ("Three Festivals . . . Their Lessons" by Z. Budapest), letters to the editor ("Editorial—Mirror Back Reality"), and advertising (for "Womantours" travel agency and "Juno Corner" with ads for special services such as psychic and tarot card readings).[8] In spite of the editorial energy, the newsletter seemed to have financial problems from the beginning.

One thousand copies were printed of the first issue. However, there is little evidence that there was a preexisting readership base for the periodical—aside from the coven itself; and the five-dollar subscription cost was expensive for the time. *Themis* accepted advertising almost from the beginning. However, special services related to witchcraft did not appear to provide much of an advertising base, and the newsletter apparently never had an advertising/sales staff. Because the newsletter was launched without adequate financial underwriting, it quickly ran into trouble. By the third issue, *Themis* was reporting financial problems and urged readers to give additional support.[9] On the positive side, the newsletter was gaining subscribers. Beginning in 1979, the newsletter started to list subscribers. In the Samhain issue, *Themis* listed sixty-six new subscribers; in the Winter Solstice issue, fifty-six were listed. The publication claimed it had ten thousand readers in 1980.[10] Subscribers came from across the nation—from Salem, Massachusetts, to Eugene, Oregon; from Tampa, Florida, to Canada. Some of the reason for this increase might have been due to Z. Budapest herself. Budapest was a kind of media star in those days, holding press conferences and appearing on talk shows not just in Los Angeles but throughout the western states.[11] Certainly, a unified organized circulation drive was not the explanation. No one was ever credited with the job of circulation solicitation.

Themis, however, was not just a periodical. It was a way of life. *Themis's* readers were involved in their publication. They met often for "Themis work parties"[12] to process letters and lay out and bundle the publication. *Themis* also started a "Tribunal of the Goddess, an alternate justice system for womon [*sic*]." Covering both criminal and civil cases, this tribunal was seen as an alternative to patriarchal courts. (In criminal cases, the "punishment" might be a demonstration or a hex. "Imagine the fear in even the most cynical criminal knowing he is being hexed by hundreds of witches!"[13])

However, readers were not just witches or followers of the "goddess movement." They were also responsible citizens. The newsletter also spoke to their other interests. The newsletter came out against the nuclear missile buildup; in favor of a healthy, primarily vegetarian diet; and for lesbian sex.[14]

Los Angeles did not seem to be the ideal home for Budapest or the newsletter. In 1980, Budapest announced plans to escape Los Angeles' pollution and life-style and move to Oakland. As Budapest explained, "Maybe it's all that warm sunshine, or lack of oxygen, but I found L.A. mentally lazy in the last couple of years. Hard to get committed wimmin to share the Goddess work, while the Sabbats were always attended very well, the work in between wasn't. I really need to work with more of a crew than just haphazard volunteer work."[15]

The move to Oakland brought little peace to Budapest. She soon had to confront legal problems. In 1980, Zeta Tau Alpha sorority in Indiana told Budapest that she would have to change the name of her newsletter. The name "Themis" was covered by a copyright held by the sorority. Since the sorority did not approve of the content of Budapest's newsletter, the name would have to be changed. "Thesmophoria," the collective name for women's festivals dedicated to the goddess Themis, was selected as the new name, although, Budapest confided, "amongst outselves we still say Themis, because it is still her paper, but on the letterhead, Thesomorphia [*sic*] will appear."[16]

Thesmophoria debuted with the Summer Solstice issue in 1981. Although the newsletter had a different look, thanks to the new graphic design by Nina Romberg Andersson of Dallas, the publication continued the numeration of *Themis* and the subtitle of the old periodical, "Voice of the New Women's Religion." The editorial focus, the content, the staff, and the editor all remained the same.

Although the name change untangled the publication's legal problems, it failed to address its financial issues. The move to Oakland did little to improve things. Circulation quickly declined from a high of ten thousand in 1980 to one thousand four years later. The financial report for 1981 showed that the periodical was not making a profit; to shore up finances, subscription rates went up, and the periodical introduced a new level of support, "Friends of the Goddess."[17] Pleas apparently did little to ease the financial crunch. With the Summer Solstice issue of 1982, the newsletter was typed in an attempt to control costs. The editor hoped that it would be a temporary measure. Not until the Spring Equinox issue in 1983 did the periodical return to set type. In that issue, however, the editor was again begging for help—in obtaining new subscriptions, in getting new advertising, in providing editorial copy.[18] On the fifth anniversary of the periodical, *Thesmophoria* writer Cindy Dunigan explained that the move to Oakland had not solved anything. There were "many problems with money, time and energy."[19]

For much of the time when *Thesmophoria* faced this financial crisis, Z. Budapest was on sabbatical. With the Lammas 1983 issue, Budapest returned and in her wake made many changes. The "Laughing Goddess Grotto," a drain on the finances and energy of the coven, was closed. She seemed to bring editorial energy back to the publication. *Thesmophoria* announced plans for special issues, including one on sex and eroticism; new ties to the women's community, including the need to get involved with the National Women's Studies Association; and a new circulation drive (for each seven names, the reader could get one free year of the newsletter).[20] Although Budapest's return had energized the publication, the newsletter remained on the edge financially. As Dunigan explained, *Thesmophoria* was marginal: "We run on marginal time, with marginal support and a very marginal budget."[21]

By 1987, even Budapest's enthusiasm could not solve the publication's problems. Two issues were skipped as the periodical moved to a new location. The Hallowmas issue was the last for *Thesmophoria*. The numeration was continued under a new name, *Thesmophoria's New Moon* in 1988. The newsletter, under Janet Roslund as editor, continues its work.

Notes

1. "Glimmerings of the Goddess: Campaign of a Religious Revolutionary, Z. Budapest," *Magical Blend.* 29, 1990, p. 40.

2. Sharon McDonald, "Z. Budapest, Witch in Progress," *Lesbian Tide,* March/April 1980, p. 6.

3. "Glimmerings of the Goddess," p. 40.

4. Z. Budapest, "Happy Winter Solstice," Winter Solstice 1980, p. 1.

5. Leslie Shephard, *Encyclopedia of Occultism and Parapsychology,* vol. 1 (Detroit: Gale Research, 1978), p. 133.

6. McDonald, "Z. Budapest," p. 7; Midsummer 1979, p. 3.

7. "Who is *Thesmis?*" Lammas 1979, p. 1.

8. Lammas 1979, pp. 1–3; Samhain 1979, p. 2; May Eve 1980, p. 2; Hallomas 1980, p. 1.

9. Samhain 1979, p. 1. See also Valerie Kirkgaard, "Prepare to Celebrate, to Adorn and Donate!!!" Candlemas 1980, pp. 1–3.

10. Z. Budapest, "Thesmophoria Needs More Subscribers," Lammas 1984, p. 1.

11. "Report from Halloween," Winter Solstice 1979.

12. "Themis Work Parties 9980," Winter Solstice 1979, p. 3.

13. Ta-Urt, "Tribune of the Goddess Is Born!" Lammas 1980, p. 1.

14. Kathy Tessmer, "We Will Stop Nuclear Madness," Autumn Equinox, p. 2; Cindy Dunigan, "Nuclear Nutrition," Spring Equinox 1983, p. 2; Georgiana Bowley, "Utopian Sex," May Eve 1984, p. 1.

15. Z. Budapest, "Happy Winter Solstice!" Winter Solstice 1980, p. 1.

16. Z. Budapest, "What Happened to Themis?" undated, p. 1.

17. "Financial Report 9981," Hallowmas 1981, p. 2; "Subscription Price," Lamas 1981, p. 3; "Friends of the Goddess," Hallowmas 1981, p. 3. The new price for subcribing was ten dollars a year (seven dollars for low-income individuals). An individual "Friend of the Goddess" paid twenty dollars a year; a matron, one thousand dollars a year.

18. "Support Thesmo!" Spring Equinox 1983, p. 2.

19. Cindy Dunigan, "MIDSUMMER," Summer Solstice 1983, p. 1.

20. "Special Notice," Lammas 1983, p. 2; Georgia Bowley "NWSA and the Goddess," Autumn Equinox 1984, p. 1; "Thesmophoria Statement of Purpose," Hallowmas 1984, p. 2.

21. Cindy Dunigan, "Spring Equinox," Spring Equinox 1985, p. 1.

Information Sources

BIBLIOGRAPHY:
Brown, Denise C. "Feminist and Witch." *WomanSpirit* 6, Fall 1979, p. 59.
Budapest, Z. "My Salem in L.A.." *WomanSpirit* 2, Fall Equinox 1975, pp. 8–9.
McDonald, Sharon. "Z Budapest, Witch in Progress." *Lesbian Tide* 9, March/April 1980, pp. 6–7.
———. "Christian Feminist vs. Goddess Movement." *WomanSpirit* 6, Summer 1980, pp. 26–27.
Shephard, Leslie, ed. *Encyclopedia of Occultism and Parapsychology.* Vol. 1. Detroit: Gale Research, 1978.
Snider, Jerry, and Michael Peter Langevin. "Glimmerings of the Goddess: Campaign of a Religious Revolutionary, Z. Budapest." *Magical Blend* 29, 1990, pp. 38–42, 97.
INDEX SOURCES: None.
LOCATION SOURCES: State Historical Society of Wisconsin, Madison, and other libraries. Holdings typically scattered.

Publication History

PERIODICAL TITLE AND TITLE CHANGES: *Themis* (1979–1981); *Thesmophoria* (1981–1987); *Thesmophoria's New Moon* (1988 to present).
VOLUME AND ISSUE DATA: Vols. 1–   (Midsummer 1979–present). Eight times a year.

PUBLISHER AND PLACE OF PUBLICATION: Susan B. Anthony Coven #1. Los
    Angeles (1979–1980); Oakland, Calif. (1980–present).
EDITORS: Zsuzsanna Budapest, Jaime Stone, Janet Roslund (1979–1980); Z. Budapest
    and others (1980–1982); Janet Roslund (1982–1983); Z. Budapest and Janet Ros-
    lund? (1983–1988); Janet Roslund (1988?–present). (Editors not always listed.)
CIRCULATION: Ulrich's, 1995: 2,000 (peak circulation: 10,000 in 1980).

Kathleen L. Endres

A TRUE REPUBLIC

Sarah M. Perkins, suffragist, temperance advocate, and moral reformer, was *A
True Republic*. That represented both a strength and a weakness. Perkins had
the strength to start the publication and edit it month after month. However, her
editorial vision was limited. Her concerns and her comments seldom reached
beyond the limits of the city of Cleveland or the state of Ohio. Although, for a
time, it was the organ of the Federal Suffrage Association of the United States,
A True Republic never gained a national stature, for it was limited by Perkins'
perspective. Nonetheless, *A True Republic* represents an interesting study of
Ohio reform journalism.

In spite of its role within the Federal Suffrage Association, *A True Republic*
was never solely a suffrage publication. Although Perkins believed that women
should have the right to vote, the editor committed her newspaper to a broader
editorial mission. In the first issue in July 1891, Perkins promised a newspaper
of *"Franchise, Temperance and Moral Reform."*[1] Throughout its fourteen years
of existence, *A True Republic* remained true to those ideals. This editorial direction was in keeping with Perkins' own eclectic reform career.

Perkins was a relative newcomer to Cleveland when she started *A True Republic*. She had been born in Cooperstown, New York, and married a clergyman,
the Reverend Orren Perkins. After living in New England for many years, she
and her husband moved back to Cooperstown to run a seminary there. The two
moved to Cleveland in 1881.

In Ohio, Perkins was best known for her work with the Woman's Christian
Temperance Union (WCTU). She was state superintendent of infirmary work
for the WCTU and often visited shut-ins at institutions. As Cleveland activist
W. A. Ingham reported, Perkins "sees many evils that ought to be remedied,
and has the moral courage to bring these things to the notice of State officials.
She believes that women should have more power to protect their homes from
intemperance and other vices, and hence ought to have the ballot."[2] Not surprisingly, Perkins was also active in the Ohio State Suffrage Association. Beyond her reform work, Perkins was also known as a lecturer and a writer with
a number of novels to her credit.

Perkins had found that suffragists and reformers were scattered in towns and
cities throughout Ohio, working in isolation. Without a newspaper, they had no

means to communicate. *A True Republic* was designed to be the voice for middle-class Ohio women who wanted the vote to improve society, who wanted the vote to remedy the community of liquor, who wanted the vote to protect their homes and families. "Woman Suffrage is the foundation to all reform," Perkins wrote in the newspaper's first issue, July 1891.[3]

Everything about the *True Republic* was uplifting, from the "News Notes" that offered snippets of news about women's improving society nationally and in Cleveland, to convention summaries of the WCTU, the State Suffrage Association, and the Literary Guild of Cleveland; from the poetry and serialized novels (often written by Perkins), to editorials that beseeched readers to do their part to improve the quality of life in Cleveland and Ohio.

One of the best ways to achieve that, according to Perkins' *True Republic*, was to shut down all the saloons. "Should we allow sixteen hundred saloons in our city [Cleveland] to tempt people to their ruins?" Perkins asked her readers. All kinds of ills would be eliminated if the saloons were closed—from riots to strikes. "Our voters should protect our boys and our homes, or else give women the power of the ballot that they may do the work themselves."[4]

Women did not need the vote to make some changes. They needed to visit the infirmaries of the state. They needed to serve on the state Board of Charities. They needed to monitor the number of illegitimate children born in the insane asylums and the lack of Christian services. They needed to demand improvements.[5]

In 1892, Perkins was given the chance to become a national suffrage figure. However, neither she nor her newspaper proved equal to the task. Judge Francis Minor of St. Louis wrote several articles for the *Forum* and the *Arena* that posited that Congress had the authority to pass a law to give women the right to vote for members of the House of Representatives. The Federal Suffrage Association was organized to push for a *law* giving women the right to vote.[6]

As the editor of Ohio's only "suffrage" paper, Perkins was an important recruit for the new organization. She was made chairman of the Federal Suffrage Association's executive committee and helped draft the group's constitution. In this early period of the association, both Perkins and her newspaper had important roles to play. By 1893, *A True Republic* called itself the official organ of the Federal Suffrage Association of the United States. Although it held this august title, little changed within the newspaper itself.

The monthly continued to emphasize issues and events relating to Cleveland and Ohio. For the sake of their families and especially their sons, the women of Cleveland were urged to close down the saloons of the city.[7] Women of the city, also, should not cooperate with government attempts to regulate houses of prostitution. Although Perkins believed in moral reform, she did not like how the Cleveland leadership was going about it. The names of prostitutes were to be registered, and the women would be forced to undergo medical examinations. No such requirements were put on men. "We trust our Christian women will not lend their influence to any such method of inequity," Perkins wrote.[8]

A *True Republic*'s affiliation with the Federal Suffrage Association was short-lived. Soon, the newspaper was without any "official" connection with any organization, although the newspaper regularly covered the news of the local WCTU, suffrage, and Sorosis groups. Perkins was also continuing an active lecture career. In 1893, 1894, and 1896, the editor wrote about her adventures on the lecture circuit of New York, New Jersey, and Ohio. Perkins sold subscriptions to her newspaper at those lectures. That probably represented a needed revenue source. As early as 1893, Perkins was complaining about subscribers who failed to renew on time.[9]

In 1895 and 1896, Perkins' readers shared the editor's experiences at the WCTU World Temperance Convention. Shortly after returning from Europe and embarking on yet another lecture tour, Perkins announced plans to redesign her publication. In a bold move (in light of the problems with delinquent subscriber accounts), Perkins announced that *A True Republic* would be enlarged in a new magazine format. Instead of eight pages, the monthly would grow to twenty, with a beautiful white front cover. The subscription price went up to one dollar from the earlier fifty cents.[10]

The new format allowed more local news stories on the activities of Cleveland and Ohio women's reform groups; news of suffrage progress in other states; profiles of national and local suffrage, temperance, and educational leaders (primarily women); essays by contributors; poetry and short stories by Perkins and others; and more letters from readers (primarily from Ohio). This shift in the editorial content was reflected in the publication's new mission statement: "Devoted to Literature, Philanthropy and Reform."

Although suffrage and temperance continued to be a major concern of the *Republic,* the editor began addressing other issues. She came out against lynching ("Truly such scenes [lynching] are a disgrace to our country, and any official who cannot enforce the law had better resign and let a better man take his place"[11]); proposed a sort of urban renewal plan ("Give them [the poor within the city of Cleveland] the use of the vacant lots and let them be self-reliant"[12]); endorsed enlightened treatment of servants ("brighten lonely hours and make life a pleasure instead of a burden"[13]); and opposed Cleveland plans to displace women workers with voting men.[14]

In 1900, Perkins again went to the WCTU's world conference. After the conference in Edinburgh, Scotland, she traveled in Europe, writing back about the amount of liquor consumed on the continent. ("I saw so much wine and beer drinking abroad that I felt that our best efforts in the temperance cause was but a pebble cast upon the seashore. The people looked at us [the WCTU women] as harmless lunatics."[15]) While Sarah Perkins was away, her daughter Emma edited the magazine. Emma Perkins, a teacher of Latin in the Woman's College of Western Reserve University of Cleveland, had been active in the magazine ever since she graduated from Vassar. She had written essays, and her activities at the college had been regularly reported in the *Republic.* Eventually, she, along with prominent reformer Sarah K. Bolton of Cleveland and the Reverend O. P. Gifford of Buffalo, were listed as contributors. (That list was extended to Harriet Stanton Blatch of Ithaca, New York, daughter of Elizabeth Cady Stanton, a longtime friend of Sarah Perkins.)[16]

Perkins' return from the world WCTU conference marked the final stage of the life of the *Republic.* The redesign and the slight editorial shift that accompanied that change had brought the magazine a certain measure of financial stability. Advertising increased, although Perkins still wanted more readers and even offered a copy of her new temperance book, *Six of Them,* with every new prepaid subscription. When Perkins returned from that world WCTU, meeting, the editorial mix remained the same—with essays, poetry, short stories, news, and editorials designed to be a "strong, healthy influence in the home."[17] However, the tenor of some of the editorials had been radicalized.

Perkins, the wife of a clergyman, began criticizing men of the cloth. "Every new man of the cloth," she wrote, needed to settle the question of "woman's sphere." "The latest idea is that woman is encroaching upon man's sphere, and in so doing is not entitled to the deference usually given to the sex." That seemed "strange advice" to Perkins, especially since the congregation would not survive if women left. A woman would never define man's sphere, and a man of "good taste" should not define woman's. "A wise man would not attempt it,"[18] she concluded. In this instance, she took only one unnamed minister to task. In January 1904, she complained about the city's entire religious community, the press, and the lawmakers.

> While one hundred thousand men are stumbling down to drunkards' grave each year and to a drunkards' eternity and the churches are silent and the law-makers are silent, the press should cry aloud and spare not. The people should be warned.[19]

Perkins, the mother of a professor, began criticizing college teachers. She bemoaned young female college graduates who fail to take their places within their families and within their communities. Perkins blamed some of the college teachers for the selfishness of these women. "Too many of these teachers are 'shut ins' and take little interest in our common humanity. They live in the past and are looking backward and not forward."[20]

In 1904, Perkins ended the year on a positive note, forecasting the continuing success of her magazine. The *Republic,* as it entered its fifteenth year, had increased the number of its subscriptions.[21] The quality of contributions never seemed better. Yet, in spite of Perkins' optimism, the *Republic* never made it to 1905. The December 1904 issue was apparently its last.[22] Sarah M. Perkins, eighty-one, died shortly after.[23]

A True Republic had a surprisingly long life in light of its reform base and the lack of institutional financial support. Although it never achieved a national stature, the monthly did have a role to play in the Ohio and especially the Cleveland reform community. It was the only "suffrage" publication in the state at the time, and it was also the only state publication that intertwined a range of reforms. The *Republic* gave a voice to middle-class, reform-minded Ohio women, as the letters to the editor indicated. It kept those same women informed on local, state, and (to a lesser extent) national developments. By and large, this information was not readily available in the general newspapers of the day. Thus, *A True Republic* fulfilled its local and state mission, if not a national one.

Notes

1. July 1891, p. 4.
2. W. A. Ingham, *Women of Cleveland and Their Work* (Cleveland: W. A. Ingham, 1893), p. 287.
3. "Salutatory," July 1891, p. 4.
4. "Darkest Cleveland," January 1862, p. 4.
5. "Women Needed on Our State Board of Charities," November 1891, p. 4.
6. In this regard, the association differed from the National Woman Suffrage Association (NWSA) in that the NWSA wanted a national *amendment.* The federal suffrage group believed that Congress had the authority to pass a *law* to allow women to vote for members of the House of Representatives (Ida Husted Harper, *The History of Woman Suffrage,* vol. 5 [New York: National American Woman Suffrage Association, 1922], pp. 656–657).
7. "Where Is the Remedy," September 1892, p. 4.
8. "Regulating Impurity," July 1893, p. 4. See also S. M. Perkins, "The Regulation of Vice a Fallacy," January 1894, p. 4.
9. "Lecture Route," May 1893, p. 4; "Our Subscribers," May 1893, p. 5.
10. "ENLARGEMENT OF A TRUE REPUBLIC," December 1896, p. 4.
11. "Lynching," July 1897, p. 130.
12. "Vacant Lots," February 1898, p. 30.
13. "Our Hired Girls," November 1987, p. 210.
14. "The Latest," November 1898, p. 210.
15. January 1901, p. 10.
16. See front covers, January 1904 and October 1904. In Elizabeth Cady Stanton's obituary, Perkins discussed her friendship with the reformer. Admitting that she disagreed with Stanton's stance on religion, Perkins said that Stanton had been a subscriber who enjoyed the *Republic.* The newspaper often printed Stanton's lectures and letters ("Died," November 1902, pp. 241–242).
17. "A True Republic," December 1902, p. 276.
18. "Woman's Sphere," March 1902, p. 60.
19. "The New Year," January 1904, p. 12.
20. "College Girls," July 1902, p. 156.
21. "1905," December 1904, p. 276.
22. In many references to *A True Republic,* the ending date of December 1904 is followed with a question mark. However, this author has not found any other issues of this publication.
23. She had been run over by a coal wagon ("Sarah M. Perkins," *The Woman's Tribune.* December 23, 1905, p. 90).

Information Sources

BIBLIOGRAPHY:
Harper, Ida Husted. *The History of Woman Suffrage.* Vol. 5. New York: National American Woman Suffrage Association, 1922.
Ingham, W. A. *Women of Cleveland and Their Work.* Cleveland: W. A. Ingham, 1893.
"Sarah M. Perkins." *The Woman's Tribune,* December 23, 1905, p. 90.
INDEX SOURCES: None.
LOCATION SOURCES: Oberlin College; University of Pittsburgh; and other libraries.

Publication History

PERIODICAL TITLE AND TITLE CHANGES: *A True Republic.*
VOLUME AND ISSUE DATA: Vols. 1–14 (July 1891–December 1904). Monthly.
PUBLISHER AND PLACE OF PUBLICATION: Sarah M. Perkins (1891–1904). Cleveland (1891–1904).
EDITORS: Sarah M. Perkins (1891–1904).
CIRCULATION: Unknown.

Kathleen L. Endres

$$\underline{\qquad} U \underline{\qquad}$$

THE UNA

When wealthy suffragist Paulina Wright Davis introduced *The Una* in 1853, it was by no means clear that public interest would be piqued by a publication with such a narrow focus. Devoted mainly to suffrage and "the elevation of Woman," *The Una* (a mystical character from Spenser's *Fairy Queen* who symbolized truth) challenged prevailing publishing wisdom that dictated that magazines for women needed to present a broad spectrum of literature, fashion, and domestic concerns of woman's sphere. While *The Lily** had appeared a few years prior to promote temperance, *The Una* was the first publication to promote the broader goals of the woman's rights movement.[1]

Although *The Una* survived only two years and ten months, it is a landmark in suffrage history because its appearance signaled a professional approach to the battle for woman's rights and because it served as a prototype on which later suffrage publications were based. As Davis herself saw it, a journal was "the most powerful engine for the change of public sentiment."[2] At the time it first circulated, however, *The Una*'s singularly focused feminist approach as a magazine met criticism and cynicism. One prominent woman journalist commented at the time that the approach of *The Una* was flawed: "People do not want a whole meal of one dish without sauce, or a whole paper on one subject," she stated. "[I]t is better to reach the public ear through papers already established and devoted to any number of things, than to get up an auditory of their own," she added.[3] This critic apparently discounted the fact that mainstream newspapers, rather than seriously reporting on the ideas and goals of the fledgling woman's movement, mocked and satirized it. In the wake of the Seneca Falls convention in 1848, "Penny Press" newspapers routinely laughed at the suffragists. Typical of this treatment was the attitude of editor James Gordon Bennett, whose *New York Herald* chided the women after a convention in 1850:

What do the leaders of the women's rights convention want? They want to vote and hustle with the rowdies at the polls. They want to be members of Congress, and in the heat of debate subject themselves to coarse jests and indecent language. They want to fill all other posts which men are ambitious to occupy, to be lawyers, doctors, captains of vessels and generals in the field. How funny it would sound in the newspapers that Lucy Stone, pleading a cause, took suddenly ill in the pains of parturition and perhaps gave birth to a fine bouncing boy in court![4]

Recognizing this tendency by the press to mock rather than report, delegates to the earliest woman's rights conventions discussed the possibility of creating a suffrage paper but never acted upon it. This early organization also failed to give the early suffrage papers either monetary or moral support.[5] Only after a number of these periodicals, *The Una* included, failed because of financial difficulty did the suffrage organizations realize they needed vehicles to disseminate information and attract followers.

But, when Davis published the inaugural monthly issue of *The Una* on February 1, 1853, she offered her journal as an alternative to the "Ladies' Books, Ladies' Magazines, and Miscellanies," arguing that American women needed "stronger nourishment; and with a work so peculiarly their own, they need at least one paper which will give a correct history of its progress and be a faithful exponent of its principles." She promised that her journal would "discuss with candor and earnestness, the Rights, Relations, Duties, Destiny and Sphere of Woman. Her Education—Literary, Scientific, and Artistic.—Her Avocation—Industrial, Commercial, and Professional. Her Interests—Pecuniary, Civil and Political."

Davis cautioned that *The Una* would "not cover so wide a field as the paper proposed at the convention, nor is it offered as a substitute for that." Showing uncanny public relations savvy for her day, Davis stated that a journal devoted to woman's rights did not negate the real "necessity of having daily and weekly journals with all the appliances for creating public sentiment and elevating the tone of the female mind, that would be used in a political campaign, or in awakening an interest on any other question."[6]

When Davis delved into publishing, she already was one of the leaders of the woman's rights movement and a primary organizer of the first National Woman's Rights Convention, which was held in October 1850 in Worcester, Massachusetts. Like many of the early suffragists, Davis came to the woman's rights movement by way of antislavery activism. Born Paulina Kellogg in New York in 1813, she married a wealthy merchant, Francis Wright, in 1833. Together, they resigned from the local Baptist church to protest its conservative politics and helped arrange an antislavery convention in Utica, New York. Around this time, she met woman's rights leader Elizabeth Cady Stanton and became interested in woman's rights. She also studied anatomy and physiology, and, when her husband died, she became the first woman to lecture on the previously unmentionable subject of woman's anatomy and, as such, was the source for some women of the only accurate information they had about their own bodies.[7] She even used a naked mannequin as a visual aid. She was one of the promoters of the controversial costume for women, bloomers.[8]

She married Thomas Davis, a well-to-do jewelry manufacturer, and moved to his home in Providence, Rhode Island, in 1849.[9] From there Davis began her venture into publishing. She financed the project herself but appealed in print to personal friends "for long subscription lists, and for aid with thought and pen."[10] Her journal published the writing of noted woman authors of the day, including Sara Clarke Lippincott ("Grace Greenwood"), Sara Payson Willis Parton ("Fanny Fern"), and Elizabeth Cady Stanton. She also provided space for published "calls" to woman's rights conventions that were held around the nation and then reported on the meetings after they occurred. The back pages of her magazine included notices for women physicians and publicity for medical colleges that accepted women and other schools that also would accept women.

Although specific circulation figures were never published, Davis noted that she had exhausted the supply of copies of the first issue. During the year 1853, she also published the names of subscribers who contributed the one dollar annual fee, including many of the prominent names in the woman's rights movement. By the end of the first year, about six hundred people had been named as subscribers. Not surprisingly, the lists included Susan B. Anthony, Lucy Stone, Elizabeth Cady Stanton, and Lucretia Mott. Some supporters sent more than the one dollar subscription fee to help the publication. Davis herself conceded that *The Una*'s readers were a select group. "For though it did not number its readers by 'several' thousands, it has had a spontaneous patronage that has plainly indicated its need," she stated.[11] In another reference to circulation, Davis wrote that editing her journal had established "pleasant relations with hundreds whose faces we have never seen."[12] She stated that *The Una* had circulated to all of the states and territories of the United States and also had subscribers in Europe.

During 1853, when *The Una* was first published, Davis' husband also was elected to Congress, and she accompanied him to Washington, D.C. There, however, her reputation preceded her, and she was, at first, ostracized by the women because of her activities.[13]

The first issue of *The Una* set the editorial tone for subsequent numbers. Inspirational fiction by a woman writer was serialized; an essay by the Reverend A. D. Mayo discussed "The Real Controversy between Man and Woman"; a critique of Charles Dickens' current novel *Bleak House* lamented his treatment of women; short articles publicized action by leaders of the suffrage movement and improvements for women's health and education; an editorial page began a lengthy discussion of "Woman as Physically Considered"; an essay argued the "Reasons Why Woman Should Define Her Own Sphere"; and numerous letters were published. Adhering somewhat to the traditional fare for magazines of the day, the journal included poetry and was peppered with quotes as filler from renowned philosophers and literary figures. Yet, it was clear that this inaugural suffrage publication had a pointed agenda. The editorial on "Woman as Physically Considered" set out "to prove that woman is not man's inferior." The essay conceded that men were physically more impressive than women but noted, in the flowery, metaphoric language of the day, that "[t]he rank weed overshadows the modest flower and prevents its natural development."[14] The essay on sphere argued that woman needed to become concerned in the more public avenues previously denied to her. "She needs to have her whole nature developed and strengthened by exercise; her attention directed to a larger circle of wants than those of her own household. She needs fully to apprehend the condition of the world; in fact, to realize the actual of the life she wishes her children to fill. This she cannot do, without some experience in its struggles and its triumphs."[15] Throughout the life of the publication, articles included such topics as "Emancipated Women" and "Woman the Reformer" and consistently sought to illustrate the important roles for women in society.

After publishing twelve issues in an eleven-month period (in order to begin volume 2 with the January number), Davis reflected that the editorial content might not have been as strident as some people would have wanted. Davis, however, said she envisioned a "slow revolution" toward equal rights for women. "If woman was intended for the place we claim for her, the stern rigidity of established institutions and prejudices may retard for a while the practical recognition of her rights; but as surely as the rivulet seeks the distant sea, she shall emerge at last into the full fruition of her glorious destiny," she wrote.[16]

Although Davis might have worried that the editorial content was too subtle, she tackled subjects that even today are considered important feminist issues. One article, for example, discussed the horror of wife abuse. The article cited specific instances of abuse, including a woman who had been beaten to death and another woman who had been tied to her bed before her husband poured sulfuric acid down her throat. "Woman is blest with a power of endurance which eminently fits her for the situation she occupies in the domestic circle, where, with few exceptions, she is treated as a drudge, or a doll, an abused tool of passion, or a nonentity," the article stated. "But there is a point beyond which endurance ought not to go."[17] Another article stated that there were three classes of women: the rich, who were "the idols of men, their play things"; the poor woman, who was "not out of her sphere sawing wood, picking rags in the gutters, peddling fish in the street, in short doing any hard drudgery which will give her a subsistence"; and, finally, "a class of 'strong minded women' who will not consent to be slaves or toys."[18]

By December 1854, Davis was exhausted from the strenuous burden of publishing the sixteen-page monthly journal. Davis lamented in print that she had tried "in vain to convince women that they needed an organ which could give to the future a correct history of this revolution."[19] Davis announced that she would suspend publication until she could find a publisher and restore herself to sufficient health so that she could write again. Yet, she also voiced her concern that, minus *The Una,* the woman's rights movement was left without any "other medium of communication than the chance notices of political or other papers."[20] Reports of *The Una*'s death, however, were premature. Davis regrouped and recruited new blood to assist her. She called upon Caroline Healy Dall to assist her as coeditor, while Davis herself temporarily moved her editorial base to Washington, D.C., for several months. The next edition—vol. 3.1— appeared only three weeks late, despite the editorial changes.[21] Dall wrote later that she was as surprised as *The Una*'s readers to see that she had been listed as one of the editors, but, apparently willing to assume the duties, she immediately began contributing lengthy editorial features that obviously helped ease the writing responsibilities for Davis. Born in 1822, Dall, a former teacher turned missionary, had written articles and fiction for *The Una* prior to assuming some editorial duties. But, her entrée into the editor position signaled for Dall the beginning of her full-time commitment to the cause of woman's rights.

With the January 1855 issue, the publishing duties were transferred to S. C. Hewitt in Boston. Although the task of publishing shifted to Hewitt, the financial burden of the struggling monthly was carried by Davis herself throughout the publication's life.[22] Davis's personal resources were sufficient to carry the magazine for a time, but clearly the publication was not in a healthy financial situation. Several notices were published in the magazine noting that subscribers had lapsed in payment of their one dollar annual fee and that "the hundreds needed to carry on an enterprise of this kind, are made up on single one dollars."[23] The new publisher solicited workers to canvass for *The Una* in the hope of increasing its circulation base and also announced that the publication would begin printing a small number of "choice advertisements." The June issue, for example, devoted the last two pages to advertisements for such products as the *New York Tribune,* medicated vapor baths, carpeting, and recently published books.

With volume 3, Davis also began publishing a list of regular contributors: Mrs. E. Oakes Smith, Mrs. F. D. Gage, Mrs. E. Cheney, Mrs. Peter, Elizabeth C. Stanton, Elizabeth P. Peabody, and Lizzie Linn.

Publishing difficulties, however, continued to plague the journal. In May 1855, an unsigned editorial lamented the arduous task of compiling editorial matter for publication: "Please furnish copy, says our Publisher," the editorial stated. "Yes sir, we wish we were made of copy." The author then noted how difficult it was both to maintain a proper household and to find the energy needed to write sufficient copy to fill an issue. "We cannot write, Mr. Publisher, till, in New England parlance, we have put everything to rights."[24]

Throughout its short life (only thirty-four issues were printed), *The Una* advocated a firm and steady course toward equal rights for women and saw full woman suffrage as the most important symbol of that goal. Even after Dall joined Davis as editor, they reiterated their editorial philosophy. *The Una* was politically independent and officially represented no one organization. The editors themselves promoted civil and religious freedom, education for women, equal compensation for women, and the right of women to work in any area they wanted. They advocated property rights for women and, most important to them, full suffrage for women.

The Una also published fiction designed to illustrate the truths and principles to which the publication ascribed. A serialized version of George Sand's *Spiridion* began in July 1855 after a note by Dall, who had translated the work from the original. She urged readers not to condemn the author as a woman "who dishonors her sex, who holds no common faith nor hope with us." Readers were asked to withhold judgment of her character until they completed reading the serial. "Whatever else she is, she is a devoted seeker after truth, and whoever reads *Spiridion* to the end, will find it a work worthy of a noble woman and an upright soul."[25]

Throughout its last year of publication, the magazine showed signs of ill health, despite the infusion of nearly one hundred new subscribers, paid in advance, who had been recruited by the prominent suffragist Lucy Stone.[26] The new publisher had promised when he took the reins in January 1855 that *The Una* would be published for at least another year. He also voiced lofty hopes of then perhaps publishing more frequently. But the journal ceased publication without explanation in October 1855. In fact, the serialized version of George Sand's *Spiridion* was incomplete. In that last number, the publisher apologized for the lateness in which it was issued and promised, falsely, as it happened, that the next month's edition would "be issued in better season."[27]

After *The Una* folded, Davis continued her activism for suffrage. She wrote occasionally for the subsequent suffrage publication, *The Revolution,** and helped found the New England Woman Suffrage Association. When she died in 1876 of rheumatism and heart disease, Stanton was the chief speaker at her memorial service. Davis's coeditor, Caroline Dall, spoke and wrote extensively on the subject of woman's rights until 1867 and then turned her attention to preaching, authoring children's stories, and writing her memoirs. She died of pneumonia at the age of ninety in 1912.

Notes

1. Mari Boor Tonn, "*The Una,* 1853–1855: The Premiere of the Woman's Rights Press," in Martha M. Solomon, ed. *A Voice of Their Own: The Woman Suffrage Press, 1840–1910* (Tuscaloosa: University of Alabama Press, 1991), p. 48.

2. P.W.D., "Regrets," February 1855, p. 25.

3. Jane Swisshelm as quoted in P.W.D., "Regrets."

4. As quoted in Eleanor Flexner, *Century of Struggle: The Woman's Rights Movement in the United States* (Cambridge, Mass.: Belknap, 1959), p. 82.

5. Linda Steiner, "Finding Community in Nineteenth Century Suffrage Periodicals," *American Journalism* 1, 1983, p. 6.

6. "The Introduction," February 1, 1853, p. 4.

7. Carol Hymowitz and Michaele Weissman, *A History of Women in America* (New York: Bantam, 1978), p. 99.

8. Ibid., p. 103.

9. E.C.S., "Reminiscences of Paulina Wright Davis," in Elizabeth Cady Stanton, Susan B. Anthony, and Matilda Joslyn Gage, eds., *History of Woman Suffrage,* vol. 1, 1848–1861 (Rochester, N.Y.: Charles Mann, 1889), pp. 283–286.

10. P.W.D., "The Introduction," February 1, 1853, p. 4.

11. P.W.D., "Regrets."

12. "To Our Readers," December 1854, p. 376.

13. E.C.S. "Reminiscences of Paulina Wright Davis," p. 286.

14. "Woman As Physically Considered," February 1, 1853), p. 8.

15. A. H. Price, "Reasons Why Woman Should Define Her Own Sphere," February 1, 1853), p. 10.

16. Paulina W. Davis, "Ending and Beginning," December 1853, p. 182.

17. "For the Una," July 1853, p. 84.

18. Untitled letter from Paulina Wright Davis, May 1853, p. 63.

19. December 1854, p. 376.

20. Ibid.

21. P.W.D., "Regrets."

22. E.C.S., "Reminiscences of Paulina Wright Davis," p. 287.

23. "A Word in Private to Subscribers," June 1854, p. 281.

24. Unsigned editorial, May 1855, p. 72.

25. Caroline H. Dall, "Appeal," July 1855, p. 97.

26. April 1855, p. 57.

27. "This Number Late," October 1855, p. 160.

Information Sources

BIBLIOGRAPHY:

Flexner, Eleanor. *Century of Struggle: The Woman's Rights Movement in the United States.* Cambridge, Mass.: Belknap Press, 1959.

Hymowitz, Carol, and Michaele Weissman. *A History of Women in America.* New York: Bantam, 1978.

James, Edward T., Janet Wilson James, and Paul S. Boyer, eds. *Notable American Women, 1607–1950.* Cambridge, Mass.: Belknap Press, 1971.

Mott, Frank L. *A History of American Magazines.* Vol. 2. Cambridge: Harvard University Press, 1957.

Solomon, Martha M., ed. *A Voice of Their Own: The Woman Suffrage Press, 1840–1910.* Tuscaloosa: University of Alabama Press, 1991.

Stanton, Elizabeth Cady, Susan B. Anthony, and Matilda Joslyn Gage, eds. *History of Woman Suffrage.* Vol. 1, 2d ed. Rochester, N.Y.: Charles Mann, 1889.

Stearns, Bertha Monica. "New England Magazines for Ladies, 1830–1860." *The New England Quarterly* 3.4, 1930, pp. 627–656.

Steiner, Linda. "Finding Community in Nineteenth Century Suffrage Periodicals." *American Journalism* 1, 1983, pp. 1–15.

INDEX SOURCES: Not indexed.

LOCATION SOURCES: Library of Congress and other libraries.

Microfilm available in American Periodical Series.

Publication History

PERIODICAL TITLE AND TITLE CHANGES: *The Una,* (1853–1855).
VOLUME AND ISSUE DATA: Vols. 1–3 (February 1853–October 1855). Monthly.
PUBLISHER AND PLACE OF PUBLICATION: Paulina Wright Davis (1853–1854); S.
    C. Hewitt (1855). Providence, R.I. (1853–1854); Boston (1855).
EDITORS: Paulina Wright Davis (1953–1854); Paulina Wright Davis and Caroline Healy
    Dall (1855).
CIRCULATION: Unknown.

Agnes Hooper Gottlieb

UNION SIGNAL

In the years following the Civil War, a variety of cultural, political, and even technological forces combined to bring about the creation of the Woman's Christian Temperance Union (WCTU) and its flagship publication, the *Union Signal.* From its inception, the *Union Signal* has commented on, and supported, a number of causes, including woman suffrage, labor matters, peace and disarmament issues, and child welfare. It has never lost sight of its original purpose: exploration of the moral, physical, social, and economic costs of alcohol use.

Even before the formation of the WCTU in 1874, temperance organizations had been active in American life. By the early 1800s, public drunkenness had become a "serious cultural problem" in the country, and temperance organizations were formed to deal with it.[1] These early prohibitionist groups, however, were largely dominated by men, who often did not understand or consider the special problems men's drinking created for women. For women, drinking was often an issue of personal and familial safety that threatened their well-being and very often their lives.[2] Not only were women the victims of domestic alcohol-related violence, but they were commonly harassed in public—sometimes even in churches—by drunken men. Although after the Civil War some states allowed women to divorce alcoholic husbands, most women lacked the financial means to do so or to raise their children alone.[3] Drunken men stood in powerful contrast to the relative powerlessness of American women; as historian Ruth Bordin put it, "Nothing was as destructive to a powerless woman's existence as a drunken husband."[4] Women had little legal/political power to take control of their own lives; the WCTU, however, offered women, many of whom had directly experienced the negative effects of alcohol, an opportunity finally to exert some control.[5] The *Union Signal* was their voice.

Although, from 1883 to 1903, the *Union Signal* was owned and published by the Woman's Temperance Publishing Association, not the WCTU, the latter group has had editorial control of the publication since its inception.[6] Consequently, it is not unfair to view the *Union Signal* primarily in terms of the goals and objectives of the WCTU, as it is "a repository of information suitable to be disseminated among various national [and local] affiliates."[7] Indeed, the

Union Signal has been "the major force holding the WCTU together between conventions" and provides readers "a comprehensive view of the activities of the Union and its work across the country."[8]

The first issue of the *Union Signal* was published on January 4, 1883,[9] and it set the tone for the first few years of publication. Combining "education, proselytizing, and entertainment,"[10] articles routinely discussed the physical effects of alcoholism,[11] equated prohibitionism with abolitionism as a campaign against moral evil,[12] planned the best ways to encourage temperance in the home and to enact prohibitionist laws,[13] and commented on the economic aspect/waste of alcohol consumption.[14] Early on, the periodical advocated instruction in the public schools about the medical/health effects of alcohol on the body (efforts that would eventually develop into modern-day "health classes").[15] Considerable space was given in each issue to correspondence and news from local WCTU chapters, as well as Sunday school exercises (always drawing a lesson about temperance) and the regular Band of Hope Lesson ("scientific" discussions regarding alcohol production and the like). Poems, short stories, puzzles and word games, and small news items recounting murders and other crimes committed by people under the influence of alcohol rounded out each issue. A small number of advertisements (food products, cards and sheet music, cookbooks, travel information) appeared weekly, growing steadily through the first couple of years of publication to fill two to three pages (of sixteen) by 1885. Circulation by the fall of 1885 was fifteen thousand.[16]

Although the topic of woman suffrage had been featured in the *Union Signal* from the beginning, editorial content in the periodical's first two years seemed somewhat to reflect the influence of the WCTU's first president, Annie Wittenmyer (1874–1879), whose interest and focus were almost exclusively temperance.[17] After editorship of the periodical passed to Mary Allen West in 1885, however, the sentiments of then-president Frances Willard (1879–1898) began to be asserted more strongly as the WCTU and the *Union Signal* became increasingly aligned with the suffrage movement as well as other feminist causes, even those unrelated to temperance.[18]

The WCTU perceived the suffrage movement as a vital ally, primarily because members believed that men would never pass prohibitionist legislation on their own. As Frances Willard stated in the *Union Signal*'s first issue, "For every man who professes allegiance to Christ, who has a voice in making the laws that so carefully protect the rum-power, there are two women professing allegiance to Christ, who do not have a voice."[19] Throughout the 1880s and into the 1890s (Willard herself became editor in 1892), articles and editorials linking temperance and suffrage movements appeared in virtually every issue of the *Union Signal,* culminating in a long series on suffrage by suffrage leader Alice Stone Blackwell in 1894.[20] Pro-suffrage comments from WCTU officers/members were also given ample coverage; for example, Ella J. Fifield opined that national prohibition "will be soonest accomplished by the ballot in the hands of women," while Fanny L. Chunn stated that "until we get the ballot we will keep on doing the moulding sentiment work that we have been engaged in for over twenty years."[21]

As Frances Willard's views became increasingly prominent in the pages of the *Union Signal,* so, too, did the view that women were the main moral agents in home and society,[22] not merely in relation to temperance issues; by the 1890s, the *Union Signal* could assert that "war will be put away in exact mathematical proportion to the degree of influence that women attain in government."[23] Indeed, a sharply feminist tone emerged throughout the mid-1880s to mid-1890s, from condemnations of women's "long habit of subjection to men in all matters of money,"[24] to the chastisement of the "mental vision that has made reasonable men squint at the human race—seeing but half of it."[25] Women's accomplishments, temperance-related or not, were given considerable exposure (particularly in the regular "Some of Our Women" feature).

Under Willard's presidency, the *Union Signal* strongly supported many leftist social causes; for instance, a series of articles by W. Howatt Gardiner on Christian socialism ran from February to April 1891. Labor conditions in America were frequently decried, and personal property ownership was often blamed for the poverty and economic inequities in American society.[26] These sentiments most likely resulted from Willard's view that poverty caused intemperance, rather than its being caused *by* intemperance—a radical shift from party-line WCTU thinking.[27]

Throughout the 1880s the WCTU experienced great membership growth, spurred to an exceptional degree by the *Union Signal,* whose readership naturally reflected the makeup of the WCTU itself—white, upper-middle-class, well-educated Protestant women.[28] As of January 1891, the periodical's circulation had grown to eighty-five thousand,[29] and advertisements for all manner of books, pamphlets, and health and household items often filled four or five pages. But all was not well with the WCTU or the *Union Signal.* By 1894, circulation had dropped off to about sixty-seven thousand, and the periodical's parent company (the Woman's Temperance Publishing Association [WTPA]) faced financial difficulty.[30] Frances Willard's death in 1898 ushered in sweeping changes within the WCTU and the pages of the *Union Signal* as Lillian Stevens assumed control of both the organization and the periodical.[31]

At the WCTU's 1898 convention, issues of peace, international arbitration, labor, and equal pay for women were not addressed for the first time in many years; the tenor of the convention sounded an almost exclusively temperance theme—a stance that would immediately be reflected in the *Union Signal* under Stevens.[32] Despite an occasional article such as "The Importance of Child Safety" or "The Disarmament Congress,"[33] and although woman suffrage continued to be championed, the long articles and series about feminist and labor issues began to be replaced with pointedly Christian-tinged articles on temperance themes.[34] Sunday school lessons, which had quietly been dropped under Frances Willard's editorship, reappeared, and although the "About Women" column continued to report non-temperance-related accomplishments by women, by 1903 the feature (along with world news blurbs) had been relegated to the back pages (both had appeared in the front of the periodical under Willard). Such recurring features as "Reform News" and "At Home and Abroad," which dealt almost exclusively with temperance themes, formed the backbone of the *Union Signal* under Stevens.[35]

At least two explanations have been offered about the *Union Signal*'s sudden change in tone under Lillian Stevens. It could be that Frances Willard's leftism simply did not reflect the views of most rank-and-file WCTU members, who had grown irritated with her politics, her inattention to the financial problems of the WTPA, and her apparent lack of Christian commitment (reflected in her advocacy of the ecumenical Parliament of Religion).[36] Under this scenario, Lillian Stevens simply moved the WCTU and the *Union Signal* back to where its members wanted it to be. It has also been theorized, though, that the more "radical" members of the WCTU simply began leaving the group during the 1890s to join other social reform groups that had sprung up since the establishment of the WCTU, thus leaving a conservative core group with little interest in any other reform but prohibition.[37] In any event, the public perception of the WCTU under Stevens' leadership began to change from that of "the best, most respected, most forward-looking women in town to narrow-minded antilibertarians riding a hobbyhorse."[38]

In the years leading up to the passage of national Prohibition in 1919, the *Union Signal* was unsurprisingly full of articles on that topic, to the virtual exclusion of any other matter. The periodical routinely provided blank pro-Prohibition petitions for readers to sign, clip, and mail to government representatives, and the text of various Prohibition bills and resolutions was regularly printed, as were maps and lists showing the states that had passed their own antiliquor laws or that had ratified the national Prohibition amendment. Special effort was put into arguing that national Prohibition would not be unconstitutional or a violation of individual rights.[39] Many articles described how conditions had improved in the states that had outlawed liquor[40] and, after national Prohibition's passage, in the country as a whole.[41]

Until the United States became involved with World War I in 1917, the only *regular* departure from the constant drumbeat of antiliquor messages during this period was the periodical's continued support of suffrage, reflected in a major 1915 article entitled "Enfranchisement of Women Indication of Advance of Civilization."[42] During American involvement in the war, the *Union Signal* mixed patriotism with its prohibitionism, describing how antiliquor laws were helping the war effort.[43] By 1914–1915, the *Union Signal* was running far fewer ads than before the turn of the century, and most of those hawked temperance-related posters, songs, and books; there were fewer ads for secular books, dictionaries, or encyclopedias or leisure/food items than under Frances Willard. By 1918–1919, virtually *no* ads appeared in the *Union Signal.*

After the passage of national Prohibition, a broader social consciousness returned to the pages of the *Union Signal,* as the periodical began again to address nontemperance-related issues, particularly those related to peace/disarmament, immigration, and child welfare.[44] However, as it began to seem possible, and then likely, that Prohibition was going to be repealed, the periodical again focused almost exclusively on this single issue—pleading with authorities to enforce Prohibition laws, defiantly denying the failure of the amendment, and quoting prominent citizens' support for Prohibition.[45] The periodical consistently asserted that most Americans, in fact, were Prohibitionists, citing an analysis of 131 wet-dry elections that found that "drys always win when more than 70% of adults vote."[46] The interesting exception to the increasingly desperate attempt to save the Eighteenth Amendment from repeal was the consistently strong focus on peace and disarmament issues, perhaps reflected most strikingly by the antiwar statements of scientist Albert Einstein and political leaders David Lloyd George and Herbert Hoover that were prominently featured on the cover of the October 24, 1931, issue.[47]

For many years following the repeal of Prohibition, the *Union Signal* devoted most of its space on the deleterious effects of alcohol, narcotics, and cigarettes, with occasional complaints against vices such as gambling or sexual license and an underlying worry about the overall decline in Christian values. Liquor advertisements received strong opposition, as did the Sunday sale of alcohol, the serving of alcohol on airplane flights, and the raising of legal drinking ages:[48] the 1964 surgeon general's report on smoking received extensive exposure.[49] While the legacy of Frances Willard and her disdain of "one-sided movements" was frequently invoked,[50] little evidence of her brand of social activism (or even a sustained breadth of interest in non-alcohol-related topics) appeared in the pages of the *Union Signal* for almost three decades following Prohibition's repeal.

Though the periodical has always included reprinted material, the present-day *Union Signal* has become very much of a "digest-style" publication; virtually all of its editorials and feature articles are reprints from other sources. A typical issue contains three or four features on a wide variety of topics, such as smoking, drug abuse, sexual abstinence and AIDS prevention, child abuse and domestic violence, and—as always—alcohol abuse,[51] along with recurring departments such as the "Noontide Hour of Prayer," the "President's Page," the "Washington Letter," devotional lessons, and discussions of WCTU affairs. Apart from items available from the WCTU's publishing arm, the Signal Press, the current *Union Signal* carries no advertisements.

While the *Union Signal's* politics can fairly be called conservative—reprints of editorialist Cal Thomas's columns frequently appear,[52] and editor in chief Rachel B. Kelly was nominated as the 1996 vice presidential candidate for the Prohibition Party[53]—there has been movement in recent years to broaden the appeal of both the publication and the WCTU itself.[54] According to the managing editor, the *Union Signal* is geared toward members *and* nonmembers.[55] The periodical is not included with membership in the WCTU but must be requested as a separate subscription. However, the current circulation of four thousand does not necessarily reflect the number of readers, as the periodical is distributed to many schools, libraries, and doctors' offices throughout the country. According to the managing editor, the *Union Signal* is more popular with, and more widely read by, non-WCTU members than members.[56]

The WCTU and the *Union Signal* have been criticized by some historians for abandoning social reform advocacy and settling into "a parochial, conservative attempt to prevent fundamental change,"[57] but such a view must be balanced with an acknowledgment of the group's role in making women aware of their own abilities. As Ruth Bordin puts it, "Before 1873 most Union women had worked only in their churches. By 1900 they had a full generation's experience behind them in political action, legislation, lobbying, and running private charitable institutions."[58] It is quite true, as some critics have pointed out, that the WCTU did not advocate the dismantling of the patriarchal family structure; however, the WCTU's ideal family gave *women's* concerns special prominence, and arguments to improve family life for women "represented a direct response to the interests of the vast majority of women."[59]

Notes

1. Randall C. Jimerson, "The Temperance and Prohibition Movement in America, 1830–1933," p. 1, in Randall C. Jimerson, Francis X. Blouin, and Charles A. Isetts, eds., *Guide to the Microfilm Edition of Temperance and Prohibition Papers* (Ann Arbor: University of Michigan, 1977), pp. 1–21. For information on other factors contributing to the formation of temperance groups, see Jack Blocker, *American Temperance Movements: Cycles of Reform* (Boston: Twayne, 1989), pp. 65, 67; Helen E. Tyler, *Where Prayer and Purpose Meet: The WCTU Story, 1874–1949* (Evanston, Ill.: Signal Press, 1949), p. 1.

2. Blocker, *American Temperance Movements,* pp. 76, 78.

3. Ibid., p. 74.

4. Ruth Bordin, *Woman and Temperance: The Quest for Power and Liberty, 1873–1900* (Philadelphia: Temple University Press, 1981), p. 162.

5. Ibid., pp. 161–162.

6. Martha M. Folk, "Series XXI: *The Union Signal* 1883–1933," p. 368, in Jimerson, Blouin, and Isetts, eds., *Guide to the Microfilm Edition of Temperance and Prohibition Papers,* pp. 368–370.

7. Ian Tyrrell, *Woman's World/Woman's Empire: The Woman's Christian Temperance Union in International Perspective* (Chapel Hill: University of North Carolina Press, 1991), p. 50.

8. Bordin, *Woman and Temperance,* p. 91.

9. The *Union Signal* resulted from a merger of two temperance publications: the national WCTU publication, the *Woman's Temperance Union* (1875–1878; name changed to *Our Union,* 1878–1882) and an Illinois WCTU publication, the *Signal* (1880–1882).

10. Bordin, *Woman and Temperance,* p. 91.

11. J. J. Ridge, "No. V—Injury to the Body," February 1, 1883, p. 7; Henry M. Hurd, "The Hereditary Influence of Alcoholic Indulgence upon the Production of Insanity," August 6, 1883, pp. 7–8.

12. Mary B. Willard, "Old Methods and New Laws," March 22, 1883, p. 8; "Slavery," letter from Virginia J. Kent, November 13, 1884, p. 5.

13. Mrs. W. A. Ingham, "The Church, God's Agency," January 4, 1883, p. 3; W. G. Eliot, "The Temperance Cause, and the Best Methods for Its Advancement," January 18, 1883, pp. 2–4.

14. "Does Drink Make Hard Times?" June 4, 1885, p. 2; "Who Pays for It?" June 25, 1885, p. 2.

15. Emily V. Keever, "Scientific Instruction," June 5, 1884, p. 5; interview with Michael Vitucci, managing editor, August 15, 1995.

16. Jane L. McKeever, "The Woman's Temperance Publishing Association," *Library Quarterly* 55, 1985, p. 372.

17. Randall C. Jimerson, "Series III: Woman's Christian Temperance Union: 1853–1934," p. 56, in Jimerson, Blouin, and Isetts, eds. *Guide to the Microfilm Edition of Temperance and Prohibition Papers* pp. 55–100.

18. Bordin, *Woman and Temperance,* pp. 91–92.

19. Frances E. Willard, "Christ in Government," January 1, 1883, p. 2.

20. Alice Stone Blackwell, "Dr. Buckley on Equal Suffrage," weekly from September 6, 1894 to October 11, 1894.

21. "What State W.C.T.U. Presidents Think," October 11, 1894, pp. 3–4.

22. "Is Womens [*sic*] Work Done in the States' [*sic*] Where Prohibition Is Enforced?" June 25, 1885, p. 5.

23. Untitled news report, January 27, 1892, p. 1.

24. "Woman and Business," June 11, 1885, p. 2.

25. Untitled article, July 26, 1894, p. 1; "Sex in the Sunday-School," October 18, 1894, pp. 7–8.

26. S.E.V. Emery, "Significance of Labor Troubles," November 24, 1892, p. 4; C. H. Zimmerman, "The Eight Hours Day and the Unemployed," August 3, 1893, p. 3; "The [Pullman] Strike," July 26, 1894, p. 8; "An Old Author on the Social Problems of Today," September 13, 1894, p. 8.

27. Jimerson, "Series III," p. 57.

28. Bordin, *Woman and Temperance,* pp. 94, 160.

29. McKeever, "The Woman's Temperance Publishing Association," p. 374.

30. Bordin, *Woman and Temperance,* p. 142.

31. The editorship of the *Union Signal* cannot readily be determined simply by consulting the masthead, particularly in the Mary Allen West and Frances Willard eras and in the period immediately following Lillian Stevens' death in 1914. Joint editorships are sometimes credited to a variety of individuals, and the names of West and Stevens were retained in the masthead for a period after their deaths. It must be noted that, since at least the days of Prohibition, the editor in chief title has been honorarily given to the sitting WCTU president; the actual day-to-day operations of the publication are run by the managing editor.

32. Bordin, *Woman and Temperance,* pp. 151–152.

33. April 27, 1899, pp. 4–5, 8.

34. "The Power of Truth," January 12, 1899, p. 8; "Beer in the Army," April 13, 1899, p. 2; John F. Cowan, "Christian Endeavor and Temperance," April 13, 1899, pp. 4–5.

35. Bordin reports that only eight of sixty-eight "Reform News" pieces in October

1899 did not concern temperance. This was a typical percentage (Bordin, *Woman and Temperance,* p. 152).

36. Jimerson, "Series III," p. 58.

37. Bordin, *Woman and Temperance,* p. 154.

38. Ibid., p. 155.

39. Richmond P. Hobson, "National Constitutional Prohibition Not an Invasion of States' Rights," May 14, 1914, p. 1; Richmond P. Hobson, "Would National Prohibition Involve an Encroachment upon the Police Powers of the State?" May 21, 1914, pp. 3–4.

40. "First-Hand Testimony from Governors of Prohibition States," May 21, 1914, p. 5; "Prohibition in West Virginia Surpasses Expectations," September 3, 1914, p. 3.

41. "Prohibition Led Jewelry Manufacturers into Adoption of Valuable Process," September 3, 1925, p. 9; James Stevens, "Sober Workingmen under Prohibition," January 30, 1926, pp. 5, 7; "Fewer Children Forced to Labor since Prohibition," January 30, 1926, p. 7.

42. John M. Evans, March 18, 1915, p. 7.

43. Elizabeth P. Anderson, "Food Will Win the War," June 6, 1918, p. 5; Emma Sanford Shelton, "Prohibition a God-Send to War Workers in Washington," July 25, 1918, p. 5.

44. Representative articles on peace and disarmament include Lella A. Dillard, "Consciousness of World Citizenship Will Bring World Peace," July 2, 1925, p. 2; "Seek Justice, Supremacy of Law and Social Harmony in Paths of Peace, President Coolidge Urges," October 24, 1925, p. 4; Lella A. Dillard, "Armistice Day Appropriate for Peace and Arbitration Programs," November 6, 1926, p. 6. Immigration articles include Ella A. Boole, "Americanization the Imperative Need of the Hour," June 6, 1918, p. 5; "American Citizens in the Making," January 23, 1919, pp. 6, 7, 13; Rose A. Davidson, "What Some of Our Centers Are Doing," October 24, 1925, p. 7. Typical child welfare articles include Edith F. Lee, "Child Welfare a Live Issue in Forty-Eight States," May 27, 1925, p. 7; Edith F. Lee, "Work through Child Welfare for Law Observance and Law Enforcement," January 30, 1926, p. 6; Valeria H. Parker, "Traffic in Women and Children," October 22, 1927, p. 652.

45. "Prominent Citizens of America Reaffirm Belief in Prohibition," May 27, 1925, pp. 4–6; Gifford Pinchot, "Eighteenth Amendment Not a Failure," October 24, 1925, p. 3; Theodore Christianson, "Failure to Enforce Prohibition Threatens State Sovereignty," April 26, 1930, p. 262; Ella A. Boole, "Observance and Enforcement—Not Repeal," November 29, 1930, pp. 723–724, 729–730, 733.

46. October 29, 1932, p. 663.

47. Carrie Chapman Catt, "Joining Hands for Peace," October 17, 1931, p. 606; May Bell Harper, "Eight Conferences for Cause and Cure of War," February 4, 1933, p. 71; "Blessed Are the Peacemakers," November 11, 1933, p. 680.

48. Izora Scott, "Into the Laws of the Land," October 14, 1939, p. 619; Mrs. Glenn G. Hays, "What WCTU Women Propose," April 3, 1954, pp. 206, 212; Mrs. Glenn G. Hays, "The President's Page," February 11, 1956, p. 5; Mildred B. Harman, "Churches Lobby, Too," November 28, 1964, pp. 6–7.

49. "The Surgeon General's Report," February 8, 1964, p. 3; Mildred B. Harman, "The Report on Smoking—A Design for Learning," February 8, 1964. pp. 6–7.

50. For example, see Emma Kidd Hulbert, "Teamwork with a Genius," February 12,

1966, pp. 3–4, or any of the special Willard issues that appeared annually in February for many years.

51. For a concise description of current WCTU concerns, see "The 1994 National WCTU Presidential Address: The Things That Matter Most," by Rachel B. Kelly, September/October 1994, pp. 10–15.

52. "The Ghost of 'Winter Holiday' Present Haunts America," January/February 1993, p. 28; "Biggest Media Gods See the Light on Conservative Christians," September/October 1994, p. 28; "Values Are Lost without God," November/December 1994, pp. 12–13.

53. Rachel B. Kelly, "National Prohibition Convention," July/August 1995, pp. 8–9.

54. Rachel B. Kelly, "Reengineering for the 21st Century," May/June 1994, pp. 6, 23.

55. Michael Vitucci, Interview.

56. Ibid.

57. Jimerson, "The Temperance and Prohibition Movement in America," p. 20.

58. Bordin, *Woman and Temperance,* p. 157.

59. Blocker, *American Temperance Movements,* pp. 83–84.

Information Sources

BIBLIOGRAPHY:

Blocker, Jack. *American Temperance Movements: Cycles of Reform.* Boston: Twayne, 1989.

Bordin, Ruth. *Woman and Temperance: The Quest for Power and Liberty, 1873–1900.* Philadelphia: Temple University Press, 1981.

Folk, Martha M. "Series XXI: *The Union Signal* 1883–1933." In Randall C. Jimerson, Francis X. Blouin, and Charles A. Isetts, eds., *Guide to the Microfilm Edition of Temperance and Prohibition Papers.* Ann Arbor: University of Michigan, 1977, pp. 368–370.

Jimerson, Randall C. "Series III: Woman's Christian Temperance Union: 1853–1934." In Randall C. Jimerson, Francis X. Blouin, and Charles A. Isetts, eds., *Guide to the Microfilm Edition of Temperance and Prohibition Papers.* Ann Arbor: University of Michigan, 1977, pp. 55–100.

———. "The Temperance and Prohibition Movement in America, 1830–1933." In Randall C. Jimerson, Francis X. Blouin, and Charles A. Isetts, eds., *Guide to the Microfilm Edition of Temperance and Prohibition Papers.* Ann Arbor: University of Michigan, 1977, pp. 1–21.

McKeever, Jane L. "The Woman's Temperance Publishing Association." *Library Quarterly* 55, 1985, pp. 365–397.

Tyler, Helen E. *Where Prayer and Purpose Meet: The WCTU Story, 1874–1949.* Evanston, Ill.: Signal Press, 1949.

Tyrrell, Ian. *Woman's World/Woman's Empire: The Woman's Christian Temperance Union in International Perspective.* Chapel Hill: University of North Carolina Press, 1991.

INDEX SOURCES: Union List of Serials.

LOCATION SOURCES: Ohio Historical Society Museum; Frances E. Willard Memorial Library; and other libraries.

Publication History

PERIODICAL TITLE AND TITLE CHANGES: The *Union Signal* (1883–present). (The *Union Signal* resulted from a merger of two temperance publications: the national WCTU publication, the *Woman's Temperance Union* [1875–1878; name changed to *Our Union,* 1878–1882] and an Illinois WCTU publication, the *Signal* [1880–1882].)

VOLUME AND ISSUE DATA: Vols. 4–   (January 4, 1883–present. Weekly (January 4, 1883–April 3, 1954; no publication from August–December 1903); biweekly (April 17, 1954–February 22, 1969); monthly (March 1969–December 1991); bimonthly (January/February 1992–present). (The first ten issues of the *Union Signal* continued volume numbering from the *Signal;* numbering then changed to volume 9, reflecting that of *Our Union.*)

PUBLISHER AND PLACE OF PUBLICATION: Woman's Temperance Publishing Association (1883–1903); Woman's Christian Temperance Union (1903–present). Chicago (1883–1903); Evanston Ill. (1903–present).

EDITORS: Mary B. Willard (1883–1885); Mary Allen West (1885–1892); Frances E. Willard (1892–1898); Lillian M. N. Stevens (1898–1914); Julia F. Deane (1914); Anna A. Gordon (1914–1926); Ella Boole (1926–1933); Ida Wise Smith (1933–1944); D. Leigh Colvin (1944–1953); Mrs. Glenn G. Hays (1953–1959); Ruth E. Tooze (1959–1974); Edith K. Stanley (1974–1980); Mrs. Kermit Edgar (1980–1988); Rachel B. Kelly (1988–present)

CIRCULATION: Vitucci interview: 4,000.

Thomas N. Lewis

UNION W.A.G.E.

The history of *Union W.A.G.E.* is inseparable from the history of the organization that published it, the Union Women's Alliance to Gain Equality (WAGE). Union W.A.G.E. was founded in March 1971 following a California state convention of the National Organization for Women at which labor activists objected to efforts to pass a state equal rights amendment (ERA) without an amendment extending California's protective legislation to men.[1] This conflict continued a decades-old debate within the Women's Trade Union League (WTUL) over the then-newly proposed equal rights amendment and the implications of "equality" for efforts to protect child and women workers through protective legislation. Like their WTUL predecessors, the women who founded Union W.A.G.E. believed that protective legislation was essential to protect the majority of women workers who were not unionized and thus had no other protection against employers' efforts to require them to work long hours under dangerous conditions for wages insufficient to sustain life. While trying to maintain this legislative floor under women workers' conditions, the WTUL and Union W.A.G.E. simultaneously worked to organize women into unions capable of enforcing better conditions than those reluctantly yielded by state legislators.[2]

Within weeks of its founding, Union W.A.G.E. launched the monthly mimeographed *Union W.A.G.E. Newsletter,* which was converted to a bimonthly tabloid and rechristened *Union W.A.G.E.* after seven months. From its origins, *Union W.A.G.E.* campaigned against the ERA and for stronger California legislation governing hours, minimum wages, and health and safety standards. In order to protect existing legislation from challenges of sex discrimination, it campaigned to extend existing legislation to male workers. But while legislation was the primary emphasis in the *Newsletter,* there was from the start also a strong emphasis on support for women workers in the process of organizing or striking for their rights, even when this brought them into conflict with union officials. The very first issue reported on a five-month-old strike by clerical workers against a local of the International Brotherhood of Electrical Workers (IBEW), comparing the IBEW's efforts to break the union to those of an antilabor firm notorious in the area, and criticized the International Labor Press Association for holding its annual meeting in the Playboy Club Hotel.[3]

The Statement of Purpose and Goals (reprinted in every subsequent issue, with some changes over the years) called for "[e]qual rights, equal pay, and equal opportunities for working women," announcing that Union W.A.G.E. was an organization of women trade unionists "organized to fight discrimination on the job, in unions and in society." Like their counterparts in the WTUL at the turn of the century, Union W.A.G.E.'s founders were committed to working within the established trade union movement. But they were also committed to challenging that movement when (as it often did, in their view) it failed to defend women workers' interests vigorously enough and to demanding that women be advanced into positions of responsibility and authority. Joyce Maupin, like other founders a veteran socialist, recalled the organization's independence with pride:

> The newspaper at times was very critical of the labor movement, and my articles were some of the worst, in labor's opinion. I had one famous one: all the office workers in San Francisco Local 2 were on strike against the union officers and I had a headline that said "Office Workers Score, Union Bosses Strike Out."[4]

Nor did the alliance hesitate to take on others in the women's movement. Several articles in *Union W.A.G.E.* criticized feminist organizations and publications for ignoring the needs of low-paid workingwomen and poor women. In one early issue Union W.A.G.E. cofounder Anne Draper offered pointed criticism of *Ms. Magazine:*

> We point away from the preoccupations and obsessions that fill the pages of *Ms.* written by career-women who identify their own minority life-situation with the "sisterhood" of the mass. . . . The most important place to organize women for their liberation is at their work place. *This means*

putting the spotlight on a goal which is unfortunately alien to the feminist "star" movement: the goal of integrating the women's liberation movement and the women's trade union movement—integrating the organization of women against social exploitation (sexism) and the organization of women against economic exploitation.

Draper conceded that many union leaders were shortsighted sexists but insisted that their sexism needed to be confronted, not avoided:

When women professionals encounter sexism in (say) a university administration, they dig their heels in and fight. . . . That is because they have no doubt that they want *in.* If the existence of sexism in the union movement . . . is utilized for the purpose of repudiating trade unionism as such, then it is only because it is being used as an excuse by people who are really expressing their alienation from the very idea of working-class struggle.[5]

The alliance staked out an unmistakably radical position. Union W.A.G.E. opposed the Vietnam War, supported "free abortion on demand," and demanded a shorter workweek, free national, comprehensive health care, "jobs for all who want them . . . and greater worker control over the workplace."[6] As time went on, Union W.A.G.E. moved beyond this issue-specific agenda to call for sweeping social transformation: "We in Union WAGE believe that women's oppression is related to the social and economic system of capitalism and can be ended only by a strong, united working-class movement."[7]

Union W.A.G.E. was a bimonthly tabloid, gradually expanding from four to twelve and finally sixteen pages with transfer letter headlines. The first (January–February 1972) newspaper-format issue bore the slogan, "For equal rights, equal pay, and equal opportunities," on top of the flag. It offered an account of the organization's first year, called for a labor ERA, reported on an organizing campaign at Blue Cross, and printed the first in a series of articles on women's labor history that continued throughout most of the newspaper's run. The paper only rarely listed its editor, elected each year by Union W.A.G.E. members, in its staff box, instead listing contributors to each issue (a list that only sometimes included the editor). Articles included first-person accounts of efforts to organize unions, articles on women's labor history, how-to guides, health and safety, labor law, working conditions in industries employing large numbers of women workers and efforts to organize them, and reports on women's caucuses in labor unions and their efforts to pressure union leaders to pay more attention to women's needs and to bring women into positions of union leadership. In the mid-1970s, the paper began a series of special sections on topics such as the electronics industry (March–April 1976), health and safety (January–February 1977), sexism and workingwomen (September–October 1977), clerical work (January–February 1978), reproductive rights (March–April 1978), the family

(March–April 1979), women and the health industry (January–February 1980), and "irregular work" (temporary, freelance, and part-time) (January–February 1981). The July 1980 *Union W.A.G.E.* reprinted excerpts from *La Razon Mestiza: Trabajemos Unidos,* a one-shot paper coproduced by Union W.A.G.E. and Chicana activists for distribution at a Chicana issues conference. Other articles reported on organizing drives, health-and-safety concerns, legislation affecting women workers, and strikes and other struggles for comparable worth. Reflecting Union W.A.G.E.'s membership, most news was from northern California, but the newspaper always had a broader reach—regularly publishing articles on women's struggles throughout the United States and Canada and occasional reports on women workers' struggles in other countries.

While Union W.A.G.E. maintained its position over the years as a working, class–based, feminist organization, disputes over the precise form that it should take twice led to major conflicts within the organization and undermined the alliance's efforts to spread from its original northern California base to become a national organization.

The formation of the Coalition of Labor Union Women (CLUW) was the first turning point. Union W.A.G.E. was highly critical of CLUW when it formed in 1974, both because of CLUW's dominance by union staffers and officials and because of its decision to limit membership to those women already in unions. (The alliance was open to all women workers, whether or not they were presently union members.)[8] Several members withdrew when *Union W.A.G.E.* published several critical articles about CLUW. But new chapters formed around the country, bringing in women drawn to its more independent stance. Union W.A.G.E. added a section to its statement of "Purpose and Goals" stating that it was "dedicated to building an organization which will properly represent working women on a national level." Alliance membership peaked at some four hundred members, with new chapters in Indiana, New York, Oregon, Washington, and southern California.[9] Efforts to tie Union W.A.G.E. to particular socialist tendencies were turned back with a compromise barring chapters from supporting governments or ideologies associated with particular governments but permitting stands in solidarity with struggles of working people in other countries.[10]

However, in 1979 a fierce battle broke out over the efforts of the newspaper's editor and other members to transform the organization into a broad socialist, feminist organization with much less emphasis on union issues. Union W.A.G.E. had already lost its New York and Seattle chapters when editor Pam Allen brought the simmering internal debate to the newspaper in an article calling for more emphasis on theoretical analysis and suggesting that work within the established unions was doomed to failure. Union W.A.G.E. cofounder Joyce Maupin responded, drawing on labor history to suggest that "Everything Can Change":

Unions are a tool, something like a hammer. You can use a hammer to drive in nails. You can use it to smash skulls. Or you can bang it against a garbage can and make noise. In the long run, people belonging to unions will determine what they do. For unions are the Achilles heel of the system.[11]

The debate extended from editorial focus, to organizing strategy, to the format of the newspaper, with the labor activists battling Allen's proposal to devote large sections of *Union W.A.G.E.* to special theme issues. Instead:

We would like to see the paper emphasize activities such as organizing drives, strikes, job actions and caucus work. . . . We need to talk about why a strike failed, what works and doesn't work in caucus building, and what new ways women are creating to get around old problems. . . .

To develop a newspaper that is more reflective of unions and workplace activities could be a very stimulating experience for WAGE. It involves actively encouraging WAGE members, nonmembers and chapters to write up and think about their experiences. When the paper becomes so intrinsically linked to our activities it is not a burden . . . but an extension of chapter activities. It then becomes the organizing tool that we need.[12]

Editor Pam Allen countered with a proposal for focus issues almost entirely devoted to education, health, and the family, arguing that this was a necessary part of deepening the alliance's theoretical analysis. But the paper's production manager insisted that "Union WAGE should primarily be concerned with women's concerns at the workplace."[13]

Alliance members tried to reconcile these increasingly entrenched tendencies at their 1979 convention, agreeing to four focus issues (but tying them to the alliance's activities and giving them less space than Allen proposed), changing the editor from an elected to an appointed position, and reaffirming their commitment to building a national, working-class women's organization.[14] However, the compromise did not hold. The Union W.A.G.E. Executive Board soon voted not to reappoint Allen as editor, citing issues ranging from the alliance's inability to afford a paid editor (Allen was the first and last editor to draw a paycheck), to differing conceptions of the role of the alliance and its newspaper, to professionalization of what the board believed should be a grassroots, collective process:

We have serious differences with Pam's conception of the newspaper and its relationship to the organization. Politically and structurally, our newspaper is part of Union WAGE. The newspaper is not a substitute for organizing, but a tool for helping women organize, and a reflection of the activities and struggles of our members and other working women. Pam, and her supporters, openly object to the Board making decisions about the content of the newspaper.[15]

Allen responded that several board members "distrusted [her] commitment to union organizing" and rejected efforts at a compromise:

> The majority of the Executive Board has said no! Concretely the Executive Board is challenging the rights of Third World, unemployed and poor women to share their concerns and their struggles because these do not fit into a trade union context.[16]

The conflict continued in the newspaper and in Union W.A.G.E.'s internal newsletter. Allen's supporters formed a Women's Work Caucus to push their perspectives, while veteran activists such as Joyce Maupin insisted that they were creating a false dichotomy since Third World women were overwhelmingly workingwomen, and many were union members:

> Tying our newspaper to actual struggle is the key to achieving [our] goals. . . . The newspaper is not a literary publication. It is a tool providing information and support to working women as they confront both employers and union bureaucrats.[17]

That was Allen's last issue as editor; the next issue announced the appointment of three coeditors—Debbie Farson, Joyce Maupin, and Peg Stone—and urged readers to join in writing and producing the newspaper.[18] A few months later a proposal by the Woman's Work Caucus to produce the focus issue on Third World women was defeated, and the caucus quickly dropped from sight.[19] But although the labor activists won, the battle left the alliance seriously weakened and increasingly dependent upon grants to keep its doors open.

These conflicts were probably inevitable, given the diverse political commitments and personal backgrounds that Union W.A.G.E. members brought to the organization. Alliance founders included veterans of U.S. communist and Trotskyist organizations, labor and New Left activists, and feminists looking for a way to make feminist concerns more directly relevant to women workers. While Union W.A.G.E.'s founding members had years of experience within the labor movement, many of the women who later joined the organization came out of the New Left and lacked the founders' commitment to working within the unions. Pam Allen, for example, who was at the center of the 1979 split, had no union experience when she joined the organization, first as a volunteer and then as a member of its two-person paid staff. Rather, her background was in feminist organizations and academe, and her vision of the organization spoke to women workers not as current or potential unionists but as the constituency for a more radical women's movement.[20]

Union W.A.G.E. was also hampered by its inability to forge an effective strategy for transforming the unions, within which it was committed to working, into organizations more responsive to the needs of women workers. Given the entrenched, bureaucratic structures in many local and national unions, the need for more democratic and accountable structures was clear. But at the same time, unremitting warfare against the bureaucrats coexisted uncomfortably with appeals to those same bureaucrats to devote increased resources to organizing women workers and to allow those workers a greater voice within their unions. The newspaper published tips on organizing reform and women's caucuses or organizing single-issue campaigns around particular grievances and cheered every effort to elect militant women to union office.[21] When two Bay Area feminist union organizers were fired, Union W.A.G.E. initially supported their efforts to build an independent union, until their efforts to secure resources led them into a union at least as corrupt and undemocratic as the one they had left. Several years later a women elected to the executive board of a Service Employees local as the sole winner on a reform ticket found her "leadership" position intensely frustrating:

> Merely calling for union democracy is a hollow cry unless we understand *why* we must support our organization. . . . Unions are a power over our lives; I think we cannot ignore them; yet how to deal with them is unclear. We must help union members deal with their apathy because every moment we remain silent . . . the union, and thus capitalism, wins. Today the working class has two enemies; only one of which is management.[22]

But if unions were part of the problem, then how was Union W.A.G.E. to accomplish its objectives? While the alliance actively lobbied for legislation and regulations to improve the conditions of women workers, it never believed these could truly empower women. Rather, its founders placed their faith in (transformed or at least reinvigorated) unions, a faith that many members found increasingly difficult to sustain. Some members turned to independent unions, such as the feminist Service, Office and Retail Workers Union of Canada, but it collapsed, having overextended itself in a struggle to organize bank workers. Others sought a rapprochement with more progressive union leaders, supporting projects such as the Service Employees International Union–affiliated 9 to 5 clerical workers organizing project. But the majority never reached a satisfactory resolution.[23]

In July 1982 an undated four-page newsletter-format issue announced, "WAGE Punches Out." Although the need for a militant workingwomen's organization remained, a letter signed by ten Union W.A.G.E. activists announced, the increasingly antilabor climate, the difficulty of securing funding, and a scarcity of new volunteers had exhausted its activists. "The time for organizing working women must come some day. We hope that we have made a significant contribution to this struggle, and we urge others to keep fighting.

... Speaking for ourselves, we have seen ceaseless injustice perpetrated on working women, and we will never forget it."[24]

An obituary published in another San Francisco women's newspaper described the alliance as "a Bay Area group that ... encouraged women to organize for power. At the same time it lambasted unions for failing to improve job conditions for women and for shutting women out of leadership posts. ... Thanks to its newspaper, the group's reputation for scrappiness in fights where rights for women workers were at stake stretched far beyond its dues-paying members."[25] That scrappiness kept *Union W.A.G.E.* lively and vibrant. But in the end, it was not sufficient to pull the organization through the decline of the labor movement within which it was committed to working.

Notes

1. Both the newspaper and the organization shared the same name. Italicized references refer to the newspaper. Although the *Union W.A.G.E.* masthead always included the periods, the newspaper usually dropped them in its articles, and in its final years often referred to the organization simply as WAGE, dropping the "Union."

2. For the Women's Trade Union League, see *Life and Labor* in this volume and Anelise Orleck's *Common Sense and a Little Fire: Women and Working-Class Politics in the United States, 1900–1965* (Chapel Hill: University of North Carolina Press, 1995).

3. "Five Months on Strike!" May 1971, p. 6; untitled news brief, p. 2. Other articles in that issue reported on a new union contract extending equal pay to men and women retail clerks, a victory in a union-backed lawsuit for equal pay for Denver newspaper workers, and an organizing drive at the University of California. The second issue (June 1971) reprinted an American Federation of Labor–Congress of Industrial Organizations (AFL-CIO) statement critical of the equal rights amendment with this introductory comment: "Union WAGE is for 'Equal Rights legislation through Congress to ban discrimination and maintain existing state legislation benefiting women workers by extending them to men.'" That statement, written by AFL-CIO staffer Doris Hardesty, focused on the ERA's potential implications for protective legislation and suggested that the campaign was ultimately a waste of time: "Perhaps the ladies of the lib should direct their efforts" to challenging the customs and laws that limited women's progress. The July 1971 issue carried an open letter to Dianne Feinstein of the San Francisco Board of Supervisors protesting the passage of a resolution endorsing the ERA as an antilabor measure, urged readers to send similar protests, and backed efforts to persuade the American Federation of Teachers (AFT) to reverse its support of the ERA: "It is essential that the AFT adopt a progressive position, one of opposition to the ERA in its present form" (pp. 7,8). The January–February 1972 issue included an article headed "For a Labor ERA," p. 3. Although Union W.A.G.E. never endorsed the ERA, the issue gradually receded from its pages. But several years later the alliance still insisted that the road to equality lay in extending greater rights to all rather than in stripping women of the few rights they possessed, strongly criticizing National Organization for Women for its position that if men were drafted, women should be, too. A front-page editorial said Union W.A.G.E. opposed registration and the draft of anyone, male or female (Debbie Farson, "No Registration, No Draft, No War," May–June 1980, p. 1).

4. Barbara Mahan, "'The Unions Wouldn't Let Women Walk the Picketline,'" *Plexus,* August 1982, p. 6.

5. Anne Draper, "Women in Struggle," March–April 1971, pp. 6–8; Lois Weiner, "The Invisible Woman: Union WAGE Looks at Ms. Magazine," November–December 1972, pp. 4–5.

6. October 1971, p. 1; "Purpose and Goals," March–April 1979, p. 13.

7. Union W.A.G.E. Executive Board, "Which Way the Women's Movement?" March–April 1977, p. 1.

8. See, for example, Joyce Maupin, "Rank and File Victory," May–June 1974, p. 5; Kay Eisenhower, "Open Membership!" May–June 1974, p. 5.; Anita Reinthaler, "Reply to Coalition of Labor Union Women, ITU Caucus," January–February 1977, p. 2 (Reinthaler said CLUW was "under the direction and control of the labor establishment" and criticized a campaign to persuade the Typographical Union to change its union emblems as trivial).

9. "Purpose and Goals," September–October 1975. In 1977, Michelle Celarier ("Union WAGE Organizes Women," *In These Times,* September. 21, 1977, p. 8) reported the alliance had grown from thirty-two founding members to three hundred. Barbara Mahan (*"Union WAGE Folds: Working Women Lose Ally,"* *Plexus* 9.6, August 1982, p. 1) reported that Union W.A.G.E. had four hundred to five hundred members at its peak in the 1970s.

10. "WAGE Moves Forward," November–December 1976, p. 3.

11. Pam Allen, "Working in Unions: For a Broader Vision," January–February 1979, p. 1; Joyce Maupin, "Everything Can Change," January–February 1979, pp. 1, 2; Geraldine Daesch, "Keeping the 'Union' in Union WAGE," January–February 1979, p. 4.

12. Deborah Farson, et al., "Focus Issues for the Paper?" January–February 1979, pp. 14–15.

13. Pam Allen, "Focus Issues for the Paper?"; Sally Floyd, "News for Working Women"; both January–February 1979, p. 14.

14. Jan Arnold, "WAGE Convention: Putting Humpty Dumpty Back Together Again," March–April 1979, pp. 12–13.

15. Jan Arnold, "From the President," July–August 1979, p. 14.

16. Pam Allen, "From the Editor," July–August 1979, p. 14. A treasurer's report (Maja Argue, "Help!") appeared on the next page, noting that the alliance was spending three times as much money as it was bringing in and suggesting that the newspaper was a major contributor to the fiscal crisis. Accordingly, the board requested a newspaper budget, eliminated the paid editor position, and raised subscription and single-copy rates.

17. Joyce Maupin, "Third World Women Lead in Organizing," September–October 1979, p. 15; Pam Allen et al., "Women's Work Caucus," September–October 1979, p. 14.

18. "Join Us," November–December 1979, p. 15. The notice listed a series of upcoming deadlines and meetings and invited readers to a layout session at which they could "[s]tart a love affair with press type!"

19. "Union WAGE Referendum: Results," March–April 1980, p. 15. The Women's Work Caucus proposal received fourteen votes, thirty-two, against for a proposal by Sally Floyd and Joyce Maupin. Ten voted for both proposals, apparently unable to distinguish between them. While there was a clear difference between the two tendencies on the relative importance to attach to efforts to work within the established trade unions, the debates on peripheral issues, while heated, often turned on seemingly minute distinctions.

20. Pam Allen, May–June 1977, pp. 6–7. This was one of several short biographical statements introducing the organization's new officers.

21. "Jenkins/Statzer Betray City Clerks," September–October 1975, p. 1. For examples of coverage of rank-and-file reform efforts, see Joyce Maupin, "Time for the Rank and File," May–June 1978, p. 1. The January–February 1977 issue announced a Union W.A.G.E. pamphlet by cofounder Jean Maddox: "The Fight for Rank and File Democracy." Endorsing reform candidates posed its own problems; the May–June 1982 (page 14) issue included a letter from Union W.A.G.E. member Laura Sanchez announcing her resignation in protest of a Union W.A.G.E. leaflet endorsing a reform slate (Sanchez was a candidate on a different slate).

22. Pat Hendricks, "Can Unions Be Changed?" November–December 1977, p. 6.

23. Karen Nussbaum, "Strategies for Clerical Workers," January–February 1976, p. 3.

24. Carla Cassler et al., "An Open Letter to Our Friends: WAGE Punches Out," (July 1982), p. 1.

25. Mahan, "*Union WAGE* Folds."

Information Sources

BIBLIOGRAPHY:
Mahan, Barbara. "*Union WAGE* Folds: Working Women Lose Ally." *Plexus* 9.6, August 1982, pp. 1, 6.
INDEX SOURCES: None.
LOCATION SOURCES: Northwestern University library and Schlesinger Library, Radcliffe College–Harvard University.

Publication History

PERIODICAL TITLE AND TITLE CHANGES: *Union W.A.G.E. Newsletter* (1971); *Union W.A.G.E.* (1972–1982).
VOLUME AND ISSUE DATA: Vols. 1–12 (1971–1982). Monthly (1971); bimonthly (1972–1982) (skipped September–October 1981 issue).
PUBLISHER AND PLACE OF PUBLICATION: Union Women's Alliance to Gain Equality. Berkeley, Calif. (1971–1976); San Francisco (1977–1982).
EDITORS: Gretchen Mackler (1971–1973); Maxine Jenkins (1973–1974); not reported (1974–1975); Pam Schechter (1975–1976); Lenore Weiss (1976–1977); Pam Allen (1977–1979); Debbie Farson, Joyce Maupin, and Peg Stone (1979–1980); Naomi Groeschel and Debbie Farson (1980–1981), Debbie Farson and Peg Stone (1981–1982).
CIRCULATION: 1,100 subscribers (1979).

Jon Bekken

V

VOICE OF THE WOMEN'S LIBERATION MOVEMENT

In its brief tenure, *Voice of the Women's Liberation Movement* (*VWLM*) played a pivotal role in the fledgling modern woman's rights era. "It gave the movement its name," says Jo Freeman,[1] who, under the name Joreen, edited the first national women's newsletter, published seven times from March 1968 to June 1969.

The birth of the National Organization for Women (NOW) in 1966 and the rise of a new feminist movement heralded a growth in national women's organizations. While NOW represented what Freeman has called "the older branch" of the movement,[2] a branch of younger, radical women also emerged. The latter segment lacked a national organization but included small groups involved in a wide range of activities. *Voice of the Women's Liberation Movement* represented the ideas of this younger branch.

"It (*VWLM*) seemed a form of communication. It was an early communication mechanism," stated Freeman, who was in her early twenties when she helped found the newsletter in Chicago. According to author June Sochen, Freeman became a feminist after finding that her colleagues in the civil rights movement discriminated against her because of her sex. "I had to face being turned down simply for being a woman," she is quoted as saying. "I became a raging gut feminist."[3]

Chicago had what Florida-based feminist Beverly Jones called "the first" of the small, independent discussion groups for leftist women. Known as the Chicago Westside Group, its founders included Freeman, Naomi Weisstein, Shulamith Firestone, Heather Booth, Amy Kesselman, Fran Rominski, and Laya Firestone.[4] Weisstein noted that "we were afraid to call ourselves feminists, since in the New Left that was hopelessly 'bourgeois.' We finally came up with 'women's liberation,' an analogy with Third World struggles (since we couldn't yet imagine the legitimacy of our own)."[5]

From this small group came the editor (Freeman) and some contributors for a national newsletter that would attract writers and readers from across the country. The mimeographed *Voice of the Women's Liberation Movement,* typed on 8½" × 11" paper, debuted in March 1968 and initially lacked a title. "This is the space for the bannerline," read the copy at the top of the six-page first issue. "We left it blank. Because this newsletter, like its sponsoring organizations, has no name."[6]

The issue's readers were asked to send in suggestions for a title, but Freeman received no responses. So, for the next issue three months later, she merely moved up the words from the first issue's one-line folio: *voice of the women's liberation movement.*

The initial issue was distributed free at bookstores and through local organizations to "those who have exercised an interest in women's liberation." Subscriptions—three dollars for twelve issues—were solicited, but readers unable to pay were invited to "write us a letter claiming poverty."[7] The mastheads proclaimed that *Voice of the Women's Liberation Movement* was printed as often as time and money permitted.

The keynote article in the first issue featured the headline, "What the Hell Is Women's Lib Anyway?" While it carried no byline, the piece was reprinted and credited to Joreen in a 1970 work, "Sisterhood Is Powerful," edited by feminist Robin Morgan.

Freeman, as Joreen, is listed as editor of the first issue of *VWLM.* She recalled also having served as editor of issues 2 and 5.[8] The remaining issues were organized under the editorial jurisdiction of others in the movement, but no reference is made to the editor's names in any issue other than the first. *VWLM* always listed Chicago-based addresses for correspondence.

VWLM reached radical women, according to author Flora Davis, and "generally presented the politico point of view."[9] Jones wrote that the newsletter was circulated among the "scattered knots of left-wing feminists. It was called the *Voice of the Women's Liberation Movement*—a title that was somewhat expansive, since nothing that could rightfully be called a movement existed yet."[10]

Freeman wrote that the newsletter's purpose

> was to reach any potential sympathizer in order to let her know that there were others who thought as she did and that she was not isolated or crazy. It also functioned to put women in contact with other like-minded women in the same area and thus stimulated the formation of new groups.[11]

Articles came from movement members throughout the country. "Things would show up in the mail," stated Freeman, who remembered typing the initial issues and spending "a lot of time" working on *VWLM* and dealing with concomitant tasks. In each issue, an appeal was made to readers to send in unsolicited articles, news and letters.

Subscribers were listed on individual 3" × 5" note cards, which indicated when they first made contact with the women's movement in Chicago; Freeman, now a Brooklyn resident and self-professed "Jane of all arts," retains some of the cards and address labels to this day.

VWLM featured articles dealing with upcoming conferences, movement news, and essays penned by feminists from Chicago and other cities. The first issue included the selection of "Male Chauvinist of the Month," with the honors being given to *Ramparts* editor Warren Hinkle III "for contributions to the cause of the oppression of women too numerous to describe herein but obvious to anyone who read the February issue of the 'Playboy' of the left."[12] Most of the newsletter's cartoons were credited to the offbeat humor and artistic bent of Weisstein.

Bylines included Kesselman, other Chicago group founders, and women's liberation movement representatives from major cities. But the newsletter also featured articles whose "authors" or titles were names representing a play on words. A "Dear John" column, for example, was signed with the name "John Magnus Fallus."[13] "Playmeat of the Month" called the Playboy bunny "an affront to human sexual dignity."[14] New Yorker Anne Koedt wrote an article that listed some male reactions to keeping women's consciousness down; the piece was titled "Cocktales."[15] In a letter to the editor, published in a later issue, Koedt objected to the title—"it seemed kind of crude, and not in context with what I tried to describe."[16]

Most issues included a list of suggested readings, including books, speeches, and essays on topics of interest to those in the women's movement. Copies of some of the works were available for a small fee.

Special events in the women's struggle garnered attention of *VWLM* writers. A 1968 demonstration against the Miss America pageant—the "first major action of the current Women's Movement"[17]—was reported in the October 1968 issue. A front-page story by Judith Duffett of New York featured this headline: "VWLM vs. Miss America"; the subhead read, "Atlantic City Is a Town with Class—They Raise Your Morals While They Judge Your Ass." The author proclaimed that the 150 women protestors had a goal: "No More Miss America!"[18] Several paragraphs into the story, however, she argued that "our purpose was *not* to put down Miss America but to attack the male chauvinism, commercialization of beauty, racism and oppression of women symbolized by the Pageant."[19]

VWLM also covered the firing of University of Chicago professor Marlene Dixon, an activist and Marxist, as well as the activities of the Society for Democratic Students and other organizations. National news about women's groups/activities/conferences became regular fare in the newsletter, with correspondence coming from individuals throughout the country. Although the production did not change—*VWLM* remained a typed newsletter, often with handwritten headlines—the issues increased in size. The June 1969 edition totaled twenty-five pages, replete with cartoons, letters, and movement news. But its final page· brought a surprising notice to readers:

> We who publish this newsletter must announce that this will be our last issue. We have decided to divest ourselves of responsibility for a national newsletter (a major responsibility for some of us) because we wish to concentrate on building a women's movement in the Chicago area. We feel regional organizing is the most important priority at this stage of our movement's history.
>
> It has also become increasingly clear to us that the newsletter was not, in fact, the "Voice of the Women's Liberation Movement." Nor do we think that any national newsletter could do justice to the role of "voice" at the present time.[20]

Readers were informed that leftover money would be used to build a women's movement in the Chicago area but that subscribers who wanted their money back could write and request it.

VWLM, which had grown from two hundred to two thousand copies and from 6 to 25 pages, was "killed," according to Freeman, because producing it proved a "herculean task."[21] At the end, she was not involved in work with *VWLM* and, in her own words, "dropped out of the movement in 1969."[22] Those putting out the final issue wrote that "we hope our decision will be viewed sympathetically and understood as a political decision. We believe it is a step toward enlisting many more Chicago women in the struggle."[23]

Notes

1. Jo Freeman, interview, July 24, 1995.
2. Jo Freeman, *The Politics of Women's Liberation* (New York: David McKay, 1975), p. 49.
3. June Sochen, *Herstory* (New York: Alfred, 1974), p. 388.
4. Beverly Jones, "Towards a Female Liberation Movement," in Miriam Schneir, ed., *Feminism in Our Time* (New York: Vintage Books, 1994), p. 108.
5. Naomi Weisstein, "Chicago '60s' Ecstasy as Our Guide," *Ms.* September–October, 1990, p. 65, as quoted in ibid, p. 108.
6. March 1968, p. 1.
7. Ibid.
8. Freeman interview.
9. Flora Davis, *Moving the Mountain* (New York: Simon and Schuster, 1991), p. 79.
10. Jones, *"Towards a Female Liberation Movement,"* p. 109.
11. Freeman, *Politics of Women's Liberation,* p. 110.
12. March 1968, p. 1.
13. June 1968.
14. February 1969, p. 5.
15. January 1969, p. 5.

16. February 1969, p. 13.
17. Robin Morgan, *Going Too Far* (New York: Random House, 1977), p. 62.
18. October 1968, p. 1.
19. October 1968, p. 4.
20. June 1969, p. 25.
21. Freeman, *The Politics of Women's Liberation,* p. 110.
22. Freeman interview.
23. June 1969, p. 25.

Information Sources

BIBLIOGRAPHY:
Davis, Flora. *Moving the Mountain.* New York: Simon and Schuster, 1991.
Freeman, Jo. *The Politics of Women's Liberation.* New York: David McKay, 1975.
Morgan, Robin. *Sisterhood Is Powerful.* New York: Random House, 1970.
———. *Going Too Far.* New York: Random House, 1977.
Schneir, Miriam, ed. *Feminism in Our Time.* New York: Vintage Books, 1994.
Sochen, June. *Herstory.* New York: Alfred, 1974.
———. *Movers and Shakers.* New York: Quadrangle/New York Times Books, 1975.
INDEX SOURCES: None.
LOCATION SOURCES: Newark (N.J.) Public Library; William Paterson College Sarah
    B. Askew Library; and other libraries. Microfilm available in the Herstory Col-
    lection.

Publication History

PERIODICAL TITLE AND TITLE CHANGES: *Voice of the Women's Liberation Move-
    ment* (March 1968–June 1969).
VOLUME AND ISSUE DATA: Vol. 1 (March 1968–June 1969). Irregular.
PUBLISHER AND PLACE OF PUBLICATION: Women's liberation movement mem-
    bers. Chicago.
EDITORS: Joreen (Jo Freeman) and (unnamed) others in movement.
CIRCULATION: Freeman, *Politics of Women's Liberation,* 1969: 2,000, including sub-
    scription copies and those distributed free.

Tina Lesher

W

WESTERN WOMAN VOTER

The *Western Woman Voter* was born in the flush of suffrage success in the state of Washington. For decades, the suffragists had struggled to regain the vote. The women in the Washington territory had the vote, but suffrage was snatched away just as the territory was to win statehood.[1] Although the measure was introduced again and again in the state legislature, not until November 1910 did women prevail and suffrage win. One of the heroines of that contest was Adella Parker, a popular Seattle lawyer and a prominent suffragist who was one of the editors of the campaign journal *Votes for Women.* In the progressive optimism of the day, Parker and several suffragists from Washington and California launched the *Western Woman Voter* as a journal to serve all the women voters throughout the West.[2]

Adella Parker is the key to understanding the launch, the editorial direction, and the demise of this monthly. She had been enormously active in the Washington suffrage campaign, acting as a member of the executive committee of the state suffrage association and president of the College Suffrage League. She was also a popular lecturer on the issue and wrote for eastern suffrage publications. She even contributed the story on the Washington state suffrage victory to the *Woman's Journal** in Boston.[3] Her good reputation within the state and regional suffrage circles meant that her publication was probably warmly received among these women. Parker was also experienced in editing a publication. That meant that she was at least familiar with the problems of production and financing. Her professional career as an attorney meant that she was familiar with issues, laws, and candidates. Thus, any publication she was associated with would address political matters in a knowledgeable manner. Her newspaper would also likely follow a Progressive Party line, a reflection of Parker's own political sentiment. She came by that reform, third-party orientation through her family. Her father, William Elbridge Parker, had supported unsuccessful Democratic presidential candidate William Jennings Bryan on his silver plank and socialist candidate Eugene V. Debs.[4] Parker's background ensured that the *Western Woman Voter* would be committed to political and social reform and would be aimed at well-educated, liberal, urban women. Those lofty aspirations and that readership demanded a high-quality publication; Parker seldom let them down.

From the front cover of the first issue to page 12, the publication seemed to fulfill its promises. The front cover carried a cartoon of a band playing on the bandwagon of "Votes for Women," driven by a man. The "band" members carried pennants reading "Idaho," "Colorado," "Washington," "Utah," and "Wyoming." Page 12 carried advertising for products designed to appeal to the thinking, affluent woman. In between were departments like "Good Government News," a column covering enlightened political measures throughout the United States, and "Correspondence," with letters from suffragists local and from as far away as Ohio and notes of congratulations from such well known suffragists as Harriet Taylor Upton of Ohio and Abigail Scott Duniway of Oregon. Features focused on the Washington state win and included "Press Comment on the Victory in Washington" and "What It Cost to Carry Washington."

There was much editorial comment; but, most important, the editors promised a different type of publication:

> a publication primarily designed to be a journal of information for the women voters of the West. It will discuss questions relating to the government of city and state, questions dealing with the legal rights of women and with the home, the child and the school insofar as they are affected by law. It will aim to keep the women of each of the suffrage states informed as to the civic activities of women voters elsewhere, and will make a special feature of "good government news" from everywhere.[5]

Readers were invited to ask questions on civics, economics, and law, thus adding an educational aspect to the publication.[6] This, however, never developed as a meaningful dimension of the publication. Instead, the *Western Woman Voter* remained a publication of news and opinion.

Adella Parker was listed first in the "staff of editors." Although she was never formally identified as the editor, she wrote the few "signed" editorials and referred to herself as the "managing editor" when the publication revived after a lapse of several months.[7] The other original editors were Alice Park, a prominent suffragist in California, and Londa Stebbins Fletcher, also from California. Maud Parker, Adella's sister, and Elizabeth Baker were also listed as editors. Four months later, Lucia Ames Mead, the Massachusetts suffragist and peace advocate, was added to the staff.[8] Late in 1911, Elsie Wallace Moore was also listed as an editor. It is difficult to determine exactly what woman contributed which stories; the *Western Woman Voter* seldom carried bylines.

It also seldom skirted controversial issues. By the second issue, the magazine endorsed the recall of the mayor of Seattle ("Mayor Gill has been a disappointment to his friends, a humiliation to those who opposed him and a menace to the fair name of the city"[9]), endorsed a candidate if the recall succeeded,[10] condemned Seattle's plans to restrict vice to one particular geographical area (this would offer "a very desirable opportunity to the white slavers"[11]), and choked with political advertising. The *Western Woman Voter* was becoming known for its courage and its provocative ideas.

By April 1911, the *Western Woman Voter* was ready to assert itself as the voice of the region. A whole set of features outlined the "Progressive Legislation of the West" and the campaign for woman suffrage in California.[12] Those features illustrated that the *Western Woman Voter* was clearly in favor of all the Progressive legislation of the West, from initiative, referendum, and recall to the direct primary, from the eight-hour day for women to workman's compensation.

The monthly was already enjoying a measure of success. Advertising—especially political advertising—was on the upswing, and circulation was growing quickly. By April 1911, the *Voter* reported that it already had readers in twenty-seven states. Not all were women; the *Western Woman Voter* boasted it had a male readership in the "hundreds."[13]

By May 1911, the interests of the magazine even seemed to be extending beyond the West. The publication profiled "America's Best Mayors" and began with Cleveland Mayor Tom Johnson and reprinted coverage of the two factory fires that killed so many women (one in New York and the other in New Jersey).[14] The monthly was soon carrying news of the New York City suffrage pageant. The eastern suffragists seemed especially intrigued by this new publication. Ida Husted Harper, the historian of the movement, wrote the editor that the *Western Woman Voter* alone provided accurate information on the women voters of the West. "I cannot put into words the inspiration and assistance this [accurate news of the West] has already been to the suffrage movement of the eastern states."[15]

This is not to say that the monthly ignored the news of its sister states in the West. The publication extensively covered the California campaign—produced primarily by its two California editors, Alice Park and Londa Stebbins Fletcher.[16] As the campaign heated up in Oregon, the *Voter* covered the race there. Often, the news was provided by one of the most important figures in that campaign, Abigail Scott Duniway.[17]

However, there were problems behind the scenes of the *Voter*. In November 1911, the publication carried news of the death of William Elbridge Parker, the father of Adella and Maud. While the quality of the writing itself did not decline, the focus of the publication shifted. The publication was now concentrating almost solely on Seattle and Washington. The publication was issued in December 1911 and January and February 1912. Then the publication lapsed, to be revived in January 1913 in a slightly altered form. The publication would reappear, but this time as a bimonthly. The editors promised that they had special issues planned covering the "Single Tax," "Anti Militarism," and "Anti Saloon." However, readers had to do something in return. The *Voter* needed one thousand subscribers at fifty cents a year to put the publication back on a sound financial footing.[18] Parker explained that the *Voter*'s lapse was "unavoidable." Her father's death as well as settling the complex estate did not allow her the time to get the publication out. It had not, however, erased the need for the monthly, an "independent political journal giving to the world accurate news of women voters of the west and their activities," she insisted.[19] Nor had the lapse hurt the writing or comment within the publication. The January 1913 issue was as editorially strong as it had always been. The *Western Woman Voter* had returned to its strong coverage within the region and within the nation. Nonetheless, the January 1913 issue was its last.

The *Western Woman Voter* held great promise. It was well written and well edited. It was built on the idea that women, once enfranchised, would vote together to achieve reform. As the death of the *Western Woman Voter* and subsequent history have shown, that idea had little to do with reality.

Notes

1. Sandra L. Myres, *Westering Women and the Frontier Experience, 1800–1915* (Albuquerque: University of New Mexico Press, 1982), p. 225.

2. Parker faced immediate competition. Mrs. M. T. Hanna, who had been publisher of *Votes for Women*, started her own publication, *The New Citizen*. Little is known about the publication other than it was established in 1911. Hanna had been publisher of the campaign journal *Votes for Women*.

3. Ida Husted Harper, ed., *The History of Woman Suffrage*, vol. 5, 1900–1920 (New York: National American Woman Suffrage Association, 1922), pp. 674–678, 681, 686.

4. "William Elbridge Parker—A Genial Philosopher," November 1911, p. 11.

5. "Announcement," January 1911, p. 6.

6. Ibid.

7. January 1913, p. 8.

8. Her involvement was probably minimal, limited to peace stories or news from eastern states.

9. "The Mayoralty of Seattle—An Opportunity," February 1911, p. 3.

10. "The Record Geo. W. Dilling in the Legislature in 1903," February 1911, p. 5.

11. "The Protection of Vice," February 1911, p. 6.

12. See front cover, April 1911.

13. "Confidential Chat between the Publisher and the Subscribers and Advertisers of the Western Woman Voter," April 1911, p. 9.

14. "America's Best Mayors—1. Tom Johnson," May 1911, p. 3; "Lest We Forget," May 1911, p. 5.

15. "Correspondence," June 1911, p. 11. Harper also credited the publication for much of the material on the Washington suffrage campaign that appeared in her *History of Woman Suffrage*, vol. 5, p. 677n.

16. See front cover, September 1911, and "The California Campaign—by Alice Park," November 1911, p. 5.

17. See, for example, Abigail Scott Duniway, "Portland Women Ask for Ballot,"
September 1911, p. 8.
18. "The Western Woman Voter," January 1913, p. 2.
19. January 1913, p. 8.

Information Sources

BIBLIOGRAPHY:
Duniway, Abigail Scott. *Path Breaking: An Autobiographical History of the Equal Suf-
frage Movement in Pacific Coast States.* Portland: James, Kerns and Abbott, 1914.
Harper, Ida Husted, ed. *The History of Woman Suffrage.* Vol. 5, 1900–1920. New York:
National American Woman's Suffrage Association, 1922.
Larson, T. A. "The Woman Suffrage Movement in Washington." *Pacific Northwest
Quarterly* 67. 2, April 1976, pp. 49–62.
Mead, Lucia True Ames. *What Women Might Do with the Ballot. The Abolition of the
War System.* New York: National American Woman Suffrage Association, 1909.
Myres, Sandra L. *Westering Women and the Frontier Experience, 1800–1915.* Albu-
querque: University of New Mexico Press, 1982.
Park, Alice L. *Women under California Laws.* San Francisco: California Equal Suffrage
Association, 1911.
Schwantes, Carlos A. *Radical Heritage: Labor, Socialism, and Reform in Washington
and British Columbia, 1885–1917.* Seattle: University of Washington Press, 1979.
INDEX SOURCES: None.
LOCATION SOURCES: Kent State University Library (Ohio) and many other libraries.
(Microfilmed on "Periodicals on Women and Women's Rights" Series I, Green-
wood Publishing.)

Publication History

PERIODICAL TITLE AND TITLE CHANGES: *Western Woman Voter.*
VOLUME AND ISSUE DATA: Vols. 1–3 (January 1911–January 1913. No issues
March 1912 to December 1912). Monthly.
PUBLISHER AND PLACE OF PUBLICATION: Western Woman Voter Publishing Co.
(1911–1913). Seattle.
EDITORS: Adella Parker (entire staff of editors includes Adella Parker, Alice Park,
Elizabeth Baker, Maud Parker, and Londa Stebbins Fletcher. Lucia Ames Mead
added in April, and Elsie Wallace Moore in October) (1911–1913).
CIRCULATION: Unknown.

Kathleen L. Endres

THE WISCONSIN CITIZEN

The road to woman suffrage in Wisconsin was far from smooth and certainly
gave little indication of progress during the seventy-three years between the
territory's first constitutional convention in 1846 and the state's ratification of
the Nineteenth Amendment in June 1919. During those years, the Wisconsin
movement lurched forward in fits and starts, with long periods of inactivity

between shorter bursts of intense lobbying and campaigning. But for the last three decades of the movement, its one constant was the suffrage sheet *The Wisconsin Citizen.*[1]

The paper, which was published continuously from 1887 to 1917, kept suffragists up-to-date on the latest suffrage developments, reported news concerning state and national suffragists, and commented on press coverage of the movement. Not only did it serve as a bulletin board for suffrage activities, but it often reflected, sometimes unwittingly, conflicts and struggles for leadership within the movement. Distributed to newspapers and suffrage organizations across the country, its news reached a constituency far larger than the Wisconsin suffrage membership.[2]

The Wisconsin Citizen was founded in 1887 by the Rev. Olympia Brown, a charter member of the American Equal Rights Association and the New England Woman's Suffrage Association. Born in 1835, Brown was one of the first woman ministers in the country and, in 1878, moved from Connecticut to Racine to take charge of a small Universalist congregation. She quickly became involved in local suffrage activity and in 1881 was elected vice president of the Wisconsin Woman Suffrage Association (WWSA). In 1884 she became president.[3]

Determined and outspoken, Brown soon became embroiled in controversy after voters passed a school suffrage bill that suffragists believed would allow women to vote in any elections considering school issues. When they went to the polls in 1887, however, many were prevented from voting. Brown promptly sued the state and launched a personal, statewide campaign.[4]

Developments in the case as well as her efforts were typically misrepresented in the press, and in August 1887 Brown convinced Racine suffragist Mrs. M. P. Dingee to volunteer as editor of a monthly publication, which they would call *The Wisconsin Citizen.* With the advent of the four-page paper, Brown told her readers, she would finally be able to circumvent "newspaper sensationalism and idle or malicious gossip" and see in print the correct account of events.[5]

The court case was eventually lost, and what Brown later described as a "torpor" settled over the Wisconsin movement. In the years between 1889 and 1902, county chapters died off, annual conventions were poorly attended, and in some years, *The Wisconsin Citizen* was the only evidence of a surviving suffrage sentiment.[6]

Published first in Racine and later in Brodhead at monthly or bimonthly intervals, the paper ran from four to eight pages at a yearly subscription price of twenty-five cents. Its main focus was the Wisconsin woman suffrage movement, but it also covered campaigns in other states and occasionally addressed other issues affecting women, such as temperance and labor laws. It followed press coverage of the movement and bitterly critiqued the antisuffrage position taken by many newspapers.[7]

During these years, Brown frequently absented herself from the state to work with national suffragists for passage of a federal amendment. She continued to communicate with the WWSA through *The Wisconsin Citizen,* but despite her attempts to keep both the paper and the WWSA alive, by the turn of the century the publication had only seventy subscribers, and the membership of the association had declined equally.[8]

This state of affairs persisted until the end of the next decade, when unrelenting lobbying by a handful of energetic and innovative suffragists persuaded the legislature to pass a suffrage referendum bill in spring 1911. Heartened by these developments, Brown used *The Wisconsin Citizen* to announce upcoming events, issue calls for volunteers and speakers, and solicit financial support. The paper boosted morale, publishing good news on the campaign whenever possible and giving full coverage to any endorsement by prominent men or organizations.

The paper also covered the opposition. It frequently published items about antisuffrage activities and paid special attention to the Wisconsin German-American Alliance after that organization, which claimed thirty-seven thousand members, announced its opposition.[9] Another enemy frequently attacked was the state's powerful brewing industry, which had long opposed woman suffrage in the belief that once women got the vote, they would vote for Prohibition.[10] When the referendum was defeated in November 1912, the paper denounced the brewers and saloon keepers:

> One element in our state which was the leader in the fight against the amendment knows its henchmen now. Every anti, whether consciously or unconsciously, voted in behalf of this element. . . . It was the breweries and the saloon keepers who fighting behind the skirts of the "antis" defeated the cause both in Ohio and Wisconsin.[11]

The enemies of suffrage were not always external opponents—a very real threat to the unity of the movement was posed by a younger generation of women who in 1910 challenged Brown's low-key campaign tactics, which in the past had brought such "meager results."[12] After failing to oust the seventy-six-year-old Brown from office, the rebels formed an independent organization, the Political Equality League (PEL). *The Wisconsin Citizen* published a few articles in which Brown answered her critics but then excluded anything about the campaign activities of the rival group. The PEL then had to resort to publishing its own newsletter, a duplication of effort that often caused confusion and prolonged the dispute.[13]

The referendum of 1912 was defeated, and during the following winter a truce between the factions was reached, with the condition that new officers be elected to lead a reorganized WWSA. After thirty years as president of the WWSA, Brown unwillingly agreed to yield the gavel. Theodora Winton Youmans, who, as assistant editor of the *Waukesha Freeman,* had written weekly suffrage columns and had acted as the PEL's press correspondent throughout the 1911–1912 campaign, became president.[14]

Sensitive of the need to unify the organization, Youmans planned on using

The Wisconsin Citizen to reassure WWSA members and inform them of the changes taking place.[15] She was determined to adopt a positive tone and in her first "President's Letter" to be published in the paper, praised the merger as a strength that would contribute to the "work of the future."[16] She soon discovered, however, that while *The Wisconsin Citizen* might print her "President's Letter," she had no editorial control over the paper, for it remained under the editorship of Lena V. Newman, whom Brown had handpicked seven years before. Newman was a loyal member of the old guard and still printed Brown's columns, often giving them precedence over Youmans'. Thus, instead of reconciling the differences between the old WWSA and the new, the paper only perpetuated them. After nearly a year of this, Youmans succeeded in ousting Newman. Under the guise of cutting publication costs and concentrating administrative work under one roof, she moved the paper to Waukesha, where it could be printed at the *Freeman,* and took over as editor.[17]

Control of what had for so long been referred to as "Rev. Brown's paper" thus passed in 1914 to Youmans, who used her power as editor to publicize her goals as president. Under her leadership, campaigning for legislation took second place to keeping the association intact and educating the public on the benefits of woman suffrage.[18] After announcing her intention to make *The Wisconsin Citizen* "primarily and essentially, a medium of communication among suffrage workers in Wisconsin," she reduced the paper to four pages, cut its mailing list from fourteen hundred (many of whom received complimentary copies) to four hundred newspapers and paying subscribers, and began to sell advertising space at fifty cents per inch.[19]

Advertising was nothing new to *The Wisconsin Citizen,* but Youmans urged readers to "patronize those who patronize us" and encouraged them to solicit advertisers from their own communities. These advertisers eventually represented not only a variety of businesses but also a number of reform and general-circulation publications. Some of these helped boost circulation rates by offering package subscription rates with *The Wisconsin Citizen.*[20]

The articles in Youmans' *Wisconsin Citizen* were newsy and to the point. Not only did she write her own copy, but she began to exchange material with a network of allied reform periodicals and pro-suffrage publications.[21] Although Youmans initially limited material to the suffrage movement in Wisconsin, she eventually began to include articles on developments in other states as well. After Congress revived the Anthony Amendment in 1915, she urged readers to insist that their state and federal representatives support the amendment and to campaign against those who refused. "It is up to you, Madame Suffragist in Mr. Blank's district, to secure his vote for justice for women," she wrote in 1917.[22]

During these years, *The Wisconsin Citizen* also reflected the conflict within the national suffrage movement over whether suffragists should continue fighting for suffrage state by state or focus on winning a national amendment. The National American Woman Suffrage Association (NAWSA), which the WWSA supported, elected to pursue state suffrage only in those states that had a strong chance of winning it. Because Wisconsin had the reputation of being one of the "hopeless" states, the WWSA directed its energy toward passage of a federal amendment and campaigns in other more promising states, a move that alienated some Wisconsin suffragists.[23]

A second, perhaps more divisive, conflict was waged over the position suffragists should take on the European war. Alice Paul's Congressional Union and took a pacifist stand, while the NAWSA offered support to Wilson's position and eventually endorsed his entry into war. Once again, the WWSA fell into line with the NAWSA, thus losing some of its most active members.[24] *The Wisconsin Citizen* reported these developments but sought to highlight consensus and focus on the positive activities of Wisconsin suffragists, such as their participation in national suffrage parades and conventions.

These schisms took a toll on the WWSA leadership, especially on Youmans, who frequently found herself traveling between Waukesha, Milwaukee, Madison, New York, and Washington in addition to her duties as press chairman, *The Wisconsin Citizen* editor, and assistant editor at the *Waukesha Freeman*. One way to reduce the pressure was to streamline the WWSA organization, reduce activities within the state, and focus energies on the campaign for the national amendment.[25] *The Wisconsin Citizen* became the victim of this policy, for Youmans first reduced it from a monthly to a quarterly in June 1916 and then, in January 1917, discontinued publication altogether. In its place, a typewritten monthly bulletin that retained the name of *The Wisconsin Citizen* was sent to the press and local societies. This substitute, however, was a far cry from the neatly typeset, eight-page paper. It was hastily put together, was often sprinkled with typing errors and corrections, and presented a slapdash appearance that could hardly have impressed Wisconsin editors.[26]

Once the original *The Wisconsin Citizen* ceased publication, the WWSA had no real local voice other than the bulletin and Youmans' weekly column in the *Freeman*. Yet a dedicated cadre of organizers persisted, constantly cutting away at resistance and building support among state and congressional representatives. Thus, in 1919, the state that had been labeled four years earlier as a lost cause won a double victory—full suffrage in the state legislature and the distinction of being the first state to ratify the federal amendment.

Although *The Wisconsin Citizen* had not played a role in these final victories, Youmans later praised it as "a doughty defender of the faith for three decades" in her history of the Wisconsin movement.[27] Certainly, most members of the WWSA, especially those veterans who had joined under Brown's leadership, would have credited it for sustaining the Wisconsin movement and keeping the spirit alive over most of the years of their memory.

Notes

1. Olympia Brown, "Wisconsin's Fight for Suffrage," *Milwaukee Free Press Sunday Magazine,* July 23, 1911, p. 1; Theodora Youmans, "How Wisconsin Women Won the Ballot," *Wisconsin Magazine of History* 5, 1921, pp. 3–32.

2. Theodora Winton Youmans, "Wisconsin," in Ida Husted Harper, ed., *History of Woman Suffrage,* Vol. 6, 1900–1920 (New York: Arno and the New York Times, 1969), pp. 699–700.

3. Charles E. Neu, "Olympia Brown and the Woman's Suffrage Movement," *Wisconsin Magazine of History* 43, Summer 1960, pp. 77–81; Charlotte Cote, *Olympia Brown: The Battle for Equality* (Racine, Wis.: Mother Courage Press, 1988), p. 190.

4. Brown, "Wisconsin's Fight for Suffrage," p. 1; Youmans, "How Wisconsin Women Won the Ballot," pp. 16–17.

5. February 1888, p. 1.

6. Brown, "Wisconsin's Fight for Suffrage," p. 1.

7. Passim. Individual articles from the *Wisconsin Citizen* are cited only when directly quoted.

8. Lawrence L. Graves, "The Wisconsin Woman Suffrage Movement, 1846–1920" (Ph.D. diss., University of Wisconsin, 1954), p. 111.

9. "German-American Alliance Meets in Milwaukee," *Milwaukee Free Press,* December 5, 1911, p. 1.

10. For discussion of opposition from the liquor industry, see Eleanor Flexner, *Century of Struggle: The Woman's Rights Movement in the United States,* rev. ed. (Cambridge: Belknap Press of Harvard University Press, 1975), pp. 328–337; Carrie Chapman Catt and Nettie Rogers Shuler, *Woman Suffrage and Politics: The Inner Story of the Suffrage Movement* (New York: Charles Scribner's Sons, 1923), pp. 440–445.

11. "Not Discouraged," November 1912, p. 4.

12. Josephine Kulzick to Olympia Brown, March 23, 1911, Ada Lois James Papers, State Historical Society of Wisconsin (hereafter ALJ Papers), box 5, folder 1; Mary Swain Wagner to Ada James, March 8, 1911, ALJ Papers, box 5, folder 1; Brown to James, July 1911, ALJ Papers, box 6, folder 1.

13. Youmans, "How Wisconsin Won the Vote," p. 21.

14. The WWSA had first elected Milwaukee suffragist Lutie Stearns, who accepted the nomination on the condition that members stop bickering. When they failed to do this, Stearns resigned after six weeks, and Youmans was recruited. See Youmans, "Wisconsin," pp. 703–704; Genevieve McBride, "Theodora Winton Youmans and the Wisconsin Woman Movement," *Wisconsin Magazine of History* 71, Summer 1988, p. 248.

15. Genevieve McBride, "Echo the Glad Sound: Origins of Public Relations in Nineteenth- and Early Twentieth-Century Reform" (Ph.D. diss., University of Wisconsin, 1989), p. 297.

16. "To Suffragists," February 1913, p. 3.

17. Willis to Youmans, January 12, 1914, Wisconsin Woman Suffrage Association Papers, State Historical Society of Wisconsin (hereafter WWSA Papers), box 3, folder 1; Brown to Youmans, January 14, 1914, WWSA Papers, box 3, folder 1; "Annual Meeting of the Wisconsin Woman's Suffrage Association," *Wisconsin Citizen,* November–December 1913.

18. Despite this change of focus, suffrage bills were presented regularly to each legislature as a matter of routine.

19. "Salutatory," June 1914, p. 1.

20. Ryan to Youmans, December 19, 1914, WWSA Papers, box 6, folder 1; Harris to Curtis, March 28, 1914, and April 6, 1914, WWSA Papers, box 3, folder 4.; Lucy Huffalser, *The Masses,* to Youmans, December 10, 1913, WWSA Papers, box 2, folder 4.

21. Ryan to Youmans, January 15, 1914, WWSA Papers, box 3, folder 1; Ryan to

Youmans, December 19, 1914 box 6, folder 3; Judith W. Loewenthal to Youmans, June 26, 1916, WWSA Papers, box 10, folder 1.
    22. "Your Responsibility," January 1917, p. 1.
    23. Flexner, *Century of Struggle,* pp. 273–276; McBride, "Echo the Glad Sound," pp. 309–315.
    24. Youmans, "How Wisconsin Women Won the Ballot," p. 29; Flexner, *Century of Struggle,* pp. 298–299; McBride, "Theodora Winton Youmans," pp. 268–269.
    25. McBride, "Theodora Winton Youmans," pp. 268–270.
    26. The *Wisconsin Citizen,* 1917–1919, WWSA Papers, box 26, folder 5.
    27. Youmans, "How Wisconsin Women Won the Ballot," p. 17.

Information Sources

BIBLIOGRAPHY:
Ada Lois James Papers. State Historical Society of Wisconsin, Madison.
Brown, Olympia. "Wisconsin's Fight for Suffrage." *Milwaukee Free Press,* July 23, 1911.
Catt, Carrie Chapman, and Nettie Rogers Shuler. *Woman Suffrage and Politics: The Inner Story of the Suffrage Movement.* New York: Charles Scribner's Sons, 1923.
Cote, Charlotte. *Olympia Brown: The Battle for Equality.* Racine, Wis.: Mother Courage Press, 1988.
Flexner, Eleanor. *Century of Struggle: The Woman's Rights Movement in the United States.* Rev. ed. Cambridge: Belknap Press of Harvard University Press, 1975.
Graves, Lawrence L. "The Wisconsin Woman Suffrage Movement, 1846–1920." Ph.D. diss., University of Wisconsin, 1954.
McBride, Genevieve. "Theodora Winton Youmans and the Wisconsin Woman Movement." *Wisconsin Magazine of History* 71, Summer 1988, pp. 3–32.
———. "Echo the Glad Sound: Origins of Public Relations in Nineteenth- and Early Twentieth-Century Reform." Ph.D. diss., University of Wisconsin, 1989.
Neu, Charles E. "Olympia Brown and the Woman's Suffrage Movement." *Wisconsin Magazine of History* 43, Summer 1960, pp. 77–87.
Wisconsin Woman Suffrage Association Papers. State Historical Society of Wisconsin, Madison.
Youmans, Theodora. "How Wisconsin Women Won the Ballot." *Wisconsin Magazine of History* 5, 1921, pp. 3–32.
———. "Wisconsin." In Ida Husted Harper, ed., *History of Woman Suffrage,* vol. 6, 1900–1920. New York: Arno and the New York Times, 1969, pp. 699–700.
INDEX SOURCES: None.
LOCATION SOURCES: State Historical Society of Wisconsin, Madison; Schlesinger Library on the History of Women in America.

Publication History

PERIODICAL TITLE AND TITLE CHANGES: *The Wisconsin Citizen.*
VOLUME AND ISSUE DATA: Vols. 1–31 (August 1887–January 1917). Monthly and bimonthly (1887–1914); monthly (1914–1916); quarterly (1916–1917).
PUBLISHER AND PLACE OF PUBLICATION: Wisconsin Woman's Suffrage Association (1887–1917). Racine, Wis. (August 1887–October 1894); Brodhead, Wis. (November 1894–September 1898); Evansville, Wis. (October 1898–May 1899);

Brodhead, Wis. (June 1899–May 1914); Waukesha, Wis. (May 1914–January 1917).
EDITORS: Mrs. M. P. Dingee (August 1887–October 1894); Helen H. Charleton (November 1894–September 1898); Marilla Andrews (October 1898–May 1899); Helen H. Charleton (June 1899–November 1906); Lena V. Newman (December 1906–May 1914); Mrs. Henry M. Youmans (June 1914–January 1917).
CIRCULATION: 70–1,400.

Elizabeth V. Burt

THE WOMAN CITIZEN

The Woman Citizen[1] enjoyed one major advantage over most other suffrage publications: at the beginning, this weekly was adequately funded. It was underwritten by the enormous financial resources of the Leslie Woman Suffrage Commission. Unfortunately, that financial stability did not last. In the end, *The Woman Citizen* became just one more casualty of the Great Depression.

The founding of *The Woman Citizen* is a twofold tale: one of Carrie Chapman Catt, the suffragist leader, and the Leslie Woman Suffrage Commission; and the other of Catt and the merger of three distinct suffrage publications, *Woman's Journal,** *Woman Voter,** and *National Suffrage News.*

The Leslie Woman Suffrage Commission was made possible by the bequest of Mrs. Frank Leslie, a New York magazine publisher, to Catt. Under the terms of the will, Catt was the primary heir to an estate valued at $1.8 million.[2] The estate was to be used, at Catt's discretion, for "the furtherance of the cause of Women's Suffrage."[3] After much litigation, the court began transferring assets to Catt in early 1917. At that time, Catt incorporated the Leslie Woman Suffrage Commission.[4] Shortly after, the commission purchased the *Woman's Journal* from Alice Stone Blackwell and moved it from Boston to New York.

But the *Woman's Journal* was only one of three publications that merged to form the *Citizen;* the other two were the *Woman Voter* and the *National Suffrage News.* Each made its own contributions to the new weekly. The *Woman's Journal* brought its long, respected history within the woman suffrage movement as well as a contributing editor, Alice Stone Blackwell. Blackwell was a prominent suffragist, *Journal* editor, and daughter of woman's rights activists Lucy Stone and Henry Blackwell. The *Voter* was known for its editorial and graphic excellence. However, none of the *Voter's* editorial staff joined the *Citizen.* In addition, the *Voter* gave the new weekly access to the membership lists of the Woman Suffrage Party in New York City[5] and the extensive advertising that appeared in the *Voter.* The *National Suffrage News* was best known for its news. Blackwell characterized it as "full of valuable matter as a nut is of meat."[6]

Carrie Chapman Catt was the link that brought these three publications together to form the new weekly—she was head of the Leslie Woman Suffrage Commission (and heir to the Leslie estate), organizer of the Woman Suffrage

Party in New York City, and head of the National American Woman Suffrage Association.

From the beginning, the *Citizen* reflected the strengths of each of the predecessor publications. The *Citizen* was well written, chock-full of news, and graphically appealing. It was also the publication of Catt's National American Woman Suffrage Association (NAWSA) and all its state affiliates.

The strength of this national association meant that the weekly had an important role to play within the suffrage movement. In its opening editorial, the weekly explained, "For the first time in suffrage history[,] the strength of the suffrage propaganda can be concentrated in one journal under the aegis of the 'National.' The success of The Woman Citizen meant the success of the 'National.' "[7] Catt entrusted the *Citizen* to Rose Young. As the weekly's first editor in chief, Young worked with both Alice Stone Blackwell, a contributing editor, and Catt to produce a top-quality journal.

Readers were not disappointed. From the cover of the first issue, to the editorials, from the features emphasizing the role of women throughout the world, to the advertisements, here was a journal in which a reader could take pride. The front cover of the first issue—and a large number of subsequent issues—showed how the new weekly was carrying on the *Journal* and the *Voter*'s graphic excellence. The illustration showed a woman pointing to an equal-suffrage sign with the list of countries that had already achieved it. In contrast, Uncle Sam with rifle had a sign that read, "For Democracy." The caption implored, "Uncle Sam, Take the Mock Out of Democracy."[8]

The editorials set the direction for the publication. This would be a "woman's political weekly to help secure votes for women under every flag that floats and its challenge is to the attention of the general public by right of being the official organ of a group of 2,000,000 women who are demanding exactly that link with the public."[9]

The *Citizen* attempted to deal with the many aspects of the "modern" woman's life. Feature stories covered everything from woman suffrage in Mexico, to an approval of the measure by the House of Commons in England; from the militarism and moral depravity of Germany, to women voting in Russia; from Maud Wood Park, chair of the NAWSA congressional committee, reporting on new developments in Congress, to accounts of how a U.S. suffragist helped immigrants; from fashions for garden work, to graphics illustrating how suffrage was organized.[10]

The *Citizen* reached an influential, primarily female audience.[11] Members of the NAWSA received the publication, as did the members of the Woman's Suffrage Party of New York City. In addition, the Leslie Commission sent the *Citizen* free of charge each week to the members of Congress.[12]

The early issues of the *Citizen* illustrated just how many interests the readers had. For example, the publication extensively covered the issue of child labor and how to protect children against exploitative employers.[13] However, the largest portion of the editorial content covered woman suffrage and how to achieve

it within individual states and as a constitutional amendment. The weekly
seemed to cover the topic from every conceivable angle: from relishing the great
victories when New York State finally won suffrage,[14] to analyzing the forces
of the opposition[15]; from covering women's parades for suffrage,[16] to pointing
out the downfall of antisuffrage opponents[17]; from emphasizing President Woodrow Wilson's support of woman suffrage,[18] to castigating the woman suffrage
pickets at the White House.[19]

This is not to say, however, that the weekly ignored current events. It was
difficult to ignore World War I. Although Catt and the editorial staff of the
Citizen found war reprehensible as an abstract, they editorially supported U.S.
involvement in the war.

> Obnoxious as war is to women, there can be no half-hearted endorsement
> by women of America's stand in this war. Of every mother's daughter it
> is required that she stand and deliver in loyalty, in service, in money and
> in life itself.[20]

During the course of the war, the weekly emphasized women's role as it published stories and editorials recounting the heroism and war work of females
and front covers that showed "Win the War Woman" in such occupations as
physician, farmer, conductor, munitions worker, and knitter.[21] However, the *Citizen* editor never missed an opportunity to link the war with the need for suffrage. As one front cover illustrated, a World War I soldier told Uncle Sam
about his mother, "She Has Given Me to Democracy; Give Democracy to
Her."[22]

The end of the war and the granting of suffrage put the *Citizen* in a quandary.
Should the weekly be discontinued? Had its mission been completed? The editors and Catt saw the need for the publication to continue, and the Leslie Commission agreed to continue its financial support of the *Citizen*. The *Citizen*
continued with a different editorial mission. The vote was only the opening
salvo. Now the weekly could address the other issues affecting women. As
Young explained, the new *Citizen* would provide political education. It would
"help clarify issues, to help interpret economic and political interplay."[23] To
that end, Catt (on behalf of the Leslie Suffrage Commission) *lent* the *Citizen* to
the newly formed League of Women Voters for 1920.[24] Young remained editor;
Catt and Blackwell stayed on as contributing editors; and the Leslie Commission
continued to underwrite the publication. During that year, the *Citizen* offered
much political education, from stories on why women joined the Democratic
and Republican parties (the publication always provided balanced coverage on
such issues), to Carrie Chapman Catt's "Citizenship Course."[25] But the publication offered more than politics. It also provided stories on the dismal economic
realities faced by workingwomen and ways to reduce the high cost of living. It
offered advice on picking the right toys for children.[26]

After the one year with the League of Women Voters, the *Citizen* began its most innovative stage. Beginning in 1921, it became an independent women's publication. The League of Women Voters was given four pages in each issue[27]; but aside from that, the *Citizen* had no formal ties with any organization and promised to cover all women's groups. As Young explained, the *Woman Citizen* "will approach its readers on its own editorial responsibility. It will in particular present such political projects as specially affect women, and its line-up on social and political questions will be that of an independent, non-partisan organ."[28] Young remained editor; Blackwell, contributing editor. Catt wrote more than in the past. The Washington bureau was strengthened. New writers dealt with new issues, such as alimony. However, some of the old features, such as "The Carrie Chapman Catt Citizen Course," continued under this new format.

Young, ill with neuritis and rheumatism, left the *Citizen* in April 1921. But in her farewell editorial, she hinted of financial problems with the magazine. Advertising did not keep pace with production costs,[29] she observed. Luckily, the Leslie Commission continued to take up the slack.

Young's resignation allowed the *Citizen* to bring in an editor trained on the consumer side of publishing. The new editor was Virginia Roderick, who had been editor of *Everybody's,* a well-regarded consumer magazine. She seemed perfectly in step with the "new" direction of the *Citizen.* As Catt explained in the editorial introducing Roderick,

> It [the *Citizen*] will gather the news concerning women and news of events that affect women and reproduce truthfully and without bias. It will continue to plead as ever for the removal of discrimination against women in law and custom. It will advocate the fullest development of every woman's individuality and demand for her an equal share of the world's duties and privileges.[30]

Immediate changes were forthcoming. The publication shifted to a biweekly frequency cycle as a way to deal with the increasing production costs. Soon the *Citizen* began an aggressive subscription campaign. It had to raise twenty-five thousand dollars if the Leslie Commission was to pay for the publication's deficits. As the editor explained, the *Citizen* cost four dollars to produce, but subscribers paid only two dollars. The publication was successful in its appeals. Between 1921 and 1924, circulation increased from eight thousand to twenty thousand. Unfortunately, it needed forty thousand for financial self-sufficiency. That meant the publication had to take a different route to cut costs. In 1924, the *Citizen* cut back to twenty-four issues a year: biweekly, September to June, and monthly, July and August. Finally in September 1925, the *Citizen* became a monthly in the hopes of appealing to more advertisers.[31]

Throughout this time, the publication aimed at becoming "*the mirror of the life of the up-to-date intelligent woman.*"[32] That meant that the publication had to deal with a wide variety of topics. The *Citizen* remained true to its reform heritage by editorially embracing and often covering the peace movement.[33] It continued its interest in child labor by covering the proposed child labor amendment from every conceivable perspective, providing features by advocates and opponents of the measure.[34] It forever stood behind Prohibition, even as the issue became more and more controversial.[35] It came out against lynching and emphasized that women within communities must demand "stern punishment of the lynchers."[36]

It also had to answer the critics of women reformers. When the Daughters of the American Revolution (DAR) tarred certain women activists in an "anti-red" campaign, Carrie Chapman Catt came to their defense in the *Citizen.*

Instead, it [DAR in its literature] has made slanderous, mendacious and brutal attacks upon thousands of Americans who never saw a Bolshevik in their lives. It has charged them with direct or indirect connection with Moscow, with plots and plans to overturn the government until a veritable wave of hysteria is sweeping the country.

Catt then went on to support such activists as social settlement leader Jane Addams and trade unionist Rose Schneiderman against the DAR charges.[37]

In spite of the strong editorial content, the aggressive subscription drives, and the cutbacks in frequency, the publication faced substantial financial problems. More subscriptions were the answer. As mentioned, at least forty thousand were needed to bring it near self-sufficiency; the *Citizen* circulation, however, was stalled at twenty thousand.[38] The circulation department advised that the name of the publication, *The Woman Citizen,* might be a drawback. The advertising department concurred. The name "conjures up the militant woman," the advertising department contended.[39] The name had become a "handicap, both in attracting new readers and in appealing to advertisers for their business. Too many people read in the name a magazine devoted to women in politics and *nothing else.*"[40] In 1927, the *Citizen* began the search for a new name. Hundreds of names were suggested; but, in the end, the *Citizen* returned to its roots. The new name, announced in November 1927, would be the *Woman's Journal.* That name "does not imply a limited political field for the magazine," the editor wrote.[41]

In 1928, the *Woman's Journal* debuted, but there was no real change to the editorial content. The League of Women Voters still had its four pages. The editor, still Virginia Roderick, carried on the same editorial tone. The *Woman's Journal* stood against child labor, for Prohibition, and for peace. Features continued to offer balanced accounts of controversial issues, and the publication still carried extensive articles on political candidates. There were some changes, however. In 1929, the magazine began offering short fiction and stories dealing with investing. By 1930, the publication was carrying stories about unemployment and public works programs. In 1931, the magazine began to venture into radio, sponsoring fifteen-minute talks on "Current Events about Women" on NBC.[42]

But there were real financial problems facing the *Journal.* In 1927, the Leslie Commission, which had consistently covered the *Citizen*'s deficits, was going out of existence. The *Citizen* reorganized under a group of stockholders called guarantors. These guarantors, who were about the best-known and most affluent activist women in the nation, bought stock in the Woman Citizen Corp. In the meantime, the name was changed to the *Journal,* and aggressive circulation and advertising campaigns followed. The publication had been successful in both campaigns, the December 1930 and January 1931 issues having near-record circulations. The May 1931 issue of the *Journal* had the largest amount of advertising ever. Yet the June 1931 issue was the *Journal*'s last. The advertising and circulation gains were not enough, and the guarantors could not provide any additional capital. The *Journal* became a victim of the Great Depression.

In his history of social feminism in the 1920s, J. Stanley Lemons called the *Woman Citizen* "the principal organ of social feminism." During the final stages of the fight for suffrage, it was perhaps the most important journal of all because it reached suffragists in all states—and every person in Congress. Its influence was primarily due to its financial backing. The Leslie Woman Suffrage Commission's funds allowed the *Citizen* to do what few other reform publications could. It could not, however, survive the Great Depression. Its work was not complete, but that work would have to wait for another magazine and another generation of women.

Notes

1. Many no doubt will argue that *The Woman Citizen* was a continuation of the *Woman's Journal.* Depending upon the circumstances, Carrie Chapman Catt, who was responsible for the launch of the *Citizen,* might agree. However, there are several reasons that *The Woman Citizen* is included separately in this volume. First, the *Journal* was only one of three publications that merged to form the *Citizen.* Second, the *Citizen* began a new numeration at the time of its launch. Third, a separate chapter allows a closer examination of this publication. Toward the end of its life, *The Woman Citizen* changed its name to the *Woman's Journal* and emphasized the pre-*Citizen* ties to the *Journal.*

2. Leslie died on September 18, 1914. The estate was appraised at $1.8 million in stocks, bonds, and real estate. However, that was not the amount that was eventually transferred to Catt in the winter of 1917. Catt had to spend a good deal of that on inheritance taxes and litigation costs. A full account of the bequest can be found in Ida Husted Harper, ed., *The History of Woman Suffrage,* vol. 5 (New York: National American Woman Suffrage Association, 1922), p. 755.

3. Harper, *The History of Woman Suffrage.*

4. Mary Gray Peck, *Carrie Chapman Catt: A Biography* (New York: H. W. Wilson, 1944), p. 225.

5. The *Voter* was the organ of the New York City Woman Suffrage Party.

6. Alice Stone Blackwell, "A Greeting," June 1, 1917, p. 7.

7. "To Subscribers and Members of the 'National,' " June 2, 1917, p. 3.

8. Front cover, June 2, 1917.

9. "A Journal of Democracy," June 2, 1917, p. 5.

10. "Votes for Women in Mexico," June 2, 1917, p. 9; "The Victory in England,"

p. 7; "The Thin Veneer," pp. 7–8; J. G. Ohsol, "Concerning Woman Suffrage in Russia," p. 12; Maud Wood Park, "The Congressional Situation," p. 14; Mrs. F. P. Bagley, "America and the Immigrant: A Suffragist Strikes the Balance," pp. 13, 18; "Keeping Up with the Plow," pp. 10–11; "How Suffrage Is Organized," pp. 16–17.

11. Exact circulation figures were not revealed in the publication until much later.

12. Harper, *The History of Woman Suffrage,* p. 556.

13. *The Woman Citizen* offered stories and editorials about the needs for labor laws to protect children. Among the first dealing with the issue was a front cover on the June 9, 1917, issue showing a woman protecting children and using the sword of "Labor Laws" against the exploiters of children who wanted these laws repealed. The caption read, "They Shall Not Pass." Other features included Alice Stone Blackwell, "Child Conservation," June 9, 1917, p. 26; "On Guard for Child-Life," April 20, 1918, p. 405.

14. "Glory, Glory Halleluia!", November 10, 1917, pp. 449–450; Alice Stone Blackwell, "Our Greatest Victory," p. 451.

15. "South Reverses Itself on State Rights," August 11, 1917, p. 179.

16. "The Woman's Parade in New York City," photo essay, November 3, 1917, pp. 434–435.

17. "Anti-Suffragist Governor Indicted," August 11, 1917, p. 179.

18. "Why a War Measure?" August 17, 1918, p. 225.

19. "The Picket and the Public," June 30, 1917, p. 79. The *Citizen* never welcomed the input of Alice Paul and the more radical suffragists.

20. "The War to End War," June 16, 1917, p. 41.

21. Mrs. James Lees Laidlaw, "War Service Activities of the New York Suffrage Party," August 25, 1917, p. 227; "An Open Letter to Women in War Time," April 13, 1918, p. 385; "Our Liberty Sandwich," May 4, 1918, p. 453. See front covers, April 13, 1918; May 11, 1918; May 18, 1918; June 1, 1918; June 8, 1918.

22. Front cover, September 29, 1917.

23. "Announcement Extraordinary," February 28, 1920, p. 911.

24. Ibid.

25. "Why I Joined My Party," February 14, 1920, p. 841; "Citizenship Course," September 18, 1920.

26. Emily Newell Blair, "Pin-Money Fallacies," February 14, 1920, pp. 850, 856–858; Elaine Hill, "A Practical Experiment with an Eye to Reducing the High Cost of Living," February 14, 1920, pp. 852–853; Louise Connolly, "Making the Plaything Fit the Child," September 4, 1920, pp. 366, 368.

27. These four pages were called "The Woman Voter" and were under the complete control of the League of Women Voters. This insert had its own editor and became known as the "official organ of the National League of Women Voters."

28. "Retrospect and Prospect," January 1, 1921, p. 837.

29. Rose Young, "Good-by Everybody, and Good Luck!" April 2, 1921, p. 1121.

30. Carrie Chapman Catt, "We March On," April 9, 1921, p. 1142.

31. Advertisement, April 9, 1921, p. 1156; "A Happy New Year," December 29, 1923, pp. 16–17; "Happy New Year!" December 27, 1924, p. 31; "Women Who Are Helping to Make The Woman Citizen," January 24, 1925, p. 31; "Heart to Heart," July 11, 1925, p. 31; "Heart to Heart," August 8, 1925, p. 31.

32. September 1925, p. 39.

33. See, for example, Carrie Chapman Catt, "Be Informed on the Peace Question,"

September 22, 1923, p. 14; "Peace Straws, December 1927, p. 26. See also the special issue on the Conference on the Cause and Cure of War, February 7, 1925.

34. See, for example, the December 27, 1924 issue; Owen Lovejoy, "The Present Child Labor Evil," pp. 9–10, 24; Grace Abbott, "The History of Child Labor Laws," pp. 11, 27; Mrs. William Lowell Putnam, "Why the Amendment Is Dangerous," pp. 12, 28; Florence Kelly, "Objections Secret and Public to the Amendment," pp. 13–14, 28; Ethel M. Smith, "Who's For? Who's Against?" pp. 14, 25.

35. In keeping with its policy of balance, the publiation provided stories by both pro- and anti-prohibitionists. But in its editorials, it remained for Prohibition (August 1928, pp. 5–7).

36. "More Lynchings," November 1926, p. 29.

37. Carrie Chapman Catt, "Open Letter to the D.A.R.," July 1927, pp. 10–12, 41–42.

38. "Heart to Heart," February 1927, p. 51. This was the same circulation that was reported in 1924 in "Happy New Year!" December 27, 1924, p. 31.

39. "Heart to Heart," September 1927, p. 43.

40. "Heart to Heart, November 1927, p. 43.

41. Ibid.

42. December 1930, p. 27.

Information Sources

BIBLIOGRAPHY:

Catt, Carrie Chapman, and Nettie Rogers Shuler. *Woman Suffrage and Politics: The Inner Story of the Suffrage Movement.* New York: Charles Scribner's Sons, 1923.

Harper, Ida Husted, ed. *The History of Woman Suffrage.* Vol. 5. New York: National American Woman Suffrage Association, 1922.

Huxman, Susan Schultz. "The *Woman's Journal,* 1870–1890: The Torchbearer for Suffrage." In Martha M. Solomon ed., *A Voice of Their Own: The Woman Suffrage Press, 1840–1910.* Tuscaloosa: University of Alabama Press, 1991.

Lemons, J. Stanley. *The Woman Citizen: Social Feminism in the 1920s.* Urbana: University of Illinois Press, 1973.

Peck, Mary Gray. *Carrie Chapman Catt: A Biography.* New York: H. W. Wilson, 1944.

"Woman's Journal Quits." *New York Times,* June 5, 1931, p. 24.

INDEX SOURCES: Indexed by the *Citizen-Journal.*

LOCATION SOURCES: Oberlin College; Schlesinger Library, Radcliffe College; and other libraries.

Publication History

PERIODICAL TITLE AND TITLE CHANGES: *The Woman Citizen* (1917–1927); *Woman's Journal* (1928–1931).

VOLUME AND ISSUE DATA: Vols. 1–16 (June 2, 1917–June 1931). Weekly (1917–1921); biweekly (1921–1924); biweekly September to June, monthly July and August (1924–1925); monthly (1925–1931).

PUBLISHER AND PLACE OF PUBLICATION: Woman Citizen Corp. (1917–1931) (underwritten by Leslie Woman Suffrage Commission 1917–1928 and guarantors 1928–1931). New York City.

EDITORS: Rose Young (1917–1921); Virginia Roderick (1921–1931).
CIRCULATION: Self-reported, 1924 and 1927: 20,000.

Kathleen L. Endres

THE WOMAN PATRIOT

In January 1918, President Woodrow Wilson, after several years of vacillation, extended his support for a federal constitutional amendment giving women the vote. Later that month, the House of Representatives passed a motion approving the amendment by the narrowest possible margin. However, the Senate did not come to grips with the issue until May 1919. The action by the upper house kicked off vicious state-by-state campaigns by both supporters and opponents, one group determined to do whatever it could to get the necessary 75 percent approval rate, the other just as determined to prevent it. When the amendment finally passed the Tennessee legislature two years later, some twenty-six million American women joined the ranks of the enfranchised.[1]

Nonetheless, the battle lines between pro- and antisuffragist forces remained ingrained. For veteran suffragist campaigners such as Alice Paul, the acquisition of the vote was only the first step in the long road to enshrining the equality of women into the sanctity of law. In 1921, just one short year after the turmoil created by the suffrage battle showed a few, but still weak, signs of waning, Paul introduced the concept of an equal rights amendment. Her timing was hardly prudent. After a battle that spread over several generations, Americans were exhausted with reform. In fact, Paul was undoubtedly tainted by the fact that she was seen primarily as a reformer living in an age when reformers were more despised than the causes they espoused.[2]

Nonetheless, she believed that in spite of acquiring legal equality in the ballot booth, American women were still denied the right to serve on juries; were not able to hold property equally with men; were unable to keep their own names after marriage; and suffered from limited rights regarding the guardianship of children and the ability to make contracts and to initiate lawsuits.[3]

Alice Paul articulated positions that forced American women to think beyond the narrow borders that defined the suffragist movement. In many ways, she inherited the mantle of Elizabeth Cady Stanton and Susan B. Anthony, owing less of her intellectual maturity to Lucy Stone and Henry B. Blackwell. Her "feminism" became as divisive in American society as the voting battles that preceded it. As the suffragist battle began to fade into history, so did the journals that grew up around it. New alliances with new causes and different class and status characteristics soon became apparent in the pages of new newspapers.

In the summer of 1916, Carrie Chapman Catt, president of the National American Woman Suffrage Association (NAWSA), approached Lucy Stone's daughter, Alice Stone Blackwell, with a proposition to create one newspaper out of three pro-suffrage journals. The following year, *The Woman's Journal,** *Woman Voter,** and *National Suffrage News* joined to form *Woman Citizen,** a moderately pro-feminist newspaper that continued to publish until 1927. On the other side of the ideological fence, three antisuffragist publications, *The Remonstrance,** *Anti-Suffrage Notes,* and The *Women's Protest,* joined forces to create the virulent, antifeminist *The Woman Patriot*.[4] The publishers moved the newspaper from New York to Washington, D.C., in the spring of 1918 to mount a last-ditch attempt to destroy the Nineteenth Amendment.

The first issue appeared on April 27. The publishers announced that like its major predecessor, *The Women's Protest,* the new publication would be sponsored by the National Association Opposed to Woman Suffrage. In the first issue, it was reported that four hundred and fifty thousand adult women who were members of the organization supported the newspaper's goals.

With the launching of the new journal, the editors declared that the "antisuffrage movement henceforth will wage unceasing war against the two great enemies of our civilization, Feminism and Socialism."[5] The editorial direction was hardly surprising, since the spirit behind the publication was the same one that drove essentially middle-class white women in the industrialized Northeast to oppose suffrage movements around the turn of the century. These were women who were wealthy, prominent in the "correct" social spheres, and deeply experienced in donating their family fortunes to worthy causes as they defined them.[6] When universal suffrage eventually became law, these determined citizens turned their attention to "new evils," with the same obsessions and drive that brought them together in the first place.

No one could accuse *The Woman Patriot* of being the kinder, gentler version of any acknowledged antisuffragist, antifeminist journal. Its "devils" were forcefully kicked in the literary teeth more than once. Without exception, it argued,

> woman suffrage means higher taxation, twice as much partisan politics, more inexperienced women in office, the perpetuation of political "frightfulness" by which women suffragists are threatening all who oppose them with "reprisals" and blacklists and a doubled Bolshevist vote, a doubled pacifist vote in time of war.[7]

Editor in chief Minnie Bronson did not abide opposition, especially from the ranks of those she detested, notably Carrie Chapman Catt, who received more than her share of attention in the journal's columns. In many ways, it was the Roaring Twenties version of a scorchy tabloid, carefully enhanced with the use of innuendo that would later be known as McCarthyism. Typical is its condemnation of a pro-suffragist university professor from Chicago. William Isaac Thomas, recently

> expelled from the faculty of the University of Chicago after his arrest on a charge of disorderly conduct for registering at a hotel under an assumed name with the wife of an absent army officer, is the same Professor Tho-

mas, who, as the special invited guest of the National American Woman Suffrage Association, created a sensation at the suffragists' famous banquet in Chicago on June 7, 1915. Professor Thomas then declared that "any unmarried girl, mentally mature, has the right to motherhood" and advocated "birth control." Anna Howard Shaw, honorary president of the suffragists, who presided, defended the professor's remarks.[8]

The unfortunate Professor Thomas would make more than one appearance in the pages of *The Woman Patriot*.

The Susan B. Anthony bill, later to become the Nineteenth Amendment, was introduced while America was still at war. The editors of *The Woman Patriot* exploited the situation to equate the campaign against suffrage with matters or persons deemed to be immoral. In a headline in the August 3, 1918, edition, the kaiser's cousin was blamed for organizing the suffrage campaign in New York City's German community. In the same issue, another headline revealed that antisuffragists were aiding needy children in war-torn Belgium. Yet a third headline noted that antisuffrage states were the most progressive in promoting child welfare.[9]

Not unlike its major ideological adversary, *Woman Citizen, The Woman Patriot* successfully bridged the end of the suffrage battles to become the voice of American female conservatism. In reality, the defeat of the antisuffragist forces in August 1920 in Tennessee brought to a close the fight against extension of the franchise, although the editors announced,

> It will be the duty of anti-suffragists to see that efforts to make double suffrage a complete success by transforming both sexes into weak neuters will be thwarted in educational channels so that this feminist disease which has already contracted twelve times in the world's history, will again subside because of women's greater love of deep instincts than of commercial careers and public competition with sons and husbands. Our fight has really just begun.[10]

Once Germany and its allies lost the war, and the Tennessee vote was registered in Washington, the Teutonic bogeyman never again suffered from attention in the pages of the journal. However, other sinister manifestations such as socialism and feminism soon took its place and, in many ways, received a much more severe deconstruction than its predecessor.

The journal argued that, in most respects, socialism and feminism posed much more of a threat to a perceived American way of life than the kaiser and his minions had ever done. At least to the editors of *The Woman Patriot,* the kaiser was naked in his military aggression, and the only threat to the unity of Allied forces facing him was a determined campaign in the United States by pacifists. Margaret C. Robinson, editor of a column titled "Anti-Suffrage Notes," once lamented in the spring of 1918 that:

It was only last August that the Women's Peace Party was sending propaganda throughout the country, importuning women to oppose the government's war plans, to oppose the draft, food control regulations, war
bond issues and a continuance of the war.[11]

In its simplest form, socialism to the people behind *The Woman Patriot* was
un-American. To them, the ideology not only was foreign in origin but had
negatively racial characteristics. It was noted that the socialist vote was concentrated in large, industrial cities from the Northeast to the Midwest. The September 7, 1918, issue reported that in New York, socialists had increased their vote
in the November elections fourfold. In Chicago, the gain (with women voting
as well), was sevenfold. Similar socialist upswings were recorded in Pittsburgh,
Cleveland, Detroit, Buffalo, Boston, San Francisco, Milwaukee, Newark, Minneapolis, Jersey City, Providence, St. Paul, Worcester, Scranton, and Fall River
and Cambridge in Massachusetts. The article noted that in all cases, less than
one-third of these urban centers were populated by Anglo-Saxons. Tainted by
an overdose of nativism, the editors noted:

It is communities of foreigners like those in which the socialist agitators
find their readiest following, and it is the women of these communities
who would flock to the polls, while the women on the farms and in the
small towns would largely stay at home. Socialism is foreign propaganda,
not American—and women suffrage is a structural part of it.[12]

The argument that socialism was foreign to American political culture was
far simpler than drawing the same parallels to the emergence of American feminism. After all, socialism was the creation of two German thinkers, one of
whom was also Jewish. As well, socialism's first major political inroads had
been made in Europe, both in the Paris Commune of 1870 and, some years
later, with the October Revolution in the Soviet Union.
    In the first major assault on feminism, the editors declared that "the entire
feminist philosophy is an insult to manhood and motherhood—a cult founded
entirely on the belief that there is no such thing as the spiritual kingdom, that
laws, votes, compulsion and force are the only agencies for securing "rights"
or redressing wrongs."[13] As pressure mounted for adoption of the equal rights
amendment, Mary G. Kilbreth, who had assumed the presidency of the National
Association Opposed to Woman Suffrage following the defeat in Tennessee,
observed:

To Feminists [*sic*], the vote, as Mrs. Catt expressed it, "was only a symbol." They did not spend millions and work for years to mark a paper
and drop it in a box. They worked for a weapon by which to achieve
certain results: the "political, social and economic independence of
women," as they called it.[14]

What was so terrifying about the independence of women? To noted radical labor leader Florence Kelley, adoption of equal rights legislation would place women under the same workplace laws as men. For Kelley, this had the potential of bringing a round of constitutional challenges to labor legislation specifically designed to protect the interests of women and children.[15] For conservative women, many of whom ended up in a strange bedfellow scenario with the likes of Kelley, feminism posed a series of more malevolent possibilities.

Antifeminists were convinced that full equality of the sexes would obliterate those barriers that existed at the time. They believed that precisely those barriers produced and protected elements of female privilege. For these people, males and females occupied separate places in the world, a phenomenon created by industrialization, which also placed dividing lines between the workplace and the home. As Susan Marshall observed:

> If the male public sphere was the realm of reason and power, the female private sphere was the realm of the heart and morality. These spheres were complementary; the home became the peaceful refuge, where higher values were nourished and comfort dispensed, both regenerating the alienated male worker and providing emotional rewards for his continued service to the industrial system.[16]

The definition of separate spheres for men and women was a little more colorful in the pages of *The Woman Patriot*. The so-called husband and father class, "these being endowed with greater strength of body and with bewhiskered toughness, must as a rule perform the outdoor work. They must provide food for the home by hunting, fishing and all the more laborious occupations by land and sea." On the other hand, "the sphere of Wives and Mothers [*sic*] is within the Home. Women are inferior in physical strength and must inevitably pass through periods of sickness and weakening of nervous power."[17]

No such set of relationships existed in the newly "feminist" state that had been created in Russia. On January 11, 1919, the journal reported that in Petrograd, all women between the ages of eighteen and forty-five would have husbands chosen for them by the town council. The article also carried the news that children produced by these unions would be raised not by their parents but by the state.

The journal used the opportunity to accuse American feminists of wanting to follow in the pathways trodden by their Soviet sisters. Editorials and articles proclaiming that female emancipation would lead to free love littered the pages of the newspaper following the victory of the Bolsheviks. American feminists, like their Soviet counterparts, were accused of distorting the meaning of words like "liberty" and "freedom." As Minnie Bronson wrote, "[T]he radicals couple some of the most beautiful words in the language into phrases that mean the vilest debasement, as applied by these same radicals."[18]

The Woman Patriot left no stone unturned in its campaign against liberal ideologies—liberal as they interpreted them. The journal wrote a review of Carrie Chapman Catt's book, *What Women Want,* in the February 22, 1919, edition. It specifically singled out the chapter in which Catt defined "The New Man." What kind of re-creation did he need?

> Every male instinct of domination and sovereignty must be bred out of the individual before he can attain the status of the new man and be a fit mate for the new woman. The new man has to unlearn those deep-rooted habits and instincts of sex.[19]

As the sounds of war faded into the past, as the battles over extension of the franchise dimmed, as tried-and-true conservatives and died-in-the-wool feminists continued to war with each other in the pages of their journals, the country was entering a new phase of economic and social development. Fortunately, or unfortunately, depending on one's point of view, neither of these images of women or the one depicting the carefree flapper who danced the Charleston rang with any sense of truth. As the 1920s dawned, the vast majority of American women "worked hard during the day, cared for their children, cleaned house and cooked meals. On summer nights, they would rest from their chores in rocking chairs on the porch or, in slum areas, on the front stoop of their tenement home."[20]

These women watched as the NAWSA voluntarily disbanded after the passing of the Nineteenth Amendment. They watched as the League of Women Voters emerged. They watched as Alice Paul continued her campaign throughout the 1920s to secure passage of an equal rights amendment. However, other activities were taking place that drew the attention of many American men and women from the gender battles of the previous decade. The Roaring Twenties became the first great decade of consumerism, bringing with it the growth of advertising as a major industry.[21] Electronic gadgetry started to make its way into everyday living as movie houses sprang up across the country, radio entered the lives of most citizens, and the promise of a personal automobile for each and every household was on the verge of reality. Both feminist and antifeminist newspapers had to compete for the attention of the American woman in a manner unknown in previous years.

What were the issues that drove *The Woman Patriot* as it made its way through the 1920s? For one, the journal continued the assault on Bolshevism in a rhetorical mode that was to repeat itself in the years following the Second World War. The New Year's Day edition in 1923 carried five headlines, all dedicated to waking a sleeping America to the dangers of communism. Quoting freely from Leon Trotsky, Vladimir Lenin, Gregory Zinoviev, and Karl Radek, the editors declared that Bolshevism would inevitably lead to the militarization of American labor. To further support the concept that Soviet communism was a clear and immediate threat to American civilization and not just some distant, strange-acting political machine, *The Woman Patriot* announced that there were "as many reds in America as communists in Russia."[22]

In an article entitled "How Reds Are Organizing Women," the journal introduced the now-familiar theme of "boring from within." Communist women should become

> members of the Feminine organizations of their communities, such as social clubs, sewing circles, etc. Entertainments should be offered to which their fellow club members should be invited and discussions of social problem should in every instance be staged. Those who express any degree of discontent with society or the government should be admired and cultivated by their Communist hosts."[23]

The newspaper's political stance became more rigidly conservative as the 1920s passed on. The editors staunchly supported the concept of states' rights to the point that most federal initiatives were interpreted as conspiracies against democracy itself. When Congress decided to introduce labor legislation regulating and, in some cases, prohibiting the employment of persons under the age of eighteen, the journal reacted with shock and horror. In a headline in the March 15, 1924, issue, a claim was made that the so-called child labor amendment would inevitably lead to federal control of the educational system. A subhead announced that Congress would also retain the power to regulate homes, guardianship, orphan's courts, and all children's institutions in the country.[24]

The next three issues were dedicated, for the most part, to fighting the child labor amendment. The editorial board, led by Mary Kilbreth, sponsored a petition against the amendment proposal. Kilbreth and her colleagues argued that the proposal was communist-inspired, since it has been promoted by labor agitator Florence Kelley. Although Kelley strongly opposed Alice Paul's equal rights amendment, Kilbreth and her colleagues regarded the unionist as a dangerous subversive, since she had translated some of Karl Marx's works and had allegedly been seen in the company of Friedrich Engels.

Essentially, the argument was based on three fundamental points. *The Woman Patriot* believed that

> denying anyone the right to work is a restriction on fundamental rights. Denying poor children the right to work would be to enforce starvation which would result in an underground labor economy out of the reach of any authority, or what the women called Bootleg Child Labor. The law would constitute an unwarranted invasion of American homes by countless bureaucrats seeking violators.[25]

It is somewhat surprising that a newspaper that espoused family values would be so opposed to federal assistance in social programs aimed precisely at this constituency. Yet, the libertarianism of the editorial board and Mary Kilbreth, specifically, took precedence over any attempt by federal politicians to shape or influence social policy. Buoyed by the defeat of the amendment at the state level, the newspaper decided to fight the extension of a piece of legislation known as the Maternity Act. A specific creation of the act, an administrative division of the Department of Labor known as the Children's Bureau, raised the ire of *The Woman Patriot.*

The intent of the legislation was to ensure that no American child would grow up without the basic fundamentals of life, including food, shelter, and medical care. The newspaper treated the activities of the Children's Bureau as an extension of a conspiracy by federal authorities to intrude on the daily lives of average Americans. Not too subtly, the journal painted a picture of communist atheism standing poised to destroy the honesty, purity, and virtue of every person calling himself or herself a citizen of the United States. However, one member of Congress, Senator Bayard of Delaware, was so incensed by the journal's scorching rhetoric that he demanded that an anti-Maternity Act document produced by the editorial board be entered in the Congressional Record. Senator Bayard noted:

> This document which spreads over thirty-five pages of the record is a mass of petty gossip, half-truths, misstatements and libelous allegations. Its purpose is to discredit the Children's Bureau and the Maternity Act. It is quite within the right of any citizen or group of citizens to oppose pending legislation and to state their case, but is neither honorable nor contributory to wise decision to see that end by slander or misrepresentation. . . . It is absurd to claim that the administration of the Children's Bureau and the Maternity Act contain anything that would give a foothold for communist principles. The conservation of mothers and children is essential to civilization and in accord with common sense.[26]

It was not characteristic of *The Woman Patriot* to be charitable to its adversaries. The publication of the senator's remarks served the sole purpose of giving its readers some insight as to why the editors despised him so much. The same issue contained a five-page rebuttal of the senator's remarks filled with the colorful and provocative language and sinister suggestions that led him to act in the first place.

What would prove to be the final battle for the minds and hearts of American women began in May 1928, when the journal decided to fight plans by the federal government to become involved in education. Mary Kilbreth appeared before the House Committee on Education under the direction of Daniel Reed on Wednesday, May 2, 1928. Kilbreth trotted out some of the timeworn arguments that had been characteristic of her campaigns in previous years. She claimed that she had proof that "radical, pacifist, minority professionals" were attempting to manipulate the proposed legislation to permit the National Education Association to "control teachers, schools and children to create a 'new world order.' "[27] In spite of her suspicions, the federal Department of Education eventually became a reality.

As the 1920s unraveled into the 1930s, and as the country faced an uncertain future. *The Woman Patriot* was beginning to look tattered and tired. From its initial heyday as a weekly publication, it had become a monthly, and even on this limited schedule, the editors were having a hard time meeting their financial obligations. In November 1931, they noted that "times are hard and the depression has struck almost everybody but office holders."[28] With a sense of resignation and some bitterness, the editors revealed that their newspaper was running a deficit of six thousand dollars per year. However, the old warhorse had enough energy to complete yet another year. In its final edition, it began a concerted campaign to paint Franklin D. Roosevelt as an unrepentant communist. In its final issue in 1932, it published what was to be the first of a series of exposes of European undesirables. Ironically, its first target was Albert Einstein.

Notes

1. Jo Freeman, "From Suffrage to Women's Liberation: Feminism in Twentieth-Century America," in Jo Freeman, ed., *Women: A Feminist Perspective,* 5th ed. (West Mountain View, Calif.: Mayfield, 1995), p. 509.

2. Mariam Darce Frenier, "American Anti-Feminist Women: Comparing the Rhetoric of Opponents of the Equal Rights Amendment with That of Opponents of Women's Suffrage," *Women's Studies International Forum,* 7, 6 1984, pp. 455–465.

3. Freeman, "From Suffrage to Women's Liberation," p. 510.

4. Susan E. Marshall, "Ladies against Women: Mobilization Dilemmas of Anti-Feminist Movements," *Social Problems* 32, No. 4, April 1985, p. 355, fn. 6.

5. April 27, 1918.

6. Susan E. Marshall, "In Defense of Separate Spheres: Class and Status Politics in the Anti-Suffrage Movement," *Social Forces* 65. 2, December 1986, pp. 330–331.

7. May 18, 1918.

8. April 27, 1918.

9. August 3, 1918.

10. August 21, 1920.

11. May 4, 1918.

12. September 7, 1918.

13. June 12, 1920.

14. June 15, 1921.

15. Jo Freeman, "From Suffrage to Women's Liberation: Feminism in Twentieth-Century America," p. 510.

16. Susan E. Marshall, "In Defense of Separate Spheres: Class and Status Politics in the Anti-Suffrage Movement," p. 333.

17. June 1, 1918.

18. January 11, 1919.

19. February 22, 1919.

20. June Sochen, *Herstory: A Woman's View of American History,* (New York: Alfred Publishing, 1974), pp. 285–286.

21. Ibid., p. 288.

22. January 1, 1923.

23. February 1, 1923.

24. March 15, 1924.

25. May 15, 1924.

26. August 19, 1926.
27. May 15, 1928.
28. November 1931.

Information Sources

BIBLIOGRAPHY:
Freeman, Jo. "From Suffrage to Women's Liberation: Feminism in Twentieth-Century America." In Jo Freeman, ed., *Women: A Feminist Perspective,* 5th ed. West Mountain View, Calif.: Mayfield, 1995.
Frenier, Mariam Darce. "American Anti-Feminist Women: Comparing the Rhetoric of Opponents of the Equal Rights Amendment with That of Opponents of Women's Suffrage." *Women's Studies International Forum* 7. 6, 1984, pp. 455–465.
Marshall, Susan E. "Ladies against Women: Mobilization Dilemmas of Anti-Feminist Movements." *Social Problems* 32.4, April 1985, pp. 348–362.
————. "In Defense of Separate Spheres: Class and Status Politics in the Anti-Suffrage Movement." *Social Forces* 65.2, December 1986, pp. 327–351.
Sochen, June. *Herstory: A Woman's View of American History.* New York: Alfred Publishing Co, 1974.
INDEX SOURCES: Union List of Serials.
LOCATION SOURCES: University of Western Ontario Library and other libraries.

Publication History

PERIODICAL TITLE AND TITLE CHANGES: *The Woman Patriot* (amalgamation of *Remonstrance, Woman Protest,* and *Anti-Suffragist Notes*).
VOLUME AND ISSUE DATA: Vols. 1–16 (1918–1932). Weekly (every Saturday) (1918–1922); Semi-monthly (1922–1931); monthly (1931–1932).
PUBLISHER AND PLACE OF PUBLICATION: Woman Patriot Publishing Company, Washington, D.C. (sponsored by the National Association Opposed to Woman Suffrage).
EDITORS: Minnie Bronson (1919–?) Editorial board: Henry Watterson, Anna Katherine Green, Octave Thanel, Annie Nathan Meyer, Elizabeth Ogden Wood, Margaret C. Robinson. Vol. 6. 9 lists Mary G. Kilbreth, former president of the National Association Opposed to Woman Suffrage, as vice president of the Woman Patriot Publishing Company. De facto, it appears that she has become the major editorial force behind the publication, although she is never listed on the masthead as editor. With the arrival of Kilbreth at the newspaper, personnel mastheads cease to exist.
CIRCULATION: Unreported.

David R. Spencer

THE WOMAN REBEL

In October 1914, birth control advocate Margaret Sanger boarded a train to Canada and from there a ship to Liverpool. "Parting from all that I held dear in life, I left New York at midnight, without a passport, not knowing whether

I could ever return,"[1] she wrote in her autobiography. She fled New York rather than face obscenity and incitement charges for publishing her magazine—*The Woman Rebel.*

The Woman Rebel was not strictly a birth control publication, although the magazine's very existence sparked the movement. Sanger's short-lived journal (only seven issues were published in 1914) also became a voice of socialist and anarchist thought, often to the dismay of readers. Sanger intended to challenge the very obscenity laws that prohibited her from printing birth control information. "I worked day and night at making it as red and flaming as possible," Sanger said.[2]

According to biographer Madeline Gray, the magazine's "primary goal was to make women, especially working women, more rebellious—rebellious about having to work such long hours in factories, rebellious about having to bear so many children, rebellious about having to be subservient to men."[3] The slogan "No Gods, No Masters" ran underneath the masthead of each issue. It was a derivation of the International Workers of the World (IWW) slogan "No God, No Master."

Sanger's first editorial supported Gray's assertion: "This paper will not be the champion of any 'ism.' All rebel women are invited to contribute to its columns. The majority of papers usually adjust themselves to the ideas of their readers but the WOMAN REBEL will obstinately refuse to be adjusted. The aim of this paper will be to stimulate working women to think for themselves and to build up a conscious fighting character."

Later in the same editorial, Sanger told readers that one of the magazine's features would be a column aimed at instructing teenage girls "of this uncertain age to know just what to do or really what constitutes clean living without prudishness." After putting forth a wandering condemnation of society's attitudes toward women and sex, Sanger said that young women were in need of knowledge and understanding of their physical nature.

"Other subjects, including the slavery through motherhood; through things, the home, public opinion and so forth, will be dealt with. It is also the aim of this paper to circulate among those women who work in prostitution; to voice their wrongs; to expose the police persecution which hovers over them and to give free expression to their thoughts, hopes and opinions. And at all times the WOMAN REBEL will strenuously advocate economic emancipation," Sanger concluded.[4] In essence, then, the journal was a soapbox for Sanger's views.

Although Sanger had spent several years prior to 1914 living her life first as a nurse, then as a quiet suburban wife and mother, she had been exposed to radical viewpoints for much of her life. Her father, Michael Higgins, was a freethinker who schooled his children in the views of single-tax proponent Henry George. Later, after Margaret married architect and painter William Sanger, the two attended a socialist party meeting in Yonkers in 1910. William Sanger had been a socialist for several years and was friends with Eugene Debs. The meeting proved to be an epiphany of sorts for Margaret Sanger. She became a socialist and devoted most of her free time to reading socialist publications and attending socialist meetings.[5]

Margaret and William Sanger moved to New York City from the affluent community of Hastings-on-Hudson in 1912. Although most of their socialist and radical friends lived in Greenwich Village, the Sangers lived in uptown Manhattan.

Socialism fueled Sanger's beliefs, but her return to work as an obstetrics nurse in 1912 awoke her to women's needs for birth control information. Sanger worked largely with Jewish immigrant women in New York's Lower East Side. Many of the women, Sanger discovered, despaired at the thought of having another baby. As one biographer wrote, "The women could not believe that she did not know the 'secret' [i.e., birth control]. Recurrent pregnancies plagued many women who were driven to desperate means to curtail them. A subterranean 'grapevine' of whispered remedies flourished in the community."[6] Many women died from botched abortion attempts.

Sanger sympathized with the women. Her own mother had given birth to eleven children, then died at the age of forty-eight. The death of a young patient, Sadie Sachs, from a failed self-abortion appears to have been a turning point in Sanger's life. She had helped nurse the woman back to health three months earlier following another self-abortion. Sachs had begged Sanger for birth control information before, only to be told that the law forbade such information from being given to patients, even from doctors and nurses. After the young woman's death, Sanger recalled: "I looked out my window and down upon the dimly lighted city. Its pains and griefs crowded in upon me, a moving picture rolled before my eyes with photographic clearness: women writhing in travail to bring forth little babies; the babies themselves naked and hungry, wrapped in newspapers to keep them from the cold; six-year-old children with pinched, pale, wrinkled faces. . . . I could bear it no longer. . . . I went to bed, knowing that no matter what it might cost, I was finished with palliatives and superficial cures; I was resolved to seek out the root of evil, to do something to change the destiny of mothers whose miseries were vast as the sky."[7]

Sanger claimed she spent most of 1913 in libraries, searching for any birth control information and finding little.[8] IWW leader Bill Haywood encouraged Sanger to go to France, where birth control information and devices were openly available. "This struck me as a splendid idea, because it would also give Bill Sanger a chance to paint instead of continuing to build suburban houses," she recalled.[9]

Upon her return to New York, Sanger decided to publish *The Woman Rebel*. "I knew something must be done to rescue those women who were voiceless; someone had to express with white hot intensity the conviction that they must be empowered to decide for themselves when they should fulfill the supreme function of motherhood. They had to be made aware of how they were being shackled, and roused to mutiny," Sanger stated in her memoirs.[10]

The Woman Rebel was not Sanger's first attempt at journalism. She had turned

a series of health talks into a column for the New York–based socialist newspaper, *The Call,* in 1912. A first series of articles, "What Every Mother Should
Know," ran successfully for several weeks, prompting a second series: "What
Every Girl Should Know." The articles ran successfully for several weeks as
well, until one Sunday readers found the column missing. In its place was a
two-column box that read: "WHAT EVERY GIRL SHOULD KNOW—NOTH-
ING—BY ORDER OF THE POST-OFFICE DEPARTMENT." The newspaper
and Sanger had run afoul of strict obscenity laws for trying to discuss syphilis
and gonorrhea.[11]

The Woman Rebel debuted in March 1914, with Sanger serving as publisher,
editor, and writer, although she did solicit contributions. Sanger's home served
as the magazine's editorial office. The magazine was small—eight pages long,
three columns per page, and printed on inexpensive paper. In her memoirs,
Sanger noted: "I was solely responsible for the magazine financially, legally,
and morally; I was editor, manager, circulation department, bookkeeper, and I
paid the printer's bill. But any cause that has not helpers is losing out. So many
men and women secretaries, stenographers, clerks, used to come in of an evening
that I could not find room for all. Some typed, some addressed envelopes, some
went to libraries and looked up things for us to use, some wrote articles, though
seldom signing their own names. Not one penny ever had to go for salaries,
because service was given freely."[12]

Under the masthead ran the slogan "A Monthly Paper of Militant Thought."
The magazine lived up to its claim. Sanger's fellow New York radicals helped
publicize the magazine at various meetings. Close to one thousand women
mailed Sanger the one dollar a year subscription price. Most hoped to receive
contraceptive advice.[13] Instead, the readers received a publication that denounced
marriage as a "degenerate institution," lobbied for the eight-hour workday,
supported socialism, and denounced capitalism and the Young Men's Christian
Association (YMCA). Typical of the articles was one attacking religion, titled
"The Pauline Ideas vs. Woman" in the May issue. "Submission, silence, and
subjection are the chief tenets of the system of religious ethics that has been
imposed upon suffering women for nearly two thousand years," the article began.[14] A similar tone was struck in an article, "Marriage and Misery," that ran
in the June issue: "The conventional marriage, nine times out of ten, as contracted among the civilized peoples of Europe, is a deeply immoral relation
fraught with the most fatal results for the future of society."[15]

Readers never received any direct contraceptive advice. The closest to such
information was a few arguments lobbying for contraception. One article, titled
"Are Preventive Means Injurious?" told readers that contraceptive devices
would not harm women. Another article, "Can You Afford a Large Family?"
told women what they already knew—that most could not. A third article told
readers abortion was more common in the United States than many women
might think. Yet another article, appearing in the April 1914 issue, called
"Man's Law," was a fictitious tale of woe concerning a young, starving woman

with three children who found she was pregnant. The woman stumbled into a hospital, asking for advice: " 'Tell me what to do,' she pleaded, frantic with fear. 'I can't,' said the nurse, averting her eyes in misery, 'the law won't allow it.' 'But you must tell me!' she begged. 'I can't bring up any more now!' 'The law—,' muttered the nurse.'' The melodramatic tale continued for the rest of a column until its inevitable conclusion: "That night the river gently washed a body to its shores. They told the nurse the next day. She crouched lower over her roll of gauze, the tears bedewing her hands. 'The law,' she wept, as she had wept so often in the same cause. 'Man's law is bitter cruel.' ''[16]

The law in question was the work of primarily one man—Anthony Comstock. Comstock, a Civil War soldier turned grocer, had an abhorrence of pornography that bordered on obsession. For forty-three years, from 1872 until his death in 1915, Comstock was given almost carte blanche authority by Congress to determine what was and was not obscene in American society. He chaired the New York Society for the Suppression of Vice and lobbied Congress to pass a law forbidding obscene materials from being distributed through the mails. Congress did so in 1873, amending Section 211 of the U.S. criminal code. The new law said that "every obscene, lewd, or lascivious and every filthy book, picture, paper, letter, writing, print, or other publication of an indecent character" could not be mailed. Anyone attempting to do so could be sentenced to five years in prison and/or fined five thousand dollars.[17] Comstock further ensured that the law would be carried out by getting himself named as a special post office inspector. Magazines like the first issue of *The Woman Rebel* were deemed unmailable and thus confiscated. Sanger, like others who violated the Comstock law, received letters from the postmaster informing them that their works were unmailable. No specific explanations were provided.[18]

Ambiguous definitions of obscenity allowed Comstock a wide berth to censor materials and prosecute individuals.[19] Even doctors who tried to give medical advice on birth control and sexually transmitted diseases ran afoul of Comstock.

Margaret Sanger purposely challenged Comstock's control, and he responded in like measure. Readers received few issues of *The Woman Rebel*. Four of the issues—March, May, July, and the joint September–October issue—were stopped by the post office. Sanger taunted Comstock and postal officials in a front-page editorial in the magazine's April issue: "It is a crime to have honest convictions in these United States. It is a crime to express them publicly. It is a crime to send them through the mails. Therefore the WOMAN REBEL has not yet been informed which of her views were so displeasing to the Postmaster, but whatever they were, she hastens to agree with the Postmaster that she was absolutely mistaken in these views. She realizes that the Post office is always 'right,' since it has the monopolized POWER to enforce that 'right.' ''

The editorial added, "In order to comply with the rules and regulations of the government, the WOMAN REBEL may be forced to become indecent and to advocate a total ignorance of Sexual Hygiene for woman.''[20]

Despite her coy apology in the April issue, or perhaps in part because of it, the May issue of *The Woman Rebel* was also stopped by the postmaster. This time the offending article told readers of the dangers of self-induced abortions. Sanger was told the issue was "[l]ewd, vile, filthy and indecent."[21]

By May, Sanger was losing her attempts at challenging Comstock and the First Amendment. Angry subscribers wanted their money back. They had received only one issue and no specific birth control information. Even Sanger's radical friends, socialists and anarchists alike, began distancing themselves and their moral and financial support from her.

But Sanger continued. "At that time I visualized the birth control movement as part of the fight for freedom of speech. How much would the postal authorities suppress? What were they really after? I was determined to prod and goad until some definite knowledge was obtained as to what was 'obscene, lewd, and lascivious.' "[22]

Sanger was skating on the proverbial thin ice with her publication, and she knew it. She broke through that ice with the July 1914 issue, in which she published an essay by Herbert A. Thorpe called "A Defense of Assassination." The article told readers that assassination was sometimes acceptable to achieve social and political reform. In one passage the author stated, "The point I wish to bring out is this—that since the great mass of people are by force of circumstances unable to use the same weapons employed by the better educated and privileged class, this does not preclude the working class from using whatever other means of defense may be at its disposal, such as the strikes, boycott, sobatage [*sic*] or assassination." The author later added, "If assassination has failed to achieve very much in the way of reform, it may be not because the method is wrong, but because it has not been practiced persistently enough."[23]

Sanger ran the article in the hope that it would startle the postmaster and Comstock enough to tell her which of the earlier articles led to her magazine's suppression.[24] She received more attention than she had expected. On August 25, 1914, two federal officials visited Sanger and handed her a subpoena. She was charged with nine counts of violating Section 211 for publishing obscene material and one count of incitement. Sanger knew that if she was convicted, she could spend as much as forty-five years in jail.[25]

Sanger charmed the judge into giving her a six-week continuance. She did little to prepare for the trial, however, preferring instead to issue a combined September–October version of *The Woman Rebel* and produce a true birth control pamphlet, *Family Limitation*.[26] The pamphlet, which also was unmailable under the Comstock laws, provided real birth control information—both verbal and pictorial. Most of the columns of the final issue of *The Woman Rebel* were devoted to publicizing Sanger's indictment. One article, "A Little Lesson," explained that birth control was not immoral, nor was it a form of race suicide. But again, the article did not provide any specifics on the issue, only an argument for birth control.[27] The final issue concluded with a series of letters from readers across the country praising Sanger for bringing the issue of birth control before the public.

When Sanger's trial date arrived, she asked for, and received, a second continuance. Not finding that enough, Sanger fled to Europe. Comstock, hoping to get Sanger to return to the United States, prosecuted her husband, William, for giving out a copy of *Family Limitation.* William Sanger received a month in jail. During William Sanger's trial, Anthony Comstock caught a cold and subsequently died. Margaret Sanger returned to the United States in September 1915, a month after Comstock's death.

Historian Lynne Masel-Walters noted that Margaret Sanger did not intend to argue her case on free speech principles. Instead, her defense would argue that banning birth control information harmed women. Sanger intended to try Comstock's law in open court. She never got the chance. Her case never came to trial. The district attorney's office issued a formal notice on February 18, 1916, announcing it would not prosecute Sanger. The case was more than a year old, more pressing cases awaited the court, and the district attorney's office did not want to make Margaret Sanger into a martyr. "Sanger lost something more than martyrdom as a result of the government's action; she lost the battle to publicize information on the desirability of and techniques for birth control," Masel-Walters noted.[28]

The Woman Rebel can best be remembered as "largely a crimson burst of anger. It was an unburdening of emotion, of pent up feelings, of hatreds and of discontent. It was anarchistic in expression, direct actionist in tone and woman liberationist in its aspirations."[29]

Notes

1. Margaret Sanger, *An Autobiography* (New York: Dover, 1971), p. 120.
2. Margaret Sanger, *My Fight for Birth Control* (New York: Farrar and Rinehart, 1931), p. 80.
3. Madeline Gray, *Margaret Sanger: A Biography of the Champion of Birth Control* (New York: Richard Marek, 1979), p. 66.
4. "The Aim," March 1914, p. 1.
5. Alex Baskin, *Woman Rebel* (New York: Archives of Social History, 1976), p. iii.
6. Ibid., p. v.
7. Sanger, *An Autobiography,* p. 92.
8. Sanger, *An Autobiography,* pp. 95–96. Historian David M. Kennedy disputed Sanger's claim. Kennedy stated that the Index Catalogue of the Library of the Surgeon-General's Office in 1898 contained two pages of citations on birth control. Despite Kennedy's findings, few women would have had access to such information or the literary ability to use it. See, however, David M. Kennedy, *Birth Control in America* (New Haven, Conn.: Yale University Press, 1970), p. 19.
9. Sanger, *An Autobiography,* p. 96.
10. Ibid., p. 106.
11. Ibid., p. 77.
12. Ibid., p. 109.
13. Gray, *Margaret Sanger,* p. 67.
14. Aegyptus, "The Pauline Ideas Vs. Woman," May 1914, p. 20.
15. "Marriage and Misery," June 1914, p. 27.

16. "Man's Law," April 1914, p. 1.

17. Mary Ware Dennett, *Who's Obscene* (New York: Vanguard Press, 1930), p. xix.

18. Sanger, *An Autobiography,* p. 110.

19. Mary Alden Hopkins, "Birth Control and Public Morals: An Interview with Anthony Comstock," *Harper's Weekly,* May 22, 1915, p. 490. See also Heywood Broun and Margaret Leach, *Anthony Comstock: Roundsman of the Lord* (New York: Albert and Charles Bone, 1927).

20. "Humble Pie," April 1914, p. 1.

21. Gray, *Margaret Sanger,* p. 70.

22. Sanger, *An Autobiography,* p. 113. Media historian Lynne Masel-Walters challenged Sanger's assertion that she viewed her publication as a First Amendment issue. See Lynne Masel-Walters, "For the 'Poor Mute Mothers?' Margaret Sanger and *The Woman Rebel,*" *Journalism History* 11.2, Spring/Summer 1984, p. 6. Most of Sanger's biographers have taken Sanger's memoirs to task for factual inaccuracies.

23. Herbert A. Thorpe, "A Defense of Assassination," July 1914, pp. 1–2.

24. Gray, *Margaret Sanger,* p. 75.

25. Sanger, *An Autobiography,* p. 114.

26. Masel-Walters, "For the 'Poor Mute Mothers?' " pp. 8–9.

27. "A Little Lesson," p. 53.

28. Masel-Walters, "For the Poor Mute Mothers," pp. 8–9.

29. Baskin, *Woman Rebel,* p. ix.

Information Sources

BIBLIOGRAPHY:

Baskin, Alex. *Woman Rebel.* New York: Archives of Social History, 1976.

Broun, Heywood, and Margaret Leach. *Anthony Comstock: Roundsman of the Lord.* New York: Albert and Charles Boone, 1927.

Dennett, Mary Ware. *Who's Obscene.* New York: Vanguard Press, 1930.

Gray, Madeline. *Margaret Sanger.* New York: Richard Marek, 1979.

Hopkins, Mary Alden. "Birth Control and Public Morals: An Interview with Anthony Comstock." *Harper's Weekly,* May 22, 1915, p. 490.

Kennedy, David M. *Birth Control in America.* New Haven, Conn.: Yale University Press, 1970.

Masel-Walters, Lynne. "For the Poor Mute Mothers?" Margaret Sanger and The Woman Rebel." *Journalism History,* 11.2, Spring/Summer 1984, pp. 3–10, 37.

Sanger, Margaret. *My Fight for Birth Control.* New York: Farrar and Rinehart, 1931.

———. *An Autobiography.* New York: Dover, 1971.

INDEX SOURCES: None.

LOCATION SOURCES: New York Public Library and other libraries. Microfilm available also in the National Register of Microfilm Masters, Washington, D.C.

Publication History

PERIODICAL TITLE AND TITLE CHANGES: *The Woman Rebel.*
VOLUME AND ISSUE DATA: Vol. 1 (March–September/October 1914). Monthly.
PUBLISHER AND PLACE OF PUBLICATION: Margaret Sanger. New York.
EDITOR: Margaret Sanger.
CIRCULATION: Unknown.

Mary M. Cronin

THE WOMAN VOTER

When the New York City Woman Suffrage Party organized, the leaders wanted
to create a political "machine"[1]—a kind of Tammany Hall[2] without graft—to
pressure the New York state legislature to enfranchise women. A "machine"
needs a voice, a newspaper or magazine, to keep its members informed. The
Woman Suffrage Party's voice in New York City was *The Woman Voter,* a
monthly publication that started out small but grew as the power of its "machine" increased. Ironically, just as the Woman Suffrage Party was ready to
win its final victory, the vote in the state of New York, *The Woman Voter* was
silenced. The *Voter* became one of the three publications[3] that became The
*Woman Citizen,** the weekly voice of the National American Woman Suffrage
Association. In large part, the birth, life, and death of the *Voter* were due to
Carrie Chapman Catt, the prominent New York suffragist.

The Woman Suffrage Party itself was Carrie Chapman Catt's idea. In October
1909, the Inter-Urban Council of twenty New York suffrage societies met at the
Convention of Disfranchised Women and founded the Woman Suffrage Party.
The idea was to create a political "machine," a hierarchical organization to
mobilize the voters in the city to support suffrage.[4] Successful the party was.
The party divided New York into sixty-three assembly districts and 2,127 election districts. Each district was under a woman leader who mobilized the women
into the geographic area. Like any New York City party, the Woman Suffrage
Party held borough and city conventions at which it elected borough and city
officers.

A party this well organized needed a voice to regularly communicate with its
membership—*The Woman Voter.* Just five months after the party was formed,
the *Voter* debuted. Its aim was the same as the party's: "The enrollment of
100,000 members this year [1910] and the attainment of woman suffrage in the
state of New York within five years."[5]

The first issue illustrated that this was a "machine" newspaper. The greatest
portion of the eight pages was devoted to party activities. The city officers were
identified (Catt was head of the party); the leaders of each borough were likewise
identified. "Party" news was organized according to borough. Readers were
also kept up-to-date on the schedule of a special train taking "delegates" and
visitors to the woman suffrage hearings in Albany. By the next issue, "party"
news continued to dominate; however, the newspaper had a stronger editorial
content.

There were more editorials, all of which dealt with suffrage. The editorials
tended to follow the standard arguments within the suffrage movement: women
would vote to bring social improvements. As one male correspondent explained,

> It is woman's right that she should have a voice in the government of the
> state, since every act of government directly or indirectly touches her

personal welfare and that of the children, in the schools, in the playgrounds, in the streets, in the factories, in the markets and in the home.[6]

The editorials also reflected the biases within society. As one writer explained,
"This movement [for suffrage] is a movement of advanced civilization. Women
vote in white men's countries; not in brown men's, black men's or yellow
men's."[7]

Editorials also focused on the specific suffrage battle raging in the New York
legislature. Often, the *Voter* editor took legislators to task for not supporting
female suffrage. For example, when the Assembly Judiciary Committee refused
to report out the suffrage bill, the *Voter* castigated the members. The rejection,
the editor wrote, represented an "outrageous autocratic interference with legitimate and honest rights of the people."[8]

This narrow editorial content was in keeping with the limited role of the early
Voter. As the editor explained in 1910, "The Woman Voter is not designed to
be a newspaper. It is too small for that. It is merely a Bulletin to announce what
is coming, to explain policies and report the progress of local work."[9]

This limited vision expanded substantially when Mary Beard took over as
editor.[10] Under Beard, the *Voter*'s editorial content began to cut across class,
age, and organizational lines. Beard transformed the *Voter* from a simple "bulletin" of the Woman Suffrage Party to a voice of New York City women who
were interested in suffrage and the advancement of their gender.

The *Voter* continued to provide specific information on the Woman Suffrage
Party's activities. However, the publication also included stories on property
rights, workingwomen, and suffrage progress in other states. In the process,
Beard expanded the *type* of contributors to the publication. Labor leader Leonora
O'Reilly and socialist Herbert R. Merrill contributed their perspectives to the
publication. Beard, hoping to influence the next generation, even added a children's page to the publication.

Beard also changed the editorial tone of the publication. The vote was not
just a way for middle-class women to improve society; it was also a tool for
the working class. The ballot represented an "instrument which may be used
by the countless thousands of working women in securing and defending better
conditions of life and labor; and as an instrument to be used by women of every
class in the realization of their political ideals."[11]

Beard introduced a measure of political radicalism to the editorials. Reasoned
arguments were no longer enough. Beard offered more options. She offered a
list of candidates for the New York legislature and their stances on suffrage.
She urged readers, "Don't let a single candidate through unscathed."[12]

Beard's hand could be seen in the graphic appearance of the publication as
well. She added editorial cartoons, a greater number of photographs, and a bright
yellow cover[13] to the *Voter*.

Beard also expanded the distribution of the *Voter* itself. No longer was the
publication available solely to subscribers. Beginning in late 1911, the *Voter*

was sold on New York City newsstands, available to anyone drawn to its vibrant yellow cover, the cartoons, and the provocative editorial mix.

Beard left the *Voter* with the April 1912 issue. The *Voter* had never been on stronger financial grounds. Advertising had never been higher, and the publication itself had never been bigger. The new editor, Florence Woolston, had only praise for the departing editor.

> Mrs. Beard brought to the VOTER a wide interest in social movements and a sympathetic understanding of the problems of women, particularly the workers. After a much-needed vacation, she will continue her work for the Party in the Wage-earners' League, which she was active in initiating and which now claims her undivided service.[14]

However, there might have been trouble brewing behind the scenes. In 1914, Beard wrote Woman's Party leader Alice Paul, referring scornfully to "those older women whose sole task has been educational."[15]

Although Beard was gone, the *Voter* never again retreated to its role of "bulletin." Woolston continued along the course that Beard had set. Features and editorials continued to point to problems affecting women within the city[16] and answered critics of suffrage.[17] The use of editorial cartoons continued and, indeed, increased. In one instance, the *Voter* offered five pages of drawings and rhymes of "Mother Goose as a Suffragette."[18] Cover designs became more interesting. They often featured innovative cartoons, including one in December 1912 in which Santa distributed presents, "Votes for Women," to three little girls named "Oregon," "Michigan," and "Arizona." One little girl, "Wisconsin," was sent away empty-handed. Santa consoled her, "Never mind, don't cry! I'll bring you one next time."[19]

In January 1913, the *Voter* carried a strange announcement. Negotiations were taking place to unite *The Woman Voter* and the newsletter of the New York State Woman Suffrage Association. This was an odd merger in light of the history of the two groups. The two had often disagreed on suffrage tactics. The New York State Woman Suffrage Association, whose strength was upstate, had emphasized school, tax, and township suffrage as opposed to state suffrage. The New York State group was reluctant to yield to the New York City group on this tactical shift.[20] Thus, the state association tended to be a different population with different tactics from the population and tactics of the New York City group. Given these differences, the merger of the two publications seemed ill fated from the start. The new publication was called *The Woman Voter and the Newsletter*. *Voter* editor Florence Woolston remained in charge, although Harriet May Mills, the state association president, was added as the state editor. Woolston promised no changes to the editorial policy of the *Voter*. However, a new four-page department, "Throughout the State" edited by Mills, was added to cover state organization news. The merged publication did have a larger circulation than the *Voter* and the newsletter separately.

In this merger, the *Voter* emerged as the dominant entity. Woolston continued to offer features on a wide range of topics that cut across class, age, and organizational lines. In July 1913, the issue covered the peace movement, a position that the publication editorially supported; the September 1913 issue was the "Labor Number," which emphasized the need for women to support wage earners.[21]

The merger, however, never proved to be satisfactory. The *Voter* got the advertising and the subscription lists of the newsletter in exchange for four pages on the state association in each issue. However, anticipated permanent increases in circulation never materialized, and the editor reported that New York City readers were "bored" with the state news, which was cut back to three pages in the summer of 1913.[22] The merger concluded at the end of 1913, but the *Woman Voter* that emerged in 1914 was different.

Woolston remained editor. However, the political environment in New York State forced a change in the *Voter's* editorial vision. The men of New York were going to vote on woman suffrage in 1915, so the editor narrowed the *Voter's* editorial focus to winning that campaign. The November 1914 issue provided a month-by-month plan to win suffrage.[23] The monthly was constantly providing articles designed to appeal to different portion of the voting population (including immigrants, unions, and Catholics), offering lists of allies in the suffrage campaign and encouraging readers never to lax in campaigning. By October 1915, the *Voter* was predicting victory. The publication was wrong. The measure was defeated. The *Voter* editor, however, put the results in the best possible light. The women had "won" half a million votes. Next time, women would just have to capture more votes.[24]

After the election, Woolston returned the *Voter* to its broader mission. The monthly covered issues that cut across class lines. In July 1916, Alyse Gregory wrote about the garment workers, who were primarily immigrants; Helen Dwight reported on child labor; and Florence Woolston outlined the "flagrant injustice to the women" in the city's night court.[25]

The publication, however, never lost sight of the next woman suffrage referendum in New York State—in November 1917. In March 1917, the *Voter* reached out to the Catholics within the city with the news that the cardinal had met with suffrage supporters. Catholic neutrality was needed if woman suffrage was going to win in New York State.[26]

Yet, just when the *Voter* was most needed to rally the forces for the November election, the word came that the publication would die. The May 1917 issue was its last. *The Woman Voter* would join the *Woman Journal* and *The National Suffrage News* to establish a new weekly to be published by the Leslie Woman Suffrage Commission.[27] However, that new weekly would be national in scope and would not be specifically associated with the New York City Woman Suffrage Party. Instead, the new publication, *The Woman Citizen,* would be the organ of the National American Woman Suffrage Association and all its affiliated state groups.

In her farewell editorial, Adaline W. Sterling, the acting editor, wrote that the "sunshine yellow journal [had been] a powerful factor in forwarding a great world movement."[28] That was an overstatement. However, *The Woman Voter* did represent an important voice for women in New York City who were interested in suffrage and equality. It differed from many suffrage publications in its coverage of issues and editorial appeals that cut across class, age, and organizational boundaries. In large part, Mary Beard, who is better known as a historian than an editor, is responsible for developing that vision. Subsequent editors continued along the lines that Beard had developed. Few other suffrage publications ever achieved such breadth.

Notes

1. The *New York World* dubbed the party a "machine," as cited by Carrie Chapman Catt and Nettie Rogers Shuler, *Woman Suffrage and Politics: The Inner Story of the Suffrage Movement* (New York: Charles Scribner's Sons, 1923), p. 283.

2. Tammany Hall was the name given the tremendously strong, although corrupt, Democratic Party machine organization in New York City.

3. The other two were the *Woman Journal** and the *National Suffrage News*.

4. Ronald Schaffer, "The New York City Woman Suffrage Party, 1909–1919," *New York History* 43.3, July 1962, pp. 269–270; Ida Husted Harper, *The History of Woman Suffrage,* vol. 4, 1900–1920 (New York: National American Woman Suffrage Association, 1922), p. 445.

5. February 1910, p. 1.

6. "An Open Letter to the Legislature by a Voter," March 1910, p. 4.

7. "Just across the Border," February 1911, p. 3.

8. "Why?" April 1910, p. 2.

9. May 1910, p. 3.

10. Mary Beard took over as editor from Minnie Reynolds, who was editor from March to May 1911. The first editors of the *Voter* were not identified in the pages of the publication. Mary Beard was identified as editor beginning with the September 1911 issue.

11. September 1911, p. 12.

12. October 1911, p. 12.

13. The official color of the suffrage movement was yellow.

14. June 1912, p. 24.

15. The comment was not directed at her work with the *Voter.* Instead it was directed at Catt's letter in the *New York Times* in which she repudiated the Congressional Union and its tactics (Aileen S. Kraditor, *The Ideas of the Woman Suffrage Movement 1890–1920* [New York: Columbia University Press, 1965], p. 232n).

16. See, for example, "An Immediate Need," June 1912, p. 25.

17. See, for example, Mary Ware Dennett, "Our Friend—The New York (Behind the) Times," June 1912, p. 25.

18. This particular offering was courtesy of the *Brooklyn Eagle* ("Mother Goose as a Suffragette," December 1912, pp. 12–14, 17–18). Occasionally, the *Woman Journal* provided a cover. See, for example, "Truth Liberty Justice," August 1912, front cover.

19. December 1912, front cover.

20. Catt and Shuler, *Woman Suffrage and Politics,* p. 284.

21. "The New Patriotism," July 1913, p. 7; "Forward to Labor Number," September 1913, pp. 7–8.

22. "The Newsletter," November 1913, p. 19.

23. "How to Win Plan of the 1915 Campaign," November 1914, pp. 12–13.

24. "Half a Million Votes Won," December 1915, p. 7.

25. Alyse Gregory, "Women and the Garment Workers," July 1916, p. 20; Helen Dwight, "The New Child Labor Law," October 1916, pp. 10; Florence Woolston, "How New York Protects Women," October 1916, p. 11.

26. Schaffer, "The New York City Woman Suffrage Party," p. 276.

27. This move was orchestrated by Carrie Chapman Catt, who was head of the Leslie Commission. Thus, Catt played a role in the history of the *Voter* throughout.

28. "A Bit of History," May 1917, p. 8.

Information Sources

BIBLIOGRAPHY:
Catt, Carrie Chapman, and Nettie Rogers Shuler. *Woman Suffrage and Politics: The Inner Story of the Suffrage Movement.* New York: Charles Scribner's Sons, 1926.
Harper, Ida Husted. *The History of Woman Suffrage.* Vol. 4, 1900–1920. New York: National American Woman Suffrage Association, 1922.
Kraditor, Aileen S. *The Ideas of the Woman Suffrage Movement, 1890–1920.* New York: Columbia University Press, 1965.
Schaffer, Ronald. "The New York City Woman Suffrage Party, 1909–1919." *New York History,* 43, July 1962, pp. 269–284.
INDEX SOURCES: None.
LOCATION SOURCES: Library of Congress; Kent State University; and many other libraries.

Publication History

PERIODICAL TITLE AND TITLE CHANGES: *The Woman Voter* (1910–1913); *The Woman Voter and the Newsletter* (1913); *The Woman Voter* (1914–1917). (*The Woman Voter* was one of three suffrage publications that were merged to create *The Woman Citizen.*)
VOLUME AND ISSUE DATA: Vols. 1–8 (February 1910–May 1917). Monthly.
PUBLISHER AND PLACE OF PUBLICATION: Woman Suffrage Party of New York City. New York.
EDITORS: Earliest editor not identified; Minnie J. Reynolds (1911); Mary R. Beard (1911–1912); Florence Woolston (1912–1917); Adaline W. Sterling (acting editor) (1916–1917).
CIRCULATION: Unknown.

Kathleen L. Endres

THE WOMAN'S COLUMN

The Woman's Column illustrates the ingenuity of the Blackwell family[1] in publicizing the woman suffrage movement. *The Woman's Column* began as a kind of news/feature service for New England newspapers. The weekly "column" was designed to keep general newspaper readers up-to-date on news about women. Six years later, the "column" became *The Woman's Column,* an inexpensive weekly suffrage newspaper. The format, content, editorial direction—and limitations—all flowed from this rather strange beginning.

In 1882 Lucy Stone and her husband, Henry Blackwell, offered every newspaper in New England a weekly column of news about women. Between one hundred and two hundred newspapers took them up on the offer. After all, there was nothing to lose; the "column" was free.[2] Six years later, the "column" took on a life of its own. The woman's "column" was transformed into a four-page, subscription-based weekly, sponsored by the American Woman Suffrage Association. *The Woman's Column,* like its sister publication *The Woman's Journal,** was edited by Alice Stone Blackwell, the brilliant daughter of Lucy Stone and Henry Blackwell.[3] Once the National and American woman suffrage associations merged in 1890,[4] the *Column* became one of the voices of the new group.[5]

Its news service beginnings helped explain the content of the *Column.* In some respects, it read like a general newspaper "column." Much of the newspaper contained short blurbs of information of and about women. Suffrage was a prominent topic. However, it was not the only subject covered by the newspaper. The weekly also covered news of women's clubs, the Woman's Christian Temperance Union, and other groups committed to the betterment of females in the United States and across the world. In addition, the newspaper offered short summaries of the comings and goings of prominent women in the nation. For example, the *Column* carried the news that Mrs. George Bowron of Chicago had patented a car coupler, that Anna C. Fall of Massachusetts had successfully argued a case between the superior court, and that the Reverend Olympia Brown's son had entered Adelbert College in Cleveland.[6] Perhaps because of its news service history, the *Column* never contained a distinct editorial page. Instead, editorial comment was woven throughout, including in some unexpected places. Of Brown's son going to Adelbert College, the editor observed, "The sons of strong-minded mothers are apt to make strong-minded men."[7] The newspaper also carried very little advertising. Sometimes the only advertising included was for its larger, better-known, and more expensive sister publication, *The Woman's Journal.*

Although the *Column* was often overshadowed by the *Journal* it had an important role to play within the suffrage movement. Because it was so inexpensive—only twenty-five cents a year to subscribe—the *Column* was a popular journal to subscribe to and to donate to interested (and disinterested) individuals. Complimentary copies often went to educators, ministers, politicians, and others sympathetic to the cause. In 1888, hundreds were sent to the Ohio Centennial Exposition. In 1891, one Illinois subscriber bought subscriptions for every member of the Illinois state legislature. In 1892 and 1893 the National American Woman Suffrage Association (NAWSA) sent fifteen hundred to prominent Alabamans.[8]

Although the low price allowed the newspaper to reach beyond the suffrage converts to a wider audience, it came at a price. In 1895, Blackwell doubled the size of the paper (to eight pages) and doubled the price (to fifty cents per year). That move proved catastrophic. As Blackwell explained, at twenty-five cents the weekly attained an "enormous circulation" and sizable debts. At fifty cents, the paper came nearer to covering its expenses but found its circulation checked. "As the main object of publishing the WOMAN'S COLUMN has always been to do missionary work, it has been thought best to put down the price again to a point that will bring it within the reach of all," she wrote. At the same time, Blackwell cut back the newspaper's frequency to fortnightly in 1897.[9]

As a fortnightly, the newspaper's focus changed somewhat. Although the paper continued to carry the short blurbs of women's news of the nation, increasingly the newspaper was providing additional, longer, in-depth coverage of specific subjects of interest to women. In 1900 and 1901, for example, the *Column* provided extensive coverage of the U.S. military's introducing state-licensed vice into the Philippines. One 1900 report, in particular, ran three of the newspaper's four pages. That story highlighted the policy, its "injustice to women," and provided a means to eradicate the prostitution (the *Column* urged women and men to write President McKinley to end the practice).[10] Most stories were neither as long nor as detailed. Some dealt with prostitution in the cities and among the Chinese.[11] Others countered criticism of women's activities or questions of women's capabilities. Henry Blackwell, who regularly contributed to the *Column,* supported the Red Cross when the military criticized the women who helped supply the hospitals. "If the regular medical and surgical army authorities had done their full duty, the private liberality of our citizens would not have been needed to fit out 'hospital ships' to supplement deficiencies," he wrote.[12] Alice Blackwell stepped in when critics contended that women were "too ignorant" to vote, pointing out that more girls graduated from public high schools than boys. "Instead of adding to the power of the ignorant vote, it is clear that equal suffrage would increase the proportion of voters who have received more than an elementary education," she argued.[13] Herein lies one of the *Column*'s greatest strengths, countering the antisuffrage propaganda and delivering the message to a relatively wide audience. For every criticism of women that surfaced, the *Column* rushed to counter it. For every argument against suffrage, the *Column* had a response. Perhaps the best example of this was in the January 10, 1903, issue, which was entirely devoted to responding to current antisuffrage arguments, from woman suffrage's doubling the foreign vote, to its overburdening women, from the threat that the vote would increase divorce, to the concern that it would spell the end of chivalry.[14]

This newspaper had a valuable life reaching out to readers in the general public as well as those within suffrage circles; yet it drained the NAWSA treasury and Blackwell's energies. The *Column* died in 1904 in its sixteenth year. That life was long by suffrage publication standards. Nonetheless, this newspaper has been generally overlooked in many accounts of suffrage publications. The *Column* often hides in the shadow of its sister publication, *The Woman's Journal*. Yet, for its day, the *Column* played the invaluable role of propagandizing for the suffrage cause. Historian Linda Steiner perhaps characterized the periodical best when she wrote of "its pithy, matter of fact, tightly edited style, and its studied avoidance of controversy and passion."[15] That type of voice was needed in the suffrage campaign.

Notes

1. Lucy Stone, Henry Blackwell, and Alice Stone Blackwell.

2. Marsha L. Vanderford, "The *Woman's Column*, 1888–1904: Extending the Suffrage Community," in Martha M. Solomon, ed., *A Voice of Their Own; The Woman Suffrage Press, 1840–1910* (Tuscaloosa: University of Alabama Press, 1991), p. 129.

3. Geoffrey Blodgett, "Alice Stone Blackwell," in Edward T. James, Janet Wilson James, and Paul S. Boyer, eds., *Notable American Women 1607–1950: A Biographical Dictionary* vol. 1 (Cambridge: Belknap Press of Harvard University Press, 1971), p. 157.

4. The merger of the National and American woman suffrage associations has been generally credited to Alice Stone Blackwell, although Eleanor Flexner points out in her book that the merger was probably inevitable. "In reality, the fact that the policies it had been advocating for twenty years had now become dominant was the main reason why the American Association, which was smaller and had done less organizing than its one-time rival, could initiate the proposal and actually take the National into camp." Negotiations began in 1887. See Eleanor Flexner, *Century of Struggle: The Woman's Rights Movement in the United States,* rev. ed. (Cambridge: Belknap Press of Harvard University Press, 1975), p. 226.

5. Blodgett, "Alice Stone Blackwell," p. 157.

6. November 14, 1891, p. 4.

7. Ibid.

8. Vanderford, "The *Woman's Column*, 1888–1904," pp. 130–132.

9. "Important Notice," December 4, 1897, p. 3.

10. "A National Disgrace," November 17, 1900, pp. 1–3. Blackwell repeatedly returned to the issue. On May 4, 1901, she reported that state-regulated vice was spreading like the "bubonic plague." "It is no time to introduce under the stars and stripes a system which was always an abomination morally, and which has long since proved itself a total failure even from the sanitary point of view. If women had had the ballot, it never could have been established" ("Like the Plague," May 4, 1901, p. 4). The *column* returned to the topic a number of times in 1901.

11. Florence Adkinson, "The New Anti-Slavery Movement in California," March 9, 1901, p. 2; Henry Blackwell, "Women Slaves in America," November 29, 1902, p. 1.

12. Henry Blackwell, "Professional Jealousy vs. the Red Cross," July 30, 1898, p. 1.

13. Alice Stone Blackwell, " 'The Ignorant Vote,' " October 4, 1902, p. 1.

14. January 10, 1903, pp. 1–4.

15. Linda Steiner, "Evolving Rhetorical Strategies/Evolving Identities," in Solomon, *A Voice of Their Own,* p. 195.

Information Sources

BIBLIOGRAPHY:
Blodgett, Geoffrey. "Alice Stone Blackwell." In Edward T. James, Janet Wilson James, and Paul S. Boyer, eds., *Notable American Women 1607–1950: A Biographical Dictionary,* vol. 1. Cambridge: Belknap Press of Harvard University Press, 1971, pp. 156–158.
Steiner, Linda. "Evolving Rhetorical Strategies/Evolving Identities." In Martha M. Solomon, ed., *A Voice of Their Own: The Woman Suffrage Press, 1840–1910.* Tuscaloosa: University of Alabama Press, 1991, pp. 183–197.
Vanderford, Marsha L. "The *Woman's Column,* 1888–1904: Extending the Suffrage Community." In Martha M. Solomon, ed., *A Voice of Their Own; The Woman Suffrage Press, 1840–1910.* Tuscaloosa: University of Alabama Press, 1991, pp. 129–152.
INDEX SOURCES: None.
LOCATION SOURCES: Library of Congress and other libraries (microfilmed by Greenwood Press).

Publication History

PERIODICAL TITLE AND TITLE CHANGES: *The Woman's Column.*
VOLUME AND ISSUE DATA: Vols. 1–17.26 (January 14, 1988–1904). Weekly (1888–1898); fortnightly (1898–1904).
PUBLISHER AND PLACE OF PUBLICATION: A. S. Blackwell. Boston.
EDITORS: Alice Stone Blackwell (1888–1904).
CIRCULATION: Unknown.

Kathleen L. Endres

WOMAN'S EXPONENT

Who are so well able to speak for the women of Utah as the women of Utah themselves? . . . that women may help each other by the diffusion of knowledge and information possessed by many and suitable to all, the publication of *Woman's Exponent,* a journal owned by, controlled by and edited by Utah ladies, has been commenced.[1]

For forty-two years, beginning in 1872, women of the Church of Jesus Christ of Latter-day Saints (commonly known as Mormons) published the *Woman's Exponent* in Salt Lake City as an eight-page, semimonthly paper, one of the earliest periodicals for women in the western United States. Although privately owned, it became the rallying point for Mormon women on issues of woman's rights, suffrage, medical care, and organizational charity. Responding to the perceived needs of its readers, it also created an atmosphere in which those needs could be recognized and articulated. In a society dominated by a male hierarchy, it bound women and their causes into an effective organizational structure.

Credit for getting the *Exponent* under way, however, must go to a man— Edward L. Sloan, editor of the *Salt Lake Herald*. He conceived the idea, chose the name, found the editor, furnished printing facilities, and undoubtedly helped with the editing of early issues. Once established, though, the paper went its independent way, bound only by its editors' mostly willing acquiescence to church doctrine and policy.

A prepublication advertisement in Sloan's paper in April 1872 solicited subscribers and stated the *Exponent*'s aims: it would discuss "every subject interesting and valuable to women" and "contain a brief and graphic summary of current news, local and general; household hints, educational matters, articles on health and dress, correspondence, editorials on leading topics of interest suitable to its columns, and miscellaneous reading." While encouraging readers to contribute and to help correct the world's misperceptions about Mormon women, it would "endeavor to defend the right, inculcate sound principles and disseminate useful knowledge."[2]

It also would serve as the organ of the Female Relief Society, the church organization for women. Its editors, as leading members of Relief Society governing boards, supported many Relief Society projects in the *Exponent*. They also reported activities of other organizations in which they had an interest, including church auxiliaries like the Young Ladies' Mutual Improvement Association and other associations, such as local and national suffrage societies, state and national Mothers' Congresses and Peace Congresses, national and international woman's councils, the Daughters of Utah Pioneers, the Utah Society of Daughters of the American Revolution, the Utah Woman's Press Club, and a local literary group called the Reapers' Club.

The *Exponent* had only two editors during its forty-two-year existence, Lula Greene Richards and Emmeline B. Wells. Sloan chose Richards after she submitted several poems to his paper. She was twenty-three years old and unmarried when she assumed the editorship, after requesting that church president Brigham Young call her to the post as a "mission." Five years later, after marriage and the births and deaths of two children, she turned the paper over to Wells, a forty-nine-year-old mother of five daughters. Wells, a regular contributor to the *Exponent* almost from its inception, remained editor and publisher until the paper's demise in 1914, assisted by her daughter, Annie Wells Cannon, during the *Exponent*'s final nine years.

The editors produced a substantial proportion of *Exponent* content, often under pen names like Geranium, Camelia, and Amethyst, perhaps partly to conceal how much of the paper came from their pens. Contributors also used pseudonyms, in spite of an appeal from the editors to overcome their diffidence and stand behind the honest opinions they entertained.[3]

Although the paper could not, as promised, discuss *every* subject of interest and value to women, it made a valiant effort in that direction. Each number contained at least one editorial, usually more. A study that examined *Exponent* content reported that more than half of its editorials concerned women and women's issues.[4] The editors believed that a woman should put her home and family first but that most women could—and should—take on additional duties. They urged women to educate themselves and cultivate their abilities in order to be both better wives and mothers and better citizens of their communities. A woman should have the same right to be a "business individual" as a man, learning and practicing "any suitable trade, art or profession."[5]

For the *Exponent,* suffrage became a religious, as well as a political, cause. Even though the Mormon priesthood excluded women, they had held voting rights in church congregations from the church's beginnings in 1830, and Utah women had received the political ballot in 1870, only three months after Wyoming's women became the first in the nation to obtain suffrage. In 1882, however, the federal Edmunds Bill denied wives of polygamous men the ballot, and five years later the Edmunds–Tucker Bill disfranchised all Utah women. Until 1896, when statehood restored woman suffrage, Mormon women conducted a continuing campaign to regain their privileged status. Between 1879 and 1897 the *Exponent* carried the motto "The Rights of the Women of Zion, and the Rights of the Women of all Nations."

Other frequent editorial topics included self-improvement, problems and goals of the paper, and the Mormon question, of which polygamy was a major component. The *Exponent* defended that practice staunchly until its discontinuance in 1890.

Exponent articles, for the most part, had the same themes as the editorials. In addition to treating woman's rights, women's place, and women's organizations, articles fostered self-improvement, provided travel reports from women journeying outside Utah, commented on local and national politics, and offered histories and biographies both sacred and secular. One author called novel reading a habit "as hurtful to the mind, as drinking tea and coffee is to the body," and others warned that puffs and rats in hair were "unwholesome for the brain . . . and likely to produce disease, if not death" and that "waltzing has become almost like an intoxicating beverage to an habitual drinker," too much of it bound to make women "frail" and "weakly."[6]

Uplifting fiction apparently did not fall under the same strictures as novels, for the *Exponent* regularly published serial stories that taught moral lessons. One contrasted the wholesome family life of a Mormon polygamist with that of a degraded U.S. congressman, but more common were chaste romances whose heroines, although tried and tested, remained true to their Mormon beliefs. Each issue also included two or three poems on subjects like nature, motherhood, friendship, church leaders, children, desirable character traits, and significant events.

Household hints provided practical suggestions on such topics as cooking, cleaning, child care, gardening, and nursing, while advertisements, occupying up to half of the last page, told readers where they might obtain anything from corsets to Studebaker wagons. Patent medicine ads appeared alongside those for sewing machines, furniture stores, and dentists.

In its early years the *Exponent,* like most newspapers of the time, used a great many miscellaneous columns of news, humor, and fascinating facts culled primarily from other publications. As it began to receive more contributions from readers, these exchanges decreased in number, but they never disappeared. They often noted accomplishments of women or news that the editors deemed of special significance for their readers, but sometimes they simply entertained.

It is difficult to determine circulation figures for the *Exponent.* It may have represented fifty thousand Utah women, as *Tullidge's Quarterly Magazine* claimed,[7] but it certainly never came close to having that number of subscribers. In 1881 it printed a Relief Society statistical report that listed, from the units reporting, 754 *Exponent* subscribers, but not all localities had responded. The earliest listing in a national directory credited it with a circulation of between five hundred and one thousand in 1885. Later estimates peaked at seven hundred in 1902 and dropped to five hundred in 1909.[8] Of course, most subscribers shared their copies with families, friends, and fellow Relief Society members, so that readers numbered many more than subscribers. Relief Society minutes reported reading of *Exponent* articles at meetings.

Like most publications of limited circulation, the *Exponent* experienced financial problems at various times during its long life, particularly after the turn of the century. Reducing the subscription price in 1889 from two dollars to one dollar a year failed to entice a substantial number of new subscribers, and Wells began to resort to combining issues; the final volume, extending from September 1912, to February 1914, contained only fourteen numbers. Advertising had disappeared, and lesson plans for Relief Society meetings, mothers' classes, and courses in domestic science and hygiene had become a staple of its content. At this point, the eighty-six-year-old Wells offered to turn the publication over to the Relief Society, with the proviso that she be retained as editor, but officers of that organization decided instead to inaugurate a new magazine and chose someone else as editor.

The editor's ''Heartfelt Farewell'' in her final issue listed what she considered the *Exponent*'s major contributions: assisting those who needed help in many different ways; providing a medium for aspiring writers; standing for high ideals in home, state, and church; proclaiming the worth and just claims of women; teaching Latter-day Saints; exerting a positive influence in the mission field; and serving as the organ of the Relief Society.[9]

Over the years, a main goal of *Exponent* editors had been to present a favorable picture of Mormon women to the outside world, but the paper undoubtedly had a larger impact on the loyal Mormons who constituted most of its audience. At a time when they were threatened by negative perceptions of their religious beliefs, moral standards, intelligence, and even appearance, it helped them maintain a more positive self-image. Editors, women of both talent and independence involved with families, church activities, civic organizations, and literary endeavors, served as role models for the way of life they advocated and attracted contributors with similar characteristics.

The editors recognized their own capabilities to accomplish significant work and expected other women to follow suit. They defended their beliefs with dignity and diplomacy. By producing a lively and attractive periodical, they helped forge networks that provided both psychological support and practical advice and made possible the successful completion of major projects, including silk production, wheat storage, and a retail store featuring products of home industry.

The *Exponent* rallied support for one cause after another during its entire forty-two years. *Tullidge's Quarterly Magazine* credited it with wielding "more real power in our politics than all of the newspapers in Utah put together."[10] Its readers learned of the concerns of church leaders, the activities of Mormon women throughout the church, the travels of their leaders, and developments in the national struggle for woman suffrage. They obtained helpful advice from editors and contributors and used the paper as an outlet for their own opinions and literary efforts. As promised in its "Salutatory," the *Exponent* gave "shape and form to ideas and hopes."[11]

Notes

1. June 1, 1872, p. 8.
2. *Salt Lake Daily Herald,* April 9, 1872, p. 3.
3. October 15, 1872, p. 76.
4. Carol Cornwall Madsen, "Remember the Women of Zion" (M.A. thesis, University of Utah, 1977), p. 127.
5. May 15, 1874, p. 187.
6. March 1, 1876, p. 147; October, 1910, p. 28; May 1, 1878, p. 177.
7. "Emmeline B. Wells," *Tullidge's Quarterly Magazine,* January 1881, p. 252.
8. George P. Rowell, *American Newspaper Directory* (New York: George P. Rowell, 1885), p. 579; N. W. Ayer and Sons, *American Newspaper Annual* (Philadelphia: N. W. Ayer and Sons, 1902 and 1909), pp. 850, 887.
9. February 1914, p. 100.
10. "Emmeline B. Wells," p. 252.
11. June 1, 1872, p. 4.

Information Sources

BIBLIOGRAPHY:

Bennion, Sherilyn Cox. "The *Woman's Exponent:* Forty-two Years of Speaking for Women." *Utah Historical Quarterly,* Summer 1976, pp. 222–239.
———. "*The New Northwest* and *Woman's Exponent:* Early Voices for Suffrage." *Journalism Quarterly* 54.2, Summer 1977, pp. 286–292.
"Emmeline B. Wells." *Tullidge's Quarterly Magazine,* January 1881, p. 252.
Madsen, Carol Cornwall. "Remember the Women of Zion." Master's thesis, University of Utah, Salt Lake City, 1977.
———. "A Mormon Woman in Victorian America." Doctoral dissertation, University of Utah, Salt Lake City, 1985.

INDEX SOURCES: None.
LOCATION SOURCES: Brigham Young University; University of Utah; Historical Department of the Church of Jesus Christ of Latter-day Saints, Salt Lake City, Utah.

Publication History

PERIODICAL TITLE AND TITLE CHANGES: *Woman's Exponent.*
VOLUME AND ISSUE DATA: Vols. 1–41 (June 1, 1872–February 1914). Semimonthly (1872–May 1902); monthly (June 1902–1914).
PUBLISHER AND PLACE OF PUBLICATION: Lula Greene Richards (1872–July 15, 1877); Emmeline B. Wells (December 1, 1875–1914). Salt Lake City, Utah.
EDITORS: Lula Greene Richards (1872–July 15, 1877); Emmeline B. Wells (December 1, 1875–1914).
CIRCULATION: *Rowell* (1885) and *Ayer* (1902, 1909) directories: 500–1,000.

Sherilyn Cox Bennion

THE WOMAN'S JOURNAL

The printed word was crucial to any one of a number of nineteenth-century social reform movements. But, unlike the larger daily presses controlled by the Hearsts, Pulitzers, and their kind, opening and operating a focused press were never an easy chore. Lucy Stone certainly discovered a number of aggravations when she decided to place her vision of woman suffrage in print.

> I wish I could rest. I am so tired today, body and soul, it seems as though I should never feel fresh again. I have been trying to get advertisements for The Woman's Journal to eke out its expenses. Yesterday I walked miles; to picture stores, crockery stores, to "special sales," going up flight after flight of stairs only to find the men out, or not ready to advertise. And for my day's toil, I did not get a cent; and when I came home at night, it was to find the house cold, the fire nearly out in the furnace, and none on the hearth; and it seemed as if the tiredness of a whole life came into my essence.[1]

When Elizabeth Cady Stanton and a congregation of like-minded, determined citizens met in a small church in Seneca Falls, New York, in 1848, they set into motion a campaign for equal rights for women that, in terms of length, ended up paralleling some of the great conflicts of Europe such as the Crusades and the Hundred Years' War. It would take more than the average nineteenth-century lifetime, seventy-two years in fact, before American women could legally report to the polls and cast a ballot for a candidate of their choice in federal elections.

Critical to the morale and cohesiveness of the suffragist cause was the maintenance of an ongoing and effective means of communication. In general, activists in one sphere became activists in another. Organizers became journalists, and journalists became organizers. However, this seamless hierarchy served neither organization nor newspaper very well. Many, such as Elizabeth Cady Stanton and Susan B. Anthony, felt pulled in two directions at once. As a consequence, with few exceptions, suffragist journalism never matured. Prior to 1911, the average circulation of the thirty-two existing journals was only 3,135.[2]

Yet, the movement had nothing to gain by remaining outside the field. Like many other groups and institutions, such as trades unions, agrarian reformers and left-wing political parties existing on the margins of American society, suffragists were, at worst, pilloried or, at least, ignored by the mainstream daily press, which, needless to say, was dominated by men. As a consequence, almost from the beginning of the fight for the right to vote, suffragists recognized the importance of owning and operating their own newspapers.

> Such journals could clearly explain the movement to the committed and convincingly explain it to the uncommitted, provide information about suffrage organizations and campaigns and suggest feminist goals and tactics.[3]

The *Woman's Journal* was by no means the first suffragist newspaper, but it outstripped its rivals in terms of longevity and circulation. Preceding the Lucy Stone–Henry Blackwell collaboration was Amelia Bloomer's pre-Civil War publication, *The Lily,** which appeared in several locations in the United States between 1849 and 1856. Pauline Kellogg Wright Davis' *The Una** was distributed from Providence, Rhode Island, between 1853 and 1855.

By 1911, *The Woman's Journal* succeeded in reaching five thousand readers per week, the first suffragist publication to break that barrier. However, by 1914, it was no longer publishing circulation figures in N. W. Ayer's newspaper and periodical directory. Throughout the history of the movement, the average life span for such endeavors was 7.52 years.[4] But the Boston-based journal published regularly until 1917, when it was amalgamated with several other suffragist publications to form *The Woman Citizen**[5]

The Woman's Journal was founded to counteract what many women considered the radical views of Elizabeth Cady Stanton and Susan B. Anthony in their journal, *The Revolution.** The newspaper, official organ of the National Woman Suffrage Association (NWSA),

> [s]elf-consciously set out to argue for a radical model for the new woman.
> . . . By *The Revolution*'s reckoning, the choice was one of ballots, brains, and babies, against bonnets, balls, and brocades. So *The Revolution* reversed the prevailing question. The issue was not whether strong-minded women were unsexed, but whether women should remain, and remain content to be—drivelling, dependent imbeciles.[6]

The ideological perspective of the Stanton–Anthony publication was not the only point of controversy between the two and Lucy Stone and Henry Blackwell.

The Revolution had been funded by one George Francis Train, a southern and pro-slavery Democrat, whose views, but not his money, presented problems for both Stanton and Anthony. His involvement with the newspaper was completely unacceptable to those around the Stone–Blackwell camp, such as Mary Ashton Livermore and William Lloyd Garrison, both of whom came to *The Woman's Journal* with unimpeachable abolitionist credentials. They were unwavering in their support of the official Republican Party platform dedicated to giving African-American males full rights of citizenship.[7]

To a significant degree, the radicalism of Stanton, Anthony, and the National Woman Suffrage Association can be attributed to the belief that women had been betrayed by the federal administration following the Civil War. Many prominent suffragists had been front and center in support for the war effort. They had high expectations when suffrage was extended to freed male slaves following defeat of the Confederacy. To their collective chagrin, they discovered that their so-called political leaders were reluctant to embark on reconstruction and female suffrage campaigns at the same time. Reconstruction and African-American emancipation became a major government priority, with the consequence that suffrage issues drifted into a political nether land for an indeterminant period of time.

With the passing of the Fourteenth and Fifteenth Amendments, the word "male" was introduced into the Constitution, and any other references to gender in respect to the right to vote were excluded. This twin legislative defeat almost sank the nascent suffragist movement in the turbulent years between 1865 and 1870. During this half decade, the movement split into two separate and warring camps, the NWSA and the American Women Suffrage Association (AWSA).

The NWSA was committed to accomplishing woman suffrage through a federal, constitutional amendment. The association was also involved in bringing to public consciousness other issues that it associated with equal rights for women, such as the right to simpler divorce, the right to hold property equally with men, and the right to unobstructed access to the workplace. On the other hand, the AWSA ignored demands for a federal amendment, concentrating instead on both the state and municipal level. Although AWSA did not ignore issues that it viewed as essential to the emancipation of women other than voting rights, its primary objective was to achieve universal suffrage for American women.[8]

The first issue of *The Woman's Journal* appeared on the streets of Boston and Chicago on January 8, 1870. Alice Stone Blackwell, Lucy Stone's daughter and successor at the journal, noted that "most of the money to start the paper was raised by Lucy Stone."[9] However, in 1883 a wealthy Boston sympathizer, Mrs. Eliza F. Eddy, left twenty thousand dollars in her will to be divided equally between Lucy Stone and Susan B. Anthony. Anthony used her legacy to publish her *History of Woman Suffrage.* Stone used hers both to cover deficits incurred in publishing *The Woman's Journal* and to sponsor a series of syndicated columns under the title "A Woman's Column," which dealt with issues ranging from news about women to comments on the suffrage question. Eventually, one thousand American papers carried the column.[10] However, very few of these journals gave editorial support to Stone and her colleagues.

Compared to other special-interest journals of the period, *The Woman's Journal* began life on solid ground. Although its early years were often marked with dust at the bottom of the money jar after each issue, the journal did not suffer from the day-to-day fight for survival that tormented Stanton and Anthony after they launched *The Revolution*. On Stone's behalf, two businessmen in the Boston area, Samuel E. Sewall and Ebenezer D. Draper, formed a joint stock company to hold the newspaper's shares. The company issued 250 shares at fifty dollars each. Lucy Stone's husband, Henry B. Blackwell, purchased the largest number, and Stone sold the remainder to the AWSA and the New England Woman's Suffrage Association (NEWSA). NEWSA also rented one room in their headquarters at 3 Tremont Street in Boston for the sole purpose of housing the journal.[11]

The journal began life with an editorial board of five persons. Ironically, its founder, Lucy Stone, declined the position of managing editor, instead attracting an experienced journalist, Mary Ashton Livermore, to the position. Livermore lived and worked in Chicago, where she had founded the suffragist journal *The Agitator*. In spite of its name, its editorial position best reflected the go-slow, nonradical perspective of Lucy Stone. Livermore agreed to accept the office of managing editor on the provision that *The Agitator* merge with *The Woman's Journal*. The journalistic marriage gave the new publication access not only to the East Coast but to the center of the country as well.[12]

Mary Livermore became the spirit by which the newspaper operated. Alice Stone Blackwell remembered her as a

> woman of magnificent ability, not only in public speaking, in which she was unsurpassed, with her majestic brows and her voice of mellow thunder, but in many other lines also—as a nurse in the Civil War, as an organizer for the Sanitary Commission, in raising money and supplies for the soldiers, and as a leader in temperance work. She had a big warm, generous heart that made her a tower of strength to many good causes, as well as a source of comfort to countless individuals.[13]

Livermore was not alone among the star-studded cast that Lucy Stone assembled. The masthead included the names of William Lloyd Garrison, who came with a three-decade pedigree as America's best-known abolitionist and founder of the abolitionist weekly *The Liberator;* Julia Ward Howe, a writer, lecturer, abolitionist, and lay preacher, composer of the "Battle Hymn of the Republic"; and Colonel Thomas Wentworth Higginson, also an abolitionist, a Unitarian clergyman, and a man with an outstanding war record and a penchant for writing witty and clever editorials. Higginson, along with contributing a weekly commentary, was also active in the equal rights movement as a lecturer in both social and literary circles. Higginson's editorials were eventually published in book form under the title *Common Sense about Women.*[14]

Frances E. Willard, the most prominent nineteenth-century American Prohibitionist, once wrote:

> *The Woman's Journal* has long been my outlook upon the great and widening world of woman's work, worth and victory. It has no peer in this noble office and ministry. Its style is pure and its spirit exalted.[15]

Its style, whether pure or not, was directly aimed at soliciting and keeping middle-class, female readers. It did not ignore men, since a number of men were able to be counted as supporters. But, as its initial masthead declared, *The Woman's Journal* was "a weekly newspaper published every Saturday in Boston and Chicago devoted to the interests of Woman, to her educational, industrial, legal and political equality and especially to her right of suffrage."[16] Throughout its columns such as "Gossips and Gleanings," "Notes and News," "Concerning Women," "Foreign Correspondence," and "Humorous," the journal seldom, if ever, mixed what it regarded as information and what it treated as enrichment. Although the front pages carried news of suffrage activities both in New England and in the country and world at large, its columns remained the sanctuary for those writers who wished to deal with those larger issues concerning American women.

For example, in the April 16, 1870, edition in a column entitled "Unsexing Women," the journal attempted to erase the sexual barriers that divided men and women, beyond that of the right to vote.

> But let us ask—what are the sacred home duties of women as distinguished from man? Must she cook? Go to any best hotel, or steamboat, or other vessel, in any part of the world, and you can learn that the "best cooks, and the most celebrated cooks, are men!" Must she wash dishes? Look into the kitchen or china-room of any of these hotels, or steamers, or other vessels, and you will find the "scullion" a man! Must she sew, make and mend clothes? Where and who are the most famous and sought for as tailors and repairers, hair dressers and shavers, shoemakers and needle and pin manufacturers? What is there sacred in any of these? They are all home duties! Which of the home duties are sacred to woman alone? . . . Sad, indeed, is that household, where the father refuses or neglects to do his full share of this duty.[17]

The appeals for equality in *The Woman's Journal* had a decidedly middle-class bias, a bias it retained throughout its lifetime. This should not be surprising. Most of those who participated in the writing and editing of suffragist journals, not to mention organizational endeavors in the various societies, were mainly middle-class women with time on their hands. They were products of the period between 1780 and 1830, a time in America when gender roles were established as a response to industrialization, immigration, and the growth of cities. Men became the leaders of business and providers for their families. Women, in contrast, were home creatures with responsibilities for organizing and caring for activities within those walls.[18]

As a result, the successful middle-class American woman during the latter half of the nineteenth century was measured by her ability to perform to perfection the roles of mother, daughter, sister, and wife-woman.[19] Only rarely did suffragist journals, *The Woman's Journal* in particular, venture into commenting on the sufferings of female domestics, female factory workers, and pieceworkers, nearly all of whom were women.[20]

In classic fashion, the February 11, 1871, edition made the case for middle-class emancipation for middle-class women.

Woman is demanding her rights in school houses, as well as in town halls. She demands her right to all the opportunities for acquiring an education which this year are held out to young men. And when, by honest toil and heroic preservation and self-sacrifice, she has fitted herself to occupy a high position in the noble army of teachers, she demands the same pay which a man would receive for the same task equally well performed. And shame on those mercenary men who would defraud woman of her just dues! Every day is demonstrating more and more clearly, not only woman's right to enter any field of labor that she may desire, but her capacity to occupy that position with honor to herself and sex.[21]

Stanton and Anthony greeted the birth of *The Woman's Journal* with a public declaration of support, while probably knowing that the well-funded Boston publication marked the end of their journalistic activities. In an article reprinted in *The Woman's Journal* on January 22, 1870, the editors of *The Revolution* stated, "The Revolution gladly welcomes this new and valiant auxiliary to the field of conflict."[22]

The artificial friendliness that marked the relationship between the two journals broke down in public in the October 22, 1870, edition of *The Woman's Journal*. Stanton and Anthony were highly critical of the approach to the suffrage question taken by Lucy Stone and her editorial team. The two veterans of the movement were convinced that Stone and company were so concerned with the suffrage question that they ignored, at their peril, the larger issues concerning female emancipation that they had addressed in *The Revolution*.

Stone was horrified at the suggestion that her newspaper and her movement were narrow-scoped. In response to the accusations, she wrote,

Such statements can only arise from an unacquaintance with the Woman's Journal, which finds space and opportunity to discuss every question, fact and interest that concerns woman. Education, work, clothing, food, health, training of children, marriage—it has turned aside from no fact of life, or problem of society in which she has an interest. The statement of The Revolution is incorrect. It is not true.[23]

The passing of *The Revolution* at the close of 1870 received narry a mention in the pages of *The Woman's Journal*. By 1871, Lucy Stone, Henry Blackwell, Julia Ward Howe, Colonel Higginson, William Lloyd Garrison, and the American Woman Suffrage Association, to all intent and purpose, had the field of suffrage journalism to themselves.

Although it has been argued that *The Woman's Journal* was primarily directed to the suffrage question,[24] it would be a mistake to reiterate the editorial perspective of *The Revolution* and pretend that other issues did not intrigue the editorial staff. Certainly, Henry B. Blackwell, in his role as editorialist, often took issue with those facts of American life that he believed mitigated against gender equality. Compiling a list of popular nineteenth-century occupations, including carpentry, printing, shoemaking, medicine, the clergy, law, and retail work, Blackwell wrote:

The whole organization of society rests on the supposition that the only proper sphere of womanly activity is marriage, and then goes on to define marriage, not as a lifelong partnership of equals with reciprocal rights and duties, but as a position of legal servitude and dependence on the part of the wife—of supremacy and mastery on the part of the husband. If ever there was a class in society subjected from the cradle to the grave to the iron heel of cruel and relentless monopoly, in every form, by another class, the instance is found where woman is the victim and man the oppressor.[25]

The editorial board became obsessed with religious questions, and it was a rare month when some comment or story did not appear with a religious theme. Generally, the outlook was favorable toward members of the clergy. Church leaders who gave support to gender equality were often singled out for special praise. As the newspaper noted, "[T]he Universalists and the Unitarians admit women to their pulpits." The journal went on to laud members of the Baptist, Congregationalist, and Episcopal churches, who, in their judgment, had acted in concert with the Universalists and the Unitarians.

In spite of the optimistic tone of the editorial, much of the so-called equality in the church was token. At a meeting of the Universalist Church's Reform League in 1875, the Reverend Elizabeth Bruce complained that the church was doing little to encourage equality of the sexes. She noted that of seven hundred ordained Universalist ministers, only ten were women. At Boston's Tufts College, where one of the Universalists' leading lights, the Reverend Thomas J. Sawyer, was dean of divinity, there were no women on campus, either in the faculty or in the student body.[26]

By 1879, the blinders had been removed from the editorial board at *The*

Woman's Journal. Organized campaigns had been prominent at both Harvard and Tufts designed to keep women from registering as students. For Stone and her compatriots, this was too much. She noted that "it is worse in men of science to treat the intellects of women with sneering contempt, and yet complain if they turn to teachers who put some faith in them."[27] By the end of 1879, Harvard announced that it would admit women undergraduates.

If mainstream religions were spared the editorial sword, Mormonism came in for more than its share of attention in *The Woman's Journal*. In the fall of 1871, the journal attempted to divorce the suffrage question from polygamy in Utah. Stone and her colleagues were concerned with charges in the daily press that the extension of the vote to women in the Mormon state would lead to the propagation of polygamist behavior. The press noted that women vastly outnumbered men in Utah, and as a consequence, polygamy was their only guarantee of marriage.

The Woman's Journal refuted the charges. It carried an article describing the activities of one William S. Godbe, a reform Mormon who was attempting to loosen Brigham Young's grip on the church and its congregations. Godbe, at a public meeting in Utah, declared that "woman suffrage, which is the legal and political expression of the doctrine of woman's equality with man, has doomed polygamy, and that nothing can save it."[28]

If one factor separates the tone and direction of *The Woman's Journal* from many of the victim-driven publications of modern day, it is the optimism that in the end, morality would prevail and that women would earn equal status in society with men. To that end, Lucy Stone and Henry Blackwell were determined to seek out and publish success stories about women and often by women. Like many other stories chosen for publication, these had a decidedly middle-class bias.

Late in 1872, the journal reported on the activities of the Woman's Tea Company. The New York–based importer had just purchased a 448-ton cargo ship appropriately named the *Madame Demorest*. The newspaper noted that it was "the first time that a ship was ever purchased, owned and sent out by women for commercial purposes."[29] Some eight years later, the journal noted the establishment of another New York enterprise, the Woman's Co-operative Dress Association. One Mrs. Sherwood, a founder of the organization, which eventually hoped to open a retail business, noted that the group had received encouragement and financial support from their husbands. In return, however, they had to perform on the same level as successful males. As Sherwood stated in her address to the Board of Directors on February 28, 1880, "[T]he store will be conducted on strictly business principles, and ten of the thirteen directors will be business men."[30] The shackles had been only partially removed.

Creativity as well as business acumen merited space in the newspaper. In 1889, women inventors were saluted, in particular, Annie Caller of Albany, New York, who patented plans for a meat broiler. Eleanor E. Howe of Bridgeport,

Connecticut, was given credit for a baby brace, and Helen S. Starkey of Sioux Falls, Dakota, was recognized for inventing a lap desk.[31]

On the question of acquiring voting rights for women, which provided the raison d'être for the existence of *The Woman's Journal,* the journal posed as a moderate, reasonable, and intellectual alternative to radical demands for instant gratification. Even when confronted with what could only be interpreted as a major insult to the movement, the journal followed the biblical incantation and often turned the other cheek. When a bill was introduced in the U.S. Senate in 1872 to extend voting rights to Native Americans, the journal responded with calm and moderation.

> Now, cannot our members of Congress find out some way by which the citizenship of woman may be as easily secured? Women have already the habits of civilized life; have given abundant proof that they can manage their own affairs. They have for a quarter of a century been asking for the rights of citizenship. They have paid taxes from the very beginning of our national existence, and are also a law-abiding class of community. Is there anything to hinder their being voters?[32]

The tone was no more strident when a bill to extend full citizenship to Native Americans in Oklahoma was introduced in the Senate in 1880. The bill provided for citizenship courts for Native Americans with the provision that a declaration of intent was sufficient to gain the right. The journal commented:

> If this bill passes, any male Indian may become a citizen by declaring his purpose to become one. But the lawmakers who so readily admit Indians, persistently shut out their own mothers from the rights of citizenship. Actions speak louder than words.[33]

In 1890, the two warring factions of the woman suffrage movement made peace. The AWSA and the NWSA joined forces and became one. Both organizations published newspapers, but the new organization declined to adopt either as its official voice. Lucy Stone died three years after the merger, to be followed by her husband in 1909. Editorial direction passed from Blackwell to Blackwell, with Alice Stone Blackwell at the helm following her mother's death. In 1910, the National American Woman Suffrage Association asked *The Woman's Journal* to once again act as its official voice. The arrangement lasted until September 30, 1912.[34] In 1917, Carrie Chapman Catt suggested that the three suffrage papers printing that year, *The Woman's Journal, Woman Voter,** and the *National Suffrage News* become one. That year, *Woman Citizen** was born. It continued to publish until 1927.

Notes

1. As cited in Alice Stone Blackwell, *Lucy Stone* (Boston: Little, Brown, 1930), p. 239.

2. Lynne Masel-Walters, "To Hustle with the Rowdies: The Organization and Functions of The American Woman Suffrage Press," in *Journal of American Culture* 3.1, Spring 1980, p. 172.

3. Masel-Walters, "To Hustle with the Rowdies," p. 168.

4. Ibid., pp. 172, 180.

5. The amalgamation included, along with *The Woman's Journal,* the *Woman Voter* and *National Suffrage News.*

6. Linda Steiner, "Evolving Rhetorical Strategies/Evolving Identities," in Martha M. Solomon, ed., *A Voice of Their Own: The Woman Suffrage Press, 1840–1910* (Tuscaloosa, Alabama: University of Alabama Press, 1991), pp. 188–190.

7. E. Claire Jerry, "The Role of Newspapers in the Nineteenth Century Woman's Movement," in Solomon, *A Voice of Their Own,* p. 22.

8. Susan Schultz Huxman, "The Woman's Journal, 1870–1890: The Torchbearer for Suffrage," in Solomon, *A Voice of Their Own,* pp. 94–95.

9. July 7, 1917.

10. Blackwell, *Lucy Stone,* p. 242.

11. Huxman, "The Woman's Journal, 1870–1890: The Torchbearer for Suffrage," p. 88.

12. July 7, 1917.

13. Ibid.

14. Ibid. Huxman, "The Woman's Journal, 1870–1890: The Torchbearer for Suffrage," pp. 92–93.

15. July 7, 1917.

16. January 8, 1870.

17. April 16, 1870.

18. Martha M. Solomon, "The Role of the Suffrage Press in the Woman's Rights Movement," in Solomon, *A Voice of Their Own,* p. 5.

19. Ibid.

20. Lynne Masel-Walters, "To Hustle with the Rowdies: The Organization and Functions of the American Woman Suffrage Press," p. 175.

21. February 11, 1871.

22. January 22, 1870.

23. October 22, 1870.

24. Claire Jerry argued that "because it was supported by the less extreme wing of the movement, the *Journal*'s audience included moderate, conservative professional women of the upper and middle class who were interested primarily in suffrage alone" (E. Claire Jerry, "The Role of Newspapers in the Nineteenth Century Woman's Movement," in Solomon, *A Voice of Their Own,* p. 22.

25. July 29, 1871.

26. David Spencer, "The Universalist and Ladies' Repository," in Kathleen L. Endres and Therese Lueck, eds., *Women's Periodicals in the United States* (Westport, Conn.: Greenwood Press, 1995), pp. 387–388.

27. June 21, 1879.

28. September 9, 1871.

29. November 9, 1872.
30. March 13, 1880.
31. March 16, 1889.
32. January 27, 1872.
33. February 28, 1880.
34. July 7, 1917.

Information Sources

BIBLIOGRAPHY:
Blackwell, Alice Stone. *Lucy Stone.* Boston: Little, Brown, 1930.
Endres, Kathleen L., and Therese Lueck, eds. *Women's Periodicals in the United States.* Westport, Conn.: Greenwood Press, 1995.
Masel-Walters, Lynne. "To Hustle with the Rowdies: The Organization and Functions of the American Woman Suffrage Press." *Journal of American Culture* 3.1, Spring 1980, pp. 167–183.
Solomon, Martha M. *A Voice of Their Own: The Woman Suffrage Press, 1840–1910.* Tuscaloosa: University of Alabama Press, 1991.
INDEX SOURCES: Union List of Serials.
LOCATION SOURCES: University of Western Ontario Library and other libraries. (Microfilm available in the Gerritsen Collection.)

Publication History

PERIODICAL TITLE AND TITLE CHANGES: *The Woman's Journal* (1870–1917).
VOLUME AND ISSUE DATA: Vols. 1–48 (1870–1917). Weekly every Saturday.
PUBLISHER AND PLACE OF PUBLICATION: Henry B. Blackwell. Boston and Chicago (1870); Boston, Chicago, and St. Louis, Mo. (1871–1878); Boston, (1879–1917); Worcester, Mass. (April 14–May 26, 1917).
EDITORS: Mary A. Livermore (1870–1871); Julia Ward Howe, Lucy Stone, Henry Blackwell (with T. W. Higginson for 1872–1873) (1880–1893); Lucy Stone (with H. B. Blackwell, Alice S. Blackwell, (1883–1893); H. B. Blackwell and Alice S. Blackwell (1883–1909); Alice S. Blackwell (1910–1917).
CIRCULATION: Unreported except for 1911: 5,000 weekly.

David R. Spencer

THE WOMAN'S TRIBUNE

The Woman's Tribune shared a common plight with many suffrage publications: lofty aspirations but meager funding. Unlike many other suffrage periodicals, Clara Bewick Colby, editor of the *Tribune,* had the fortitude and the financial resources to struggle on for twenty-six years. Between 1883 and 1909, Colby published the *Tribune* without the financial support of any suffrage organization, without an endowment, and without an advertising base large enough to sustain the publication. That gave her editorial independence; she may have liked some level of financial stability, however. Colby never planned on that type of independence.

The *Tribune* was designed to have organizational backing. It was launched as the weekly organ of the Nebraska Woman Suffrage Association. The *Tribune* seldom made the frequency promised. Finally, in 1884, Colby announced that finances prevented a weekly cycle; the newspaper would come out semimonthly (issued on the first and fifteenth). That also proved to be unrealistic; during its first year, the *Tribune* came out monthly. When the newspaper did come out, it did not dedicate itself solely to reporting the activities of the Nebraska suffrage group but included news of the state's Women's Christian Temperance Union, the Relief Corp., and the Association for the Advancement of Women. Colby was soon expanding the editorial content of the publication further. By April 1884, she was offering "Household Hints," "Our Young Friends Department" (with short stories), and "Babies Corner" (with poetry), all features designed to expand the editorial appeal and readership base of the newspaper. That expansion would be needed; by May 1884, the *Tribune* had lost the financial support of the Nebraska Woman Suffrage Association.[1] Although clearly upset by the organization's decision ("friends forgot their promises, they allowed their personal and family cares to prevent their fulfillment of their part of the contract, and it soon became evident that THE TRIBUNE must fight for every inch of ground it gained, even the well-known friends of woman suffrage and campaign workers fearing to invest a dollar in a venture so precarious"[2]), Colby retained ties with the state group and even acted as president of the association from 1885 to 1898.[3]

Colby formalized many of the changes she had already made to the periodical. Although she and her newspaper would remain committed to the suffrage cause, she saw her publication having a wider mission: "It aims to be a good family and literary paper, such that people will want, even if they do not agree with its positions."[4] Moreover, Colby moved to make hers a paper of importance within suffrage circles regionally and nationally.

To make it a "good family and literary paper," she offered features of use to any woman regardless of her political orientation. The *Tribune* provided columns on health ("Hygiene and Medical Notes"), literature ("Literary Notes"), law ("Law and Lady"), and fashion. Features dealt with a wide range of topics, from art ("The Development and Growth of Art in the West"), to nutrition ("Figs as Food"), from women ministers ("A Woman Ordained"), to the tariff ("What Is an American System of Taxation and Tariff"); from short stories for the youngsters ("A True Cat Story"), to arguments on labor issues ("Attitude of the Woman Movement to the Labor Question" by J. K. Ingalls).[5]

To make her paper a suffrage mouthpiece, Colby offered a range of news, features, and editorials. The *Tribune* carried news of suffrage activities throughout the nation. However, the greatest amount of the coverage focused on the West, both because of the early suffrage successes there and because of the *Tribune*'s original home, Nebraska. Thus, the *Tribune* covered the suffrage activities in Wisconsin, Nebraska, Kansas, Iowa, South Dakota, and Colorado.[6] Colby also covered the national suffrage organizations, even though they provided no financial support. Prior to the merger of the National and the American woman suffrage associations, Colby showed her organizational preference. The *Tribune* extensively covered the National Woman Suffrage Association (NWSA) convention, dedicating pages to verbatim reports and speeches (some of which were given by Colby[7]), while the newspaper provided only cursory reports of the conventions of the American Woman Suffrage Association (AWSA). That type of support brought its own rewards. As she stumped the western states, Susan B. Anthony, the NWSA leader, drummed up subscribers for the *Tribune,* asserting that the newspaper was the organ of the National group.[8] The *Tribune,* however, never received any formal recognition from the NWSA or the subsequent National American Woman Suffrage Association.

Features, likewise, were designed to elicit support for the suffrage cause. Maude Meredith wrote about the faulty reasoning by women who did not want suffrage; the Reverend D. P. Livermore of Massachusetts wrote on one prominent woman who opposed suffrage; Julia Carbine of Colorado Springs set forth a decidedly radical economic argument for suffrage in "Women's Work and Wages": and Florence Kelly Wischnewetzky wrote about the suffrage movement among German workingwomen.[9] To find out Elizabeth Cady Stanton's latest thoughts, suffragists had to turn to the *Tribune,* for as Colby bragged. "The WOMAN'S TRIBUNE is the only suffrage paper to which Mrs. Stanton sends regular contributions." The newspaper published Stanton's personal reminiscences and the *Woman's Bible* in serialized form.[10]

Editorials ran the gamut of woman's rights issues. To concerns that voting women might smoke, Colby assured her readers that suffrage and smoking were not related: "It is the frivolous society woman who finds life vapid and tiresome and who seeks the zest of a new diversion" who was more likely to turn to tobacco.[11] Colby resisted schemes to exclude certain types of women from suffrage. The *Tribune,* she wrote, stands "for the rights of all, even for those of the misguided women of wealth who have well nigh forfeited their claims to consideration by their criminal indifference to the welfare of the country and to their own heritage."[12] Suffrage was not the only issue that Colby addressed. She opposed laws that licensed prostitution or treated women differently from men in the crime, and she endorsed equal job opportunities (while opposing laws that give women an advantage: "A fair field and no favor is what women ought to want and have").[13] Those types of editorial stances were in keeping with the *Tribune*'s broad editorial philosophy: "The WOMAN'S TRIBUNE stands not only for woman suffrage but for all human interests which require the freedom and development of both halves of humanity."[14]

Colby also covered international issues, reporting on woman's rights in India, English social betterment groups, relief work in Cuba, and suffrage gains in Norway.[15]

In the early days of the *Tribune,* Colby seemed to have endless energy and money to spend on her newspaper. Several times she issued daily editions so the newspaper could adequately cover important women's conferences. The

Tribune became the first women's daily when it issued, from March 27 to April 5, 1888, its special International Council of Women editions. Colby also issued daily editions covering the National Woman Suffrage Association conventions in 1893 (January 16–19) and 1894 (February 15–21).

For much of its life, the *Tribune* lived a somewhat nomadic existence. From 1883 to 1889, Colby published her newspaper primarily from her home in Beatrice, Nebraska. (Her daily editions in 1888 were published in Washington, D.C.). When Colby's husband was appointed assistant attorney general in the Harrison administration, Colby and her newspaper split their time between Washington, D.C. (November to April) and Beatrice, Nebraska (May to October). That continued until 1893, when Colby, her newspaper, and her husband moved to Washington, D.C., full-time. Shortly after the Spanish American War, she and her husband separated, with Colby and her newspaper staying in Washington, D.C., and her husband returning to Nebraska. In 1904, she and her newspaper moved back west, this time to Portland.

The breakup of her marriage had many implications for the *Woman's Tribune*. The newspaper never made a profit. As early as 1888, she was pleading for additional subscribers. Colby said she needed 10,000 subscribers to make her periodical profitable.[16] With the exception of the daily editions covering the International Council of Women, when the circulation reached 12,500,[17] the *Tribune* never reached the 10,000 subscription mark. In 1888, she only had about 8,000 subscribers.[18] Colby had hoped that her six months in Washington, D.C., would bring many more subscribers, since readers would want to know about the national legislation affecting women; but, with the suffrage movement focused on states, the increase was negligible. In 1890, she reported a circulation of 9,200.[19] The *Tribune* still did not have enough subscribers to make it profitable. Indeed, Colby had to learn to set type to reduce expenses. As Olympia (Brown) Willis related.

> For a time she had her own little [printing] outfit in the basement of her house in Washington, where she did everything from writing the editorials to folding and mail[ing]. . . . Often, when subscriptions were slow in coming, she was obliged to wait for days in order to get the money to pay the expense of mailing.[20]

Willis noted that Colby was ever optimistic about the future of her newspaper. But prospects never seemed to improve. She asked for donations in 1891, when it became apparent that the *Tribune* would never be named the journal of the National American Woman Suffrage Association.[21] The *Tribune* seemed on the brink of folding in 1892 because of debts run up when Colby traveled and lectured during the South Dakota suffrage campaign. The anticipated subscription increase never materialized.[22] Colby coped by reducing the number of issues, resuming its weekly frequency in September 1892. Even then, the *Tribune* skipped issues. Nonetheless, in 1893 and 1894, the newspaper came out daily to cover the National American Woman Suffrage Association (NAWSA) convention. (The daily may have been profitable. Colby took orders for the daily in 1894 and published an extra five thousand copies, presumably to fill these requests.[23]) By the end of 1894, Colby was again reporting financial problems and could not publish a number of weekly issues in October, November, and December. She reported that she still had unpaid debts from the South Dakota campaign. In 1895, she decided not to issue a daily edition of the NAWSA convention. The *Tribune* dealt with its financial problems by reducing frequency. In 1895, the newspaper switched to a biweekly frequency from August to December and back to weekly from December to April 1896, when it became a biweekly. (The fortnightly frequency was formally announced in December.[24])

In 1901, still not on sound financial footing, the *Tribune* announced plans to become a magazine at the beginning of the next volume. "The demand of the public for something small, convenient and artistic is the inevitable reaction from, and unconscious protest against the expansion of the daily," she wrote.[25] But Colby, apparently, had not discussed her plans with supporters. Six months later she canceled the format changes. The next month, the *Tribune* announced plans to return to its weekly frequency as a newspaper.[26] That frequency was never achieved. Weeks and even months were missed as Colby lectured in the West and then faced problems renewing her second-class mailing privileges.[27]

Finally, in 1904, against the advice of her friends, Colby moved her *Tribune* to Oregon. She explained:

> I go to Oregon at this time because it is the part of the country towards which all friends of woman suffrage are looking with hope and anticipation because of the suffrage amendment which will be submitted there at the election in June, 1906.[28]

But Colby's financial prospects did not improve with her move. The *Tribune* was not well received in Oregon. Advertising, always sparse, became even less after the move. Frequency, not always consistent, became even more irregular. After the defeat of suffrage in Oregon in 1906, the *Tribune* faced uncertain times. After two lapses (one between October 9, 1907, and January 11, 1908; the other between December 12, 1908, and March 6, 1909), Colby announced that she had had enough. Many longtime subscribers had died; others had not renewed. Colby personally had paid off many of the publication's debts, but, she wrote, "The mechanical part of the work must wait until the money is in hand. The future of the paper is with you who read this notice." The publication died with that March 6, 1909, issue.[29] Without an endowment or organizational support, Colby did not have the money or energy to carry on. The subscribers apparently did not respond in numbers large enough to assure any future. Although her newspaper had died, Colby did not leave the suffrage movement. This time she dedicated most of her time to the Federal Suffrage Association, which concentrated on national action.

The *Woman's Tribune,* at twenty-six years, had the second longest life span of any periodical published by the suffrage movement of the United States.[30] Its broad-based editorial content, designed to appeal to more than die-hard suffrage proponents, set it apart from other social-movement newspapers and probably explained why it was never officially named the journal of the NWSA or the NAWSA. As Willis explained,

> Undoubtedly this very versatility and variety unfitted the Tribune to be an organ of the National American Association while it made it a most interesting and profitable family paper in which Woman's Suffrage was commended to many by the very fact that it was made interesting by being associated with other subjects.[31]

Notes

1. December 1884, p. 2.
2. Ibid.
3. Norma Kidd Green, "Clara Dorothy Bewick Colby," in Edward T. James, Janet Wilson James, and Paul S. Boyer, ed., *Notable American Women 1607–1950: A Biographical Dictionary,* Vol. 1 (Cambridge: Belknap Press of Harvard University Press, 1971), p. 355. Because of her other commitments with the *Tribune* and on the lecture circuit, Colby did not dedicate much time to her presidency. As one historian noted, "Her fourteen-year term of office marked this period of the Nebraska movement as the most inactive, ineffective, disorganized, and directionless in its history, a fact largely attributable to Mrs. Colby herself" (Dennis Anthony Fus, "Persuasion on the Plains: The Woman Suffrage Movement in Nebraska," [Ph.D. diss., Indiana University, 1972], p. 75).
4. December 1884, p. 2.
5. July 7, 1888, p. 6; August 18, 1888, p. 8; October 1886, p. 3; July 7, 1888, pp. 4, 7; August 4, 1888, p. 8; September 8, 1988, p. 3.
6. "Annual Meeting of Wisconsin WSA," November 1885, p. 1; "Kansas Department," August 22, 1888, p. 7; "Woman Suffrage Convention in Iowa," July 1885, p. 1; "To Subscribers and Friends," May 14, 1892, p. 140; "Notice to Subscribers," December 16, 1893.
7. See, for example, "The Relation of the Woman Suffrage Movement to the Labor Question," March 1886, p. 1. Almost this entire issue to dedicated to covering the NWSA convention.
8. Olympia (Brown) Willis, ed., *Democratic Ideals: A Memorial Sketch of Clara B. Colby* (N.p.: Federal Suffrage Association, 1917), p. 34. Apparently the only support the NWSA officially displayed was sending the *Tribune* to the members of the U.S. Congress for four years. That custom was continued when the National and American suffrage organizations merged. (Colby was on the committee that negotiated that merger.) Then, both the *Tribune* and the *Journal* were sent to members of Congress. That was discontinued in 1891, although Colby reported that she continued to do so (June 6, 1891, p. 180).
9. Maude Meredith, "Why," October 1886, p. 1; D. P. Livermore, "Mrs. Corbin on

Woman Suffrage,'' August 4, 1888, p. 2; Julia A. Sabine, ''Women's Work and Wages,'' August 22, 1888, p. 3; Florence Kelly Wischnewetzky, ''The Movement among German Working Women,'' March 1886, p. 1.

10. ''The Woman's Tribune,'' January 3, 1891, p. 3; Stanton's personal reminiscences were used in an appeal for subscriptions, ''The announcement which the TRIBUNE is authorized to make, that Mrs. Stanton will write her personal reminiscences as a special feature for the coming year, will be a great inducement to subscribers'' (''End of Vol. V,'' December 1, 1888, p. 4; ''The Woman's Bible,'' March 2, 1894, p. 34).

11. ''Will the Coming Woman Smoke,'' November 16, 1889, p. 281.

12. ''Working Women and the Ballot,'' December 5, 1891, p. 321.

13. ''An Infamous Bill,'' March 12, 1892, p. 76; August 21, 1897, p. 66; February 19, 1898, p. 13.

14. December 22, 1900, p. 98.

15. ''Female Rights in India,'' April 14, 1894, p. 74; ''Women's Cooperative Guild,'' September 22, 1894, p. 162; ''Relief Work in Cuba,'' September 4, 1897, p. 70; ''Universal Suffrage in Norway,'' May 28, 1898, p. 41.

16. ''HELP WANTED,'' August 4, 1888, p. 5.

17. E. Claire Jerry, ''Clara Bewick Colby and the *Woman's Tribune,* 1883–1909: The Free Lance Editor as Movement Leader,'' in Martha M. Solomon, ed., *A Voice of Their Own: The Woman Suffrage Press, 1840–1910* (Tuscaloosa: University of Alabama Press, 1991), pp. 111–112.

18. ''End of Vol. V,'' December 1, 1888, p. 4; June 15, 1889, p. 4.

19. That circulation was reported in ''The Circulation of the Tribune,'' September 27, 1890, p. 228. The *Beatrice* (Nebraska) *Express* reported the *Tribune's* circulation at ten thousand. The ninety-two hundred figure was also reported by *Ayer's* in 1889, as the *Tribune* reported on September 27, 1890, p. 228.

20. Willis, *Democratic Ideals,* p. 36.

21. June 6, 1891, p. 180.

22. ''To Subscribers and Friends,'' May 14, 1892, p. 140.

23. March 3, 1894, p. 50.

24. December 26, 1896, p. 102.

25. May 11, 1901, p. 34.

26. ''Important Notice,'' November 16, 1901, p. 74; December 14, 1901, p. 82.

27. ''Wanderings Westward,'' July 12, 1902, p. 73; July 5, 1902, p. 69.

28. ''Special Notice to Subscribers,'' August 20, 1904, p. 36.

29. ''A Word with Subscribers,'' March 6, 1909, p. 2.

30. The *Woman Journal** had the longest life span.

31. Willis, *Democratic Ideals,* p. 37.

Information Sources

BIBLIOGRAPHY:

Fus, Dennis Anthony. ''Persuasion on the Plains: The Woman Suffrage Movement in Nebraska.'' Ph.D. diss. Indiana University, 1972.

Green, Norma Kidd. ''Clara Dorothy Bewick Colby.'' In Edward T. James, Janey Wilson James, and Paul S. Boyer, eds. *Notable American Women 1607–1950: A Biographical Dictionary.* Vol. 1. Cambridge: Belknap Press of Harvard University Press, 1971, pp. 355–357.

Jerry, E. Claire. ''Clara Bewick Colby and the *Woman's Tribune:* 1883–1909: The Free

Lance Editor as Movement Leader." In Martha M. Solomon, ed., *A Voice of Their Own: The Woman Suffrage Press. 1840–1910*. Tuscaloosa: University of Alabama Press, 1991, pp. 110–128.

Willis, Olympia (Brown), ed., *Democratic Ideals: A Memorial Sketch of Clara B. Colby*. N.p.: Federal Suffrage Association, 1917.

INDEX SOURCES: The *Tribune* provided an index starting with vol. 5.

LOCATION SOURCES: Library of Congress; Boston Public Library; Oberlin College Library (Ohio); and other, primarily university, libraries.

Publication History

PERIODICAL TITLE AND TITLE CHANGES: *The Woman's Tribune*.

VOLUME AND ISSUE DATA: Vols. 1–26 (August 1883–March 6, 1909). Irregular publication, said to be weekly and biweekly but actually comes out about monthly (1883–1886); weekly (1887–1895) (fortnightly, June–October 1889–1895) (many issues not published) (daily: March 27–April 5, 1888; January 16–19, 1893; February 15–21, 1894); fortnightly (August–December 1895); weekly (December 1895–1896); fortnightly (August 1896–1901); weekly (forty issues per year) (1901–1904); fortnightly (1904–1909) (publication lapses: October 19, 1907–January 11, 1908, and December 12, 1908–March 6, 1909).

PUBLISHER AND PLACE OF PUBLICATION: Nebraska Woman Suffrage Association (1883–1884); the Tribune Co. (1884); Clara Bewick Colby (1884–1909). Beatrice, Nebr. (1883–1889); Beatrice, Nebr. (May–October); Washington, D.C. (November–April) (1889–1892); Washington, D.C. (1893–1904); Portland, Oreg. (1904–1909).

EDITORS: Nebraska Woman Suffrage Association Committee (Clara Colby, Mrs. Theron Nye, and Ida Edson) (August 1883); Clara Bewick Colby (November 1, 1883–1909).

CIRCULATION: Self-reported, 1889: 9,200.

Kathleen L. Endres

WOMANSPIRIT

Two women "on the road" in 1974 found themselves at the Country Women's collective in California helping to put together an issue of the magazine *Country Women*. Their involvement in this "Spirituality Issue"—which proclaimed that spiritual awakening was a "revolution in women's consciousness"[1]—inspired them to start their own magazine, *WomanSpirit*. The two women, Ruth and Jean Mountaingrove, as lovers and business partners, formed the soul of the magazine. Along with a production collective, they ran the magazine for a decade. Editor Jean Mountaingrove recalled the motivation: "That Spirituality issue sparked flashes in us that coalesced into a proposal to our Southern Oregon women's community that we joined in beginning a feminist spirituality quarterly."[2]

Beginning in the fall of 1974, *WomanSpirit* was issued quarterly on the lunar schedule—each equinox and solstice. "From the first we were sure that

WomanSpirit was meant to appear anew with each new season."[3] *WomanSpirit* was organized thematically.

> We women are contextual. . . . So in *WomanSpirit* we choose the material to relate: to cluster around themes. Then we arrange the clusters in a sequence that recognizes the connections among them. As we read, reread, type, proofread and correct the copy, we usually find so many relationships among them that to us the magazine eventually feels more spherical than linear.[4]

The lunar and seasonal occurrences often provided the theme for the issue, and readers were asked to send material based on the theme. For example, the Winter Solstice issue dealt with the topic, "transforming darkness and unknowns into the light of consciousness."[5]

Although spiritual, *WomanSpirit* eschewed a parochial definition of spiritualism, allowing many-voiced discussions on a broad range of spirituality issues. Its unassuming freshness was appreciated:

> As women begin to explore their spirituality, a number of publications are surfacing, but unlike many new periodicals—exponents of a particular faith, creed, or dogma—*WomanSpirit,* in helping us share and listen to our many tongues, is unique among its sister journals.[6]

The Mountaingroves attempted to translate their feminism, especially the feminist technique of consciousness-raising (c-r), to the pages of a magazine. "Our image of feminism grew from our experience with the movement in the early '70s. . . . By 1974 c-r and sisterhood had revolutionized our lives. Naturally we wanted our feminist magazine to be grounded in them."[7] Discussions emulating the structure of consciousness-raising sessions ranged through the pages. These types of discussions were also constituted on the production floor.

> As we discuss the material of the issue we all learn from each other. Together we answer these questions: "What is she saying? Is the message feminist? Why do you like (dislike) it? How will it help other women?" Some of our best times in production are these stretching, challenging times when the material we are considering leads us to talk of politics, philosophy, and touches the present issue of OUR lives.[8]

The process of production as a consciousness-raising experience made it onto the pages in diverse ways. For instance, a "Collective Poem" recorded a sentence from each woman present, the first stanza written while they read manuscripts. The second stanza was written after they "consulted the I Ching to resolve a question about including a controversial article." The third stanza "occurred after a circle of thirteen women sat on the floor together the last night of layout."[9]

From poetry to prose, lyrics to calligraphy, and rituals to chants, *WomanSpirit* integrated editorial with art. Intricate line drawings flowed across its pages. A magazine full of women's work, a typical issue incorporated the work of sixty to seventy women, often with seven or eight women represented on any one page.[10] Work was gathered from women all over the nation and from international locations. Readers were involved; their work ran unedited. The publication

> honored each woman's statement for her own mode of speaking: her style, her spelling, her form. . . . [T]hey can't all be English professors. We want *WomanSpirit* readers to think, "I could have MY work printed, too." Not all valuable ideas are developed in standard artistic forms.[11]

Each issue involved a production collective whose membership varied from issue to issue.

> The production circle has always been an open group—ranging in size from three to more than 15 women. . . . The diversity and enthusiasm of each new group gives each issue of *WomanSpirit* its freshness— a vitality and roughness which keeps *WomanSpirit* young and immediate.[12]

Beyond the production aspect, the collective ideal boiled down to the core partnership of Ruth and Jean Mountaingrove.

> Ruth and I arranged our lives so that we could work on every issue, and when an issue was done the other women had other needs and priorities— like travel, lovers, jobs and children. We found that we were the only ones left to make the necessary decisions. . . . We wanted to be a collective but in practice we were a partnership.[13]

For survival, the magazine developed a "feminist distribution system" for bookstore sales during its first year of publication. Each issue was mailed directly to about one hundred feminist bookstores, primarily in the United States.[14]

Harkening back to the reliance on *Country Women* for its creation, *WomanSpirit* never had an advertising base. "[W]e wisely decided not to rely on printing advertising. That policy was really an accident." Since Jean Mountaingrove learned her magazine craft at the knees of staff at *Country Women,* which did not carry advertising, she "didn't learn how. . . . Later we tried to imagine ads in *WomanSpirit* and realized it would be like a billboard in a woodland meadow!" Carrying advertising would have been at conflict with the magazine's mission. "No matter how lovely the ad might be, it would not fit with our intention to create a safe, caring space for our readers where they can safely open up even their most vulnerable feelings." The Mountaingroves later realized that the relative poverty of their publication gave them publishing freedom. "It is freeing to know that we can print anything we think is worthwhile without jeopardizing our ability to print another issue."[15]

Lack of an advertising base occasioned a frugal and nomadic process: no telephone, no business cards. "We drove around the countryside asking for places with electricity where we would type and layout the magazine." It also forced a reliance on kindred spirits and kind souls for much of its financial stability, particularly in the beginning. "A $1,000 gift from one woman paid our first printers' bill. . . . To pay the second and later ones we sometimes had to borrow for a month or two till the bookstore payments came in." But by the middle of their run they were solvent. By 1981, they had been able "to avoid borrowing" for three years. But they were "still careful of our spending. . . . As a result of this economy, *WomanSpirit* was able to build a barn for storage and work space at last."[16] Just because *WomanSpirit* had attained its woman-built office did not mean that it became homebound. To keep its "energy" fresh, the editors would sometimes gather collectives and put together issues while in other locations, such as San Diego and Boston.

The relative success of *WomanSpirit* put it at a crossroads in 1981.

> *WomanSpirit* has reached a place of stability. Her income is enough to enable her to continue. . . . If we stay small, we can continue at this level. But if we want to expand much, we will have to improvise some new ways of getting the extra work done. . . . We both know we want *WomanSpirit* to continue, we are just going to have to discover HOW.[17]

The Mountaingroves and their production collectives did maintain the magazine through 1984. It was seen as "part of an alternative media movement dedicated to the building of new, accessible forms of communication for political and social change."[18] The magazine rounded out its decade, having been a part of this movement through its exploration of women's spiritual dimensions. But, in 1984, it was time for the Mountaingroves to resume their own journey.

> *WomanSpirit* has served as an exploration in women's spirit both past and present. It recorded our lives and rituals, remembering women's power and essence as a guide for our future. After much soul searching, Ruth and Jean decided to end publication.[19]

Notes

1. *Country Women,* April 1974, p. 1.
2. Jean Mountaingrove, "Love and a Shoestr[i]ng: Hard Work and Miracles," *New Women's Times,* March 1981, p. 20.
3. Ibid., p. 21.
4. Ibid., p. 20.

5. "WOMANSPIRIT," Fall Equinox 1976, p. 62.

6. Kirsten Grimstad and Susan Rennie, eds., "WOMANSPIRIT Quarterly," *New Women's Survival Sourcebook* (New York: Knopf, 1975), p. 196.

7. Mountaingrove, "Love and a Shoestr[i]ng."

8. Ibid., p. 21.

9. "Collective Poem," Spring Equinox 1976, p. 27.

10. Mountaingrove, "Love and a Shoestr[i]ng," pp. 20–21.

11. Ibid.

12. Ibid., p. 21.

13. Ibid., p. 22.

14. Ibid., p. 23.

15. Ibid., p. 22.

16. Ibid.

17. Ibid., p. 23.

18. "Farewell to Comrades," *New Women's Times,* October 1983, p. 10.

19. Ibid.

Information Sources

BIBLIOGRAPHY:

"Farewell to Comrades." *New Women's Times,* October 1983, p. 10.

Grimstad, Kirsten, and Susan Rennie, eds. "WOMANSPIRIT Quarterly." *New Women's Survival Sourcebook.* New York: Knopf, 1975.

Mountaingrove, Jean. "Love and a Shoestr[i]ng: Hard Work and Miracles." *New Women's Times,* March 1981, pp. 20–23.

INDEX SOURCES: Self-indexed, Alternative Press Index.

LOCATION SOURCES: Library of Congress; University of Pittsburgh; and other libraries.

Publication History

PERIODICAL TITLE AND TITLE CHANGES: *WomanSpirit* (1974–1984).

VOLUME AND ISSUE DATA: Vols. 1–10. (Autumn Equinox 1974–Summer Solstice 1984) (numbering does not always start over with a new year). Quarterly.

PUBLISHER AND PLACE OF PUBLICATION: WomanSpirit. Wolf Creek, Oreg.

EDITORS: Collective (including Ruth and Jean Mountaingrove).

CIRCULATION: Ulrich's, 1983: 6,000.

Therese L. Lueck

WOMEN LAWYERS JOURNAL

In 1899, at a time when women were not admitted to the Bar Association of New York City or the American Bar Association, a group of women lawyers in the New York area decided to form a bar association of their own: the Women Lawyers' Club of New York. Most established bar groups in the United States would not admit women; indeed, not until 1869 had women been allowed to practice law in any state. The barrier was broken when the Iowa Bar admitted

Arabella Babb Mansfield. In 1872, Alta Hulett of Illinois became the first woman admitted to practice in a state court.[1]

The Women Lawyers' Club of New York thrived for its first half decade and sponsored several well-attended public meetings. At the time, one of the chief vehicles for women's emerging involvement in the public sphere was clubs organized along social, political, and professional lines. The Women Lawyers' Club was among these associations, and one of its leading members was well-known clubwoman Fanny Carpenter, a graduate of New York University Law School. She was a member of Sorosis, the Woman's Press Club, the Society of New England Women, and the Women's Republican Club. In 1912, she was an unsuccessful candidate for the presidency of the General Federation of Women's Clubs.[2]

Carpenter was credited with keeping the Women Lawyers' Club alive, but by 1910—with membership down to twelve—the leaders decided they needed a spark to reignite their association.

The answer was the *Women Lawyers' Journal*. It was founded in May 1911 to publicize the work of women lawyers and attract members to the club. "We hope to benefit each other and grow; we hope to further the best ends of all women lawyers in general; we hope to further the interests of all womankind," the journal declared in an unsigned article on the front page.[3]

The first issue, an eight-page tabloid, sold for fifteen cents a copy or fifty cents a year and included advertisements for law books, bonding services, and legal forms.

The publication was the idea of Edith Griswold, a club member who specialized in patent law and contributed an article on the subject to the first issue. The other movers were the president of the club, Marion Weston Cottle, a solo practitioner in lower Manhattan, and the first editor, Eugenie Raye-Smith, a law professor at New York University who was active in the suffrage movement in New York, particularly in her home borough of Queens.[4]

There were four kinds of articles in the first issue: news of club activities; uplifting reports on the accomplishments of women lawyers; articles on substantive legal issues as could be found in any legal publication; and articles about social and political issues of interest to all women. (It has been an enduring mix. Throughout its eighty-four-year-history, editors have come and gone, and formats have changed, but the articles in most editions of the journal have fitted, roughly, these four categories.)

The first issue of the journal is an artifact worth studying in the cultural history of feminism, because it illustrates the difficulties posed by the so-called equality-difference question, Can women argue for perfect equality while also arguing for sisterhood and for the notion that women have special qualities that men do not possess—qualities that are important for human progress? For the women lawyers striving to be accepted in the legal marketplace of the early twentieth century, the dilemma was solved by urging women to learn the "masculine" style that the practice of law required, while retaining the social graces of the well-bred woman: "[A]lthough we are professional women, we believe we are not of the type which the poet execrated when he spoke of those 'filtered intellects who have left their womanhood on the strainer.' " The anonymous author, in a direct plea to readers, continued, "We do not wish to assume an antagonistic feministic view. If we do seem to lean that way at any time, let us know, won't you?"[5]

The first issue included a commentary by President Cottle, which revealed how she felt about women's natural inclinations. Under a headline, "The Woman Jury Lawyer," Cottle wrote that "the principal drawbacks to woman's success when pitted against man in a legal battle are to be found in the handicaps of sex." The voice, physical appearance, and attire of the average woman lawyer does not produce the impression of authority and aggressiveness of the average male lawyer, Cottle said, advising her readers to learn self-possession through careful preparation and concentration, which will eliminate self-consciousness.

> The skillful cross-examination of her witnesses and the well-aimed attack upon the weak points in her case, which are sure to come from a quick-witted man opponent, will not only cause her to lose her head, but probably her case, unless she displays the calmness and self-control necessary to defeat the maneuvers of the enemy.[6]

From the start and continuing today, according to the current editor, Veronica Boda of Philadelphia, the *Women Lawyers' Journal* has depended on volunteer editors and articles contributed by members.[7] This has created two constants in the publication's history. First, the pages reflect the interests of the lawyers who have taken the time to contribute, unlike the pages of for-profit publications, which live and die by their ability to give readers precisely what the readers want. Second, there has been a lack of consistent ideology because of the frequent changes in editors. There have been fifty editors in eighty-four years, a turnover rate of one editor per twenty months.

From 1911 to 1922 the publication continued its eight-page format, and its success was manifested by the growing membership list published in each issue. From the nineteen New Yorkers listed in the first issue, the list grew to 334 by 1922 and included lawyers in most states.[8] In 1913, the name of the club had been changed to the Women Lawyers' Association, reflecting its national membership, and in 1923 the organization was reorganized as the National Association of Women Lawyers. Many of its members were also members of the American Bar Association, which began admitting women after passage of the Nineteenth Amendment.

While a staple of the journal remained news about women lawyers—much of it chronicled in a regular column by Cottle—women's issues and the need for reform of the justice system dominated the pages of the journal in the early years. The October 1915 edition was devoted entirely to suffrage, leading with a front-page article urging members to campaign for a "yes" vote on a woman suffrage question on the New Jersey ballot and continuing inside with arguments for women's voting rights around the country.

The lead article in the February 1915 issue advocated creation of a public defender's office for indigent criminal defendants. Beginning a theme that was to continue throughout the magazine's history, the magazine began reporting extensively in the 1920s on the proposed equal rights amendment (ERA) to the U.S. Constitution. Issue after issue chronicled the progress of the amendment through state legislatures, and the underlying assumption of most of the articles was that the amendment would be good, reflecting the association's support for the ERA.

In 1940, the journal published a three-part series exploring the issue in depth. In one of the articles, California lawyer Helen Elizabeth Brown reviewed court decisions dating to the mid-nineteenth century to explain why an amendment was needed. The journal also published an anti-ERA article railing against cluttering up the Constitution with unneeded amendments. The author was identified only by the initials L.T.S.[9]

During World War II, the journal was dominated by news of women lawyers active in the war effort. In April 1942, the journal inaugurated ''For the Duration,'' a department about women lawyers' war work. Some of the items were about how women's legal work was important to war production effort, but there also were notes about women's work outside the workplace. In a report on women lawyers in Washington, volunteer correspondent and member Beatrice Clephane wrote, ''Women lawyers here are busier than ever before, and if they cannot find time for first aid classes and have no talent for knitting, they need not feel like slackers because they have learned that they can save lives by becoming blood donors.''[10]

As early as that April 1942 issue, though, at least one author in the journal—retaining the journal's focus on social problems and women's equality—looked toward the war's end. When that came, wrote Daphne Robert of Georgia, the pendulum would swing either backward or forward. ''If it swings forward, we may see the easing of all laws which discriminate against the equal rights of women. If it swings backward, we may expect a return of the 'chatteldom' of women. We can be of great value in guiding the direction of the pendulum, but meanwhile, we must WORK, WATCH and WIN.''[11]

In the spring issue of 1947, under the supervision of the association's new president, Adele Springer, the journal appears to have made a leap forward in the number of articles. The 107-page journal included articles on marriage and divorce laws, the United Nations Commission on the Status of Women, jury service for women, congresswomen in action, the New York State Law against Discrimination, legal problems of artificial insemination, and, of course, lawyers in the news.[12]

For the first time, in the spring issue of 1951, the magazine was able to quantify the number of women practicing law. The authors of the study reported that, according to the 1949 *Martindale-Hubbell Law Directory,* the leading directory of lawyers in America, there were 169,489 lawyers in the United States, of whom 2,997, or 1.7 percent, were women. Of the women lawyers, 18 percent practiced in New York State. Rhode Island had the lowest percentage. The two women lawyers in that state represented 0.3 percent of the bar.[13]

Just as World War II had loomed large in the pages of the journal, so did the cold war. For many years, the journal's back cover contained an application form for prospective members of the association. For the first time, in the fall 1952 issue, the form included lines asking prospective members if they were members of the Communist Party or if they had been a member during the previous five years. At the 1952 convention of the association, the members considered a resolution to ban communists from the organization, but a quorum wasn't present at the meeting, and the resolution was shelved. The questions on the application form were added instead, and they remained on the form through the spring 1971 issue.[14]

In succeeding years, the journal celebrated the success of women lawyers in fields still dominated by men. The winter 1964 issue, the first after the assassination of President John F. Kennedy, profiled Sarah Hughes, the first woman U.S. district court judge and the jurist who had sworn in Lyndon Johnson as president.[15] In the spring 1964 issue, Hughes wrote an article for the journal on the pros and cons of elected and appointed judges, coming out on the side of an elected judiciary.[16] In the summer of 1964, association member Martha Griffiths, a congresswoman from Michigan, wrote about her experiences on the powerful House Ways and Means Committee.[17]

A less well known writer in the journal in 1964 was a young law professor from Columbia University, Ruth Bader Ginsburg, later to be a member of the U.S. Supreme Court. The article, on a familiar subject to readers of the journal, was titled, "The Need for the Equal Rights Amendment."[18]

In more recent years, the journal's coverage has, as always, reflected the concerns of women, women lawyers in particular. Articles on sexual harassment began cropping up in the 1970s. Some things did not change. Writers in the journal continued to show interest—as Cottle had in the first issue—in how women lawyers could present themselves in court to compete with men. An article in the winter 1985 issue reported on research by two University of Central Florida professors on how listeners evaluate the courtroom credibility of men and women lawyers. The results found evidence that female jurors tend to believe a male lawyer more than a female lawyer. "Our findings suggest that the female attorney is well-advised to devise communications strategies designed to build her credibility as a competent, reliable source of information," the authors wrote.[19]

With a circulation of 1,479 in 1995, the journal's mix of stories remained the same as always. The twenty-eight page March 1995 issue included articles on the rights of women in the Philippines, the effect of gender on the murder trial of ex-football star O. J. Simpson, and a report on news of members of the association. Conferences on such topics as "rainmaking" for women lawyers were listed.[20]

Editor Veronica Boda of Philadelphia is a busy practitioner who says she depends on volunteer writers. While the magazine champions women's rights and equality, it has always been, and will continue to be, devoid of ideology, Boda says. "The association is nearing its 100th year and we're still going strong."[21]

Notes

1. Mary H. Zimmerman, ed., *75 Year History of National Association of Women Lawyers* (Lansing, Mich.: National Association of Women Lawyers, 1975), p. 415.
2. "Mrs. Philip Carpenter," May 1912, p. 1.
3. "Our Aim," May 1911, p. 1.
4. "Eugenie Raye-Smith," October 1914, p. 76.
5. "Our Aim," p. 1.
6. "The Woman Jury Lawyer," May 1911, p. 5.
7. Veronica Boda, telephone interview, June 6, 1995.
8. Zimmerman, *75 Year History,* p. 34.
9. L. T. S. "Woman and the Law," February 1940, p. 57.
10. Beatrice Clephane, "We Work for Victory," April 1942, p. 8.
11. Daphne Robert, "Our Place in This War," April 1942, p. 7.
12. "Table of Contents," Spring 1947.
13. Albert P. Blaustein and Howard Kaplan, "America's Women Lawyers: The 1949 Lawyer Count," Spring 1951, p. 18. The survey did not include women with law degrees—numbering 4,447 in 1940, according to that year's census. See Zimmerman, *75 Year History,* p. 68.
14. Unsigned article, Fall 1952, p. 10.
15. Unsigned article, Winter 1964, p. 3.
16. Sarah Hughes, "Selection of Judges," Spring 1964, p. 43.
17. Martha Griffiths, "My First 2 Years on Ways and Means," Summer 1964, p. 100.
18. Ruth Bader Ginsburg, "The Need for the Equal Rights Amendment," Winter 1964, p. 44.
19. Shari Hodgson and Burt Pryor, "Survey of Reactions to Women Lawyers," Winter 1985, p. 7.
20. Certification Statement, U. S. Postal Service, 1995, p. 5.
21. Boda interview.

Information Sources

BIBLIOGRAPHY:
Zimmerman, Mary H., ed. *75 Year History of National Association of Women Lawyers.* Lansing, Mich.: National Association of Women Lawyers, 1975.
INDEX SOURCES: Current Law Index: Legal Resource Index (LegalTrac); Index to Legal Periodicals.
LOCATION SOURCES: Catholic University Law Library; Georgetown University Law Library; Washington College of Law; and other (primarily university law) libraries.

Publication History

PERIODICAL TITLE AND TITLE CHANGES: *Women Lawyers' Journal* (1911–1943); *Women Lawyers Journal* (1944–present).

VOLUME AND ISSUE DATA: Vols. 1– (May 1911–present). Quarterly (1911–present).

PUBLISHER AND PLACE OF PUBLICATION: Women Lawyers' Club (1911–1913); the Women Lawyers' Association (1913); Women Lawyers' Association (1914–1927); National Association of Women Lawyers (1927–present). New York (1911–mid-1920s); editorial offices moved to each individual editor's hometown (mid-1920s–early 1960s); Chicago (early 1960s–present).

EDITORS: Eugenie Raye-Smith (1911–1914); Isabel Giles (1914–1915); Mary Lilly (1915–1916); Sarah Guinan (1916–1917); Alice Parker Hutchins (1917–1921); Rose Falls Bres (1921–1926); Katharine Pike (1927–1930); Rosalind Goodrich Bates (1931); Edwina Austin Avery (1935); Rosalind Goodrich Bates (1935–1936); Frances Spooner (1936–1938); Laura Berrien (1938); Jean Smith Evans (1938–1942); Elizabeth Reed (1943); Ernestine Breisch Powell (1944); Catherine Donovan (1945); Ernestine Breisch Powell (1945); Catherine Donovan (1945); Victoria Gilbert (1946); Katherine Makielski (1947); Dorothea Blender (1947–1950); Eileen Flynn (1950–1951); Amalia Pasternacki (1951–1952); Alma Zola Groves (1952–1954); Josephine Pisani (1954–1955); Mary Connelly (1955–1956); Dorothy Yancy (1956–1957); Eva Mack (1957–1958); Maria Meuter (1958–1960); Nina Miglionico (1960–1961); Josephine Mary Brown (1961–1963); Mary Louise McLeod (1963–1964); Elizabeth Guhring (1964–1965); Adele Weaver (1965–1966); Lois Forer (1966–1967); Florence Shientag (1967–1968); Dorothy May Jones (1968–1969); Marjorie Childs (1969–1970); Phyllis Shampanier (1970–1971); Mary Jeanne Coyne (1971–1972); Lee Berger Anderson (1972–1973); Mary Pappas (1973–1974); Lee Penland (1974–1976); Helen Nassif (1976–1977); Mary Bell Hammerman (1977–1978); Ethel Danzig (1979–1980); Margaret Hawes (1981); Mattie Belle Davis (1982); Ann Lake (1983–1985); Janis Blough (1984–1985); Ann Lake (1985–1986); Janis Blough (1986–1988); Claire Morrison (1989–1990); Linda Lengyel (1990–1993); Veronica Boda (1993–present).

CIRCULATION: U.S. Postal Service, 1995: 1,479.

Henry Gottlieb

Appendix: Chronology

This chronology includes only those publications profiled in this volume. Over the course of their lives, many of these publications have had name changes. The publication names cited in this chronology are those used in the title of the profile. This chronology provides the name of the periodical; its beginning year; its publisher; its location; and ending date in parentheses if appropriate. The various name changes, publisher changes, location changes, last issue data as well as additional details are available in the individual entries.

1835   *The Advocate and Family Guardian,* American Female Guardian Society and Home for the Friendless, N.Y. (ceased publication in 1941).

1838   *The Friend of Virtue,* New England Moral Reform Society, Boston (ceased publication in 1892).

1840   *The Lowell Offering,* Harriet Farley, Lowell, Mass. (ceased publication in 1850).

1847   *Pittsburgh Saturday Visiter,* Jane G. Swisshelm, Pittsburgh (ceased publication in 1854).

1849   *The Lily,* Amelia Bloomer, Seneca Falls, N.Y. (ceased publication in 1856).

1851   *The Genius of Liberty,* Elizabeth A. Aldrich, Cincinnati (ceased publication in 1853).

1853   *The Una,* Pauline Wright Davis, Providence, R.I. (ceased publication in 1855).

1856   *The Sibyl,* John Whitbeck Hasbrouck, Middletown, N.Y. (ceased publication in 1864).

1869   *The Pioneer,* Emily Pitts Stevens, San Francisco (ceased publication in 1873).

        The Revolution, Susan B. Anthony, New York (ceased publication in 1872).

1870   *The Woman's Journal,* Alice B. Blackwell, Boston (ceased publication in 1917).

1872   *Woman's Exponent,* Emmeline B. Wells, Salt Lake City, Utah (ceased publication in 1914).

1878   *The National Citizen and Ballot Box,* Matilda Joslyn Gage, Syracuse, N.Y. (ceased publication in 1881).

1879   *The Queen Bee,* Caroline Nichols Churchill, Denver (ceased publication in 1895).

1881   *The New Northwest,* Abigail Scott Duniway, Portland, Oreg. (ceased publication in 1887).

1883   *Union Signal,* Woman's Christian Temperance Union, Evanston, Ill.

          The Woman's Tribune, Clara Bewick Colby, Beatrice, Nebr., and Washington, D.C. (ceased publication in 1909).

1887   *The Wisconsin Citizen,* Wisconsin Woman's Suffrage Association, Waukeska, Wis. (ceased publication in 1917).

1888   *Free Speech and Headlight,* Ida B. Wells, Memphis, Tenn. (ceased publication in 1892).

          The Woman's Column, Alice Blackwell, Boston (ceased publication in 1904).

1889   *The Business Woman's Journal,* Mary F. Seymour, New York (ceased publication in 1896).

          GFWC Clubwoman, General Federation of Women's Clubs, Washington, D.C.

1890   *Far and Near,* Oswald Weber Jr., New York (ceased publication in 1894).

          The Remonstrance, Women's Anti-Suffrage Association of Massachusetts, Boston (ceased publication in 1920).

1891   *Farmer's Wife,* I.W. Pack, Topeka, Kans. (ceased publication in 1894).

          A True Republic, Sarah M. Perkins, Cleveland (ceased publication in 1904).

1895   *The American Jewess,* Rosa Sonneschein, Chicago and New York (ceased publication in 1899).

          The Keystone Louise B. Poppenheim, Charleston, S.C. (ceased publication in 1913).

1908   *The Anti-Suffragist,* New York State Association Opposed to Woman Suffrage, Albany, N.Y. (ceased publication in 1912).

1909   *The Forerunner,* Charlton Publishing, New York (ceased publication in 1916).

          The Progressive Woman, the Progressive Woman Publishing Co., Chicago (ceased publication in 1914).

1910   *The Woman Voter,* Woman Suffrage Party of New York City, New York (ceased publication in 1917).

1911   *Life and Labor,* Women's Trade Union League, Chicago (ceased publication in 1921).

            Western Woman Voter, Western Woman Voter Publishing Co., Seattle (ceased publication in 1913).

            Women Lawyers Journal, National Association of Women Lawyers, New York.

1913   *The Reply,* Helen S. Harman-Brown, New Canaan, Conn. (ceased publication in 1915).

            Suffragist, National Woman's Party, Washington, D.C. (ceased publication in 1921).

1914   *The Woman Rebel,* Margaret Sanger, New York (ceased publication in 1914).

1917   *Birth Control Review,* the American Birth Control League, New York (ceased publication in 1940).

            Four Lights. New York City Woman's Peace Party, New York (ceased publication in 1919).

            The Woman Citizen, Woman Citizen Corp., New York (ceased publication in 1931).

1918   *The Woman Patriot,* The Woman Patriot Publishing Co., Washington, D.C. (ceased publication in 1932).

1919   *National Business Woman,* National Federation of Business and Professional Women's Clubs, Washington, D.C.

1923   *Equal Rights,* National Woman's Party, Washington, D.C. (ceased publication in 1954).

1933   *The Catholic Worker,* Dorothy Day, New York.

1941   *Peace and Freedom,* Women's International League for Peace and Freedom, Philadelphia.

1956   *The Ladder,* National Daughters of Bilitis, San Francisco (ceased publication in 1972).

1962   *La Wisp,* Southern California Women Strike for Peace, Los Angeles (ceased publication in 1990).

            N.Y. Peaceletter. Women Strike for Peace, New York (ceased publication in 1990).

1967   *Skirting the Capital with Marian Ash,* Marian Ash, Sacramento, Calif. (ceased publication in 1974).

1968   *No More Fun and Games,* Cell 16, Cambridge, Mass. (ceased publication in 1973).

            Voice of the Women's Liberation Movement, Women's Liberation Movement Members, Chicago (ceased publication in 1969).

1970   *Notes from the First Year,* New York Radical Women, New York (ceased publication in 1971).

            off our backs, off our backs Inc., Washington, D.C.

Red Star, Red Women's Detachment, New York (ceased publication in 1971).

1971   *Majority Report,* The Majority Report Co., New York (ceased publication in 1979).

Network News, Sociologists for Women in Society, Akron, Ohio.

Prime Time, Marjory Collins, New York (ceased publication in 1977).

1972   *Media Report to Women,* Women's Institute for Freedom of the Press, Washington, D.C.

New Directions for Women, New Directions for Women Inc., Englewood, N.J. (ceased publication in 1993).

1974   *Daughters of Sarah,* Daughters of Sarah Inc., Evanston, Ill.

Woman Spirit, Woman Spirit, Wolf Creek, Oreg. (ceased publication in 1984).

1975   *New Women's Times,* New Women's Times Inc., Rochester, N.Y. (ceased publication in 1984).

Sojourner, Sojourner Inc., Boston.

1976   *Lilith,* Lilith Publications Inc., New York.

Sinister Wisdom, Harriet Desmoines and Catherine Nicholson, Berkeley, Calif. (ceased publication in 1994).

1977   *Chrysalis,* Chrysalis collective, Los Angeles (ceased publication in 1980).

Focus: A Journal for Lesbians, Boston Chapter of Daughters of Bilitis, Boston/Cambridge (ceased publication in 1983).

Plainswoman, Plainswoman Inc., Grand Fork, N. Dak. (ceased publication in 1989).

1978   *Harvard Women's Law Journal,* Harvard Law School, Cambridge, Mass.

1979   *Thesmophoria,* Susan B. Anthony Coven #1, Oakland, Calif.

1982   *The Celibate Woman Journal,* Martha Leslie Allen, Washington, D.C. (ceased publication in 1988).

9to5 Newsletter, 9to5 National Association of Working Women, Milwaukee, Wis.

1984   *Feminist Teacher,* Ablex Publishing Corp., Norwood, N.J.

Bibliography

Adickes, Sandra. "Mind over Spindles: An Examination of Some of the Journals, Newspapers, and Memoirs of the Lowell Female Operatives." *Women's Studies* 1, 1973, pp. 279–287.

Albert, Judith Claver, and Stewart Albert, eds., *The Sixties Papers: Documents of a Rebellious Decade,* New York: Praeger, 1984.

Allen, Martha L. *1981 Index/Directory of Women's Media* Washington, D.C.: Women's Institute for Freedom of the Press, 1981.

———. *The Development of Communication Networks among Women, 1963–1983.* Ann Arbor: University Microfilms International, 1989.

Alonso, Harriet Hyman. *Peace as a Women's Issue: A History of the U.S. Movement for World Peace and Women's Rights.* Syracuse, N.Y.: Syracuse University Press, 1993.

Arthur and Elizabeth Schlesinger Library on the Holdings of Women in America: The Manuscripts, Inventories, and Catalogs of Manuscripts, Books, and Pictures. 3 vols. Boston: G. K. Hall, 1973.

Banner, Lois W. *Elizabeth Cady Stanton: A Radical for Woman's Rights* Boston: Little, Brown, 1980.

Baskin, Alex. *Woman Rebel.* New York: Archives of Social History, 1976.

Beasley, Maurine. "Donna Allen and the Women's Institute: A Feminist Perspective on the First Amendment." Paper presented at the American Journalism Historians Association, Philadelphia, October 3–5, 1991.

Beasley, Maurine, and Shelia J. Gibbons. *Taking Their Place: A Documentary History of Women and Journalism.* Washington, D.C.: American University Press, 1993.

Becker, Susan D. *The Origins of the Equal Rights Amendment: American Feminism between the Wars.* Westport, Conn.: Greenwood Press, 1981.

Bennion, Sherilyn Cox. "The *Woman's Exponent:* Forty-two Years of Speaking for Women." *Utah Historical Quarterly.* 44.3, Summer 1976, pp. 222–239.

———. "*The New Northwest* and *Woman's Exponent* Early Voices for Suffrage." *Journalism Quarterly* 54.2, Summer 1977, pp. 286–292.

————. *"The Pioneer:* The First Voice for Women's Suffrage in the West." *The Pacific Historian,* 25.4, Winter 1981, pp. 15–21.

————. *Equal to the Occasion: Women Editors of the Nineteenth-Century West.* Reno: University of Nevada Press, 1990.

Berg, Barbara J. *The Remembered Gate: Origins of American Feminism: The Woman and the City 1800–1860.* New York: Oxford University Press, 1978.

"Big Mama vs. Big Brother." *The Nation,* November 29, 1980, pp. 564–565.

Biggs, Mary. " 'Conditions' Traditions." *Women's Review of Books,* April 1984, pp. 7–8.

Blackwell, Alice Stone. *Lucy Stone: Pioneer of Women's Rights.* Boston: Little, Brown, 1930.

Blair, Karen. "The Clubwoman as Feminist: The Woman's Culture Club Movement in the United States, 1868–1914." Diss. State University of New York, Buffalo, 1976.

Blanchard, Margaret. *Revolutionary Sparks: Freedom of Expression in Modern America.* New York: Oxford University Press, 1992.

Bland, Sidney. "Techniques of Persuasion: The National Woman's Party and Woman Suffrage, 1913–1919." Diss. George Washington University, 1972.

Bloomer, Dexter C. *Life and Writings of Amelia Bloomer.* Boston: Arena, 1895.

Brady, Marilyn Dell. "Populism and Feminism in a Newspaper by and for Women of the Kansas Farmers' Alliance, 1891–1894." *Kansas History,* 7.4, Winter 1984–1985, pp. 280–290.

Brandt, Kate. "Lisa Ben: A Lesbian Pioneer." *Visibilities,* January/February 1990, pp. 8–10.

Brown, Denise C. "Feminist and Witch." *WomanSpirit,* Fall 1979, p. 39.

Brown, Olympia. "Wisconsin's Fight for Suffrage." *Milwaukee Free Press* July 23, 1911, p. 1.

Brown, Rita Mae. *A Plain Brown Rapper.* Baltimore: Diana Press, 1976.

Budapest, Z. "Christian Feminist vs. Goddess Movement." *WomanSpirit,* Summer 1980, pp. 26–27.

Buhle, Mari J. *Women and American Socialism, 1870–1920.* Urbana: University of Illinois Press, 1981.

Bularzik, Mary. "The Bonds of Belonging: Leonora O'Reilly and Social Reform." *Labor History* 24, Winter 1983, pp. 60–83.

Bunch, Charlotte, and Nancy Myron, eds. *Class and Feminism.* Baltimore: Diana Press, 1974.

Burleigh, Celia. "People Worth Knowing: Jane Grey Swisshelm." *Woman's Journal,* August 20, 1870, p. 257; August 27, 1870, p. 265; September 3, 1870, p. 274.

Busby, Linda J., and Greg Leichty. "Feminism and Advertising in Traditional and Nontraditional Women's Magazines 1950s–1980s." *Journalism Quarterly* 70.2, Summer 1993, pp. 247–264.

Butcher, Patricia Smith. "More than Just a Parlor Ornament: Women's Rights Periodicals and Women's Higher Education, 1849–1920." Diss., Rutgers University, 1986.

Camhi, Jane Jerome. *Women against Women: American Anti-Suffragism, 1880–1920.* Brooklyn, N.Y.: Carlson, 1994.

Cardinale, Susan. *Special Issues of Serials about Women, 1965–1975.* Monticello, Ill.: Council of Planning Librarians, 1976.

Catt, Carrie Chapman, and Nettie Rogers Shuler. *Woman Suffrage and Politics: The Inner Story of the Suffrage Movement.* New York: Charles Scribner's Sons, 1923.

Chafe, William. *The Paradox of Change: American Women in the Twentieth Century.* New York: Oxford University Press, 1991.

Chafetz, Janet Saltzman, and Anthony Gary Dworkin. "IN THE FACE OF THREAT: Organized Anti-Feminism in Comparative Perspective." *Gender and Society* 1.1, March 1987, pp. 33–60.

Cheda, Sherrill. "Small Mags: Feminist." *Emergency Librarian,* 4.5, May/June 1977, pp. 14–15.

———. "Women's Studies Journals." *Atlantis,* 3.2, 1978, pp. 151–155.

Churchill, Caroline Nichols. *Active Footsteps.* Colorado Springs: Mrs. C. N. Churchill, 1909.

Clardy, Andrea Fleck. *Words to the Wise: A Writer's Guide to Feminist and Lesbian Periodicals and Publishers.* 2d ed. Ithaca, N.Y.: Firebrand Books, 1986.

Cole, Diane. "A Feminist Reader's Guide." *Ms.,* October 1987, p. 73.

Coleman, Kate. " 'Country Women': The Feminists of Albion Ridge." *Mother Jones,* April 1978, pp. 23–24.

Coleman, Willie M. "The 'Woman's Era' 1894–1897: Voices from Our 'Womanist' Past." *Sage,* 1.2, Fall 1984, pp. 36–37.

Conlin, Joseph, ed. *The American Radical Press, 1880–1920.* Westport, Conn.: Greenwood Press, 1974.

Contreras, Gloria. "A Gender Balancing Resource List." *Social Education,* 51.3, March 1987, pp. 200–205.

Cook, Blanche Wiesen, ed. *Crystal Eastman on Women and Revolution.* New York: Oxford University Press, 1978.

Cooper, Nancy. "Feminist Periodicals." *Mass Comm Review* 3.3, Summer 1976, pp. 15–23.

Cote, Charlotte. *Olympia Brown: The Battle for Equality.* Racine, Wis.: Mother Courage Press, 1988.

Cott, Nancy. *The Grounding of Modern Feminism.* New Haven, Conn.: Yale University Press, 1987.

Coy, Patrick, ed. *A Revolution of the Heart: Essays on the Catholic Worker.* Philadelphia: Temple University Press, 1988.

Creedon, Pamela J., ed. *Women in Mass Communication.* 2d ed. Newbury Park, Calif.: Sage, 1993.

Croly, Jane Cunningham. *Sorosis: Its Origin and History.* New York: Press of J. J. Little, 1886.

Danky, James P. *Undergrounds: A Union List of Alternative Periodicals in Libraries of the United States and Canada.* Madison: State Historical Society of Wisconsin, 1974.

———. *Women's Periodicals and Newspapers from the 18th Century to 1981: A Union List of the Holdings of the Madison, Wisconsin Libraries.* Boston: G. K. Hall, 1982.

Davis, Flora. *Moving the Mountain: The Women's Movement in America since 1960.* New York: Simon and Schuster, 1991.

Davis, Paulina Wright. *A History of the National Women's Rights Movement for Twenty Years from 1850 to 1970.* New York: Journeymen Printers' Cooperative Association, 1871.

Day, Dorothy. *The Long Loneliness: The Autobiography of Dorothy Day.* Garden City, N.Y.: Image Books, 1959.

DeCosta-Willis, Miriam, ed. *The Memphis Diary of Ida B. Wells.* Boston: Beacon Press, 1995.

Degen, Marie Louise. *The History of the Women's Peace Party.* New York: Garland, 1972 (reprint of 1939).

Dennett, Mary Ware. *Who's Obscene.* New York: Vanguard Press, 1930.

Dobbs, Jennie. "America's First All Women's Magazine." *New England Galaxy* 19.2, 1977, pp. 44–48.

Downing, John. *Radical Media, The Political Experience of Alternative Communication.* Boston: South End Press, 1984.

DuBois, Ellen. *Feminism and Suffrage: The Emergence of an Independent Women's Movement in America, 1848–1860.* Ithaca, N.Y.: Cornell University Press, 1978.

———. *The Grounding of Modern Feminism.* New Haven, Conn.: Yale University Press, 1987.

Dunbar, Bradford. *A Checklist of American Women's Periodicals and and Newspapers through 1876.* N.p.: American Antiquarian Society Archives, Ms. Control., 1984.

Duniway, Abigail Scott. *Path Breaking: An Autobiographical History of the Equal Suffrage Movement in Pacific Coast States.* New York: Schocken Books, 1971 (reprint from James, Kerns, and Abbott, 1914).

Echols, Alice. *Daring to Be BAD: Radical Feminism in America, 1967–1975.* Minneapolis: University of Minnesota Press, 1989.

Eisenstein, Zillah, ed. *Capitalist Patriarchy and the Case for Socialist Feminism.* New York: Monthly Review Press, 1979.

Eisler, Benita, ed. *The Lowell Offering: Writings by New England Mill Women (1840–1845).* New York: J. B. Lippincott, 1977.

Ek, Richard A. "Victoria Woodhull and the Pharisees." *Journalism Quarterly* 49.3, Autumn 1972, pp. 453–459.

Endres, Kathleen L. "Jane Grey Swisshelm: 19th Century Journalist and Feminist." *Journalism History* 2.4, Winter 1975–1976, pp. 128–131.

———. "The Women's Press in the Civil War: A Portrait of Patriotism, Propaganda and Prodding." *Civil War History,* March 1984, pp. 31–53.

Endres, Kathleen L., and Therese L. Lueck, eds. *Women's Periodicals in the United States: Consumer Magazines.* Westport, Conn.: Greenwood Press, 1995

Epstein, Barbara. *The Politics of Domesticity: Women, Evangelism, and Temperance in Nineteenth Century America.* Middletown, Conn.: Wesleyan University Press, 1981.

Esterberg, Kristin Gay. "From Illness to Action: Conceptions of Homosexuality in *The Ladder* 1956–1965." *The Journal of Sex Research.* 27, February 1990, pp. 65–80.

Evans, Sara. *Personal Politics: The Roots of Women's Liberation in the Civil Rights Movement and the New Left.* New York: Vintage Books, 1979.

Farrington, Jean, and Cristine C. Rom. "Feminist Periodicals." *Serials Review* 5.4, October/December 1979, pp. 13–24.

Firestone, Shulamith. *The Dialectic of Sex: The Case for Feminist Revolution.* Rev. ed. New York: Bantam, 1970.

Fisher, S. J. "Reminiscences of Jane Grey Swisshelm." *Western Pennsylvania Historical Magazine* 4, July 1921, pp. 165–174.

Flexner, Eleanor. *Century of Struggle: The Woman's Rights Movement in the United States* rev. ed. Cambridge, Mass.: Belknap Press, 1975.

Folkerts, Jean, and Dwight L. Teeter. *Voices of a Nation: A History of the Media in the United States.* New York: Macmillan, 1989.

Fox, Louis H. "Pioneer Women's Rights Magazine." *New York Historical Society Quarterly* 48.1, January 1958, pp. 70–74.

Freeman, Jo. *The Politics of Women's Liberation: A Case Study of an Emerging Social Movement and Its Relation to the Policy Process.* New York: David McKay, 1975.

Friedan, Betty. *It Changed My Life: Writing on the Women's Movement.* New York: Random House, 1976.

Gage-Colby, Ruth. "Women Strike for Peace." *New World Review* 31.6, June 1963, pp. 5–8.

Galloway, Sue. "Women." *Wilson Library Bulletin* 47, October 1972, pp. 150–152.

Gilman, Charlotte Perkins. *Women and Economics* New York: Harper and Row, 1966.

Ginzberg, Lori. "Moral Suasion Is Moral Balderdash: Women, Politics, and Social Activism in the 1850s." *Journal of American History* 73.3, December 1986, pp. 601–622.

Goldstein, Cynthia. "The Radical Press and the Beginning of the Birth Control Movement in the United States." Paper presented at the Association for Education in Journalism and Mass Communication, Memphis, August 3–6, 1985.

Goodman, Vern. "Little Magazine May Have Big Future." *New Directions for Women,* September/October 1982, p. 18.

Gordon, Linda. *Woman's Body, Woman's Right: A Social History of Birth Control in America.* New York: Penguin, 1976.

Gordon, Suzanne. "Culture as Propaganda." *Change: The Magazine of Learning* 8, April 1976, pp. 45–47.

Gottlieb, Agnes Hooper. "Women Journalists and the Municipal Housekeeping Movement: Case Studies of Jane Cunningham Croly, Helen M. Winslow and Rheta Childe Dorr." Diss., University of Maryland 1992.

Graham, Abbie. *Grace H. Dodge: Merchant of Dreams.* New York: Woman's Press, 1926.

Gray, Madeline, *Margaret Sanger.* New York: Richard Marek, 1979.

Griffith, Elisabeth. *In Her Own Right: The Life of Elizabeth Cady Stanton.* New York: Oxford University Press, 1984.

Grimstad, Kirsten, and Susan Rennie, eds. *The New Woman's Survival Catalogue.* New York: Coward, McCann, and Geoghegan, 1973.

———. *The New Woman's Survival Sourcebook.* New York: Knopf, 1975.

Guy-Sheftall, Beverly. "Women's Studies at Spelman College: Reminiscences from the Director." *Women's Studies International Forum* 9.2, 1986, pp. 151–155.

Hady, Maureen E. *Women's Periodicals and Newspapers from the Eighteenth Century to 1981: A Union List of the Holdings of Madison, Wisconsin, Libraries.* Boston: G. K. Hall, 1982.

Harper, Ida Husted. *The History of Woman Suffrage* Vols. 4–5. New York: National American Woman Suffrage Association, 1922.

Harrison, Cynthia. *Women's Movement Media: A Source Guide* New York: Bowker, 1975.

Hartmann, Heidi I., and Ann R. Markusen. "Contemporary Marxist Theory and Practice:

A Feminist Critique." *The Review of Radical Political Economy.* 12.2, Summer 1980, pp. 87–94.

Hayes, Kathleen. "Daughters of Sarah." *The Other Side,* November 1985, pp. 10–11.

Hays, Elinor R. *Morning Star: A Biography of Lucy Stone, 1818–1893.* New York: Harcourt, Brace, and World, 1961.

———. *Those Extraordinary Blackwells: The Story of a Better World.* New York: Harcourt, Brace, and World, 1967.

Henderson, Harold. "Was Christ a Feminist?" (Chicago) *Reader,* August 27, 1993, pp. 8–9, 24–25.

Hill, Mary A. *Charlotte Perkins Gilman: The Making of a Radical Feminist, 1860–1898.* Philadelphia: Temple University Press, 1980.

"The History of 9to5." Cleveland *Plain Dealer,* June 12, 1993, p. 8A.

Hole, Judith, and Ellen Levine. *Rebirth of Feminism.* New York: Quadrangle, 1971.

Houde, Mary Jean. *Reaching Out: A Story of the General Federation of Women's Clubs.* Chicago: Mobium Press, 1989.

Hulme, Marylin A. *Sourcebook for Sex Equality: Small Presses. An Annotated Listing of Small Presses and Alternative Sources for Books and Media. Bibliographic Series I.* New Brunswick, N.J.: Rutgers, 1977.

Hummer, Patricia M. "The Decade of Elusive Promise: Professional Women in the United States, 1920–1930." Diss., Duke University, 1976.

Humphreys, Nancy K. *American Women's Magazines: An Annotated Historical Guide.* New York: Garland, 1989.

Ingham, W. A. *Women of Cleveland and Their Work.* Cleveland: W. A. Ingham, 1893.

Irwin, Inez Haynes. *The Story of the Woman's Party.* New York: Harcourt, Brace, 1921.

Jablonsky, Thomas J. "Duty, Nature, and Stability: The Female Antisuffragists 1894–1920." Diss., University of Southern California, 1978.

Jacoby, Robin Miller. "The Women's Trade Union League and American Feminism." *Feminist Studies* 3, 1975, pp. 126–140.

James. Edward T., Janet Wilson James, and Paul S. Boyer, eds. *Notable American Women, 1607–1950.* Cambridge, Mass.: Belknap Press, 1971.

Joan, Polly, and Andrea Chesman. *Guide to Women's Publishing.* Paradise, Calif.: Dustbooks, 1978.

Johnstone, Johanna. *Mrs. Satan: The Incredible Saga of Victoria Woodhull.* New York: Putnam's, 1967.

Kelly, Janis. "The Life and Times of *off our backs:* A Women's News Journal." *New Women's Times,* March 1981, pp. 25–26.

Kennedy, Susan. " 'The Want It Satisfies Demonstrates the Need of It': A Study of Life and Labor of the Women's Trade Union League." *International Journal of Women's Studies* 3.4, July/August 1980, pp. 391–406.

Kessler, Lauren. *The Dissident Press, Alternative Journalism in American History.* Beverly Hills, Calif.: Sage, 1984.

Kinnard, Cynthia D. *Antifeminism in American Thought: An Annotated Bibliography.* Boston: G. K. Hall, 1986.

Kirkby, Diane. *Alice Henry: The Power of Pen and Voice* Melbourne: Cambridge University Press, 1991.

Kisner, Arlene, ed. *Woodhull and Claflin's Weekly* Washington, D.C.: Times Change Press, 1972.

Koedt, Anne, Ellen Levine, and Anita Rapone, eds. *Radical Feminism* New York: Quadrangle, 1973.

Kraditor, Aileen, *The Ideas of the Woman Suffrage Movement: 1890–1920.* New York: Columbia University Press, 1965.

———. *The Radical Persuasion 1890–1917: Aspects of the Intellectual History and the Historiography of Three American Radical Organizations.* Baton Rouge: Louisiana State University Press, 1981.

Kranich, Kimberlie A. "Women's Media: By, for and about." *Press Woman.* November 1988, pp. 6–9.

———. "Catalysts for Change: Periodicals by U.S. Women of Color, 1968–1988." *Feminist Teacher* 5.1, Spring 1990, pp. 26–41.

Krichmar, Albert. *The Women's Rights Movement in the United States. 1848–1970: A Bibliography and Sourcebook.* Metuchen, N.J.: Scarecrow Press, 1972.

Kriegel, Phyllis. "Quarterly for Jewish Women." *New Directions for Women.* March 1986, p. 17.

Kuhlman, Erika A. "The Feminist Pacifist Challenge to Progressive Hegemony: The Debate Over U.S. Intervention in World War I." Diss., Washington State University, 1995.

Lane, Ann J. *To Herland and Beyond: The Life and Work of Charlotte Perkins Gilman.* New York: Pantheon Books, 1990.

Larcom, Lucy. *A New England Girlhood.* Boston: Houghton-Mifflin. 1889.

Larsen, T. A. "The Woman Suffrage Movement in Washington." *Pacific Northwest Quarterly* 67.2, April 1976, pp. 49–62.

Larson, Arthur J. *Crusader and Feminist: Letters of Jane Grey Swisshelm.* St. Paul: Minnesota Historical Society, 1934.

Lemons, J. Stanley. *The Woman Citizen: Social Feminism in the 1920s.* Urbana: University of Illinois Press, 1973.

Lent, John A. *Women and Mass Communications: An International Annotated Bibliography.* Westport, Conn.: Greenwood, 1991.

Lont, Cynthia M., ed. *Women and Media: Content, Careers and Criticism.* Belmont, Calif.: Wadsworth, 1995.

Lumsden, Linda. " 'Rampant Women': The Role of the Right to Peaceably Assemble in the Woman Suffrage Movement, 1908–1919." Diss., University of North Carolina at Chapel Hill, 1994.

Lunardini, Christine. *From Equal Suffrage to Equal Rights: Alice Paul and the National Woman's Party, 1910–1928.* New York: New York University Press, 1986.

Lupton, Mary Jane. " 'Conditions.' " *Women: A Journal of Liberation* 5.2, 1977, pp. 14–15.

Madsen, Carol Cornwall. "A Mormon Woman in Victorian America." Diss., University of Utah, 1985.

Manahan, Nancy. "Future Old Maids and Pacifist Agitators: The Story of Tracy Mygatt and Frances Witherspoon." *Women's Studies Quarterly* 10, Spring 1982, pp. 10–13.

Marshall, Susan E. "In Defense of Separate Spheres: Class and Status Politics in the Anti Suffrage Movement." *Social Forces* 65.2, December 1986, pp. 327–351.

Marzolf, Marion, and Nancy Bock. "The Literature of Women in Journalism History: A Supplement." *Journalism History* 3.4, Winter 1976–1977, pp. 116–120.

Marzolf, Marion, Ramona Rush, and Darlene Stein. "The Literature of Women in Journalism History." *Journalism History* 1.4, Winter 1974–1975, pp. 117–128.

Masel-Walters, Lynne. "A Burning Cloud by Day: The History and Content of the 'Women's Journal.' " *Journalism History* 3.4, Winter 1976–1977, pp. 103–110.

———. "Their Rights and Nothing More: A History of *The Revolution*. 1868–1870." *Journalism Quarterly* 53, 1976, pp. 242–251.

———. "To Hustle with the Rowdies: The Organization and Functions of the American Woman Suffrage Press." *Journal of American Culture* 3.1, Spring 1980, pp. 167–183.

———. "For the Poor Mute Mothers? Margaret Sanger and The Woman Rebel." *Journalism History* 11.2, Spring/Summer 1984, pp. 3–10, 37.

Mather, Anne. "A History of Feminist Periodicals, Part I." *Journalism History* 1.2, Summer 1974, pp. 82–85.

———. "A History of Feminist Periodicals, Part II." *Journalism History* 1.4, Winter 1974–1975, pp. 108–111.

———. "A History of Feminist Periodicals, Part III." *Journalism History* 2.1, Spring 1975, pp. 19–31.

McAlister, Kim. "Feminist Profile: 100 Years of Activism: The Feminist Press in America." *Longest Revolution* 6.1, October/November 1981, p. 10+.

McCauley, Elfrieda B. "The New England Mill Girls: Feminine Influence in the Development of Public Libraries in New England, 1820–1860." Diss., Columbia University, 1972.

McDonald, Sharon. "Z. Budapest, Witch in Progress." *Lesbian Tide* 9, March/April 1980, pp. 6–7.

Mehlman, Terry, ed. *Annotated Guide to Women's Periodicals in the United States and Canada.* Richmond, Ind.: Earlham College Women's Program Office, 1982–1985.

Mikutowicz, Sharon. "Women in the Media." *Publishers' Auxiliary.* July 25, 1975, p. 2.

Miller, William D. *A Harsh and Dreadful Love: Dorothy Day and the Catholic Worker Movement.* New York: Liveright, 1973.

———. *Dorothy Day: A Biography.* New York: Harper and Row, 1982.

Millett, Kate. *Sexual Politics* Garden City, N.Y.: Doubleday, 1970.

Mitchell, Juliet, and Ann Oakley, eds. *What Is Feminism?* New York: Pantheon, 1986.

Morgan, Robin. *Sisterhood Is Powerful.* New York: Random House, 1970.

———. *Going Too Far.* New York: Random House, 1977.

Mott, Frank L. *A History of American Magazines.* Vols. 2–4. Cambridge, Mass.: Belknap, 1957.

Moynihan, Ruth B. *Rebel for Rights.* New Haven, Conn.: Yale University Press, 1983.

Murolo, Priscilla. "Working Girls' Clubs, 1884–1928: Class and Gender on the 'Common Ground of Womanhood.' " Diss., Yale University, 1992.

Murphy, James E., and Sharon Murphy. *Let My People Know, American Indian Journalism, 1828–1978.* Norman: University of Oklahoma Press, 1981.

Murphy, Sharon. *Other Voices: Black, Chicano, and American Indian Press.* Dayton, Ohio: Pflaum Standard, 1974.

Myron, Nancy, and Charlotte Bunch, eds. *Lesbianism and the Women's Movement.* Baltimore: Diana Press, 1975.

Nestor, Agnes. *Woman's Labor Leader.* Rockford, Ill.: Bellevue Books, 1954.

Neu, Charles E. "Olympia Brown and the Woman's Suffrage Movement." *Wisconsin Magazine of History* 43, Summer 1960, pp. 77–87.

Northrup, Flora L. *The Record of a Century, 1834–1934*. New York: American Female Guardian Society and Home for the Friendless, 1934.

O'Connor, June. *The Moral Vision of Dorothy Day: A Feminist Perspective*. New York: Crossroad, 1991.

O'Neill, William. *Everyone Was Brave: The Rise and Fall of Feminism in America*. New York: Quadrangle, 1969.

"Open Letter to Our Friends: 'Wage' Punches Out." *Union W.A.G.E.* no. 71 (1982), entire issue.

Parks, Joy. " 'Sinister Wisdom': A Chronicle." *Women's Review of Books,* February 1984, pp. 14–15.

Payne, Elizabeth Anne. *Reform, Labor and Feminism*. Urbana: University of Illinois Press, 1988.

Peck, Mary Gray. *Carrie Chapman Catt: A Biography*. New York: H.W. Wilson, 1944.

Pool, Gail. "Women's Publications: Some Issues." *Massachusetts Review* 24 Summer 1983, pp. 467–473.

Porter, Jack N. "Rosa Sonnenschein [*sic*] and THE AMERICAN JEWESS: The First Independent English Language Jewish Women's Journal in the United States." *American Jewish History* 68, September 1978, pp. 57–63.

———. "Rosa Sonnenschein and *The American Jewess:* New Historical Information of an Early American Zionist and Jewish Feminist." *American Jewish Archives* 32.2, November 1980, pp. 125–131.

Potter, Clare. *The Lesbian Periodical Index*. Tallahassee, Fla.: Naiad Press, 1986.

Redstockings, ed. *Feminist Revolution*. New Paltz: Redstockings, 1975.

Roberts, Nancy. "Journalism for Justice: Dorothy Day and the *Catholic Worker*." *Journalism History* 10.½, Spring/Summer 1983, pp. 2–9.

———. *Dorothy Day and the Catholic Worker*. Albany: State University of New York Press, 1984.

Robinson, Harriet H. *Loom and Spindle*. Kailua, Hawaii: Press Pacifica, 1976.

Roff, Sandra Shoick. "A Feminine Expression: Ladies' Periodicals in the New York Historical Society Collection." *Journalism History,* Autumn/Winter 1982, pp. 92–99.

Rom, Cristine C. "Feminist Little Magazines." *Serials Review* 5, October/December 1979, pp. 31–37.

Rupp, Leila, and Verta Taylor. *Survival in the Doldrums: The American Women's Rights Movement, 1945 to the 1960s*. New York: Oxford University Press, 1987.

Rush, Ramona, and Donna Allen, eds. *Communications at the Crossroads: The Gender Gap Connection*. Norwood, N.J.: Ablex, 1989.

Ryan, Mary. "The Power of Women's Networks: A Case Study of Female Moral Reform in Antebellum America." *Feminist Studies* 5, Spring 1979, pp. 66–85.

Salper, Roberta, ed. *Female Liberation: History and Current Politics*. Old Westbury: State University of New York, 1972.

Sanger, Margaret. *My Fight for Birth Control*. New York: Farrar and Rinehart, 1931.

———. *An Autobiography*. New York: Dover, 1971.

Sarachild, Kathie. "Covering Up Women's History, An Example. Notes from the First, Second, and Third Years." *Woman's World,* July–September 1972, pp. 14–16, 24.

Schaffer, Ronald. "The New York City Woman Suffrage Party 1909–1919." *New York History* 43, July 1962, pp. 269–284.

Scharnhorst, Gary. *Charlotte Perkins Gilman: A Bibliography.* Metuchen, N.J.: Scarecrow Press, 1985.

Schneir, Miriam, ed. *Feminism in Our Time.* New York: Vintage Books, 1994.

Schwartz, Judith. *Heterodoxy: The Radical Feminists of Greenwich Village, 1912–1940.* Norwich, Vt.: New Victoria, 1986.

Searing, Susan. "Feminist Publications." *Utne Reader.* November/December 1989, pp. 134–139.

Sheppard, Alice. *Cartooning for Suffrage.* Albuquerque: University of New Mexico Press, 1994.

Small, Melvin, and William D. Hoover, eds., *Give Peace a Chance: Exploring the Vietnam Antiwar Movement.* Syracuse, N.Y.: Syracuse University Press, 1992.

Smith-Rosenberg, Carroll. *Disorderly Conduct: Visions of Gender in Victorian America.* New York: Knopf, 1985.

Sochen, June. *The New Woman: Feminism in Greenwich Village, 1910–1920.* New York: Quadrangle, 1972.

———. *Herstory.* New York: Alfred, 1974.

———. *Movers and Shakers.* New York: Quadrangle, 1975.

Solanas, Valerie. *SCUM Manifesto.* New York: Olympia Press, 1968.

Solomon, Martha M., ed. *A Voice of Their Own: The Woman Suffrage Press, 1840–1910.* Tuscaloosa: University of Alabama Press, 1991.

Soto, Shirlene Ann. "The Emerging Chicana: A Review of the Journals." *Southwest Economy and Society* 2, October/November 1976, pp. 39–45.

Stanton, Elizabeth Cady, Susan B. Anthony, and Matilda Joslyn Gage, eds. *History of Woman Suffrage.* Vol. 1, 2d ed. Rochester, N.Y.: Charles Mann, 1889.

Stanton, Elizabeth Cady. *Eighty Years and More: Reminiscences, 1815–1897.* Boston: Northeastern University Press, 1993 (originally published 1898).

Stearns, Bertha-Monica. "Early Factory Magazines in New England: The 'Lowell Offering' and Its Contemporaries." *Journal of Economic and Business History* 2, 1930, pp. 685–705.

———. "Reform Periodicals and Female Reformers, 1830–1860." *American Historical Review* 37, July 1932, pp. 678–699.

Steiner, Linda. "The Woman's Suffrage Press, 1850–1900: A Cultural Analysis." Diss., University of Illinois at Urbana–Champaign, 1979.

———. "Finding Community in Nineteenth Century Suffrage Periodicals." *American Journalism* 1, 1983, pp. 1–15.

Stephanson, Anders, Stanley Aronowitz, and Frederic Jameson, eds. *The Sixties without Apology.* Minneapolis: University of Minnesota Press, 1984.

Sterling, Dorothy. *Black Foremothers; Three Lives.* Old Westbury, N.Y.: Feminist Press, 1979.

Stevens, Doris. *Jailed for Freedom.* New York: Boni and Liveright, 1920.

Streitmatter, Rodger. "*Vice Versa:* America's First Lesbian Magazine." Paper presented at the Association for Education in Journalism and Mass Communication, Washington, D.C., August 1995.

Suggs, Henry Lewis, ed. *The Black Press in the South 1865–1979.* Westport, Conn.: Greenwood Press, 1983.

Swerdlow, Amy. *Women Strike for Peace: Traditional Motherhood and Radical Politics in the 1960s.* Chicago: University of Chicago Press, 1993.

Swisshelm, Jane Grey. *Half a Century.* Chicago: Jansen, McClurg, 1880.

Tanner, Leslie, ed. *Voices of Women's Liberation.* New York: New American Library, 1970.

Thompson, Mildred. *Black Women in United States History: Ida B. Wells-Barnett.* Brooklyn, N.Y.: Carson, 1990.

Thorpe, Margaret F. *Female Persuasion: Six Strong-Minded Women.* New Haven, Conn.: Yale University Press, 1949.

Tracy, Joan I. "Feminist Periodicals: An Annotated Bibliography of Current Publications." *The Serials Librarian* 3.4, Summer 1979, pp. 387–405.

Trinkl, John. "Left Publications: Red Ink." *Guardian,* September 1, 1982, p. 9.

Troester, Rosalie Riegle, ed. *Voices from the Catholic Worker.* Philadelphia: Temple, 1993.

van Gelder, Lindsey. "Can Feminists Sell Out . . . on the Newsstand?" *Ms.,* July 1979, p. 23.

Wachsberger, Ken, ed. *Voices from the Underground.* Tempe, Ariz; Mica Press, 1993.

Wagner, Sally M. "That Word Is Liberty: A Biography of Matilda Joslyn Gage." Diss., University of California, Santa Cruz, 1978.

Ware, Cellestine. *Woman Power: The Movement for Women's Liberation.* New York: Tower, 1970.

Ware, Susan. *Holding Their Own: American Women in the 1930s.* Boston: Twayne, 1982.

Washington, Roxanne. "9 to 5 Rally Celebrates 20th Year." Cleveland *Plain Dealer,* June 12, 1993, p. 1.

Wells, Ida B. *Crusade for Justice: The Autobiography of Ida B. Wells* Chicago: University of Chicago Press, 1972.

Wells, Mildred White. *Unity in Diversity: The History of the General Federation of Women's Clubs.* Washington, D.C.: General Federation of Women's Clubs, 1953.

Wheeler, Helen R. *Womanhood Media: Current Resources about Women.* Metuchen, N.J.: Scarecrow Press, 1972.

Whitten, Mary. *These Were the Women: U.S.A., 1776–1860.* New York: Hastings House, 1954.

Willard, Frances E. *Glimpses of Fifty Years: The Autobiography of an American Woman.* Chicago: Women's Temperance Publication Association, 1889.

Willett, Dawn. "Christian Feminists Look to Daughters." *Chicago Tribune,* August 1, 1986, sec. 2, p. 7.

Willis, Gwendolen B., ed. "Olympia Brown, An Autobiography." *Annual Journal of Universalist Historical Society* 4, 1963, pp. 1–76.

Willis, Olympia. *Acquaintances Old and New among Reformers.* Milwaukee: S. E. Tate, 1911.

Willis, Olympia (Brown), ed. *Democratic Ideals: A Memorial Sketch of Clara B. Colby.* N.p.: Federal Suffrage Association, 1917.

Winkler, Karen. "Signs of Change in Women's Studies: The Success of an Uncommon Journal." *Chronicle of Higher Education.* September 15, 1980, p. 23.

Winslow, Helen M. "Confessions of a Newspaper Woman." *Atlantic Monthly,* February 1905, pp. 206–211.

Women's Institute for Freedom of the Press. "Directory of Women's Media." Washington, D.C.: Women's Institute for Freedom of the Press, 1989.

"Women's Literature: The Feminist Press." *Newsweek,* April 26, 1971, p. 65.

Wood, Mary. *The History of the General Federation of Women's Clubs for the First Twenty Two Years of Its Organization.* New York: History Department, General Federation of Women's Clubs, 1912.

Woodroofe, Debby. " 'Notes from the Second Year.' " *International Socialist Review* 31.6, September 1970, p. 4.

Yates, Gayle Graham. *What Women Want: The Ideas of the Movement.* Cambridge: Harvard University Press, 1975.

Zophy, Angela Howard, ed. *Handbook of American Women's History.* New York: Garland, 1990.

Zuckerman, Mary Ellen, com. *Sources on the History of Women's Magazines, 1972–1960: An Annotated Bibliography.* Westport, Conn.: Greenwood Press, 1991.

Index

Page numbers in **bold** refer to main entries.

About the Contributors

MAURINE BEASLEY is professor in the College of Journalism, University of Maryland, College Park.

JON BEKKEN is instructor in the Department of Communications and Journalism, Suffolk University, Boston.

SHERILYN COX BENNION is professor in the Department of Journalism, Humboldt State University, Arcata, California.

ELIZABETH V. BURT is assistant professor in the School of Communication, University of Hartford, Connecticut.

MARY M. CRONIN is assistant professor in the Edward R. Murrow School of Communication, Washington State University, Pullman.

DAVID R. DAVIES is assistant professor in the Department of Journalism, University of Southern Mississippi, Hattiesburg.

JEAN E. DYE is adjunct professor in the Department of Communication, University of Cincinnati, Ohio.

KATHLEEN L. ENDRES is professor in the School of Communication, University of Akron, Ohio. She is the editor of *Trade, Industrial, and Professional Periodicals of the United States* (1994) and co-editor of *Women's Periodicals in the United States: Consumer Magazines* (1995).

AGNES HOOPER GOTTLIEB is assistant professor and assistant chair of the Department of Communication, Seton Hall University, South Orange, New Jersey.

HENRY GOTTLIEB is senior writer for *The New Jersey Law Journal.*

SAMMYE JOHNSON is professor in the Department of Communication, Trinity University, San Antonio, Texas.

PAULA KASSELL is founder of *New Directions for Women*. She is currently creating a new index for that publication.

ERIKA A. KUHLMAN is instructor in the History Department, Washington State University, Pullman.

SUE A. LAFKY is assistant professor in the School of Journalism and Mass Communication, University of Iowa, Iowa City.

TINA LESHER is assistant professor in the Department of Communication, William Paterson College of New Jersey, Wayne.

THOMAS N. LEWIS is a writer and editor in Cincinnati, Ohio.

THERESE L. LUECK is associate professor in the School of Communication, University of Akron, Ohio. She is coeditor of *Women's Periodicals in the United States: Consumer Magazines* (1995).

LINDA LUMSDEN is instructor in the Communication Department, Peace College, Raleigh, North Carolina.

MARION MARZOLF is professor emeritus with the Department of Communication, University of Michigan, Ann Arbor.

BEVERLY G. MERRICK is assistant professor in the Department of Journalism and Mass Communication, New Mexico State University, Las Cruces.

ANNA R. PADDON is assistant professor in the School of Journalism, Southern Illinois University at Carbondale.

DIANA PECK is associate professor in the Department of Communication, William Paterson College of New Jersey, Wayne.

PATRICIA PRIJATEL is professor in the School of Journalism and Mass Communication, Drake University, Des Moines, Iowa.

BARBARA STRAUS REED is associate professor in the Department of Journalism and Mass Media, Rutgers University, New Brunswick, New Jersey.

BARRY WISE SMITH is promotional assistant at Oxmoor House, Southern Progress Corporation, Birmingham, Alabama.

DAVID R. SPENCER is associate professor in the Graduate School of Journalism, Middlesex College, London, Ontario, Canada.

LINDA STEINER is assistant professor in the Department of Journalism and Mass Media, Rutgers University, New Brunswick, New Jersey.

PATRICIA M. ULBRICH is researcher associate, Women's Studies Program, University of Pittsburgh, Pennsylvania.

JAN WHITT is assistant professor in the School of Journalism, University of Colorado, Boulder.

KYU HO YOUM is associate professor in the Walter Cronkite School of Journalism and Telecommunications, Arizona State University, Tempe.

ISBN 0-313-28632-9

90000>

EAN

9 780313 286322

HARDCOVER BAR CODE